COLLEGE
HOCKEY
GUIDE

MEN'S EDITION

Seventeenth Printing
June 2007

Thomas E. Keegan

Athletic Guide Publishing

COLLEGE HOCKEY GUIDE
MEN'S EDITION

By Thomas E. Keegan

Published by:

Athletic Guide Publishing
PO Box 1050
Flagler Beach, FL 32136-1050 USA

Copyright © 1991, 1992, 1993, 1994, 1995, 1996, 1997, 1998, 1999, 2000, 2001, 2002, 2003, 2004, 2005, 2006 and 2007
by Thomas E. Keegan

First printing 1990/1991
Second printing 1991/1992, completely revised
Third printing 1992/1993, completely revised
Fourth printing 1993/1994, completely revised
Fifth printing 1994/1995, completely revised
Sixth printing 1995/1996, completely revised
Seventh printing 1996/1997, completely revised
Eighth printing 1997/1998, completely revised
Ninth printing 1998/1999, completely revised
Tenth printing 1999/2000, completely revised
Eleventh printing 2000/2001, completely revised
Twelfth printing 2001/2002, completely revised
Thirteenth printing 2002/2003, completely revised
Fourteenth printing 2003/2004, completely revised
Fifteenth printing 2004/2005, completely revised
Sixteenth printing 2005/2006, completely revised
Seventeenth printing 2006/2007, completely revised June 14, 2007

Publisher's Cataloging-in-Publication Data

Keegan, Thomas, 1943-
        College Hockey Guide / by Thomas E. Keegan, - 17th ed.
        562 p.   14x22 cm.
ISBN 10: 1-60179-100-3   ISBN 13: 978-1-60179-100-9   ISSN 1092-9312
1. college reference - admissions, enrollment, tuition, scholarships, financial aid, recruiting, planning, etc. 2. college hockey - rosters, schedules, standings, statistics, etc. 3. college contacts - hockey coaches, athletic directors, sports information, admissions, rinks, etc. I. title

91-662232

Athletic Guide Publishing
PO Box 1050
Flagler Beach, FL 32136-1050
386.439.2250 phone
386.439.2249 fax

Thomas E. Keegan   *Publisher / Senior Editor*

(agp@flaglernet.com)

William A. Cross   *Editor*

Carrie Lathan   *Editor*

www.hockeycenter.com

Cover photo: Michigan State University

Disclaimer

TABLE OF CONTENTS

GOVERNING BODY INDEX

LEAGUE INDEX

COLLEGE INDEX

ADVERTISERS INDEX

Introduction

INTRODUCTION

By Tom Keegan

The College Hockey Guide has always been somewhat of a "work in progress". The very first edition, published in 1990 was 176 pages. The concept was successful and now, seventeen annual editions later, this College Hockey Guide Men's Edition is well over 500 pages.

That first edition included full page coverage of all the NCAA programs and twenty pages of listings of club programs. Also included were several articles to assist prospective student-athletes in the college evaluation and recruiting process. The content growth which has tripled the size of the College Hockey Guide has been information to assist in the process of getting an opportunity to play at the college level.

This year we are providing additional resources in the areas of academics, skill and strength training, marketing and recruiting and we are in the process of completing an expanded survey of the NCAA and ACHA coaches. After all, who better to offer advice to prospects than the coaches that may eventually recruit them.

We have also recently analyzed the probabilties of playing NCAA hockey, playing NCAA Division I hockey and finally earning a full hockey scholarship at the NCAA Division I level. This important information follows in STRICTLY BY THE NUMBERS.

This section shows how difficult it is to advance to college hockey. Only 1% of prospective student-athletes currently playing bantam, midget, junior, high school or prep school hockey will ever play at the NCAA level.

That 1% probability of playing varsity college hockey can be discouraging to prospective student-athletes. You can however increase your chances of being in that 1%, or possibly even in the one-quarter of 1% that will earn a full scholarship in an NCAA Division I program.

Over the last four years we have published The Student-Athlete and College Recruiting by Rick Wire. Rick's book provides valuable information in the areas of marketing and recruiting. Rick recommends a pro-active approach which includes "player profile forms", "highlight video tapes", newspaper articles etc. and a full fledged marketing campaign for your product in this case a prospective college hockey player.

Returns from our survey of college hockey coaches indicates that the coaches prefer to deal directly with the player, avoiding recruiting services. Recruiting services are also quite expensive, often impersonal and usually not very effective. They will usually accept any candidate willing to pay for their service. of Recruiting Services, with control over the distribution of materials as well as immediate feedback of the results.

We feel that the College Hockey Guide improves every year and this edition is no exception. If you use the information contained in the College Hockey Guide you will increase the probability of success at the college level. Good luck!

Strictly
By The Numbers

STRICTLY BY THE NUMBERS

Male College Hockey Prospects (Estimated for 2006/2007)

Participation Level	Participants
USA Hockey 13-14	55,000
USA Hockey 15-16	40,000
USA Hockey 17-19	30,000
US High School	50,000
US Prep School	10,000
CHA Bantam	75,000
CHA Midget	50,000
CHA Juvenile	10,000
CHA Junior	20,000
Canadian High School	5,000
European	5,000
Total	350,000

NCAA Participants (Actual for 2006/2007)	3,731
	(1.06 %)
NCAA Division 1 Participants (Actual for 2006/2007)	1,552
	(0.44 %)
NCAA Division 2 Participants (Actual for 2006/2007)	202
	(0.06 %)
NCAA Division 3 Participants (Actual for 2006/2007)	1,978
	(0.56 %)
NCAA Division 1 Full Scholarships (Projected for 2006/2007)	840
	(0.24%)

NCAA ROSTER STATISTICS

If your goal is to play college hockey it is important to play where the combination of hockey development and exposure is within an environment which allows for academic development and success.

How are you to know where your son should play to have the greatest chance to satisfy these criteria?

This College Hockey Guide includes rosters of all NCAA 1, 2 and 3 teams. Each of the rosters includes pertinent information about all of the players who have successfully navigated the hockey development level and are playing at the college level. Each of these players found a way to develop their skills and get noticed. I think it is important for you to know how they succeeded so that you can plot your own course.

There are 1,551 players on NCAA Division 1 rosters, 202 players on NCAA Division 2 rosters and 1,978 players on Division 3 rosters for 2006/ 2007. How did they get there? Which programs provided the development and exposure?

NCAA Players (2006/07)	D1	D2	D3	T
ACHA Transfers	4	0	4	8
AEHL	0	2	7	9
AEL	0	0	1	1
AHL	5	3	5	13
AJHL	91	0	22	113
AtJHL	9	11	53	73
AWJHL	6	0	0	6
BCHL	171	0	54	225
CCHA Transfers	4	0	3	7
CEHL	0	0	3	3
CHA Transfers	7	0	9	16
CIAU	0	0	1	1
CJHL	48	1	39	88
ContHA	0	0	1	1
CSHL	1	2	24	27
ECAC Transfers	3	0	7	10
ECAC (3) Transfers	0	2	31	33
EJHL	142	22	184	348
EmJHL	2	6	13	21
EOJHL	0	1	3	4
FEL	2	0	0	2
GHJHL	7	0	12	19
HEA Transfers	14	0	6	20
HS	24	35	254	313
IJHL	0	4	18	22
KIJHL	1	0	0	1
MAAC Transfers	2	0	0	2
ManJHL	20	1	23	44
MarJHL	3	0	4	7
MCHA Transfers	1	0	0	1
MIAC Transfers	0	0	7	7
Midget AAA	4	1	18	23
Midget AA	0	0	3	3
Midget A	0	0	3	3
MJHL	2	9	45	56
MnJHL	3	1	38	42
MWJHL	11	0	15	26
NAHL	251	1	187	439
NCHA	1	0	9	10
NE10 Transfers	0	0	1	1
NEL	0	0	2	2
NEPSAC	109	59	320	488
NJCAA	0	6	16	22
NOJHL	6	0	16	22
NPJHL	0	0	10	10
NWJHL	0	0	1	1
OCAA	0	0	3	3
OPJHL	98	1	132	231
PS	73	26	170	269
QJAHL	10	0	6	16
SEL	3	0	11	14
SIJHL	2	0	11	13
SJHL	31	0	25	56
SUNYAC Transfers	0	1	10	11
USHL	343	0	30	373
VIJHL	0	0	2	2
WCHA Transfers	5	0	3	8
WOJHL	19	0	16	35
WSHL	0	1	11	12
MISC	10	6	77	93

Of the 3,731 players on NCAA roster for 2006/07 - 2,960, or about 80% last played in just ten leagues or levels:

NCAA Players	D1	D2	D3	T
NEPSAC & PS	282	85	490	857
NAHL	251	1	187	439
USHL	343	0	30	373
EJHL	142	22	184	348
HS	24	35	254	313
OPJHL	98	1	132	231
BCHL	171	0	54	225
AJHL	91	0	22	113
CJHL	48	1	39	88
AtJHL	9	11	53	73

These numbers are based on the roster information provided by the NCAA programs sponsoring ice hockey. This information has been verified but we still were unable to determine last team for 93 NCAA players.

The other part of this equation is the player population of each of these leagues or levels. Our data for overall player population is not as easy to verify.

Our best estimate of NEPSAC and other private school players in the United States is 10,000 (freshman through senior). Based on this estimate 8.57% of prep and private school players continue playing hockey at the NCAA level.

If there are 50,000 public high school players in the United States then about 0.6 % of public high school players continue playing hockey at the NCAA level.

At the junior level it is more reliable to determine how many players per year move on to NCAA hockey. The top leagues are:

NAHL	110 players per year
USHL	93 players per year
EJHL	87 players per year

College Listing
State & SAT

COLLEGES LISTED BY STATE

ALABAMA (1)
Alabama-Huntsville, University of

ALASKA (2)
Alaska Anchorage, University of
Alaska Fairbanks, University of

ARIZONA (1)
Arizona, University of

CALIFORNIA (1)
Southern California, University of

COLORADO (3)
Colorado College
Denver, University of
United States Air Force Academy

CONNECTICUT (7)
Connecticut College
Connecticut, University of
Quinnipiac College
Sacred Heart University
Trinity College
Wesleyan University
Yale University

ILLINOIS (3)
Illinois-Champaign, University of
Lake Forest College
Robert Morris College

INDIANA (1)
Notre Dame, University of

IOWA (1)
Iowa State University

MAINE (5)
Bowdoin College
Colby College
Maine, University of
New England, University of
Southern Maine, University of

MARYLAND (2)
Towson University
United States Naval Academy

MASSACHUSETTS (28)
American International College
Amherst College
Assumption College
Babson College
Becker College
Bentley College
Boston College
Boston University
Curry College
Fitchburg State College
Framingham State College
Harvard University
Holy Cross, College of the
Massachusetts-Amherst, University of
Massachusetts-Boston, University of
Massachusetts-Dartmouth, University of
Massachusetts-Lowell, University of
Merrimack College
Nichols College
Northeastern University
Salem State College
Stonehill College
Suffolk University
Tufts University
Wentworth Institute of Technology
Western New England College
Williams College
Worcester State College

MICHIGAN (12)
Adrian College
Eastern Michigan University
Ferris State University
Finlandia University
Lake Superior State University
Michigan-Ann Arbor, University of
Michigan-Dearborn, University of
Michigan State University
Michigan Technological University
Northern Michigan University
Wayne State University
Western Michigan University

MINNESOTA (16)
Augsburg College
Bemidji State University
Bethel University
Concordia College
Gustavus Adolphus College
Hamline University
Minnesota-Crookston, University of
Minnesota-Duluth, University of
Minnesota-Twin Cities, University of
Minnesota State University-Mankato
Saint Cloud State University
Saint John's University
Saint Mary's University of Minnesota
Saint Olaf College
Saint Scholastica, College of
Saint Thomas, University of

MISSOURI (2)
Lindenwood University
Saint Louis University

NEBRASKA (1)
Nebraska-Omaha, University of

NEW HAMPSHIRE (7)
Dartmouth College
Franklin Pierce College
New England College
New Hampshire, University of
Plymouth State College
Saint Anselm College
Southern New Hampshire University

NEW JERSEY (2)
Princeton University
Rutgers University

NEW YORK (25)
Canisius College
Clarkson University
Colgate University
Cornell University
Elmira College
Hamilton College
Hobart College
Manhattanville College
Niagara University
Rensselaer Polytechnic Institute
Rochester Institute of Technology

Saint Lawrence University
Skidmore College
State Univ of New York-Brockport
State Univ of New York-Buffalo State
State Univ of New York-Cortland
State Univ of New York-Fredonia
State Univ of New York-Geneseo
State Univ of New York-Morrisville
State Univ of New York-Oswego
State Univ of New York-Plattsburgh
State Univ of New York-Potsdam
Union College
United States Military Academy
Utica College

NORTH CAROLINA (3)
Duke University
North Carolina-Chapel Hill, Univ of
North Carolina State University

NORTH DAKOTA (1)
North Dakota, University of

OHIO (5)
Bowling Green State University
Kent State University
Miami University
Ohio University
Ohio State University

PENNSYLVANIA (8)
Lebanon Valley College
Mercyhurst College
Neumann College
Pennsylvania State University
Pittsburgh, University of
Robert Morris University
Scranton, University of
West Chester University

RHODE ISLAND (5)
Brown University
Johnson & Wales University
Providence College
Rhode Island, University of
Salve Regina University

VERMONT (5)
Castleton State College
Middlebury College
Norwich University
St. Michael's College
Vermont, University of

VIRGINIA (3)
George Mason University
Virginia Polytech. Inst. & State Univ.
Virginia, University of

WASHINGTON DC (1)
Georgetown University

WISCONSIN (12)
Concordia University Wisconsin
Lawrence University
Marian College of Fond du Lac
Milwaukee School of Engineering
Northland College
St. Norbert College
Wisconsin-Eau Claire, University of
Wisconsin-Madison, University of
Wisconsin-River Falls, University of
Wisconsin-Stevens Point, University of
Wisconsin-Stout, University of
Wisconsin-Superior, University of

COLLEGES LISTED BY SAT/ACT SCORE
(VERBAL & MATH ONLY)

SAT 1400 +
Brown University
Dartmouth College
Harvard University
Middlebury College
Princeton University
Wesleyan College
Yale University

SAT 1300 - 1399
Amherst College
Boston College
Boston University
Bowdoin College
Colby College
Colgate University
Connecticut College
Connecticut, University of
Cornell University
Duke University
Georgetown University
Hamilton College
Michigan-Ann Arbor, University of
Notre Dame, University of
Rensselaer Polytechnic Institute
Southern California, University of
Saint Olaf College
Trinity College
Tufts University
Virginia, University of
Williams College

SAT 1200 - 1299
Babson College
Bentley College
Colorado College
Holy Cross, College of the
Illinois-Champaign, University of
Iowa State University
Lawrence University
Miami University
Michigan Technological University
Milwaukee School of Engineering
Minnesota-Twin Cities, University of
North Carolina-Chapel Hill, University of
Northeastern University

Pittsburgh, University of
Providence College
Rochester Institute of Technology
Rutgers University
Skidmore College
State University of New York-Geneseo
Union College
United States Air Force Academy
United States Military Academy
United States Naval Academy
Wisconsin-Madison, University of

SAT 1100 - 1199
Alabama-Huntsville, University of
Arizona, University of
Augsburg College
Bethel University
Canisius College
Clarkson University
Concordia College
Denver, University of
Elmira College
Gustavus Adophus College
Hamline University
Hobart College
Lake Forest College
Lebanon Valley College
Massachusetts-Amherst, University of
Michigan State University
New Hampshire, University of
North Carolina State University
Ohio State University
Pennsylvania State University
Quinnipiac College
Rhode Island, University of
Scranton, University of
Saint Anselm College
Saint John's University
Saint Lawrence University
Saint Louis University
Saint Michael's College
Saint Norbert College
Saint Thomas, University of
Stonehill College
State University of New York-Buffalo State

State University of New York-Oswego
Vermont, University of
Virginia Polytech. Inst. & State University
Wisconsin-Eau Claire, University of
Wisconsin-Superior, University of

SAT 1000 - 1099
Adrian College
Alaska Anchorage, University of
Alaska Fairbanks, University of
Assumption College
Bemidji State University
Bowling Green State University
Concordia University Wisconsin
Eastern Michigan University
Fitchburg State College
Framingham State College
George Mason University
Kent State University
Lake Superior State University
Lindenwood University
Maine, University of
Manhattanville College
Massachusetts-Dartmouth, University of
Massachusetts-Lowell, University of
Mercyhurst College
Merrimack College
Michigan-Dearborn, University of
Minnesota-Crookston, University of
Minnesota-Duluth, University of
Nebraska-Omaha, University of
New England, University of
Niagara University
North Dakota, University of
Northern Michigan University
Northland College
Norwich University
Ohio University
Robert Morris University
Sacred Heart University
Salve Regina University

Southern Maine, University of
Saint Cloud State University
Saint Mary's University of Minnesota
Saint Scholastica College
State University of New York-Brockport
State University of New York-Cortland
State University of New York-Fredonia
State University of New York-Plattsburgh
State University of New York-Potsdam
Suffolk University
West Chester University
Western Michigan University
Western New England College
Wisconsin-River Falls, University of
Wisconsin-Stevens Point, University of
Worcester State College

SAT 900 - 999
American International College
Castleton State College
Curry College
Ferris State University
Finlandia University
Franklin Pierce College
Johnson & Wales University
Marian College of Fond du Lac
Massachusetts-Boston, University of
Minnesota State University-Mankato
Neumann College
New England College
Nichols College
Plymouth State College
Robert Morris College
Salem State College
Southern New Hampshire University
State University of New York-Morrisville
Towson University
Utica College
Wayne State University
Wentworth Institute of Technology
Wisconsin-Stout, University of

Making Informed College Decisions

COLLEGE HOCKEY SELECTION GUIDELINES

NCAA DIVISION I - II - III - ACHA DIVISION I - II - III - NJCAA - CLUB

By Tom Keegan

This <u>College Hockey Guide</u> contains information on hundreds of college level hockey programs. A number of these programs have either junior varsity or other second levels which brings the number of potential intercollegiate playing possibilities to well over five hundred.

The opportunities range from NCAA Division I to NCAA Division III, ACHA, NJCAA or club level hockey. Some frequently asked questions include: Where do I fit? Do I also want an education? Do I want to graduate in four years or five? Do I want to play or will I be satisfied to sit on the bench for the first few years? Can I get a scholarship or financial aid? These are but a few of the questions that must be answered before you can select a school.

The standard recommendation from most concerned educators and parents over the years has been to pick a school where you will be happy for four years in the unfortunate event you don't make the hockey team. We subscribe 100% to this recommendation. This still leaves you with many alternatives. We assume that the overriding influence on your college decision is hockey. You want to play at the college level. So, should you select the best school or the best hockey team?

If you are one of the talented few prospects that is unofficially offered a guaranteed full scholarship for four years from a quality NCAA Division I program, then you probably have the talent to play at any school you choose. You must then select the school which provides you with the best combination of educational opportunities, location, social experience, cost, hockey, etc. based upon the importance of each factor to you.

Athletic scholarships are technically renewed annually and not awarded for four years. If you are not quite at the talent level to be offered full scholarships for the duration, you may be offered either a full or partial scholarship for the first year, with the balance of the scholarship dependent upon your performance your first year. Or, you may be told that a scholarship will be available to you, but not until you prove yourself during that first season. If the school is not interested in providing you with a four year scholarship, then the school probably is not certain that you will be successful in their program. This situation should suggest to you that your value to that particular school may not be as great as you had thought. Given this situation, you may want to explore schools that have teams which are not quite at the same competition level. If the top NCAA Division I schools are not able to commit to you for four years, maybe some schools in the lower echelon of Division I are willing to make the full commitment. A player considered marginal at one of the schools which routinely goes to the NCAA tournament may be an impact player at another Division I institution.

As we review preseason Division I rosters it is not unusual to find forty to fifty varsity prospects. In this kind of a numbers game we know that from ten to twenty-five players are going to be disappointed by the time final cuts are made. Even after those cuts the squad may still include from five to ten players that will not normally dress for games. Most of the players cut probably could have had an impact at the NCAA Division II/III or ACHA Division I level.

The preseason rosters of NCAA Division III programs may bulge to 75 or more and it is obvious that only about one-third of those players trying out will actually make the squad, much less the travel squad. Here again many players could have opted for a team playing at a slightly lower competition level and made the team.

Division I coaches have problems picking their teams, but those problems are generally resolved in the spring. The typical Division I program will have about thirty to thirty five returning or recruited players and from five to fifteen walk-ons. All of the recruited players and quite possibly most of the walk-ons have been seen by one or more of the coaches, usually more than two or three times. The Division I coach can pretty well predict his team makeup by the beginning of summer with very little movement after that.

NCAA Division III coaches may have a more difficult time. Since they normally do not have the luxury of scholarships and early and regular signing periods, they must actually recruit many more players than they really need. Just to make it a little tougher add the fact that the typical coach will not get a chance to see most of his prospects on the ice. He depends primarily upon recommend-ations from other coaches. He knows the positions that must be filled for the coming season, but he will not be able to make up his preseason roster until he checks the dorms in September to find out which prospects actually enrolled.

Depending upon his particular school situation he may have to dramatically over recruit. If he is the coach at a very selective school that accepts an average of only fifteen percent of applicants, he may have to recruit two hundred players to get thirty admitted. Of course those thirty admittees will not result in thirty players because many of those were also admitted to other schools and he may be lucky to get half. So, in this situation, two hundred recruits may actually result in just fifteen players on the ice.

Now, if his recruits don't fit his historical admissions patterns he may have other problems. If he gets lucky and the admissions office accepts twenty percent of his prospects, and seventy-five percent accept he could end up with thirty quality players vying for fifteen positions. Great for team competition but there will be fifteen unhappy former players wandering around campus that fall.

When you are filing applications for colleges one method calls for applying to two or three schools that offer certain admission, two or three to which you should be admitted, and two or three to which you might be admitted. Add hockey to the formula. Make sure that at least one school at each level is one where you know you can play.

We stated earlier that the typical NCAA Division III coach will not see most of his prospects play. The burden then falls to you. If you are going to spend four years at a school, take the time to visit and get a good feel for the school and the hockey program. Attend a game and a practice, stay overnight and spend some time with the team. You can't learn too much about the school if you are considering the commitment of time and money involved. A good weekend visit to one school is far more worthwhile than visiting two or three schools over a weekend and learning nothing about the schools. We recommend visiting from Thursday through Saturday when the hockey team has a Friday home game. Arrive early enough to watch the entire Thursday practice and spend Thursday evening with the team. Stay overnight, have your interview and tour and dine in the cafeteria. Also attend some classes on Friday and the game on Friday night. Spend as much time as possible around the team and the coach. When you depart on Friday night or Saturday morning you should know not only if you are good enough to play on that team, but if you fit in with the character of the team and the school.

As a prospective college player you should visit enough schools to feel comfortable with your eventual choice. Visit schools at several competition levels. Consider all of the options. Prep school, high school, midget and junior hockey players should seriously consider teams at all levels. A visit to an ACHA game at Penn State, Illinois - Champaign, Iowa State, Colorado, Arizona or Towson might offer a real surprise. They often play in front of capacity crowds in large modern rinks.

If you seriously want to play college hockey there is a place for you to play. The College Hockey Guide provides you with a fairly detailed page on every NCAA and many ACHA men's programs. In addition to all of the programs listed there are club level or junior varsity programs at many schools at all levels. Club level contacts change frequently and it is difficult to maintain communications at this level. If you are attempting to locate a specific club program, contact College Hockey Guide directly for current contact information.

If you are realistic about your own hockey ability, and you take the time to evaluate the various hockey programs and schools, you will find a place to play.

DEVELOPING OPTIONS
AND MAKING INFORMED CHOICES

By Joe Battista - Executive Director, Nittany Lion Club & former Head Hockey Coach
The Pennsylvania State University

I have been fortunate to be involved in hockey as a player, coach or administrator in Juniors, High School, Prep School, NCAA, ACHA, USA Hockey and the National Hockey League with the Pittsburgh Penguins. I am constantly amazed at how poorly prepared and ill-informed high school players and parents are when it comes to choosing a college and a college hockey program. This is one of the single most important decisions a young man and his family will make yet, unfortunately, most people spend more time researching the purchase of a new car than they do a college education.

The purpose of this article is to provide you with a game plan for developing a list of options for your choice of schools. There is no way to touch on everything; this is simply intended to whet your appetite, to provide a spark to get you motivated to become informed. I offer this information to help you to take a new look at choosing the best options for you based on informed decisions. Most young players aspire to earn a hockey scholarship and play NCAA Division I hockey, to represent their country on a national team or in the Olympics, and to play professional hockey at some level. These are all lofty goals for most student-athletes and only a very few exceptional athletes ever realize these dreams. So what is a hockey player to do? Give up? Certainly not! The answer is to get to work and start gathering the facts about college hockey programs and college admissions so that you can make informed choices. There is a school out there for everyone. There are excellent NCAA Division III, ACHA Division I and II, Intercollegiate Club and Intramural programs at some of the best schools in the country. Don't forget to consider them. The key is to find the college that offers you the best combination of academic and athletic options. Get a realistic evaluation from an unbiased source, work hard in school and on the ice, and develop a list of options.

The guiding principle in all your decisions should be academics. Academics comes first, hockey second and social life third. The first questions most coaches ask you will probably be about your grade point average, class standing and SAT/ACT scores. Athletic ability does not guarantee admission to a college. More and more, public pressure is forcing colleges to re-evaluate their admissions standards for athletes.

Former Notre Dame Basketball Coach Digger Phelps comments, "We have a serious problem with sports in our society. We forget that an athletic career is very short and team championships are just moments. Education is something that lasts a lifetime." Your academic record begins in 9th grade and is based on college preparatory courses. These include English, math, physical sciences and social science. (Physical education, health, shop etc. don't count) Make sure that you work closely with your guidance counselors throughout your high school years. The better your academic record, the more options are open for you.

Call or write to schools and coaches and get current facts. Request academic, athletic, financial and campus life materials. Do your homework! You must keep hockey in proper per-spective and select a school for the right reasons.

What if you step on the ice the first day of practice and blow out your knee? Will you still be happy at the school? Some kids will attend a school, tryout for the hockey team, get cut and then realize they don't like the school and it doesn't have the major they wanted in the first place! The key to choosing a school is to develop options. Many factors will play a part in your decision on which college you will choose. You should consider: cost, academic requirements, location, size, public vs. private, academic reputation, graduation and job placement rates, majors offered, financial aid available, social setting, student body makeup etc. Make a chart that will help you to compare various schools.

You should then divide the list of schools into three groups:

1. Those where you are certain to be admitted.

2. Those where you have a good chance to be admitted.

3. Those where you are a long shot to be admitted.

Plan to apply to at least two or three schools in each category. Find out the application deadlines (they are sooner than you think). Seniors should be applying in early fall and making plans to visit the campus and to set up meetings with the admissions office and the hockey coach.

How many Division I or III games or practices have you gone to lately? How about your coach who has been telling you that you're "varsity" and "scholarship" material? If he hasn't seen a game at these levels in several years then how can you have faith in his advice? The answer is to go and see for yourself. Go to a practice and a game at the schools where you want to make an application.

When you go for your campus visit have a list of questions prepared for the admissions counselor and the coach. You must do your homework prior to your visit or you're wasting time and money. Ask questions about faculty to student ratios, national rankings of the department, where do the faculty come from, what kind of financial aid is available, etc. Don't take anyone's word for granted. Ask for proof. Coaches will tell you that their business school is one of the best in the country. According to whom? Business Week? The Gourman Report? There are many publications which rank academic programs. Ask them to prove it to you in writing!

Once on campus ask about housing, food services, social and recreational activities, etc. You should also talk to members of the hockey team. Talk to a top player and a fifth line player. A kid cut from the team is probably going to have nothing good to say about the coaches, but if you keep that in mind, you may still learn something of value.

When you meet the coach, wear appropriate attire. The first impression will last a long time! Ask him intelligent questions. How many players will graduate this year? What positions do they play? Do you allow walk-ons to tryout? Where do you do most of your recruiting? Do you have a JV team and/

or an intramural program? Do you have an academic support program? When does the team practice? Ask him to describe his style of coaching.

Warning! Beware the coach who makes "guarantees". Recruiting is an inexact science and you really don't know how many other kids have received the same guarantee. Your recruiting "stock" may rise and fall as the coach finds better prospects or as other recruits find better opportunities elsewhere. The thing to remember is that there are no "guarantees".

You should call or write to coaches and get current information prior to meeting with them. Get a copy of a game program or media guide and see where the majority of players come from. Compare the number of Americans/Canadians on the team. Is the rink on campus? Does the team have its own locker room? What equipment is provided? Are all road expenses covered?

What type of student and community support is there? Is there extensive media coverage? Is there a team physician, trainers and access to a training room? What kind of strength training facilities are available?

Remember that coaches see hundreds of players during the course of the recruiting process and they may not recognize you or your parents after just one meeting. Also they may recognize you in your uniform but not in street clothes. So if you run into them at a rink or at a tournament, go up and reintroduce yourself.

When most high school hockey players talk about playing college hockey the only level mentioned is NCAA Division I. In reality, very few of

you will ever reach that goal. There are many NCAA Division III, ACHA Division I and II, Intercollegiate Club and Junior College teams that may make more sense academically, athletically, financially, geographically and socially.

Effective 2006/2007 there are fifty-eight NCAA Division I programs. Division I includes the Atlantic, CCHA, CHA, ECAC, Hockey East and WCHA.

How hard is it to play Division I hockey?

Number of Division I players   1,551

Positions open each year   380
    (equal distribution after transfers)

Current rosters indicate that this group of 380 will normally include approximately:

USHL (USA Hockey Tier 1)	8 5
NAHL (USA Hockey Tier 2 Jr A)	6 5
EJHL (USA Hockey Tier 3 Jr A)	3 5
All Canadian Junior A	1 2 0
NEPSAC & PS	4 5
Total	3 5 0

This leaves just 30 positions available for everyone else in North America, Europe, Asia, etc.

The facts are very clear. Only the very best will make it to Division I. Preseason rosters at most Division I schools include 20 returning players, 5 - 10 "blue-chip" recruits, 5 - 10 "recruited" walk-ons and another 15 - 20 walk-ons for a total of 50 - 60 players. At least 20 - 30 will be cut and since only 20 can dress each game, another 6 - 10 will be sitting in the stands watching.

The most unfortunate part is that many players cut or riding the bench at Division I schools might have been outstanding players on Division III or ACHA Division I, II or III teams. Worse yet, these other schools may make more sense academically, financially, etc.

My intention is not to discourage anyone, but to open up people's eyes to the facts so that you are better informed and can therefore make a better choice. Besides, if you truly are Division I material, chances are you'll know it because you'll be "recruited". Although parents are well-meaning, it's a good idea to get an unbiased evaluation of your talent to get an idea of what level you should shoot for. There is a joke among recruiters that says a player should always play one level below where his parents think he should! The sad fact is that it isn't always a joke.

There are currently 75 Division II-III programs throughout the country. The scope of each program in terms of budget, commitment from the school, fan and media support, quality of the rink, equipment supplied, etc. varies greatly from school to school as does the quality of the academic programs offered.

If you like a small school atmosphere, the traditional liberal arts education, then look no further. Schools like Williams, Amherst, Colby and Middlebury in New England and Gustavus Adolphus, Bethel, St. John's and Augsburg in Minnesota have excellent hockey programs, offer an exceptional education and also come with a hefty price tag approaching and in some cases exceeding $30,000 a year.

You need to do your homework to find out which of these programs/schools suits you. Are they among the best in the country? (Lately it's been Wisconsin-Stevens Point, Elmira, Babson, Middlebury, Bowdoin and St. Norberts, to name a few.) Some of the top Division III programs are more competitive than some of the less competitive Division I schools. These schools offer the athlete almost everything that the Division I program offers with the exception of athletic scholarships (There is financial aid available, especially at the more selective schools). On the other end of the spectrum are the bare-bones varsity programs. They typically have to travel to an off campus rink for practice, and play at odd hours (some at 5:00 am, others at 10:00 pm), offer little in the way of equipment, meal money and fan support and often play a very limited schedule. Some of these programs do not have the budgets of, nor are they competitive with many of the ACHA programs. Needless to say you must shop around and get the answers.

There are currently about 180 ACHA Division I and II programs playing at all sizes of schools across the country. These non-varsity programs are typically well organized, receive significant school funding, get tremendous community and student support and in many ways are like some of the better NCAA Division III programs. Many of these teams play in front of standing-room only crowds, have their own TV and radio broadcasts, provide players with most of their own equipment and have budgets that rival the best NCAA Division III programs. Once again it is your job to hunt these schools down.

There are currently over 100 ACHA Division III teams playing at schools across the country. These range from the well organized, well funded programs run through the athletic or club sports departments to the loosely organized programs running on shoestring budgets with player fees paying for equipment, expenses and ice costs.

In closing I encourage you to set your goals high and to go after your dreams. I hope you will be honest with yourself when evaluating your abilities and potential. There are a lot of great universities out there and one of them is going to make sense for you academically and athletically. Do your homework and develop options which make sense.

COLLEGE HOCKEY:
TRULY A NUMBERS GAME

By Tom Keegan

This <u>College Hockey Guide</u> includes a listing of all college hockey programs by average SAT score. As you review this chart and compare your results to the school averages, you should discover that the stronger you are academically, the greater your playing opportunities.

At the low end of the chart, you will find the least selective schools. Most prospective student athletes that are NCAA Clearinghouse eligible will find themselves admissable to these institutions. So, if you have a low grade point average and a low SAT/ACT score, you are competing with virtually all prospects for these positions.

At the other end of the spectrum you will find schools which require SAT average in the 1,400 plus range. These schools are not able to pick from the general population of prospective college hockey players. They may only be able to consider the top 5% to 10% of the prospective players.

If you are in this category, you will find that your prospects are more favorable because ninety to ninety-five percent of prospective hockey players have already eliminated themselves academically from consideration. For this reason, the stronger you are academically, the weaker you can be as a player and still play college hockey.

This becomes very evident when you observe college coaches at tournaments which provide profiles of all participants.

A typical coach will make a cursory examination of the academic qualifications of all of the players in the tournament and highlight the players that appear to be appropriate academic candidates for his school.

A very selective college coach may highlight less than 10% of the players in the tournament. When the games begin, the coach only seriously considers his predetermined candidates.

If you want to dramatically increase your chances of playing college hockey, make yourself academically attractive to even the most selective schools.

SCHOLARSHIPS AND FINANCIAL AID

By Tom Keegan

College Hockey programs register with the NCAA or the ACHA as Division I, II or III or with the NJCAA as a junior college program. Additionally there are many college club programs which do not register with the NCAA, ACHA or the NJCAA. Every prospective college hockey player is probably aware that the NCAA Division I schools are permitted eighteen full scholarships. These can be broken up to provide any combination of full and partial scholarships which do not exceed the value of eighteen full scholarships.

Division I programs may award the limit, or in some cases may not award any hockey scholarships at all. For example, the Ivy League schools do not provide any hockey scholarships. If the Division I status is required due to the overall athletic program, and the hockey program is actually competing at the Division II or III competition level, it is quite likely that few, if any, hockey scholarships are awarded.

NCAA Division II programs are only permitted thirteen and one-half full scholarships. As in Division I, the number of full scholarships actually awarded may vary anywhere from zero to the limit. NCAA Division II programs can also award partial scholarships to more individuals as long as the limit of thirteen and one -half full scholarship equivalencies is not exceeded. Other awards and financial aid are also available at NCAA Division I and II institutions but if awarded in conjunction with an athletic scholarship the entire amount is charged against the athletic scholarship fund for the purpose of calculating equivalencies.

Note that on our college pages we indicate the number of full scholarships available for each NCAA Division I or II program. In some situations the number of scholarships has been intentionally overstated to compensate for other awards available to hockey players which must be included in the amount of hockey scholarship dollars reported to the league and the NCAA.

Division III programs have chosen to award no athletic scholarships so need-based financial aid is the only source for funds. This type of aid may take the form of a campus job, student loans, financial grants or a combination of all three. ACHA programs generally award only financial aid but many also provide hockey equipment and supplies, travel expenses, lodging and meal money. Club programs usually offer no scholarships, equipment or supplies.

If paying for college is a major concern, review the costs carefully. You may be better off financially paying full tuition, room and board at an in-state school, than receiving a half scholarship at an expensive out of state school. Note that all costs shown in this guide are in state/out of state. As an in-state resident you may get a significant break.

Financial aid is available at most private institutions and many state schools. It is very important to check with each institution to determine the type and amount of aid available. Schools will give you either an estimate or the actual aid package prior to acceptance deadlines. School A and School B may both have total costs of $15,000, but if A offers $5,000 in aid and B offers $10,000 in aid, that may influence your decision. The information is available through the schools and it is typically part of the information packet available through the admissions office.

Qualifying for financial aid requires the completion of a form which will be used to produce the Student Aid Report. The form required will vary by school, but the most common are the FAF, FFS and USA Funds Form. Some states may require a specific state form and the college may also require it's own form. If you follow the detailed instructions, the forms are pretty straight forward. If you have a choice, the USA Funds Single File form is free and ap-pears to be somewhat easier to complete than either the FAF or the FFS. The various financial aid forms are normally available through your high school college advisor as well as college admission offices.

For fall financial aid awards you will need to complete your financial aid form early in the calendar year. This will be based upon income from your last federal tax return. The keys to receiving the financial aid award which you are entitled to are 100% completion and meeting the deadlines. All of the forms have deadlines, but most of the schools have more restrictive deadlines. It is critical to meet the deadlines.

Once the available aid has been allocated, it can't be reallocated. There are a number of publications which supply detailed information on colleges. Your public library, school library, college advising office and local bookstore all should have quite a variety of reference material on individual college costs and financial aid.

Academics

NCAA GUIDE FOR THE
COLLEGE BOUND STUDENT ATHLETE

Before you begin...

This Guide for the College-Bound Student-Athlete will lead you through a number of important topics, including your academic eligibility, amateurism eligibility, registration with the NCAA Initial-Eligibility Clearinghouse, financial aid and recruiting rules.

We addressed issues for three important groups of readers:

- High school students who hope to participate in college athletics at an NCAA college or university;

- Parents and legal guardians; and

- High school counselors and athletics administrators.

What is the NCAA?

The NCAA, or National Collegiate Athletic Association, was established in 1906 and serves as the athletics governing body for more than 1,280 colleges, universities, conferences and organizations. The national office is in Indianapolis, but the member colleges and universities develop the rules and guidelines for athletics eligibility and athletics competition for each of the three NCAA divisions. The NCAA is committed to the student-athlete and to governing competition in a fair, safe, inclusive and sportsmanlike manner.

The NCAA's membership includes:

- 326 active Division I members;

- 281 active Division II members; and

- 421 active Division III members.

One of the differences among the three divisions is that colleges and universities in Divisions I and II may offer athletics scholarships, while Division III colleges and universities may not.

What is the NCAA Initial-Eligibility Clearinghouse?

The NCAA Initial-Eligibility Clearinghouse (the clearinghouse) is an organization that works with the NCAA to determine a student's eligibility for athletics participation in his or her first year of college enrollment. Students who want to participate in college sports during their first year of enrollment in college must register with the clearinghouse.

Located in Iowa City, Iowa, the clearinghouse staff follows NCAA bylaws and regulations in analyzing and processing a student's high school academic records, ACT or SAT scores, and key information about amateurism participation, to determine the student's initial eligibility.

When to call the clearinghouse

Please contact the clearinghouse when you have questions like these:

- How do I register?

- I have forgotten my PIN. Can I get a new one?

- Some of my classes are not on my high school's list. How can I get a class added?

- My clearinghouse report shows I am missing some material. What is missing?

- Where do I send my transcripts?

- What do the codes on my clearinghouse report mean?

- I have been home schooled. What do I have to do to register?

- I am a high school counselor and I do not know my high school's PIN. Can I find out what it is?

- I am a high school administrator and want to add some core courses to our high school list. How do I do that?

NCAA Initial-Eligibility Clearinghouse
301 ACT Drive
PO Box 4043
Iowa City, IA 52243-4043
www.ncaaclearinghouse.net
877.262.1492 (customer service Monday – Friday, 8 a.m. – 5 p.m. CST)
319.337.1492 (international callers)
319.337.1556 (fax)

When to call the NCAA
Please contact the NCAA when you have questions like these:

- What are the rules and regulations related to initial eligibility?

- What are the rules and regulations related to amateurism?

- What are the regulations about transferring from one college to another?

- What are the rules about athletics scholarships and how can they be reduced or canceled?

- I have a learning disability. Are there any other requirements for me?

NCAA
PO Box 6222
Indianapolis, IN 46206-6222
317.917.6222
(Monday – Friday, noon – 4 p.m. EST)

Division I Core GPA and Tes Score Sliding Scale

Core GPA	SAT	ACT
3.550 & above	400	37
3.525	410	38
3.500	420	39
3.475	430	40
3.450	440	41
3.425	450	41
3.400	460	42
3.375	470	42
3.350	480	43
3.325	490	44
3.300	500	44
3.275	510	45
3.250	520	46
3.225	530	46
3.200	540	47
3.175	550	47
3.150	560	48
3.125	570	49
3.100	580	49
3.075	590	50
3.050	600	50
3.025	610	51
3.000	620	52
2.975	630	52
2.950	640	53
2.925	650	53
2.900	660	54
2.875	670	55
2.850	680	56
2.825	690	56
2.800	700	57
2.775	710	58
2.750	720	59
2.725	730	59
2.700	730	60
2.675	740-750	61
2.650	760	62
2.625	770	63
2.600	780	64
2.575	790	65

2.550	800	66
2.525	810	67
2.500	820	68
2.475	830	69
2.450	840-850	70
2.425	860	70
2.400	860	71
2.375	870	72
2.350	880	73
2.325	890	74
2.300	900	75
2.275	910	76
2.250	920	77
2.225	930	78
2.200	940	79
2.175	950	80
2.150	960	80
2.125	960	81
2.100	970	82
2.075	980	83
2.050	990	84
2.025	1000	85
2.000	1010	86

What are core courses?

For a definition of core courses, see information below. See your high school's core-course list at www.ncaaclearinghouse.net.

Academic-Eligibility Requirements

Division I

2006 - 2007

If you enroll in a Division I college between 2006 and 2007 and want to participate in athletics or receive an athletics scholarship during your first year, you must:

• Graduate from high school;

• Complete these 14 core courses:
  - 4 years of English
  - 2 years of math (algebra 1 or higher)
  - 2 years of natural or physical science (including one year of lab science if offered by your high school)
  - extra year of English, math or natural or physical science
  - 2 years of social science
  - 3 years of extra core courses (from any category above, or foreign language, nondoctrinal religion or philosophy);

• Earn a minimum required grade-point average in your core courses; and

• Earn a combined SAT or ACT sum score that matches your core-course grade-point average and test score sliding scale on this page (for example, a 2.400 core-course grade-point average needs a 860 SAT).

Note: Computer science courses can be used as core courses only if your high school grants graduation credit in math or natural or physical science for them, and if the courses appear on your high school's core-course list as a math or science courses.

You will be a qualifier if you meet the academic requirements listed above. As a qualifier, you:

• Can practice or compete for your college or university during your first year of college;

• Can receive an athletics scholarship during your first year of college; and

• Can play four seasons in your sport if you maintain your eligibility from year to year.

You will be a nonqualifier if you do not meet the academic requirements listed above. As a nonqualifier, you:

• Cannot practice or compete for your

college or university during your first year of college;

- Cannot receive an athletics scholarship during your first year of college, although you may receive need-based financial aid; and

- Can play only three seasons in your sport if you maintain your eligibility from year to year (to earn a fourth season you must complete at least 80 percent of your degree before beginning your fifth year of college).

Division I

2008 and Later

If you enroll in a Division I college in 2008 or later and want to participate in athletics or receive an athletics scholarship during your first year, you must:

- Graduate from high school;

- Complete these 16 core courses:
  - 4 years of English
  - 3 years of math (algebra 1 or higher)
  - 2 years of natural or physical science (including one year of lab science if offered by your high school)
  - 1 extra year of English, math or natural or physical science - 2 years of social science
  - 4 years of extra core courses (from any category above, or foreign language, nondoctrinal religion or philosophy);

- Earn a minimum required grade-point average in your core courses; and

- Earn a combined SAT or ACT sum score that matches your core-course grade-point average and test score

sliding scale on page 9 (for example, a 2.400 core-course grade-point average needs a 860 SAT).

Note: Computer science courses can be used as core courses only if your high school grants graduation credit in math or natural or physical science for them, and if the courses appear on your high school's core-course list as a math or science courses.

Remember

Meeting the NCAA academic rules does not guarantee your admissions into a college. You must apply for admission.

Division II

2005 and Later

If you enroll in a Division II college in 2005 or later and want to participate in athletics or receive an athletics scholarship during your first year, you must:

- Graduate from high school;

- Complete these 14 core courses:
  - 3 years of English
  - 2 years of math (algebra 1 or higher)
  - 2 years of natural or physical science (including one year of lab science if offered by your high school)
  - 2 extra years of English, math or natural or physical science
  - 2 years of social science
  - 3 years of extra core courses (from any category above, or foreign language, nondoctrinal religion or philosophy);

- Earn a 2.000 grade-point average or better in your core courses; and

- Earn a combined SAT score of 820 or

an ACT sum score of 68. There is no sliding scale in Division II.

Note: Computer science courses can be used as core courses only if your high school grants graduation credit in math or natural or physical science for them, and if the courses appear on your high school's core-course list as a math or science courses.

You will be a qualifier if you meet the academic requirements listed above. As a qualifier, you:

- Can practice or compete for your college or university during your first year of college;

- Can receive an athletics scholarship during your first year of college; and

- Can play four seasons in your sport if you maintain your eligibility from year to year.

You will be a partial qualifier if you do not meet all of the academic requirements listed above, but you have graduated from high school **and** meet one of the following:

- The combined SAT score of 820 or ACT sum score of 68; OR

- Completion of the 14 core courses with a 2.000 core-course grade-point average.

As a partial qualifier, you:

- Can practice with your team at its home facility during your first year of college;

- Can receive an athletics scholarship during your first year of college;

- Cannot compete during your first year of college; and

- Can play four seasons in your sport if you maintain your eligibility from year to year.

You will be a nonqualifier if you did not graduate from high school, or, if you graduated and are missing both the core-course grade-point average or minimum number of core courses and the required ACT or SAT scores. As a nonqualifier, you:

- Cannot practice or compete for your college or university during your first year of college;

- Cannot receive an athletics scholarship during your first year of college, although you may receive need-based financial aid; and

- Can play four seasons in your sport if you maintain your eligibility from year to year.

Division III

Division III does not use the NCAA Initial-Eligibility Clearinghouse. Contact your Division III college regarding its policies on financial aid, practice and competition.

Core Courses, Grade Point Average, Tests & Special Conditions

The amateurism and academic rules will be used to determine whether you may participate in sports during your first year in college. These rules are not a guide for your admission to college. Each college has its own admission requirements. **Remember, meeting the NCAA academic rules does not guarantee your admission into a college. You must still apply for admission.**

Core Courses

A core course must:

- Be an academic course in one or a combination of these areas: English, mathematics, natural/physical science, social science, foreign language, nondoctrinal religion or philosophy;

- Be four-year college preparatory; and

- Be at or above your high school's regular academic level (no remedial, special education or compensatory courses).

Not all classes you take to meet high school graduation requirements may be used as core courses.

Check your high school's list of approved core courses at the clearinghouse Web site at www.ncaaclearinghouse.net or ask your high school counselor.

Grade-Point Average

How Your Core-Course Grade-Point Average is Calculated

The clearinghouse will calculate the grade-point average of your core courses on a 4.000 scale. The best grades from your NCAA core courses will be used. Grades from additional core courses you took will be used only if they improve your grade-point average.

The clearinghouse will assign the following values to each letter grade:

A - 4 points	C - 2 points
B - 3 points	D - 1 point

Special High School Grades and Grade-Point Average

If your high school uses numeric grades (like 92 or 93), those grades will be changed to your high school's letter grades (such as A or B).

See your high school's grading scale by pulling up your school's list of approved core courses at www.ncaaclearinghouse.net.

If your high school uses plus and minus grades (such as A+ or B–), the plus or minus will not be used to calculate your core-course grade-point average.
If your high school normally "weights" honors or advanced courses, these weighted courses may improve your core-course grade-point average. Your high school must notify the clearinghouse of such weighting. To see if your high school has a weighted scale that is being used for calculating your core-course grade-point average, visit www.ncaaclearinghouse.net for an explanation of how these grade weights are handled

ACT and SAT Tests

Test-Score Requirements

You must achieve the required score on an SAT or ACT test before your full-time college enrollment. You must do this whether you are a citizen of the United States or of a foreign country. You must take the national test given on one or more of the dates shown below.

National Testing Dates

SAT	ACT
October 6, 2007	September 16, 2007
November 3, 2007	October 27, 2007
December 1, 2007	December 8. 2007
January 26, 2008	February 9, 2008
May 3, 2008	April 12, 2008
June 7, 2008	June 14, 2008

Taking Tests More than Once

You may take the SAT or the ACT more than one time. If you take either test more than once, you may use your best subscore from different tests to meet the minimum test-score requirements. Here is an example:

	Math	Verbal/ Critical Reading	Total Score
SAT (10/06)	350	**470**	820
SAT (12/06)	**420**	440	860
Scores used	**420**	**470**	**890**

Your test score will continue to be calculated using the math and verbal/ critical reading subsections of the SAT and the math, science, English and reading subsections of the ACT. **The writing component of the ACT or SAT will not be used to determine your qualifier status.**

IMPORTANT CHANGE:

All SAT and ACT test scores **must** be reported to the clearinghouse **directly** from the testing agency. Test scores will **not** be accepted if reported on a high school transcript.

When registering for the SAT or ACT, input the clearinghouse code of 9999 to make sure the score is reported directly to the clearinghouse.

Students With Disabilities: Special Conditions

A student with a disability must meet the same requirements as all other students, but is provided certain accommodations to help meet these requirements. **If you are a student with a diagnosed disability, you will need to let the NCAA know about your disability only if you plan on using core courses after your eighth semester of high school and you plan on attending a Division I college.**

To Document Your Disability

Send the following to the NCAA at the address found on page 2. Do not send this information to the clearinghouse:

- Copy of your professional diagnosis; and

- Copy of your IEP, ITP, 504 plan or statement of accommodations. (One of the above documents should be dated within the last three years.)

Note: Please include home address, telephone number, student's social security number, and the year of the student's high school graduation.

Core Courses
If you are a high school student with a disability and have received help (for example, taken special classes or received extra time for tests) because of that disability, you are eligible for the following:

- You may use a course that your high school has designed for students with disabilities, if it appears on your high school's list of approved core courses.

- You may take core courses any time

before your enrollment as a full-time student in college, even during the summer after your last high school year. Remember, for Division I, you must document your disability with the NCAA to receive this accommodation.

Nonstandard Tests

If you have a disability, you may also take a nonstandard test to satisfy test-score requirements. Follow these guidelines:

- Register for nonstandard testing as described by ACT or SAT, submitting a properly documented and confirmed diagnosis.

- Follow procedures governed by ACT or SAT. (The test may not be administered by a member of your high school athletics department or any NCAA school's athletics department.)

- If you take a nonstandard ACT or SAT, you may take the test on a date other than a national testing date, but you still must achieve the required test score.
- Your high school counselor can help you register to take a nonstandard test.

The GED

The General Education Development (GED) test may, under certain conditions, satisfy the graduation requirement, but it will not satisfy core-course grade-point average, or test-score requirements. Contact the NCAA for information about GED submission.

Home School

Home-schooled students who plan to

enroll in a Division I or Division II college must register with the clearinghouse and must meet the same requirements as all other students.

Important

You pick your own PIN. Write your PIN downand keep it handy. You will need it when you are contacting the clearinghouse.

To register, go to www.ncaaclearinghouse.net. Click on **Prospective Student-Athletes, then Domestic Student Release Form,** and follow the prompts.

Eligibility Waivers

If you don't meet the academic requirements to be a qualifier, a waiver of the requirements may be filed on your behalf by an NCAA school. Contact the NCAA or the college you will attend for information about the waiver process.

More Questions about Academic Requirements Here are some questions you may still have after reviewing the previous sections.

Q: How do I know which courses are core courses?

A: You may view your high school's list of NCAA-approved core courses at www.ncaaclearinghouse.net. (On the **General Information** page of that Web site, select **List of Approved Core Courses**). Or, you can ask your high school counselor for the list.

Q: May courses taken in eighth grade satisfy core-course requirements?

A: No. Courses taken in eighth grade will not satisfy core-course requirements.

Q: **What is the lowest grade that will be used for a course to count as a core course?**

A: The lowest grade is D.

Q: **How is my core-course GPA calculated?**

A: Your core-course GPA is the average of your best grades achieved for all required core courses. If you have taken extra core courses, those courses will be used in your GPA, only if they improve your GPA.

Q: **Will courses taken after my senior year meet core-course requirements?**

A: **For Division I, no.** Only courses completed in grades nine through 12 will qualify as core courses for Division I. Courses taken in summer school after your fourth (senior) year cannot be used. If you are missing one or more core courses after high school graduation, you must return to your high school during its regular academic year to take any missing courses and you can't enroll in a Division I college until the fall of the following year. For Division I, you may also retake any core course during that additional year at the same high school and substitute the new grade earned in that repeated year to recalculate your grade-point average.

For Division II, yes. All core courses completed before your full-time enrollment at a Division II college may be used by the clearinghouse.

For Division I students with diagnosed disabilities, yes. If you have a properly diagnosed and documented disability, as described on page 13, you may use one or more core courses completed after high school but before full-time enrollment in college. See page 13 for more information.

Remember:

The clearinghouse does not use plus or minus grades when figuring out your core-course grade-point average. For example, grades of B+, B and B- will each be worth 3 quality points.

Q: **May independent-study, Internet and correspondence courses count as core courses?**

A: Yes, if the following four conditions are met:

• The course meets core-course requirements (see pages 9 and 10);

• You and the instructor have access to each other during the course so that the instructor can teach, evaluate and provide assistance to you;

• Appropriate academic authorities evaluate your work according to the high school's academic policies; and

• The course is acceptable for any student to take and is placed on your high school transcript.

Q: **Do pass-fail grades count?**

A: Yes, these grades may satisfy your core-course requirements. The clearinghouse will assign your high school's lowest passing grade for a pass-fail class.

Q: May college courses count as core courses?

A: Yes, a college course may be used as a core course if it is accepted by your high school and if the course:

- Would be accepted for any other student;

- Is on your high school transcript (Division I only) Any college transcripts should also be sent to the clearinghouse, and

- Meets all other requirements for a core course.

Q: How are courses taken over two years counted?

A: A one-year course that is spread over a longer period of time is considered one course and will receive a maximum of one core-course credit (Example: Algebra 1, spread over two years, would receive one unit of credit.)

Q: How does the NCAA treat courses similar in content?

A: Some approved core courses might be considered duplicates. That is, the content of one course is the same as that of another, even though the classes might have different titles. If you have taken two classes considered to be duplicates, you will receive only one core-course credit (typically for the course with the higher grade). Please ask your high school counselor if you have questions about duplicate courses.

Q: Do courses for students with disabilities count as core courses?

A: Yes. If you have a diagnosed disability, you may use courses designed for students with disabilities to meet NCAA core-course requirements. These courses must appear on the high school's list of approved core courses for a student to receive NCAA credit for the course. These courses must be similar in content and scope as a regular core course offered in that academic area. Check with your high school counselor.

Q: Will credit-by-exam courses meet core-course requirements?

A: No. Courses completed through credit-by-exam may not be used.

Q: Are vocational courses acceptable?

A: No. Traditional vocational courses (e.g., typing, auto mechanics, driver's education and health) are not acceptable.

Q: May my study in a foreign country help me meet core-course requirements?

A: If you attended a secondary school outside the United States for all or part of grades nine through 12, different evaluation procedures will be applied to your international education documents. You must register with the clearinghouse if you completed course work outside the United States and you must submit original-language documents with certified translations for clearinghouse evaluation.

Division I Worksheet

This worksheet is provided to assist you in monitoring your progress in meeting NCAA initial-eligibility standards. The clearinghouse will determine your official status after you graduate. Remember to check your high school's list of approved courses for the classes you have taken. Use the following scale: A = 4 quality points; B = 3 quality points; C = 2 quality points; D = 1 quality point

English (4 years required)

Course Title Example: English 9	Credit .5	X Grade = A	Quality Points (multiply credit by grade) (.5 x 4) = 2
Total English Units			**Total Quality Points**

Mathematics (2 years required 2006 – 2007; 3 years required 2008 and after)

Course Title Example: Algebra 1	Credit 1.0	X Grade = B	Quality Points (multiply credit by grade) (1.0 x 3) = 3
Total Mathematics Units			**Total Quality Points**

Natural/physical science (2 years required)

Course Title	Credit	X Grade =	Quality Points (multiply credit by grade)
Total Natural/Physical Science Units			**Total Quality Points**

Additional year in English, mathematics or natural/physical science (1 year required)

Course Title	Credit	X Grade =	Quality Points (multiply credit by grade)
Total Additional Units			**Total Quality Points**

Social Science (2 years required)

Course Title	Credit	X Grade =	Quality Points (multiply credit by grade)
Total Science Units			**Total Quality Points**

Additional Academic Courses (3 years required 2006 – 2007; 4 years required 2008 and after)

Course Title	Credit	X Grade =	Quality Points (multiply credit by grade)
Total Additional Academic Units			**Total Quality Points**

Core Course GPA (14 Credits required 2006 – 2007; 16 required 2008 and after)

Total Quality Points	Total Number of Credits	Core-Course GPA (Total Quality Points/Total Credits)

Division II Worksheet

This worksheet is provided to assist you in monitoring your progress in meeting NCAA initial-eligibility standards. The clearinghouse will determine your official status after you graduate. Remember to check your high school's list of approved courses for the classes you have taken. Use the following scale: A = 4 quality points; B = 3 quality points; C = 2 quality points; D = 1 quality point

English (3 years required)

Course Title	Credit	X Grade =	Quality Points (multiply credit by grade) (.5 x 4) = 2
Example: English 9	.5	A	
Total English Units			Total Quality Points

Mathematics (2 years required)

Course Title	Credit	X Grade =	Quality Points (multiply credit by grade) (1.0 x 3) = 3
Example: Algebra 1	1.0	B	
Total Mathematics Units			Total Quality Points

Natural/physical science (2 years required)

Course Title	Credit	X Grade =	Quality Points (multiply credit by grade)
Total Natural/Physical Science Units			Total Quality Points

Additional year in English, mathematics or natural/physical science (2 years required)

Course Title	Credit	X Grade =	Quality Points (multiply credit by grade)
Total Additional Units			Total Quality Points

Social Science (2 years required)

Course Title	Credit	X Grade =	Quality Points (multiply credit by grade)
Total Science Units			Total Quality Points

Additional Academic Courses (3 years required)

Course Title	Credit	X Grade =	Quality Points (multiply credit by grade)
Total Additional Academic Units			Total Quality Points

Core Course GPA (14 Credits required)

Total Quality Points	Total Number of Credits	Core-Course GPA (Total Quality Points/Total Credits)

NCAA Initial-Eligibility Clearinghouse

The clearinghouse evaluates your academic record to determine if you are eligible to participate at a Division I or II college as a freshman student-athlete. (The clearinghouse is not the NCAA, but an organization that performs academic evaluations for the NCAA.)

Clearinghouse Contact Information

NCAA Initial-Eligibility Clearinghouse:
PO Box 4043
301 ACT Drive
Iowa City, IA 52243-4043

Package or overnight delivery:
301 ACT Drive
Iowa City, IA 52243-4043

Web address:
www.ncaaclearinghouse.net

Clearinghouse customer service
Representatives are available from 8 a.m. to 5 p.m., Central time, Monday through Friday.

U.S. callers (toll-free):
877.262.1492

International callers:
319.337.1492
Fax

319.337.1556

Clearinghouse Registration

Complete the Student Release Form

To register with the clearinghouse, you must complete the Student Release Form (SRF), after your junior year, online, and send the clearinghouse the registration fee ($50 for domestic and $75 for international students). This SRF does two things:

- It authorizes each high school you have attended to send the clearinghouse your transcript, test scores, proof of graduation and other necessary academic information.

- It authorizes the clearinghouse to send your academic information to all colleges that request your eligibility status.

Online registration: The only method is to register online. Go online to www.ncaaclearinghouse.net. Select **Prospective Student-Athletes** and click on **Domestic Student Release Form** or **Foreign Student Release Form.** Complete the SRF form online, and include your credit or debit card information to pay the fee. Then follow instructions to complete the transaction.

Print a copy of your completed registration form and both Copy 1 and Copy 2 of the transcript release form. Sign the transcript release forms, and give both to your high school counselor.

When completing the SRF sections, please follow the step-by-step instructions outlined below.

Section I: Student Information

Enter all information accurately, including your Social Security number (SSN) and date of birth. This information must match exactly other data the clearinghouse receives for you (such as high school transcripts and requests from colleges seeking your eligibility status). Be sure you provide an e-mail address that will be active even after you complete high school.

Section II: High School You Now Attend

Enter the name, address and code

number of the high school you now attend, along with your expected date of high school graduation. Get your high school code from your counselor or use the code look-up at www.ncaaclearinghouse.net. Click on Prospective Student-Athletes, then List of Approved Core Courses.

Section III: Schools You Previously Attended

If you have attended more than one school (including summer school) during grades nine, 10,11 or 12, complete Section III. List all schools you previously attended, starting with the most recent. Make sure to include all schools, whether or not you received grades or credits. If you attended ninth grade in a junior high school located in the same school system in which you later attended high school, do not list the ninth-grade school. If you need to list more schools than space allows, use a separate sheet of paper.

Special instructions for Web users: If you need to enter more than six high schools, contact the clearinghouse at 877.262.1492. Or, once you've registered with the clearinghouse, select **Prospective Student-Athletes,** then **Registered Student Login,** then add information for the additional schools on yourrecord.

Section IV: Personal Identification Number (PIN)

Create a personal identification number (PIN) of four digits (numbers between 0 and 9) that you can easily remember. Do not choose a PIN that might be easily guessed (like your birthday or street address). Record your PIN in the space provided below and keep it in a safe place.

PIN

Check your file status. Once you have submitted your SRF and PIN, you may check your status in one of two ways:

• Visit www.ncaaclearinghouse.net. On the home page, click on Prospective Student-Athletes, then Registered Student Login (enter your SSN and PIN).

• Call the clearinghouse customer service line at 877.262.1492.

If you have forgotten your PIN, fax or mail your new PIN choice to the clearinghouse, along with your name, address, SSN, date of birth and signature.

Section V: Clearinghouse Communication Method

The clearinghouse may communicate with you by e-mail or regular mail. This will include most correspondence and certification **reports. E-mail correspondence will require that you have submitted a valid e-mail address in Section I of your SRF.** You will need to indicate the option you prefer. We encourage you to select the e-mail option. E-mail will enable you to receive correspondence from the clearinghouse up to two weeks earlier than regular mail.

You may change your communication option or update your e-mail address at www.ncaaclearinghouse.net, or by writing or faxing the clearinghouse.

Section VI: Pay Your Fee (or submit fee waiver)

Your form will be eligible for processing only with payment of an application fee of $50 for domestic students or $75 for international students (or submission of a fee waiver if you have been granted a waiver). You must pay by debit or credit card.

You are eligible for a waiver of the registration fee only if you have already received a waiver of the ACT or SAT fee. Your SRF fee waiver section must then be completed by an authorized high school official and include the school seal. Your waiver may also be submitted online by an authorized high school official. If you have not yet been granted a fee waiver by ACT or SAT, you are not yet eligible for a waiver of the registration fee.

Section VII: Authorization Signature

Carefully examine the entire SRF to make sure you have completed it correctly, included your fee payment authorization and signed it. If you are younger than 18 years old, your parent or legal guardian also must sign.

You will be asked to verify your signature by checking a box to certify your identity. A similar check box and name field is also included for your parent or guardian, who must provide a signature if you are younger than 18.

Section VIII: SRF Completion by Your High School

Your high school will complete your registration by sending Copy 1, along with your high school transcript, to the clearinghouse. After graduation, but before your high school closes for the summer, your high school must send Copy 2 to the clearinghouse, along with a copy of your final transcript confirming your high school graduation.

Online registrants also will answer several questions about their amateur status and their past experiences in organized competition. It is important to answer these questions honestly to ensure that your amateur status can be determined.

Keep Track Of Your Courses, Units & Credits

Elsewhere in this guide are two tables to help you keep track of your completed core courses, units, grades and credits you received for them, plus your ongoing grade-point average. Generally, you will receive the same credit at the clearinghouse as you received from your high school. Examples are provided in the English and math sections of both worksheets:

1 trimester unit = 0.33 units
1 semester unit = 0.50 units
1 year = 1.0 unit

Keep Grade-Point Totals for Each Course

Determine your points earned for each course. Multiply the points for the grade by the amount of credit earned. Use the following scale unless your high school has a different scaleon file with the clearinghouse:

A - 4 quality points
B - 3 quality points
C - 2 quality points
D -1 quality point

Remember:The clearinghouse does not use plus or minus grades when figuring your core-course grade-point average. For example, grades of B+, B and B- will each be worth 3 quality points.

Examples of total quality point calculation:

- An A grade (4 points) for a trimester course (0.33 units): 4 points x 0.33 units = 1.32 total quality points

- An A grade (4 points) for a semester course (0.50 units): 4 points x 0.50 units = 2.00 total quality points

- An A grade (4 points) for a full-year course (1.00 units): 4 points x 1.00 units = 4.00 quality points

Calculate Your Overall Grade-Point Average

To calculate your estimated core-course grade-point average, divide the total number of points for all your core courses by the total number of core-course units you have completed.

Note: Your calculation helps you keep track of your grade-point average. The clearinghouse will calculate your official core-course grade-point average once it has received your final transcript.

Example of core-course grade-point average calculation:

- 42 quality points and 14 core-course units, 42/14=3.000 grade-point average

Compare Your Core-Course Grade-Point Average to Division I or II College Requirements

You can check to see if you will meet the academic requirements listed on pages 9 through 11 of this guide by comparing these requirements to the core courses you have completed or are currently taking, and the core-course grade-point average you have calculated based on those core courses.

- If you lack core-course units, which

is likely if you have not yet completed high school, make sure you enroll in and complete the courses you still need.

- If you complete more core-course units than you need, the clearinghouse will select the highest grades that meet initial-eligibility requirements to calculate your core-course grade-point average. Please note that it is still necessary to complete the required number of core-course units in each area (for example, two units of social science).

- Contact the clearinghouse staff toll-free at 877.262.1492 if you need help.

- Please talk to your parents or guardians and high school counselor if you have questions.

Check Your Status with the Clearinghouse

After you have registered with the clearinghouse, paid the fee and sent your transcript and SAT or ACT score(s), you may check your status.

- Online by following these simple steps:

  1. Go online to www.ncaaclearinghouse.net;

  2. Click on **Prospective Student-Athlete**;

  3. Click on **Registered Student Login**; and

  4. Input SSN and PIN.

- Call customer service at 877.262.1492 from 8 a.m. to 5 p.m. Central time Monday through Friday.

Clearinghouse Questions

Here are some questions you may still have after reviewing the previous section.

Q: Do I have to register with the clearinghouse?

A: Yes. If you want to participate in Division I or II athletics as a freshman, you must register with the clearinghouse. See the first section of this guide for amateurism and academic-eligibility standards that apply to you.

Q: Is clearinghouse certification the same as college admission?

A: No. Initial-eligibility certification from the clearinghouse does not guarantee your admission to any Division I or II college. You must apply for college admission separately. The clearinghouse only determines whether you meet NCAA requirements as a freshman student-athlete in a Division I or II college to be able to compete, practice and receive an athletics scholarship.

Q: May I send my academic information directly to the clearinghouse?

A: No. Transcripts must come to the clearinghouse by mail directly from the high school – not from you. Give Copies 1 and 2 of the transcript release form to the counselors at the high school you have attended.

Note: The clearinghouse will not accept faxed transcripts.

Q: Who may see my academic information?

A: The clearinghouse will provide eligibility information only to colleges that request your academic information. If no NCAA college requests your eligibility status, the clearinghouse may not process an eligibility-status certification.

Q: When is the best time for me to register with the clearinghouse?

A: Register after your junior year in high school. If you do not submit all required documents, your file will be incomplete and will be discarded after three years. After that time, you will need to re-register and pay your fee again.

Q: Is there a registration deadline?

A: No. However, you must be certified as a qualifier before you can receive an athletics scholarship or practice or compete at a Division I or II college during your first year of enrollment.

Q: What if I have attended more than one high school?

A: If you have attended multiple high schools since ninth grade, the clearinghouse must receive an official transcript for each school. Transcripts can come directly from each school or from the high school from which you are graduating. Check with your high school counselor.

Q: How may I arrange for the testing agency to send my scores directly to the clearinghouse?

A: When you register to take the ACT or the SAT, mark code "9999" so that the testing agency will send your scores to the clearinghouse. Test scores must be reported to the clearinghouse directly from SAT or ACT. The clearinghouse will not accept test scores reported on high school transcripts.

If you have questions:
Contact the clearinghouse staff toll-free at 877.262.1492; or check the clearinghouse web site: www.ncaaclearinghouse.net.

Questions to Ask as You Consider Colleges

You may want to ask your prospective college coaches the following questions as you consider colleges.

Athletics

1. **What positions will I play on your team?** It is not always obvious. Most coaches want to be flexible, so you might not receive a definite answer.

2. **What other players may be competing at the same position?** The response could give you an idea of when you can expect to be a starter.

3. **Will I be redshirted my first year?** The school's policy on redshirting may impact you both athletically and academically.

4. **What expectations do you have for training and conditioning?** This will reveal the institution's commitment to a training and conditioning program.

5. **How would you best describe your coaching style?** Every coach has a particular style that involves different motivational techniques and discipline. You need to know

if a coach's teaching style matches your learning style.

6. **When does the head coach's contract end? How long does the coach intend to stay?** The answer could be helpful. Do not make any assumptions about how long a coach will be at a school. If the coach leaves, does this change your mind about the school/program?

7. **What are preferred, invited and uninvited walk-on situations?** How many do you expect to compete? How many earn a scholarship? Situations vary from school to school.

8. **Who else are you recruiting for my position?** Coaches may consider other student-athletes for every position.

9. **Is medical insurance required for my participation?** Is it provided by the college? You may be required to provide proof of insurance.

10. **If I am seriously injured while competing, who is responsible for my medical expenses?** Different colleges have different policies.

11. **What happens if I want to transfer to another school?** You may not transfer without the permission of your current school's athletics administration. Ask how often coaches grant this privilege and ask for an example of a situation in which permission was not granted.

12. **What other factors should I consider when choosing a college?** Be realistic about your

athletics ability and the type of athletics experience you would enjoy. Some student-athletes want to be part of a particular athletics program, even if that means little or no playing time. Other considerations include coaching staff and style. Of course, the ideal is to choose a college or university that will provide you with both the educational and athletics opportunities you want.

Academics

1. **How good is the department in my major? How many students are in the department? What credentials do faculty members hold? What are graduates of the program doing after school?**

2. **What percentage of players on scholarship graduate?** The response will suggest the school's commitment to academics. You might want to ask two follow-up questions:

3. **What percentage of incoming students eventually graduate?** The response will suggest the school's commitment to academics. You might want to ask two follow-up questions:

    1) What percentage of incoming students eventually graduate?

    2) What is the current team's grade-point average?

3. **What academic support programs are available to student-athletes?** Look for a college that will help you become a better student.

4. **If I have a diagnosed and documented disability, what kind of academic services are available?** Special academic services may help you achieve your academic goals.

5. **How many credit hours should I take in season and out of season?** It is important to determine how many credit hours are required for your degree and what pace you will follow to obtain that degree.

6. **Are there restrictions in scheduling classes around practice?** NCAA rules prevent you from missing class for practice.

7. **Is summer school available? If I need to take summer school, will it be paid for by the college?** You may need to take summer school to meet academic and/or graduation requirements.

College Life

1. **What is a typical day for a student-athlete?** The answer will give you a good idea of how much time is spent in class, practice, study and travel. It also will give you a good indication of what coaches expect.

2. **What are the residence halls like?** The response should give you a hint of how comfortable you would be in your room, in study areas, in community bathrooms and at the laundry facilities. Also ask about the number of students in a room, co-ed dorms and the rules governing life in the residence halls.

3. **Must student-athletes live on campus?** If"yes,"ask about exceptions.

Financial Aid

1. **How much financial aid is available for both the academic year and summer school? What does your scholarship cover?**

2. **How long does my scholarship last?** Most people think a "full ride" is good for four years, but athletics financial aid is available on a one-year, renewable basis.

3. **What are my opportunities for employment while I am a student?** Find out if you can be employed in season, out of season or during vacation periods.

4. **Exactly how much will the athletics scholarship be? What will and will not be covered?** It is important to understand what college expenses your family is responsible for so you can arrange to pay those. Educational expenses can be paid with student loans and government grants, but it takes time to apply for these. Find out early so you can get something lined up.

5. **Am I eligible for additional financial aid? Are there any restrictions?** Sometimes a student-athlete cannot accept a certain type of scholarship because of NCAA limitations. If you will be receiving other scholarships, let the coach and financial aid officer know so they can determine if you may accept additional dollars.

6. **Who is financially responsible if I am injured while competing?** You need to understand your financial obligations if you suffer an injury while participating in athletics.

7. **Under what circumstances would my scholarship be reduced or canceled?** Coaches should be able to give you some idea of how players are evaluated from year to year and how these decisions are made. The institution may have a policy governing renewal of athletics aid. Ask if such a policy exists and read it.

8. **Are there academic criteria tied to maintaining the scholarship?** Some institutions add academic requirements to scholarships (e.g., minimum grade-point average).

9. **What scholarship money is available after eligibility is exhausted to help me complete my degree?** It may take longer than four years to complete a college degree program. Some colleges assist student-athletes financially as they complete their degrees. Ask how such aid is awarded. You may have to work with the team or in the athletics department to qualify for this aid.

10. **What scholarship money is available if I suffer an athletics career-ending injury?** Not every institution continues to provide an athletics scholarship to a student-athlete who can no longer compete because of a career-ending injury.

11. **Will my scholarship be maintained if there is a change in coaches?** A coach may not be able to answer this, but the athletics director may.

Information for Parents and Guardians

If you are the parent or legal guardian of a potential student-athlete, please pay special attention to the amateurism and academic eligibility and clearinghouse sections.

Amateurism and Academic Eligibility

If your child plans to compete, practice or receive an athletics scholarship at a Division I or II college, he or she must meet the eligibility requirements on pages 5-11 of this guide.

Clearinghouse Registration: Transcript and Test-Score Submissions

It is best for your son or daughter to register with the clearinghouse after completion of his or her junior year. Once registered, your son or daughter must ask the high school counselor or registrar to send his or her academic transcripts to the clearinghouse. ACT or SAT test score(s) also must be submitted to the clearinghouse. Your son or daughter must list the clearinghouse as a separate recipient of his or her ACT or SAT scores when he or she takes the test The test scores must come directly from SAT or ACT The clearinghouse will not accept test scores reported on the high school transcript.

The clearinghouse will typically review your son's or daughter's high school record and send a preliminary report to him or her, with notification of any missing requirements. A final report may be issued once your son's or daughter's high school submits a final transcript showing high school graduation. Please call the clearinghouse at 877.262.1492 if you have any questions.

How to Monitor Your Son's or Daughter's Eligibility

You may check the clearinghouse Web site at www.ncaaclearinghouse.net to make sure your son or daughter is taking approved courses. A list of core courses should have been submitted to the clearinghouse by your son's or daughter's high school. Check your son's or daughter's schedule before each year in high school to make certain that he or she is taking the required courses.

NCAA colleges may obtain information from the clearinghouse about your son's or daughter's status and progress only if his or her information is specifically requested by that college.

Financial Aid

If your son or daughter is academically eligible to participate in intercollegiate athletics and is accepted as a full-time student at a Division I or II school, he or she may receive athletics-based financial aid from the school. Division I or II financial aid may include tuition and fees, room and board, and books.

Division III institutions do not award financial aid based on athletics ability. A Division III college may award need-based or academically related financial aid.

A nonqualifier may receive only need-based financial aid (aid unrelated to athletics). A nonqualifier also may receive nonathletics aid from private sources or government programs (such as Pell grants).The college financial aid office can provide further information.

It is important to understand several points about athletics scholarships from Divisions I and II schools:

- All athletics scholarships awarded by NCAA institutions are limited to one year and are renewable annually. There is no such award as a four-year athletics scholarship.

- Athletics scholarships may be renewed annually for a maximum of five years within a six-year period of continuous college **attendance. Athletics aid may be canceled or reduced at the end of each year.**

- Athletics scholarships are awarded in a variety of amounts, ranging from full scholarships (including tuition, fees, room and board, and books) to very small scholarships (e.g., books only).

- The total amount of financial aid a student-athlete may receive and the total amount of athletics aid a team may receive can be limited. These limits can affect whether a student-athlete may accept additional financial aid from other sources. Ask financial aid officials at the college or university about any other financial aid your son or daughter might be eligible to receive, and how this aid impacts his or her athletics aid limit **You must inform the college financial aid office about scholarships received from all sources, such as local civic or booster clubs.**

An athletics scholarship is a tremendous benefit to most families, but you should also have a plan to pay for college costs that are not covered by a scholarship (such as travel between home and school). You should also consider how you will finance your son's or daughter's education if the athletics scholarship is reduced or canceled.

National Letter of Intent

The National Letter of Intent (NLI) is a voluntary program administered by the Collegiate Commissioners Association, not by the NCAA. By signing an NLI, your son or daughter agrees to attend the institution for one academic year. In exchange, that institution must provide athletics financial aid for one academic year.

Restrictions are contained in the NLI itself. Read them carefully. These restrictions may affect your son's or daughter's eligibility.

If you have questions about the National Letter of Intent visit the NLI Web site at www.national-letter.org or call 205.458.3013.

Agents

During high school, your son or daughter might be contacted by an agent who is interested in representing your son or daughter in contract negotiations or for commercial endorsements. Some agents may not identify themselves as agents, but may simply say they are interested in your son's or daughter's general welfare and athletics career. They may offer gifts or other benefits to you and your family.

NCAA rules do not prevent meetings or discussions with an agent. However, your son or daughter will jeopardize his or her eligibility in a sport if he or she agrees, verbally or in writing, to be represented by an agent while attending high school or college, regardless of whether the agreement becomes effective immediately or after his or her last season of college eligibility.

Your son or daughter will also endanger his or her college athletics eligibility if he or she, or your family, accepts benefits or gifts from an agent If an individual contacts your son or daughter about marketing his or her athletics ability, be careful. If you have concerns, contact your high school coach, director of athletics or the NCAA.

Recruiting

See summary of recruiting rules and terms.

Scouting/Recruiting Services

During high school, your family might be contacted by a scouting/ recruiting service. The NCAA does not sanction or endorse any of these services. Remember, a scouting/recruiting service cannot base its fee on the amount of a student's college scholarship. For example, it is impermissible for a recruiting/scouting service to offer a money-back guarantee. If you have any questions, please call the NCAA.

All-Star Contests – Basketball and Football

After your son or daughter completes high school eligibility, but before graduating, he or she may participate in two high school all-star football or basketball contests in each sport. If you have any questions, please call the NCAA.

Transfer Students

If your son or daughter transfers from a two-year or four-year college to an NCAA school, he or she must meet certain requirements before being eligible for practice, competition or financial aid at that college. Order the NCAA Transfer Guide by calling 888.388.9748 or download it from the NCAA Web site at www.NCAA.org. Call the NCAA if you have questions about transfer requirements.

Home School

Home-schooled students who plan to enroll in a Division I or Division II college must register with the clearinghouse, and must meet the same requirements as all other students.

After registering, the home-schooled student must send the following information to the clearinghouse:

- Standardized test score(s) must be on an official transcript from a traditional high school OR be sent directly from the testing agency;

- Transcript listing credits earned and grades (home-school transcript and any other official transcript from other high schools, community colleges, etc.);

- Proof of high school graduation;

- Evidence that home schooling was conducted in accordance with state law; and

- List of texts used throughout home schooling (including text titles, publisher and in which courses the text was used).

Details for High School Counselors and Athletics Administrators

Initial Eligibility

Why an Initial-Eligibility Clearinghouse?

NCAA colleges and institutions agree that it is important for all high school students to meet minimum academic standards to practice or compete in college athletics. The clearinghouse evaluates student courses, grades and test scores, to determine whether students meet NCAA minimum academic requirements. The NCAA membership is committed to academic success and graduation of its student-athletes.

NCAA Initial Eligibility and College Admission are Both Needed

Admission to an NCAA college or university is not the same as NCAA initial eligibility. Each institution decides which students to admit, based on its admissions criteria. Keep in mind that if a student-athlete meets NCAA initial-eligibility standards, that student still may not be admitted to the institution. Likewise, a student-athlete who gains admission to a college or university may not meet NCAA initial-eligibility standards.

Help Students Select Courses Grades Eight-12

If students take a rigorous college-preparatory curriculum, they are more likely to be successful. Help your students select courses that:

- Meet high school graduation requirements;

- Adequately prepare them for rigorous college work; and

- Meet NCAA initial-eligibility requirements.

Grade 11

- Encourage students to take the ACT or SAT or both.

- When registering for the test, students must should select the clearinghouse (code 9999) as a score recipient

- After completing grade 11, students

who plan to participate in college sports at a Division I or II college should register with the clearinghouse. The clearinghouse registration form is available online at www.ncaaclearinghouse.net. **The student should not register before the end of the junior year,** because the clearinghouse cannot process a student's certification until it has received a transcript that shows at least six semesters.

- After the student registers, send the student's transcript to the clearinghouse. The transcript may be sent by regular mail or overnight delivery. **The clearinghouse will not accept faxed transcripts.**

Grade 12

- After graduation, review the student's transcript carefully. Make sure the transcript is accurate before you mail it. Once the clearinghouse receives a final transcript, it will not use an amended final transcript. Remember, faxed transcripts are not acceptable.

- You may check online the list of your graduating high school students who have registered with the clearinghouse, at www. ncaaclearinghouse.net. On the home page, click on **High School Administration,** then on **High School Administrator Login.**

After logging in, click on Graduation List Reports.

Your High School's List of NCAA-Approved Core Courses

What is the list?

Each high school has its own list of NCAA-approved core courses. For the clearinghouse to use a course in a student's evaluation, the course on the transcript must be on your high school's list.

Where can I find my high school's list?

- Go to www.ncaaclearinghouse.net.

- Select **High School Administration.**

- Click on **List of Approved Core Courses.**

- Follow the prompts.

How can I update my high school's list?

- Go to www.ncaaclearinghouse.net.

- Select **High School Administration.**

- Click on **High School Administrator Login.**

- You will be required to input your high school six-digit code and your high school PIN. If your high school did not select a PIN, or you don't remember your high school PIN, see the login page for directions on how to obtain a PIN.

- After logging in, click on Submit Core-Course Modifications. From there, follow the prompts.

Why is this important?

- It is vital that your high school's list of approved core courses is kept up to date.

- This will ensure that your students are given appropriate credit by the clearinghouse for the courses they have taken.

- If you have not reviewed and updated

your list in the past year, the eligibility of your students may be affected.

- You must review your list at least once per year.

Core-Course Requirements

Core Courses

A core course is a recognized college-preparatory course taught by a qualified instructor. The course must fulfill a graduation requirement in the appropriate academic area at your high school. Remedial or basic-level courses are not core courses. Your high school's list of approved core courses, once submitted to the clearinghouse, will be available for anyone who wishes to view it on the clearinghouse Web site at www.ncaaclearinghouse.net.

Eighth-grade courses.

Eighth-grade courses do not satisfy initial-eligibility requirements.

Courses completed after high school graduation.

Courses taken after a student's eighth semester (fourth year) of high school will not satisfy Division I initial-eligibility requirements. In contrast, for Division II, all core courses completed after high school, but before initial full-time enrollment in college, may meet NCAA requirements.

Pass-fail grades.

Pass-fail grades may be used to satisfy initial-eligibility requirements, but will be given the high school's lowest passing grade.

Independent study and courses taught on the Internet.

ndependent-study and Internet courses may satisfy initial eligibility requirements if these courses meet core-course requirements. The instructor and student must have access to one another throughout the course, the student's work must be evaluated by appropriate authorities, and the course must appear on the student's high school transcript.

Credit-by-exam and vocational-school courses.

Credit-by -exam and vocational-school courses do not satisfy initial-eligibility requirements.

Duplicate course work.

If a student completes two classes that are considered to be duplicates (e.g., algebra I and algebra A/B), he or she will only receive core-course credit for one of the classes (typically the course with the higher grade).

Courses for students with disabilities.

Students with disabilities may use courses specifically designed for such students.The course must be comparable to a core course in the mainstream curriculum and must appear on your high school's list of approved core courses.

Submit courses for students with disabilities online at www.ncaaclearinghouse.net.

ACT and SAT Scores

Test-score requirements.

Students must achieve a required SAT or ACT score (See page 9 for the Division I grade-point average/ test-score that corresponds with their core-course grade-point average sliding

scale. See Division II requirements.). Students must take the tests under standard testing conditions on a national testing date before their initial, full-time enrollment at college. See the SAT Web site at www.collegeboard.com and the ACT Web site at www.act.org for national testing dates.

Calculation of highest score.

If a student has taken the ACT or SAT more than once, that student's highest score from each subtest or subsection will be used to determine his or her score, provided all scores are submitted to the clearinghouse.

NEW INFORMATION.

All SAT and ACT test scores must be reported directly from the testing agency to the clearinghouse. The clearinghouse will not accept test scores reported on the high school transcript.

Nonstandard tests.

Nonstandard tests are available for students with a diagnosed disability. Please visit the SAT or ACT Web sites for more information on registering for nonstandard tests.

Writing component.

The writing component of the ACT and SAT will not be used by the clearinghouse to determine initial eligibility.

NCAA Core-Course Grade-Point Average

Calculation of core-course grade-point average.

The NCAA core-course grade-point

average is calculated using only those core courses that are accepted and appear on the student's clearinghouse certification report.

Grade values.

The following grade values are used in determining a student's grade-point average:

> A - 4 quality points
> B - 3 quality points
> C - 2 quality points
> D - 1 quality point

If your high school uses plus and minus grades (such as A+ or B-), the plus or minus will not be used to calculate your core-course grade-point average.

Division I and II core-course grade-point average requirements.

Students must achieve a minimum core-course grade-point average to compete at the Division I or II level. The core-course grade-point average for Division I students must correspond with the ACT or SAT score based on the core-course grade-point average and test-score qualifier index on page 9 of this guide. In Division II, a student-athlete must have a minimum core-course grade-point average of at least 2.000.

International students.

If you have a student who has been educated in part at a international secondary school, it will be necessary to obtain transcripts from the international institution and send those transcripts and translations, along with the domestic transcript, to the clearinghouse. Students who graduate from high school in the United States will be evaluated under the same rules as all other domestic students.

Computer science reminder.

The NCAA no longer accepts computer science courses, unless those courses receive graduation credit in mathematics or natural/physical science, and appear as such on the high school's list of NCAA-approved core courses.

Home school.

Students who have been home schooled in whole or in part in grades nine through 12 must register with the clearinghouse. To determine what documents must be submitted to the clearinghouse, please visit the clearinghouse Web site at www.ncaaclearinghouse.net.

Clearinghouse Web Site Features

The following features are available to you as a high school administrator on the clearinghouse Web site.

- **Core-course modifications.** Submit revisions to your high school's core-course list.

- **Updates to clearinghouse contact data.** Update your school's contact name, graduation date, e-mail address, PIN or demographic data.

- **Graduation list reports.** Print a list of registered students from the current graduating class. After graduation, send the clearinghouse a final transcript with proof of graduation for each student on your roster.

- **Contact the clearinghouse.** E-mail inquiry to the clearinghouse is the easiest contact method.

- **Submit a fee waiver.** High school administrators may submit fee waiver verifications for eligible students only if the student received a fee waiver from SAT or ACT.

More information. For more information online, see the clearinghouse Web site at www.ncaaclearinghouse.net.

Recruiting Regulations

Introduction

College coaches must follow the rules outlined in this section. You are expected to follow these rules as well.

Recruiting Terms Contact.

A contact occurs any time a coach has any face-to-face contact with you or your parents off the college's campus and says more than hello. A contact also occurs if a coach has any contact with you or your parents at your high school or any location where you are competing or practicing.

Contact period.

During this time, a college coach may have in-person contact with you and/or your parents on or off the college's campus. The coach may also watch you play or visit your high school. You and your parents may visit a college campus and the coach may write and telephone you during this period.

Dead period.

The college coach may not have any in-person contact with you or your parents at any time in the dead period. The coach may write and telephone you or your parents during this time.

Evaluation.

An evaluation is an activity by a coach to evaluate your academic or athletics ability. This would include visiting your high school or watching you practice or compete.

Evaluation period.

The college coach may watch you play or visit your high school, but cannot have any in-person conversations with you or your parents off the college's campus. You and your parents can visit a college campus during this period. A coach may write and telephone you or your parents during this time.

Official visit. Any visit to a college campus by you and your parents paid for by the college. The college may pay the following expenses:

- Your transportation to and from the college;

- Room and meals (three per day) while you are visiting the college; and

- Reasonable entertainment expenses, including three complimentary admissions to a home athletics contest.

- Before a college may invite you on an official visit, you will have to provide the college with a copy of your high school transcript (Division I only) and SAT, ACT or PLAN score.

Prospective student-athlete.

You become a "prospective student-athlete"when:

- You start ninth-grade classes; or

- Before your ninth-grade year, a college gives you, your relatives or your friends any financial aid or other benefits that the college does not provide to students generally.

Quiet period.

The college coach may not have any in-person contact with you or your parents off the college's campus. The coach may not watch you play or visit your high school during this period. You and your parents may visit a college campus during this time. A coach may write or telephone you or your parents during this time.

Unofficial visit.

Any visit by you and your parents to a college campus paid for by you or your parents. The only expense you may receive from the college is three complimentary admissions to a home athletics contest. You may make as many unofficial visits as you like and may take those visits at any time. The only time you cannot talk with a coach during an unofficial visit is during a dead period.

Recruiting Calendars

To look at recruiting calendars for all sports, go to www.NCAA.org.

Amateurism
Clearinghouse

AMATEURISM ELIGIBILITY REQUIREMENTS

In response to the NCAA membership's concern about amateurism issues related to both international and domestic students, the clearinghouse will determine the amateurism eligibility of all freshmen and transfer prospective student-athletes for initial participation at an NCAA Division I or II member institution. In Division III, certification of an individual's amateurism status is completed by each institution, not the clearinghouse.

If you plan to participate in intercollegiate athletics at an NCAA Division I or II institution in fall 2007 or thereafter, you must have both your academic and amateurism status certified by the clearinghouse before representing the institution in competition.

Beginning in 2006 when you register with the clearinghouse, you will be asked about benefits and activities that might impact your status as an amateur. [Note: If you register with the clearinghouse before the amateurism-related questions are added to the system, you will be asked to return to the clearinghouse Web site and answer the following questions. You will not be charged a second registration fee for returning to answer these questions, but you will need the PIN number you created when you initially registered with the clearinghouse.] The information you provide about your athletics participation will be reviewed and a determination will be made as to whether your amateurism status should be certified or if a penalty should be assessed before certification. If a penalty is assessed, you will have an opportunity to appeal the decision.

The following precollegiate enrollment activities will be reviewed:

1. Contracts with a professional team.

2. Salary for participating in athletics.

3. Prize money.

4. Play with professionals.

5. Tryouts, practice or competition with a professional team.

6. Benefits from an agent or prospective agent.

7. Agreement to be represented by an agent.

8. Delayed initial full-time collegiate enrollment to participate in organized sports competition.

Additional information regarding NCAA amateurism rules is available on the NCAA's Web site (www.NCAA.org).

Questions About the Certification of Amateur Status

Who will be certified?

Every prospective student-athlete, both domestic and international, who is attending an NCAA Division I or II institution for the first time, must be certified by the clearinghouse. This includes prospective student-athletes who are transferring from any two-or-four year institutions (including international institutions) that are not members of NCAA Division I or II. Thus if an individual wants to participate in athletics at an NCAA Division I or II institution, the prospective student-athlete must register with the clearinghouse and submit the appropriate documentation to receive a certification decision.

Do transfer prospective student-athletes also have to register with the clearinghouse?

Every prospective student-athlete who is attending an NCAA Division I or II institution for the first time must be certified by the clearinghouse.

When should I register with the clearinghouse?

Register for the clearinghouse at the beginning of your junior year in high school. The athletics participation section should be updated regularly so that institutions recruiting you will have up-to-date information about you. Be sure to send your high school transcript to the clearinghouse after you have completed at least six semesters of high school coursework.

Is there a registration deadline?

No. However, prospective student-athletes must be certified as an amateur before they may receive an athletics scholarship or practice or compete at a Division I or II institution.

Is there an additional fee to register with the clearinghouse because of the additional questions on athletics participation?

No, there is only one fee to register for the clearinghouse, which covers both the academic and amateurism certification. In addition, there is no reduction of the fee if the prospect does not need an academic certification (e.g., has already served an academic year in residence at a collegiate institution).

May I receive a fee waiver?

Yes, you are eligible for a waiver of the initial-eligibility certification fee if you have already received a fee waiver (not a state voucher) for the ACT or SAT. If you have not been granted a fee waiver by ACT or SAT, then you will NOT be eligible for a waiver of the certification fee. If you are seeking a waiver of the certification fee, you should confirm your eligibility with your high school counselor. Your high school counselor MUST submit an electronic fee waiver confirmation before your registration may be processed.

How often can I update my information?

You cn update your information as often as you need until you request a final certification of your amateurism status. At that point you will no longer be able to update your amateurism information.

Can I receive different amateurism certifications for Division I and Division II?

Yes, Division 1 and II have different rules, so it is possible that your certification status may be different for each division.

Who can help me complete the amateurism registration process?

Anyone can assist you in completing the process. However, when you have completed the registration process, YOU will be the only person allowed to submit the information to the clearinghouse.

Will a paper copy of the amateurism form be available?

No, the registration form will only be available on the NCAA Initial Eligibility Clearinghouse Web site and must be completed online.

Questions Relating to the Athletics Participation Section of the Amateurism Clearinghouse

What if I enroll in an NCAA Division 1 or Division II institution and decide to participate in a sport other than one of the three I had listed on the amateurism clearinghouse registration form?

If you decide to participate in a sport other than the three you listed on the registration form, the institution in which you enroll will be responsible for certifying your amateurism status in that sport.

If I have been participating in events related to my sport for a significant period of time, what events do I need to list on the amateruism registration form?

You should include all events in which you participated, beginning with the ninth grade and thereafter.

Am I automatically ineligible if I violated the amateurism rules?

No, The clearinghouse will review your athletics participation history. If there are violations of the NCAA's amateurism rules, the clearinghouse may certify you with conditions, which must be fulfilled before you are eligible for competition. The conditions will be set based on which rule was violated and the severity of the violation. Such conditions may include repayment of money or sitting out of competition for specified number of games, or both. In some cases, the clearinghouse may determine that the violations are such that permanent ineligibility for competition is the appropriate penalty.

Can I appeal a certification decision regarding my amateur status?

Yes. The NCAA has an appeals process in place if you choose to appeal the certification decision. You will need to work with an NCAA institution since all appeals must be filed by a member institution.

OVERVIEW OF NCAA DIVISIONS I AND II PRES-ENROLLMENT AMATEURISM BYLAWS		
	Permissible in Division I? (Student-athletes first enrolling on or after August 1, 2002.)	Permissible in Division II? (Student-athletes first enrolling on or after August 1, 2001.)
Enters into a Contract with a Professional Team	No	Yes
Accepts Prize Money	Yes. If it is an open event, and does not exceed actual and necessary expenses.	Yes
Enters Draft	Yes	Yes
Accepts Salary	No	Yes
Receives Expenses from a Professional Team	No	Yes
Competes on a Team with Professionals	No	Yes
Tryouts with a Professional Team Before Initial Collegiate Enrollment	Yes	
May receive actual and necessary expenses for one visit (up to 48 hours) from each professional team. Self-financed tryouts may be for more than 48 hours.	Yes	
Receives Benefits from an Agent	No	No
Enters into Agreement with an Agent (oral or written)	No	No
Delays Full-Time Collegiate Enrollment and Participates in Organized Competition [If you are charged with season(s) of competition under this rule, you will also have to serve an academic year in residence at the NCAA institution.]	Tennis and Swimming & Diving: Have one year after high school graduation to enroll full time in a collegiate institution or will lose one season of intercollegiate competition for each calendar year during which you continue to participate in organized competition. All Other Sports: Any participation in organized sports competition during each 12-month period after the student's 21st birthday and prior to initial full-time enrollment in a collegiate institution shall count as one year of varsity competition.	All Sports: Must enroll at the next opportunity (excluding summer) immediately after the date that your high school class normally graduates (or the international equivalent) or you will use a season of intercollegiate competition for each calendar year or sports season (subsequent to that date) in which you have participated in organized competition.

The chart summarizes the Divisions I and II pre-enrollment rules. In order to assist you in understanding the rules, we have included the following definitions:

Definition of a Professional Team

In Divisions I and II, a team is considered professional if it declares itself to be professional or provides any player more than actual and necessary expenses for participation on the team.

Actual and necessary expenses are limited to the following:

(a) Meals and lodging directly tied to competition and practice held in preparation for competition;

(b) Transportation (i.e., expenses to and from practice and competition, cost of transportation between home and the training/practice site at the beginning and end of the season);

(c) Apparel, equipment and supplies related to participation on the team;

(d) Coaching and instruction, use of facilities and entry fees;

(e) Health insurance, medical treatment and physical therapy; and

(f) Other reasonable expenses (e.g., laundry money).

Definition of Organized Competition

In Division I, athletics competition is considered organized if any one of the following conditions exists:

(a) Competition is scheduled and publicized in advance;

(b) Official score is kept;

(c) Individual or team standings are maintained;

(d) Official timer or game officials are used;

(e) Admission is charged;

(f) Teams are regularly formed or team rosters are predetermined;

(g) Team uniforms are used;

(h) A team is privately or commercially sponsored; or

(i) The competition is either directly or indirectly sponsored, promoted or administered by an individual, an organization or any other agency.

In Division II, athletics competition is considered organized if any one of the following criteria are met:

(a) Any team or individual competition or training in which payment (including expenses) is provided to any participant;

(b) Any competition as a result of signing a contract for athletics participation;

(c) Any competition as a result of involvement in a professional draft;

(d) Any competition funded by a professional sports organization;

(e) Any competition funded by a representative of an institution's athletics interest that is not an open event; or

(f) Any practice with a professional athletics team (excluding a 48-hour tryout).

National
Letter of Intent

National Letter of Intent

The National Letter of Intent is a document administered by the Collegiate Commissioners Association, not the NCAA. The basic premise of the **National Letter of Intent (NLI)** program is to provide finality to the recruiting process. Most colleges that offer NCAA Division I and II athletic scholarships use the NLI. No Division III schools, junior colleges or preparatory schools are members of the NLI Program. However, many junior colleges do use a Letter of Intent, implemented either by the national association, their individual conferences, or even individual schools.

Signing the National Letter of Intent, in effect, ends the recruiting process. Member schools agree to not pursue a student-athlete once they sign a NLI with another institution. However, not all college coaches abide by this part of the agreement. After signing the NLI, the prospect is also ensured an athletic scholarship for one academic year. An institutional financial aid tender accompanies the NLI. If the student-athlete does not enroll at that school for a complete academic year, they could be penalized, with the possibility of losing up to two seasons of eligibility.

A student-athlete signs a National Letter of Intent with an institution and not with a specific coach. If the coach who recruited the student-athlete leaves that institution, the NLI is still valid and they are legally bound to the school for one full year. If a high school prospect signs a National Letter of Intent and then reneges on the contract and does not attend the school or does not satisfy the terms of the NLI Program, they lose two years of eligibility at the next NLI institution. But,

if the school they leave agrees to enter into a Qualified Release Agreement, the penalty is reduced from two years to one. The original school is not required to provide the student-athlete with the Qualified Release Agreement. However, many coaches will grant a release if a player wishes to leave. If a student-athlete signs it on a day outside of the early or late signing period, the NLI agreement is null and void.

There is a big difference between the National Letter of Intent and other Letters of Intent, such as those used by junior colleges. If a recruit signs an NLI and later decides to instead en-roll at a junior college, there are no penalties. The reverse is also true – if a student-athlete signs a Letter of In-tent at a junior college, they can change their mind and later sign a National Letter of Intent without hav-ing to sit out for a year. Only after sign-ing an NLI and then changing from one NCAA Division I or II institution to an-other would they lose a season or seasons of eligibility.

When a prospect signs a National Letter of Intent, **they are guaranteed athletic financial aid for one academic year at that institution** and nothing more. By attending the college with which the student-athlete signed for at least one academic year, and not just by completing one playing season at that school, they satisfy the NLI. A student-athlete only signs a National Letter of Intent one time, but they sign the financial tender every year.

Division I Men's Ice Hockey Signing Periods:

April 11 - August 1, 2007
November 14 - November 21, 2007
April 9 - August 1, 2008

Q. When I sign a National Letter of Intent what do I agree to do?

When you sign the National Letter of Intent you agree to attend for one academic year the institution listed on the Letter in exchange for that institution awarding athletics financial aid for one academic year.

Q. By signing a National Letter of Intent am I guaranteed that I will play on a team?

No. Signing a National Letter of Intent does not guarantee you playing time or a spot on the team. Rather, by signing a National Letter of Intent, the institution with which you sign agrees to provide you athletics financial aid for the academic year.

Q. How do I fulfill the National Letter of Intent?

You fulfill the National Letter of Intent in one of two ways: (1) By attending the institution with which you sign for at least one academic year; or, (2) By graduating from a junior college if you signed a National Letter of Intent while in high school or during your first year at the junior college.

Q. If I complete the playing season at the institution with which I sign, have I fulfilled the National Letter of Intent?

No. Completing a playing season alone does not fulfill the National Letter of Intent. You must complete the academic year in residence.

Q. Do I sign a National Letter of Intent every year?

No, while under NCAA rules you must be notified annually regarding whether your athletics aid has been renewed. You only sign an NLI when you first enroll in a four-year institution or if you are a four-two-four transfer student.

Q. Once I sign a National Letter of Intent may I be recruited by other institutions?

Once you sign a National Letter of Intent, all other participating conferences and institutions are obligated to cease recruiting you. Accordingly, you have an obligation to notify any recruiter from a National Letter of Intent institution of the fact you have signed a National Letter of Intent.

Q. Am I required to sign a National Letter of Intent?

No. You are not required to sign a National Letter of Intent but many student-athletes sign a National Letter of Intent because they want to create certainty in the recruiting process. Specifically, by signing a National Letter of Intent, you agree to attend the institution for one year in exchange for the institution's promise, in writing, to provide you athletics financial aid for the entire academic year. Simply, by signing a National Letter of Intent you are given an award including athletics aid for the upcoming academic year provided you are admitted to the institution and you are eligible for athletics aid under NCAA rules. Furthermore, by signing a National Letter of Intent you effectively end the recruiting process. Once you sign a National Letter of Intent, a recruiting ban goes into effect and you may no longer be recruited by any other National Letter of Intent school.

Q. If I sign with an NCAA Division I institution may I still sign with a Division II institution?

The true issue is not whether a school is a Division I or Division II institution but whether an institution is a member of the National Letter of Intent Program. With more than 500 participating institutions, the NLI program is truly national in scope. Briefly, all Division I institutions, with the exception of the Service Academies, half of the Patriot League and schools in the Ivy League, are members of the program, and all fully active Division II institutions participate in the program. No Division III institutions, NAIA schools, preparatory schools, junior colleges, or community colleges participate in the National Letter of Intent program.

Q. Who signs a National Letter of Intent?

Generally, only prospective student-athletes enrolling in a four-year institution for the first time sign a National Letter of Intent. Student-athletes who start their academic career at a four-year institution and then transfer to a junior college may also sign a National Letter of Intent if they plan on entering a second four-year institution.

Q. If I sign a National Letter of Intent in one sport may I sign a National Letter of Intent in a different sport?

No. You may only sign one valid National Letter of Intent annually. Furthermore, when you sign a National Letter of Intent, the Letter is signed with an institution and not with a coach or with a specific sports team.

Q. Is a National Letter of Intent considered valid if I submit it to the institution via facsimile?

Yes. When you sign the National Letter of Intent, you enter into an agreement with the institution. Faxing only represents the means by which you transmit the National Letter. Accordingly, a National Letter of Intent transmitted by facsimile is considered valid. In addition to sending the fax, you should also return the hard copy of the National Letter to the signing institution.

Q. If I do not live with a parent or legal guardian, is it necessary that a parent or legal guardian sign the National Letter of Intent?

If you are under the age of 21, your parent or legal guardian must sign the National Letter of Intent in order for it to be considered valid. If you are 21 years of age or older, it is not necessary for your parent or legal guardian to sign the document.

Q. If my parent or legal guardian lives at a different location than I do, is it permissible to sign a letter sent by facsimile?

While not ideal, it is permissible to obtain signatures on a National Letter of Intent via fax. From a procedural stand point, you should make three copies of the fax and sign the document in triplicate. Once signed, you should retain a copy for your records and return the other two copies to the institution. When the institution receives the copies, they will retain a copy and forward a copy to their conference office for filing.

Q. Can a coach be present when I sign the National Letter of Intent off-campus?

No. A coach cannot be present when you sign a National Letter of Intent off-campus. Pursuant to NCAA Bylaw 13.1.6.2, any in-person, off-campus contact made with a prospect for the purpose of signing a National Letter of Intent or attendance at activities related to the signing of the National Letter of Intent is prohibited.

Q. Is it permissible to receive a National Letter of Intent while on campus for an official visit?

Yes. While under the terms of the National Letter of Intent program a coach or institutional representative may not hand-deliver a National Letter of Intent off-campus, there is nothing that precludes you from receiving a National Letter of Intent while on campus for an official visit. Please remember that you may only sign a National Letter of Intent during a permissible signing period. Furthermore, signing a National Letter of Intent is a big commitment. Accordingly, it is strongly suggested that you consult your parent or legal guardian in this decision-making process.

Q. If I am going to walk-on to the team, may I sign a National Letter of Intent?

No. Under the terms of the National Letter of Intent program, an institution is strictly prohibited from allowing you to sign a National Letter of Intent if you are a non-scholarship walk-on. In order for a National Letter of Intent to be considered valid, it must be accompanied by an athletics financial aid award letter, which lists the terms and conditions of the award, including the amount and duration of the financial aid. Simply put, there must be an athletics aid award including athletics aid for a National Letter of Intent to be valid.

Q. May I sign a National Letter of Intent before I am certified as eligible by the NCAA Clearinghouse?

Yes. You may sign a National Letter of Intent before you receive your final certification determination from the Clearinghouse. In fact, it is very common for a prospect to sign a National Letter of Intent during the course of his/her senior year. When you sign a National Letter of Intent you agree to submit the necessary information and documents to the NCAA Clearinghouse. If you are classified by the NCAA Clearinghouse as either a Qualifier or Partial Qualifier, the National Letter of Intent is considered valid. If by the institution's opening day of classes for the fall term you are classified as a nonqualifier pursuant to NCAA Bylaw 14.3, your National Letter of Intent is rendered null and void.

Q. When is the permissible time period for signing a National Letter of Intent?

You may sign a National Letter of Intent only during the designated signing period. If you sign a National Letter of Intent outside the appropriate signing period, the National Letter of Intent shall be considered null and void. Presuming you are within the permissible signing period, you and your parent or legal guardian must sign the NLI within 14 days of issuance.

Q. Where is my signed National Letter of Intent filed? Who is responsible for filing the document?

You should sign your National Letter of Intent in triplicate. Once you have signed the Letter in triplicate, you should retain one copy of the signed

Letter for your records. You should then send the remaining two documents to the institution listed on the Letter. When the institution receives your Letters, it will keep one copy and forward one copy to its conference office. The institution must file your NLI with its conference office within 21 days after the date of final signature. If this filing deadline is not met, the Letter will be invalid. Once the conference office receives your Letter, it will notify the National Letter of Intent office via mail or computer of the fact you have signed a National Letter of Intent.

Q. Is a National Letter of Intent binding if the coach of my sport leaves the institution to take another position?

Yes. The National Letter of Intent you signed with an institution is valid if the coach that recruited you leaves the institution with which you signed. When you sign a National Letter of Intent you sign with an institution and not with a coach or a specific team.

Q. Do I sign a National Letter of Intent if I transfer to another four-year institution?

No. A student-athlete transferring from one four-year institution to another four-year institution may not sign a National Letter of Intent.

Q. What happens if I change my mind and do not want to attend the institution with which I sign and want to attend another National Letter of Intent institution?

If you do not attend the institution with which you signed, or if you do not fulfill the terms of the National Letter of Intent, the basic penalty is that you lose two years of eligibility and must serve two years in residence at your next National Letter of Intent institution.

Q. Can the Basic Penalty, which calls for the loss of two years of eligibility and requires that I serve two years in residence at the next National Letter of Intent Institution, be reduced?

Yes. The Basic Penalty under the National Letter of Intent agreement may be reduced by entering into a Qualified Release Agreement with the signing institution. By entering into a Qualified Release Agreement, the institution and the student-athlete mutually agree to release each other from any commitment and liability related to signing a National Letter of Intent. Pursuant to the Qualified Release Agreement, you may not represent a second National Letter of Intent institution in any sport during your first year of residence and you will be charged with the loss of one season of eligibility in all sports

Q. Who executes the Qualified Release Agreement?

The Qualified Release Agreement must be executed by the Director of Athletics (or a designee), your parent or legal guardian and yourself. Your coach does not sign the Qualified Release Agreement. Furthermore, your coach does not have the authority to release you from your National Letter of Intent obligations.

Q. Is the Qualified Release Agreement the same as the One-Time Transfer Exception as set forth in NCAA Bylaw 14.5.5.2.10?

No. The Qualified Release Agreement and the NCAA One-Time Transfer Exception are two different policies. Pursuant to NCAA Bylaw 14.5.5.2.10 (One-Time Transfer Exception), a student-athlete who has not previously transferred from a four-year institution and does not participate in Division I men's ice hockey, may transfer and not have to serve a year in residence under NCAA rules. To use the One-Time Transfer Exception, the student-athlete must have been in good academic standing and fulfilled progress toward degree requirements at the previous institution. Furthermore, the student-athlete must have been eligible at the previous institution and the previous institution must have no objection to the student being granted an exception to the NCAA residence requirement. The fact that a student is eligible for the NCAA One-Time Transfer Exception does not mean a student-athlete has received a Qualified Release Agreement pursuant to the National Letter of Intent program, nor does the One-Time Transfer Exception eliminate the penalty provisions of the National Letter of Intent.

Q. Is an institution required to grant a Qualified Release Agreement if requested?

No. Just as the National Letter of Intent is a voluntary agreement, the Qualified Release Agreement is voluntary in nature. An institution is not required to provide you with a Qualified Release Agreement. If an institution denies your request for a Qualified Release Agreement, you may petition the National Letter of Intent Steering Committee for such an agreement. In order to petition the NLI Steering Committee, you must document in writing that you requested a Qualified Release Agreement from the Director of Athletics of the signing institution and that your request was denied. Once proper documentation has been submitted, the NLI Steering Committee will consider your request. Petitions to the NLI Steering Committee should be sent to the NLI Program, 2201 Richard Arrington, Jr. Blvd. N., Birmingham, Alabama 35203.

Q. If I do not satisfy my National Letter of Intent agreement, may I practice or receive athletics aid at another National Letter of Intent institution?

Yes. Signing a National Letter of Intent does not impact your ability to practice or receive athletics aid at another National Letter of Intent institution. The Basic Penalty under the National Letter of Intent program is the loss of two years of eligibility in all sports and the requirement of two years in residence at the next National Letter of Intent institution.

Q. If I fail to honor my NLI commitment and do not attend the institution with which I signed, may another NLI member institution recruit me?

Yes, but only if you have received a Qualified Release Agreement from the institution with which you signed, or the institution that desires to recruit you is granted permission to do so by the institution with which you signed. (If permission to contact is granted, it is not limited to certain institutions, but to all institutions seeking to recruit the student-athlete.)

Q. If my request for a Qualified Release Agreement is denied, is the institution obligated to provide me an opportunity for a hearing as to why the request was denied?

No.

Q. May a mid-year enrollee sign a National Letter of Intent?

Under the terms of the National Letter of Intent program, a written award of athletics aid for the entire academic year must accompany a National Letter of Intent. Accordingly, the National Letter of Intent program does not allow for prospective student-athletes enrolling at midyear to sign a National Letter of Intent. The National Letter of Intent program has created an exception to this general rule for midyear junior college transfer students in the sport of football. A midyear junior college transfer student in the sport of football may sign a National Letter of Intent during the designated signing period.

Q. If I sign a letter of intent with a junior college may I sign a National Letter of Intent?

Yes. You may sign a National Letter of Intent if you have already signed a letter of intent with a junior college or an NAIA school. The National Letter of Intent program is a voluntary program with over more than participating institutions, all of which are members of either NCAA Division I or II. By entering the National Letter of Intent program, participating institutions agree to honor one another's commitments. Make certain you understand the difference between a NAIA or junior college letter and the National Letter of Intent before you sign more than one letter.

Q. If I sign a National Letter of Intent, may I attend a junior college or a school that does not participate in the NLI program without incurring any National Letter of Intent penalties?

If you sign a National Letter of Intent, you may attend any institution that does not belong to the National Letter of Intent program without incurring any National Letter of Intent penalties while at the non-participating school. Please note, though, if you ever transfer to an institution participating in the National Letter of Intent program, the National Letter of Intent penalties would be applied at your next National Letter of Intent institution.

Q. If I call the NCAA can I get more information about the National Letter of Intent?

No. The National Letter of Intent program is not administered by the NCAA. Rather, the National Letter of Intent program is administered by the Collegiate Commissioners Association (CCA). The CCA was formed in 1939 to promote uniformity in football officiating and mechanics and to standardize interpretations of playing rules throughout the nation. Over the years the CCA has grown, but its mission has remained consistent over time, promoting uniformity and standard treatment of issues. By promoting uniform treatment of prospective student-athletes, the National Letter of Intent program reduces and limits recruiting pressure on student-athletes and promotes and preserves the amateur nature of collegiate athletics. Conferences, on behalf of their member institutions, join the National Letter of Intent program and are knowledgeable about National Letter of Intent rules and regulations. The Southeastern Conference handles the daily administrative duties of the National Letter of Intent program on behalf of the CCA.

Q. Where can I find more information about the National Letter of Intent?

While certainly this web site is an excellent place to find information regarding the National Letter of Intent, the best way to learn about the document is to read the actual letter. All the terms of the National Letter of Intent have been published on the document so you can have time to read and understand the terms of the agreement. Signing a National Letter of Intent is a very important step and you owe it to yourself to read the document and to review it with your parent or legal guardian. When you sign a National Letter of Intent you are agreeing to attend the institution with which you sign for one academic year. Accordingly, you should be certain about your choice of institution before you sign a National Letter of Intent.

New England Preparatory School Athletic Council

2006 - 2007 Directory

- Listings of 165 New England private preparatory schools, their athletic directors, coaches, headmasters, enrollment, phone numbers and more.

- Also lists New England championship teams by sport and NEPSAC policies and regulations, etc.

- The 2006 - 2007 directories are available for $20.

Send order to:

Kate Turner - NEPSAC
Brewster Academy
80 Academy Drive
Wolfeboro, NH 03894
nepsac_kateturner@brewsteracademy.org
Make check payable to: NEPSAC

NCAA
Academic
Progress

NCAA APR PROGRESS REPORT

By Tom Keegan

A new consideration for prospective student-athletes is the NCAA Academic Progress Rate and the resulting penalties for underachieving college teams. It is clear that the trend in college athletics is toward requiring student-athletes to be students first. College teams that don't perform will be sanctioned. Sanctioning will result in reduced scholarships and reduced practice time, etc.

It would appear that colleges will become even less likely to accept the student-athlete with a questionable academic history and / or future. Prospective student-athletes will want to select programs that will have their full complement of scholarships and no practice restrictions.

The NCAA released its Academic Progress Rate (APR) data for 2005-06, which now gives a three-year picture of each school's progress.

Alaska-Anchorage is the only Division I men's ice hockey program that is in jeopardy of being sanctioned, although it is temporarily exempted because the APR data is not yet complete. RIT is also below the threshold, but its data is only based upon one year, and thus is also temporarily exempted.

The APR is meant to be a gauge for academic progress for each team at each school. Generally, if a player is progressing 20 percent towards graduation each year over a five-year period, they are considered in good standing.

A score of 925 represents the minimum to be considered in good standing. Scores below that subject an athletic program to sanctions. However, the APR is meant to be a four-year rolling average, and with only three years of data, some programs that fall below 925 are given temporary exemptions because of the smaller sample size.

The average of all Division I men's ice hockey teams is 970, which is better than any men's sport except fencing. The women's ice hockey average is 977. The men's basketball average is 927, and football is 931.

A complete list of Division I men's teams is below:

US Air Force Academy	988
Alabama Huntsville, University of	946
Alaska Anchorage, U of	(+) 919
Alaska-Fairbanks, University of	949
American International College	994
US Military Academy	969
Bemjidi State University	973
Bentley College	995
Boston College	986
Boston University	970
Bowling Green State University	983
Brown University	997
Canisius College	961
Clarkson University	972
Colorado College	985
Connecticut College	950
Cornell University	983
Dartmouth College	990
Ferris State University	970
Harvard University	1000
Holy Cross, College of the	1000
Lake Superior State University	945
Maine, University of	959
Massachusetts Lowell, U of	959
Massachusetts Amherst, U of	951
Mercyhurst College	950
Merrimack College	957

Miami University	980	St. Cloud State University	943
Michigan Ann Arbor, University of	984	St. Lawrence University	975
Michigan State University	986	Union College	988
Minnesota Crookston, U of	954	Vermont, University of	968
Minnesota Duluth, University of	945	Wisconsin	969
Minnesota State U Mankato	942	Wayne State University	966
Nebraska Omaha, University of	941	Western Michigan University	974
New Hampshire, University of	961	Yale University	1000
Niagara University	965		
Northeastern University	977		
North Dakota, University of	930		
Northern Michigan University	982		
Notre Dame, University of	996		
Ohio State University	965		
Princeton University	984		
Providence College	966		
Quinnipiac College	972		
Rensselaer Polytecnic Institute	1000		
Robert Morris College (2 years)	945		
Rochester Inst of Tech (1 year)	913		
Sacred Heart University	1000		

+ APR that does not subject the team to contemporaneous penalties due to the squad-size adjustment. The "upper confidence boundary" of a team's APR must be below 925 for that team to be subject to contemporaneous penalties. Squad-size adjustments will be eliminated when the fourth year of APR data is collected, provided the team's multiyear cohort includes 30 or more student-athletes.

Other

AGENTS

During high school, you might be contacted by a player agent. A player-- agent may want to represent you in contract negotiations or for commercial endorsements if you show the potential to be a professional athlete. Agents may contact you during your high school years to gain an advantage over other individuals who may wish to represent you when your college eligibility expires. Many times, these individuals will not represent themselves as agents, but rather as someone interested in your overall welfare and athletics career. These individuals also may try to give gifts or benefits to you and your family.

NCAA rules don't prohibit meetings or discussions with an agent. However, you jeopardize your college eligibility in a sport if you agree (orally or in writing) to be represented by an agent while in high school or college, regardless of whether the agreement becomes effective immediately or after your last season of college eligibility. Also, receiving any benefits or gifts by you, your family or friends from a player agent would jeopardize your college eligibility.

If an individual contacts you about marketing your athletics ability, please be careful. If you have concerns about a player agent, contact your high-school coach, director of athletics or the NCAA national office for assistance.

DRUG TESTING

NCAA institutions are dedicated to the ideal of fair and equitable competition as well as the protection of the health and safety of the student athletes. The NCAA drug testing program was created so that no participant has an artificially induced advantage, that no participant might be pressured to use chemical substances to remain competitive and to safeguard the health and safety of participants.

The NCAA has a list of banned drugs. This list can be found on the NCAA Web page at www.ncaa.org/sportssciences/drugtesting/. The NCAA has issued warnings about the use of dietary supplement products. Because of the lack of regulation in the production, distribution and sale of these products, the purity is unknown; some may contain banned substances. Students should check with coaches, physicians and the Dietary Supplement Resource Exchange Center (877.202.0769 toll free) before taking any of these products. Some supplements contain substances such as ephedrine (ma huang), DHEA, androstenedione and norandrostenedione, which are banned by the NCAA but are sold in health food stores.

Each academic year in Divisions I and II sports in which the NCAA conducts year round drug testing (currently Divisions I and II football and Division I track and field), you must sign a drug testing consent form when you report for practice or before the Monday of your college's fourth week of classes, whichever occurs earlier. In all other Division I and II sports and in Division III each academic year, you must sign a drug testing consent form before you compete. Drug testing occurs randomly on a year round basis in Divisions I and II football and track and field. Drug testing also is conducted at NCAA championships and football bowl games. If you test positive, you will lose a season of competition in all sports if the season of competition has not yet started. If the season of competition has started, you will lose one full season of competition in all sports (i.e., remaining contests in the current season and contests in the following season up to the time that you were declared ineligible during the previous year). In addition, many colleges have their own drug use policies that may affect your participation.

Further, the use of tobacco products is prohibited for coaches, game officials and student athletes in all sports during practice and competition. A student athlete who uses tobacco products during practice or competition automatically is disqualified for the remainder of that practice or game.

GRADUATION RATES

To help you in selecting a college, the NCAA national office annually makes available Divisions I, II and III admissions and graduation rate information. To make the information easy to get, the Division I or II college recruiting you must provide its graduation rate information to you, as well as your parents, at the earlier of the following opportunities: (1) upon request by you or your parents, or (2) after the school's first arranged in person meeting with you (or your parents) but not later than the day before you sign a National Letter of Intent or an offer of admission and/or financial aid.

In addition, the NCAA national office makes graduation rate information available annually to your high school.

WHAT TO ASK

The following questions and information were developed by the NCAA Student Athlete Advisory Committee. The committee urges prospective student athletes to ask these types of questions during their recruitment.

Athletics

What positions will I play on your team?

• It's not always obvious.

• Most coaches want to be flexible so that you are not disappointed.

Describe the other players competing at the same position.

• If there is a former high-school all-American at that position, you may want to take that into consideration.

• This will give you clues as to what year you might be a starter.

Can I " redshirt " my first year?

• Find out how common it is to redshirt and how that will affect graduation.

• Does the school redshirt you if you are injured?

What are the physical requirements each year?

• Philosophies of strength and conditioning vary by institution.

• You may be required to maintain a certain weight.

How would you best describe your coaching style?

• Every coach has a particular style that involves different motivational techniques and discipline.

• You need to know if a coach's teaching style does not match your learning style.

What is the game plan?

• For team sports, find out what kind of offense and defense is employed.

• For individual sports, find out how you are seeded and how to qualify for conference and national championships

When does the coach's contract end?

• Don't make any assumptions about how long a coach will be at a school.

• If the coach is losing and the contract ends in two years, you may have a new coach.

Describe the preferred, invited and uninvited walk-on situation. How many make it, compete and earn a scholarship?

• Different teams treat walk-ons differently.

Academics

How good is the department in my major?

• Smaller colleges can have very highly rated departments.

- A team's reputation is only one variable to consider.

What percentage of players on scholarship graduate in four years?

- This will tell you about the quality of their commitment to academics.

- The team's grade point average also is a good indicator of the coach's commitment to academics.

College Life

Describe the typical class size.

- At larger schools, classes are likely to be larger and taught by teaching assistants.

- Average class size is important to the amount of attention you receive.

Describe in detail your academic support program. For example: Study hall requirements, tutor availability, staff, class load, faculty cooperation.

- This is imperative for marginal students.

- Find a college that will take the 3.000 students and help them get a 3.500 GPA.

Describe the typical day for a student athlete.

- This will give you a good indication of how much time is spent in class practice, studying and traveling.
- It also will give you a good indication of what coaches expect.

What are the residence halls like?

- Make sure you would feel comfortable in study areas, community bath-rooms and laundry facilities.

- Number of students in a room and coed dorms are other variables to consider.

Will I be required to live on campus throughout my athletics participation?

- If the answer is yes, ask whether there are exceptions.

- Apartment living may be better than dorm living.

Financial Aid

How much financial aid is available for summer school?

- There is no guarantee. Get a firm commitment.

- You may need to lighten your normal load and go to summer school in order to graduate in four years. You can take graduate courses and maintain your eligibility.

What are the details of financial aid at your institution?

- What does my scholarship cover?

- What can I receive in addition to the scholarship and how do I get more aid?

How long does my scholarship last?

- Most people think a "full ride" is good for four years.

• Financial aid is available on a one year renewable basis.

If I'm injured, what happens to my financial aid?

• A grant-in-aid is not guaranteed past a one year period even for injuries.

• It is important to know if a school has a commitment to assist student-athletes for more than a year after they have been injured

What are my opportunities for employment while I'm a student?

• Find out if you can be employed in season, out of season or during vacation periods.

ADDITIONAL COMMENTS

Scouting Services

- During high school, you might be contacted by a scouting service. NCAA rules prohibit scouting services from receiving payment based on the amount of your college scholarship. The NCAA does not sanction or endorse any scouting service. Therefore, attempt to determine whether the scouting service meets NCAA requirements.

All Star Contests

- After your high school eligibility is completed and before graduation, you can participate in two high school all star football or basketball contests in each sport.

Transfer Students

- If you transfer from a two year or four year college to an NCAA school, you must satisfy certain requirements before being eligible to participate in athletics at that college. Call the NCAA office if you have questions about transfer requirements. You can order free of charge the NCAA Student Athlete Transfer Guide by calling 800.638.3731.

Student Athlete Statement

- Each academic year, you must sign a statement about your eligibility, recruitment, financial aid and amateur status under NCAA rules. Don't jeopardize your eligibility by violating NCAA rules.

Conference Regulations

- Conferences may have additional regulations about recruiting, eligibility and financial aid. Ask your recruiter or the conference office about these rules.

Reporting Rules Violations

- If you think you have been improperly or unfairly recruited, notify the conference office or the NCAA. Knowingly furnishing the NCAA or your college false or misleading information about your involvement or knowledge of a rules violation will make you ineligible.

Video Conferences

- The NCAA produces a fall and spring video conference each year. The video conferences are intended to help high school athletes, their parents and athletics administrators understand NCAA initial eligibility services for students with disabilities and the recruiting process. Please check the NCAA Web site at www.ncaa.org for additional information

NCAA eligibility rules are sometimes complex as they apply to certain students. This guide should not be relied upon exclusively. Contact the NCAA office or appropriate conference office for proper interpretations in specific cases. Your inquiries should be addressed to the NCAA membership services staff at the address on the contents page of this brochure.

How Do You
Get Noticed

HOW DO YOU GET NOTICED?

By Tom Keegan

One of the most commonly asked questions relates to players exposure. Coaches, parents and players all want to know how to increase players exposure to college coaches at all levels.

A common response to the question is, "Don't worry, if someone is good enough to play NCAA Division I, the coaches will find them." While this certainly may occur, I don't subscribe to this theory 100%.

There are over 6,000 midget, junior and high school teams in North America. If each team plays 40 games, there are 120,000 games in a typical season. Assuming 60 NCAA Division I programs and one scout on the road per team, each scout would have to see 2,000 games for each game to be scouted. Just to have each team scouted one time during the season each scout would have to see over 50 games.

These are only averages. Programs that have historically been successful training grounds for NCAA Division I will attract significantly more attention. So if you see twenty college scouts at a Prep School game featuring Shattuck-St. Mary's and Culver or Avon Old Farms and Berkshire, a USHL game between Omaha and Lincoln or an NAHL game between St. Louis and Springfield, you can assume that many other programs will get no attention.

According to the college coaches we surveyed the most heavily scouted leagues in the United States were:

TIER I
United States Hockey League

TIER II JUNIOR A
North American Hockey League

TIER III JUNIOR A
Eastern Junior Hockey League
Atlantic Junior Hockey League

TIER III JUNIOR B
Empire Junior Hockey League
Metropolitan Junior Hockey League
Minnesota Junior Hockey League

HIGH SCHOOLS / PREP SCHOOLS
Connecticut Prep Schools
Maine Prep Schools
Massachusetts High Schools
Massachusetts Prep Schools
Minnesota High Schools
Minnesota Prep Schools
New Hampshire Prep Schools
New York High Schools
New York Prep Schools
North Dakota High Schools
Ohio High Schools
Pennsylvania High Schools
Rhode Island High Schools
Rhode Island Prep Schools
Vermont Prep Schools
Wisconsin High Schools

It is likely that 80% to 90% of the scouting will be devoted to just 10% of the 6,000 programs. So what are you to do if you don't play for one of the 600 top programs? Give up? No, but you do need to find other avenues to get the exposure you require.

Additional options are available in spring and summer, after the traditional hockey season. Several organizations conduct College Evaluation/Exposure Camps throughout North America.

These camps are typically weekend programs which run Friday through Sunday but some are week long camps and some run for a number of weeks. Some of these camps are by invitation only and don't advertise, while others actually have tryouts to get into the camp. Most of these evaluation camps feature scrimmages or games to evaluate the players.

Quality summer exposure opportunities available in the United States are pretty limited with the notable exception of USA Hockey Select Tryouts.

For additional summer exposure opportunities we suggest that you visit www.hockeycenter.com.

OPPORTUNITIES IN HOCKEY SEMINAR

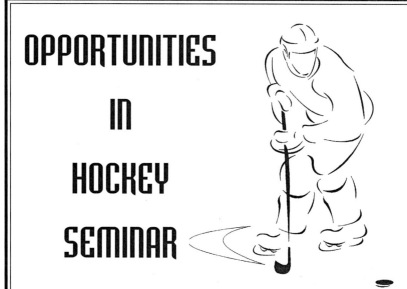

Since 1990 The Hockey Guides have been the ultimate reference for hockey players, parents, counselors, educational consultants, coaches and administrators as they investigate college hockey opportunities by providing valuable resource information, support and seminars.

Now bring this proven educational program to your association, league, team or school by scheduling an Opportunities In Hockey seminar at your location. Our program is designed to prepare student-athletes academically, athletically and mentally for college hockey and the recruiting process. This seminar will provide valuable information to assist your players and their parents evaluate their options and make informed decisions in the college investigation and selection process.

For additional information, or to schedule a seminar, please contact Tom Keegan at The Hockey Guides.

For further information please contact:
The Hockey Guides
PO Box 1050 • Flagler Beach, FL 32136
386.439.2250
Email agp@flaglernet.com

Coach
Surveys

COACH SURVEYS

By Tom Keegan

During the sixteen years that we have published The College Hockey Guide we have often been asked the same questions by prospective college players and their parents. Rather than provide our interpretations of the answers to these frequently asked questions we conducted a survey of college hockey coaches at all levels.

The following section provides reponses from a cross section of NCAA I and III, ACHA I and NJCAA head and assistant coaches. As you review this section you will find that the responses are pretty consistent.

These coaches provide a list of leagues and tournaments which they scout and also recommend specific leagues to assist in player development.

This should effectively answer the two questions we are asked most often:

Where will a player best develop the skills to play college hockey?

and

Where will a prospective college player have the best chance for exposure?

You may get the same advice from a recruiter for a junior team or from the director of an exposure camp or an exposure tournament. They may have a great situation available for you, but they also have a vested interest in promoting their program. You need to explore the options and do your own research.

The surveys also review both the good qualities that successful student-athletes bring to the college program and the qualities absent in players that fail. If all of the coach responses talk about character, academic success and hard work then work on developing the traits that the coaches desire. If lack of organization, effective time-management and study skills are major causes for failure to succeed, work on developing better skills in these areas.

The great majority of college hockey coaches are more than willing to help prospective student-athletes succeed. These surveys answer some general questions that should assist all players that aspire to play at the college level. If you have more specific questions you should communicate with college coaches and ask for their advice. If they have seen you play they can certainly be more specific in suggesting playing opportunities to develop your skills.

—— Concordia College ——

Steve Baumgartner, Head Coach

Which leagues do you regularly "scout" to locate prospective players for your college?
SJHL; USHL; Minnesota High Schools; North Dakota High School; Junior College Teams.

What specific events do you "scout" to locate prospective players for your college?
Minnesota State High School tournament; North Dakota State High School tournament; USHL Championships.

What developmental level and/or league do you recommend to prospective college players?
USHL.

What qualities do you look for in prospects during the recruiting process?
Good students, good skills.

What qualities are lacking in most of the prospects which you reject?
Probably skill level of the players from high school and maturity.

What is the most difficult part of recruiting?
Convincing people to come and then waiting for financial aid to come in before they can make a final decision.

What traits do your successful student athletes bring to the program?
Strong work ethic, will to succeed and to influence other people.

What advice can you offer to high school "age" hockey players that aspire to play at the college level?
Work hard in the off-season to become a better player. Clinics, summer leagues and specialty camps are all over the place. Bigger, faster, stronger is still highly looked at. Take care of your academics. Be a champion in the classroom as well as the ice!!

—— Lake Forest College ——

Tony Fritz, Head Coach

Which leagues do you regularly "scout" to locate prospective players for your college?
OHL -Tier II Jr. A; NAHL; AWHL; USHL; Eastern Prep School; Midwest Jr. B.

What specific events do you "scout" to locate prospective players for your college?
Prep School Christmas tournaments; HNIB; Newmarket Jr. A tournament; Buc Bowl USHL; Chicago Showcase; NAHL - Compuware.

What developmental level and/or league do you recommend to prospective college players?
PG Prep Schools; Triple A Midget; Jr. A - Tier II.

What qualities do you look for in prospects during the recruiting process?
Academic ability - Can he get into school? Skating ability, speed, strength, vision of the ice, hands, understanding of the game.

What qualities are lacking in most of the prospects which you reject?
Hands - passing ability, creativity, seeing the ice, understanding the game.

What is the most difficult part of recruiting?
The repetition; endless hours on the phone; false promises made by Jr. and D I coaches who lead players on instead of being honest about their ability.

What traits do your successful student athletes bring to the program?
Coachability, work ethic, self-motivation, discipline.

Why do some of your recruited athletes fail to succeed?
Don't understand that they have to go to class and study. Underestimate the quality of D III, overestimate their own ability, lack of perseverance, lack of physical strength and training.

What advice can you offer to high school "age" hockey players that aspire to play at the college level?
Be a good student; work hard; get an honset evaluation of your ability from someone knowledgeable; play at the highest level possible; market yourself; go where you can play, visit the coach and campus, be honest with yourself, go to the school that meets your academic needs.

— Mercyhurst College —

Rick Gotkin, Head Coach

Which leagues do you regularly "scout" to locate prospective players for your college?
All Jr. B and A leagues in U.S. and Canada.

What specific events do you "scout" to locate prospective players for your college?
All.

What developmental level and/or league do you recommend to prospective college players?
Jr. A or prep school.

What qualities do you look for in prospects during the recruiting process?
Character and skating.

What traits do your successful student athletes bring to the program?
Character.

Why do some of your recruited athletes fail to succeed?
Character.

What advice can you offer to high school "age" hockey players that aspire to play at the college level?
Work hard and study.

——— Milwaukee School of Engineering ———

Mark Ostapina, Head Coach

Which leagues do you regularly "scout" to locate prospective players for your college?
NH High Schools: Ontario; Quebec; Sweden; EJHL; New England Prep Schools.

What specific events do you "scout" to locate prospective players for your college?
HNIB; Alliance tourney; NECDL; USA Regionals/Nationals.

What developmental level and/or league do you recommend to prospective college players?
USA Developmental Camps.

What qualities do you look for in prospects during the recruiting process?
1A. Good person. 1B. Good player.

What qualities are lacking in most of the prospects which you reject?
Character, conviction.

What traits do your successful student athletes bring to the program?
Strong mentally, character individual.

Why do some of your recruited athletes fail to succeed?
Easily distracted, finds it easy to quit on game.

What advice can you offer to high school "age" hockey players that aspire to play at the college level?
To seek highest level of competition possible.

—— University of Minnesota-Twin Cities ——

Mike Guentzel, Assistant Coach

Which leagues do you regularly "scout" to locate prospective players for your college?
USHL; Minnesota State H.S. League.

What specific events do you "scout" to locate prospective players for your college?
All-Star tournaments; USA Hockey camps; USHL League games; MSHSL games; MSHSL tournaments.

What developmental level and/or league do you recommend to prospective college players?
USHL.

What qualities do you look for in prospects during the recruiting process?
Speed, skill, smarts, character, size, academics, social qualities.

What qualities are lacking in most of the prospects which you reject?
Character and social concerns, bad students.

What is the most difficult part of recruiting?
None.

What traits do your successful student athletes bring to the program?
Quality academic selling points. Usually very focused individuals.

Why do some of your recruited athletes fail to succeed?
Poor time management, difficult to adjust to moving away from home and bad decisions.

What advice can you offer to high school "age" hockey players that aspire to play at the college level?
Work hard.

—— University of Nebraska-Omaha ——

Mike Kemp, Head Coach

Which leagues do you regularly "scout" to locate prospective players for your college?
USHL; SJHL; BCHL; OHL; CJHL; AJHL; MJHL.

What specific events do you "scout" to locate prospective players for your college?
Select 15, 16, 17; Prospect Camps; Hockey Night in Boston; Minn. Model Camp.

What developmental level and/or league do you recommend to prospective college players?
Junior hockey which best suits their living arrangements.

What qualities do you look for in prospects during the recruiting process?
Hard working-consistent, talent level, academics.

What qualities are lacking in most of the prospects which you reject?
Talent, discipline.

What is the most difficult part of recruiting?
Trying to convince a prospect that our program will better suit him than other programs.

What traits do your successful student athletes bring to the program?
Enjoyable to be with on the ice and off. Good with public.

Why do some of your recruited athletes fail to succeed?
Could not adjust to rigors of classroom and of college hockey all at once.

What advice can you offer to high school "age" hockey players that aspire to play at the college level?
Make sure you improve your talent level at every stage but not at the expense of your grades.

—— Pennsylvania State University ——

Joe Battista, Head Coach

Which leagues do you regularly "scout" to locate prospective players for your college?
NAHL; New York H.S. (Western); Metro Toronto; Metro Jr. B (Atlantic); Prep Schools; EJHL (New England); PA High Schools; Ohio High Schools.

What specific events do you "scout" to locate prospective players for your college?
Chicago Showcase; Key Stone games; Compuware tourney; HNIB; Metro Jr. A Showcase; PA H.S. All-Star Games; Liberty Bell-NJ; Metro Jr. B Showcase; Lawrenceville-NJ.

What developmental level and/or league do you recommend to prospective college players?
Post Grad. Prep; NAHL; EJHL; USHL.

What qualities do you look for in prospects during the recruiting process?
Grades, character, work ethic, finances (must pay own way), team players.

What qualities are lacking in most of the prospects which you reject?
Grades, physical attributes, speed, size, skill.

What is the most difficult part of recruiting?
Getting up to date academic info. Getting to tournaments in season. Players looking at Division 1 only.

What traits do your successful student athletes bring to the program?
Good time management skills, academics, first class on and off the ice.

Why do some of your recruited athletes fail to succeed?
Poor time management-easily distracted. Too many parties, lack of respect for our level of play, not focused, not used to competing for their ice time.

What advice can you offer to high school "age" hockey players that aspire to play at the college level?
Develop options and keep them all open. Consider a year of Post High School Hockey. Don't play more than 40-50 games so you can develop academics. Strength training, etc. Buy the College Hockey Guide! Be realistic in assessing your abilities.

——— Quinnipiac College ———

Rand Pecknold, Head Coach

Which leagues do you regularly "scout" to locate prospective players for your college?
BCHL; N.E. high schools; USHL; AJHL; SJHL; NAHL; EJHL; N.E. Prep Leagues.

What specific events do you "scout" to locate prospective players for your college?
Buc Bowl; Royal Bank; Hayward Cup.

What developmental level and/or league do you recommend to prospective college players?
All of the above except the high schools.

What qualities do you look for in prospects during the recruiting process?
Talent, character, grit & competitiveness. Academics.

What qualities are lacking in most of the prospects which you reject?
Academics, talent, grit.

What traits do your successful student athletes bring to the program?
Competitiveness.

Why do some of your recruited athletes fail to succeed?
Lack of maturity.

What advice can you offer to high school "age" hockey players that aspire to play at the college level?
Don't take anything for granted. Respect how difficult it is to compete at the Division I level and make the commitment.

—— St. John's University ——

John Harrington, Head Coach

Which leagues do you regularly "scout" to locate prospective players for your college?
MN H.S.; USHL; NAHL; AWHL.

What specific events do you "scout" to locate prospective players for your college?
Buc Bowl; Regular Season USHL; Regular Season MN State H.S.; MN State H.S. Tournament, Hayward Invitational.

What developmental level and/or league do you recommend to prospective college players?
USHL.

What qualities do you look for in prospects during the recruiting process?
Good students, good players, speed.

What qualities are lacking in most of the prospects which you reject?
Good academics.

What is the most difficult part of recruiting?
Finding good students that are good athletes that can pay a large amount of money to go to school.

What traits do your successful student athletes bring to the program?
Good athletes. Good well rounded students. Quality people.

Why do some of your recruited athletes fail to succeed?
Lack of discipline. Balancing school with hockey.

What advice can you offer to high school "age" hockey players that aspire to play at the college level?
Worry about academics early, we are past the days where sports will carry you through. Do as well as you can in school, it gives you more options.

—— Tufts University ——

Brian F. Murphy, Head Coach

Which leagues do you regularly "scout" to locate prospective players for your college?
I.S.L.-New England Prep; Greater Boston league-MA; Middlesex league-MA.

What specific events do you "scout" to locate prospective players for your college?
Holiday tourneys; Summer tourneys-HNIB; NECDL; Spring tourneys; State tourneys; ISL tourney; Regular season games.

What developmental level and/or league do you recommend to prospective college players?
Weight lifting/skills clinic.

What qualities do you look for in prospects during the recruiting process?
High academic achievement, maturity, ability to improve as a player.

What qualities are lacking in most of the prospects which you reject?
Academics; hockey skill level is low.

What is the most difficult part of recruiting?
Not having a rink on campus to show prospective athletes.

What traits do your successful student athletes bring to the program?
Strong work ethic, confidence in self, ability to succeed without constant guidance from coaches, parents, teachers, etc.

Why do some of your recruited athletes fail to succeed?
Lack of ability to self organize and motivate.

What advice can you offer to high school "age" hockey players that aspire to play at the college level?
1. Concentrate on school work. 2. Get realistic advice from your coach, other coaches, college coaches as to realistic level you can play at. 3. Choose a school you would be happy at if you weren't going to play hockey.

— United States Air Force Academy —

Frank Serratore, Head Coach

Which leagues do you regularly "scout" to locate prospective players for your college?
USHL; Minnesota High School; NAHL; ECHL; New England and Eastern High Schools; Michigan Midget.

What specific events do you "scout" to locate prospective players for your college?
League games (above leagues).

What developmental level and/or league do you recommend to prospective college players?
Junior Hockey: USHL, NAHL, ECHL.

What qualities do you look for in prospects during the recruiting process?
Athletic abililty, character, academics.

What qualities are lacking in most of the prospects which you reject?
Academic.

What is the most difficult part of recruiting?
Finding - Sorting process, identifying players who possess the ability, character, and academics needed to qualify for the academy.

What traits do your successful student athletes bring to the program?
Must be well rounded (athletic, character, academic).

Why do some of your recruited student athletes fail to succeed?
A few have a difficult time adjusting to the untraditional environment at the academy, but not many.

What advice can you offer to high school "age" hockey players that aspire to play at the college level?
Live clean, take pride in academics, work hard - compete - and have fun in athletics.

—— Wayne State University ——

Bill Wilkinson, Head Coach

Which leagues do you regularly "scout" to locate prospective players for your college?
USHL; Southern Ontario Jr. B; SJHL; Western Ontario Jr. B; BCHL; CJHL; NAHL; OPJHL; AJHL.

What specific events do you "scout" to locate prospective players for your college?
Buc Bowl-Des Moines, Iowa; Mac Midget tournament; Compuware tournament; Hockey Night in Boston; Hasting Early Bird; Early Bird tournaments through Canada/USA; Chicago Showcase; King of the Hill; Hayword tournament.

What developmental level and/or league do you recommend to prospective college players?
USHL, NAHL, SJHL, BCHL, or any one that has quality schedule. Jr. A or prep schools.

What qualities do you look for in prospects during the recruiting process?
Hockey skills-speed, intelligence, puck skills. Quality of the individual-confidence, honest and trust worthy. Character; skating.

What qualities are lacking in most of the prospects which you reject?
Intelligence.

What traits do your successful student athletes bring to the program?
Leadership both on and off the ice, academic achievements; character.

Why do some of your recruited athletes fail to succeed?
Committment to both academics and athletics is not strong enough. Players must understand it takes some longer than others to achieve. Lack of goals; definition of success.

What advice can you offer to high school "age" hockey players that aspire to play at the college level?
Don't go to college too soon! Be prepared both athletically as well as academically in order to achieve. A year out of school playing and getting prepared brings a better rounded student/athlete to our program. Be ready to play at the next level-take your time to emerge.

Skill Development

THE NEED FOR SKILL DEVELOPMENT

By Tom Keegan

One of the constants which the college coaches highlight in the coach survey section is the need for more skill development, especially in the formative years of hockey. Without advanced levels of skating, stickhandling and shooting skills prospective college players will have a difficult time earning a spot on any team.

Much like a student must demonstrate in prep school or high school that he has the academic skills to succeed in a selective college or university, a hockey player must usually already demonstrate satisfactory hockey skills to get the opportunity to play at the NCAA Division I level or, for that matter, any level of college hockey.

According to hockey skills coaches such as Bob Richardson, Real Turcotte and Jack Blatherwick these skills are best learned at an early age. An athlete is able to improve these skills more rapidly in the mite, squirt and peewee years than as a bantam, midget or junior player.

During these early years it is more important to play in a skill-oriented environment than in a program which concentrates on system development and building a winning record. System development is almost always at the expense of skill development.

How many players do you know that have won numerous championships but never played beyond midget or junior? On the other hand how many players do you know that were never good enough to play on the winning youth hockey team but somehow played four years in college and eventually some minor pro or in the NHL?

In addition to finding a youth hockey association in your area which stresses skill development we recommend that you seek out summer programs which also stress development of individual hockey skills.

Summer used to be a great time to work on hockey skills. That was before tournament operators found that they could run hockey tournaments and hockey showcase events all summer so that the best players would have an opportunity to play with and against other "elite" players.

USA Hockey monitored puck touches, passes and possession time during the recent Olympics. Even at this, the highest level of hockey, the average player only had possession of the puck for 1:07 per game. That is in a sixty-minute game. Now how much time do you think that the average youth hockey player touches the puck in a game or even in a four game tournament? Instead of travelling hours to a summer tournament where development will be practically non-existent why not spend the time and resources in a quality skills-oriented hockey school.

You will find that you have far more opportunities in hockey if you are the fastest skater, the most accomplished stickhandler or the player with the quickest, hardest and most accurate shots.

While most college hockey coaches probably feel that bigger is better, they are always looking for the player with the best skills. Your knowledge of the neutral zone trap or the left wing lock is great but you better be able to skate, stickhandle and shoot.

SKILL DEVELOPMENT

By Bob Richardson

Why aren't we producing skilled players anymore?

Some of the brightest minds in hockey at the highest levels, pro and college, are asking the same questions. Where are the skilled players? One of the answers is that the players are playing too many games and having far too few productive practice sessions.

In the games players rarely handle the puck. Even when a coach encourages a player to handle the puck in a game, that player does not have the puck on his (her) stick longer than twenty - thirty seconds maximum. That player is probably only skating twelve - eighteen minutes in a thirty-six minute game. So how can you improve? To improve you need repetition of skill.

The window of opportunity to develop not only physical skill, but read and react skills is gone when wasting time teaching systems. It is well known through current research that the "wiring of the brain", the connections made between events, and how to assimilate that information are best made while young. It is the same as learning a foreign language which is much easier when you are young. Why take this tremendous opportunity for growth and waste it on teaching systems that may or may not help you win a 10 year old game on a Saturday afternoon?

"If the neurons are used, they become integrated into the circuitry of the brain by connecting to other neurons, if they are not used, they may

die. It is the experiences of childhood, determining which neurons are used, that wire the circuits of the brain"... (this) "determines whether the child grows up to be intelligent or dull, fearful or self-assured, articulate or tongue tied," as written by Sharon Begley in <u>Newsweek</u>, February 19, 1996. The advancement of the brain is incumbent upon a wide range of experiences. It is through these experiences, some which succeed, some which do not, that enhances a young player's hockey sense.

The Europeans have well known about the window of opportunity for the development of the neurological system. They act upon this knowledge with a heavy emphasis on skill and hockey sense at a young age.

Mike Boyle, strength and conditioning coach for Boston University and the Massachusetts Satellite Program, believes that the accumulation of skating for the whole year has made many of today's young players inflexible. Without a full range of motion, skaters become too tight and cannot get full power into their skating strides. Mike feels that young players need to play other sports, particularly running sports, to cross train and to take time away from skating.

There is too much evaluation of ten year old teams and players. What is the instrument of evaluation? It is wins, goals, assists. Panic sets in when those criteria are not met. The reality is this usually precludes fun and skill development, so in the end those players fall far short of their potential.

The pressure to win, to score points as indicators of "success" are false and shallow. They lead to players who, in the future, have trouble handling pressure. The best players are oblivious to pressure because they have the necessary skills to get the job done. Skills, confidence, mental toughness and hockey sense is what wins in the long run. Success in terms of wins, championships, trophies or personal point totals mean nothing. The chances have become slim for those elusive scholarships. More fun is needed. More skill is needed. More dedication is needed. More creativity should be encouraged.

(Excerpt reprinted with permission of Hockey USA)

Major Camp
Prep and Junior • July 14-19, 2007

Hockey development camp, designed exclusively for top-level prep and junior players born between 1988-1991. All players skate in six training sessions and compete in six games. Each training session is devoted to developing specific skills, with time reserved for a small-games tournament. All camp participants attend seminars that focus on leadership skills and the development of character. The program is limited to 8 teams of 18 players (10 forwards, 6 defense, 2 goalies). This camp includes cost of room and board.

Minor Camp
July 8-12, 2007

Hockey development camp, designed exclusively for top-level players born in 1992 and 1993 and aspire to play with top prep and junior programs in the United States. All players skate in six training sessions and compete in six games. Each training session is devoted to developing specific skills, with time reserved for a small-games tournament. All camp participants attend seminars that focus on leadership skills and the development of character. The program is limited to 6 teams of 18 players (10 forwards, 6 defense, 2 goalies). This camp includes cost of room and board.

Goaltender Program

We will provide five goaltender sessions throughout the Major, Minor and Girls Camps. Goaltending sessions focus on maximizing the potential of each goaltender. Training programs are personalized based on experience and ability.

Camp Location:

National Hockey Training Camps are held at the University of Southern Maine in Gorham, Maine.

Information

Jim Ward 860-739-7333 (after July 1st 860-235-7031)
National Hockey Training Camps
860-235-7031
E-Mail Us - nhtcamps@sbcglobal.net

Nothing But Net
Hockey Skills Camp

August 2008

Rockville Ice Arena

Rockville, Maryland

Our program is designed to develop and improve your individual skills. Special emphasis will be placed on overspeed training, power skating, puck control & scoring techniques

Be Ready For Tryouts!

For more information call:
301.874.0027

Nothing But Net Hockey Skills
P.O. Box 7243
Gaithersburg, MD 20898-7243

Showcase Events

SHOWCASE EVENTS

By Tom Keegan

The ability to showcase ones hockey skills is an important step in the road to playing college hockey. The college coach survey section provides many suggestions from current college coaches. Most of these opportunities are the results of team events during the regular hockey season.

USA Regional and National Tournaments provide some opportunity for exposure. Midget, Prep School and Junior Tournaments attract college scouts as well as Major Junior and Junior A, B & C scouts.

Most of these in-season opportunities are usually the result of team entries or team accomplishments.

The spring and summer provide the best opportunities for individuals to get additional exposure.

USA Hockey Regional and National Select Camps and the Chicago Showcase provide individuals the opportunity for reasonably-priced exposure.

For-Profit Showcase Events include:

Atlantic Hockey Showcase

Chowder Cup

Global Sports Camps

Hockey Night In Boston - Atlantic

Hockey Night In Boston - Midwest

Hockey Night In Boston - Pacific

National Collegiate Development Camp

National Prep School Development Camp

Pre-Prep Showcase

There seems to be quite a bit of growth in spring and summer Showcase Events. With the growing number of opportunities for out of season exposure we recommend that you communicate directly with the coaches of specific colleges to find out which events they plan to attend during their off-season. If you have the academic and hockey credentials to play at Yale and that is your first choice then you should find out where the Yale staff will be scouting.

The Showcases will typically include in their advertising which coaches will be present at their events. We suggest that you avoid disappointment by verifying with the coach that he, or one of his assistants, will in fact be there.

At the same time you should find out if your grade level is being scouted. If you are attending a Showcase during the summer after your high school graduation you may find that schools are not looking at graduates. If however you will be doing a post-graduate year at a New England Prep School the schools may be interested. The spring or summer between your junior and senior years is probably the best time to invest in a Showcase.

August 2007

Boys and Girls
(1991, 1992, 1993 Birth Years)
Co-Directors:
Jeff Quebec & Bob Rotondo

Pre-Prep Showcase®

P.O. Box #80480
Stoneham, Massachusetts 02180
TEL #: (781) 279-0859
FAX #: (781) 397-0847
info@preprepshowcase.com
www.preprepshowcase.com

*"Last years attendance and participation
included student-athletes from thirty states and
provinces along with admissions officers and
ice hockey coaches from fifty private schools.
Don't be overlooked—sign-up today!"*

DEDICATIO ~ EXECELLENTIA ~ PROSPERITAS ~ LAUREOLA

HNIB

HOCKEY NIGHT IN BOSTON

ATLANTIC TRYOUT CAMPS
BOYS TRYOUTS
APRIL , 2008
ICEPLEX
MONCTON, NEW BRUNSWICK

CONTACT:
Fred Englehart
Hockey Night In Boston - Atlantic
POB 1551, Station A, Frederickton, NB, E3B 5G2, CANADA
hnib@nbnet.nb.ca

MIDWEST TRYOUT CAMPS
BOYS TRYOUTS
JUNE 21, 22 & 23, 2007
ANN ARBOR ICE CUBE
ANN ARBOR, MICHIGAN

CONTACT:
Bill Nook
Hockey Night In Boston - Midwest
23200 Commerce Park Road, Cleveland, OH 44122
216.464.6321

PACIFIC TRYOUT CAMPS

BOYS TRYOUTS
JUNE 16 & 17, 2007
GLACIAL GARDENS
LAKEWOOD, CALIFORNIA

CONTACT:
Bill Nook
Hockey Night In Boston - Pacific
23200 Commerce Park Road, Cleveland, OH 44122
216.464.6321

2008

"America's Premier High School Hockey Event"

Teams from across the United States
consisting of the top high school
age players representing over forty states
will compete and showcase their talents to scouts
from every major hockey institution in the country.

April 2008

Make your plans now to attend and scout the
top high school players in the country
as they compete for the national crown.

For more information write to:
Jim Smith
Showcase Director
859 Oakton Street
Elk Grove Village, Illinois 60007

Educational
Consultants

EDUCATIONAL CONSULTANTS

By Tom Keegan

The average cost of an education at private or out-of-state public U.S. colleges and universities probably exceeds $120,000. If it doesn't today, it surely will by the time the average high school age hockey player has his degree. On the five-year plan that number gets even higher.

I have had numerous conversations with educational consultants over the past few years and the family of an average hockey player should be able to get all of the assistance required for anywhere from $ 500 to $5,000.

If the bar is set at $120,000 then that works out to be anywhere from half a percent to 5% depending on the consultant, your needs and the length of time you use the services.

Most home buyers budget some amount for an inspection before making a large investment in property. Your investment in an education is also of a magnitude that may require some professional guidance.

A good consultant may very easily save you much more that his or her fee because of the special knowledge acquired over years of helping students with their college investigation and selection. Most of us have but one or two hockey players to offer and we can't afford too much of a learning curve in the college selection process.

Now if the educational consultant also has a background or extensive knowledge of hockey then he becomes even more valuable.

The next few pages contain information on several educational consultants. Each of these consultants has been invited to be included here because we feel that they have the expertise to assist you in this all-important process. Some have hockey playing backgrounds and can also assist you with an evaluation of your hockey abilities and recommendations for additional hockey development.

In addition to this group we have information on other educational consultants with excellent credentials in other areas.

We suggest that you communicate with educational consultants to determine if there is a value in using their services. Many will offer you an initial session before making any committment. You may talk to several before you find one that is a good fit for you and your situation.

"Player Development is the Key to Hockey in College"

- Lots of tools exist to help
- Many of them are here
- Review this guide carefully

- *You can find your own way through the player development process but it will take determination.*
- *I have provided coaching through the process to many players who are skating on prep school, junior and college teams*

MY THREE RULES FOR PLAYERS WHO WISH TO PLAY IN COLLEGE:

1. Live and play in control on and off the ice (Mind-Body-Attitude-Drugs-etc.!)
2. Achieve your academic potential — earn a solid classroom G.P.A. and a strong set of national test scores (SAT or ACT)!
3. Enhance your playing skills — not the game count!

If you believe you need help and want some low-cost guidance contact:

Coach Steve Malley
1792 Reading Street
Crofton, MD 21114

stevemalley@hockeycenter.com
www.veryserioushockey.com

THE SCHOOL COUNSELING GROUP, INC.

Which school is the right school?
Let us help you decide.

202.333.3530

www.schoolcounseling.com
guidance@schoolcounseling.com

Ethna Hopper, MA, IECA, CEP
Director
Carol R. Shabe, MEd
Jenifer Rideout, BS, IECA
Alexandra Ruttenberg, EdM, IECA, CEP
Peter Sturtevant, Jr., MA

4725 MacArthur Blvd. NW, Washington, DC 20007-1904
Providing educational counseling for
American and international families since 1979.

Prep School Route
to College Hockey

THE PREP SCHOOL ROUTE TO COLLEGE HOCKEY

By Jim Ward, Head Coach, Connecticut College

Student athletes who aspire to play college hockey have many options that can help them reach their goal. Programs can offer quality coaches, schedules and resources to aid in the development of their players. Each student athlete and his family must evaluate their long-term goals and decide which program will help them reach those goals. If the family agrees that an academic focus is desirable along with a strong athletic program, then the private school experience is worth serious consideration. Prep school hockey in New England is considered by many, as the best route for the student-athlete to pursue admission to top colleges and universities and play a significate role with its varsity hockey program. Prep school student-athletes learn to balance rigorous academic and athletic schedules so that they have the ability to reach their potential both in the classroom and in the rink. College recruiters know that if a prospect has the ability to handle the academic and social pressures of the classroom and dormitory they will have a focused player on the ice!

There are currently fifty-six private boarding and day schools that support varsity ice hockey programs in New England. Twenty-seven of these schools compete at the Division I level and the remainder have Division II programs. There are another 18 prep programs throughout the country that compete as independent programs. Each school has its own unique identity and charter. Private schools set their own admission standards, meaning each member of the student body has to meet a certain academic criteria in order to be admitted. Many of these schools may offer either a boarding or day school environment. All will promote the fact that their students attend classes that are smaller in size and work closely and intimately with faculty with a low student to faculty ratio. Diverse academic curriculum, structured study hall and dormitory policy are unique with each school. Preparation of students for admission to the strongest college or university is the common goal of all.

One who explores the option of attending a prep school, boarding or day, should do so with a holistic viewpoint. Focus on the quality and type of classroom, social and athletic components that each school has to offer. A student-athlete will not be able to attain peak performance academically or athletically if he is uncomfortable in the environment in which he lives. A personalized and disciplined environment is one that allows students to build trust in themselves and with the faculty, coaches and dorm parents around them. Student athletes can exceed their previous accomplishments and raise the quality of their performance to another level.

Brian Leetch (Avon Old Farms-New York Rangers), Marty Reasoner (Deerfield Academy-St Louis Blues), Mike Dunham (Canterbury-Nashville), Mike Ricter (Northwood Prep-New York Rangers) and Matt Herr (Hotchkiss-Washington Capitals) each made the decision to attend their alma mater for the educational value they would get from boarding school. No doubt, for the teenage boys making the decision, hockey served as the carrot, while their parents focused on the high caliber of the classroom and overall experience.

Prep programs with traditional schedules will start tryouts at the end of the fall sports season allowing hockey players to participate in fall sports. Chris Bala, Harvard Sophomore and Ottawa Senator draft played football and baseball at Hill School. The season will be completed in time for spring sports. Brian Leetch threw a 90 mile per hour fastball and Mike Mottau, Boston College; NY Ranger draft played lacrosse at Avon Old Farms School. This allows prep school student athletes be athletes first and hockey players second. Playing several sports best develops balance, agility, quickness, coordination, competitiveness and a better awareness of your body.

The majority of the schools have rinks on campus allowing teams to practice daily for one and half to two hours. Most competitive prep hockey programs have schedules that are challenging and rigorous, regularly attracting college recruiters and pro scouts. Teams will participate in at least one tournament, usually during the Christmas vacation. The pace of the season is intense. Qualification criteria for the New England Tournament is tight so each game is critical and must be played at the highest tempt. Many traditional rivalries in prep hockey have existed between these schools since the beginning of the century.

Athletics are important to private schools as sports instill qualities in student that are essential to be successful in life. The game of ice hockey, more than any sport, teaches individuals how to play competitively with passion, discipline and sportsmanship: these qualities are not always a natural combination for adolescents to utilize in their daily lives. Most Prep coaches are educators first and foremost, taking pride in his commitment to educate and develop the whole athlete. The classroom and the rink are not separate. Most coaches are members of the faculty and communicate with their player's teachers daily to monitor academic progress. College counselors and coaches together advise and market their student-athletes when it comes time to file applications. Coaches often contact college coaches who have programs that best compliments the student athlete's profile.

Students will take advantage of an additional year of high school as a post graduate student or may repeat a year in order to add an additional year of maturation and building a larger base of knowledge to take into college. Typically, prep teams are more physically and emotionally mature than public school teams and they consist of players who have set high academic and athletic standards for themselves.

Boarding schools compete with one another for the top students. Each must stay abreast of changes in curriculum development at their school and offer opportunities that will best prepare them for a rapidly changing world. What most boarding schools offer is an education that is relevant to our changing world. Jay Ward (Director of Northfield Mount Hermon Summer School) feels that schools are focusing on the following themes that will shape education in the next century:

• Educate students how to effectively

and efficiently deal with large amounts of information made available by technology.

- Prepare students to deal intelligently with social and ethical decisions.

- Address issues of multiculturalism and tolerance, as communities in the United States increasingly consist of a variety of ethnic backgrounds.

- Prepare students to think globally and to be internationally aware. Familiarity and respect for other cultures is going to be important for our students as they enter a work world that will be more international in nature.

It is difficult to imagine that a student playing a sixty game schedule will have the opportunity or the time to be fully engaged in his academics. Members of a private school community are busy individuals with a need for strong time management skills. Sandwiched around practice is class, hours of homework and other extracurricular commitments. After graduating from prep school and gaining admission to a selective college, some opt for a year of junior hockey. Those who are fortunate to be a member of a private school community will have a greater enrichment of the mind and strengthened intellectual base.

Financial aid based on family need is available at the prep school level. How aid packages are determined will vary from school to school. The sacrifice that a family makes to send their son to prep school will pay off if he is prepared academically, emotionally and athletically. The bottom line is that prep school, with the student-athletes dedication and hard work, will create more opportunities for admission to colleges or universities than he would have otherwise.

If considering a private school that offers a competitive ice hockey program, do not make a judgment based solely by last years record or the number of college scholarships offered to it's alumni. Do your homework in researching the academic curriculum, residential life policies and extracurricular offerings to be sure that each will be compatible with your needs. Prep school and prep hockey is not for everyone but those who have taken advantage of this opportunity find that the experience has changed and shaped their lives in a most positive manner.

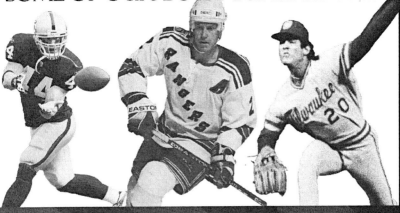

"RESIDENTIAL PROGRAM OF HOCKEY & SCHOLASTIC EXCELLENCE"

Celebrating Our 10th Anniversary

SEPTEMBER - JUNE

BANFF HOCKEY ACADEMY

1-888-423-6369 • Box 2242, Banff, Alberta, Canada T1L 1B9

Berkshire School

Great Place.

Great Program.

Great Preparation.

Founded in 1907, Berkshire School is a coeducational college prep school offering a unique educational experience to 375 boys and girls from across the country and around the world.

• Located on a 500-acre campus just over two hours from Boston or New York and just one hour from Hartford or Albany.

• The 2003 New England Champions Girls' Varsity Champions. Made the playoffs all six years in Division I. Recent graduates have gone on to play for such schools as BC, BU, Brown, Clarkson, Colgate, UConn, Elmira, Middlebury, UNH, Princeton, St. Lawrence.

• The Boys' Varsity: made the Division I playoffs two of the last five years. Recent graduates have gone on to play for such schools as Connecticut College, Hamilton College, Skidmore, Trinity, Tufts, UVM, Wesleyan and West Point.

Varsity Girls' Coach
Lori Charpentier
(413) 229-1292
lcharpentier@berkshireschool.org

Varsity Boys' Coach
Dan Driscoll
(413) 229-1003
ddriscoll@berkshireschool.org

Berkshire School
Sheffield, Massachusetts
www.berkshireschool.org
We learn not for school, but for life.

Lori Charpentier
Girls' Varsity Coach & Athletic Director

Berkshire's six year record under her direction is 137-22-7, including a Division I Championship in 2003. They have also made it to the final four four straight seasons. In 2000-2001 she led the Bears to an undefeated regular season at 22-0-3 and was named the NIHOA Coach of the Year. Hockey night in Boston has named her the Division I Coach of the Year four times, as well as Division II Coach of the Year. Her career record now stands at 204-31-10. Charpentier is the second all-time leading goal scorer at Dartmouth College, leading the team to an Ivy League title as a junior, and being named captain in her senior year. She was also named Academic All-Ivy as a senior.

Coach Charpentier can be contacted by e-mail at lcharpentier@berkshireschool.org.

Dan Driscoll
Boys' Varsity Coach & Associate Director of Admission

A graduate of the University of Connecticut, spent the past five years in the admissions office at Pomfret School, including the last two as director. In addition to enrolling new students, Mr. Driscoll was also the head coach of the boys' varsity hockey team, a position he will also hold at Berkshire. Prior to Pomfret, he spent five years at the Winchendon School, where he served in a variety of roles, including admissions director, athletic director, hockey coach and history teacher. Mr. Driscoll is the house head in Buck. His wife, Dory, a High School All-American track athlete from the University of Connecticut, will lend her expertise as an assistant in our track program. The Driscolls have five children – Anna, Dan, Mark, Kathryn and Meghan. Coach Driscoll can be contacted by email at ddriscoll@berkshireschool.org.

BERKSHIRE SCHOOL
245 N. Undermountain Road
Sheffield, Massachusetts 01257
Phone: 413.229.1003
e-mail: admission@berkshireschool.org
www.berkshireschool.org

College Hockey Guide Men's Edition

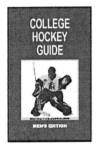

The College Hockey Guide contains over 500 pages of important information for prospective college hockey players including articles to assist in the college selection process, including admission, SAT/ACT, enrollment, campus tuition, room and board, financial aid and scholarship information as well as rosters and records. College coaches provide information on how to get recruited and what it takes to succeed.

To Order by Phone Call:

800.255.1050

www.hockeybookstore.com

To order by Mail
Send Check or Money Order in the amount of $45.95 U.S. to:
Athletic Guide Publishing
PO Box 1050
Flagler Beach, FL 32136
386.439.2250

College Hockey Guide Women's Edition
$42⁹⁵

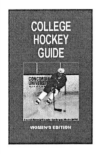

The College Hockey Guide contains over 300 pages of important information for prospective college hockey players including articles to assist in the college selection process, including admission, SAT/ACT, enrollment, campus tuition, room and board, financial aid and scholarships information as well as rosters and records. College coaches provide information on how to get recruited and what it takes to succeed.

To Order by Phone Call:

800.255.1050

www.hockeybookstore.com

To order by Mail
Send Check or Money Order in the amount of $42.95 U.S. to:
Athletic Guide Publishing
PO Box 1050
Flagler Beach, FL 32136
386.439.2250

Canterbury School

Canterbury School is a private lay Catholic coeducational boarding and day school for grades 9-12.

Our tradition is strong and proud, and each student carries on that tradition by being an active participant three seasons a year at his or her level. This athletic requirement underscores our goal to prepare well-balanced and healthy individuals who understand that what really matters are sportsmanship, hard work, and cooperation.

Canterbury School
101 Aspetuck Avenue
New Milford, CT 06776-2825
860-210-3832 • www.cbury.org
admissions@cbury.org

A commitment to accept, to challenge, to inspire

THE CULVER ACADEMIES

WITH AN EYE ON THE GOAL . . . ON ICE, IN LIFE

Our mission at the Culver Academies is to develop the whole individual- mind, character, spirit and body. To accomplish this, Culver has spent over 100 years creating integrated academic, leadership, religious, and athletic programs that are unrivalled in the United States. This mission has guided both Culver Boys' and Girls' Hockey Programs since their inceptions, and the programs have benfited from facilities that are second to none.

The John W. Henderson Ice Arena is home to the Academies' nationally recognized hockey program. It houses two sheets of ice, one NHL-sized and one Olyumpic, nine locker rooms, a weight room, and a training room. With this facility, the five teams (three boys' and two girls') have the opportunity to skate and train for an average of two hours each day during the season and to play nationally competitive schedules. With individual develpment as the main emphasis, the program has helped such current or former NHP players as Gary Suter, Kevin Dean, Barry Richter, and Aris Brimanis fulfill their dreams. In total, the NRL has drafted 17 Culver players while over 100 others have gone on to compete at the collegiate level at institutions such as Princeton, New Hampshire, Vermont, Wisconsin, Colorado College, Miami University, Williams, and Middlebury. While, in just three seasons, the girl's program has nine graduates playing at institutions such as Yale, New Hampshire, St. Lawrence, Ohio State, Minnesota, and Wisconsin.

The Culver Academies
1300 Adademy Road #147
Culver, Indiana 46511-1291
800-5-CULVER
(219)842-8092 (FAX)

⊕ Gilmour Academy

An independent, coeducational, college preparatory day (PK - 12) and boarding school (7 - 12) in the Holy Cross tradition

- 13 Advanced Placement courses and 20 different sports

- 100% of graduating seniors have strong college options

- Competitive Prep Hockey Program

- Daily ice time in our NHL-size ice arena located on campus

- Schedule includes midwestern and eastern prep school teams

For admissions information contact:

Devin Schlickmann
Dean of Admissions

Mike McNeill
Boys Hockey Coach

Rick Filighera
Girls Hockey Coach

34001 Cedar Road
Gates Mills, Ohio 44040
Phone: 440.473.8050
Fax: 440.473.8010
admissions@gilmour.org
www.gilmour.org
www.gilmourhockey.org

Gilmour Academy's motto
"Success to those who persevere"
will serve you well in our classrooms, on our ice,
and in your life beyond Gilmour.

THE HILL SCHOOL

A co-educational boarding school in grades 9-12 and postgraduate. The Hill School provides academically able young men and women both a well-structured college preparatory course of studies and a superb athletic tradition.

- 7:1 Student/Teacher Ratio
- Advanced Placement and Honors Courses
- Excellent College Placement
- Financial Aid Available

- Edward T. Hall Arena on Campus
- Competitive Division I Independent Mid-Atlantic/New England Schedule
- 15 Interscholastic Sports Offered

The Hill currently has 3 alumni playing in the NHL, and at highly competitive collegiate levels, including Amherst, Connecticut College, Elmira, Fairfield, Hamilton, Harvard, Hobart, Holy Cross, Middlebury, Penn State, Trinity, Union and Williams

For information, contact:

Matt Mulhern, Boys' Hockey Coach
Lindsay Barton, Girls' Hockey Coach
The Hill School
Pottstown, PA 19464
Phone   610.326.1000
Fax   610.705.1753

HOOSAC SCHOOL

Founded 1889

- Student-teacher ratio 5:1

- Mastery teaching for all students

- Individualized college counseling

- Advanced placement courses available

- Proactive advisor system

- SAT prep course

- Strong varsity teams in ice hockey, lacrosse, and soccer

For more information contact:
Dean Foster
Assistant Headmaster & Director of Admission
Hoosac School
Hoosick, NY 12089

800.822.0159
518.686.3370 fax
www.hoosac.com • email: info@hoosac.com

KENT

Excellence in the American Prep School Tradition

Kent School
Kent, CT 06757
1-800-538-5368
www.kent-school.edu

Kents Hill School

KENTS HILL, MAINE

THE PROGRAM
N.E. Prep, Div. II &
Maine Class B Schedule
30 Games & Playoffs
2 All-Star Team Opportunties
4 Position-Specific Coaches

THE FACILITY
New $7 Million Rink &
Field House in 2000
State-of-the-Art Fitness
Center & Weight Room

THE SCHOOL
Co-ed, College Preparatory
Grades 9-12, Postgraduate
Learning Skills Center
Small Classes; 6:1 Ratio

Boys' Coach - Larry Cockrell
Girls' Coach - Amy Smucker

P.O. Box 257
Kents Hill, ME 04349
207.685.4914
www.kentshill.org

National Sports Academy
at Lake Placid

Co-ed College Preparatory Boarding School

• Alpine • Ice Hockey • Nordic • Ski Jumping
• Snowboarding • Freestyle • Luge

Northfield Mount Hermon

A coeducational, college preparatory school, Northfield Mount Hermon enrolls 950 boarders and 200 day students in grades 9 – 12 and postgraduate. With an innovative educational program (called the NMH Plan), incredibly diverse and talented people, and world-class resources, the school enables students to learn better and grow more as individuals.

Athletic Program

NMH has over 65 teams (nicknamed the Hoggers) competing in approximately 15 sports each for boys and girls. The school's athletic facilities include a new eight-lane track, a fitness center and training room on each campus, and an indoor climbing wall.

NMH Hockey

Our program gives players the best possible preparation for college hockey. We do this by having the highest caliber coaches, top-tier student players from around the world, and a rigorous in-and-out-of-season training program. NMH is a member of the newly formed New England Prep School Ice Hockey Conference. Check our team Web pages at
www.nmhschool.org/hockey/boys
www.nmhschool.org/hockey/girls

NMH
Northfield Mount Hermon
S C H O O L

Admission Office • 206 Main Street • Northfield, MA 01360-1089
Phone: (413) 498-3227 • Web site:www.nmhschool.org

NORTHWOOD SCHOOL

ICE HOCKEY

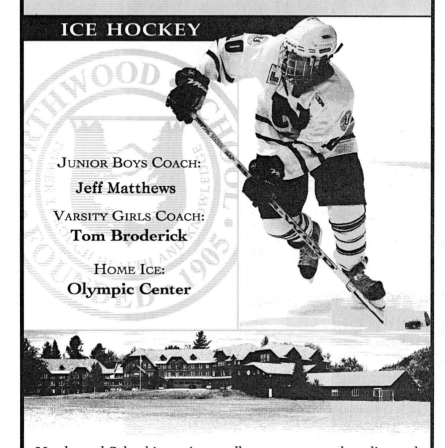

JUNIOR BOYS COACH:
Jeff Matthews

VARSITY GIRLS COACH:
Tom Broderick

HOME ICE:
Olympic Center

Northwood School is a private college preparatory boarding and day school for young men and women in grades 9 through post graduate year. The student-to-faculty ratio is 6:1 and faculty members reside on campus; as a result students receive individual academic and interpersonal guidance in all areas of the living and learning experience.

p: 518.523.3382   f: 518.523.3405
e: admissions@northwoodschool.com
www.northwoodschool.com

Phillips
Academy

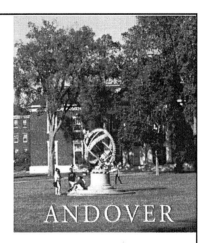

ANDOVER

Phillips Academy, a residential secondary school, seeks students of intelligence and integrity from diverse cultural, racial, socioeconomic and geographic backgrounds.

The school's residential structure enables faculty to support students in their personal, social and intellectual development. The academic program fosters excellence in all disciplines within the liberal arts tradition. Faculty members guide students in mastering skills, acquiring knowledge and thinking critically, creatively and independently. The school strives to help young people achieve their potential not only intellectually, but also artistically, athletically and morally, so that they may lead responsible and fulfilling lives.

The academy is committed to establishing a community that encourages people of diverse backgrounds and beliefs to understand and respect one another and to be sensitive to differences of gender, ethnicity, class and sexual orientation. In its programs the school seeks to promote a balance of leadership, cooperation and service, together with a deeper awareness of the global community and the natural world.

Phillips Academy
180 Main Street
Andover, Massachusetts 01810-4161
Telephone 978.749.4000 ♦ Fax 978.749.4068
www.andover.edu

Dean Boylan - Boys' Hockey Coach
dboylan@andover.edu

Martha Fenton - Girls' Hockey Coach
mfenton@andover.edu

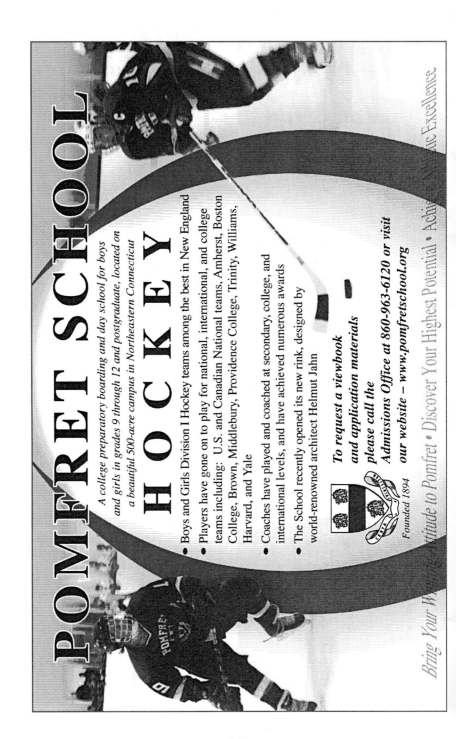

Proctor Academy

Founded in 1848, Proctor is a coeducational boarding community of 325 students known for it's innovative academic programs and student-centered approach to education. The curriculum is broad and includes traditional courses including Honors and Advanced Placement (AP) classes as well as electives in such diverse subjects as Environmental Social Science, Boat Building, Forestry and Digital Animation. Students matriculate to outstanding 4 year colleges.

Most students participate in one of the school's trimester long off-campus programs which include: Ocean Classroom, Mountain Classroom, Language Abroad in either Aix-en-Provence, France or Segovia, Spain or at the American School in Tangier, Morocco.

The village campus is surrounded by over 2300 acres of forest lands and includes an on campus ice hockey arena, the Blackwater Ski area, and a new 420 seat performing arts center. 20 Dormitories average 12 students each and the campus is fully networked for use with new wireless technologies.

For more information please call or write the admission office or contact our hockey coaches directly:

Admissions
P.O. Box 500
Andover, NH 03216
Phone: 603.735.6312
Fax: 603.735.6284
email: admissions@proctornet.com

Emily McKissock, Girls' Coach
emily_mckissock@proctornet.com
Mike Walsh, Boys' Coach
mike_walsh@proctornet.com

www.proctoracademy.org

- 147 -

hockey & academics

Shattuck-St. Mary's offers students a solid college preparatory academic program AND a nationally recognized hockey development experience. We call it "the AND experience." For our students, it means physical, intellectual, and leadership growth. It also means great preparation for college and life.

• College Prep
• Coeducational
• Boarding and Day
• Grades 6-12
• Shuttle options from Twin Cities
• Average class size: 14 students

SHATTUCK·ST.MARY'S
Faribault, Minnesota
800-421-2724
admissions@s-sm.org

TILTON
SCHOOL

NEPSAC Division II Champions

2000 • 2001 • 2002

COEDUCATIONAL • COLLEGE PREPARATORY • GRADES 9-PG

For information, contact our Admission Office at (603) 286-1733, or visit our Web site at www.tiltonschool.org.

TRINITY-PAWLING SCHOOL

Take aim on your success!

... in a traditional and supportive
environment that combines challenging
academics and Division I Hockey in the highly
competitive Founders' League, showcasing some
of the finest talent in the country.

TRINITY-PAWLING SCHOOL
700 ROUTE 22
PAWLING, NEW YORK 12564
845.855.3100
www.trinitypawling.org

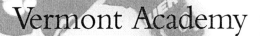

Go Blue Knights!

WYOMING SEMINARY

Founded in NE Pennsylvania in 1844, Wyoming Seminary is one of the oldest continuously coeducational day/boarding schools in the country. Offering a rigorous academic program and extensive fine and performing arts, Wyoming Seminary's Upper School is well known for competitive athletic teams.

COMPETITION • COMMITMENT • COMMUNITY

Hockey Program
- Competitive varsity and junior varsity programs
- 40-45 game Division I Nat'l Independent schedule exposes players to colleges and competition from the East Coast to the Midwest.
- Full-time strength and conditioning coordinator for off-season development
- Annual European trip (e.g. the Czech Republic, Austria)

Athletics
Twenty sports offered –
FALL: field hockey, football, golf*, cross country*, soccer*
SPRING: baseball, softball, lacrosse*, tennis*
Sports offered for boys and for girls
Two fitness rooms, pool, stadium, tennis courts and athletic fields

Academics
More than 140 courses available
24 AP courses
Skilled, experienced teachers
8:1 student/teacher ratio (average class size is 13)
Personalized college counseling begins in 10th grade
75% of graduates accepted by *most, highly* and *very competitive* colleges
Diverse student body: 20+ countries
Science center with 5 labs, 20,000+ volume library, three computer labs

Arts
Vocal, instrumental music at all levels
Visual art studio and gallery space
One dance, three theatrical performances annually
Two performing arts centers
Summer *Performing Arts Institute,* internationally known faculty

WYOMING SEMINARY
founded 1844

COLLEGE PREPARATORY SCHOOL

1-570-270-2160 • toll free 1-877-WYOSEM1 • www.wyomingseminary.org
Upper School Grades 9 - 12 plus postgraduate

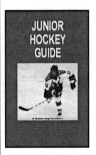
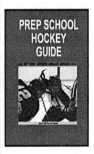

U. S. Junior Route
to College Hockey

THE U. S. JUNIOR ROUTE TO COLLEGE HOCKEY

By Tom Keegan

For many prospective college hockey participants the best route to college is through one of the many junior teams that provide opportunities to improve and showcase individual and team skills. Junior Hockey usually affords the opportunity for an expanded schedule of competitive games. Junior opportunities in the United States include a wide variety of Tier 1, Tier 2 Junior A and Tier 3 Junior A, B and C leagues and teams and you need to investigate carefully before you commit to any league or team.

If your goal is to play hockey at the college level, United States Tier 1, Tier 2 Junior A and Tier 3 Junior A provide excellent experience and exposure which should increase your potential for playing college hockey.

In the past the most successful junior leagues were in Canada. Now the United States Hockey League, the North American Hockey League, and the Eastern Junior Hockey League have become dominant as college feeder leagues and are attracting top junior players from the United States. There are also a number of US Junior B Teams and Leagues which spend a great deal of time and effort providing exposure for players.

Investigate your junior options just as you would your college options. You will probably be spending two seasons with the same team and you want to make sure that you will be happy and successful in that situation. Talk to others that have played for the organization and the coach. Will the team provide the development and exposure which you desire or are they interested only in winning the league or provincial championship?

If you hope to attend a specific college, talk to the college coaching staff before you decide upon your junior team. Many colleges have specific teams and leagues which they recommend for a variety of reasons. They may want to place you in one situation to improve in a specific skill or in another situation because they scout that team often and can monitor your improvement. They may also want to place you on a team which will provide you with development while at the same time keeping you in an organizational situation which supports your return to that particular college coach.

Many Junior Leagues have college nights or college weekends during which all league teams play at the same location to increase the number of scouts that will attend the games. These are usually held early in the season and can be a real advantage if you have a great weekend. NCAA Division I coaches are not going to normally offer you a scholarship based upon one game or one weekend, but rather based upon several different exposures. If your league has a college weekend and you play well you may be included in future scouting trips. If your play is below expectations you should still have other opportunities as the college coaches scout other players on your team or in your league.

If your goal is to play junior hockey make sure that your team plays in tournaments which are scouted by junior teams. Most United States

Midget AAA players receive the exposure necessary to get a tryout with a junior team. You can certainly improve your odds by contacting junior teams directly. Place a greater emphasis on contacts with teams that meet your needs.

If you are playing Prep School, Midget AA, A or High School hockey in the United States you will want to initiate contact with junior organizations and junior leagues. Junior teams normally have several tryout camps and they will often allow you to attend the preliminary camp if you ask. The final tryout camp is usually limited to returning players and those that have survived the preliminary camps.

In summary we suggest that you really investigate the variety of junior opportunities available to you. Get information from the teams and leagues and talk to former players. Determine which junior organizations can best help you attain your long term goals in hockey and beyond hockey. Consider all of the options and evaluate the strengths and weaknesses of each just as you would in choosing a college. If you feel that you need assistance in the investigation and evaluation process with junior programs contact an educational consultant with a background in this specific area. We have included some of the most knowledgeable sources in this guide.

ATLANTIC JUNIOR HOCKEY LEAGUE
PO Box 1151
McAfee, NJ 07428
O 201.670.9370
ajhlhockey@aol.com
www.ajhlhockey.org

BINGHAMTON JR SENATORS
Neil Fuiles - General Manager
PO Box 627
Binghamton, NY 13902
O 607.343.0458
neilfuiles@binghamtonjrsenators.com
www.binghamtonjrsenators.com

NEW YORK BOBCATS
Ron Kinnear General Manager
40 Underhill Blvd., Suite 1B
Syosset, NY 11791
O 516.680.7642
rkinnear@mindspring.com
www.nybobcats.com

BOSTON BULLDOGS
Mike Addesa - GM / Head Coach
962 Lord Road
Wakefield, NH 03872
O 603.522.3813
coachaddesa@bulldogshockey.com
www.bulldogshockey.com

NORTHERN CYCLONES
Bill Flanagan: President & Head Coach
1 Mountain Road
Burlington, MA 01803
O 781.425.6778
bflanagan@northernmasshockey.com
www.northernmasshockey.com

CONNECTICUT WOLFPACK
Bob Crawford - President
6 Progress Drive
Cromwell, CT 06416
O 860.632.0323x25
rcraw1959@aol.com
www.jrwolfpack.com

PHILADELPHIA LITTLE FLYERS
John Giacobbo - President
827 Hunters Drive
Deptford, NJ 08096
O 215.901.0440
jsgflyers@aol.com
www.littleflyers.org

HUDSON VALLEY EAGLES
Keith McAdams - GM / Head Coach
595 New Loudon Rd, #148
Latham, NY 12180
O 631.796.8453
keithhockeygoal@aol.com
www.hudsonvalleyeagles.org

PORTLAND JUNIOR PIRATES
Sean O'Brien - President
PO Box 5033
Biddeford, Maine 04007
O 207.282.8484
sean@portlandjuniorpirates.com
www.portlandjuniorpirates.com

LACONIA LEAFS
Joshua Bourdon - General Mgr.
444 Province Road
Laconia, NH 03246
O 603.528.0789
coachbourdon@laconiaicearena.com
www.laconialeafs.com

WALPOLE EXPRESS
Rob Barletta - General Manager
2130 Providence Highway
Walpole, MA 02801
O 508.660.5423x220
rob@walpoleexpress.com
www.walpoleexpress.com

NEW JERSEY ROCKETS
Peggy Del Mauro - President
PO Box 126
Berkeley Heights, NJ 07922
O 908.753.1856
info@njrockets.com
www.njrockets.com

WASHINGTON JR. NATIONALS
Jeff Nygaard - General Manager
8107 Hampton Meadows Lane
Chesterfield, VA 23832
O 540.330.1357 / F 301.774.5372
washingtonlittlecaps@comcast.net
www.jrnationals.org

29 Cummings Park, Suite 404
Woburn, MA 01801
Phone: 781.938.4400 • Fax 781.938.4448
www.easternjunior.com

APPLE CORE MAJOR JUNIOR
GM: Henry Lazar
35 Seacoast Terrace, Apt 6U
Brooklyn, NY 11235
O 718.332.4555

JERSEY HITMEN
GM: Peter Masters
PO Box 2100
Framingham, MA 01703
O 508.820.1600

BAY STATE BREAKERS
President: John Cashman
PO Box 1178
Marshfield, MA 02066
O 781.792.2946

JUNIOR BRUINS
GM: Peter Masters
PO Box 2100
Framingham, MA 01703
O 508.820.1600

BOSTON HARBOR WOLVES
GM: Christian George
PO Box 290658
Boston, MA 02129
O 617.242.3006

NEW ENGLAND HUSKIES
President: Leo Gould
PO Box 405
Tyngsboro, MA 01879
O 508.634.3746

BRIDGEWATER BANDITS
GM: Mike McLaughlin
20 Bedford Park
Bridgewater, MA 02324
O 508.697.6804

NEW ENGLAND FALCONS
GM: Gary Dineen
Enfield Twin Rinks, 1 Prior Road
Enfield, CT 06082
O 860.745.5588

CAPITAL DISTRICT SELECTS
GM: Jim Salfi
19 Oakwood Blvd
Clifton Park, NY 12065
O 518.371.3795

NEW HAMPSHIRE MONARCHS
GM: Sean Tremblay
Tri-Town Arena, 311 West River Road
Hooksett, NH 03106
O 603.270.1013

FOXBORO STARS
President / GM: Fred Lane
2130 Providence Hwy., PO Box 227
Walpole, MA 02081
O 401.723.6134

SYRACUSE STARS
Owner / President: Don Kirnan
5679 Thompson Road
Dewitt, NY 13214
O 315.446.7363

GREEN MOUNTAIN GLADES
GM: Dennis Himes
81 Peterson Lane
Williston, VT 05495
O 802.879.3665

VALLEY JUNIOR WARRIORS
President: John Gilmartin
654 South Union Street
Lawrence, MA 01842
O 978.557.5517x11

ADMINISTRATION & TEAM ORGANIZATION
Commissioner: DAN ESDALE • danesdale@aol.com
Secretary/Treasurer: JIM PRIOR • jimprior@easternjunior.com

NY APPLE CORE MINOR JUNIOR
GM: Henry Lazar
lizard77@prodigy.net
O 718.332.4555

JUNIOR BRUINS
GM: Chris Masters
chris@bostonjuniorbruins.com
O 781.820.1600

BAY STATE BREAKERS
GM: David McCauley
baystatebreakers@verizon.net
O 781.878.7500x14

MAKSYMUM HOCKEY
GM: Tony Maksymiu
tony@maksymumhockey.com
O 585.426.8488

BREWSTER BULLDOGS
GM: Steve Santini
brewstericearena@aol.com
O 845.279.2229x10

NEW ENGLAND FALCONS
GM: Lincoln Flagg
jrcoyotecoach@cs.com
O 413.786.6063

BRIDGEWATER BANDITS
GM: Todd Stirling
tstirling@bridgewaterbandits.com
O 508.279.0600x111

NEW HAMPSHIRE MONARCHS
GM: Ryan Frew
ryan@tri-townicearena.com
O 603.270.1018

BUFFALO STARS
GM: Peter Preteroti
sportsniag@aol.com
O 716.685.1122

PITTSBURGH JUNIOR PENGUINS
GM: George Kelly
pghjrb@aol.com
O 412.977.4634

CAPITAL DISTRICT MINOR
Owner / GM: Jim Salfi
jpsalfi@aol.com
O 518.371.3795

SALEM ICE DOGS
GM: Mark Latham
salemicedogs@aol.com
O 978.745.3489

FITCHBURG HUSKIES
Head Coach: Jon Gardner
coachjongardner@yahoo.com
O 781.883.6437

SYRACUSE STARS
GM: Tony Herrick
tony@syracusestars.net
O 315.446.1238

FOXBORO STARS
GM: Rick Touzos
rtouzos@foxborosportscenter.com
O 508.698.0505

TRI-STATE SELECTS
President: Mike Palmer
eskimo66@aol.com
O 610.513.7378

GREEN MOUNTAIN GLADES
Head Coach: Justin Martin
peacvt@hotmail.com
O 802.233.3612

VALLEY JUNIOR WARRIORS
GM: Andy Heinze
aheinze@jrwarriors.com
O 978.557.5518x17

JERSEY WILDCATS
President: Jim Stanlick, Jr.
jimweld@aol.com
O 973.214.1065

VIRGINIA STATESMEN
GM: Paul Veillette
pveillette@skatequest.com
O 443.527.3802

METROPOLITAN JUNIOR HOCKEY LEAGUE
Glenn Hefferan, President
PO Box 1151 • McAfee, NJ 07428
O (973) 823-8147 • F (973) 823-8215
email: metleag@aol.com • web: www.metleague.org

BETHLEHEM BLAST

Jack Keefe - President
320 East First Street
Bethlehem, PA 18015
Phone: 610.625.4774
jkeefe@comcast-spectacor.com
www.bethlehemblast.org

CENTRAL PENN PANTHERS

Ray Ferry - President
Regency Sports Rink
2155 Ambassador Circle
Lancaster, PA 17603
Phone: 717.391.6065
manager@pennpanthers.org
www.pennpanthers.org

CONNECTICUT CLIPPERS

Bob Crawford - President
6 Progress Drive
Cromwell, CT 06416
Phone: 860.632.0323 Ext 25
rcraw1959@aol.com
www.clippershockey.com

CONNECTICUT WOLVES

Dan McCarthy - President
1346 Wolf Hill Road
Cheshire, CT 06410
Phone: 203.272.1069
dmccar1238@aol.com
www.ctwolveshockey.com

HUDSON VALLEY EAGLES

Keith McAdams - GM/Head Coach
Knickerbacker Arena
103rd Street and 8th Avenue
Troy, NY 12180
Phone: 631.796.8453
keithhockeygoal@aol.com
www.hudsonvalleyeagles.org

MASS CONN BRAVES

Jim Callahan - President
95 Prospect Street
East Longmeadow, MA 01028
Phone: 413.525.4205
jdcallahan@charter.net
www.massconnhockey.com

JUNIOR TITANS

George Haviland - Owner
c/o Wall Sports Arena
1215 Wyckoff Road
Farmingdale, NJ 07727
admin@jrtitans.com
www.jrtitans.com

NEW JERSEY ROCKETS

Peggy Del Mauro - President
PO Box 126
Berkeley Heights, NJ 07922
Phone: 908.753.1856
info@njrockets.com
www.njrockets.com

NORTHERN MASS CYCLONES

Bill Flanagan - President
One Mountain Road
Burlington, MA 01803
Phone: 781.425.6778
bflanagan@northernmasshockey.com
www.northernmasshockey.com

PHILADELPHIA JUNIOR FLYERS

Bud Dombrowski - GM / Head Coach
700 Lawrence Drive
West Chester, PA 19380
Phone: 610.436.9670
hockey@iceline.info
www.iceline.info/flyers/default.htm

PHILADELPHIA LITTLE FLYERS

John Giacobbo - President
827 Hunters Drive
Deptford, NJ 08096
Phone: 215.901.0440
jsgflyers@aol.com
www.littleflyers.org

PORTLAND JUNIOR PIRATES

Sean O'Brien - President
PO Box 5033
Biddeford, ME 04007
Phone: 207.282.8484
sean@portlandjuniorpirates.com
www.portlandjuniorpirates.com

SUFFOLK PAL
Jim Wright - GM/Head Coach
27 Laurel Drive
Sayville, NY 11782
Phone: 631.344.4606
puck@bnl.gov
www.suffolkpalhockey.com

VALLEY FORGE MINUTEMEN

Jerry Domish - GM/Head Coach
87 Brower Avenue
PO Box 1070
Oaks, PA 19456
Phone: 610.650.9690
jerry@oakscenterice.com
www.oakscenterice.com

WASHINGTON JR. CAPITALS
John Osidach - President
10220 Democracy Lane
Potomac, MD 20854
nick.carso@jrnats.com
www.jrnats.com

Commissioner
Bob Breu
717 Lincoln Avenue North
Faribault, MN 55021
C 507.210.1566
F 507.334.7801
bob@mnjhl.com

President
Ken Gaber
14450 288th Avenue NW
Zimmerman, MN 55398
C 563.580.2693
O 763.389.5779
mnjhlpres@aol.com

Vice President
Len Mankowski
PO Box 793
South St. Paul, MN 55075
O 651.451.1453
F 651.451.1508
len@mnjhl.com

Secretary
Mike Fatis
46807 Cape Horn Road
Cleveland, MN 56017
O 507.931.3797
F 507.931.0157
mike@mnjhl.com

Treasurer
Ross Smith
8109 Bryant Avenue South
Bloomington, MN 55420
O / F 952.888.4311
ross@mnjhl.com

Director of Media Relations
Brian McDonough
PO Box 24024
Edina, MN 55424
O 612.915.1644
C 612.220.4402
F 612.920.8326
brian@mnjhl.com

Minnesota Ice Hawks
Minnesota Owls
St. Louis Lightning
St. Paul Lakers
Twin Cities Northern Lights
Wisconsin Mustangs

NORTH AMERICAN HOCKEY LEAGUE
2601 Avenue of the Stars, Suite 400
Frisco, TX 75034
O 214.387.5650 / F 214.975.2250
www.nahl.com
nahl@nahl.com

Chairman
Jason Martel

| **Commissioner** | **Deputy Commissioner** |
| Eric Krupka | Mark Frankenfeld |

Director of Media & | **Director of Administration**
Communications | David Lee
Brian McDonough

Alaska Avalanche   North Iowa Outlaws
Alexandria Blizzard   Santa Fe Roadrunners
Alpena IceDiggers   Southern Minnesota Express
Bismarck Bobcats   Springfield Junior Blues
Fairbanks Ice Dogs   St. Louis Bandits
Fargo-Moorhead Jets   Texas Tornado
Mahoning Valley Phantoms   Traverse City North Stars
Marquette Rangers   Wichita Falls Wildcats
U.S. National U-18 Team

UNITED STATES HOCKEY LEAGUE
300 North 5th Street, Suite 2
Grand Forks, ND 58203
O 701.775.7334 / F 701.775.2684
www.ushl.com
ushl@ushl.com

Commissioner
John "Gino" Gasparini
O 701.775.6839
F 701.775.2684
ushl@ushl.com

Deputy Commissioner
Bill Bredin
bredin.ushl@midconetwork.com

Director of Hockey Operations
Scott Brand
215 South Kipling Street, #272
St. Paul, MN 55119
O 651.501.8724
F 651.501.8725

Director of Communications
& Media Relations
Andrew Leapaldt
leapaldt.ushl@midconetwork.com

Cedar Rapids RoughRiders

Chicago Steel

Des Moines Buccaneers

Green Bay Gamblers

Indiana Ice

Lincoln Stars

Ohio Junior Blue Jackets

Omaha Lancers

Sioux City Musketeers

Sioux Falls Stampede

Tri-City Storm

Waterloo Black Hawks

WESTERN STATES HOCKEY LEAGUE
1000 East Cerritos Avenue
Anaheim, CA 92805
O 714.502.9185 x240 / F 714.502.9375
www.wshl.org
wshloffice@aol.com

Chairman
Don R. Thorne
O 949.474.5915
F 949.474.5917
wshlhky@aol.com

Commissioner / President
Ron White
O 714.502.9185 x240
F 714.502.9375
wshloffice@aol.com

Deputy Commissioner
M.F. Schurman
O 619.990.3812
F 760.745.8427
mfschurman@sbcglobal.net

Secretary
Laura Ellis

Director of Publicity
Carl Brown

Cajun Catahoulas
Capital Thunder
Dallas Hawks
El Paso Rhinos
Peoria Coyotes
Phoenix Polar Bears
San Antonio Diablos
San Diego Surf
SoCal Bombers
Tulsa Rampage
Valencia Vipers

Canadian Jr. Route
to College Hockey

THE CANADIAN JUNIOR ROUTE TO COLLEGE HOCKEY

By Tom Keegan

Another option for college hockey exposure is through one of the Canadian Junior "A" Hockey Leagues. It is important to note that at this time, Major Junior Hockey is not an option. Players with Major Junior Hockey experience are virtually ineligible to participate at the college level in the United States. This may change in the near future so prospective college hockey players should monitor the progress of changes to the NCAA Amateurism Rules and Regulations. At the time this article is prepared, and this guide published, Major Junior Hockey is not an option for the prospective U. S. college hockey player.

Some of the Canadian Junior "A" Leagues have a long history of providing talent to U. S. Colleges. Despite the travel considerations Canadian Junior "A" Leagues are well scouted and generally do an excellent job of preparing players for the college game and beyond.

Most, if not all, of the Canadian Junior "A" Hockey Leagues also have their own league and/or team Educational Representatives that work with the teams and players to insure players meet the academic requirements of U. S. colleges and universities.

As we mentioned several times in the U.S. Junior article, it is important to investigate the leagues and teams to determine how each specific situation has done historically in preparing and placing players in U. S. college hockey programs.

In addition to the many Canadian Junior "A" Hockey Programs there are also many Canadian Junior "B" Hockey Leagues and Teams that have demonstrated their ability to both prepare and market their players over the years. We feel that you must investigate these successes more on a team by team basis as some teams in a league may consistently place most of their players while other teams in the same league may have very little success in the placement of players.

Canadian Junior Hockey is well supported by fans throughout the country. Teams generally have a strong fan base which often supports the local team both at home and on the road.

Many players from the United States have had great experiences playing both Junior "A" and Junior "B" hockey in Canada.

Once again, we encourage you to review the college hockey rosters contained in this guide to see the results. You will find that some college hockey programs are made up almost entirely of players with Canadian Junior Hockey experience.

SHAPE YOUR FUTURE THROUGH
EDUCATION
AND THE

The Alberta Junior Hockey League is dedicated to furnishing its athletes with the best available opportunities for future development and growth.

Our League supports its players through assistance in their academic, athletic and personal lives throughout their pursuit of individual goals.

WWW.AJHL.CA

AJHL ALUMNI ON 2006-07 NCAA ROSTERS

BONNYVILLE PONTIACS
Jean-Marc Beaudoin	St. Paul, AB
Karson Gillespie	Mankota, SK
Jon Kalinski	Lacorey, AB
Mark Letestu	Elk Point, AB
Connor Shields	Edmonton, AB
Rob Sirianni	Edmonton, AB

BROOKS BANDITS
Bryan Brunton	Colorado Spgs, CO
Brendan Connolly	Canmore, AB
Chad Johnson	Calgary, AB
Chris Meagher	Victoria, BC
Rob Turnville	Olds, AB

CALGARY CANUCKS
Dave Barton	Calgary, AB
Tyler Gotto	Calgary, AB
Jon Grecu	Calgary, AB
Pat Inglis	Calgary, AB
Kevin McLeod	Calgary, AB
Rob Smith	Brooks, AB

CALGARY ROYALS
Jay Beagle	Calgary, AB
Nathan Fornataro	Calgary, AB
Matt Forsyth	Calgary, AB
TJ Galiardi	Calgary, AB
John Gibson	Okotoks, AB
Kurtis Kisio	Calgary, AB
Mike Kneeland	Calgary, AB
Brian Lee	Toronto, ON
Jeff MacPhee	Calgary, AB
Mark Matheson	Calgary, AB
Mat Robinson	Calgary, AB
Brett Wilson	Calgary, AB

CAMROSE KODIAKS
Dan Bertram	Calgary, AB
Matt Boyd	St. Alber, AB
Ryan Donald	St. Albert, AB
TJ Fast	Calgary, AB
Dan Glover	Delburne, AB
Logan Gorslitz	Ft McMurray, AB
Lee Jubinville	Edmonton, AB
Matt McKnight	Selkirk, AB
Ryan Muspratt	Calgary, AB
Mason Raymond	Cochrane, AB
MacGregor Sharp	Red Deer, AB
David Thompson	Wainwright, AB
Chris Wanchulak	Edson, AB

CANMORE EAGLES
Jordan Alford	Red Deer, AB
Chris Berry	Calgary, AB
Mark Bomersback	Rochester, AB
Scott Kalinchuk	Sylvan Lk, AB
Joey Martini	Calgary, AB

CROWSNEST PASS
Brock Sheahan	Lethbridge, AB

DRAYTON VALLEY THUNDER
Taylor Davenport	Okotoks, AB
Cam French	St. Albert, AB
Dan Henningson	Edmonton, AB
Daryl Marcoux	Slave Lake, AB
Kael Mouillierat	Edmonton, AB
Jason Nopper	Calgary, AB
Jeremy Russell	St. Albert, AB
Braden Walls	Calgary, AB

DRUMHELLER DRAGONS
Brandon Knelsen	Three Hills, AB
Dion Knelsen	Three Hills, AB
AJ Mikkelson	Chestermere, AB

FORT MCMURRAY OIL BARONS
Lane Caffaro	Slave Lake, AB
TJ Campbell	Ft McMurray, AB
Matt Glasser	Calgary, AB
Matt Lamirande	Calgary, AB
Brad Mills	Olds, AB
Rob Nolan	Sherwood Pk, AB
Jody Pederson	Smithers, BC
Brandon Sadlowski	St. Paul, AB
Mike Schreiber	Sherwood Pk, AB
John Schwarz	Calgary, AB
Matt Strickland	Leduc, AB
Tyler Webb	Austin, TX
Chevan Wilson	St. Albert, AB

FORT SASKATCHEWAN TRADERS
Glenn Fisher	Edmonton, AB

GRANDE PRAIRIE STORM
Gabriel Chenard-Poirier	St. Augustin, QC
Ryan Chrenek	Grande Prairie, AB
Malcolm Gwilliam	Kamloops, BC
Mark Malekoff	Grande Prairie, AB
Scott McCulloch	Lacombe, AB
Kyle Radke	Bashaw, AB
Jordan Wakefield	Spruce Gr, AB
Chris Wilson	Prince Albert, SK

LLOYDMINSTER BOBCATS
Nick Kary   Wetaskiwin, AB

OKOTOKS OILERS
Neil Graham   Calgary, AB
Dallas Hand   Spruceview, AB

OLDS GRIZZLYS
Parker Burgess   Calgary, AB
Darcy Campbell   Airdrie, AB
Dave Cowan   Calgary, AB
Rob Cowan   Calgary, AB
Braden Desmet   Strathmore, AB
Tyler Hilbert   Okotoks, AB
Brett Hopfe   Didsbury, AB
Jimmy Kerr   Leduc, AB
Nathan Lawson   Calgary, AB
Landis Stankievech   Trochu, AB

SHERWOOD PARK CRUSADERS
Gregory Copeland   Lloydminster, SK
Braydon Cox   Sherwood Pk, AB

SHERWOOD PARK CRUSADERS (cont'd)
Sean Dersch   Edmonton, AB
Aaron Lee   Calgary, AB
Jeff Lee   Calgary, AB
Jeff Pasemko   Redwater, AB
Mark Smith   Edmonton, AB
Jase Weslosky   St. Albert, AB

SPRUCE GROVE SAINTS
Ryan Berry   Edmonton, AB
Jordan Erickson   Ft McNeill, BC
Blake Hamilton   Edmonton, AB
Ben Scrivens   Spruce Gr, AB
Nathan Sigmund   San Diego, CA
Nick Sirota   Fox Lake, WI

ST. ALBERT SAINTS
Kevin Du   Spruce Gr, AB
Nick Johnson   Calgary, AB
Brian McNary   Edmonton, AB
Justin Mills   Edgerton, AB

NCAA DIVISION I HOME ATTENDANCE

2005-2006

	Institution	Attendance	G	Avg		Institution	Attendance	G	Avg
1	Wisconsin	270,228	20	13,511	31	Providence	41,451	17	2,438
2	North Dakota	261,875	24	10,911	32	Clarkson	42,554	18	2,364
3	Minnesota	220,903	22	10,041	33	Bowling Green	47,165	20	2,358
4	Colorado	154,590	23	6,721	34	St. Lawrence	42,257	18	2,347
5	Michigan	140,350	21	6,683	35	Harvard	34,132	15	2,275
6	New Hampshire	118,627	19	6,243	36	Lake Superior State	41,346	19	2,176
7	St. Cloud State	109,975	18	6,109	37	Notre Dame	40,080	19	2,109
8	Denver	118,331	20	5,916	38	Army	33,849	17	1,991
9	Boston College	100,191	17	5,893	39	Princeton	27,492	14	1,963
10	Boston University	100,248	18	5,569	40	Alabama Huntsville	23,268	12	1,939
11	Nebraska Omaha	116,318	21	5,538	41	Quinnipiac	30,005	16	1,875
12	Ohio State	109,576	20	5,478	42	Colgate	36,104	20	1,805
13	Maine	107,696	20	5,384	43	Bemidji State	25,968	15	1,731
14	Michigan State	106,652	21	5,078	44	Merrimack	27,533	16	1,720
15	Minnesota Duluth	89,271	18	4,959	45	Union	32,547	19	1,713
16	Mass. Amherst	70,630	16	4,414	46	Ferris State	30,030	18	1,668
17	Dartmouth	64,260	16	4,016	47	Air Force	20,668	13	1,589
18	Vermont	72,054	18	4,003	48	Brown	11,406	9	1,267
19	Alaska Fairbanks	62,418	16	3,901	49	Holy Cross	18,198	16	1,137
20	Cornell	65,212	17	3,836	50	Niagara	17,461	16	1,091
21	Alaska Anchorage	64,999	18	3,611	51	Mercyhurst	15,184	18	843
22	Minn. State Mankato	64,177	18	3,565	52	Connecticut	10,866	14	776
23	Rensselaer	65,413	20	3,270	53	Robert Morris	8,556	16	534
24	Northern Michigan	67,659	21	3,221	54	Wayne State	6,902	13	530
25	Yale	43,332	14	3,095	55	Sacred Heart	6,652	15	443
26	Mass. Lowell	48,760	16	3,047	56	Bentley	5,577	17	328
27	Northeastern	39,906	14	2,850	57	Canisius	5,085	16	317
28	Western Michigan	47,178	17	2,775	58	American Int'l	3,409	16	213
29	Miami	47,768	18	2,653	NR	Rochester Institute	18,949	12	1,579
30	Michigan Tech	41,810	17	2,459		(reclassifying to DI)			

Governing Bodies

American Collegiate
Hockey Association
2475 Archdale
West Bloomfield, MI 48324-3607
O 248.366.7914 • Fax 248.366.7915
acha@achahockey.org
www.achahockey.org

Executive Director **Christian Wilk** chriswilk@achahockey.org	**President** **Marshall Stevenson** — Towson University — Linthicum Hall Towson, MD 21252 Office: 410.704.2963 Fax: 410.704.4702 mstevenson@achahockey.org
Vice President Division I **John Bosch** jbosch@achahockey.org	**Vice President Division II** **Paul Hebert** phebert@achahockey.org
Vice President Division III **Sam Kelly** kelly@achahockey.org	**Past President** **Josh Brandwene** jbrandwene@achahockey.org
Treasurer **Brian Moran** — Eastern Michigan University — 2475 Archdale West Bloomfield, MI 48324-3607 Office: 248.366.7914 Fax: 248.366.7915 bmoran4@achahockey.org	**Secretary** **Jim Martin** — Michigan State University — jmartin@achahockey.org

**American Collegiate
Hockey Association**
2475 Archdale
West Bloomfield, MI 48324-3607
O 248.366.7914 • Fax 248.366.7915
acha@achahockey.org
www.achahockey.org

Commissioner Division I
Brian Moran
— Eastern Michigan University —
2475 Archdale
West Bloomfield, MI 48324-3607
Office: 248.366.7914
Fax: 248.366.7915
bmoran4@achahockey.org

Commissioner Division II
Mike Radakovich
— University of Michigan —
18717 Golfview
Livonia, MI 48152
Office: 248.476.4203
d2commissioner@achahockey.org

Commissioner Division III
Tom Vanderlaan
d3commish@achahockey.org

Referee-in-Chief
Shane Hanlon
2308 Overland Avenue
Sinking Spring, PA 19608
Office: 610.621.5629
shanlon@achahockey.org

USA Hockey Representative
Ken Fikis
kfikis@achahockey.org

ACHA MEN'S PROGRAMS

Division I (50)

University of Arizona	Tucson, AZ
Arizona State University	Tempe, AZ
Binghamton University	Binghamton, NY
University at Buffalo	Buffalo, NY
Central Oklahoma University	Buffalo, NY
Cornell University	Ithaca, NY
University of Delaware	Newark, DE
Drexel University	Philadelphia, PA
Duquesne University	Pittsburgh, PA
Eastern Michigan University	Ypsilanti, MI
University of Illinois	Champaign, IL
Indiana University of Pennsylvania	Indiana, PA
Iowa State University	Ames, IA
Ithaca College	Ithaca, NY
John Carroll University	Cleveland, OH
Kent State University	Kent, OH
Lehigh University	Bethlehem, PA
Liberty University	Lynchburg, VA
Lindenwood University	Saint Charles, MO
University of Maryland	College Park, MD
Mercyhurst College	Erie, PA
University of Michigan Dearborn	Dearborn, MI
Minot State University	Minot, ND
United States Naval Academy	Annapolis, MD
Niagara University	Niagara, NY
North Dakota State University	Fargo, ND
Oakland University	Rochester, MI
Oswego State University	Oswego, NY
Ohio University	Athens, OH
University of Oklahoma	Norman, OK
Penn State University	State College, PA
University of Pittsburgh	Pittsburgh, PA
University of Rhode Island	Kingston, RI
Robert Morris College	Chicago, IL
Robert Morris University	Moon Township, PA
University of Rochester	Rochester, NY
Rutgers University	New Brunswick, NJ
Saint Louis University	St. Louis, MO
University of Scranton	Scranton, PA
Slippery Rock University	Slippery Rock, PA
St. Bonaventure University	St. Bonaventure, NY
Syracuse University	Syracuse, NY
Towson University	Towson, MD
Villanova University	Philadelphia, PA

www.achahockey.org

Washington & Jefferson College	Washington, PA
Weber State University	Ogden, UT
West Chester University	West Chester, PA
West Virginia University	Morgantown, WV
Western Michigan University	Kalamazoo, MI
Youngstown State University	Youngstown, OH

Division II (130)

Bates College	Lewiston, ME
Bowling Green State University	Bowling Green, OH
Bradley University	Peoria, IL
Bridgewater State College	Bridgewater, MA
Brigham Young University	Provo, UT
Bryant University	Smithfield, RI
C.W. Post, Long Island University	Brookville, NY
University of California Berkeley	Berkeley, CA
University of California Los Angeles	Los Angeles, CA
California State University Long Beach	Long Beach, CA
Central Connecticut State University	New Britain, CT
Central Michigan University	Mount Pleasant, MI
Clark University	Worcester, MA
University of Colorado	Boulder, CO
Colorado State University	Fort Collins, CO
Columbia Basin College	Pasco, WA
Connecticut College	New London, CT
University of Connecticut	Storrs, CT
Daniel Webster College	Nashua, NH
Davenport University	Grand Rapids, MI
University of Dayton	Dayton, OH
University of Denver	Denver, CO
DePaul University	Chicago, IL
Duke University	Durham, NC
Eastern Illinois University	Charleston, IL
Eastern Washington University	Cheney, WA
Endicott College	Beverly, MA
Ferris State University	Big Rapids, MI
Franklin & Marshall College	Lancaster, PA
Georgetown University	Washington, DC
Gonzaga University	Spokane, WA
Grand Valley State University	Allendale, MI
College of the Holy Cross	Worcester, MA
University of Idaho	Moscow, ID
University of Illinois	Champaign, IL
Indiana University	Bloomington, IN
University of Iowa	Iowa City, IA
University of Kansas	Lawrence, KS
La Salle University	Philadelphia, PA
Lafayette College	Easton, PA

 *www.achahockey.org*

Liberty University	Lynchburg, VA
Lindenwood University	St. Charles, MO
Loyola Marymount University	Los Angeles, CA
Lyndon State College	Lyndonville, VT
Marist College	Poughkeepsie, NY
Marquette University	Milwaukee, WI
University of Maryland Baltimore County	Baltimore, MD
Massachusetts Institute of Technology	Cambridge, MA
McKendree College	Lebanon, IL
Metropolitan State College of Denver	Denver, CO
Miami University (OH)	Oxford, OH
University of Michigan	Ann Arbor, MI
Michigan State University	East Lansing, MI
Michigan Technological University	Houghton, MI
Millersville University	Millersville, PA
Minnesota State University Mankato	Mankato, MN
University of Minnesota	Minneapolis, MN
Missouri State University- Maroon	Springfield, MO
Missouri State University - White	Springfield, MO
University of Missouri Columbia	Columbia, MO
Montana State University	Bozeman, MT
Montclair State University	Montclair, NJ
Muhlenberg College	Allentown, PA
University of Nebraska Lincoln	Lincoln, NE
University of Nevada - Las Vegas	Las Vegas, NV
University of New Hampshire	Durham, NH
The College of New Jersey	Ewing, NJ
New York University	New York, NY
University of North Carolina	Chapel Hill, NC
North Carolina State University	Raleigh, NC
Northern Illinois University	De Kalb, IL
Northern Michigan University	Marquette, MI
University of North Texas	Denton, TX
Northwestern University	Evanston, IL
Oakland University	Rochester Hills, MI
Ohio State University	Columbus, OH
University of Oregon	Eugene, OR
Palmer College of Chiropractic	Davenport, IA
University of Pennsylvania	Philadelphia, PA
Pennsylvania State University	State College, PA
University of Pittsburgh	Pittsburgh, PA
Princeton University	Princeton, NJ
University of Puget Sound	Tacoma, WA
Purdue University	West Lafayette, IN
Rhode Island College	Providence, RI
Rider University	Lawrenceville, NJ
Robert Morris College Chicago - Maroon	Chicago, IL
Robert Morris College Chicago - White	Chicago, IL
Robert Morris College Springfield	Springfield, IL

 *www.achahockey.org*

Rowan University	Glassboro, NJ
Saint Cloud State University	Saint Cloud, MN
Saint Joseph's University	Philadelphia, PA
Saint Norbert's College	DePere, WI
University of Saint Thomas	St. Paul, MN
San Jose State University	San Jose, CA
University of Scranton	Scranton, PA
Seton Hall University	South Orange, NJ
Siena College	Loudonville, NY
University of Southern California	Los Angeles, CA
Southern Illinois University Edwardsville - Gold	Edwardsville, IL
Southern Illinois University Edwardsville - Silver	Edwardsville, IL
Springfield College	Springfield, MA
Stanford University	Stanford, CA
University at Stony Brook	Stony Brook, NY
SUNY - Cortland	Cortland, NY
Temple University	Philadelphia, PA
University of Texas	Austin, TX
Texas A & M University	College Station, TX
Texas Tech University	Lubbock, TX
Union College	Schenectady, NY
University of Toledo	Toledo, OH
United States Coast Guard Academy	New London, CT
Utah State University	Logan, UT
Utah Valley State College	Orem, UT
University of Vermont	Burlington, VT
University of Virginia	Charlottesville, VA
Virginia Polytechnic Institute and State University	Blacksburg, VA
Wagner College	Staten Island, NY
Walla Walla College	Walla Walla, WA
University of Washington	Seattle, WA
Washington State University	Pullman, WA
Weber State University	Ogden, UT
West Virginia University	Morgantown, WV
Western Connecticut State University	Danbury, CT
Western Washington University	Bellingham, WA
Westfield State College	Westfield, MA
Wheaton College (IL)	Wheaton, IL
William Paterson University	Wayne, NJ
University of Wisconsin - Platteville	Platteville, WI
Worcester Polytechnic Institute	Worcester, MA

Division III (133)

University of Akron	Akron, OH
University of Alabama	Tuscaloosa, AL
Albany State University	Albany, NY
Albion College	Albion, MI
Community College of Allegheny County	Pittsburgh, PA
Alpena Community College	Alpena, MI

www.achahockey.org

Alvernia College	Reading, PA
Appalachian State University	Boone, NC
Arizona State University	Tempe, AZ
Baylor University	Waco, TX
Belmont University	Nashville, TN
Berklee College of Music	Boston, MA
Briarcliffe College	Bethpage, NY
Bryn Athyn College of the New Church	Bryn Athyn, PA
Butler University	Indianapolis, IN
University of California Davis	Davis, CA
University of California San Diego	San Diego, CA
California State University Northridge	Northridge, CA
California University of Pennsylvania	California, PA
Calvin College	Grand Rapids, MI
Carleton College	Northfield, MN
College of the Canyons	Santa Clarita, CA
Case Western Reserve University	Cleveland, OH
Catholic University of America	Washington, DC
University of Central Florida	Orlando, FL
Christopher Newport University	Newport News, VA
University of Cincinnati	Cincinnati, OH
The Citadel	Charleston, SC
Clemson University	Clemson, SC
University of Colorado	Boulder, CO
Colorado College	Colorado Springs, CO
Colorado School of Mines	Golden, CO
Creighton University	Omaha, NE
Dordt College	Sioux Center, IA
East Carolina University	Greenville, NC
Eastern Kentucky University	Richmond, KY
East Stroudsburg University	East Stroudsburg, PA
Edinboro University	Edinboro, PA
Embry-Riddle Aeronautical University	Daytona Beach, FL
Fairfield University	Fairfield, CT
Farmingdale State University	Farmingdale, NY
Ferris State University	Big Rapids, MI
University of Florida	Gainesville, FL
Florida Atlantic University	Boca Raton, FL
Florida Gulf Coast University	Fort Myers, FL
Florida Institute of Technology	Melbourne, FL
Florida Southern College	Lakeland, FL
Florida State University	Tallahassee, FL
Fordham University	Bronx, NY
Fort Lewis College	Durango, CO
Fresno State University	Fresno, CA
Frostburg State University	Frostburg, MD
George Washington University	Washington, DC
University of Georgia	Athens, GA
Georgia Tech University	Atlanta, GA

 *www.achahockey.org*

Grand Valley State University	Atlantic, GA
Hofstra University	Hempstead, NY
Hope College	Holland, MI
Indiana University of Pennsylvania	Indiana, PA
Indiana University Purdue University Indianapolis	Indianapolis, IN
Iowa State University	Ames, IA
Jackson Community College	Jackson, MI
Johns Hopkins University	Baltimore, MD
Kalamazoo College	Kalamazoo, MI
Kennesaw State University	Kennesaw, GA
Kutztown University	Kutztown, PA
Lansing Community College	Lansing, MI
Lawrence Technological University	Southfield, MI
Lincoln Land Community College	Springfield, IL
University of Louisville	Louisville, KY
Loyola College	Baltimore, MD
Lynn University	Boca Raton, FL
University of Mary Washington	Fredericksburg, VA
Middle Tennessee State University	Murfreesboro, TN
Monmouth University	West Long Branch, NJ
Moorpark College	Moorpark, CA
Mount Saint Mary's College	Newburgh, NY
Muhlenberg College	Allentown, PA
Muskegon Community College	Muskegon, MI
Nassau Community College	Garden City, NY
University of North Carolina Charlotte	Charlotte, NC
University of North Carolina Wilmington	Wilmington, NC
University of North Texas	Denton, TX
University of Northern Arizona	Flagstaff, AZ
University of Northern Colorado	Greeley, CO
University of Northern Iowa	Cedar Falls, IA
Northwood University	Midland, MI
Oakland University	Rochester Hills, MI
Oklahoma State University	Stillwater, OK
Old Dominion University	Norfolk, VA
Pennsylvania State University Altoona	Altoona, PA
Pennsylvania State University Behrend	Erie, PA
Pennsylvania State University Berks/Lehigh Valley College	Reading, PA
Pennsylvania State University Delaware County	Media, PA
University of Pittsburgh	Pittsburgh, PA
University of Pittsburgh Johnstown	Johnstown, PA
Radford University	Radford, VA
Richard Stockton College	Pomona, NJ
University of Richmond	Richmond, VA
Robert Morris University	Moon Township, PA
Rowan University	Glassboro, NJ
University of Rutgers-Camden	Camden, NJ
Sacramento State University	Sacramento, CA
San Diego State University	San Diego, CA

 www.achahockey.org

Saginaw Valley State University	Saginaw, MI
St. Clair County Community College	Port Huron, MI
St. Olaf College	Northfield, MN
Saint Vincent College	Latrobe, PA
Salisbury University	Salisbury, MD
Santa Rosa Junior College	Santa Rosa, CA
Shippensburg University	Shippensburg, PA
University of South Carolina	Columbia, SC
University of South Dakota	Vermillion, SD
South Dakota State University	Brookings, SD
University of South Florida	Tampa, FL
Southern Connecticut State University	New Haven, CT
University of Southern Indiana	Evansville, IN
Southern Methodist University	Dallas, TX
State University of New York Farmingdale	Farmingdale, NY
Suffolk County Community College	Seldon, NY
University of Tennessee	Knoxville, TN
University of Texas Austin	Austin, TX
Texas A&M University	College Station, TX
Texas Tech University	Lubbock, TX
Tulane University	New Orleans, LA
Vanderbilt University	Nashville, TN
Virginia Commonwealth University	Richmond, VA
Virginia Military Institute	Lexington, VA
Washington College	Chestertown, MD
Widener University	Chester, PA
College of William and Mary	Williamsburg, VA
Wright State University	Dayton, OH
University of Wyoming	Laramie, WY

 www.achahockey.org

AMERICAN COLLEGIATE HOCKEY ASSOCIATION

The American Collegiate Hockey Association (ACHA) is an organization of College/University affiliated programs, which provides structure, regulates operations and promotes the quality of collegiate ice hockey. The ACHA is a chartered non-profit corporation and is classified as a 501 (c) (3) organization with the Internal Revenue Service.

The ACHA was established on April 20, 1991. Fifteen charter members met during the Chicago Showcase in Skokie, IL at the North Shore Hilton. These member teams had been playing college hockey for many years but wished to legitimize its play by standardizing some of its procedures.

The members that created the organization were: Tom Keegan (ACHA), Al Murdoch (Iowa State), Joe Battista (Penn State), Jim Gilmore (Ohio), Ernie Ferrari (Stanford), Howard Jenks (California-Berkeley), Jeff Aikens (North Dakota State), Don Spencer (West Virginia), Jim Barry (Navy), Scott Fuller (Navy), Leo Golembiewski (Arizona), Ron Starr (DePaul), Cary Adams (PCHA), Jim Warden (PCHA), and Jack White (UCLA).

The inaugural year of the ACHA was the 1991-1992 season. The goal of the organization was to create an impartial governing body to monitor national tournaments, player eligibility, and general oversight. Over the years, this initial goal has evolved into the organization's mission statement: The ACHA's primary mission is to support the growth of two-year and four-year collegiate hockey programs nationwide; The ACHA identifies standards that serve to unite and regulate teams at the collegiate level; The ACHA shall emphasize academic performance, institutional sanction, eligibility criteria, and standards of play and opportunities for national competition; and the ACHA promotes all aspects of collegiate hockey stressing the personal development of individual athletes as well as national recognition for member organizations.

All ACHA teams are members of USA Hockey and joined the American Hockey Coaches Association (AHCA) in 1999.

The ACHA has both men's and women's teams. The men's side is made up of three divisions of men's teams: Division I, II, and III. Each of the separate divisions has its own distinguishing set of guidelines. The women's side has two divisions, with its inaugural season started in 2000 with 15 teams.

By the 10th anniversary season in 2001-2002 season, the ACHA had a total of 179 teams registered with 33 teams in Division I, 100 teams in Division II, 18 teams in Division III, and 20 teams in the Women's Division. Continued growth through the 2006-2007 season (15th anniversary) the total number of teams has increased to over 350 teams, with 50 teams in Division I, 146 teams in Division II, 119 teams in Division III, 32 teams in Women's Division I and 9 teams in the newly formed Women's Division II.

ACHA DIVISION I NATIONAL TOURNAMENT
2006-2007

YOUNGSTOWN, OHIO

FIRST ROUND *(2.28.07)*

University of Rhode Island	5 West Virginia University	3
Oklahoma University	1 University of Delaware	2
Ohio University	2 University of Michigan Dearborn	3 *(ot)*
Lindenwood University	4 Oakland University	5
Penn State University	2 Robert Morris College	1 *(ot)*
University of Illinois	5 Washington & Jefferson	0
Liberty University	9 Kent State University	1
Iowa State University	3 West Chester University	6

QUARTER-FINALS *(3.1.07)*

University of Rhode Island	3 University of Delaware	4
Oakland University	5 University of Michigan Dearborn	1
University of Illinois	8 West Chester University	3
Penn State University	2 Liberty University	1

SEMI-FINALS *(3.3.07)*

Penn State University	5 University of Delaware	2
University of Illinois	2 Oakland University	3

NATIONAL CHAMPIONSHIP *(3.4.07)*

Penn State University	1 Oakland University	5

ACHA DIVISION I NATIONAL TOURNAMENT
2006-2007

FINAL 2007 RANKIINGS
1. Oakland University
2. Pennsylvania State University
3. University of Illinois
4. University of Delaware
5. University of Rhode Island
6. Liberty University
7. West Chester University
8. University of Michigan-Dearborn
9. Oklahoma University
10. Ohio University
11. Lindenwood University
12. Iowa State University
13. West Virginia University
14. Kent State University
15. Robert Morris College
16. Washington & Jefferson University

ACHA DIVISION I NATIONAL CHAMPIONS

1983	University of Alabama Huntsville*
1984	University of Alabama Huntsville*
1985	Penn State University*
1986	University of Arizona*
1987	North Dakota State University*
1988	North Dakota State University*
1989	North Dakota State University*
1990	Penn State University*
1991	North Dakota State University*
1992	Iowa State University
1993	North Dakota State University
1994	North Dakota State University
1995	Ohio University
1996	Ohio University
1997	Ohio University
1998	Penn State University
1999	Vacated
2000	Penn State University
2001	Penn State University
2002	Penn State University
2003	Penn State University
2004	Ohio University
2005	University of Illinois
2006	University of Rhode Island
2007	Oakland University

*   ACHA established in 1991. NIT Champions for 1983-1990 inluded in list.

ACHA DIVISION II NATIONAL TOURNAMENT
2006-2007

POOL A RECORDS

Michigan State University	3 - 0 - 0
Stony Brook	2 - 1 - 0
Florida Gulf Coast University	1 - 2 - 0
San Jose State University	0 - 3 - 0

POOL B RECORDS

Eastern Washington University	2 - 1 - 0
Pennsylvania State University	2 - 1 - 0
University of Michigan	2 - 1 - 0
Ohio State University	0 - 3 - 0

POOL C RECORDS

Colorado State University	2 - 1 - 0
Miami University	1 - 1 - 1
Grand Valley State University	1 - 1 - 1
Siena University	1 - 2 - 1

POOL D RECORDS

Davenport University	3 - 0 - 0
University of Colorado	2 - 1 - 0
Wagner University	1 - 2 - 0
New York University	0 - 3 - 0

SEMI-FINALS

Davenport University	3	Eastern Washington University	0
Michigan State University	7	Colorado State University	3

NATIONAL CHAMPIONSHIP

Michigan State University	5	Davenport University	4

ACHA DIVISION II NATIONAL TOURNAMENT
2006-2007

FINAL 2007 RANKIINGS
1. Michigan State University
   2. Davenport University
3. Colorado State University
3. Eastern Washington University

ACHA DIVISION II NATIONAL CHAMPIONS

1994	Ferris State University
1995	Colorado State University
1996	Western Michigan University
1997	Life College
1998	Life College
1999	Life College
2000	Miami University
2001	Life College
2002	Life College
2003	University of Colorado
2004	Oakland University
2005	Michigan State University
2006	Oakland University
2007	Michigan State University

ACHA DIVISION III NATIONAL TOURNAMENT
2006-2007

NATIONAL CHAMPIONSHIP *(3.03.07)*

Kennesaw State University 5 SUNY Albany 1

ACHA DIVISION III NATIONAL CHAMPIONS

2000	Butler University
2001	University of Wyoming
2002	Robert Morris College
2003	Muskegon Community College
2004	Calvin College
2005	University of Colorado
2006	Wright State University
2007	Kennesaw State University

BOB JOHNSON AWARD

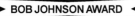

BOB JOHNSON AWARD

Presented annually by the Bob Johnson Foundation and College Hockey Guide to the player that best demonstrates hockey ability as well as achievement, leadership, good sportsmanship and enthusiasm, as well as academic and community service accomplishments.

Bob Johnson

March 4, 1931 - November 26, 1991

"The thing you remember is the enthusiasm which he brought to life. Everyday he would come to the rink, Bob would say, 'It's a great day for hockey'. I think that's how Bob wants to be remembered and that's how the hockey world will remember him."

Jeff Sauer
Head Coach
University of Wisconsin

BOB JOHNSON AWARD RECIPIENTS

1993 Ross Cowan
(Pennsylvania State University)

1994 Bill Ward
(Iowa State University)

1995 Jesse Hubenschmidt
(University of Michigan-Dearborn)

1996 Rob Keegan
(Pennsylvania State University)

1997 Doug Borud
(Iowa State University)

1998 Rob Howitt
(Iowa State University)

1999 Sam Eaton
(University of Illinois)

2000 Alon Eizenman
(Pennsylvania State University)

2001 Glenn Detulleo
(Iowa State University)

2002 Josh Mandel
(Pennsylvania State University)

2003 Tim Danlow
(University of Illinois)

2004 Glenn Zuck
(Pennsylvania State University)

2005 Mike Roesch
(University of Illinois)

2006 Anthony Feyock
(University of Rhode Island)

**American Hockey
Coaches Association**
7 Concord Street
Gloucester, MA 01930
www.ahcahockey.com

**Executive Director
Joe Bertagna**
7 Concord Street
Gloucester, MA 01930
Phone: 781.245.4177
Fax: 781.245.2492
jbertagna@hockeyeastonline.com

**Treasurer
Bruce Delventhal**
SUNY - Plattsburgh
101 Broad Street
Plattsburgh, NY 12901
Phone: 518.564.3140
delvenbw@plattsburgh.edu

**President
George Gwozdecky**
University of Denver

**Vice President
Sponsorships
Mike Schafer**
Cornell University

**Vice President
Membership
Paul Pearl**
College of Holy Cross

**Vice President
Convention Planning
Kevin Patrick**
University of Wisconsin

**Past President
Roger Grillo**
Brown University

**63rd Annual AHCA Convention & Exhibits
Naples, Florida
April 2007**

Coaches: contact Joe Bertagna
for membership information

AHCA

The American Hockey Coaches Association was formed in May of 1947 in Boston, MA, by a handful of college coaches concerned about the game they loved. It has grown to include professional, junior, high school, and youth hockey coaches, as well as referees, administrators, sales representatives, journalists, and fans. It is open to men and women alike. Perhaps the best way to understand the AHCA is to read its formal goals, as written in the AHCA Constitution:

The object of this Association shall be:

1. To help maintain the highest possible standards in hockey and the hockey profession.

2. To discuss matters of mutual interest.

3. To submit to the proper organizations, suggestions for the improvement of hockey.

4. To discuss various phases of hockey.

5. To place at the disposal of coaches sources of hockey information.

6. To work together for the improvement of conditions in American hockey.

7. To have a representative group of hockey people before whom hockey problems of general interest may be discussed and to whom others may be referred for the friendly interchange of ideas.

8. To establish good fellowship and social contact.

9. To maintain high educational standards when coaching the game of ice hockey

To reach its stated goals, the AHCA is led by a slate of Officers and a Board of Governors, elected by the AHCA membership. In addition, the following Standing Committees assist in the identification and implementation of projects for the association. The committees are:

· Awards Committee

· Convention Planning Committee

· Ethics Committee (Exec. Committee)

· High School-Professional Committee

· Legislative Committee

· Rules Recommendation

· Committee Sponsorship-Liaison Committee

· Women's Committee

Through this structure, the AHCA will honor both its post and present, through awards recognizing individuals and teams who have achieved a unique place in the game.

shape the on-ice playing rules used by the NCAA.

encourage sportsmanship through its 'Code of Conduct' for coaches and athletes.

· share information on coaching and training strategies and methods.

· assist the NCAA and college hockey conference commissioners in promoting the game.

· provide a forum for the exchange of ideas on hockey, through regular publications during the hockey season and through clinics for coaches, as well as the annual AHCA Convention in the spring.

**National Collegiate
Athletic Association**
700 West Washington Street
PO Box 6222
Indianapolis, Indiana 46206-6222
www.ncaa.org

**Division I
Tom Jacobs**
Office: 317.917.6222
Fax: 317.917.6888
tjacobs@ncaa.org

**Division III
Keisha Campbell**
Office: 317.917.6222
Fax: 317.917.6888
kcampbell@ncaa.org

**Playing Rules / Publications
Ty Halpin**
Office: 317.917.6222
Fax: 317.917.6888
thalpin@ncaa.org

**Media
Mark Bedics**
Office: 317.917.6222
Fax: 317.917.6888
mbedics@ncaa.org

**Records / Statistics
Bonnie Senappe**
Office: 317.917.6222
Fax: 317.917.6888
bsenappe@ncaa.org

**Records / Statistics
J. D. Hamilton**
Office: 317.917.6222
Fax: 317.917.6888
jhamilton@ncaa.org

NCAA MEN'S PROGRAMS

Division I (59)

University of Alabama, Huntsville	CHA
University of Alaska Anchorage	WCHA
University of Alaska Fairbanks	CCHA
American International College	AHA
Bemidji State University	CHA
Bentley College	AHA
Boston College	HEA
Boston University	HEA
Bowling Green State University	CCHA
Brown University	ECAC
Canisius College	AHA
Clarkson University	ECAC
Colgate University	ECAC
Colorado College	WCHA
University of Connecticut	AHA
Cornell University	ECAC
Dartmouth College	ECAC
University of Denver	WCHA
Ferris State University	CCHA
Harvard University	ECAC
College of the Holy Cross	AHA
Lake Superior State University	CCHA
University of Maine, Orono	HEA
University of Massachusetts, Amherst	HEA
University of Massachusetts at Lowell	HEA
Mercyhurst College	AHA
Merrimack College	HEA
Miami University	CCHA
University of Michigan	CCHA
Michigan State University	CCHA
Michigan Technological University	WCHA
Minnesota State University Mankato	WCHA
University of Minnesota Duluth	WCHA
University of Minnesota, Twin Cities	WCHA
University of Nebraska at Omaha	CCHA
University of New Hampshire	HEA
Niagara University	CHA
University of North Dakota	WCHA
Northeastern University	HEA
Northern Michigan University	CCHA
University of Notre Dame	CCHA
Ohio State University	CCHA
Princeton University	ECAC
Providence College	HEA
Quinnipiac University	AHA
Rensselaer Polytechnic Institute	ECAC
Robert Morris University	CHA
Rochester Institute of Technology	AHA
Sacred Heart University	AHA
St. Cloud State University	WCHA
St. Lawrence University	ECAC
U.S. Air Force Academy	CHA
U.S. Military Academy	AHA

Union College	ECAC
University of Vermont	ECAC
Wayne State University	CHA
Western Michigan University	CCHA
University of Wisconsin, Madison	WCHA
Yale University	ECAC

Division II (7)

Assumption College	ECAC Northeast
Franklin Pierce College	ECAC Northeast
University of Minnesota, Crookston	Independent
Southern New Hampshire University	Northeast-10
Saint Anselm College	ECAC
Saint Michael's College	ECAC East
Stonehill College	ECAC Northeast

Division III (70)

Adrian College *(2007/2008)*	MCHA
Amherst College	NESCAC
Augsburg College	MIAC
Babson College	ECAC East
Becker College	Independent
Bethel University	MIAC
Bowdoin College	NESCAC
Castleton State College	ECAC East
Colby College	NESCAC
Concordia College, Moorhead	MIAC
Concordia University Wisconsin *(2007/2008)*	MCHA
Connecticut College	NESCAC
Curry College	ECAC Northeast
Elmira College	Independent
Finlandia University	Independent
Fitchburg State College	ECAC Northeast
Framingham State College	ECAC Northeast
Gustavus Adolphus College	MIAC
Hamilton College	NESCAC
Hamline University	MIAC
Hobart College	ECAC
Johnson and Wales University	ECAC Northeast
Lake Forest College	NCHA
Lawrence University	Independent
Lebanon Valley College	ECAC Northeast
Manhattanville College	ECAC-III
Marian College	Independent
University of Massachusetts, Boston	ECAC East
University of Massachusetts, Dartmouth	ECAC Northeast
Middlebury College	NESCAC
Milwaukee School of Engineering	Independent
Neumann College	ECAC-III
New England College	ECAC East
University of New England *(2010/2011)*	
Nichols College	ECAC Northeast
Northland College	Independent
Norwich University	ECAC East
Plymouth State College	ECAC Northeast
Salem State College	ECAC East

Salve Regina University	ECAC Northeast
University of Scranton	Independent
Skidmore College	ECAC East
University of Southern Maine	ECAC East
Saint John's University	MIAC
Saint Mary's University of Minnesota	MIAC
Saint Norbert College	NCHA
Saint Olaf College	MIAC
College of Saint Scholastica	NCHA
University of Saint Thomas	MIAC
State University of New York Brockport	SUNYAC
State University of New York Buffalo State	SUNYAC
State University of New York Cortland	SUNYAC
State University of New York Fredonia	SUNYAC
State University of New York Geneseo	SUNYAC
State University of New York Oswego	SUNYAC
State University of New York Plattsburgh	SUNYAC
State University of New York Potsdam	SUNYAC
Suffolk University	ECAC Northeast
Trinity College	NESCAC
Tufts University	NESCAC
Utica College	ECAC
Wentworth Institute of Technology	ECAC Northeast
Wesleyan University	NESCAC
Western New England College	ECAC Northeast
Williams College	NESCAC
University of Wisconsin, Eau Claire	NCHA
University of Wisconsin, River Falls	NCHA
University of Wisconsin, Stevens Point	NCHA
University of Wisconsin, Stout	NCHA
University of Wisconsin, Superior	NCHA
Worcester State College	ECAC Northeast

NCAA DIVISION I CHAMPIONSHIP
2006-2007

FIRST ROUND *(3.23.07 - 3.24.07)*

University of Minnesota Twin Cities	4	Air Force Academy	3
University of North Dakota	8	University of Michigan	5
Boston College	4	St. Lawrence University	1
Miami University	2	University of New Hampshire	1 *ot*
Clarkson University	0	University of Massachusetts	1 *ot*
University of Maine	4	St. Cloud State University	1
Boston University	1	Michigan State University	5
University of Alabama Huntsville	2	University of Notre Dame	3 *ot*

SECOND ROUND *(3.24.07 - 3.25.07)*

University of North Dakota	3	University of Minnesota Twin Cities	2 *(ot)*
Boston College	4	Miami University	0
University of Massachusetts	1	University of Maine	3
Michigan State University	2	University of Notre Dame	1

SEMI FINALS *(4.5.07)*

University of North Dakota	4	Boston College	6
University of Maine	2	Michigan State University	4

NATIONAL CHAMPIONSHIP *(4.7.07)*

Boston College	1	Michigan State University	3

NCAA DIVISION III CHAMPIONSHIP

2006-2007

PLAY-IN *(3.7.07)*

University of Wisconsin River Falls	1	Bethel College	2
Middlebury College	9	SUNY Fredonia	1

QUARTER FINALS *(3.10.07)*

St. Norbert College	4	Bethel College	1
SUNY Oswego	3	Norwich University	0
Manhattanville College	5	Babson College	3
Univ. of Massachsetts Dartmouth	2	Middlebury College	3

SEMIFINALS *(3.17.07)*

St. Norbert College	3	SUNY Oswego	4(*ot*)
Manhattanville College	2	Middlebury College	3

NATIONAL CHAMPIONSHIP *(3.18.07)*

SUNY Oswego	4	Middlebury College	3 *(ot)*

HOBEY BAKER MEMORIAL AWARD

The Hobey Baker Memorial Award is presented annually to the outstanding NCAA college hockey player in the United States by the Decathlon Club of Bloomington, Minnesota. The award has become recognized as U.S. college hockey's premier individual honor. As such, it has helped promote U.S. college hockey, the skills needed to play the game and the ideals for which the original Hobey Baker lived and died.

Hobey Baker had all the attributes of a fabulous athlete; a great physique, fantastic reflexes, instant coordination of hand and eye, iron discipline, blazing courage. But he was different. Hobey Baker was the college athlete supreme. The gentleman sportsman, the amateur in the pure sense, playing the game for the sport, who never fouled, despised publicity and refused professional offers. To this day, he is offered as a striking example of the finest that America has produced. In his era, Hobey Baker was universally recognized as the best amateur hockey player in the United States.

HOBEY BAKER AWARD WINNERS

1981	Neal Broten *University of Minnesota*
1982	George McPhee *Bowling Green State University*
1983	Mark Fusco *Harvard University*
1984	Tom Kurvers *University of Minnesota-Duluth*
1985	Bill Watson *University of Minnesota-Duluth*
1986	Scott Fusco *Harvard University*
1987	Tony Hrkac *University of North Dakota*
1988	Robb Stauber *Univ. of Minnesota-Twin Cities*
1989	Lane MacDonald *Harvard University*
1990	Kip Miller *Michigan State University*
1991	David Emma *Boston College*
1992	Scott Pellerin *University of Maine*
1993	Paul Kariya *University of Maine*
1994	Chris Marinucci *University of Minnesota-Duluth*
1995	Brian Holzinger *Bowling Green State University*
1996	Brian Bonin *Univ. of Minnesota-Twin Cities*
1997	Brendan Morrison *University of Michigan-Ann Arbor*
1998	Chris Drury *Boston University*
1999	Jason Krog *University of New Hampshire*
2000	Mike Mottau *Boston College*
2001	Ryan Miller *Michigan State University*
2002	Jordan Leopold *University of Minnesota*
2003	Peter Sejna *Colorado College*
2004	Junior Lessard *University of Minnesota-Duluth*
2005	Marty Sertich *Colorado College*
2006	Matt Carle *Denver University*
2007	Ryan Duncan *University of North Dakota*

NCAA DIVISION I RECORDS 2006-2007

	W	L	T	Win %
Notre Dame	32	7	2	.798
Minnesota - Crookston	31	10	3	739
Norwich	20	8	0	.714
Clarkson	25	9	5	.705
Castleton	17	6	4	.704
Boston College	29	12	1	.702
New Hampshire	26	11	2	.692
Michigan State	26	13	3	.655
Rochester Institute of Technology	21	11	2	.647
Michigan	26	14	1	.646
Sacred Heart	21	11	4	.639
St. Cloud State	22	11	7	.638
Boston University	20	10	9	.628
New England College	17	10	1	.625
Miami	24	14	4	.619
North Dakota	24	14	5	.616
St. Lawrence	23	14	2	.615
Massachusetts - Amherst	21	13	5	.603
Maine	23	15	2	.600
Dartmouth	18	12	3	.591
Quinnipiac	21	14	5	.588
Denver	21	15	4	.575
United States Military Academy	17	12	5	.574
Niagara	18	13	6	.568
United States Air Force Academy	19	16	5	.538
Vermont	18	16	5	.526
Nebraska - Omaha	18	16	8	.524
Lake Superior	21	19	3	.523
Cornell	14	13	4	.516
Colorado	18	17	4	.513
Michigan Tech	18	17	5	.512
Wisconsin - Madison	19	18	4	.512
Bemidji State	14	14	5	.500
Western Michigan	18	18	1	.500
Princeton	15	16	3	.485

Ohio State	15	17	5	.473
Connecticut	16	18	2	.472
Harvard	14	17	2	.455
Brown	11	15	6	.438
Northeastern	13	18	5	.431
Union	14	9	3	.431
Robert Morris	14	19	2	.429
Colgate	15	21	4	.425
Minnesota - Mankata	13	19	6	.421
Alabama - Huntsville	13	20	3	.403
Yale	11	17	3	.403
Ferris State	14	22	3	.397
Minnesota - Duluth	13	21	5	.397
Alaska - Anchorage	13	21	3	.392
Northern Michigan	15	24	2	.390
Rensselaer	10	18	8	.389
Wayne State	12	21	2	.371
Alaska - Fairbanks	11	22	6	.359
Bentley	12	22	1	.357
Holy Cross	10	20	5	.357
Mercyhurst	9	20	6	.343
Massachusetts - Lowell	8	21	7	.319
Providence	10	23	3	.319
Cansius	9	23	3	.300
American International College	8	25	1	.250
Bowling Green	7	29	2	.211
Merrimack	3	27	4	.147

NCAA DIVISION III RECORDS 2006-2007

	W	L	T	Win %
Massachusetts - Dartmouth	25	3	1	.879
Oswego	23	3	3	.845
Manhattanville	21	2	5	.839
St. Norbert	25	4	2	.839
Wisconsin - Stout	21	5	2	.786
Wisconsin - River Falls	21	6	2	.759
Wisconsin - Superior	20	6	1	.759
Milwaukee School of Engineering	19	6	2	.741
Neumann	17	5	5	.722
Norwich	20	8	0	.714
Finlandia	19	8	0	.704
Castleton	17	6	4	.704
Middlebury	20	8	3	.694
Bowdoin	16	7	3	.673
Skidmore	16	8	2	.654
Babson	18	10	1	.638
Bethel	18	10	1	.638
St. Thomas	17	10	0	.630
Curry	16	9	2	.630
New England College	17	10	1	.625
Wentworth	16	9	3	.625
Geneseo	16	10	0	.615
Southern Maine	15	9	2	.615
Plattsburgh	14	8	6	.607
Colby	14	9	2	.600
Hobart	13	8	5	.596
Fredonia	15	10	4	.586
Amherst	14	10	1	.580
Utica	13	9	3	.580
Fitchburg State	14	10	3	.574
Wesleyan	11	8	5	.562
Elmira	13	10	4	.556
St. Scholastica	15	12	2	.552
Nichols	13	11	1	.538
Augsburg	12	10	4	.538
Stonehill	14	12	1	.537
Marian	14	12	3	.534
St. Anslem	13	2	3	.518
Buffalo State	12	12	2	.500
Johnson & Wales	12	12	1	.500
Lawrence	13	14	2	.483
Southern New Hampshire	12	14	1	.463
Gustavus Adolphus	11	13	2	.462
Plymouth State	11	13	2	.462

St. Olaf	11	14	2	.444
Connecticut College	10	13	2	.440
Salve Regina	10	14	1	.420
Wisconsin - Eau Claire	9	14	4	.407
Brockport	7	12	7	.404
St. John's	9	14	2	.400
Trinity	8	13	4	.400
Cortland	8	14	3	.380
Williams	8	14	2	.375
Western New England	8	15	0	.348
Salem State	9	17	0	.346
Suffolk	7	15	2	.333
Minnesota - Crookston	7	16	3	.327
Hamilton	7	16	1	.312
St. Mary's	7	17	1	.300
Assumption	7	18	2	.296
Wisconsin - Stevens Point	7	18	2	.296
Worcester State	6	16	1	.283
Concordia	7	18	0	.280
Hamline	7	18	0	.280
Tufts	6	18	0	.250
Franklin Pierce	5	17	2	.250
St. Michael's	6	20	0	.231
Potsdam	5	19	1	.220
University of Massachusetts - Boston	5	20	1	.212
Lake Forest	3	21	3	.167
Framingham State	2	20	1	.109
Lebanon Valley	2	22	1	.100
Northland	0	26	1	.019

**National Junior College
Athletic Association**
PO Box 7305
Colorado Springs, CO 80933-7305
www.njcaa.org

**Executive Director
Wayne Baker**
Office: 719.590.9788
Fax: 719.590.7324
wbaker@njcaa.org

**Associate Executive Director
Mary Ellen Leight**
Office: 719.590.9788
Fax: 719.590.7324
meleight@njcaa.org

**NJCAA Ice Hockey Coaches Association President
Pat Martin
(SUNY - Canton)**

NJCAA MEMBER COLLEGES

Erie Community College
Hudson Valley Community College
Minot State University - Bottineau
Mohawk Valley Community College
Monroe Community College
Country College of Morris
North Country Community College
SUNY - Canton

NATIONAL JUNIOR COLLEGE ATHLETIC ASSOCIATION
TOURNAMENT CHAMPIONS

1972	Itasca State Junior College	1990	College of DuPage
1973	Canton Agricultural Tech. College	1991	North Dakota State Univ.-Bottineau
1974	Canton Agricultural Tech. College	1992	Canton Agricultural Tech. College
1975	Canton Agricultural Tech. College	1993	University of Minnesota-Crookston
1976	Canton Agricultural Tech. College	1994	University of Minnesota-Crookston
1977	Rainy River Community College	1995	North Country Community College
1978	Canton Agricultural Tech. College	1996	SUNY-Canton
1979	Canton Agricultural Tech. College	1997	SUNY-Canton
1980	College of DuPage	1998	Minot State University - Bottineau
1981	Canton Agricultural Tech. College	1999	Rainy River Community College
1982	Canton Agricultural Tech. College	2000	SUNY-Canton
1983	Canton Agricultural Tech. College	2001	Hudson Valley Community College
1984	Hibbing Community College	2002	Morrisville State College
1985	Hibbing Community College	2003	Minot State University - Bottineau
1986	North Dakota State Univ.-Bottineau	2004	Morrisville State College
1987	SUNY-Canton	2005	Morrisville State College
1988	College of DuPage	2006	Morrsiville State College
1989	Canton Agricultural Tech. College	2007	Minot State University - Bottineau

Leagues

Atlantic Hockey Association
591 North Avenue, #2
Wakefield, MA 01880
781.246.2595 • Fax 781.246.2576
www.atlantichockeyonline.com

Commissioner
Robert M. DeGregorio, Jr.
Office: 781.246.2595
Fax: 781.246.2576
rdegregorio@atlantichockeyonline.com

Director of Media Relations
David Rourke
Office: 781.246.2595
Fax: 781.246.2576
drourke@atlantichockeyonline.com

Director of Officiating
Eugene Binda
Office: 781.246.2575
Fax: 781.246.2576

American International College

Bentley College

Canisius College

University of Connecticut

College of the Holy Cross

Mercyhurst College

Rochester Institute of Technology

Sacred Heart University

United States Air Force Academy

United States Military Academy

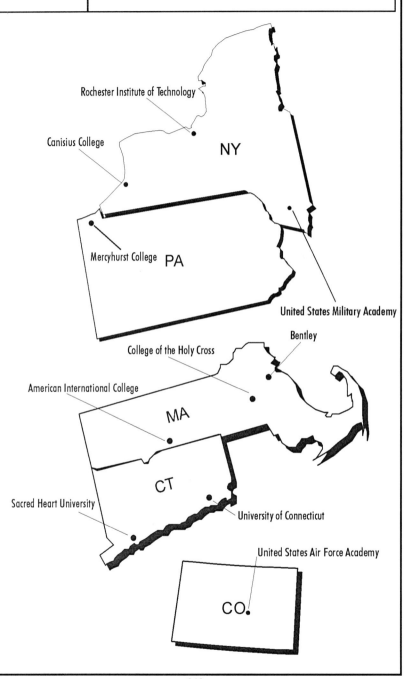

Rochester Institute of Technology

Canisius College

NY

Mercyhurst College PA

United States Military Academy

Bentley

College of the Holy Cross

American International College

MA

CT

Sacred Heart University

University of Connecticut

United States Air Force Academy

CO

ATLANTIC HOCKEY ASSOCIATION
FINAL 2006-2007 CONFERENCE STANDINGS

		Pts	GP	Record	Win%	GF- GA	GP	Record	Win%	GF- GA
1	RIT	41	28	20- 7- 1	0.732	116- 71	34	21-11- 2	0.647	132- 93
2	Sacred Heart	38	28	17- 7- 4	0.679	91- 74	36	21-11- 4	0.639	118- 99
3	Army	35	28	15- 8- 5	0.625	82- 69	34	17-12- 5	0.574	94- 87
4	Connecticut	32	28	15-11- 2	0.571	90- 89	36	16-18- 2	0.472	108-126
5	Air Force	31	28	13-10- 5	0.554	94- 70	40	19-16- 5	0.538	132-107
6	Holy Cross	23	28	9-14- 5	0.411	87- 94	35	10-20- 5	0.357	96-123
7	Mercyhurst	22	28	9-15- 4	0.393	98-106	35	9-20- 6	0.343	114-134
	Bentley	22	28	11-17- 0	0.393	75-101	35	12-22- 1	0.357	90-136
9	Canisius	21	28	9-16- 3	0.375	76- 95	35	9-23- 3	0.300	86-130
10	American International	15	28	7-20- 1	0.268	68-108	34	8-25- 1	0.250	74-134

2007 ATLANTIC HOCKEY TOURNAMENT

PLAY-IN GAME *(3.03.07)*

American International College	2	Canisius College	1

QUARTER FINALS *(3.10.07)*

Bentley College	2	United States Military Academy	6
American International College	0	Sacred Heart University	4
College of the Holy Cross	0	United States Air Force Academy	3
Mercyhurst College	4	University of Connecticut	5

SEMI FINALS *(3.16.07)*

United States Air Force Academy	5	Sacred Heart University	4
University of Connecticut	1	United States Military Academy	3

CHAMPIONSHIP *(3.17.07)*

United States Air Force Academy	6	United States Military Academy	1

ATLANTIC HOCKEY ASSOCIATION CHAMPIONS

	REGULAR	TOURNAMENT
2004	College of the Holy Cross	College of the Holy Cross
2005	Quinnipiac University	Mercyhurst College
2006	College of the Holy Cross	College of the Holy Cross
2007	Rochester Institute of Technology	United States Air Force Academy

ATLANTIC HOCKEY LEAGUE SCORING (OVERALL):

					GP	PPG	G - A - P
1	Eric Ehn	Air Force	JR	F	40	1.60	24-40-64
2	Andrew Ramsey	Air Force	SR	F	36	1.33	23-25-48
3	James Sixsmith	Holy Cross	SR	F	35	1.34	17-30-47
4	Pierre-Luc O'Brien	Sacred Heart	SR	F	36	1.28	16-30-46
5	Steve Pinizzotto	RIT	SO	F	34	1.29	13-31-44
	Mike Phillipich	Air Force	SO	F	37	1.19	16-28-44
7	Simon Lambert	RIT	JR	F	34	1.26	17-26-43
8	Bear Trapp	Sacred Heart	SO	F	36	1.11	17-23-40
9	Alexandre Parent	Sacred Heart	JR	F	36	1.06	15-23-38
10	Luke Flicek	Army	JR	F	34	1.09	14-23-37
11	Matt Scherer	Connecticut	SR	F	35	1.03	22-14-36
12	Ben Cottreau	Mercyhurst	JR	F	28	1.25	14-21-35
	Matt Smith	RIT	JR	F	34	1.03	17-18-35
14	Dale Reinhardt	Holy Cross	JR	F	35	0.97	16-18-34
	Josh Heidinger	Canisius	FR	F	35	0.97	8-26-34
	Cole Koidahl	Connecticut	SR	F	36	0.94	13-21-34
17	Jeff Gumaer	Bentley	SO	F	34	0.97	18-15-33
	Kyle Gourgon	Mercyhurst	SR	F	35	0.94	11-22-33
19	Trevor Stewart	Connecticut	SR	F	36	0.89	9-23-32
20	Chris Myhro	Connecticut	SO	F	34	0.91	20-11-31
21	Al Mazur	RIT	FR	D	29	1.00	6-23-29
	Tim Manthey	Army	SO	D	34	0.85	11-18-29
23	Jereme Tendler	American Intern.	JR	F	32	0.88	15-13-28
	Brent Patry	RIT	JR	D	34	0.82	9-19-28
	Dain Prewitt	Bentley	SO	F	35	0.80	13-15-28
	Eric Giosa	Sacred Heart	SO	F	36	0.78	12-16-28
27	Scott Champagne	Mercyhurst	SR	F	26	1.04	10-17-27
	Jon Landry	Holy Cross	SR	D	27	1.00	9-18-27
	Owen Meyer	Army	FR	F	32	0.84	11-16-27
	Bryce Hollweg	Army	JR	F	34	0.79	10-17-27
	Jeff Hajner	Air Force	FR	F	40	0.68	13-14-27
32	Anton Kharin	RIT	FR	F	34	0.76	14-12-26
	Jason Weeks	Canisius	FR	F	35	0.74	15-11-26
	Anthony Canzoneri	Bentley	SO	F	35	0.74	9-17-26
35	Matt Pierce	Mercyhurst	SO	F	35	0.71	11-14-25
	David Grimson	Sacred Heart	SO	D	36	0.69	4-21-25
37	Dave Jarman	Sacred Heart	FR	F	34	0.65	11-11-22
	Casey Bickley	Army	SR	D	34	0.65	6-16-22
39	Ryan Toomey	Mercyhurst	JR	F	32	0.66	12- 9-21
	Carl Hudson	Canisius	FR	D	34	0.62	10-11-21
	Michael Cohen	Canisius	SR	F	35	0.60	10-11-21
	Cody Collins	Mercyhurst	FR	F	35	0.60	6-15-21
	Josh Schaffer	Air Force	JR	F	38	0.55	7-14-21
44	Dan Ringwald	RIT	FR	D	30	0.67	4-16-20
	Marc Menzione	Bentley	FR	F	34	0.59	7-13-20
	Ricky Walton	RIT	JR	F	34	0.59	6-14-20
47	David Kasch	Canisius	JR	F	27	0.70	6-13-19
	Marc Zwicky	Bentley	JR	F	32	0.59	5-14-19
	Chris Forsman	Canisius	FR	D	34	0.56	6-13-19
50	Chris Trafford	Mercyhurst	SO	F	25	0.72	9- 9-18
	Mark Pavli	American Intern.	JR	F	27	0.67	7-11-18
	Robb Ross	Army	JR	F	33	0.55	6-12-18
	Matt Burke	Holy Cross	JR	D	35	0.51	2-16-18
	Scott Marchesi	Sacred Heart	JR	D	36	0.50	5-13-18
	Sean Erickson	Connecticut	SO	D	36	0.50	1-17-18
56	Tom Dickhudt	Bentley	SO	F	29	0.59	6-11-17
	Ryan Driscoll	Holy Cross	FR	F	33	0.52	6-11-17
	Jeremy Leroux	American Intern.	SR	D	33	0.52	3-14-17

	Pat Percella	Bentley	SO	F	35	0.49	9- 8-17
60	Michael Mayra	Air Force	SO	D	26	0.62	1-15-16
	Brad Harris	RIT	SR	F	30	0.53	4-12-16
	Dewey Thomson	Holy Cross	SO	F	31	0.52	7- 9-16
	Sean Nappo	Holy Cross	SR	F	34	0.47	7- 9-16
	Brennan Sarazin	RIT	SO	F	34	0.47	7- 9-16
	Matt Fennell	Mercyhurst	FR	D	34	0.47	2-14-16
	Cullen Eddy	Mercyhurst	FR	D	35	0.46	5-11-16
67	Nick Johnson	Sacred Heart	FR	F	30	0.50	5-10-15
	Charles Solberg	Connecticut	JR	F	32	0.47	4-11-15
	Bryan Jurynec	American Intern.	JR	F	34	0.44	6- 9-15
	Darrell Draper	RIT	JR	F	34	0.44	5-10-15
	Peter Ferraro	Sacred Heart	SR	F	36	0.42	5-10-15
	Billy Devoney	Air Force	SR	D	40	0.38	5-10-15
	Theo Zacour	Air Force	SR	F	40	0.38	4-11-15
74	Chris Ochoa	Connecticut	FR	F	32	0.44	6- 8-14
	Mike McMillan	American Intern.	FR	F	32	0.44	5- 9-14
	Brett Robinson	Mercyhurst	SO	F	33	0.42	5- 9-14
	Greg Genovese	American Intern.	JR	F	34	0.41	4-10-14
	Nick Vandenbeld	Mercyhurst	FR	F	35	0.40	7- 7-14
	Michael Coppola	Connecticut	FR	F	36	0.39	6- 8-14
	Brian Gineo	Air Force	SR	D	38	0.37	4-10-14
	Greg Flynn	Air Force	SO	D	39	0.36	1-13-14
82	Matt Warren	Mercyhurst	JR	F	26	0.50	5- 8-13
	Brodie Sheahan	Holy Cross	FR	F	29	0.45	5- 8-13
	Kyle Bushee	Canisius	JR	D	29	0.45	3-10-13
	Chris Risi	Mercyhurst	FR	F	35	0.37	6- 7-13
	Matt Charbonneau	Air Force	JR	D	35	0.37	3-10-13
	Brian Burns	Connecticut	SR	F	35	0.37	0-13-13
88	Steven Matic	RIT	FR	F	30	0.40	5- 7-12
	Joey Coccimiglio	Canisius	SR	F	32	0.38	6- 6-12
	Alec Kirschner	Connecticut	FR	F	33	0.36	6- 6-12
	Scott McDougall	Connecticut	SR	F	33	0.36	5- 7-12
	Zach McKelvie	Army	SO	D	34	0.35	3- 9-12
	Jaye Judd	Bentley	JR	D	34	0.35	2-10-12
	Josh Print	Air Force	JR	F	36	0.33	4- 8-12
	Josh Frider	Air Force	SO	F	39	0.31	9- 3-12
96	Bobby Phillips	Mercyhurst	SO	D	28	0.39	1-10-11
	Neil Graham	Mercyhurst	FR	F	30	0.37	4- 7-11
	Erik Boisvert	Sacred Heart	FR	F	30	0.37	4- 7-11
	Jarrett Scarpaci	Connecticut	SR	F	32	0.34	3- 8-11
	Rob Forshner	Holy Cross	FR	F	32	0.34	3- 8-11
	Matt Woodard	American Intern.	SO	D	33	0.33	4- 7-11
	Rob Godfrey	Holy Cross	SR	D	33	0.33	4- 7-11
	Justin Hofstetter	RIT	SO	D	34	0.32	6- 5-11
	Jeff Fearing	Army	JR	F	34	0.32	5- 6-11
	Frankie DeAngelis	American Intern.	FR	D	34	0.32	3- 8-11
	Casey Russell	Bentley	SO	D	35	0.31	4- 7-11
	Kalen Wright	Sacred Heart	SR	D	36	0.31	2- 9-11
	Matt Fairchild	Air Force	FR	F	39	0.28	5- 6-11
109	Jesse Newman	RIT	SO	F	24	0.42	2- 8-10
	Will Ryan	Army	SO	F	28	0.36	5- 5-10
	Chad Richardson	American Intern.	SO	F	30	0.33	3- 7-10
	Matt Crowell	RIT	FR	F	31	0.32	6- 4-10
	Jeason Lecours	American Intern.	SR	F	32	0.31	5- 5-10
	Frank Schiavone	Air Force	JR	D	33	0.30	3- 7-10
	Frank O'Grady	Holy Cross	JR	D	33	0.30	2- 8-10
	Brady Dolim	Army	SR	F	34	0.29	4- 6-10
	Chris Bolognino	American Intern.	JR	D	34	0.29	3- 7-10
	Chase Podsiad	Army	JR	D	34	0.29	1- 9-10

	Thomas Spencer	Sacred Heart	SR	D	34	0.29	0-10-10
	Matt Gordon	Sacred Heart	FR	F	35	0.29	4- 6-10
	Kyle Tyll	Sacred Heart	SO	F	36	0.28	7- 3-10
	Drew Sanders	Sacred Heart	SR	F	36	0.28	2- 8-10
123	Cal St. Denis	Holy Cross	JR	F	25	0.36	1- 8- 9
	Rob Tarantino	RIT	SR	F	28	0.32	3- 6- 9
	Ken Rowe	Army	JR	F	31	0.29	6- 3- 9
	Spencer Churchill	Canisius	SO	F	34	0.26	3- 6- 9
	Billy Irish-Baker	Canisius	SR	F	35	0.26	3- 6- 9
128	Brent Olson	Air Force	SO	F	22	0.36	1- 7- 8
	Brian Reese	Air Force	SR	F	23	0.35	4- 4- 8
	Matt Werry	Holy Cross	JR	F	28	0.29	5- 3- 8
	Joel Kitchen	Canisius	JR	F	30	0.27	0- 8- 8
	Neil Sullivan	American Intern.	SR	F	33	0.24	6- 2- 8
	Lyle Gal	Army	JR	F	34	0.24	4- 4- 8
	Bobby Raymond	RIT	SO	D	34	0.24	2- 6- 8
	David Cianfrini	Canisius	FR	D	34	0.24	1- 7- 8
	Brett Nylander	Air Force	FR	F	39	0.21	3- 5- 8
137	Paul Ferraro	Sacred Heart	SO	D	19	0.37	5- 2- 7
	Mike Floyd	Mercyhurst	SO	F	20	0.35	2- 5- 7
	Mark Fuqua	American Intern.	SR	F	22	0.32	3- 4- 7
	William Crum	Connecticut	SR	D	30	0.23	4- 3- 7
	Brendan Olinyk	Connecticut	FR	D	34	0.21	3- 4- 7
	Mark Zarbo	Bentley	FR	D	34	0.21	1- 6- 7
	Greg Brown	Canisius	JR	F	35	0.20	3- 4- 7
	Nick Kary	Sacred Heart	JR	F	36	0.19	2- 5- 7
145	Ryan Hawkins	Connecticut	SO	F	16	0.38	2- 4- 6
	Jay Medenwaldt	Air Force	SR	F	22	0.27	2- 4- 6
	Marty Dams	Holy Cross	SO	D	25	0.24	1- 5- 6
	Shane McAdam	Holy Cross	SO	D	25	0.24	0- 6- 6
	Paul Scalici	Bentley	JR	F	29	0.21	5- 1- 6
	David Turco	American Intern.	SO	F	31	0.19	3- 3- 6
	Kirk Medernach	Mercyhurst	SO	D	32	0.19	1- 5- 6
	Blake Hamilton	Bentley	FR	F	33	0.18	2- 4- 6
153	Vincent Amigone	Canisius	FR	F	17	0.29	3- 2- 5
	Chris Hepp	Air Force	FR	D	18	0.28	0- 5- 5
	Kane Osmars	Bentley	FR	F	20	0.25	1- 4- 5
	Brian Kolb	Holy Cross	JR	F	21	0.24	5- 0- 5
	Nick DeCroo	Bentley	FR	F	22	0.23	2- 3- 5
	Stephen Burns	RIT	JR	D	29	0.17	2- 3- 5
	Brendan Harrison	Bentley	FR	F	31	0.16	3- 2- 5
	Tanner Fogarty	Holy Cross	SR	F	31	0.16	3- 2- 5
	Chris Colvin	Army	JR	D	32	0.16	1- 4- 5
	Nick Schneider	Connecticut	SO	D/F	34	0.15	1- 4- 5
163	Aaron Anderson	Army	JR	F	14	0.29	0- 4- 4
	Alec Wright	Canisius	FR	F	15	0.27	1- 3- 4
	Tristan Fairbarn	RIT	SR	F	17	0.24	2- 2- 4
	Josh Froese	American Intern.	FR	F	18	0.22	0- 4- 4
	Chris Angelo	Canisius	SR	F	21	0.19	3- 1- 4
	Michael Picone	Army	SR	F	21	0.19	2- 2- 4
	Anders Olson	Bentley	FR	F	21	0.19	1- 3- 4
	Ben Ellsworth	American Intern.	SR	F	27	0.15	0- 4- 4
	Jaymie Harrington	Canisius	SR	F	28	0.14	1- 3- 4
	Joe Cucci	Bentley	JR	D	32	0.12	1- 3- 4
	Pat Henk	Mercyhurst	SR	D	32	0.12	0- 4- 4
	Mike Field	American Intern.	JR	F	34	0.12	1- 3- 4
	Chris Trovato	Holy Cross	JR	F	34	0.12	1- 3- 4
176	Eric Sefchik	Army	FR	F	18	0.17	2- 1- 3
	Matt Hickey	Army	SO	F	19	0.16	1- 2- 3
	Eric St. Arnauld	Connecticut	SR	F	19	0.16	1- 2- 3

	Jay Holladay	American Intern.	FR D	20	0.15	0- 3- 3
	Jim Tselikis	Holy Cross	JR F	21	0.14	0- 3- 3
	Derek Fisher	Mercyhurst	FR D	23	0.13	0- 3- 3
	Corey Laurysen	Sacred Heart	FR D	26	0.12	0- 3- 3
	Bill Leahy	Army	SO F	27	0.11	2- 1- 3
	Michael Olmstead	Connecticut	FR D	33	0.09	0- 3- 3
	Bobby Preece	Bentley	FR D	34	0.09	0- 3- 3
	Scott Follett	Canisius	JR D	35	0.09	2- 1- 3
187	John Stockler	Connecticut	JR F	10	0.20	1- 1- 2
	Brent Alexin	RIT	FR F	10	0.20	1- 1- 2
	Brent Franklin	Holy Cross	JR D	12	0.17	0- 2- 2
	Jamie Coghlan	Mercyhurst	JR D	15	0.13	1- 1- 2
	Denis Kirstein	Mercyhurst	SR D	16	0.12	0- 2- 2
	David Martinson	Air Force	FR F	17	0.12	0- 2- 2
	Charles Veilleux	Sacred Heart	SR D	18	0.11	1- 1- 2
	Anthony Pellarin	Bentley	JR F	18	0.11	0- 2- 2
	Kerry Bowman	Mercyhurst	JR F	19	0.11	2- 0- 2
	B.J. Bayers	Connecticut	SO F	21	0.10	1- 1- 2
	Jay Bletzer	Bentley	JR D	22	0.09	0- 2- 2
	Ray Jean	Bentley	SR G	25	0.08	0- 2- 2
	Jason Smith	Sacred Heart	SR G	28	0.07	0- 2- 2
	Peter MacDougall	Canisius	FR F	31	0.06	2- 0- 2
	Ian McDougall	Army	JR D	33	0.06	0- 2- 2
202	Bryce Nantes	Holy Cross	JR F	3	0.33	1- 0- 1
	Matt Richards	Sacred Heart	FR F	6	0.17	0- 1- 1
	Louis Gentile	Sacred Heart	SR F	7	0.14	1- 0- 1
	Joe Walchessen	Connecticut	FR D	7	0.14	0- 1- 1
	Bill Pinel	Holy Cross	FR D	8	0.12	0- 1- 1
	Stefan Drew	Sacred Heart	SO G	8	0.12	0- 1- 1
	Matt Harris	RIT	JR D	9	0.11	1- 0- 1
	Bryan Becker	Air Force	JR F	9	0.11	0- 1- 1
	Brandon Johnson	Air Force	FR D	9	0.11	0- 1- 1
	Frederic Jean	Connecticut	FR F	10	0.10	0- 1- 1
	Andrew Goberstein	Bentley	SO F	11	0.09	0- 1- 1
	Brent Griffin	American Intern.	JR D	12	0.08	0- 1- 1
	Scott Tomes	Connecticut	SR G	12	0.08	0- 1- 1
	Eric Dahlberg	Connecticut	SO D	12	0.08	0- 1- 1
	Dean Yakura	American Intern.	FR F	13	0.08	1- 0- 1
	Andy Gevorkyan	American Intern.	FR F	14	0.07	1- 0- 1
	John Patera	Canisius	SO D	14	0.07	0- 1- 1
	Kai Magnussen	Holy Cross	SO F	17	0.06	1- 0- 1
	Ian Dams	Holy Cross	FR G	18	0.06	0- 1- 1
	Keith Rodger	American Intern.	SO D	20	0.05	1- 0- 1
	Jesse Williams	Bentley	FR D	20	0.05	1- 0- 1
	Jordan Wakefield	Mercyhurst	SR G	20	0.05	0- 1- 1
	Bret Norris	Canisius	SR D	34	0.03	0- 1- 1

GOALS AGAINST AVERAGE:

				MINUTES	GA	GAA
1	Josh Kassel	Army	SO	1913:15:00	76	2.38
2	Jocelyn Guimond	RIT	JR	1163:01:00	48	2.48
3	Louis Menard	RIT	FR	815:53:00	34	2.5
4	Jason Smith	Sacred Heart	SR	1703:22:00	79	2.78
5	Andrew Loewen	Canisius	FR	1486:21:00	71	2.87
6	Beau Erickson	Connecticut	FR	1149:15:00	56	2.92
7	Peter Foster	Air Force	SR	856:20:00	43	3.01
8	Ian Dams	Holy Cross	FR	985:27:00	53	3.23
9	Jordan Wakefield	Mercyhurst	SR	1150:23:00	66	3.44
10	Tom Fenton	American Intern.	SO	1471:02:00	92	3.75
11	Ray Jean	Bentley	SR	1455:07:00	97	4
12	Tyler Small	Mercyhurst	SO	832:24:00	56	4.04

Minimum 33% of Team Minutes Played

SAVE PERCENTAGE:

				SAVES	GA	PCT
1	Jocelyn Guimond	RIT	JR	567	48	0.922
2	Louis Menard	RIT	FR	366	34	0.915
3	Jordan Wakefield	Mercyhurst	SR	689	66	0.913
4	Josh Kassel	Army	SO	790	76	0.912
5	Andrew Loewen	Canisius	FR	738	71	0.912
6	Beau Erickson	Connecticut	FR	548	56	0.907
7	Jason Smith	Sacred Heart	SR	755	79	0.905
8	Tyler Small	Mercyhurst	SO	485	56	0.896
9	Ian Dams	Holy Cross	FR	419	53	0.888
10	Ray Jean	Bentley	SR	711	97	0.88
11	Tom Fenton	American Intern.	SO	650	92	0.876
12	Peter Foster	Air Force	SR	274	43	0.864

Minimum 33% of Team Minutes Played

WINNING PERCENTAGE:

				W- L- T	PCT
1	Louis Menard	RIT	FR	11- 3- 0	0.786
2	Jason Smith	Sacred Heart	SR	16- 9- 3	0.625
3	Josh Kassel	Army	SO	17-11- 4	0.594
4	Beau Erickson	Connecticut	FR	10- 7- 2	0.579
	Jocelyn Guimond	RIT	JR	10- 7- 2	0.579
6	Ian Dams	Holy Cross	FR	8- 9- 0	0.471
7	Andrew Loewen	Canisius	FR	9-12- 3	0.438
8	Peter Foster	Air Force	SR	4- 6- 3	0.423
9	Ray Jean	Bentley	SR	9-15- 1	0.38
10	Tom Fenton	American Intern.	SO	8-16- 1	0.34
11	Tyler Small	Mercyhurst	SO	3- 8- 3	0.321
12	Jordan Wakefield	Mercyhurst	SR	5-12- 2	0.316

Minimum 33% of Team Minutes Played

**Atlantic Coast
Collegiate Hockey League**
204 Beagle Gap Run
Waynesboro, VA 22980
www.acchockey.com

**Commissioner
Mark Henderson**
hend028@adelphia.com

**SID & Board Member
Roger Voisinet**
Phone: 434.974.1500 / Fax 434.974.7750
roger@cvilleproperties.com

**Referee-In-Chief
Keith Rosenfeld**
Phone: 434.220.0489
keithros@hotcakesgourmet.com

**Board Member
Steve Malley**
Phone: 410.721.3599
steve-malley@comcast.net

**Board Member
Michael Dettmers**
Phone: 321.277.9931
mdettmers@msn.com

**League Statistician & Treasurer
Matt Hodges**
Phone: 434.817.5120
hodges@cstone.net

Duke University

Georgetown University

George Mason University

University of North Carolina

North Carolina State University

University of Virginia

Virginia Polytechnic Institute

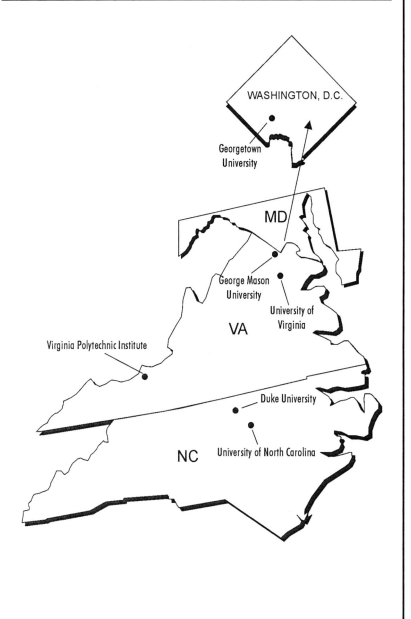

ATLANTIC COAST COLLEGIATE
HOCKEY LEAGUE

ACCHL

WASHINGTON, D.C.

Georgetown
University

MD

George Mason
University

University of
Virginia

VA

Virginia Polytechnic Institute

Duke University

University of North Carolina

NC

ATLANTIC COAST
COLLEGIATE HOCKEY LEAGUE
FINAL 2006-2007 CONFERENCE STANDINGS

		Pts	GP	Record	Win%	GF- GA	GP	Record	Win%GF-GA
1	Georgetown	24	12	12-0-0			22	20-2-0	
2	Duke	16	12	8-4-0			18	10-8-0	
3	Virginia Tech	13	12	6-5-1			18	8-9-1	
4	Virginia	12	12	6-6-0			12	10-11-0	
5	Norrth Carolina State	11	12	6-5-1			25	16-8-1	
6	North Carolina	6	12	3-9-0			20	6-13-1	
7	George Mason	0	12	0-12-0			18	2-16-0	

2007 ATLANTIC COAST COLLEGIATE HOCKEY LEAGUE TOURNAMENT

FIRST ROUND *(2007)*

Duke University	5	George Mason University	0
Virginia Tech University	6	University of North Carolina	2
North Carolina State	7	University of Virginia	4

SEMI FINALS *(2007)*

Georgetown University	9	North Carolina State University	2
Duke University	3	Virginia Tech University	2

CHAMPIONSHIP *(2007)*

Georgetown University	6	Duke University	3

ATLANTIC COAST COLLEGIATE HOCKEY LEAGUE CHAMPIONS

	REGULAR		TOURNAMENT
1996	Virginia Polytechnic Institute	1996	University of Virginia
1997	University of Virginia	1997	Liberty University
1998	University of Virginia	1998	Duke University
1999	University of Virginia	1999	University of Maryland
2000	University of Virginia	2000	University of Virginia
2001	North Carolina State University	2001	University of Maryland
2002	Liberty University	2002	Liberty University
2003	North Carolina State University	2003	North Carolina State University
2004	Duke University	2004	Duke University
2005	University of Virginia	2005	Georgetown University
2006	Duke University	2006	Duke University
2007	Georgetown University	2007	Georgetown University

**Central Collegiate
Hockey Association**
23995 Freeway Park Drive, Suite 101
Farmington Hills, MI 48335-2817
248.888.0600 • Fax 248.888.0664
www.ccha.com

**Commissioner
Tom Anastos**
tanastos@ccha.com

**Director of Communications
Fred Pletsch**
fpletsch@ccha.com

**Director of Officials
Brian Hart**
ccha@ccha.com

**Communications Manager
Courtney Welch**
cwelch@ccha.com

**University of Alaska Fairbanks
Bowling Green State University
Ferris State University
Lake Superior State University
Miami University
University of Michigan
Michigan State University
University of Nebraska Omaha
Northern Michigan University
University of Notre Dame
Ohio State University
Western Michigan University**

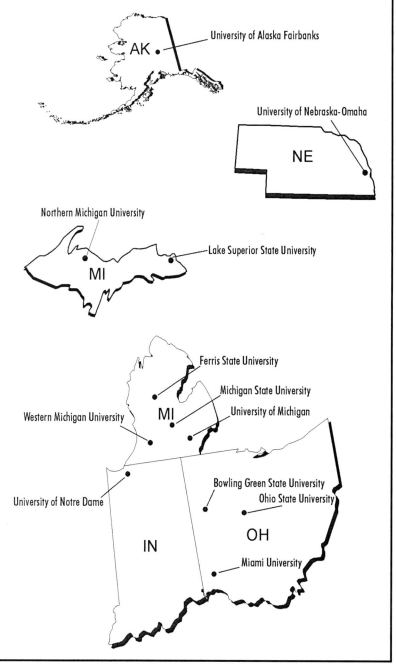

CCHA	**CENTRAL COLLEGIATE HOCKEY ASSOCIATION**

AK • University of Alaska Fairbanks

University of Nebraska-Omaha

NE •

Northern Michigan University

MI

Lake Superior State University

Ferris State University

Michigan State University

Western Michigan University

MI

University of Michigan

University of Notre Dame

Bowling Green State University

Ohio State University

IN

OH

Miami University

CENTRAL COLLEGIATE HOCKEY ASSOCIATION
FINAL 2006-07 CONFERENCE STANDINGS

		Pts	GP	Record	Win%	GF- GA	GP	Record	Win%	GF- GA
1	Notre Dame	45	28	21- 4- 3	0.804	90- 51	42	32- 7- 3	0.798	143- 70
2	Michigan	37	28	18- 9- 1	0.661	119- 85	41	26-14- 1	0.646	174-129
3	Miami	36	28	16- 8- 4	0.643	93- 70	42	24-14- 4	0.619	135-107
4	Michigan State	33	28	15-10- 3	0.589	81- 65	42	26-13- 3	0.655	137-102
5	Nebraska-Omaha	30	28	13-11- 4	0.536	100- 85	42	18-16- 8	0.524	153-128
6	Western Michigan	29	28	14-13- 1	0.518	85- 93	37	18-18- 1	0.500	120-126
7	Ohio State	28	28	12-12- 4	0.500	89- 86	37	15-17- 5	0.473	120-120
8	Lake Superior	25	28	11-14- 3	0.446	65- 74	43	21-19- 3	0.523	111-110
9	Ferris State	22	28	10-16- 2	0.393	70- 92	39	14-22- 3	0.397	107-126
10	Northern Michigan	21	28	10-17- 1	0.375	66- 80	41	15-24- 2	0.390	96-123
11	Alaska Fairbanks	19	28	7-16- 5	0.339	70- 90	39	11-22- 6	0.359	100-128
12	Bowling Green	11	28	5-22- 1	0.196	51-108	38	7-29- 2	0.211	75-147

2007 CCHA SUPER 6 CHAMPIONSHIP

FIRST ROUND (3.02.07-3.04.07)

Northern Michigan University	2	Ohio State University	6
Northern Michigan University	3	Ohio State University	2
Northern Michigan University	3	Ohio State University	2
Bowling Green State University	2	University of Nebraska Omaha	3
Bowling Green State University	5	University of Nebraska Omaha	7
Ferris State University	4	Lake Superior State University	3
Ferris State University	3	Lake Superior State University	4
Ferris State University	2	Lake Superior State University	3
University of Alaska Fairbanks	3	Western Michigan University	2
University of Alaska Fairbanks	2	Western Michigan University	6
University of Alaska Fairbanks	3	Western Michigan University	1

SECOND ROUND (3.09.07-3.10.07)

University of Nebraska Omaha	2	Michigan State University	4
University of Nebraska Omaha	1	Michigan State University	4
Lake Superior State University	2	University of Miami	1
Lake Superior State University	2	University of Miami	1
Northern Michigan University	1	University of Michigan	4
Northern Michigan University	3	University of Michigan	8
University of Alaska Fairbanks	1	University of Notre Dame	7
University of Alaska Fairbanks	1	University of Notre Dame	3

SEMI FINALS (3.16.07)

Lake Superior State University	0	University of Notre Dame	3
Michigan State University	2	University of Michigan	5

THIRD PLACE (3.17.07)

Lake Superior State University	6	Michigan State University	7

MASON CUP CHAMPIONSHIP (3.17.07)

University of Michigan	1	University of Notre Dame	2

CENTRAL COLLEGIATE HOCKEY ASSOCIATION CHAMPIONS

	REGULAR	TOURNAMENT
1972	Ohio State University	Ohio State University
1973	Saint Louis University	Bowling Green State University
1974	Lake Superior State University	Saint Louis University
1975	Saint Louis University	Saint Louis University
1976	Bowling Green State University	Saint Louis University
1977	Saint Louis University	Bowling Green State University
1978	Bowling Green State University	Bowling Green State University
1979	Bowling Green State University	Bowling Green State University
1980	Northern Michigan University	Northern Michigan University
1981	Northern Michigan University	Northern Michigan University
1982	Bowling Green State University	Michigan State University
1983	Bowling Green State University	Michigan State University
1984	Bowling Green State University	Michigan State University
1985	Michigan State University	Michigan State University
1986	Michigan State University	Western Michigan University
1987	Bowling Green State University	Michigan State University
1988	Lake Superior State University	Bowling Green State University
1989	Michigan State University	Michigan State University
1990	Michigan State University	Michigan State University
1991	Lake Superior State University	Lake Superior State University
1992	University of Michigan	Lake Superior State University
1993	Miami University	Lake Superior State University
1994	University of Michigan	University of Michigan
1995	University of Michigan	Lake Superior State University
1996	Lake Superior State University	University of Michigan
1997	University of Michigan	University of Michigan
1998	Michigan State University	Michigan State University
1999	Michigan State University	University of Michigan
2000	University of Michigan	Michigan State University
2001	Michigan State University	Michigan State University
2002	University of Michigan	University of Michigan
2003	Ferris State University	University of Michigan
2004	University of Michigan	Ohio State University
2005	University of Michigan	University of Michigan
2006	University of Miami	Michigan State University
2007	University of Notre Dame	University of Notre Dame

CCHA LEAGUE SCORING (OVERALL):

					GP	PPG	G - A - P
1	T.J. Hensick	Michigan	SR	F	41	1.68	23-46-69
2	Kevin Porter	Michigan	JR	F	41	1.41	24-34-58
3	Scott Parse	Nebraska-Omaha	SR	F	40	1.30	24-28-52
4	Andrew Cogliano	Michigan	SO	F	38	1.32	24-26-50
	Nathan Davis	Miami	JR	F	42	1.19	21-29-50
6	Ryan Jones	Miami	JR	F	42	1.14	29-19-48
	Erik Condra	Notre Dame	SO	F	42	1.14	14-34-48
8	Mike Santorelli	Northern Michigan	JR	F	41	1.15	30-17-47
9	Mark Letestu	Western Michigan	FR	F	37	1.24	24-22-46
10	Paul Szczechura	Western Michigan	SR	F	37	1.22	19-26-45
	Chad Kolarik	Michigan	JR	F	41	1.10	18-27-45
12	Alex Nikiforuk	Nebraska-Omaha	SR	F	41	1.05	14-29-43
	Tim Kennedy	Michigan State	SO	F	42	1.02	18-25-43
14	Kyle Greentree	Alaska	JR	F	39	1.08	21-21-42
15	Ryan Thang	Notre Dame	FR	F	42	0.98	20-21-41
16	Jack Johnson	Michigan	SO	D	36	1.08	16-23-39
	Kevin Deeth	Notre Dame	FR	F	42	0.93	17-22-39
18	Bryan Marshall	Nebraska-Omaha	JR	F	38	0.95	11-25-36
	Bryan Lerg	Michigan State	JR	F	41	0.88	23-13-36
20	Curtis Fraser	Alaska	SR	F	37	0.95	19-16-35
21	Jeff LoVecchio	Western Michigan	SO	F	37	0.92	19-15-34
	Brandon Scero	Nebraska-Omaha	JR	F	38	0.89	18-16-34
	David Rohlfs	Michigan	SR	F	41	0.83	17-17-34
	Darin Olver	Northern Michigan	SR	F	41	0.83	14-20-34
	Mark Van Guilder	Notre Dame	JR	F	42	0.81	18-16-34
26	Jeff Pierce	Western Michigan	JR	F	35	0.94	12-21-33
	Justin Abdelkader	Michigan State	SO	F	38	0.87	15-18-33
	Jonathan Matsumoto	Bowling Green	JR	F	38	0.87	11-22-33
	Dan Charleston	Nebraska-Omaha	SO	F	41	0.80	14-19-33
30	Chris Mueller	Michigan State	JR	F	42	0.76	16-16-32
	Marty Guerin	Miami	SR	F	42	0.76	12-20-32
32	Jim McKenzie	Michigan State	JR	F	35	0.86	12-18-30
	Zac Pearson	Ferris State	SR	F	37	0.81	9-21-30
	Troy Schwab	Lake Superior	SO	F	41	0.73	6-24-30
	Jarod Palmer	Miami	FR	F	42	0.71	11-19-30
	Tomas Klempa	Nebraska-Omaha	SO	F	42	0.71	10-20-30
	Trent Campbell	Lake Superior	SR	F	43	0.70	12-18-30
	Derek Smith	Lake Superior	JR	D	43	0.70	10-20-30
39	Derek Whitmore	Bowling Green	JR	F	38	0.76	19-10-29
40	Sean Collins	Ohio State	SR	D	37	0.76	9-19-28
	Jeffrey Rainville	Lake Superior	SR	F	42	0.67	13-15-28
42	Mick Lawrence	Nebraska-Omaha	JR	F	38	0.71	13-14-27
	Matt Hunwick	Michigan	SR	D	41	0.66	6-21-27
44	Tommy Goebel	Ohio State	JR	F	32	0.81	12-14-26
	Andrew Schembri	Ohio State	SR	F	34	0.76	9-17-26
	Brian Bicek	Western Michigan	JR	F	37	0.70	15-11-26
	Garrett Regan	Notre Dame	SO	F	42	0.62	14-12-26
	Tyler Howells	Michigan State	SR	D	42	0.62	4-22-26
	Josh Sim	Lake Superior	SO	F	43	0.60	15-11-26
50	Mathieu Beaudoin	Ohio State	SR	F	37	0.68	14-11-25
	Matt Christie	Miami	SR	F	37	0.68	8-17-25
	Jason DeSantis	Ohio State	JR	D	37	0.68	5-20-25
	Matt Verdone	Ferris State	SR	F	39	0.64	11-14-25
	Justin Mercier	Miami	SO	F	40	0.62	10-15-25
	Tim Crowder	Michigan State	SO	F	41	0.61	14-11-25
56	Brian Kaufman	Miami	SO	F	34	0.71	7-17-24
	Darcy Campbell	Alaska	JR	D	39	0.62	4-20-24
	Nick Sucharski	Michigan State	SO	F	41	0.59	9-15-24

	Tim Miller	Michigan	SO F	41	0.59	7-17-24
	Alec Martinez	Miami	SO D	42	0.57	9-15-24
61	Cody Chupp	Ferris State	FR F	37	0.62	8-15-23
	Brandon Naurato	Michigan	SO F	40	0.57	12-11-23
	Juha Uotila	Nebraska-Omaha	SO D	40	0.57	5-18-23
64	Dion Knelsen	Alaska	FR F	35	0.63	5-17-22
	Brendan Connolly	Ferris State	SO F	38	0.58	11-11-22
	Tyler Eckford	Alaska	SO D	39	0.56	5-17-22
	Nathan Perkovich	Lake Superior	FR F	42	0.52	15- 7-22
	Jason Paige	Notre Dame	SR F	42	0.52	11-11-22
	Noah Babin	Notre Dame	SR D	42	0.52	2-20-22
70	Eddie Del Grosso	Nebraska-Omaha	FR D	37	0.57	4-17-21
	Wes O'Neill	Notre Dame	SR D	42	0.50	3-18-21
72	Domenic Maiani	Ohio State	JR F	28	0.71	8-12-20
	Matt Siddall	Northern Michigan	JR F	37	0.54	4-16-20
	Adam Naglich	Alaska	SO F	39	0.51	6-14-20
	Nick Sirota	Northern Michigan	SO F	41	0.49	10-10-20
	Zach Tarkir	Northern Michigan	SR D	41	0.49	7-13-20
	Raymond Eichenlaub	Miami	SO D	42	0.48	4-16-20
78	Adam Bartholomay	Nebraska-Omaha	SO D	29	0.66	10- 9-19
	Mitch Ganzak	Miami	JR D	36	0.53	4-15-19
	Kenny Bernard	Ohio State	SR F	37	0.51	7-12-19
	Kyle Lawson	Notre Dame	FR D	38	0.50	4-15-19
82	Josh Sciba	Notre Dame	SR F	33	0.55	8-10-18
	Tyson Strachan	Ohio State	SR D	35	0.51	7-11-18
	Mark Mitera	Michigan	SO D	41	0.44	1-17-18
85	Brett Blatchford	Notre Dame	FR D	30	0.57	2-15-17
	Matt McIlvane	Ohio State	JR F	36	0.47	6-11-17
	Tomas Petruska	Bowling Green	FR F	37	0.46	8- 9-17
	Matt Waddell	Ohio State	SR D	37	0.46	5-12-17
	Ryan Mahrle	Western Michigan	SR D	37	0.46	2-15-17
	Travis Turnbull	Michigan	SO F	41	0.41	8- 9-17
91	Mark Bomersback	Ferris State	SR F	20	0.80	9- 7-16
	Matt Maunu	Northern Michigan	SR D	41	0.39	5-11-16
	Rob Lehtinen	Northern Michigan	SR F	41	0.39	2-14-16
94	Patrick Galivan	Western Michigan	SO F	22	0.68	7- 8-15
	Justin White	Notre Dame	SO F	29	0.52	2-13-15
	Adam Miller	Ferris State	JR F	31	0.48	9- 6-15
	Aaron Lewicki	Ferris State	FR F	32	0.47	9- 6-15
	Todd McIlrath	Bowling Green	FR F	34	0.44	5-10-15
	John Dingle	Ohio State	JR F	37	0.41	7- 8-15
	Lucas Burnett	Alaska	SR F	39	0.38	3-12-15
	Pat Bateman	Northern Michigan	SR F	41	0.37	7- 8-15
	Dominic Osman	Lake Superior	SR F	43	0.35	6- 9-15
	Derek R. Smith	Lake Superior	SR F	43	0.35	3-12-15
104	Corey Elkins	Ohio State	SO F	26	0.54	7- 7-14
	Chris Zarb	Ferris State	SO D	29	0.48	1-13-14
	Brandon Svendsen	Bowling Green	SO F	35	0.40	6- 8-14
	TJ Miller	Northern Michigan	FR D	37	0.38	2-12-14
	Nathan Fornataro	Alaska	SR D	39	0.36	6- 8-14
	Braden Walls	Alaska	SO F	39	0.36	6- 8-14
	Joe Van Culin	Ferris State	SR D	39	0.36	5- 9-14
	Dan Eves	Lake Superior	JR F	41	0.34	6- 8-14
	Chris Summers	Michigan	FR D	41	0.34	6- 8-14
113	Tom Fritsche	Ohio State	JR F	19	0.68	5- 8-13
	Bill Bagron	Nebraska-Omaha	JR F	26	0.50	2-11-13
	Jeremy Scherlinck	Ferris State	SR D	28	0.46	2-11-13
	Ethan Graham	Michigan State	SR D	35	0.37	1-12-13
	Brandon Knelsen	Alaska	FR F	39	0.33	2-11-13
	Simon Gysbers	Lake Superior	FR D	41	0.32	4- 9-13

	Barnabas Birkeland	Lake Superior	SR	D	43	0.30	5- 8-13
120	Dan Riedel	Ferris State	SO	F	19	0.63	3- 9-12
	Jay Sprague	Michigan State	FR	F	32	0.38	3- 9-12
	Chris Frank	Western Michigan	SO	D	36	0.33	2-10-12
	Tyler Ludwig	Western Michigan	FR	D	37	0.32	1-11-12
	Nino Musitelli	Miami	JR	F	38	0.32	5- 7-12
	Mike Ratchuk	Michigan State	FR	D	40	0.30	4- 8-12
	Daniel Vukovic	Michigan State	JR	D	42	0.29	7- 5-12
127	Chris Snavely	Michigan State	SR	D	27	0.41	2- 9-11
	Mathieu Picard	Ohio State	FR	F	32	0.34	3- 8-11
	Jeff Dunne	Michigan State	JR	D	33	0.33	1-10-11
	Kai Kantola	Bowling Green	FR	F	36	0.31	5- 6-11
	John Mazzei	Bowling Green	JR	F	36	0.31	2- 9-11
	Brian Lebler	Michigan	FR	F	37	0.30	7- 4-11
	Aaron Lee	Alaska	JR	F	37	0.30	6- 5-11
	Mike Nesdill	Bowling Green	JR	D	37	0.30	1-10-11
	Jason Dest	Michigan	SR	D	39	0.28	1-10-11
	Mark Bernier	Nebraska-Omaha	FR	D	42	0.26	3- 8-11
	Michael Bartlett	Notre Dame	SR	F	42	0.26	3- 8-11
138	Jim Jorgensen	Ferris State	JR	D	20	0.50	3- 7-10
	James Unger	Bowling Green	SR	F	21	0.48	7- 3-10
	Kyle Hood	Ohio State	JR	D/F	29	0.34	5- 5-10
	Matt Case	Ferris State	FR	D	29	0.34	4- 6-10
	Andrew Sarauer	Northern Michigan	JR	F	30	0.33	5- 5-10
	Tim Hartung	Northern Michigan	SO	F	31	0.32	0-10-10
	Kevin Roeder	Miami	SO	D	36	0.28	1- 9-10
	Johann Kroll	Ohio State	JR	D	37	0.27	1- 9-10
	Tim Maxwell	Bowling Green	SO	D	38	0.26	0-10-10
	Eric Vesely	Ferris State	SR	F	39	0.26	8- 2-10
148	Matt Martello	Lake Superior	FR	F	18	0.50	2- 7- 9
	Dan Kissel	Notre Dame	FR	F	22	0.41	6- 3- 9
	Nick Fanto	Nebraska-Omaha	FR	F	30	0.30	5- 4- 9
	Brent Kisio	Nebraska-Omaha	SR	F	32	0.28	5- 4- 9
	Blair Riley	Ferris State	FR	F	34	0.26	3- 6- 9
	Trevor Hyatt	Alaska	SO	F	35	0.26	4- 5- 9
	Kevin Schmidt	Bowling Green	SO	D	35	0.26	3- 6- 9
	Phil Angell	Nebraska-Omaha	SR	D	36	0.25	1- 8- 9
	T.J. Jindra	Notre Dame	SR	F	41	0.22	2- 7- 9
157	Corey Couturier	Ferris State	SO	F	22	0.36	3- 5- 8
	Sam Campbell	Ohio State	JR	F	27	0.30	2- 6- 8
	Christian Hanson	Notre Dame	SO	F	33	0.24	6- 2- 8
	Dan Swanson	Nebraska-Omaha	FR	F	36	0.22	3- 5- 8
	Jason Moul	Western Michigan	SR	F	36	0.22	3- 5- 8
	Matt Clackson	Western Michigan	SO	F	36	0.22	0- 8- 8
	Bryce Anderson	Ohio State	SR	F	37	0.22	4- 4- 8
	Adam Welch	Ferris State	JR	D	39	0.21	2- 6- 8
	Tom Sawatske	Notre Dame	SR	D	41	0.20	3- 5- 8
	Gary Steffes	Miami	FR	F	42	0.19	5- 3- 8
	Brock Sheahan	Notre Dame	JR	D	42	0.19	3- 5- 8
	Steven Kaunisto	Lake Superior	FR	D	42	0.19	1- 7- 8
169	Nenad Gajic	Nebraska-Omaha	SO	F	6	1.17	2- 5- 7
	Jeric Agosta	Nebraska-Omaha	FR	F	29	0.24	4- 3- 7
	Chris Clackson	Western Michigan	FR	F	30	0.23	3- 4- 7
	Evan Rankin	Notre Dame	JR	F	31	0.23	4- 3- 7
	J.T. Dahlinger	Ferris State	SO	F	31	0.23	1- 6- 7
	Ryan Baird	Lake Superior	FR	D	34	0.21	0- 7- 7
	Nathan Ansell	Western Michigan	JR	D	34	0.21	0- 7- 7
	Dan Knapp	Nebraska-Omaha	SR	D	35	0.20	2- 5- 7
	Michael Hodgson	Bowling Green	JR	D	35	0.20	1- 6- 7
	Kevin Labatte	Western Michigan	SR	F	36	0.19	5- 2- 7

	Steve Vanoosten	Alaska	SO	D	38	0.18	1- 6- 7
	Chris Lawrence	Michigan State	SR	F	40	0.17	1- 6- 7
181	Justin Binab	Alaska	SO	F	21	0.29	2- 4- 6
	Dan Sturges	Michigan State	JR	F	21	0.29	1- 5- 6
	Christiaan Minella	Notre Dame	FR	F	21	0.29	1- 5- 6
	Ryan Muspratt	Alaska	JR	F	23	0.26	4- 2- 6
	Brandon Warner	Michigan State	SR	D	23	0.26	2- 4- 6
	Charley Fetzer	Miami	JR	D	30	0.20	0- 6- 6
	Nik Sellers	Lake Superior	FR	F	33	0.18	4- 2- 6
	Jeff Lee	Alaska	FR	F	34	0.18	2- 4- 6
	Mike Eickman	Nebraska-Omaha	SR	D	36	0.17	1- 5- 6
	T.J. Campbell	Alaska	JR	D	38	0.16	0- 6- 6
	Geoff Smith	Miami	SR	F	40	0.15	3- 3- 6
	Dusty Collins	Northern Michigan	SR	F	41	0.15	4- 2- 6
	Danny Fardig	Michigan	SO	F	41	0.15	2- 4- 6
194	Justin Lewandowski	Ferris State	SO	F	17	0.29	1- 4- 5
	Kevin Montgomery	Ohio State	FR	D	17	0.29	1- 4- 5
	Matt Schepke	Michigan State	SO	F	23	0.22	3- 2- 5
	Alan Dorich	Northern Michigan	FR	D	24	0.21	0- 5- 5
	John Scrymgeour	Lake Superior	FR	F	26	0.19	3- 2- 5
	Mike Lesperance	Western Michigan	JR	F	26	0.19	2- 3- 5
	James Perkin	Bowling Green	FR	F	27	0.19	2- 3- 5
	Alex Spezia	Ferris State	JR	D	29	0.17	0- 5- 5
	Casey Haines	Ferris State	FR	F	31	0.16	3- 2- 5
	Bill Loupee	Miami	SO	F	34	0.15	1- 4- 5
	Kyle Page	Bowling Green	FR	D	37	0.14	0- 5- 5
	Pat Aubry	Lake Superior	FR	F	41	0.12	3- 2- 5
	Nathan Sigmund	Northern Michigan	SO	F	41	0.12	1- 4- 5
207	Marty Gurnoe	Lake Superior	SO	D	12	0.33	0- 4- 4
	Dave Krisky	Western Michigan	SO	F	16	0.25	1- 3- 4
	Morgan Ward	Michigan	SR	F	16	0.25	0- 4- 4
	Dan VeNard	Notre Dame	JR	D	17	0.24	0- 4- 4
	Kevin O'Connor	Western Michigan	SO	D	18	0.22	1- 3- 4
	Jordan Emmerson	Alaska	SR	F	22	0.18	1- 3- 4
	Blake Cosgrove	Northern Michigan	JR	D	25	0.16	1- 3- 4
	Dave Barton	Ohio State	SR	F	27	0.15	2- 2- 4
	Evan Case	Ferris State	SO	D	28	0.14	1- 3- 4
	Tommy Dee	Bowling Green	FR	F	29	0.14	2- 2- 4
	Steve Silver	Western Michigan	SO	D	29	0.14	2- 2- 4
	Matt Frank	Ferris State	SO	F	33	0.12	1- 3- 4
	Steve Kampfer	Michigan	FR	D	35	0.11	1- 3- 4
	Joe Cooper	Miami	SR	F	36	0.11	3- 1- 4
	Tim Cook	Michigan	SR	D	36	0.11	0- 4- 4
	Steven Oleksy	Lake Superior	SO	D	39	0.10	2- 2- 4
	Brad Robbins	Miami	JR	D	39	0.10	0- 4- 4
	Matt Butcher	Northern Michigan	FR	F	40	0.10	0- 4- 4
	Brandon Gentile	Michigan State	SO	D	41	0.10	0- 4- 4
	Bobby Selden	Northern Michigan	SR	D	41	0.10	0- 4- 4
227	Kyle Jones	Alaska	SO	F	16	0.19	1- 2- 3
	Jerad Kaufmann	Nebraska-Omaha	SO	G	16	0.19	0- 3- 3
	JJ Koehler	Nebraska-Omaha	FR	F	18	0.17	2- 1- 3
	Dane Hetland	Miami	FR	F	22	0.14	0- 3- 3
	Zach Pelletier	Ohio State	JR	F	24	0.12	1- 2- 3
	Michael Findorff	Miami	SO	D	26	0.12	1- 2- 3
	Jonathan Lupa	Western Michigan	JR	D	31	0.10	0- 3- 3
	Ray Kaunisto	Northern Michigan	FR	F	41	0.07	3- 0- 3
235	Rich Meloche	Bowling Green	SR	F	13	0.15	2- 0- 2
	Kurt Kivisto	Michigan State	SO	F	14	0.14	1- 1- 2
	Jacques Lamoureux	Northern Michigan	FR	F	16	0.12	1- 1- 2
	Sean Weaver	Western Michigan	SO	F	16	0.12	1- 1- 2

	Charlie Effinger	Miami	JR	G	17	0.12	0- 2- 2
	Jordan Pernarowski	Alaska	FR	D	19	0.11	1- 1- 2
	Anthony Ciraulo	Michigan	FR	F	24	0.08	1- 1- 2
	Zak McClellan	Michigan State	JR	F	27	0.07	0- 2- 2
	Jon Erickson	Bowling Green	JR	F	28	0.07	0- 2- 2
	Brandon Gawryletz	Alaska	JR	D	30	0.07	1- 1- 2
	Brett John	Western Michigan	SR	F	30	0.07	1- 1- 2
	Ryan Turek	Michigan State	FR	D/F	31	0.06	0- 2- 2
	Jason Blain	Lake Superior	JR	F	38	0.05	1- 1- 2
	Jeff Lerg	Michigan State	SO	G	42	0.05	0- 2- 2
249	Eric Aarnio	Nebraska-Omaha	JR	G	1	1.00	0- 1- 1
	Brett Molnar	Bowling Green	FR	F	3	0.33	0- 1- 1
	Alexandre Lacombe	Miami	SO	F	7	0.14	1- 0- 1
	Pat Inglis	Lake Superior	FR	G	10	0.10	0- 1- 1
	Bobby Henderson	Nebraska-Omaha	SR	D	11	0.09	0- 1- 1
	Josh Boyd	Bowling Green	FR	F	12	0.08	1- 0- 1
	Chris Wilson	Nebraska-Omaha	FR	F	15	0.07	0- 1- 1
	Spencer Dillon	Northern Michigan	SO	D	15	0.07	0- 1- 1
	Justin Gutwald	Lake Superior	JR	D	23	0.04	0- 1- 1
	Riley Gill	Western Michigan	FR	G	23	0.04	0- 1- 1
	Jeff Zatkoff	Miami	SO	G	26	0.04	0- 1- 1
	Ben Geelan	Bowling Green	JR	F	28	0.04	0- 1- 1
	Jimmy Spratt	Bowling Green	SO	G	31	0.03	0- 1- 1
	Bill Zaniboni	Northern Michigan	JR	G	35	0.03	0- 1- 1
	Russ Sinkewich	Bowling Green	SO	D	37	0.03	0- 1- 1
	Billy Sauer	Michigan	SO	G	40	0.03	0- 1- 1

GOALS AGAINST AVERAGE:

				MINUTES	GA	GAA
1	David Brown	Notre Dame	SR	2389:40:00	63	1.58
2	Jeff Zatkoff	Miami	SO	1541:35:00	58	2.26
3	Jeff Jakaitis	Lake Superior	SR	2055:24:00	79	2.31
4	Jeff Lerg	Michigan State	SO	2465:06:00	99	2.41
5	Charlie Effinger	Miami	JR	988:37:00	44	2.67
6	Bill Zaniboni	Northern Michigan	JR	1903:27:00	85	2.68
7	Riley Gill	Western Michigan	FR	1333:03:00	62	2.79
8	Jeremie Dupont	Nebraska-Omaha	FR	1688:26:00	80	2.84
9	Joseph Palmer	Ohio State	FR	1968:00:00	97	2.96
10	Mitch O'Keefe	Ferris State	SO	1681:58:00	85	3.03
11	Billy Sauer	Michigan	SO	2353:52:00	119	3.03
12	Wylie Rogers	Alaska	JR	1312:55:00	67	3.06
13	Chad Johnson	Alaska	SO	1002:10:00	52	3.11
14	Jimmy Spratt	Bowling Green	SO	1730:10:00	105	3.64
15	Daniel Bellissimo	Western Michigan	JR	893:51:00	58	3.89

Minimum 33% of Team Minutes Played

SAVE PERCENTAGE:

				SAVES	GA	PCT
1	Jeff Jakaitis	Lake Superior	SR	1059	79	0.931
2	David Brown	Notre Dame	SR	844	63	0.931
3	Jeff Zatkoff	Miami	SO	662	58	0.919
4	Jeff Lerg	Michigan State	SO	1042	99	0.913
5	Riley Gill	Western Michigan	FR	645	62	0.912
6	Bill Zaniboni	Northern Michigan	JR	807	85	0.905
7	Billy Sauer	Michigan	SO	1028	119	0.896
8	Charlie Effinger	Miami	JR	380	44	0.896
9	Wylie Rogers	Alaska	JR	548	67	0.891
10	Joseph Palmer	Ohio State	FR	782	97	0.89
11	Jeremie Dupont	Nebraska-Omaha	FR	637	80	0.888
12	Jimmy Spratt	Bowling Green	SO	817	105	0.886
13	Mitch O'Keefe	Ferris State	SO	654	85	0.885
14	Chad Johnson	Alaska	SO	393	52	0.883
15	Daniel Bellissimo	Western Michigan	JR	379	58	0.867

Minimum 33% of Team Minutes Played

WINNING PERCENTAGE:

				W- L- T	PCT
1	David Brown	Notre Dame	SR	30- 6- 3	0.808
2	Jeff Lerg	Michigan State	SO	26-13- 3	0.655
3	Billy Sauer	Michigan	SO	25-14- 1	0.638
4	Jeff Zatkoff	Miami	SO	14- 8- 3	0.62
5	Charlie Effinger	Miami	JR	10- 6- 1	0.618
6	Riley Gill	Western Michigan	FR	13- 8- 1	0.614
7	Jeremie Dupont	Nebraska-Omaha	FR	13-10- 6	0.552
8	Jeff Jakaitis	Lake Superior	SR	16-16- 3	0.5
	Joseph Palmer	Ohio State	FR	15-15- 4	0.5
10	Chad Johnson	Alaska	SO	5- 6- 2	0.462
11	Bill Zaniboni	Northern Michigan	JR	12-21- 2	0.371
12	Daniel Bellissimo	Western Michigan	JR	5-10- 0	0.333
13	Wylie Rogers	Alaska	JR	6-15- 4	0.32
14	Mitch O'Keefe	Ferris State	SO	7-19- 3	0.293
15	Jimmy Spratt	Bowling Green	SO	6-22- 1	0.224

Minimum 33% of Team Minutes Played

**Central States
Collegiate Hockey League**
2475 Archdale
West Bloomfield, MI 48324-3607
248.366.7914 • Fax 248.366.7915
www.cschl.com

Commissioner / Treasurer / Statistician / Webmaster
Brian Moran
2475 Archdale
West Bloomfield, MI 48324-3607
O 248.366.7914 / F 248.366.7915
bmoran4@achahockey.org

President	**Vice-President**
Chris Wilk	**Paul Fassbender**
chriswilk@achahockey.org	paulfassbender@emuhockey.com

Secretary	**Past President**
Erik Turngren	**John Bosch**
turngren@achahockey.org	jbosch@achahockey.org

Eastern Michigan University

University of Illinois

Iowa State University

Kent State University

Lindenwood University

University of Michigan Dearborn

Ohio University

Robert Morris College

Saint Louis University

Western Michigan University

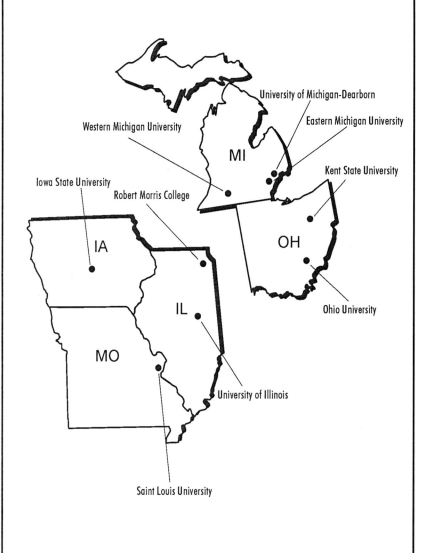

CSCHL

CENTRAL STATES COLLEGIATE HOCKEY LEAGUE

University of Michigan-Dearborn

Eastern Michigan University

Western Michigan University

MI

Kent State University

Iowa State University

Robert Morris College

IA

OH

IL

Ohio University

MO

University of Illinois

Saint Louis University

CENTRAL STATES
COLLEGIATE HOCKEY LEAGUE
FINAL 2006-07 CONFERENCE STANDINGS

		Pts	GP	Record	Win%	GF- GA	GP	Record
1	Ohio	58	22	18- 4- 0		126- 49	35	27- 7- 1
2	Illinois	56	18	14- 4- 0		99- 32	30	26- 4- 0
3	Lindenwood	48	18	12- 6- 0		84- 64	36	25-11- 0
4	Iowa State	46	18	11- 6- 1		75- 60	36	26- 8- 2
5	Kent State	34	20	9-11- 0		92-105	38	26-11- 1
6	Robert Morris	34	20	9- 9- 2		76- 84	35	14-15- 6
7	Eastern Michigan	30	24	10-14- 0		83-106	35	16-17- 2
8	Michigan Dearborn	30	20	8-12- 0		91-115	36	16-18- 2
9	Western Michigan	26	22	7-13- 2		87-102	38	19-16- 3
10	Saint Louis	8	18	2-16- 0		50-146	39	4-24- 0

2007 CSCHL PLAYOFFS

QUARTER FINALS *(2.16.07)*

Kent State University	2	Iowa State University	8
Robert Morris University	5	Lindenwood University	9
Eastern Michigan University	1	University of Illinois	10
University of Michigan Dearborn	1	Ohio University	3

SEMI FINALS *(2.17.07)*

| Lindenwood University | 4 | University of Illinois | 8 |
| Iowa State University | 4 | Ohio University | 3 |

CONSOLATION FINAL *(2.18.07)*

| Lindenwood University | 3 | Ohio University | 2 |

CHAMPIONSHIP *(2.18.07)*

| Iowa State University | 5 | University of Illinois | 3 |

CENTRAL STATES COLLEGIATE HOCKEY LEAGUE CHAMPIONS

	REGULAR	TOURNAMENT
1972		Lewis College
1973		Iowa State University
1974		Chicago State University
1975		Loyola University (Chicago)
1976		University of Illinois Chicago
1977		Chicago State University
1978		Chicago State University
1979		Illinois State University
1980		Iowa State University
1981		Iowa State University
1982		Illinois State University
1983		Marquette University
1984		Iowa State University
1985		Iowa State University
1986		University of Illinois
1987		Iowa State University
1988		University of Illinois
1989		Iowa State University
1990		Iowa State University
1991		Iowa State University
1992	University of Michigan - Dearborn Iowa State University	University of Illinois
1993	University of Michigan - Dearborn	Eastern Michigan University
1994	Ohio University	Eastern Michigan University
1995	Ohio University	Ohio University
1996	Ohio University	Ohio University
1997	Iowa State University	Iowa State University
1998	University of Michigan - Dearborn	University of Michigan - Dearborn
1999	University of Michigan - Dearborn	(Vacated)
2000	Ohio University	Ohio University
2001	Eastern Michigan University	Eastern Michigan University
2002	Iowa State University	Iowa State University
2003	University of Illinois	University of Illinois
2004	Ohio University	Ohio University
2005	Ohio University	Ohio University
2006	Ohio University	University of Illinois
2007	Ohio University	Iowa State University

CSCHL SCORING STATISTICS (OVERALL):			GP	G - A - P
Jason O'Bannon	LIND	F	20	18-29-47
Steve Rademacher	ISU	F	20	26-16-42
Derek Porter	ISU	F	24	17-18-35
Brandon Hanley	OU	F	20	13-18-31
Chris Hourigan	KSU	F	20	11-20-31
Matthew Chromy	ISU	D	20	11-19-30
Chris Tasic	OU	F	20	14-16-30
Dave Fitzgerald	WMU	F	20	9-20-29
Jim Fuhs	UM-D	F	16	10-19-29
Shawn Wilson	LIND	F	20	17-12-29
Sean McWhorter	RMC	F	20	15-13-28
Jeff Jepson	OU	F	20	7-19-26
Joel Kuehn	ILL	F	16	4-21-25
Kevin Lee	LIND	F	20	14-11-25
Michael Podelnyk	ILL	F	15	13-12-25
Daniel Olgren	OU	F	24	11-13-24
Jordan Pringle	LIND	F	18	11-13-24
Steve LaFrenier	ISU	F	20	11-12-23
Dan McNabb	LIND	F	17	17-6-23
Mike Murtaugh	SLU	F	16	11-12-23
Jason Nemeth	ISU	F	16	12-11-23
Ryan Nawrocki	KSU	F	19	10-12-22
Brandon Fackey	KSU	F	19	10-11-21
Kelly Koester	ILL	F	22	14-7-21
Clay LaBrosse	EMU	F	15	8-13-21
Aaron Moss	SLU	F	19	11-10-21
Larry Kopecky	ILL	F	15	8-12-20
David Moyer	EMU	D	19	8-12-20
T.J. Murphy	ISU	F	19	7-13-20
Alex Park	KSU	F	18	12-8-20
Paul Warriner	OU	F	19	11-9-20
Quinn Henry	RMC	F	14	6-13-19
Matt Jennings	UM-D	F	17	5-14-19
Johnny Liang	ILL	F	12	7-12-19
Nathan Hucker	OU	D	18	1-17-18
Matt Opyd	SLU	F	24	2-16-18
Jayson Peterson	SLU	F	16	9-9-18
John Yasak	OU	D	18	6-12-18
Chris Goerdt	EMU	F	16	6-11-17
JJ Heredia	EMU	F	16	5-12-17
Ryan Wood	LIND	F	15	8-9-17
Dave Bruder	RMC	F	19	4-12-16
Nick Fabbrini	ISU	F	16	10-6-16
Drew Heredia	WMU	F	10	4-12-16
Derek Makula	WMU	D	19	8-8-16
Henri St. Arnault	UM-D	F	18	2-14-16
Steve Galvan	UM-D	F	20	7-8-15
Kyle Rickermann	SLU	D	17	3-12-15
Brandon Steffek	SLU	F	19	8-7-15
Matt Widing	UM-D	F	17	5-10-15
Jason Brown	OU	F	16	5-9-14
Gary Gardner	ILL	F	18	6-8-14
Peter Katowicz	LIND	F	19	2-12-14
Patrick (PJ) Pinkerton	WMU	D	22	4-10-14
JJ Plutt	KSU	F	19	7-7-14
Steve Schue	UM-D	F	18	7-7-14
Kevin Thompson	EMU	F	19	6-8-14
Travis Bokina	RMC	F	13	5-8-13

Ryan Connolly	LIND	F	21	6-7-13
Michael Crowley	ILL	F	19	6-7-13
Brian Gahagan	KSU	D	19	7-6-13
EddieMartin	ILL	F	9	8-5-13
Rob Tauer	OU	F	16	6-7-13
Justin Althof	OU	F	17	5-7-12
Marshall Chubirka	OU	F	12	7-5-12
Pat Clark	OU	F	16	7-5-12
Josh Daugherty	KSU	F	15	5-7-12
Allen Raushel	OU	F	11	5-7-12
Joey Resch	KSU	F	17	4-8-12
Adam Stoner	UM-D	F	17	1-11-12
Teddy Theodoroff	LIND	F	18	8-4-12
Tom Ciaverilla	LIND	F	13	3-8-11
Mike Kincaid	LIND	F	18	7-4-11
Steve Koich	LIND	F	20	5-6-11
Brandon Moran	WMU	F	12	3-8-11
Bill Adolph	ILL	F	14	6-4-10
Nick Cross	RMC	F	19	3-7-10
Brian Hopper	KSU	D	10	0-10-10
Peter Majkozak	ILL	F	16	5-5-10
Pat Mannina	KSU	D	9	3-7-10
Justin Petruska	SLU	F	14	5-5-10
Matt Verdoni	WMU	D	16	3-7-10
Ryan Bond	WMU	F	16	3-6-9
Mike Guentner	LIND	F	17	3-6-9
Brian Hopper	SLU	D	10	4-5-9
Shane Mytnik	OU	F	16	3-6-9
Mike Paulsen	ISU	F	8	2-7-9
Kyle Thistle	EMU	D	19	2-7-9
James Donovan	OU	F	12	3-5-8
Brad Hoelzer	EMU	F	16	3-5-8
Brad Kerch	RMC	F	24	4-4-8
Mike Mannina	EMU	D	17	2-6-8
Kevin McAvoy	LIND	F	18	3-5-8
Phil Oberlin	ILL	F	21	4-4-8
Mike Peota	ILL	D	21	2-6-8
Bobby Prest	LIND	F	14	3-5-8
Nick Robillard	UM-D	D	17	1-7-8
Adam Saito	ILL	F	18	4-4-8
Ryan Tomassoni	SLU	D	11	0-8-8
Mike Wolff	LIND	F	11	4-4-8
Matt Androne	EMU	F	16	1-6-7
Mike Coomer	UM-D	D	20	2-5-7
Craig Drdek	KSU	F	22	4-3-7
Chris Malik	LIND	F	18	1-6-7
Bryan Moss	OU	D	18	1-6-7
Ricky Simmons	SLU	F	14	1-6-7
Jon Canniff	EMU	F	16	1-5-6
Scott Cortwright	LIND	F	8	4-2-6
Dave Easterbrook	UM-D	F	16	3-3-6
Zach Han	LIND	F	16	5-1-6
Joel Herr	ILL	D	7	2-4-6
Will Hux	EMU	F	15	4-2-6
Steve Kardel	OU	F	20	2-4-6
Nick Kostel	ISU	F	20	4-2-6
Brad Krueger	WMU	F	16	2-4-6
Aleks Perrin	EMU	F	15	2-4-6
Jim Roach	EMU	F	20	4-2-6
Ben Ruffolo	WMU	D	20	3-3-6

Michael Sholler	RMC	F	14	1-5-6
Jeff Snook	EMU	F	14	3-3-6
Ryan Tallon	SLU	F	18	1-5-6
Joshua Thompson	ILL	F	20	2-4-6
Jason Vella	EMU	D	15	0-6-6
Kevin Wicklin	ILL	F	12	1-5-6
Ryan Behnke	WMU	F	8	3-2-5
Chris Carlson	LIND	F	20	1-4-5
Grady Clingan	RMC	F	18	2-3-5
Brent Cornelius	WMU	D	16	3-2-5
Kahlin Dawson	ISU	F	20	0-5-5
Joe Diebold	UM-D	F	20	1-4-5
Phil Gerber	OU	D	14	1-4-5
Worthe Holt	RMC	D	13	1-4-5
AJ Jensen	SLU	D	8	0-5-5
Derek Krause	UM-D	D	18	2-3-5
JohnLaub	SLU	D	10	3-2-5
Rob MacInnes	EMU	F	14	3-2-5
Chris Meegan	RMC	D	17	2-3-5
Geoff Miller	RMC	D	12	3-2-5
Mike Nelson	ILL	F	17	2-3-5
Derek Purvis	LIND	D	5	3-2-5
Alex Tauchen	SLU	D	15	1-4-5
Brian Thompson	ISU	F	10	3-2-5
Andy Betourne	RMC	D	13	0-4-4
Tom Burke	KSU	D	23	2-2-4
Kyle Cook	ISU	D	18	3-1-4
Bryan Czajka	RMC	D	18	0-4-4
Tim Gardner	RMC	F	11	1-3-4
Tony Genualdi	OU	D	18	2-2-4
Ryan Gregory	ILL	D	8	1-3-4
Jim Guzzardi	ILL	F	14	2-2-4
Charles Harvey	EMU	F	5	1-3-4
Ian Heinzen	OU	D	17	2-2-4
Dustin Henning	KSU	D	13	1-3-4
Bobby Mayes	SLU	F	24	0-4-4
Adam Mueller	EMU	D	16	1-3-4
Mike Pangrazzi	WMU	D	18	2-2-4
Mike Ross	ISU	F	20	1-3-4
Andrew Schmidt	WMU	F	16	2-2-4
BrianSpring	LIND	F	6	2-2-4
Jason TerAvest	WMU	F	18	3-1-4
Wolff Volet	WMU	F	18	4-0-4
Andrew Baron	RMC	F	12	2-1-3
Dennis Belkin	RMC	F	13	2-1-3
Corey Bise	KSU	F	12	2-1-3
PierceButler	ISU	D	8	1-2-3
Ricky Gomez	LIND	D	18	1-2-3
Kyle Hagerman	UM-D	D	17	2-1-3
Gary Hupp	SLU	D	12	1-2-3
Matt McLin	RMC	D	16	1-2-3
Steve Nelson	WMU	D	8	3-0-3
Chris Serra	WMU	G	20	0-3-3
Mark Skeels	OU	F	13	1-2-3
Josh Westbrook	ISU	D	14	1-2-3
Sean Baltazar	KSU	D	16	0-2-2
Barry Baxter	ISU	F	4	0-2-2
Sean Breneman	ILL	F	11	0-2-2
Blake Busse	ISU	D	14	2-0-2
Skipper Clark	ISU	D	16	0-2-2

Justin Farmer	KSU	D	10	1-1-2
Casey Fitzpatrick	UM-D	F	14	0-2-2
JamesFrazier	KSU	F	4	0-2-2
Eric Gebhardt	ILL	F	7	1-1-2
Zach Hargis	ISU	D	13	0-2-2
Lucas Hartman	EMU	D	14	0-2-2
Adam Lesko	KSU	D	20	1-1-2
Phil Lombardo	EMU	F	14	2-0-2
Aaron Neville	KSU	F	10	1-1-2
Joakim Nilsson	OU	F	17	1-1-2
Josh Nummerdor	EMU	F	21	1-1-2
Ted Parran	EMU	D	8	0-2-2
Greg Pellegrin	RMC	F	14	1-1-2
Sean Preston	UM-D	D	10	0-2-2
Marino Santi	ILL	D	20	0-2-2
Joe Schaber	SLU	D	8	1-1-2
Carl Seitz	ISU	D	6	0-2-2
Rex Szyper	UM-D	D	15	1-1-2
ColinTrulock	EMU	D	7	1-1-2
Evan Visuri	OU	F	16	2-0-2
Brett Wills	UM-D	D	18	2-0-2
Trent Baker	SLU	G	15	0-1-1
Derek Bol	ISU	D	2	0-1-1
Kye Budziszewski	SLU	D	15	0-1-1
Corry Daus	EMU	F	15	0-1-1
Kyle Everett	OU	D	3	0-1-1
Matt Hattie	WMU	F	19	0-1-1
Steve Jacobs	EMU	D	18	0-1-1
Ken Jacobsmeyer	OU	F	12	0-1-1
Derek Janssen	LIND	F	7	0-1-1
Geoff Kienzle	EMU	D	10	0-1-1
Max Malone	ILL	D	12	1-0-1
Jim Matela	KSU	F	14	1-0-1
Aaron Merkle	KSU	G	20	0-1-1
John Mihalik	UM-D	F	16	0-1-1
Mark Myers	LIND	D	15	0-1-1
Roch Naert	ISU	D	16	0-1-1
Adam Perkins	KSU	F	11	0-1-1
Zach Reis	LIND	F	2	1-0-1
Dave Schmitt	ILL	D	10	1-0-1
Andrew Smith	LIND	F	13	1-0-1
Dan Solakiewicz	OU	F	6	0-1-1
Jerry Taylor	RMC	D	16	0-1-1
Kyle Whitehead	WMU	F	10	0-1-1
Ross Wimer	KSU	D	14	0-1-1
Stephen Yu	UM-D	G	16	0-1-1
Marco Zenere	WMU	F	20	1-0-1

GOALS AGAINST AVERAGE:

		MINUTES	GA	GAA
Mike Burda	ILL	160	4	1.50
Chris Carlson	OU	809	23	1.71
Mike DeGeorge	ILL	1560.55	50	1.92
Derek Defelice	OU	203.25	9	2.66
Ryan Baksh	OU	948.43	42	2.66
Jeff Reed	KSU	253.07	12	2.85
Geoff Miller	ISU	80	4	3.00
Nick Roberts	WMU	136.37	7	3.08
Christian Johansson	ISU	757.45	39	3.09
Jeremy Kaleniecki	EMU	986.16	52	3.16
Paul Marshall	OU	148.92	8	3.22
Trent Baker	ISU	1102.18	63	3.43
Graham Lippert	LIND	1748.32	105	3.60
Matt Dennison	LIND	361.94	22	3.65
Ryan Gregory	KSU	1209.06	75	3.72
Aaron Merkle	RMC	1853.52	115	3.72
Kyle Nova	KSU	770.87	49	3.81
Andrew Karie	WMU	183.1	12	3.93
Chris Serra	WMU	1378.67	91	3.96
Kyle Johnson	WMU	598.49	40	4.01
Brian Markowicz	EMU	835.6	63	4.52
Stephen Yu	UM-D	1555.6	119	4.59
Nick Hill	UM-D	185.95	18	5.81
Joe Rutherford	EMU	285.67	28	5.88
Micah Robbins	RMC	240	24	6.00
Matthew Janiga	UM-D	419.62	49	7.01
Trey Spiller	SLU	613.33	79	7.73
Joe Siepka	SLU	646.67	88	8.16
Ron Michalek	RMC	20	4	12.00

SAVE PERCENTAGE:

		SAVES	GA	PCT
D.J. Kohler	ILL	20	0	1.000
Chris Carlson	OU	282	23	0.925
Mike DeGeorge	ILL	593	50	0.922
Christian Johansson	ISU	444	39	0.919
Mike Burda	ILL	44	4	0.917
Aaron Merkle	RMC	1097	115	0.905
Jeremy Kaleniecki	EMU	486	52	0.903
Trent Baker	ISU	574	63	0.901
Ryan Gregory	KSU	678	75	0.900
Jeff Reed	KSU	101	12	0.894
Kyle Nova	KSU	396	49	0.890
Ryan Baksh	OU	332	42	0.888
Chris Serra	WMU	716	91	0.887
Kyle Johnson	WMU	310	40	0.886
Matt Dennison	LIND	165	22	0.882
Graham Lippert	LIND	770	105	0.880
Paul Marshall	OU	58	8	0.879
Nick Roberts	WMU	50	7	0.877
Brian Markowicz	EMU	431	63	0.872
Stephen Yu	UM-D	813	119	0.872
Andrew Karie	WMU	76	12	0.864
Nick Hill	UM-D	113	18	0.863
Geoff Miller	ISU	25	4	0.862
Derek Defelice	OU	55	9	0.859
Micah Robbins	RMC	143	24	0.856

Matthew Janiga	UM-D	262	49	0.842
Joe Siepka	SLU	452	88	0.837
Trey Spiller	SLU	394	79	0.833
Joe Rutherford	EMU	120	28	0.811
Ron Michalek	RMC	12	4	0.750

WINNING PERCENTAGE: W- L- T

Mike DeGeorge	ILL	23-4-0
Graham Lippert	LIND	17-10-2
Ryan Gregory	KSU	14-8-0
Ryan Baksh	OU	12-2-2
Aaron Merkle	RMC	12-17-2
Stephen Yu	UM-D	11-13-3
Trent Baker	ISU	10-4-3
Chris Carlson	OU	10-4-0
Chris Serra	WMU	10-10-2
Jeremy Kaleniecki	EMU	9-8-1
Kyle Nova	KSU	9-3-1
Christian Johansson	ISU	7-4-2
Brian Markowicz	EMU	5-8-0
Matt Dennison	LIND	5-1-0
Kyle Johnson	WMU	5-5-1
Jeff Reed	KSU	3-0-0
Joe Rutherford	EMU	2-2-0
Mike Burda	ILL	2-0-0
Geoff Miller	ISU	2-0-0
Derek Defelice	OU	2-0-1
Micah Robbins	RMC	2-2-0
Joe Siepka	SLU	2-8-0
Nick Hill	UM-D	2-0-0
Matthew Janiga	UM-D	2-5-0
Andrew Karie	WMU	2-1-0
D.J. Kohler	ILL	1-0-0
Paul Marshall	OU	1-1-0
Trey Spiller	SLU	1-10-0
Nick Roberts	WMU	1-1-0
Chris Abbott	LIND	0-0-0
Ron Michalek	RMC	0-0-0
Brendan Swearingen	SLU	0-0-0

College Hockey America
1500 Birchmont Drive, #29
Bemidji, MN 56601
www.collegehockeyamerica.com

Commissioner
R. H. "Bob" Peters
3229 Birchmont Drive NE
Bemidji, MN 56601
Office: 218.755.2767
Fax: 218.760.4146
email: rpeters@bemidjistate.edu

Assistant Commissioner Operations
Deb Slough
1500 Birchmont Drive, #29
Bemidji, MN 56601
Office: 218.755.2942
Fax: 218.755.3898
dslough@bemidjistate.edu

Assistant Commissioner Media Relations
Jeff Weiss
5101 John C. Lodge, 101 Mattaei
Detroit, MI 48202
Office: 313.577.7542
Fax: 313.577.5997
jeff.weiss@wayne.edu

Supervisor of Officials
Greg Shepherd
Office: 651.330.5131
Fax: 651.330.5131

University of Alabama Huntsville

Bemidji State University

Niagara University

Robert Morris University

Wayne State University

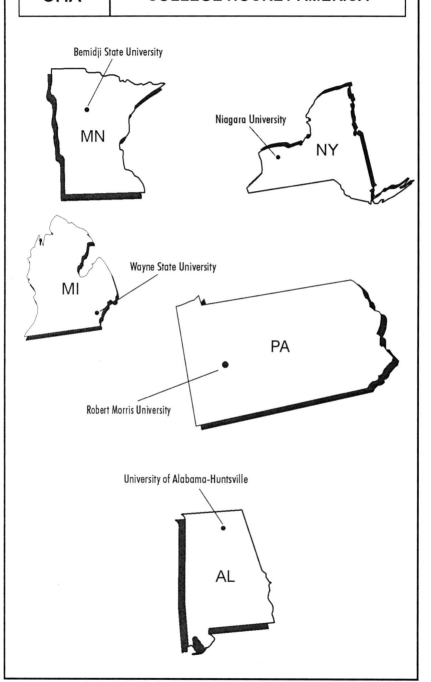

CHA

COLLEGE HOCKEY AMERICA

Bemidji State University

MN

Niagara University

NY

Wayne State University

MI

Robert Morris University

PA

University of Alabama-Huntsville

AL

COLLEGE HOCKEY AMERICA
FINAL 2006-07 CONFERENCE STANDINGS

		Pts	GP	Record	Win%	GF- GA	GP	Record	Win%	GF- GA
1	Niagara	24	20	9- 5- 6	0.6	70- 62	37	18-13- 6	0.568	126-128
2	Bemidji State	23	20	9- 6- 5	0.575	56- 54	33	14-14- 5	0.500	97-109
3	Robert Morris	19	20	9-10- 1	0.475	67- 72	35	14-19- 2	0.429	110-129
4	Wayne State	18	20	8-10- 2	0.45	64- 63	35	12-21- 2	0.371	97-125
5	AlabamaHuntsville	16	20	7-11- 2	0.4	63- 69	36	13-20- 3	0.403	112-137

2007 COLLEGE HOCKEY AMERICA PLAYOFFS

QUATER FINAL (3.09.07)

University of Alabama-Huntsville	4	Wayne State University	3

SEMIFINALS (3.10.07)

University of Alabama Huntsville	5	Niagara University	3
Robert Morris University	7	Bemidji State University	5

CHAMPIONSHIP (3.11.07)

University of Alabama Huntsville	5	Robert Morris University	4

COLLEGE HOCKEY AMERICA CHAMPIONS

	REGULAR		TOURNAMENT
2000	Niagara University	2000	Niagara University
2001	University of Alabama-Huntsville	2001	Wayne State University
2002	Wayne State University	2002	Wayne State University
2003	University of Alabama-Huntsville	2003	Wayne State University
2004	Bemidji State University	2004	Niagara University
2005	Bemidji State University	2005	Bemidji State University
2006	Niagara University	2006	Bemidji State University
2007	Niagara University	2007	University of Albama Huntsville

COLLEGE HOCKEY AMERICA LEAGUE SCORING (OVERALL):

					GP	PPG	G - A - P
1	Ted Cook	Niagara	SO	F	37	1.3	32-16-48
2	Sean Bentivoglio	Niagara	SR	F	37	1.24	16-30-46
3	Les Reaney	Niagara	SO	F	37	1.19	16-28-44
4	Chris Moran	Niagara	FR	F	37	1.08	9-31-40
5	Matt Caruana	Niagara	JR	F	37	1.03	14-24-38
6	Ryan Cruthers	Robert Morris	JR	F	34	1.09	17-20-37
7	Aaron Clarke	Robert Morris	SR	F	35	1.03	11-25-36
	David Nimmo	Alab-Huntsville	SR	F	36	1	14-22-36
9	Grant Selinger	Alab-Huntsville	SR	F	36	0.92	17-16-33
10	Doug Conley	Robert Morris	SR	F	35	0.86	7-23-30
11	Travis Winter	Bemidji State	SO	F	33	0.88	12-17-29
	Rob Sirianni	Bemidji State	SR	F	33	0.88	11-18-29
13	Brett McConnachie	Alab-Huntsville	SR	F	35	0.8	12-16-28
14	Sean Berkstresser	Robert Morris	JR	F	34	0.76	9-17-26
	Vince Rocco	Niagara	SO	F	37	0.7	9-17-26
16	Nate Higgins	Wayne State	SR	F	35	0.71	13-12-25
17	Blaine Jarvis	Bemidji State	JR	F	33	0.73	10-14-24
	Jason Bloomingburg	Wayne State	SR	F	35	0.69	11-13-24
19	Mike Salekin	Alab-Huntsville	SR	D	34	0.68	7-16-23
	Jared Katz	Wayne State	FR	F	35	0.66	11-12-23
21	Dan Iliakis	Wayne State	SR	D	32	0.69	6-16-22
	Shaun Arvai	Alab-Huntsville	SR	D	35	0.63	2-20-22
23	Tyler Scofield	Bemidji State	SO	F	27	0.78	7-14-21
	Chris Margott	Robert Morris	SO	F	31	0.68	12- 9-21
	Steve Canter	Alab-Huntsville	SR	F	35	0.6	12- 9-21
	Derek Bachynski	Wayne State	JR	F	35	0.6	7-14-21
	Pat Oliveto	Niagara	SR	D	36	0.58	2-19-21
28	Joey Moggach	Bemidji State	FR	F	27	0.74	4-16-20
	Jason Baclig	Wayne State	SR	F	33	0.61	8-12-20
30	Logan Bittle	Robert Morris	JR	F	32	0.59	5-14-19
31	Jason Towsley	Robert Morris	SO	F	25	0.72	7-11-18
	Mark Nebus	Wayne State	SR	F	35	0.51	6-12-18
	Egor Mironov	Niagara	FR	F	37	0.49	10- 8-18
34	David Boguslawski	Robert Morris	JR	F	32	0.53	10- 7-17
35	Luke Erickson	Bemidji State	SR	F	18	0.89	13- 3-16
	Scott Kalinchuk	Alab-Huntsville	SO	D	35	0.46	6-10-16
	Josh Murray	Alab-Huntsville	SO	F	35	0.46	6-10-16
	Jeff Caister	Wayne State	FR	D	35	0.46	2-14-16
	Tyler Gotto	Niagara	FR	D	36	0.44	2-14-16
40	Jon Grabarek	Wayne State	SO	F	27	0.56	5-10-15
	Ryan Miller	Bemidji State	SR	F	29	0.52	5-10-15
42	Chris Kaufman	Robert Morris	JR	D	25	0.56	6- 8-14
	Jake Sparks	Robert Morris	JR	D	30	0.47	3-11-14
	Tyler Hilbert	Alab-Huntsville	JR	F	33	0.42	5- 9-14
45	Joel Gasper	Robert Morris	JR	F	32	0.41	4- 9-13
	Matt Pope	Bemidji State	JR	F	33	0.39	5- 8-13
	Kyle Rogers	Niagara	SO	F	35	0.37	6- 7-13
	Kevin Morrison	Alab-Huntsville	FR	F	36	0.36	9- 4-13
	Dominik Rozman	Alab-Huntsville	SR	F	36	0.36	6- 7-13
50	Mike Forgie	Wayne State	JR	F	30	0.4	6- 6-12
	Tylor Michel	Wayne State	JR	F	31	0.39	8- 4-12
52	Kyle Frieday	Robert Morris	FR	F	22	0.5	3- 8-11
	Shane Holman	Bemidji State	SR	F/D	26	0.42	7- 4-11
	Brandon Marino	Bemidji State	SO	F	29	0.38	2- 9-11
	Cody Bostock	Bemidji State	SO	D	33	0.33	3- 8-11
	Stavros Paskaris	Wayne State	JR	F	34	0.32	3- 8-11
	Ryan Bernardi	Wayne State	FR	D	35	0.31	3- 8-11
	Brandon Roshko	Alab-Huntsville	FR	D	36	0.31	3- 8-11

59	Joe Federoff	Alab-Huntsville	SO	F	20	0.5	3- 7-10
	John Vadnais	Bemidji State	FR	D	31	0.32	2- 8-10
	Jeff Gilbert	Robert Morris	JR	D	34	0.29	4- 6-10
	Matt Sweazey	Alab-Huntsville	SO	F	34	0.29	2- 8-10
63	Brett Hopfe	Robert Morris	JR	F	29	0.31	2- 7- 9
	Ryan Annesley	Niagara	FR	D	31	0.29	3- 6- 9
	Matt Krug	Wayne State	SO	D	35	0.26	3- 6- 9
	Rob Cowan	Robert Morris	JR	D	35	0.26	1- 8- 9
67	Tom Biondich	Robert Morris	JR	F	24	0.33	5- 3- 8
	Garrett Roth	Bemidji State	SR	F	28	0.29	3- 5- 8
	Riley Weselowski	Bemidji State	JR	D	31	0.26	3- 5- 8
	Derek Punches	Wayne State	SO	F	35	0.23	1- 7- 8
71	Tyler Lehrke	Bemidji State	FR	F	20	0.35	5- 2- 7
	Tom Train	Alab-Huntsville	FR	F	30	0.23	3- 4- 7
	Nate Bostic	Niagara	FR	F	35	0.2	3- 4- 7
74	Dave Cowan	Robert Morris	FR	D	19	0.32	1- 5- 6
	Chris Peluso	Bemidji State	FR	D	26	0.23	0- 6- 6
	Mark Cannon	Wayne State	SR	F	29	0.21	2- 4- 6
	Travis Anderson	Niagara	JR	D	37	0.16	0- 6- 6
78	Cale Tanaka	Alab-Huntsville	FR	F	27	0.19	2- 3- 5
	Jake Bluhm	Bemidji State	JR	F	30	0.17	2- 3- 5
	Dave Deterding	Bemidji State	JR	D	33	0.15	1- 4- 5
	Matt Boldt	Wayne State	SR	D	34	0.15	1- 4- 5
82	Taylor Donohoe	Wayne State	SR	D	24	0.17	1- 3- 4
	Kevin Galerno	Alab-Huntsville	SO	F	28	0.14	2- 2- 4
	Scott Langdon	Niagara	JR	D	33	0.12	2- 2- 4
	Andrew Bonello	Robert Morris	JR	D	34	0.12	0- 4- 4
	Dan Sullivan	Niagara	SO	D	36	0.11	0- 4- 4
87	Matt Allen	Bemidji State	SO	F	17	0.18	1- 2- 3
	Jake Obermeyer	Robert Morris	SO	D	20	0.15	2- 1- 3
	Brennan Barker	Alab-Huntsville	FR	D	20	0.15	1- 2- 3
	Davide Nicoletti	Alab-Huntsville	FR	D	24	0.12	0- 3- 3
	Nathan Schwartzbauer	Bemidji State	SR	D	33	0.09	0- 3- 3
92	Armando Scarlato	Niagara	SO	D	8	0.25	1- 1- 2
	Jim Burichin	Niagara	FR	D	17	0.12	0- 2- 2
	Bryan Mills	Robert Morris	SR	D	28	0.07	1- 1- 2
	A.J. Larivee	Alab-Huntsville	SR	D	28	0.07	0- 2- 2
96	Kyle Hardwick	Bemidji State	FR	D	2	0.5	0- 1- 1
	Parker Burgess	Robert Morris	FR	F	5	0.2	0- 1- 1
	Tim Madsen	Niagara	JR	F	7	0.14	0- 1- 1
	Joey Olson	Robert Morris	JR	F	8	0.12	0- 1- 1
	Graham McManamin	Bemidji State	FR	D	10	0.1	0- 1- 1
	Chris McKelvie	Bemidji State	FR	F	11	0.09	1- 0- 1
	Eric Trax	Robert Morris	JR	D	11	0.09	0- 1- 1
	Chevan Wilson	Niagara	FR	F	12	0.08	0- 1- 1
	Adam Drescher	Wayne State	SR	D	13	0.08	0- 1- 1
	Joe Tuset	Robert Morris	SR	G	14	0.07	0- 1- 1
	Cliff Ketchen	Niagara	JR	F	24	0.04	1- 0- 1
	Ryan Olidis	Niagara	FR	F	24	0.04	0- 1- 1

GOALS AGAINST AVERAGE:

				MINUTES	GA	GAA
1	Matt Climie	Bemidji State	JR	1665:35:00	84	3.03
2	Joe Tuset	Robert Morris	SR	701:49:00	36	3.08
3	Juliano Pagliero	Niagara	SO	1610:09:00	83	3.09
4	Will Hooper	Wayne State	SR	1064:14:00	60	3.38
5	Marc Narduzzi	Alab-Huntsville	JR	1478:16:00	86	3.49
6	Brett Bothwell	Wayne State	FR	1043:19:00	62	3.57
7	Christian Boucher	Robert Morris	JR	1406:11:00	84	3.58

Minimum 33% of Team Minutes Played

SAVE PERCENTAGE:

				SAVES	GA	PCT
1	Juliano Pagliero	Niagara	SO	889	83	0.915
2	Joe Tuset	Robert Morris	SR	376	36	0.913
3	Christian Boucher	Robert Morris	JR	744	84	0.899
4	Matt Climie	Bemidji State	JR	733	84	0.897
5	Marc Narduzzi	Alab-Huntsville	JR	729	86	0.894
6	Brett Bothwell	Wayne State	FR	499	62	0.889
7	Will Hooper	Wayne State	SR	437	60	0.8798

Minimum 33% of Team Minutes Played

WINNING PERCENTAGE:

				W- L- T	PCT
1	Juliano Pagliero	Niagara	SO	14-11- 3	0.554
2	Matt Climie	Bemidji State	JR	11-10- 5	0.519
3	Brett Bothwell	Wayne State	FR	8- 9- 1	0.472
4	Joe Tuset	Robert Morris	SR	5- 6- 0	0.455
5	Christian Boucher	Robert Morris	JR	9-13- 2	0.417
6	Marc Narduzzi	Alab-Huntsville	JR	8-16- 2	0.346
7	Will Hooper	Wayne State	SR	4-12- 1	0.265

Minimum 33% of Team Minutes Played

2007

COLLEGE / PREP SHOWCASE EVENTS

NATIONAL COLLEGIATE DEVELOPMENT CAMP
PRINCETON SPORTS CENTER
MONMOUTH JUNCTION, NEW JERSEY
JULY 15 - 22, 2007

NATIONAL PREP DEVELOPMENT CAMP
PRINCETON SPORTS CENTER
MONMOUTH JUNCTION, NEW JERSEY
JULY 15 - 22, 2007

PRE PREP SHOWCASE
SALEM ICENTER
SALEM, NEW HAMPSHIRE
AUGUST 2-5, 2007

HOCKEY NIGHT IN BOSTON - MIDWEST
ANN ARBOR ICE CUBE
ANN ARBOR, MICHIGAN
JUNE 21-23, 2007

HOCKEY NIGHT IN BOSTON - PACIFIC
GLACIAL GARDENS
LAKEWOOD, CALIFORNIA
JUNE 21-23, 2007

NATIONAL HOCKEY TRAINING
UNIVERSITY OF SOUTHERN MAINE
GORHAM, MAINE
JULY 2007

ECAC Hockey League
Pepsi Arena
51 S Pearl Street
Albany, NY 12207
www.ecachockeyleague.com

Commissioner
Steve Hagwell
Office: 518.487.2289
Fax: 518.487.2290
shagwell@ecachockeyleague.com

Assistant Commissioner
Laura Stange
Office: 518.487.2288
Fax: 518.487.2290
lstange@ecachockeyleague.com

Brown University
Clarkson University
Colgate University
Cornell University
Dartmouth College
Harvard University
Princeton University
Quinnipiac University
Rensselaer Polytechnic Institute
St. Lawrence University
Union College
Yale University

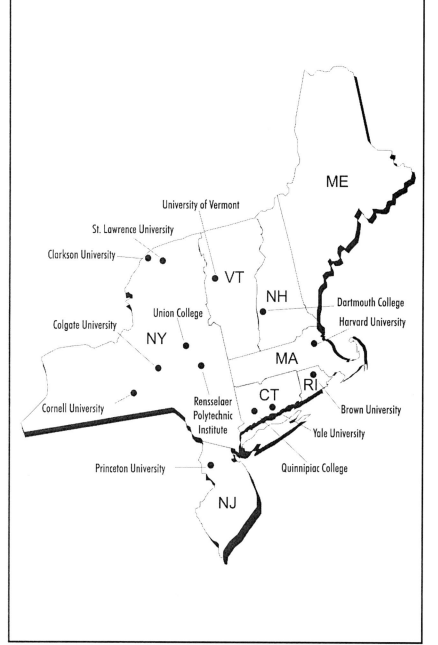

ECAC

ECAC HOCKEY LEAGUE

University of Vermont

St. Lawrence University

Clarkson University

ME

VT

NH

Dartmouth College

Colgate University

Union College

Harvard University

NY

MA

Cornell University

Rensselaer
Polytechnic
Institute

CT

RI

Brown University

Princeton University

Yale University

Quinnipiac College

NJ

ECAC HOCKEY LEAGUE
FINAL 2006-07 CONFERENCE STANDINGS

		Pts	GP	Record	Win%	GF-GA	GP	Record	Win%	GF-GA
1	St. Lawrence	33	22	16- 5- 1	0.75	73- 55	39	23-14- 2	0.615	122-104
2	Clarkson	30	22	13- 5- 4	0.682	74- 53	39	25- 9- 5	0.705	136- 93
3	Dartmouth	27	22	12- 7- 3	0.614	69- 60	33	18-12- 3	0.591	105- 93
4	Cornell	24	22	10- 8- 4	0.545	64- 55	31	14-13- 4	0.516	90- 78
	Quinnipiac	24	22	10- 8- 4	0.545	74- 63	40	21-14- 5	0.588	140-106
6	Princeton	22	22	10-10- 2	0.500	69- 63	34	15-16- 3	0.485	102-100
	Harvard	22	22	10-10- 2	0.500	67- 65	33	14-17- 2	0.455	88- 90
8	Colgate	17	22	7-12- 3	0.386	53- 60	40	15-21- 4	0.425	100-105
	Rensselaer	17	22	6-11- 5	0.386	55- 84	36	10-18- 8	0.389	88-130
	Yale	17	22	8-13- 1	0.386	56- 72	31	11-17- 3	0.403	78- 98
11	Brown	16	22	6-12- 4	0.364	65- 69	32	11-15- 6	0.438	96- 95
12	Union	15	22	7-14- 1	0.341	54- 74	36	14-19- 3	0.431	103-119

2007 ECAC HOCKEY LEAGUE PLAYOFFS

FIRST ROUND (3.2.07 - 3.4.07)
(Best of Three Series)

Rensselaer Polytechnic Institute	0	Colgate University	2
Yale University	0	Harvard University	2
Brown University	1	Princeton University	2
Union College	0	Quinnipiac University	2

QUARTERFINALS (3.09.07 - 3.10.07)
(Best of Three Series)

Quinnipiac University	2	Cornell University	0
Harvard University	0	Clarkson University	2
Colgate University	0	St. Lawrence University	2
Princeton University	0	Dartmouth College	2

SEMIFINALS (3.16.07)

Quinnipiac University	4	St. Lawrence University	0
Dartmouth College	4	Clarkson University	5

THIRD PLACE (3.17.07)

Dartmouth College	3	St. Lawrence University	5

CHAMPIONSHIP (3.17.07)

Quinnipiac University	2	Clarkson University	4

ECAC HOCKEY LEAGUE CHAMPIONS

	REGULAR	**TOURNAMENT**
1962	St. Lawrence University	
1963	Harvard University	
1964	Providence College	
1965	Boston College	
1966	Clarkson University	
1967	Cornell University	
1968	Cornell University	
1969	Cornell University	
1970	Cornell University	
1971	Harvard University	
1972	Boston University	
1973	Cornell University	
1974	Boston University	
1975	Boston University	
1976	Boston University	
1977	Boston University	
1978	Boston College	
1979	University of New Hampshire	
1980	Cornell University	
1981	Providence College	
1982	Northeastern University	
1983	Harvard University	
1984	Rensselaer Polytechnic Institute	
1985	Rensselaer Polytechnic Institute	Rensselaer Polytechnic Institute
1986	Harvard University	Cornell University
1987	Harvard University	Harvard University
1988	Harvard University	St. Lawrence University
1989	Harvard University	St. Lawrence University
1990	Colgate University	Colgate University
1991	Clarkson University	Clarkson University
1992	Harvard University	St. Lawrence University
1993	Harvard University	Clarkson University
1994	Harvard University	Harvard University
1995	Clarkson University	Rensselaer Polytechnic Institute
1996	University of Vermont	Cornell University
1997	Clarkson University	Cornell University
1998	Yale University	Princeton University
1999	Clarkson University	Clarkson University
2000	St. Lawrence University	St. Lawrence University
2001	Clarkson University	St. Lawrence University
2002	Cornell University	Harvard University
2003	Cornell University	Cornell University
2004	Colgate University	Harvard University
2005	Cornell University	Cornell University
2006	Colgate University	Harvard University
	Dartmouth College	
2007	St. Lawrence University	Clarkson University

					GP	PPG	G - A - P
1	David Jones	Dartmouth	JR	F	33	1.33	18-26-44
	Brandon Wong	Quinnipiac	FR	F	40	1.10	27-17-44
3	Reid Cashman	Quinnipiac	SR	D	40	1.02	3-38-41
4	Shawn Weller	Clarkson	JR	F	39	1.03	19-21-40
	Tyler Burton	Colgate	JR	F	40	1.00	18-22-40
6	Nick Dodge	Clarkson	JR	F	36	1.08	18-21-39
	Marc Fulton	Colgate	SR	F	38	1.03	15-24-39
8	T.J. Fox	Union	SO	F	36	1.03	13-24-37
	Jesse Winchester	Colgate	JR	F	37	1.00	16-21-37
	David Cayer	Clarkson	JR	F	39	0.95	11-26-37
	Jamie Bates	Quinnipiac	JR	F	40	0.93	14-23-37
12	Steve Zalewski	Clarkson	JR	F	39	0.87	16-18-34
13	Jeff Prough	Brown	JR	F	32	1.03	16-17-33
	Kyle Rank	St. Lawrence	SR	F	39	0.85	15-18-33
	Ben Nelson	Quinnipiac	JR	F	40	0.82	17-16-33
16	Kevin DeVergilio	St. Lawrence	SO	F	36	0.89	9-23-32
	Bryan Leitch	Quinnipiac	SO	F	40	0.80	12-20-32
18	Sean Backman	Yale	FR	F	29	1.07	18-13-31
	T.J. Galiardi	Dartmouth	FR	F	33	0.94	14-17-31
	Josh Coyle	Union	JR	F	33	0.94	14-17-31
	Shea Guthrie	Clarkson	SO	F	36	0.86	8-23-31
	Max Taylor	St. Lawrence	SR	F	39	0.79	13-18-31
23	Nick Johnson	Dartmouth	JR	F	33	0.91	14-16-30
24	Lee Jubinville	Princeton	SO	F	32	0.91	11-18-29
25	Tanner Glass	Dartmouth	SR	F	32	0.88	8-20-28
	Darroll Powe	Princeton	SR	F	34	0.82	13-15-28
27	Kirk MacDonald	Rensselaer	SR	F	33	0.82	12-15-27
	Jason Walters	Union	FR	F	35	0.77	8-19-27
	Jake Luthi	Rensselaer	SR	D	36	0.75	4-23-27
	Matt Beca	Clarkson	FR	F	38	0.71	10-17-27
31	Grant Goeckner-Zoeller	Princeton	SR	F	33	0.79	8-18-26
	Matt Cook	Union	SO	F	36	0.72	12-14-26
	Chris D'Alvise	Clarkson	SO	F	37	0.70	16-10-26
	David Marshall	Quinnipiac	SO	F	39	0.67	17- 9-26
35	Mike McKenzie	St. Lawrence	FR	F	31	0.81	12-13-25
	Topher Scott	Cornell	JR	F	31	0.81	4-21-25
	Kevin Du	Harvard	SR	F	33	0.76	5-20-25
	Brock McBride	St. Lawrence	SO	F	34	0.74	9-16-25
	Lane Caffaro	Union	SO	D	34	0.74	7-18-25
	Drew Bagnall	St. Lawrence	SR	D	39	0.64	6-19-25
41	Mark Arcobello	Yale	FR	F	29	0.83	10-14-24
	Byron Bitz	Cornell	SR	F	29	0.83	8-16-24
	Brian McNary	Brown	JR	F	30	0.80	6-18-24
	Sean Hurley	Brown	JR	D	32	0.75	10-14-24
	J.T. Wyman	Dartmouth	JR	F	33	0.73	13-11-24
	Kevin Westgarth	Princeton	SR	F	33	0.73	8-16-24
	Doug Rogers	Harvard	FR	F	33	0.73	7-17-24
48	Oren Eizenman	Rensselaer	SR	F	28	0.82	9-14-23
	Ryan Maki	Harvard	SR	F	32	0.72	12-11-23
	Ben Lovejoy	Dartmouth	SR	D	32	0.72	7-16-23
	Mark Magnowski	Princeton	FR	F	33	0.70	10-13-23
	Brett Wilson	Princeton	SO	F	33	0.70	8-15-23
	Mario Valery-Trabucco	Union	FR	F	35	0.66	12-11-23
	Nick St. Pierre	Colgate	SO	D	40	0.57	7-16-23
55	Kevin Swallow	Dartmouth	SO	F	32	0.69	8-14-22
56	Raymond Sawada	Cornell	JR	F	31	0.68	10-11-21
	Mike Taylor	Harvard	JR	F	33	0.64	10-11-21
	Andrei Uryadov	Rensselaer	SO	F	35	0.60	8-13-21

	Olivier Bouchard	Union	SR	F	36	0.58	12- 9-21
	Seth Klerer	Rensselaer	SO	F	36	0.58	9-12-21
	Tom Riley	Colgate	SO	F	38	0.55	10-11-21
62	Mark McCutcheon	Cornell	SR	F	29	0.69	10-10-20
63	Tony Romano	Cornell	FR	F	29	0.66	9-10-19
	Colin Greening	Cornell	FR	F	31	0.61	11- 8-19
	Alex Meintel	Harvard	JR	F	32	0.59	14- 5-19
	Paul Kerins	Rensselaer	FR	F	34	0.56	7-12-19
	Jake Morissette	Rensselaer	JR	F	36	0.53	7-12-19
	Grant Clitsome	Clarkson	JR	D	38	0.50	7-12-19
	Jean-Marc Beaudoin	Quinnipiac	FR	F	40	0.47	8-11-19
	Eric Lampe	Quinnipiac	FR	F	40	0.47	8-11-19
71	Sean Dersch	Brown	SR	F	27	0.67	5-13-18
	Matt Vokes	Brown	SO	F	29	0.62	10- 8-18
	Bill LeClerc	Yale	SR	D	29	0.62	6-12-18
	Blake Gallagher	Cornell	FR	F	29	0.62	3-15-18
	Rob Pritchard	Dartmouth	SO	F	33	0.55	10- 8-18
	Dylan Reese	Harvard	SR	D	33	0.55	9- 9-18
	Jon Pelle	Harvard	JR	F	33	0.55	7-11-18
	Alex Biega	Harvard	FR	D	33	0.55	6-12-18
	Mike Schreiber	Union	FR	D	35	0.51	3-15-18
	Greg Holt	Quinnipiac	FR	F	38	0.47	6-12-18
81	Charlie Giffin	St. Lawrence	JR	F	25	0.68	8- 9-17
	Mitch Carefoot	Cornell	SR	F	27	0.63	9- 8-17
	Chris Cahill	Yale	FR	F	31	0.55	8- 9-17
	Sean Muncy	Brown	SO	F	32	0.53	8- 9-17
	Matt Angers-Goulet	Rensselaer	SO	F	35	0.49	9- 8-17
	Mike Sullivan	Clarkson	SR	F	39	0.44	8- 9-17
	David McIntyre	Colgate	FR	F	40	0.42	9- 8-17
	Jason Williams	Colgate	FR	F	40	0.42	5-12-17
89	Antonin Roux	Brown	SR	F	26	0.62	4-12-16
	Jimmy Fraser	Harvard	SO	F	29	0.55	6-10-16
	Connor Shields	Dartmouth	SO	F	33	0.48	1-15-16
	Jonathan Ornelas	Rensselaer	JR	F	34	0.47	7- 9-16
	Dan Henningson	Quinnipiac	SO	D	39	0.41	2-14-16
94	Jared Seminoff	Cornell	SO	D	23	0.65	1-14-15
	Grant Lewis	Dartmouth	SR	D	24	0.62	1-14-15
	Sean Flanagan	St. Lawrence	FR	F	29	0.52	5-10-15
	Brian McCafferty	Harvard	SO	D	29	0.52	1-14-15
	Chris Poli	Brown	JR	F	30	0.50	4-11-15
	Doug Krantz	Cornell	JR	D	31	0.48	5-10-15
	Brodie Rutherglen	Clarkson	SR	F	37	0.41	8- 7-15
	Casey Parenteau	St. Lawrence	SO	F	37	0.41	6- 9-15
	Matt Sorteberg	Quinnipiac	JR	D	37	0.41	4-11-15
	Jason Fredricks	Colgate	SO	D	37	0.41	3-12-15
104	Dan Travis	Quinnipiac	JR	F	18	0.78	4-10-14
	Brian Ihnacak	Brown	SR	F	27	0.52	3-11-14
	Brendon Nash	Cornell	FR	D	29	0.48	2-12-14
	Michael Grenzy	Clarkson	SR	D	30	0.47	2-12-14
	Thomas Dignard	Yale	FR	D	31	0.45	4-10-14
	David Robertson	Brown	JR	D	31	0.45	3-11-14
	Mike Moore	Princeton	JR	D	32	0.44	4-10-14
	Jeremy Russell	Brown	FR	D	32	0.44	3-11-14
	Max Cousins	Princeton	SR	D	32	0.44	3-11-14
113	Ryan Garbutt	Brown	SO	F	29	0.45	9- 4-13
	Robert Page	Yale	JR	D	31	0.42	3-10-13
	Cam MacIntyre	Princeton	FR	F	32	0.41	9- 4-13
	Jon Grecu	Dartmouth	JR	F	32	0.41	3-10-13
	Torren Delforte	Union	JR	F	35	0.37	4- 9-13
118	Jean-Francois Boucher	Yale	JR	F	30	0.40	3- 9-12

	Chris Potts	Union	SO	F	34	0.35	6- 6-12
	Michael Beynon	Union	JR	D	34	0.35	2-10-12
	Zach Miskovic	St. Lawrence	SO	D	39	0.31	2-10-12
	Tyrell Mason	Clarkson	SO	D	39	0.31	1-11-12
123	Evan Barlow	Cornell	SO	F	28	0.39	6- 5-11
	Chris Myers	Quinnipiac	SO	F	30	0.37	3- 8-11
	Jeremiah Cunningham	St. Lawrence	FR	F	32	0.34	7- 4-11
	Devin Timberlake	Brown	FR	F	32	0.34	3- 8-11
	Brett Westgarth	Princeton	SR	D	33	0.33	0-11-11
	Kurt Colling	Rensselaer	SO	F	34	0.32	3- 8-11
	Travis Vermeulen	St. Lawrence	FR	F	39	0.28	3- 8-11
130	Jordan Hack	St. Lawrence	JR	F	22	0.45	5- 5-10
	Dan Bartlett	Princeton	FR	F	26	0.38	5- 5-10
	Peter Bogdanich	Colgate	SO	F	28	0.36	3- 7-10
	Mark Wallmann	St. Lawrence	JR	F	34	0.29	4- 6-10
	Alex Curran	St. Lawrence	FR	F	36	0.28	3- 7-10
	Peter Merth	Rensselaer	FR	D	36	0.28	0-10-10
	Shawn Fensel	St. Lawrence	SO	D	37	0.27	3- 7-10
	Jared Ross	St. Lawrence	SO	D	38	0.26	5- 5-10
138	Dan Shribman	Dartmouth	SR	F	25	0.36	4- 5- 9
	Michael Karwoski	Yale	SO	F	25	0.36	4- 5- 9
	Chad Morin	Harvard	FR	D	29	0.31	2- 7- 9
	Jody Pederson	Princeton	FR	D	32	0.28	1- 8- 9
	David Sloane	Colgate	SO	D	35	0.26	4- 5- 9
	Matt Generous	St. Lawrence	SO	D	37	0.24	3- 6- 9
144	Brad Mills	Yale	SR	F	20	0.40	2- 6- 8
	Blair Yaworski	Yale	JR	F	21	0.38	1- 7- 8
	Andrzej Sandrzyk	St. Lawrence	SR	F	24	0.33	2- 6- 8
	Will Engasser	Yale	JR	F	25	0.32	7- 1- 8
	Brandan Kushniruk	Princeton	SO	F	26	0.31	4- 4- 8
	Mark Anderson	Colgate	SO	D	29	0.28	1- 7- 8
	Matt Cohen	Yale	SR	D	31	0.26	3- 5- 8
	Landis Stankievech	Princeton	JR	F	32	0.25	5- 3- 8
	Adam Bellows	Clarkson	SO	D	33	0.24	0- 8- 8
	Derek Keller	St. Lawrence	FR	D	33	0.24	0- 8- 8
	Kevin Broad	Rensselaer	SR	F	35	0.23	3- 5- 8
155	Augie DiMarzo	Union	SO	F	7	1.00	1- 6- 7
	Jeff Christiansen	Union	FR	F	16	0.44	5- 2- 7
	Aaron Volpatti	Brown	FR	F	23	0.30	5- 2- 7
	Eric Slais	Brown	SO	F	25	0.28	2- 5- 7
	Paul Dufault	Harvard	JR	F	26	0.27	1- 6- 7
	Reed Kipp	Rensselaer	SO	D	28	0.25	1- 6- 7
	Michael Kennedy	Cornell	SO	F	30	0.23	5- 2- 7
	Mike Campaner	Colgate	SR	D	30	0.23	0- 7- 7
	Andrew Lord	Rensselaer	JR	F	32	0.22	2- 5- 7
	Daryl Marcoux	Princeton	SR	D	34	0.21	3- 4- 7
	Philippe Paquet	Clarkson	SO	D	37	0.19	3- 4- 7
	Dustin Gillanders	Colgate	JR	F	37	0.19	1- 6- 7
	Ben Camper	Colgate	JR	F	39	0.18	2- 5- 7
	Max Kolu	Clarkson	SR	F	39	0.18	1- 6- 7
169	Sean McMonagle	Brown	FR	F	16	0.38	3- 3- 6
	John Doherty	Quinnipiac	JR	D	16	0.38	2- 4- 6
	Mike Atkinson	Quinnipiac	FR	F	23	0.26	4- 2- 6
	Steve Rolecek	Harvard	SO	F	26	0.23	2- 4- 6
	Mark Agnew	Quinnipiac	JR	F	27	0.22	3- 3- 6
	Dan Lefort	Quinnipiac	JR	D	27	0.22	2- 4- 6
	Dave Watters	Harvard	JR	F	28	0.21	1- 5- 6
	Kyle Hagel	Princeton	JR	F	29	0.21	4- 2- 6
	Tyler Mugford	Cornell	SO	F	29	0.21	1- 5- 6
	Justin Krueger	Cornell	FR	D	31	0.19	1- 5- 6

	Steve Mandes	Harvard	SR	F	33	0.18	3- 3- 6
	Brendan Milnamow	Union	SO	D	33	0.18	2- 4- 6
	Andrew Meyer	Quinnipiac	SO	D	36	0.17	2- 4- 6
	Tim Marks	Clarkson	FR	F	37	0.16	1- 5- 6
183	Greg Beller	Yale	FR	F	24	0.21	2- 3- 5
	Patrick Brosnihan	Yale	SO	F	27	0.19	3- 2- 5
	John Gibson	Dartmouth	SO	D	28	0.18	0- 5- 5
	Matt Nelson	Yale	SO	F	30	0.17	2- 3- 5
	Paul Baier	Brown	JR	D	32	0.16	1- 4- 5
	Garrett Vassel	Rensselaer	FR	F/D	32	0.16	1- 4- 5
189	Tom Bardis	St. Lawrence	FR	F	12	0.33	2- 2- 4
	Peter Boldt	Dartmouth	FR	D	17	0.24	0- 4- 4
	Dan Tuttle	Clarkson	SO	F	20	0.20	3- 1- 4
	Kevin Kaiser	Princeton	FR	F	21	0.19	2- 2- 4
	Justin Milo	Cornell	FR	F	24	0.17	3- 1- 4
	Christian Jensen	Rensselaer	FR	D	24	0.17	1- 3- 4
	Taylor Davenport	Cornell	SO	D	27	0.15	2- 2- 4
	Jack Christian	Harvard	SO	D	32	0.12	0- 4- 4
	Mike Werner	Colgate	JR	F	33	0.12	2- 2- 4
	Tyler Magura	Harvard	JR	F	33	0.12	0- 4- 4
	Sean Streich	Union	SR	D	36	0.11	1- 3- 4
	Liam Huculak	Colgate	SR	F	39	0.10	2- 2- 4
201	Mike Stuart	Brown	SO	D	10	0.30	1- 2- 3
	Tommy Green	Rensselaer	SR	F	15	0.20	1- 2- 3
	Mike Wakita	Union	FR	D	20	0.15	0- 3- 3
	Jason Shaffer	Union	FR	F	21	0.14	1- 2- 3
	Dan Peace	Rensselaer	JR	F	22	0.14	1- 2- 3
	Michael Bordieri	Quinnipiac	SR	F	24	0.12	1- 2- 3
	Mike Harr	Union	SO	D	24	0.12	0- 3- 3
	Ryan Donald	Yale	FR	D	25	0.12	1- 2- 3
	Brandon Harrington	Dartmouth	SO	F	31	0.10	1- 2- 3
	Mike Hartwick	Dartmouth	SR	D	33	0.09	0- 3- 3
	Ethan Cox	Colgate	FR	F	35	0.09	2- 1- 3
	Jake Schwan	Union	JR	F	36	0.08	0- 3- 3
	Matt Curley	Clarkson	SR	D	39	0.08	2- 1- 3
	Mark Nelson	Quinnipiac	SO	F	40	0.07	0- 3- 3
215	Ryan Bellows	Dartmouth	SO	F	8	0.25	0- 2- 2
	Shawn Mole	Yale	SR	D	9	0.22	1- 1- 2
	Cam French	Princeton	FR	F	12	0.17	1- 1- 2
	Josh Gillam	Dartmouth	FR	F	13	0.15	2- 0- 2
	Keith Shattenkirk	Princeton	JR	F	13	0.15	0- 2- 2
	JD McCabe	Harvard	JR	D	15	0.13	1- 1- 2
	Tyler Eaves	Rensselaer	JR	F	15	0.13	1- 1- 2
	Hunter Thunell	Brown	FR	D	15	0.13	0- 2- 2
	Nick Coskren	Harvard	SO	F	15	0.13	0- 2- 2
	Joe Gaudet	Dartmouth	FR	F	16	0.12	1- 1- 2
	Dan Glover	Cornell	SR	D	16	0.12	0- 2- 2
	Kevin Crane	Princeton	FR	D	16	0.12	0- 2- 2
	Jordan Pietrus	Brown	FR	F	17	0.12	0- 2- 2
	Zane Kalemba	Princeton	FR	G	21	0.10	0- 2- 2
	Erik Burgdoerfer	Rensselaer	FR	D	23	0.09	1- 1- 2
	Troy Davenport	Cornell	SO	G	24	0.08	0- 2- 2
	Sam Bowles	Union	JR	F	25	0.08	0- 2- 2
	Dave MacDonald	Harvard	JR	D	26	0.08	0- 2- 2
	Robert Burns	Yale	SR	F	27	0.07	0- 2- 2
	Matt Palmer	Brown	SO	D	29	0.07	0- 2- 2
	Mike Devine	Dartmouth	JR	G	32	0.06	0- 2- 2
	Alex Greig	Colgate	SR	D	35	0.06	0- 2- 2
237	Bill Keenan	Harvard	SO	F	5	0.20	1- 0- 1
	Jordan Zitoun	Quinnipiac	FR	D	5	0.20	1- 0- 1

Tyler Beachell	Princeton	FR	F	7	0.14	1- 0- 1
Mike Arciero	Clarkson	JR	F	7	0.14	0- 1- 1
Kevin McLeod	Cornell	SR	D	8	0.12	0- 1- 1
Brad Schroeder	Princeton	FR	D	11	0.09	1- 0- 1
Jordan Cyr	Rensselaer	FR	F	11	0.09	1- 0- 1
Scott Van der Linden	Brown	FR	D	11	0.09	0- 1- 1
Christian Read	Princeton	SR	F	12	0.08	1- 0- 1
Mike Willemsen	Clarkson	SO	F	13	0.08	1- 0- 1
David Inman	Yale	SO	D	13	0.08	0- 1- 1
B.J. Mackasey	Princeton	SR	D	14	0.07	0- 1- 1
Jonathan Lareau	Union	FR	D	15	0.07	0- 1- 1
David Germain	Yale	JR	F	17	0.06	0- 1- 1
Justin Tobe	Harvard	SR	G	18	0.06	0- 1- 1
Josh Duncan	Quinnipiac	FR	D	19	0.05	0- 1- 1
Jeremiah Crowe	Clarkson	FR	D	22	0.05	1- 0- 1
Alec Richards	Yale	SO	G	26	0.04	0- 1- 1
Dan Rosen	Brown	FR	G	27	0.04	0- 1- 1
Matthew Thomey	Yale	JR	F	27	0.04	0- 1- 1
Andrew Estey	Union	FR	F	28	0.04	0- 1- 1
Alex Petizian	St. Lawrence	FR	G	29	0.03	0- 1- 1
Ryan Swanson	Rensselaer	SR	D	33	0.03	0- 1- 1
Mark Dekanich	Colgate	JR	G	36	0.03	0- 1- 1
Bud Fisher	Quinnipiac	SO	G	39	0.03	0- 1- 1

GOALS AGAINST AVERAGE:

				MINUTES	GA	GAA
1	David Leggio	Clarkson	JR	2166:53:00	78	2.16
2	Justin Tobe	Harvard	SR	984:18:00	37	2.26
3	Alex Petizian	St. Lawrence	FR	1698:42:00	65	2.3
4	Mark Dekanich	Colgate	JR	2135:35:00	83	2.33
5	Troy Davenport	Cornell	SO	1293:44:00	52	2.41
6	Bud Fisher	Quinnipiac	SO	2307:38:00	97	2.52
7	B.J. Sklapsky	Princeton	SR	739:20:00	32	2.6
8	Mike Devine	Dartmouth	JR	1927:31:00	85	2.65
9	Dan Rosen	Brown	FR	1597:21:00	73	2.74
10	Kyle Richter	Harvard	FR	992:02:00	47	2.84
11	Zane Kalemba	Princeton	FR	1161:26:00	56	2.89
12	Justin Mrazek	Union	JR	1933:05:00	97	3.01
13	Alec Richards	Yale	SO	1518:02:00	79	3.12
14	Jordan Alford	Rensselaer	JR	880:47:00	46	3.13

Minimum 33% of Team Minutes Played

SAVE PERCENTAGE:

				SAVES	GA	PCT
1	David Leggio	Clarkson	JR	1037	78	0.93
2	Mark Dekanich	Colgate	JR	993	83	0.923
3	Dan Rosen	Brown	FR	839	73	0.92
4	Alex Petizian	St. Lawrence	FR	706	65	0.916
5	Mike Devine	Dartmouth	JR	911	85	0.915
6	B.J. Sklapsky	Princeton	SR	327	32	0.911
7	Justin Tobe	Harvard	SR	364	37	0.908
8	Justin Mrazek	Union	JR	916	97	0.904
9	Kyle Richter	Harvard	FR	437	47	0.903
10	Bud Fisher	Quinnipiac	SO	898	97	0.903
11	Troy Davenport	Cornell	SO	461	52	0.899
12	Jordan Alford	Rensselaer	JR	380	46	0.892
13	Zane Kalemba	Princeton	FR	459	56	0.891
14	Alec Richards	Yale	SO	646	79	0.891
15	Mathias Lange	Rensselaer	SO	543	77	0.876

Minimum 33% of Team Minutes Played

WINNING PERCENTAGE:

				W-L-T	PCT
1	David Leggio	Clarkson	JR	24- 7- 5	0.736
2	Alex Petizian	St. Lawrence	FR	19- 9- 1	0.672
3	B.J. Sklapsky	Princeton	SR	7- 4- 1	0.625
4	Troy Davenport	Cornell	SO	11- 7- 2	0.6
5	Mike Devine	Dartmouth	JR	17-12- 3	0.578
6	Bud Fisher	Quinnipiac	SO	20-14- 5	0.577
7	Mark Dekanich	Colgate	JR	15-17- 4	0.472
8	Kyle Richter	Harvard	FR	7- 8- 2	0.471
9	Dan Rosen	Brown	FR	9-12- 4	0.44
10	Justin Tobe	Harvard	SR	7- 9- 0	0.438
11	Jordan Alford	Rensselaer	JR	5- 7- 2	0.429
12	Justin Mrazek	Union	JR	13-18- 3	0.426
13	Zane Kalemba	Princeton	FR	8-11- 1	0.425
14	Alec Richards	Yale	SO	9-15- 2	0.385
15	Mathias Lange	Rensselaer	SO	5-11- 6	0.364

Minimum 33% of Team Minutes Played

	Eastern College
	Athletic Conference

EAST

Eastern College
Athletic Conference
1311 Craigville Beach Road
P.O. Box 3
Centerville, MA 02632
www.ecac.org

Commissioner
Rudy Keeling
Office: 508.771.5060
Fax: 508.771.9481
rkeeling@ecac.org

Senior Associate Commissioner
Steve Bamford
Office: 508.771.5060 x 215
Fax: 508.771.9481
sbamford@ecac.org

Coordinator Operations & Services
Michael Letzeisen
Office: 508.771.5060 x 236
Fax: 508.771.9481
mletzeisen@ecac.org

Administrative Assistant - Hockey
Anne Glover
Office: 508.771.5060 x 222
Fax: 508.771.9481
aglover@ecac.org

Babson College
Castleton State College
University of Massachusetts Boston
New England College
Norwich University
St. Anselm College
St. Michael's College
Salem State College
Skidmore College
University of Southern Maine

(St. Anselm & St. Michael's not eligible for league tournament)

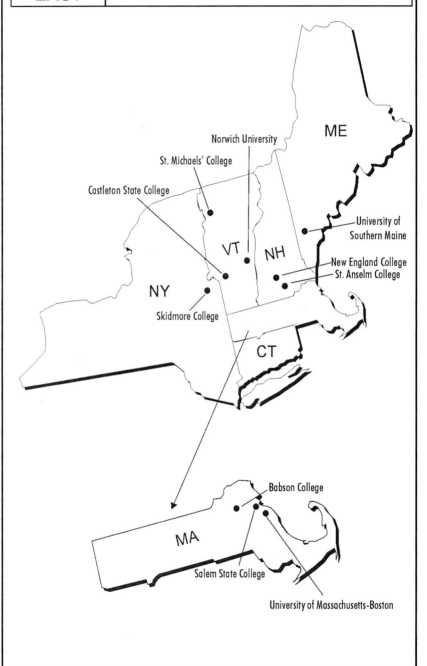

ECAC EAST

EASTERN COLLEGE ATHLETIC CONFERENCE - EAST

ME

Norwich University

St. Michaels' College

Castleton State College

VT

NH

NY

Skidmore College

University of Southern Maine

New England College
St. Anselm College

CT

MA

Babson College

Salem State College

University of Massachusetts-Boston

EASTERN COLLEGE ATHLETIC CONFERENCE EAST

FINAL 2006-07 CONFERENCE STANDINGS

		Pts	GP	Record	Win%	GF-GA	GP	Record	Win%	GF-GA
1	Norwich	28	19	14- 5- 0	0.737	75- 40	28	20- 8- 0	0.714	116- 62
2	New England	27	19	13- 5- 1	0.711	79- 48	28	17-10- 1	0.625	108- 82
3	Skidmore	26	19	12- 5- 2	0.684	56- 49	26	16- 8- 2	0.654	89- 72
	Southern Maine	26	19	12- 5- 2	0.684	72- 47	26	15- 9- 2	0.615	102- 69
	Castleton	26	19	11- 4- 4	0.684	68- 47	27	17- 6- 4	0.704	114- 67
6	Babson	23	19	11- 7- 1	0.605	71- 51	29	18-10- 1	0.638	112- 81
7	Saint Anselm	19	19	8- 8- 3	0.500	55- 55	28	13-12- 3	0.518	99- 81
8	Salem State	10	19	5-14- 0	0.263	41- 68	26	9-17- 0	0.346	67- 84
9	UMass Boston	6	19	3-16- 0	0.158	36- 92	26	5-20- 1	0.212	48-115
10	Saint Michael's	4	19	2-17- 0	0.105	39-100	26	6-20- 0	0.231	72-122

2007 EASTERN COLLEGE ATHLETIC CONFERENCE EAST PLAYOFFS

QUARTER FINALS (2.24.07)

Babson College	5	Skidmore College	4
Castleton State College	3	University of Southern Maine	2
Salem State College	3	New England College	4
University of Massachusetts Boston	2	Norwich University	8

SEMI FINALS (3.03.07)

Babson College	4	Norwich University	1
Castleton State College	2	New England College	3

CHAMPIONSHIP (3.04.07)

Babson College	5	New England College	3

EASTERN COLLEGE ATHLETIC CONFERENCE
EAST TOURNAMENT CHAMPIONS

1966	Colby College	1987	Merrimack College
1967	Merrimack College	1988	Merrimack College
1968	Merrimack College	1989	Merrimack College
1969	American International College	1990	American International College
1970	University of Vermont	1991	Middlebury College
1971	Bowdoin College	1992	Babson College
1972	University of Massachusetts-Boston	1993	Bowdoin College
1973	University of Vermont	1994	Salem State College
1974	University of Vermont	1995	Salem State College
1975	Bowdoin College	1996	Amherst College
1976	Bowdoin College	1997	Colby College
1977	Merrimack College	1998	Hamilton College
1978	Bowdon College	1999	Norwich University
1979	University of Massachusetts-Lowell	2000	Norwich University
1980	Merrimack College	2001	New England College
1981	University of Massachusetts-Lowell	2002	Norwich University
1982	University of Massachusetts-Lowell	2003	Norwich University
1983	University of Massachusetts-Lowell	2004	Norwich University
1984	Babson College	2005	New England College
1985	Salem State College	2006	Norwich University
1986	Bowdoin College	2007	Babson College

					GP	PPG	G - A - P
1	Mark Carragher	Southern Maine	SR	F	26	1.81	22-25-47
2	Rick Cleaver	Norwich	JR	F	28	1.57	24-20-44
3	Chris Sparkes	Southern Maine	SR	F	26	1.50	18-21-39
4	Eric Lauriault	Norwich	JR	F	28	1.36	11-27-38
5	Brad Baldelli	Babson	SO	F	29	1.24	16-20-36
6	Brandon Heck	Castleton	SO	F	27	1.22	14-19-33
7	Rob Hutchison	Skidmore	SR	F	26	1.15	11-19-30
	Steve Culbertson	Castleton	FR	F	27	1.11	17-13-30
	Mark Ehl	New England	FR	F	28	1.07	13-17-30
10	Jared Silver	Saint Michael's	SR	F	22	1.27	15-13-28
	Matt Czerkowicz	Skidmore	FR	F	26	1.08	11-17-28
12	Joe Huchko	Castleton	SR	D	27	1.00	11-16-27
	Travis Martell	Castleton	JR	D	27	1.00	7-20-27
	Mike Mullen	New England	JR	F	28	0.96	11-16-27
15	Raphael Robitaille	Norwich	JR	F	24	1.08	11-15-26
	Mike Foley	Saint Anselm	JR	F	26	1.00	13-13-26
	Mike Stevens	Southern Maine	JR	F	26	1.00	4-22-26
	Nikita Kashirsky	Norwich	SO	F	28	0.93	17- 9-26
	Jason Schneider	Babson	FR	F	29	0.90	14-12-26
20	Ryan Mero	Saint Michael's	SO	F	19	1.32	10-15-25
	Shane Farrell	Babson	FR	F	24	1.04	10-15-25
	Pat Forshner	Saint Anselm	JR	F	27	0.93	11-14-25
23	Colin Fitzpatrick	Saint Anselm	JR	F	28	0.86	9-15-24
	John Geverd	Babson	JR	F	29	0.83	16- 8-24
25	David Pazzaglia	Salem State	SO	F	26	0.88	5-18-23
	Paul Ruta	New England	SR	F	28	0.82	10-13-23
27	JT Balben	Babson	SO	F	24	0.92	7-15-22
	Ryan Bartlett	Castleton	SO	F	27	0.81	6-16-22
	Casey Fazekas	Babson	FR	D	29	0.76	3-19-22
30	Brian Pouliot	New England	JR	F	17	1.24	8-13-21
	John Burns	Saint Michael's	SO	D	24	0.88	1-20-21
	Sean Ferguson	Salem State	SR	F	26	0.81	9-12-21
33	Mike Carmody	New England	JR	F	22	0.91	10-10-20
	Kirk Bolduc	Castleton	FR	F	26	0.77	5-15-20
	Mickey Serra	New England	JR	F	28	0.71	13- 7-20
	Eric Ouellette	Norwich	JR	F	28	0.71	7-13-20
	Pat McLaughlin	Babson	SO	F	28	0.71	6-14-20
	Trevor Turner	New England	FR	D	28	0.71	4-16-20
39	Alex DiPietro	Babson	SO	D	24	0.79	6-13-19
	Teddy Gowan	Skidmore	SO	F	26	0.73	9-10-19
	Brett Smith	Saint Anselm	SR	D	28	0.68	6-13-19
42	Bobby Siers	Southern Maine	SR	F	25	0.72	3-15-18
	Anthony Ferri	Skidmore	FR	F	26	0.69	10- 8-18
	Chris McInnis	Salem State	FR	F	26	0.69	6-12-18
	Dane Marshall	Southern Maine	JR	D	26	0.69	3-15-18
46	Pat Noonan	Southern Maine	FR	F	15	1.13	10- 7-17
	Ross Carmichael	Castleton	SO	F	27	0.63	6-11-17
	Evan Romeo	Castleton	FR	F/D	27	0.63	4-13-17
	Anders Lusth	New England	JR	F	28	0.61	7-10-17
	Brian Hartigan	Saint Anselm	SO	D	28	0.61	2-15-17
51	Rocco Dabecco	UMass Boston	SO	F	17	0.94	2-14-16
	Matt Johnson	Norwich	FR	F	22	0.73	6-10-16
	Jon Bellonio	New England	SR	F	25	0.64	4-12-16
	Matt Hall	Saint Michael's	JR	D/F	26	0.62	8- 8-16
	Nick Sacca	Saint Anselm	SR	F	28	0.57	7- 9-16
56	Adam Larrabee	UMass Boston	FR	F	18	0.83	7- 8-15
	Alex Muse	New England	FR	F	20	0.75	3-12-15
	Eric Curtis	Castleton	FR	F	21	0.71	8- 7-15

	James Duhamel	Norwich	JR	F	21	0.71	7- 8-15
	Chris Travis	Southern Maine	FR	F	23	0.65	4-11-15
	Jeff Armando	New England	FR	F	24	0.62	10- 5-15
	Derek Evjenth	Saint Anselm	SR	F	24	0.62	8- 7-15
	Mike Gibbons	Skidmore	SO	F	25	0.60	10- 5-15
	Steve Smiddy	Castleton	FR	F	25	0.60	9- 6-15
	Zach Doyen	Salem State	SO	F	26	0.58	10- 5-15
	Jeff Chillson	Salem State	SO	F	26	0.58	7- 8-15
	Chris Helms	Southern Maine	SR	D	26	0.58	6- 9-15
	Danny Ohlson	Saint Anselm	SR	F	27	0.56	5-10-15
69	Jim Koehler	Norwich	SO	F	23	0.61	7- 7-14
	Kyle Smith	Southern Maine	SO	F	24	0.58	7- 7-14
	Mike Venit	Babson	JR	F	25	0.56	8- 6-14
	Derek Girouard	Saint Michael's	SR	F	25	0.56	8- 6-14
73	Kris Kranzky	UMass Boston	FR	F	17	0.76	6- 7-13
	Ryan Daust	UMass Boston	FR	F	21	0.62	7- 6-13
	Shane Masotta	Saint Anselm	JR	D	22	0.59	2-11-13
	Phil Sbrocchi	Norwich	JR	D	25	0.52	2-11-13
	Pat Tyman	Skidmore	SO	F	26	0.50	6- 7-13
	Steve Keady	Skidmore	SO	D	26	0.50	5- 8-13
	Aaron Blades	Salem State	FR	F	26	0.50	4- 9-13
	Phil McDavitt	Skidmore	SO	D	26	0.50	3-10-13
	Quinn MacNulty	Skidmore	SR	D	26	0.50	1-12-13
	Jon Globke	New England	FR	F/D	28	0.46	3-10-13
	Gabriel Chenard-Poirier	Babson	FR	D	29	0.45	4- 9-13
84	Tom Galiani	Southern Maine	FR	F	25	0.48	6- 6-12
	Cody Austin	UMass Boston	FR	F	26	0.46	5- 7-12
	Andrew O'Neill	Salem State	SR	F	26	0.46	3- 9-12
	Rico Piatelli	Norwich	SO	F	27	0.44	5- 7-12
88	DJ Fimiani	Norwich	FR	F	18	0.61	4- 7-11
	Erik Caron	Saint Michael's	JR	F	19	0.58	4- 7-11
	Jeff Tellier	Salem State	FR	F	21	0.52	2- 9-11
	Jared Lavender	Castleton	SO	D	27	0.41	5- 6-11
	Mike Curtis	Saint Anselm	SR	F	27	0.41	5- 6-11
	Joe Garofalo	New England	JR	D	28	0.39	1-10-11
94	Tim Daley	Skidmore	FR	F	19	0.53	2- 8-10
	Jeff Alexander	Castleton	FR	F/D	21	0.48	5- 5-10
	Jonathan Fecteau	Salem State	SO	D	22	0.45	3- 7-10
	CJ Viso	Norwich	SO	F	23	0.43	2- 8-10
	Andrew Gartman	Saint Anselm	SR	F	25	0.40	6- 4-10
	Bill Glynn	Salem State	SO	D	25	0.40	5- 5-10
	Scott Schaub	Skidmore	SR	F	26	0.38	6- 4-10
	Tyler Stitt	Norwich	FR	D	26	0.38	0-10-10
	Matt Harrington	Babson	SO	F	27	0.37	5- 5-10
	Seth Goodrich	Saint Anselm	FR	D	27	0.37	2- 8-10
	Ryan Farrell	Babson	SR	F	28	0.36	5- 5-10
105	Russ Peterson	UMass Boston	FR	D/F	17	0.53	4- 5- 9
	Tom Kerwin	Saint Anselm	SO	F	20	0.45	5- 4- 9
	Mike Nunziato	Saint Anselm	SO	D	25	0.36	4- 5- 9
	Chris Healey	Saint Michael's	SO	F	26	0.35	4- 5- 9
	Ben Loss	Southern Maine	SO	D/F	26	0.35	4- 5- 9
	Brett Yancey	Southern Maine	SR	D	26	0.35	2- 7- 9
111	Brian Shea	New England	SO	F	16	0.50	4- 4- 8
	Drew LaCombe	UMass Boston	FR	F	17	0.47	4- 4- 8
	Craig Serino	Norwich	FR	D	20	0.40	5- 3- 8
	Joe Loiselle	New England	JR	F/D	21	0.38	2- 6- 8
	Eric Tallent	Norwich	FR	F	22	0.36	2- 6- 8
	Nick Quagliani	Norwich	FR	F	25	0.32	4- 4- 8
	Joe Fernald	Saint Anselm	SO	F	25	0.32	3- 5- 8
	Matthew Link	Castleton	SR	D	25	0.32	2- 6- 8

	Nick Petrangelo	Skidmore	FR	D	25	0.32	2- 6- 8
	Marc Santuccio	Southern Maine	SR	F	26	0.31	2- 6- 8
	Jonathan Silver	Saint Michael's	FR	F	26	0.31	1- 7- 8
122	Matt Grazioso	Saint Anselm	JR	F	15	0.47	3- 4- 7
	Tim Welsh	Skidmore	SO	D	18	0.39	1- 6- 7
	Jeff Lazeren	Castleton	SO	F	22	0.32	6- 1- 7
	Jean-Maxime Legare	Saint Michael's	FR	F	22	0.32	4- 3- 7
	Tom Maregni	Babson	JR	F	22	0.32	3- 4- 7
	Michael Muolo	UMass Boston	SO	F	24	0.29	4- 3- 7
	Steve Ebbole	UMass Boston	FR	D	24	0.29	1- 6- 7
	Jordan Skinner	Southern Maine	FR	D	25	0.28	3- 4- 7
	Chris Sabo	Babson	FR	F	25	0.28	2- 5- 7
	Chris Webb	Skidmore	FR	F	26	0.27	2- 5- 7
	David Vorozilchak	Saint Michael's	FR	D	26	0.27	0- 7- 7
	Brian Dobler	Saint Anselm	SR	D	27	0.26	3- 4- 7
	Justin Wissman	Norwich	SO	D	27	0.26	0- 7- 7
135	Tim Dancey	Saint Michael's	JR	F	12	0.50	5- 1- 6
	Billy Kasper	Norwich	FR	D	20	0.30	0- 6- 6
	Jeff Beecher	Castleton	JR	F	21	0.29	3- 3- 6
	Josh Giordani	Southern Maine	SO	F	25	0.24	3- 3- 6
	Ryan Hayes	Salem State	JR	F	25	0.24	2- 4- 6
	Andrew Ward	UMass Boston	JR	D	25	0.24	1- 5- 6
	Billy Langmaid	UMass Boston	SO	D	25	0.24	0- 6- 6
	Mike Ciardullo	Saint Michael's	SR	F	26	0.23	4- 2- 6
	Andrick Deppmeyer	Saint Michael's	JR	D	26	0.23	1- 5- 6
	Brett Noll	Salem State	FR	D	26	0.23	1- 5- 6
	Chris Wood	Babson	FR	F	27	0.22	3- 3- 6
146	Nate Smith	Babson	JR	F	9	0.56	1- 4- 5
	Pat Melillo	New England	JR	F	18	0.28	4- 1- 5
	Andrew Riddell	New England	FR	D	20	0.25	1- 4- 5
	Dan Anctil	Saint Michael's	JR	F	20	0.25	1- 4- 5
	Mike Anderson	Castleton	SO	D	22	0.23	1- 4- 5
	Matt Davis	Salem State	FR	D	23	0.22	2- 3- 5
152	Chris O'Brien	Saint Anselm	JR	F	4	1.00	1- 3- 4
	Chris MacPhee	Saint Anselm	FR	F	10	0.40	2- 2- 4
	Brent Swanson	Castleton	FR	F	11	0.36	2- 2- 4
	Igor Karlov	Southern Maine	FR	F	15	0.27	2- 2- 4
	Alex Higgins	Saint Michael's	FR	F	19	0.21	3- 1- 4
	Patrick McGuirk	Saint Michael's	FR	F	20	0.20	1- 3- 4
	Eric Lampman	Skidmore	SR	F	23	0.17	3- 1- 4
	Damen Nisula	Salem State	FR	F	24	0.17	2- 2- 4
	Taylor McKenna	Skidmore	SR	F	24	0.17	2- 2- 4
	Kyle Simpson	UMass Boston	JR	F	26	0.15	3- 1- 4
	Nick Westcott	Castleton	FR	D	26	0.15	0- 4- 4
	Andy DiMasi	Saint Michael's	SR	D	26	0.15	0- 4- 4
164	Ernie Economides	Skidmore	FR	F	5	0.60	1- 2- 3
	Craig Richardson	Castleton	SO	D	8	0.38	2- 1- 3
	Ryan Ferguson	Babson	JR	F	8	0.38	1- 2- 3
	Matt Baron	Babson	JR	D	15	0.20	1- 2- 3
	Jeff Harris	Saint Michael's	SR	F	23	0.13	2- 1- 3
	Nick Jones	Babson	SO	D	25	0.12	0- 3- 3
	Luke Williams	Salem State	SR	F	26	0.12	3- 0- 3
	Eric Morgani	Southern Maine	SO	F/D	26	0.12	3- 0- 3
	Kevin Hughes	Salem State	FR	D	26	0.12	1- 2- 3
	Bryan Dodge	Saint Michael's	SO	D	26	0.12	0- 3- 3
	Tim Ivers	Saint Anselm	FR	D	27	0.11	1- 2- 3
	Evan Erdmann	New England	JR	D/F	28	0.11	0- 3- 3
176	David Allen	UMass Boston	FR	F/D	3	0.67	0- 2- 2
	Chris Manemeit	Castleton	JR	F	5	0.40	0- 2- 2
	Matt Vredenburgh	Skidmore	SO	F/D	6	0.33	1- 1- 2

Liam Chatterton	Babson	FR	D	7	0.29	1- 1- 2
Joey Peller	Skidmore	SO	D	8	0.25	1- 1- 2
Marcus Fajardo	UMass Boston	SO	F	8	0.25	0- 2- 2
Dallas Hand	New England	FR	F/D	8	0.25	0- 2- 2
James Hall	UMass Boston	SO	F/D	10	0.20	0- 2- 2
Brad Flynn	Southern Maine	FR	F	10	0.20	0- 2- 2
Viktor Berfelt	New England	FR	D	11	0.18	0- 2- 2
Pat McCarthy	Babson	SO	D	15	0.13	0- 2- 2
Dana Thibault	Norwich	JR	D	15	0.13	0- 2- 2
Mike McMahon	Babson	FR	D	17	0.12	0- 2- 2
Jeff Swanson	Castleton	SO	G	20	0.10	0- 2- 2
Matt Gosselin	New England	JR	D	22	0.09	0- 2- 2
Charlie Moroni	Skidmore	FR	D	24	0.08	0- 2- 2
David Thompson	Norwich	FR	G	25	0.08	0- 2- 2
193 Steve Martorana	Skidmore	SR	D	4	0.25	1- 0- 1
Peter Langella	Norwich	SR	D	5	0.20	1- 0- 1
Brady Greco	Skidmore	SR	D	5	0.20	0- 1- 1
Joe Doherty	Salem State	SO	D	6	0.17	1- 0- 1
Andrew Woodford	Saint Anselm	SO	D	6	0.17	0- 1- 1
Jimmy Santacroce	Skidmore	FR	G	6	0.17	0- 1- 1
Robert Carbone	UMass Boston	SO	F	7	0.14	1- 0- 1
Sean Gray	New England	SO	D	7	0.14	0- 1- 1
Adam Gaudreau	Norwich	FR	D	8	0.12	1- 0- 1
Kevin Ciborowski	Salem State	FR	F	9	0.11	1- 0- 1
Ben Gunn	Saint Anselm	SO	F	9	0.11	0- 1- 1
Brian Hopper	Saint Michael's	SO	D	9	0.11	0- 1- 1
Alex Prough	Salem State	FR	F	9	0.11	0- 1- 1
Cam Clark	Skidmore	JR	F	10	0.10	1- 0- 1
Dustin Hayes	Salem State	FR	F	10	0.10	0- 1- 1
Derek Jackson	Saint Michael's	SR	G	11	0.09	0- 1- 1
Bryan McGrath	Salem State	JR	F	11	0.09	0- 1- 1
Taylor Bergeron	Babson	FR	F	12	0.08	0- 1- 1
Jake Carlson	UMass Boston	FR	F	13	0.08	1- 0- 1
Tyler White	Castleton	JR	F	15	0.07	1- 0- 1
Michael Jordan	UMass Boston	FR	F	15	0.07	0- 1- 1
Jake Berube	Southern Maine	FR	F	15	0.07	0- 1- 1
Kevin Corley	Saint Anselm	SR	D	16	0.06	1- 0- 1
Filip Bjork	New England	FR	D	16	0.06	0- 1- 1
Hunter Dowd	UMass Boston	JR	D	18	0.06	1- 0- 1
Chris Flaherty	UMass Boston	SO	F	18	0.06	0- 1- 1
Jonathan Lechance	Norwich	SR	D	18	0.06	0- 1- 1
Noah Lucia	Norwich	JR	D	19	0.05	0- 1- 1
Jeff Diehl	UMass Boston	FR	F	21	0.05	1- 0- 1
Aaron Burke	UMass Boston	SO	F	22	0.05	0- 1- 1
Skylar Nipps	Babson	SO	G	23	0.04	0- 1- 1
David Beckles	Southern Maine	SR	G	23	0.04	0- 1- 1
Wade Collins	UMass Boston	SO	D	26	0.04	0- 1- 1

GOALS AGAINST AVERAGE:

				MINUTES	GA	GAA
1	David Thompson	Norwich	FR	1381:48:00	45	1.95
2	Jason Zuck	Saint Anselm	FR	1055:33:00	40	2.27
3	D.J. Delbuono	Skidmore	FR	1252:10:00	53	2.54
4	Jeff Swanson	Castleton	SO	1172:34:00	52	2.66
5	Skylar Nipps	Babson	SO	1346:27:00	60	2.67
6	David Beckles	Southern Maine	SR	1365:40:00	61	2.68
7	Ron Baia	New England	FR	1140:51:00	52	2.73
8	Ryan Hatch	Salem State	SO	1416:01:00	71	3.01
9	Jason Rafuse	Saint Anselm	SR	573:13:00	32	3.35
10	Ryan Donovan	UMass Boston	FR	1404:33:00	93	3.97
11	Derek Jackson	Saint Michael's	SR	590:42:00	40	4.06
12	Erik Smith	Saint Michael's	SR	797:44:00	64	4.81

Minimum 33% of Team Minutes Played

SAVE PERCENTAGE:

				SAVES	GA	PCT
1	D.J. Delbuono	Skidmore	FR	629	53	0.922
2	Jason Zuck	Saint Anselm	FR	427	40	0.914
3	Jeff Swanson	Castleton	SO	509	52	0.907
4	David Thompson	Norwich	FR	436	45	0.906
5	Ryan Donovan	UMass Boston	FR	898	93	0.906
6	David Beckles	Southern Maine	SR	587	61	0.906
7	Ron Baia	New England	FR	500	52	0.906
8	Ryan Hatch	Salem State	SO	672	71	0.904
9	Skylar Nipps	Babson	SO	556	60	0.903
10	Jason Rafuse	Saint Anselm	SR	247	32	0.885
11	Derek Jackson	Saint Michael's	SR	304	40	0.884
12	Erik Smith	Saint Michael's	SR	428	64	0.87

Minimum 33% of Team Minutes Played

WINNING PERCENTAGE:

				W- L- T	PCT
1	David Thompson	Norwich	FR	17- 6- 0	0.739
2	Ron Baia	New England	FR	13- 5- 1	0.711
3	Jeff Swanson	Castleton	SO	11- 5- 3	0.658
4	Jason Zuck	Saint Anselm	FR	10- 5- 2	0.647
5	D.J. Delbuono	Skidmore	FR	13- 7- 2	0.636
6	Skylar Nipps	Babson	SO	14- 8- 1	0.63
7	David Beckles	Southern Maine	SR	13- 8- 2	0.609
8	Ryan Hatch	Salem State	SO	9-15- 0	0.375
9	Derek Jackson	Saint Michael's	SR	4- 7- 0	0.364
10	Jason Rafuse	Saint Anselm	SR	3- 7- 1	0.318
11	Ryan Donovan	UMass Boston	FR	5-19- 1	0.22
12	Erik Smith	Saint Michael's	SR	2-11- 0	0.154

Minimum 33% of Team Minutes Played

HOCKEY
NORTHEAST

Eastern College
Athletic Conference Northeast
1311 Craigville Beach Road
P.O. Box 3
Centerville, MA 02632
www.ecac.org

Commissioner
Rudy Keeling
Office: 508.771.5060
Fax: 508.771.9481
rkeeling@ecac.org

Senior Associate Commissioner
Steve Bamford
Office: 508.771.5060 x 215
Fax: 508.771.9481
sbamford@ecac.org

Coordinator Ops & Services
Michael Letzeisen
Office: 508.771.5060 x 236
Fax: 508.771.9481
mletzeisen@ecac.org

Administrative Assistant
Anne Glover
Office: 508.771.5060 x 222
Fax: 508.771.9481
aglover@ecac.org

Assumption College
Curry College
Fitchburg State College
Framingham State College
Franklin Pierce College
Johnson & Wales University
University of Massachusetts - Dartmouth
Nichols College
Plymouth State College
Salve Regina University
Southern New Hampshire University
Stonehill College
Suffolk University
Wentworth Institute of Technology
Western New England College
Worcester State College

(Assumption, Franklin Pierce, So.New Hampshire & Stonehill not tournament eligible)

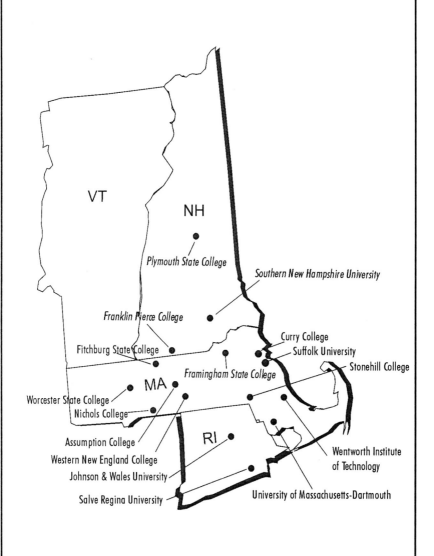

VT

NH

Plymouth State College

Southern New Hampshire University

Franklin Pierce College

Curry College

Fitchburg State College

Suffolk University

Stonehill College

Framingham State College

Worcester State College

MA

Nichols College

Assumption College

RI

Western New England College

Wentworth Institute of Technology

Johnson & Wales University

Salve Regina University

University of Massachusetts-Dartmouth

EASTERN COLLEGE ATHLETIC CONFERENCE NORTHEAST

FINAL 2006-07 CONFERENCE STANDINGS

		Pts	GP	Record	Win%	GF-GA	GP	Record	Win%	GF-GA
1	UMass Dartmouth	28	15	14- 1- 0	0.933	73- 29	29	25- 3- 1	0.879	148- 58
2	Curry	27	15	13- 1- 1	0.9	102- 29	27	16- 9- 2	0.630	141- 83
3	Wentworth	24	15	11- 2- 2	0.8	71- 35	28	16- 9- 3	0.625	116- 94
4	Plymouth State	21	15	10- 4- 1	0.7	62- 44	26	11-13- 2	0.462	86-100
5	Fitchburg State	20	15	9- 4- 2	0.667	62- 48	27	14-10- 3	0.574	99- 93
6	Johnson & Wales	18	15	9- 6- 0	0.6	56- 57	25	12-12- 1	0.500	86-117
7	Nichols	17	15	8- 6- 1	0.567	69- 54	26	13-11- 2	0.538	104-103
8	Salve Regina	16	15	8- 7- 0	0.533	44- 46	25	10-14- 1	0.420	68- 94
9	Suffolk	13	15	6- 8- 1	0.433	62- 66	24	7-15- 2	0.333	88-104
10	Worcester State	8	15	4-11- 0	0.267	44- 76	23	6-16- 1	0.283	69-110
11	Western N.E.	4	15	2-13- 0	0.133	36- 78	23	8-15- 0	0.348	64- 98
12	Framingham State	1	15	0-14- 1	0.033	46- 83	23	2-20- 1	0.109	68-122
	Division II									
1	Southern N.H.	18	15	9- 6- 0	0.6	59- 59	27	12-14- 1	0.463	99-121
2	Stonehill	13	15	6- 8- 1	0.433	57- 64	27	14-12- 1	0.537	114-104
3	Assumption	8	15	3-10- 2	0.267	42- 67	27	7-18- 2	0.296	77-134
4	Franklin Pierce	4	15	1-12- 2	0.133	31- 81	24	5-17- 2	0.250	66-130

2007 EASTERN COLLEGE ATHLETIC CONFERENCE NORTHEAST PLAYOFFS

QUARTER FINALS (2.24-25.07)

Salve Regina University	2	University of Mass. Dartmouth	9
Nichols College	2	Curry College	7
Fitchburg State College	3	Plymouth State College	2
Johnson & Wales University	1	Wentworth College	5

SEMI FINALS (2.28.07)

Fitchburg State College	3	University of Mass. Dartmouth	7
Wentworth College	4	Curry College	3

CHAMPIONSHIP (3.03.07)

Wentworth College	3	University of Mass. Dartmouth	4

EASTERN COLLEGE ATHLETIC CONFERENCE
NORTHEAST TOURNAMENT CHAMPIONS

	DIVISION II	**DIVISION III**
2004	Stonehill College	Curry College
2005	Southern New Hampshire University	Curry College
2006	Southern New Hampshire University	University of Massachusetts Dartmouth
2007	University of Massachusetts Dartmouth	University of Massachusetts Dartmouth

ECAC NORTHEAST LEAGUE SCORING (OVERALL):

					GP	PPG	G - A - P
1	Jeff Grant	UMass Dartmouth	JR	F	29	1.86	25-29-54
2	Kyle McCullough	UMass Dartmouth	SR	F	28	1.71	17-31-48
3	Brandon Hammermeister	Southern N.H.	JR	F	27	1.74	21-26-47
4	Brendan O'Brien	Stonehill	SO	F	23	1.96	12-33-45
5	Matt Curran	Stonehill	JR	F	26	1.69	30-14-44
	Dominic DiMarzo	Southern N.H.	JR	F	27	1.63	23-21-44
7	John Rocchio	Suffolk	SO	F	23	1.87	13-30-43
8	Ryan Moore	Fitchburg State	SR	F	27	1.56	23-19-42
9	Bill McCreary	Curry	SR	F	26	1.58	12-29-41
10	Dan Pencinger	Suffolk	JR	F	24	1.67	21-19-40
11	Mike Dryer	Fitchburg State	SR	F	27	1.44	13-26-39
12	Eddie Chlanda	Curry	JR	F	26	1.46	15-23-38
13	Anthony Monte	Nichols	SO	F	26	1.42	26-11-37
14	Ross Enmark	Curry	FR	F	26	1.31	23-11-34
	Chris Chambers	Plymouth State	FR	F	26	1.31	17-17-34
16	Kyle Cook	Nichols	SO	F	26	1.27	18-15-33
	Ryan Singer	Wentworth	SR	F	28	1.18	12-21-33
	Dave Lewandowski	Wentworth	SO	F	28	1.18	10-23-33
19	Zeke Costello	Nichols	FR	F	26	1.23	3-29-32
	Jeff Olitch	Wentworth	FR	F	28	1.14	18-14-32
	Jim Foley	UMass Dartmouth	SR	F	29	1.10	18-14-32
22	Matt McGilvary	Johnson & Wales	JR	F	25	1.20	17-13-30
23	Philip Lamy	Western N.E.	SO	F	23	1.22	12-16-28
	Zach Cobb	Johnson & Wales	SR	F	25	1.12	11-17-28
	Deni Bojadzic	Plymouth State	JR	F	26	1.08	13-15-28
	Peter Lindner	UMass Dartmouth	SR	F	29	0.97	12-16-28
27	Jason Ledo	Fitchburg State	SR	F	26	1.04	10-17-27
	Jeff Bieber	Nichols	SO	D	26	1.04	10-17-27
29	Tom Ford	Worcester State	SO	F	23	1.13	13-13-26
30	Joseph Fields	Franklin Pierce	JR	F	22	1.14	6-19-25
	Chris Krawczyk	Worcester State	SR	F	23	1.09	8-17-25
	James Florentino	Stonehill	SO	D	27	0.93	7-18-25
33	Atte Uola	Assumption	FR	F	25	0.96	13-11-24
	Jim Trahon	Assumption	JR	F	27	0.89	5-19-24
	Paul Carr	UMass Dartmouth	SR	D	28	0.86	6-18-24
36	Nicholas Glum	Framingham State	JR	F	23	1.00	14- 9-23
	Brian DelSavio	Franklin Pierce	SR	F	23	1.00	14- 9-23
	Ryan Jacobs	Johnson & Wales	JR	F	25	0.92	14- 9-23
	George Cademartori	Curry	SR	F	26	0.88	11-12-23
	Pete Roundy	Stonehill	FR	F	27	0.85	6-17-23
41	Mark Rintel	Worcester State	FR	F	21	1.05	9-13-22
	Ethan Porter	Southern N.H.	SR	F	24	0.92	4-18-22
	Adam Frew	Johnson & Wales	JR	F	25	0.88	6-16-22
	Jeremy Hmura	Curry	SO	F	26	0.85	7-15-22
	Joey Sides	Wentworth	SO	F	28	0.79	8-14-22
	Tyler Vrolyk	UMass Dartmouth	JR	F	29	0.76	13- 9-22
47	Jay Londer	Plymouth State	SR	F	26	0.81	10-11-21
	Ryan Gervais	Nichols	SO	F	26	0.81	9-12-21
	Goose LaCroix	Plymouth State	SR	F	26	0.81	9-12-21
	Paul Garabedian	UMass Dartmouth	JR	F	27	0.78	10-11-21
	Stephen Owens	Wentworth	SO	F	28	0.75	10-11-21
	Nick Paquin	UMass Dartmouth	SO	F	29	0.72	9-12-21
53	James Pentecost	Curry	SO	F	24	0.83	9-11-20
	Robert Sequeira	Curry	SR	D	25	0.80	7-13-20
	Martin Winzer	Wentworth	FR	D	28	0.71	7-13-20
56	Chuck Matthews	Franklin Pierce	SR	F	23	0.83	5-14-19
	Mike Mallette	Salve Regina	JR	F	24	0.79	11- 8-19
	Nick Davis	Suffolk	FR	D	24	0.79	4-15-19

	Cole Ruwe	Nichols	SO	D	26	0.73	5-14-19
	Eric Cremer	Nichols	FR	F	26	0.73	3-16-19
61	Dan Surette	Assumption	SR	D	24	0.75	5-13-18
	Travis Hampton	Salve Regina	SR	F	25	0.72	9- 9-18
	Matt Arsenault	Fitchburg State	SO	F	27	0.67	9- 9-18
	Paul Reissfelder	Stonehill	SO	F	27	0.67	7-11-18
	Chris Shore	UMass Dartmouth	SO	F	29	0.62	11- 7-18
66	Alex Olson	Suffolk	SO	F	13	1.31	9- 8-17
	Ray Kirby	UMass Dartmouth	SR	F	18	0.94	6-11-17
	Craig Houle	Johnson & Wales	FR	F	19	0.89	9- 8-17
	Matt Haddock	Western N.E.	FR	F	22	0.77	8- 9-17
	Hank Levin	Western N.E.	SO	F	23	0.74	7-10-17
	Tim Richard	Framingham State	JR	F	23	0.74	6-11-17
	Josh McClellan	Worcester State	SR	D	23	0.74	5-12-17
	Anthony Zanetti	Stonehill	JR	F	26	0.65	5-12-17
74	John Durkin	Stonehill	JR	F	19	0.84	7- 9-16
	Ryan Doyle	Salve Regina	SR	F	22	0.73	6-10-16
	Jonathan Lamken	Framingham State	JR	F	23	0.70	10- 6-16
	Pat Turcotte	Plymouth State	SO	D	26	0.62	3-13-16
	Trevor Spiridi	Curry	JR	F	27	0.59	5-11-16
	Tyler Crocker	UMass Dartmouth	JR	D	29	0.55	3-13-16
80	Ben Colby	Framingham State	SR	D	21	0.71	6- 9-15
	Donald Rankin	Curry	FR	D	22	0.68	8- 7-15
	Nathan Perreault	Worcester State	JR	F	22	0.68	5-10-15
	Mitch Sabo	Suffolk	SO	D	24	0.62	6- 9-15
	Mike O'Malley	Johnson & Wales	SO	D	25	0.60	3-12-15
	Greg Mailloux	Fitchburg State	SR	F	26	0.58	6- 9-15
	Billy Ninteau	Stonehill	SO	D	26	0.58	5-10-15
	Jason Arrighie	Nichols	SR	F	26	0.58	2-13-15
	Matt Paget	Assumption	JR	F	27	0.56	6- 9-15
	Derek Rupert	Wentworth	SO	F	28	0.54	7- 8-15
	Matt Gilman	Wentworth	SO	F	28	0.54	5-10-15
91	Brian Davis	Stonehill	JR	F	19	0.74	6- 8-14
	Jason Akstin	Framingham State	JR	F	21	0.67	5- 9-14
	Dave Carroll	Southern N.H.	SO	D	21	0.67	3-11-14
	Josh Morgan	Worcester State	JR	F	22	0.64	6- 8-14
	Mike Majesty	Western N.E.	SO	F	23	0.61	7- 7-14
	Jake Pickard	Salve Regina	SO	F	23	0.61	6- 8-14
	Jason Tarbell	Curry	SO	D	23	0.61	5- 9-14
	Shawn Longley	Western N.E.	JR	F	23	0.61	4-10-14
	Chris Cadieux	Plymouth State	JR	F	26	0.54	8- 6-14
	Frank Amato	Stonehill	SO	F	26	0.54	7- 7-14
	Andrew Hutton	Fitchburg State	FR	F	27	0.52	6- 8-14
102	Dave Gault	Curry	FR	F	16	0.81	4- 9-13
	Luke McDonough	Assumption	JR	F	20	0.65	6- 7-13
	Chris Hanson	Worcester State	FR	F	21	0.62	4- 9-13
	Joe Balog	Western N.E.	SO	D	22	0.59	8- 5-13
	Shawn Roach	Johnson & Wales	JR	F	23	0.57	7- 6-13
	DJ McNaughton	Johnson & Wales	FR	F	23	0.57	7- 6-13
	Tyler Trott	Salve Regina	FR	F	23	0.57	6- 7-13
	John Routhier	Assumption	JR	F	24	0.54	6- 7-13
	Sean Staid	Assumption	SO	F	25	0.52	6- 7-13
	Frank Bova	Assumption	SO	F	26	0.50	6- 7-13
	Michael O'Brien	Wentworth	FR	F	28	0.46	5- 8-13
	Francis Gunn	UMass Dartmouth	SO	D	28	0.46	1-12-13
114	Ricky Helmbrecht	Curry	FR	D	9	1.33	5- 7-12
	Rocco Dabecco	Nichols	SO	F	11	1.09	3- 9-12
	Andrew Redvanly	Suffolk	JR	F	16	0.75	6- 6-12
	Jonathan Whitham	Curry	JR	D	18	0.67	2-10-12
	Chris Rogers	Stonehill	FR	F	20	0.60	5- 7-12

	Ryan DiBartolomeo	Southern N.H.	FR	F	21	0.57	5- 7-12
	Greg Demerjian	Wentworth	SO	D	23	0.52	6- 6-12
	Jeremy Schmidt	Framingham State	FR	F	23	0.52	5- 7-12
	Jeff Kasper	Franklin Pierce	SO	F	24	0.50	6- 6-12
	Kent Honeyman	Southern N.H.	FR	D	24	0.50	4- 8-12
	Derek Avakian	Plymouth State	SR	F	24	0.50	2-10-12
	Kevin Marchesi	Johnson & Wales	FR	F	25	0.48	4- 8-12
	Topo LaCroix	Plymouth State	JR	F	26	0.46	4- 8-12
	Nate Gardner	Plymouth State	SR	F	26	0.46	2-10-12
	Chris Gunn	Southern N.H.	JR	F	27	0.44	8- 4-12
	Chase Feole	Stonehill	JR	F	27	0.44	7- 5-12
	Russ Hanson	Wentworth	SO	F	28	0.43	5- 7-12
131	Kris Kranzky	Nichols	FR	F	11	1.00	6- 5-11
	Scott Zanolli	Suffolk	SO	F	20	0.55	5- 6-11
	Coursen Schneider	Franklin Pierce	SO	F	22	0.50	5- 6-11
	Ben Reynolds	Franklin Pierce	JR	F	22	0.50	2- 9-11
	Mike Mondello	Suffolk	FR	F	23	0.48	7- 4-11
	Dan McLaughlin	Worcester State	SR	D	23	0.48	5- 6-11
	Kyle Bousquet	Southern N.H.	SR	D	23	0.48	1-10-11
	Conor McCahill	Salve Regina	SO	F	24	0.46	5- 6-11
	John Frey	Southern N.H.	FR	F	24	0.46	4- 7-11
	Mike Rust	Assumption	JR	F	26	0.42	6- 5-11
	Steve Kelleher	Curry	SR	F	27	0.41	4- 7-11
	Dillon Rioux	Wentworth	SO	D	28	0.39	2- 9-11
143	Josh Barboza	Suffolk	JR	F	10	1.00	5- 5-10
	Louis Hoey	Curry	SO	F	13	0.77	1- 9-10
	Colin Goodwin	Framingham State	FR	D	13	0.77	1- 9-10
	Nathaniel Robie	Curry	JR	D	20	0.50	3- 7-10
	Sean Sylvester	Curry	FR	F	20	0.50	3- 7-10
	Steven Murphy	Curry	FR	F	22	0.45	5- 5-10
	Joe McCarthy	Franklin Pierce	FR	F	23	0.43	4- 6-10
	Mike Kravchuk	Salve Regina	JR	D	23	0.43	1- 9-10
	Chet Riley	Southern N.H.	SR	F	24	0.42	3- 7-10
	Mykul Haun	Plymouth State	SR	F	25	0.40	1- 9-10
	Billy Carroll	UMass Dartmouth	FR	F	26	0.38	7- 3-10
	Zach Lindsay	Nichols	SR	F	26	0.38	5- 5-10
	Bobby Dashner	Plymouth State	JR	D	26	0.38	5- 5-10
	Bob Kalousian	Fitchburg State	SO	F	27	0.37	7- 3-10
	Joshua Douglas	Southern N.H.	JR	F	27	0.37	6- 4-10
	Pat Welch	UMass Dartmouth	FR	F	27	0.37	3- 7-10
	Evan Spencer	Stonehill	SR	D	27	0.37	2- 8-10
	Rob Carpenter	Stonehill	JR	F	27	0.37	2- 8-10
	Matt Serino	UMass Dartmouth	FR	F	29	0.34	3- 7-10
162	Matt Sayer	Southern N.H.	FR	F	6	1.50	4- 5- 9
	Mark Malone	Nichols	SR	D	11	0.82	3- 6- 9
	Jeff Oddleifson	Wentworth	JR	F	13	0.69	5- 4- 9
	Steve Carkin	Fitchburg State	SR	D	14	0.64	2- 7- 9
	Graeme Bourne	UMass Dartmouth	FR	D	16	0.56	1- 8- 9
	Andrew Broughton	Curry	SO	F	20	0.45	4- 5- 9
	Chris Genovese	Assumption	SO	D	22	0.41	3- 6- 9
	Kyle Kruse	Franklin Pierce	FR	D	24	0.38	3- 6- 9
	Ryan Moreau	Plymouth State	JR	F	25	0.36	5- 4- 9
	James Capulli	Assumption	FR	F	25	0.36	1- 8- 9
	Matt Farley	Southern N.H.	FR	F	26	0.35	6- 3- 9
	Corey Horner	Nichols	SR	F	26	0.35	5- 4- 9
	Andrew Affronti	Wentworth	FR	F	28	0.32	1- 8- 9
175	Matt Koehler	Wentworth	JR	F	10	0.80	5- 3- 8
	Dave Notartomaso	Johnson & Wales	SO	F	10	0.80	1- 7- 8
	Ross Goff	Fitchburg State	JR	D	20	0.40	2- 6- 8
	Joseph Mulvey	Framingham State	FR	F	21	0.38	5- 3- 8

	Jakub Kubrak	Johnson & Wales	JR	D	21	0.38	3- 5- 8
	Ken Burlage	Southern N.H.	SR	D	21	0.38	1- 7- 8
	Eric Quinlan	UMass Dartmouth	FR	D	22	0.36	1- 7- 8
	Mike Amato	Western N.E.	SR	F	23	0.35	4- 4- 8
	Kyle Hallett	Framingham State	SO	F	23	0.35	3- 5- 8
	Eric Bouchard	Salve Regina	FR	F	24	0.33	6- 2- 8
	Patrick Bambery	Salve Regina	FR	F	25	0.32	5- 3- 8
	Bryan Goodwin	Salve Regina	JR	D	25	0.32	1- 7- 8
	Patrick Ciummo	Assumption	JR	F	26	0.31	5- 3- 8
	Ron Carlucci	Fitchburg State	FR	F	27	0.30	1- 7- 8
	Dave Kaloustian	Fitchburg State	SR	D	27	0.30	0- 8- 8
190	Stephen Schofield	Fitchburg State	SR	F	4	1.75	3- 4- 7
	Casey Goodell	Franklin Pierce	FR	F	17	0.41	5- 2- 7
	Ryan Sullivan	Framingham State	FR	D	17	0.41	1- 6- 7
	Zach Sufilka	Salve Regina	SO	D	18	0.39	3- 4- 7
	Stephen Butler	Framingham State	JR	F	19	0.37	1- 6- 7
	Ryan Collins	Suffolk	SO	F	20	0.35	4- 3- 7
	John Delaney	Suffolk	SR	F	20	0.35	2- 5- 7
	Geoffrey Ferreira	Curry	SR	D/F	21	0.33	1- 6- 7
	Matt Auwarter	Worcester State	JR	F	23	0.30	6- 1- 7
	Chad Larkowski	Fitchburg State	JR	F	23	0.30	5- 2- 7
	Zachary Cantin	Stonehill	FR	F	23	0.30	3- 4- 7
	Jake Noonan	Salve Regina	JR	F	24	0.29	4- 3- 7
	Ryan Paglinco	Plymouth State	FR	F	26	0.27	3- 4- 7
	Kyle Allen	Plymouth State	SR	F	26	0.27	2- 5- 7
	Paul Moran	UMass Dartmouth	FR	D	27	0.26	0- 7- 7
205	Mark Cerretani	Curry	FR	F	10	0.60	4- 2- 6
	Phil Gabriele	Wentworth	JR	D	12	0.50	1- 5- 6
	Dean Smith	Western N.E.	SO	F	14	0.43	1- 5- 6
	Randy Morin	Assumption	JR	D	20	0.30	2- 4- 6
	Jason Remsbecker	Western N.E.	SO	F	20	0.30	2- 4- 6
	Peter Wilson	Franklin Pierce	JR	F	21	0.29	4- 2- 6
	John Madsen	Johnson & Wales	FR	D	21	0.29	1- 5- 6
	Matt Whitney	Franklin Pierce	SO	F	23	0.26	3- 3- 6
	Evan Williams	Southern N.H.	JR	F	23	0.26	2- 4- 6
	Mark Bucci	Worcester State	JR	C	23	0.26	2- 4- 6
	Tyler Bickford	Johnson & Wales	SO	D	23	0.26	0- 6- 6
	Mark Baker	Nichols	FR	D	26	0.23	3- 3- 6
	Colby Jones	Nichols	FR	D	26	0.23	2- 4- 6
	Ryan Tierney	Fitchburg State	JR	F	27	0.22	4- 2- 6
	Matt Buono	Wentworth	SR	F	28	0.21	3- 3- 6
220	Chris Galvin	Suffolk	FR	F	14	0.36	1- 4- 5
	Sean Boudreau	Framingham State	SO	F	15	0.33	2- 3- 5
	Brett Casavant	Framingham State	FR	F	15	0.33	2- 3- 5
	Ed Kus	Franklin Pierce	SO	D	15	0.33	1- 4- 5
	Doug Martin	Wentworth	FR	F	17	0.29	4- 1- 5
	Stephen Ficaro	Framingham State	FR	D	18	0.28	1- 4- 5
	Nick Bartelloni	Salve Regina	SO	D	19	0.26	1- 4- 5
	Lee Belisle	Worcester State	FR	F	21	0.24	2- 3- 5
	Joshua Williams	Framingham State	FR	D	22	0.23	1- 4- 5
	Christopher Brecken	Fitchburg State	FR	D	23	0.22	2- 3- 5
	Bill Galvin	Suffolk	SO	F	23	0.22	2- 3- 5
	Phil Demers	Assumption	JR	D	23	0.22	1- 4- 5
	Ed Achilles	Worcester State	JR	F	23	0.22	1- 4- 5
	James Killeen	Stonehill	SO	D	26	0.19	0- 5- 5
234	Ryan Lord	Johnson & Wales	JR	F	5	0.80	0- 4- 4
	Michael Goulet	Fitchburg State	JR	F	9	0.44	2- 2- 4
	Mike McNulty	UMass Dartmouth	JR	D	10	0.40	0- 4- 4
	Nick Stevenson	Southern N.H.	FR	D	12	0.33	0- 4- 4
	Jonathan Finn	UMass Dartmouth	JR	F/D	13	0.31	1- 3- 4

	Name	Team	Yr	Pos			
	Justin Liut	Curry	SO	F	14	0.29	2- 2- 4
	Nick Sampson	Western N.E.	JR	F	16	0.25	1- 3- 4
	Ross Bennett-Bonn	Western N.E.	JR	F	17	0.24	4- 0- 4
	Joseph Hurley	Framingham State	FR	F	19	0.21	3- 1- 4
	Stephen Murphy	Franklin Pierce	FR	D	19	0.21	0- 4- 4
	Wayne Bonkowski	Fitchburg State	SO	D	20	0.20	1- 3- 4
	Jake Rinaldo	Western N.E.	SO	D	20	0.20	0- 4- 4
	Joe Willard	Western N.E.	SO	F	21	0.19	3- 1- 4
	Rob Perretta	Franklin Pierce	SO	D	22	0.18	3- 1- 4
	Tim Recio	Suffolk	JR	D	22	0.18	0- 4- 4
	Aaron Tiernan	Fitchburg State	SO	D	23	0.17	2- 2- 4
	Chris Hill	Salve Regina	SO	F	23	0.17	2- 2- 4
	Nick Klassen	Western N.E.	JR	D	23	0.17	1- 3- 4
	Josh Goodman	Southern N.H.	JR	D	24	0.17	1- 3- 4
	Thomas Ohlson	Southern N.H.	FR	F	24	0.17	1- 3- 4
	Nathaniel Burns	Salve Regina	FR	D	25	0.16	0- 4- 4
	Steve Milley	Plymouth State	SR	D	26	0.15	1- 3- 4
	Glenn Cacaro	Nichols	SO	D	26	0.15	0- 4- 4
	Frank Cavaliere	Stonehill	SO	D	27	0.15	2- 2- 4
	Mike LaRoche	Fitchburg State	SR	F	27	0.15	0- 4- 4
259	Michael Sabo	Southern N.H.	JR	F	8	0.38	1- 2- 3
	Bryan Smusz	Suffolk	FR	F	16	0.19	2- 1- 3
	Tyler Cleary	Assumption	FR	F	16	0.19	1- 2- 3
	Dominic Cavallaro	Southern N.H.	SR	D	16	0.19	0- 3- 3
	Justin Graziano	Western N.E.	FR	F	17	0.18	1- 2- 3
	Brandon Goodnow	Salve Regina	FR	F	18	0.17	1- 2- 3
	Pat Tamez	Western N.E.	JR	D	18	0.17	0- 3- 3
	Jack Nagle	Worcester State	FR	D	20	0.15	1- 2- 3
	John Coutts	Fitchburg State	SO	F	21	0.14	1- 2- 3
	Dan Drinkwater	Worcester State	FR	F	22	0.14	2- 1- 3
	Tim Dupuis	Assumption	FR	D	22	0.14	1- 2- 3
	William Knauber	Worcester State	SO	D	22	0.14	0- 3- 3
	Ryan Strayer	Franklin Pierce	JR	F	24	0.12	2- 1- 3
	Jon Retelle	Assumption	FR	D	25	0.12	1- 2- 3
	John Curley	Johnson & Wales	SR	F/D	25	0.12	0- 3- 3
274	Steve Wardynski	Southern N.H.	JR	F/D	3	0.67	0- 2- 2
	Adam Ysasi	Wentworth	SR	F	3	0.67	0- 2- 2
	Scott May	Suffolk	FR	F	4	0.50	0- 2- 2
	Josh Lupinek	Franklin Pierce	SO	D	5	0.40	2- 0- 2
	Thomas Harrison	Curry	FR	D	5	0.40	0- 2- 2
	Neil Donahue	Framingham State	SO	F	5	0.40	0- 2- 2
	Brett Bilodeau	Franklin Pierce	SR	F	7	0.29	1- 1- 2
	Bryan Myers	Suffolk	SO	D	8	0.25	0- 2- 2
	Paul Forselius	Salve Regina	FR	D	9	0.22	0- 2- 2
	Matt Berard	UMass Dartmouth	FR	F	10	0.20	0- 2- 2
	Mike St. Lawrence	Assumption	FR	F	11	0.18	1- 1- 2
	Chris Fraterrigo	Fitchburg State	JR	F	11	0.18	0- 2- 2
	C.J. Demmons	Franklin Pierce	SR	F	11	0.18	0- 2- 2
	Richie Rice	Salve Regina	JR	F	11	0.18	0- 2- 2
	Stephan Davis	Framingham State	FR	D	12	0.17	1- 1- 2
	David Trantin	Framingham State	SO	D	15	0.13	1- 1- 2
	Matt Broadhead	Nichols	SO	F/D	15	0.13	0- 2- 2
	Corey Glynn	Stonehill	FR	D	15	0.13	0- 2- 2
	Sean Maguire	Framingham State	SO	F	19	0.11	0- 2- 2
	Jeff Spencer	Johnson & Wales	FR	D	19	0.11	0- 2- 2
	Colin Brophy	Johnson & Wales	SR	D	20	0.10	1- 1- 2
	Derek Whitney	Assumption	FR	D	21	0.10	0- 2- 2
	Shane Poulin	Johnson & Wales	FR	D	22	0.09	1- 1- 2
	Stephen Pfeiffer	Johnson & Wales	FR	F	24	0.08	0- 2- 2
	Pat Keenan	Assumption	FR	D	25	0.08	1- 1- 2

	Name	School	Yr	Pos			
	Andrew Goduco	Southern N.H.	JR	F	26	0.08	1- 1- 2
	Rob Pagani	Wentworth	SO	D	28	0.07	1- 1- 2
301	Mark Trahan	UMass Dartmouth	SO	F	1	1.00	1- 0- 1
	Brendan Healey	Wentworth	FR	F	1	1.00	0- 1- 1
	Jarrett Sousa	Curry	SO	D	2	0.50	0- 1- 1
	Joe Diorio	Suffolk	JR	F	2	0.50	0- 1- 1
	Tucker Callen	Curry	FR	F	3	0.33	0- 1- 1
	AJ Maulucci	Johnson & Wales	FR	F	5	0.20	1- 0- 1
	Neil Walsky	Wentworth	FR	F	5	0.20	1- 0- 1
	James Wood	Assumption	JR	F	6	0.17	1- 0- 1
	Trevor Moss	Suffolk	FR	F	6	0.17	0- 1- 1
	Mike Cafferty	Stonehill	SO	F	7	0.14	1- 0- 1
	Dan Conklin	Suffolk	FR	F	7	0.14	0- 1- 1
	Andrew Dinkelmeyer	Western N.E.	FR	D	7	0.14	0- 1- 1
	Patrick Haley	Curry	SO	F	8	0.12	1- 0- 1
	Mark Lodge	Southern N.H.	FR	D	8	0.12	0- 1- 1
	Bryan Calabro	Worcester State	JR	F	8	0.12	0- 1- 1
	Andrew Rosser	Western N.E.	SO	D	9	0.11	1- 0- 1
	Shane Murphy	Franklin Pierce	SO	F	9	0.11	0- 1- 1
	Chris Carpenter	UMass Dartmouth	SO	F/D	9	0.11	0- 1- 1
	Neal Gerber	Nichols	FR	F	9	0.11	0- 1- 1
	Bryan Radomski	Plymouth State	FR	D	9	0.11	0- 1- 1
	Carmine Vetrano	Southern N.H.	FR	G	9	0.11	0- 1- 1
	Mike Daraio	Stonehill	FR	F	9	0.11	0- 1- 1
	Andrew Christopher	Suffolk	SO	D	9	0.11	0- 1- 1
	Andrew Lisi	Curry	FR	G	10	0.10	0- 1- 1
	Matt Gassman	Nichols	FR	G	10	0.10	0- 1- 1
	Ryan Daly	Suffolk	FR	F	10	0.10	0- 1- 1
	Jim Mellon	Suffolk	FR	F	11	0.09	0- 1- 1
	Kyle Taylor	Suffolk	FR	D	12	0.08	1- 0- 1
	Steven Della Calce	Franklin Pierce	FR	F	12	0.08	0- 1- 1
	Steve Nims	Worcester State	SO	D	12	0.08	0- 1- 1
	Phil LaCasse	Southern N.H.	FR	D	13	0.08	0- 1- 1
	John Sommers	Stonehill	SO	F	13	0.08	0- 1- 1
	Charlie Bacon	Johnson & Wales	JR	G	15	0.07	0- 1- 1
	Patrick Dolan	Fitchburg State	SO	D	16	0.06	0- 1- 1
	Rich Walters	Nichols	FR	D	18	0.06	1- 0- 1
	Petter Adeberg	Plymouth State	FR	F	18	0.06	1- 0- 1
	Drew Vrolyk	Western N.E.	FR	D	18	0.06	0- 1- 1
	Zachary Cardella	Curry	FR	G	20	0.05	0- 1- 1
	Jason Richardson	Worcester State	SO	G	20	0.05	0- 1- 1
	Trevor Clark	Franklin Pierce	JR	F	21	0.05	0- 1- 1
	Keith Fink	Nichols	SO	G	21	0.05	0- 1- 1
	Joe Drago	Suffolk	FR	D	21	0.05	0- 1- 1
	Sam Kessler	Suffolk	FR	D	21	0.05	0- 1- 1
	Bryn Sneddon	Salve Regina	SR	F	23	0.04	1- 0- 1
	Mike Anderson	Franklin Pierce	SR	D	23	0.04	0- 1- 1
	Brandt Nelson	Salve Regina	JR	D	23	0.04	0- 1- 1
	Devan McConnell	Fitchburg State	JR	G	25	0.04	0- 1- 1

GOALS AGAINST AVERAGE:

				MINUTES	GA	GAA
1	Jeff Green	UMass Dartmouth	SO	1707:57:00	54	1.9
2	Erik Shields	Plymouth State	FR	871:12:00	44	3.03
3	Zachary Cardella	Curry	FR	1093:51:00	57	3.13
4	Justin Marriott	Wentworth	FR	1338:58:00	77	3.45
5	Devan McConnell	Fitchburg State	JR	1502:05:00	87	3.48
6	Chase Goodrich	Salve Regina	SO	1167:47:00	68	3.49
7	Josh Green	Stonehill	SR	753:46:00	46	3.66
8	Matt Gorman	Stonehill	SR	870:21:00	55	3.79
9	Kyle Sagnella	Western N.E.	SO	538:45:00	35	3.9
10	Matt Courchesne	Southern N.H.	SO	1337:48:00	90	4.04
11	Keith Fink	Nichols	SO	1081:47:00	74	4.1
12	Sean Bertoni	Suffolk	SR	684:33:00	47	4.12
13	Charlie Bacon	Johnson & Wales	JR	773:43:00	54	4.19
14	Jamie DiGiulio	Assumption	FR	1003:00:00	71	4.25
15	Mick Fitzpatrick	Plymouth State	FR	616:27:00	44	4.28
16	Jason Richardson	Worcester State	SO	1184:35:00	87	4.41
17	Brandon Gervais	Western N.E.	JR	771:03:00	57	4.44
18	Andy Joyce	Framingham State	FR	555:54:00	44	4.75
19	Spencer Utman	Franklin Pierce	JR	975:53:00	78	4.8
20	Brian Noiles	Johnson & Wales	SO	736:01:00	62	5.05
21	Matthew Trusz	Framingham State	SO	614:22:00	54	5.27

Minimum 33% of Team Minutes Played

SAVE PERCENTAGE:

				SAVES	GA	PCT
1	Jeff Green	UMass Dartmouth	SO	649	54	0.923
2	Devan McConnell	Fitchburg State	JR	824	87	0.905
3	Erik Shields	Plymouth State	FR	411	44	0.903
4	Justin Marriott	Wentworth	FR	707	77	0.902
5	Mick Fitzpatrick	Plymouth State	FR	366	44	0.893
6	Zachary Cardella	Curry	FR	470	57	0.892
7	Jason Richardson	Worcester State	SO	712	87	0.891
8	Jamie DiGiulio	Assumption	FR	581	71	0.891
9	Chase Goodrich	Salve Regina	SO	539	68	0.888
10	Sean Bertoni	Suffolk	SR	366	47	0.886
11	Charlie Bacon	Johnson & Wales	JR	419	54	0.886
12	Matt Gorman	Stonehill	SR	416	55	0.883
13	Josh Green	Stonehill	SR	345	46	0.882
14	Brian Noiles	Johnson & Wales	SO	442	62	0.877
15	Brandon Gervais	Western N.E.	JR	396	57	0.874
16	Keith Fink	Nichols	SO	514	74	0.874
17	Matthew Trusz	Framingham State	SO	374	54	0.874
18	Matt Courchesne	Southern N.H.	SO	614	90	0.872
19	Spencer Utman	Franklin Pierce	JR	526	78	0.871
20	Kyle Sagnella	Western N.E.	SO	229	35	0.867
21	Andy Joyce	Framingham State	FR	272	44	0.861

Minimum 33% of Team Minutes Played

WINNING PERCENTAGE:

				W- L- T	PCT
1	Jeff Green	UMass Dartmouth	SO	25- 3- 1	0.879
2	Josh Green	Stonehill	SR	8- 3- 1	0.708
3	Erik Shields	Plymouth State	FR	8- 4- 1	0.654
4	Justin Marriott	Wentworth	FR	14- 7- 2	0.652
5	Zachary Cardella	Curry	FR	11- 7- 1	0.605
	Keith Fink	Nichols	SO	11- 7- 1	0.605
7	Brian Noiles	Johnson & Wales	SO	6- 4- 0	0.6
8	Devan McConnell	Fitchburg State	JR	12-10- 3	0.54
9	Chase Goodrich	Salve Regina	SO	9-10- 0	0.474
10	Matt Courchesne	Southern N.H.	SO	11-13- 0	0.458
11	Charlie Bacon	Johnson & Wales	JR	6- 8- 1	0.433
12	Matt Gorman	Stonehill	SR	6- 9- 0	0.4
13	Kyle Sagnella	Western N.E.	SO	3- 5- 0	0.375
14	Brandon Gervais	Western N.E.	JR	5- 9- 0	0.357
15	Jason Richardson	Worcester State	SO	6-13- 1	0.325
16	Jamie DiGiulio	Assumption	FR	5-11- 1	0.324
17	Spencer Utman	Franklin Pierce	JR	4-11- 2	0.294
18	Mick Fitzpatrick	Plymouth State	FR	3- 8- 1	0.292
	Sean Bertoni	Suffolk	SR	3- 8- 1	0.292
20	Matthew Trusz	Framingham State	SO	1- 8- 1	0.15
21	Andy Joyce	Framingham State	FR	1- 8- 0	0.111

Minimum 33% of Team Minutes Played

Eastern College
Athletic Conference Northeast
1311 Craigville Beach Road
P.O. Box 3
Centerville, MA 02632
www.ecac.org

Commissioner
Rudy Keeling
Office: 508.771.5060
Fax: 508.771.9481
rkeeling@ecac.org

Senior Associate Commissioner
Steve Bamford
Office: 508.771.5060 x 215
Fax: 508.771.9481
sbamford@ecac.org

Coordinator Operations & Services
Michael Letzeisen
Office: 508.771.5060 x 236
Fax: 508.771.9481
mletzeisen@ecac.org

Administrative Assistant - Hockey
Anne Glover
Office: 508.771.5060 x 222
Fax: 508.771.9481
aglover@ecac.org

Elmira College
Hobart College
Lebanon Valley College
Manhattanville College
Neumann College
Utica College

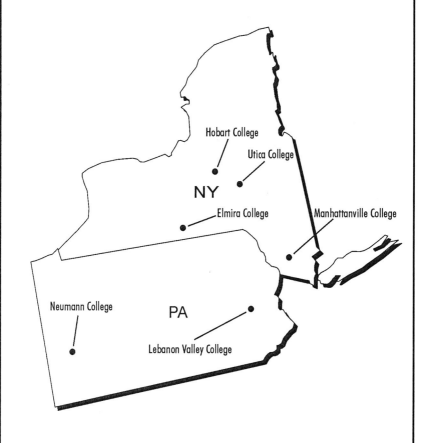

EASTERN COLLEGE ATHLETIC CONFERENCE WEST

FINAL 2006-07 CONFERENCE STANDINGS

		Pts	GP	Record	Win%	GF-GA	GP	Record	Win%	GF-GA
1	Manhattanville	23	15	9- 1- 5	0.767	71- 29	28	21- 2- 5	0.839	151- 54
2	Neumann	20	15	8- 3- 4	0.667	80- 41	27	17- 5- 5	0.722	137- 74
3	Utica	17	15	7- 5- 3	0.567	52- 39	25	13- 9- 3	0.580	87- 61
4	Elmira	16	15	7- 6- 2	0.533	55- 50	27	13-10- 4	0.556	96- 86
5	Hobart	13	15	5- 7- 3	0.433	50- 51	26	13- 8- 5	0.596	106- 79
6	Lebanon Valley	1	15	0-14- 1	0.033	26-124	25	2-22- 1	0.100	58-174

2007 EASTERN COLLEGE ATHLETIC CONFERENCE WEST PLAYOFFS

QUARTER FINAL *(2.21.07)*

Hobart College	4	Elmira College	5

SEMIFINALS *(2.24.07)*

Utica College	1	Neumann College	2
Elmira College	3	Manhattanville College	5

CHAMPIONSHIP *(3.3.07)*

Neumann College	4	Manhattanville College	5

EASTERN COLLEGE ATHLETIC CONFERENCE WEST CHAMPIONS

	TOURNAMENT
1978	Elmira College
1979	Middlebury College
1980	SUNY - Oswego
1981	SUNY - Plattsburgh
1982	SUNY - Plattsburgh
1983	SUNY - Oswego
1984	Rochester Institute of Technology
1985	Union College
1986	Rochester Institute of Technology
1987	SUNY-Plattsburgh
1988	Elmira College
1989	Rochester Institute of Technology
1990	Elmira College
1991	Elmira College
1992	SUNY - Plattsburgh
1993	Elmira College
1994	Rochester Institute of Technology
1995	Mercyhurst College
1996	Rochester Institute of Technology
1997	Elmira College
1998	Niagara University
1999	Rochester Institute of Technology
2000	Rochester Institute of Technology
2001	Rochester Institute of Technology
2002	Rochester Institue of Technology
2003	Elmira College

REGULAR

2004	Hobart College	2004	Hobart College
2005	Utica College	2005	Manhattanville College
2006	Manhattanville College	2006	Elmira College
2007	Manhattanville College	2007	Manhattanville College

					GP	PPG	G - A - P
1	Neil Trimm	Neumann	JR	F	27	2.48	18-49-67
2	Mike Hedden	Neumann	SO	F	26	2.00	31-21-52
3	Mark Van Vliet	Neumann	JR	F	27	1.89	18-33-51
4	Chris Mills	Manhattanville	SR	F	28	1.57	14-30-44
5	Matt Ward	Neumann	FR	F	24	1.71	14-27-41
6	Justin Rohr	Manhattanville	SR	F	27	1.48	14-26-40
7	Mike Ruberto	Manhattanville	JR	F	27	1.41	17-21-38
8	Kyle Casey	Neumann	SO	F	27	1.37	16-21-37
9	Conor Bradley	Hobart	SR	F	25	1.36	14-20-34
10	Michael Richard	Elmira	JR	F	27	1.22	9-24-33
11	Jason Murfitt	Manhattanville	JR	F	27	1.15	18-13-31
12	Mike Gooch	Neumann	JR	D	27	1.11	5-25-30
13	Alex Beatrice	Lebanon Valley	SR	F	25	1.08	15-12-27
14	Shawn Houde	Hobart	JR	F	25	1.04	16-10-26
15	Rusty Masters	Elmira	FR	F	26	0.96	12-13-25
16	Jared Allison	Utica	SR	F	21	1.14	11-13-24
	Stefan Schoen	Elmira	SO	F	24	1.00	13-11-24
	Matt Piegza	Manhattanville	FR	F	24	1.00	12-12-24
19	Mike McCarthy	Hobart	SR	F	24	0.96	7-16-23
20	Mike Polsonetti	Hobart	SR	D	20	1.10	8-14-22
	AJ Mikkelsen	Manhattanville	FR	D	26	0.85	7-15-22
22	Dave Werner	Utica	FR	F	23	0.91	11-10-21
	Derek Lynden	Manhattanville	SO	F	24	0.88	12- 9-21
	Arlen Marshall	Manhattanville	FR	F	25	0.84	11-10-21
	Dave McKenna	Elmira	SO	F	25	0.84	8-13-21
	Nicolas Dumoulin	Elmira	SO	D	26	0.81	8-13-21
	Niklas Berntsson	Manhattanville	FR	F	27	0.78	8-13-21
28	Jonathan Swift	Hobart	SR	F	25	0.80	5-15-20
	Brian Cibelli	Hobart	JR	F	25	0.80	5-15-20
	Jeff Smith	Lebanon Valley	SR	F	25	0.80	5-15-20
	Justin Joy	Elmira	SR	F	27	0.74	6-14-20
32	Bryce Dale	Utica	SO	F	24	0.79	7-12-19
	Andrew Brennan	Hobart	SO	D	25	0.76	6-13-19
34	Colin Kingston	Utica	SO	F	21	0.81	5-12-17
	Jarred Frey	Lebanon Valley	SO	F	23	0.74	7-10-17
	Mike Manos	Hobart	SR	D	26	0.65	5-12-17
	B.J. Greaves	Manhattanville	SR	F	28	0.61	6-11-17
38	Brandon Laidlaw	Utica	FR	F	21	0.76	8- 8-16
	Matt Fitzgibbons	Utica	FR	F	23	0.70	7- 9-16
	Matt Ruberto	Manhattanville	JR	D	24	0.67	5-11-16
41	Kevin Krogol	Utica	SR	F	20	0.75	9- 6-15
	Matt Rowe	Lebanon Valley	SO	F	23	0.65	4-11-15
	Jesse Cole	Neumann	SO	F	25	0.60	9- 6-15
	Jason Merritt	Hobart	SO	F	26	0.58	6- 9-15
45	Troy Maleyko	Manhattanville	SR	D	24	0.58	5- 9-14
	Darcy Pettie	Elmira	SR	F	27	0.52	6- 8-14
47	Dillon Henningson	Manhattanville	FR	F	17	0.76	5- 8-13
	Jeff Pappalardi	Utica	FR	F	24	0.54	1-12-13
	Rick Lynch	Elmira	SR	D	26	0.50	1-12-13
	Zeke Hume	Manhattanville	JR	D/F	27	0.48	7- 6-13
51	Joe Watson	Utica	JR	F	21	0.57	8- 4-12
	Edward Brzek	Hobart	JR	F	22	0.55	4- 8-12
	Andrew Bedford	Elmira	JR	F	23	0.52	7- 5-12
	Bert Malloy	Lebanon Valley	SO	D	24	0.50	7- 5-12
	Blake Bonham	Hobart	FR	F	25	0.48	5- 7-12
	Russell Smith	Elmira	JR	D/F	26	0.46	5- 7-12
	Chris Wanchulak	Manhattanville	JR	D	28	0.43	2-10-12
58	Scott Goheen	Manhattanville	SR	F	10	1.10	5- 6-11

	Name	Team	Yr	Pos	Games	Avg	G-A-Pts
	Casey Mignone	Lebanon Valley	FR	F	25	0.44	4- 7-11
60	Mike Lane	Utica	FR	D	19	0.53	0-10-10
	Jan Velich	Elmira	FR	F	21	0.48	6- 4-10
	Sean Cryer	Neumann	JR	D	23	0.43	0-10-10
63	Nick Lynch	Utica	JR	F	12	0.75	2- 7- 9
	Ryan Adler	Hobart	SO	D	24	0.38	4- 5- 9
	Brock Van Slyke	Neumann	SO	D	27	0.33	3- 6- 9
66	Vincent Nucci	Utica	FR	F	9	0.89	4- 4- 8
	Noel Lortie	Elmira	FR	F	10	0.80	4- 4- 8
	Aleksey Koval	Hobart	FR	F	14	0.57	2- 6- 8
	Scott Phelps	Utica	FR	F	19	0.42	3- 5- 8
	Erik Stoyanvich	Neumann	SO	F	21	0.38	2- 6- 8
	Ryan Heickert	Neumann	SO	F	22	0.36	4- 4- 8
	TJ Schneider	Utica	SO	F	24	0.33	3- 5- 8
	Gregg Johannesen	Utica	SR	D	25	0.32	2- 6- 8
	Greg Moore	Elmira	FR	D	27	0.30	0- 8- 8
75	Brendan McIntyre	Manhattanville	JR	F	18	0.39	2- 5- 7
	Sean Wilson	Lebanon Valley	FR	D	20	0.35	1- 6- 7
	Donavon Hall	Neumann	SO	F	22	0.32	3- 4- 7
	Michael Steiner	Hobart	SO	D	24	0.29	3- 4- 7
	Josh Merson	Utica	SO	D	25	0.28	4- 3- 7
80	Gregory Alberti	Hobart	FR	F	17	0.35	2- 4- 6
	Derrick Ryan	Elmira	SO	F	23	0.26	1- 5- 6
	Randy Bauer	Utica	SR	D	25	0.24	0- 6- 6
	Kyle Branson	Elmira	SO	D	26	0.23	2- 4- 6
	Adam Scott	Hobart	SR	F	26	0.23	2- 4- 6
	Danny Genovese	Manhattanville	FR	D	27	0.22	0- 6- 6
86	Joe DiCamillo	Manhattanville	FR	F	13	0.38	1- 4- 5
	Aaron Laycock	Hobart	SR	F	16	0.31	3- 2- 5
	Ryan Merritt	Lebanon Valley	SR	D	16	0.31	0- 5- 5
	Aaron Jeffery	Utica	FR	F	17	0.29	1- 4- 5
	Kirk Golden	Hobart	SO	F	18	0.28	5- 0- 5
	Keleigh Schrock	Neumann	SO	F	19	0.26	3- 2- 5
	Albert Mitchell	Elmira	SO	F	20	0.25	1- 4- 5
	Bryant Harris	Hobart	SO	D	24	0.21	2- 3- 5
	Tony Wiseman	Utica	JR	D	25	0.20	0- 5- 5
	Charles Paterson	Neumann	FR	D	26	0.19	0- 5- 5
	Scott Gamble	Elmira	FR	D	27	0.19	1- 4- 5
97	Bobby Cahill	Hobart	FR	F	9	0.44	2- 2- 4
	Marc Borden	Hobart	SR	F	11	0.36	0- 4- 4
	Zach Gieszler	Utica	SO	D	13	0.31	1- 3- 4
	Phil Boots	Utica	SR	F	13	0.31	0- 4- 4
	Anthony Longo	Lebanon Valley	FR	F	14	0.29	2- 2- 4
	Stewart Sjoberg	Neumann	SO	F	14	0.29	2- 2- 4
	Andy Orsini	Lebanon Valley	FR	F	20	0.20	4- 0- 4
	Dayne Bihn	Neumann	JR	F	20	0.20	3- 1- 4
	Nick Harris	Lebanon Valley	SO	F	21	0.19	2- 2- 4
	Rob Scales	Lebanon Valley	JR	F	23	0.17	1- 3- 4
	Andrew Gallant	Manhattanville	SR	G	26	0.15	0- 4- 4
108	Josh Jacobs	Neumann	SO	F	8	0.38	0- 3- 3
	Peter Vaisanen	Neumann	SO	F	10	0.30	2- 1- 3
	Pat Skehan	Lebanon Valley	FR	F	12	0.25	1- 2- 3
	Eli Facchinei	Lebanon Valley	SO	F	16	0.19	1- 2- 3
	Anthony Scales	Lebanon Valley	JR	D	22	0.14	0- 3- 3
	Ryan Arnone	Elmira	JR	F	24	0.12	2- 1- 3
	Nick Kiella	Elmira	SR	F	26	0.12	2- 1- 3
115	Mike Demarchi	Neumann	SO	F	8	0.25	1- 1- 2
	Dan Miller	Hobart	FR	D	9	0.22	0- 2- 2
	Matt Jimenez	Utica	FR	D	10	0.20	0- 2- 2
	John Giacobbo	Neumann	SO	D	11	0.18	0- 2- 2

Vinny Ciardullo	Manhattanville	SO F	12	0.17	0- 2- 2
Darin Pandovski	Elmira	FR F	13	0.15	1- 1- 2
Jeff Nuttall	Neumann	JR F	15	0.13	1- 1- 2
Doug Slipacoff	Neumann	SO D	16	0.12	1- 1- 2
Rocky Romanella	Lebanon Valley	FR F	17	0.12	0- 2- 2
Spiros Anastas	Lebanon Valley	FR F	18	0.11	2- 0- 2
Ryan Horgan	Lebanon Valley	FR D	18	0.11	0- 2- 2
Dave Gooch	Neumann	FR D	18	0.11	0- 2- 2
Pete Rossi	Lebanon Valley	JR F/D	25	0.08	1- 1- 2

128
Chris Asplund	Elmira	SO F	3	0.33	1- 0- 1
Kyle Sibley	Utica	JR D	7	0.14	0- 1- 1
Kyle Smith	Lebanon Valley	FR F	8	0.12	1- 0- 1
Todd Gilmore	Neumann	SO F	8	0.12	1- 0- 1
Jacob Cline	Manhattanville	SO F	8	0.12	0- 1- 1
Phil Hotarek	Manhattanville	FR D	9	0.11	0- 1- 1
Tyler Rivers	Neumann	FR D	14	0.07	0- 1- 1
Chris Galiotti	Manhattanville	SO D	18	0.06	0- 1- 1
E.J. Smith	Lebanon Valley	SO D	19	0.05	0- 1- 1
Adam Dekker	Utica	JR G	24	0.04	0- 1- 1
Mike Collichio	Neumann	JR G	25	0.04	0- 1- 1

GOALS AGAINST AVERAGE:

				MINUTES	GA	GAA
1	Andrew Gallant	Manhattanville	SR	1509:00:00	48	1.91
2	Adam Dekker	Utica	JR	1353:21:00	56	2.48
3	Keith Longo	Hobart	SO	997:22:00	43	2.59
4	Casey Tuttle	Elmira	FR	1150:13:00	52	2.71
5	Mike Collichio	Neumann	JR	1515:14:00	69	2.73
6	Aaron Miller	Lebanon Valley	FR	1132:24:00	125	6.62

Minimum 33% of Team Minutes Played

SAVE PERCENTAGE:

				SAVES	GA	PCT
1	Andrew Gallant	Manhattanville	SR	617	48	0.928
2	Keith Longo	Hobart	SO	475	43	0.917
3	Adam Dekker	Utica	JR	574	56	0.911
4	Mike Collichio	Neumann	JR	668	69	0.906
5	Casey Tuttle	Elmira	FR	354	52	0.872
6	Aaron Miller	Lebanon Valley	FR	763	125	0.859

Minimum 33% of Team Minutes Played

WINNING PERCENTAGE:

				W- L- T	PCT
1	Andrew Gallant	Manhattanville	SR	19- 2- 5	0.827
2	Mike Collichio	Neumann	JR	14- 5- 5	0.688
3	Casey Tuttle	Elmira	FR	11- 5- 3	0.658
4	Adam Dekker	Utica	JR	12- 9- 3	0.562
5	Keith Longo	Hobart	SO	7- 6- 5	0.528
6	Aaron Miller	Lebanon Valley	FR	1-18- 1	0.075

Minimum 33% of Team Minutes Played

Hockey East Association
591 North Avenue, #2
Wakefield, Massachusetts 01880
781.245.2122
www.hockeyeastonline.com

Commissioner
Joe Bertagna
Office: 781.245.2122
Fax: 781.245.2492
jbertagna@hockeyeastonline.com

Associate Commissioner
Kathy Wynters
Office: 781.245.2122
Fax: 781.245.2492
kwynters@hockeyeastonline.com

Director of Public Relations
Brion O'Connor
Office: 781.245.2122
Fax: 781.245.2492
info@hockeyeastonline.com

Supervisor of Officials
Brendan M. Sheehy
Office: 781.245.2122
Fax: 781.245.2492
bsheehy@hockeyeastonline.com

Boston College
Boston University
University of Maine
University of Massachusetts Amherst
University of Massachusetts Lowell
Merrimack College
University of New Hampshire
Northeastern University
Providence College
University of Vermont

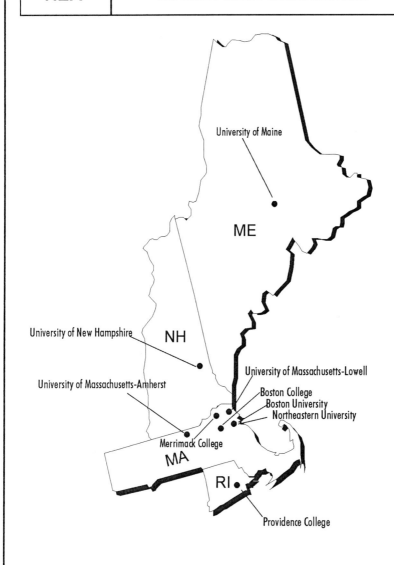

| HEA | HOCKEY EAST ASSOCIATION |

University of Maine

ME

University of New Hampshire

NH

University of Massachusetts-Lowell

University of Massachusetts-Amherst

Boston College
Boston University
Northeastern University

Merrimack College

MA

RI

Providence College

HOCKEY EAST ASSOCIATION
FINAL 2006-07 CONFERENCE STANDINGS

		Pts	GP	Record	Win%	GF-GA	GP	Record	Win%	GF-GA
1	New Hampshire	38	27	18- 7- 2	0.704	96- 62	39	26-11- 2	0.692	139- 89
2	Boston College	37	27	18- 8- 1	0.685	89- 65	42	29-12- 1	0.702	142- 94
3	Boston University	34	27	13- 6- 8	0.630	69- 51	39	20-10- 9	0.628	99- 78
4	Massachusetts	33	27	15- 9- 3	0.611	71- 63	39	21-13- 5	0.603	109- 91
5	Maine	29	27	14-12- 1	0.537	80- 69	40	23-15- 2	0.600	133- 99
	Vermont	29	27	12-10- 5	0.537	55- 56	39	18-16- 5	0.526	87- 78
7	Northeastern	23	27	9-13- 5	0.426	60- 66	36	13-18- 5	0.431	84- 94
8	Providence	21	27	9-15- 3	0.389	66- 71	36	10-23- 3	0.319	76-108
9	UMass Lowell	18	27	7-16- 4	0.333	51- 76	36	8-21- 7	0.319	74-104
10	Merrimack	8	27	3-22- 2	0.148	28- 86	34	3-27- 4	0.147	37-111

2007 HOCKEY EAST PLAYOFFS

QUARTER FINALS *(3.08.07 - 3.10.07)*
(Best of Three Series)

University of Vermont	1	Boston University	2
Northeastern University	0	Boston College	2
Providence College	0	University of New Hampshire	2
University of Maine	0	University of Massachusetts	2

SEMI FINALS *(3.16.07)*

University of Massachusetts	2	University of New Hampshire	3
Boston University	2	Boston College	6

CHAMPIONSHIP *(3.17.07)*

Boston College	5	University of New Hampshire	2

HOCKEY EAST ASSOCIATION CHAMPIONS

	REGULAR	TOURNAMENT
1985	Boston College	Providence College
1986	Boston College	Boston University
1987	Boston College	Boston College
1988	University of Maine	Northeastern University
1989	Boston College	University of Maine
1990	Boston College	Boston College
1991	Boston College	Boston University
1992	University of Maine	University of Maine
1993	University of Maine	University of Maine
1994	Boston University	Boston University
1995	University of Maine	Boston University
1996	Boston University	Providence College
1997	Boston Universtiy	Boston University
	University of New Hampshire	
1998	Boston University	Boston College
1999	University of New Hampshire	Boston College
2000	Boston University	University of Maine
2001	Boston College	Boston College
2002	University of New Hampshire	University of New Hampshire
2003	University of New Hampshire	University of New Hampshire
2004	Boston College	University of Maine
2005	Boston College	Boston College
2006	Boston University	Boston University
2007	University of New Hampshire	Boston College

					GP	PPG	G-A-P
1	Brian Boyle	Boston College	SR	F	42	1.26	19-34-53
2	Nathan Gerbe	Boston College	SO	F	41	1.15	25-22-47
3	Benn Ferriero	Boston College	SO	F	42	1.10	23-23-46
4	Josh Soares	Maine	SR	F	40	1.12	20-25-45
	Michel Léveillé	Maine	SR	F	40	1.12	19-26-45
	Brock Bradford	Boston College	SO	F	42	1.07	19-26-45
7	Trevor Smith	New Hampshire	SO	F	39	1.10	21-22-43
	Teddy Purcell	Maine	FR	F	40	1.07	16-27-43
9	Joe Rooney	Boston College	SR	F	42	1.00	16-26-42
10	Matt Fornataro	New Hampshire	JR	F	39	1.03	13-27-40
11	Jacob Micflikier	New Hampshire	SR	F	36	1.06	11-27-38
12	Mike Radja	New Hampshire	JR	F	33	1.12	19-18-37
13	Pete MacArthur	Boston University	JR	F	39	0.92	16-20-36
14	Chris Capraro	Massachusetts	SR	F	35	1.00	10-25-35
	Torrey Mitchell	Vermont	JR	F	39	0.90	12-23-35
16	Billy Ryan	Maine	JR	F	40	0.82	13-20-33
17	Brett Hemingway	New Hampshire	SR	F	36	0.89	13-19-32
	Chris Higgins	Boston University	SO	F	39	0.82	13-19-32
19	Cory Quirk	Massachusetts	SO	F	39	0.79	13-18-31
	Dean Strong	Vermont	SO	F	39	0.79	13-18-31
	Jerry Pollastrone	New Hampshire	SO	F	39	0.79	9-22-31
22	Kenny Roche	Boston University	SR	F	38	0.76	12-17-29
23	Brett Motherwell	Boston College	SO	D	42	0.67	3-25-28
24	Matt Gilroy	Boston University	SO	D	39	0.67	9-17-26
	Bret Tyler	Maine	JR	D	40	0.65	6-20-26
26	Jon Rheault	Providence	JR	F	35	0.71	12-13-25
	Bryan Ewing	Boston University	JR	F	35	0.71	9-16-25
	P.J. Fenton	Massachusetts	JR	F	39	0.64	10-15-25
	Dan Bertram	Boston College	JR	F	40	0.62	8-17-25
30	Keith Johnson	Maine	SR	F	37	0.65	10-14-24
	Mark Matheson	Massachusetts	SR	D/F	38	0.63	13-11-24
32	Kevin Jarman	Massachusetts	SR	F	35	0.66	9-14-23
	Brad Flaishans	New Hampshire	JR	D	39	0.59	4-19-23
34	Chad Costello	Northeastern	FR	F	32	0.69	11-11-22
	Keenan Hopson	Maine	JR	F	38	0.58	7-15-22
	Chris Murray	New Hampshire	SR	D	39	0.56	9-13-22
	Mike Hamilton	Maine	SR	F	40	0.55	9-13-22
38	Jason Tejchma	UMass Lowell	SR	F	36	0.58	10-11-21
	Nick Mazzolini	Providence	SO	F	36	0.58	5-16-21
	Will Ortiz	Massachusetts	FR	F	38	0.55	7-14-21
41	Matt Anderson	Massachusetts	SR	F	38	0.53	10-10-20
	Mike Lundin	Maine	SR	D	40	0.50	6-14-20
43	Kyle Kraemer	Northeastern	FR	F	33	0.58	7-12-19
	Brayden Irwin	Vermont	FR	F	33	0.58	7-12-19
	Chris Davis	Massachusetts	SO	F	35	0.54	8-11-19
	Peter Lenes	Vermont	SO	F	38	0.50	8-11-19
47	Mike Morris	Northeastern	SR	F	20	0.90	7-11-18
	Kory Falite	UMass Lowell	FR	F	34	0.53	10- 8-18
	Jason Lawrence	Boston University	SO	F	39	0.46	5-13-18
	Mike Kostka	Massachusetts	JR	D	39	0.46	3-15-18
	Ben Smith	Boston College	FR	F	42	0.43	10- 8-18
52	Colin McDonald	Providence	SR	F	36	0.47	13- 4-17
	Jeremy Hall	UMass Lowell	SR	F	36	0.47	8- 9-17
	Corey Carlson	Vermont	SO	F	37	0.46	9- 8-17
	Craig Switzer	New Hampshire	JR	D	39	0.44	3-14-17
56	Steve Birnstill	Northeastern	SR	D	32	0.50	3-13-16
	Brent Shepheard	Maine	SR	F	35	0.46	8- 8-16
	Joe Vitale	Northeastern	SO	F	35	0.46	7- 9-16

	Name	Team	Yr	Pos	GP	Avg	G-A-Pts
	Jeremy Dehner	UMass Lowell	FR	D	36	0.44	3-13-16
	Kenny Macaulay	Vermont	SR	D	39	0.41	3-13-16
61	Mark Roebothan	UMass Lowell	SO	F	34	0.44	7- 8-15
	Josh Ciocco	New Hampshire	SR	F	38	0.39	6- 9-15
	Sean Sullivan	Boston University	SR	D	38	0.39	3-12-15
	Colin Vock	Vermont	FR	F	39	0.38	10- 5-15
	Viktor Stålberg	Vermont	FR	F	39	0.38	7- 8-15
	Ryan Gunderson	Vermont	SR	D	39	0.38	1-14-15
67	Ryan Ginand	Northeastern	SO	F	29	0.48	6- 8-14
	Cody Wild	Providence	SO	D	32	0.44	6- 8-14
	Dennis McCauley	Northeastern	SO	F	33	0.42	5- 9-14
	Jimmy Russo	Northeastern	JR	F	33	0.42	4-10-14
	Nick Schaus	UMass Lowell	FR	D	36	0.39	1-13-14
	Justin Braun	Massachusetts	FR	D	39	0.36	4-10-14
	Mark Lutz	Vermont	JR	D	39	0.36	3-11-14
74	Alex Berry	Massachusetts	SO	F	29	0.45	7- 6-13
	Ben Holmstrom	UMass Lowell	FR	F	30	0.43	4- 9-13
	Wes Clark	Maine	JR	F	32	0.41	8- 5-13
	Greg Collins	Providence	FR	F	33	0.39	5- 8-13
	Bryan Esner	Northeastern	SR	F	36	0.36	8- 5-13
	Tony Zancanaro	Providence	SR	F	36	0.36	5- 8-13
	Thomas Fortney	New Hampshire	SO	F	39	0.33	6- 7-13
81	Paul Worthington	UMass Lowell	FR	F	28	0.43	2-10-12
	Jason Bergeron	UMass Lowell	FR	F	34	0.35	7- 5-12
	Chris Auger	UMass Lowell	FR	F	34	0.35	2-10-12
	Mark Fayne	Providence	FR	D	36	0.33	5- 7-12
	Bobby Butler	New Hampshire	FR	F	38	0.32	9- 3-12
	David Leaderer	Massachusetts	JR	D	39	0.31	4- 8-12
87	Joe Santilli	Northeastern	SR	F	17	0.65	2- 9-11
	Brandon Yip	Boston University	SO	F	18	0.61	5- 6-11
	John Cavanagh	Providence	FR	C	24	0.46	1-10-11
	Pierce Norton	Providence	SO	F	31	0.35	6- 5-11
	Greg Collins	New Hampshire	SO	F	33	0.33	4- 7-11
	Pat Kimball	Merrimack	FR	F	34	0.32	5- 6-11
	Ray Ortiz	Northeastern	SR	F	36	0.31	2- 9-11
	Kyle Laughlin	Providence	SO	F	36	0.31	2- 9-11
	Jamie Fritsch	New Hampshire	SO	D	39	0.28	2- 9-11
	Mike Brennan	Boston College	JR	D	42	0.26	0-11-11
97	Kevin Schaeffer	Boston University	SR	D	33	0.30	6- 4-10
	Matt Byrnes	Merrimack	SR	F	34	0.29	3- 7-10
	Carl Sneep	Boston College	FR	D	38	0.26	1- 9-10
	Matt Duffy	Maine	SO	D	39	0.26	5- 5-10
	Luke Popko	Boston University	FR	F	39	0.26	4- 6-10
102	Eric Thomassian	Boston University	SR	F	18	0.50	0- 9- 9
	Anthony Aiello	Boston College	SO	D	22	0.41	1- 8- 9
	Chase Watson	Providence	SR	F	29	0.31	2- 7- 9
	J.C. Robitaille	Merrimack	FR	F	30	0.30	3- 6- 9
	Cleve Kinley	UMass Lowell	SR	D	31	0.29	3- 6- 9
	Brian Roloff	Vermont	FR	F	38	0.24	4- 5- 9
	Andrew Orpik	Boston College	SO	F	38	0.24	3- 6- 9
109	Chris Myers	Vermont	SR	F	20	0.40	3- 5- 8
	Mike Alexiou	Merrimack	SR	F	24	0.33	2- 6- 8
	Matt Burto	Massachusetts	JR	F	27	0.30	5- 3- 8
	Mike Potacco	UMass Lowell	SO	F	32	0.25	5- 3- 8
	J.R. Bria	UMass Lowell	SR	D	32	0.25	2- 6- 8
	Randy Guzior	Northeastern	FR	F	36	0.22	6- 2- 8
	Rob Bellamy	Maine	JR	F	37	0.22	1- 7- 8
	Matt Greene	Boston College	JR	F	39	0.21	5- 3- 8
	Ryan Weston	Boston University	JR	F	39	0.21	2- 6- 8
	Travis Ramsey	Maine	JR	D	40	0.20	0- 8- 8

119	Jamie Carroll	Providence	SR	F	31	0.23	3- 4- 7
	Matt Taormina	Providence	SO	D	35	0.20	5- 2- 7
121	Chris Donovan	Northeastern	FR	F	24	0.25	4- 2- 6
	Rob Rassey	Northeastern	SO	F	29	0.21	2- 4- 6
	Christopher Hahn	Maine	SO	F	29	0.21	0- 6- 6
	Bryan Horan	Providence	SR	F	30	0.20	3- 3- 6
	Matt Jones	Merrimack	FR	F	32	0.19	4- 2- 6
	Todd Fletcher	UMass Lowell	SR	F	32	0.19	1- 5- 6
	Pat Bowen	Merrimack	FR	D	32	0.19	0- 6- 6
	Frank Stegnar	UMass Lowell	FR	F	34	0.18	3- 3- 6
	Derek Pallardy	Merrimack	JR	F	34	0.18	2- 4- 6
	Brian Strait	Boston University	FR	D	36	0.17	3- 3- 6
	Dinos Stamoulis	Providence	SR	D	36	0.17	2- 4- 6
	Louis Liotti	Northeastern	SO	D	36	0.17	0- 6- 6
	Shawn Vinz	New Hampshire	SR	F	38	0.16	4- 2- 6
	Kevin Kapstad	New Hampshire	SO	D	38	0.16	4- 2- 6
	Simon Danis-Pepin	Maine	SO	D	40	0.15	2- 4- 6
136	Ian Schaser	UMass Lowell	FR	F	20	0.25	2- 3- 5
	Kyle Kucharski	Boston College	SO	F	26	0.19	2- 3- 5
	Matt Price	Boston College	FR	F	26	0.19	2- 3- 5
	Tim Kunes	Boston College	SO	D	27	0.19	1- 4- 5
	Dan McGoff	Boston University	JR	D	32	0.16	4- 1- 5
	Justin Mills	Merrimack	SR	F	33	0.15	1- 4- 5
	Chris Eppich	Providence	FR	F	34	0.15	0- 5- 5
	Patrick Cullity	Vermont	FR	D	34	0.15	0- 5- 5
	Brian O'Hanley	Boston College	JR	D	36	0.14	2- 3- 5
	Brian McGuirk	Boston University	JR	F	36	0.14	1- 4- 5
	John McCarthy	Boston University	SO	F	39	0.13	2- 3- 5
	Scott Crowder	Massachusetts	SO	F	39	0.13	1- 4- 5
	Brett Watson	Massachusetts	FR	F	39	0.13	1- 4- 5
	Peter LeBlanc	New Hampshire	FR	F	39	0.13	1- 4- 5
150	Greg Costa	Northeastern	FR	F	10	0.40	2- 2- 4
	Dan Rossman	New Hampshire	FR	F	18	0.22	1- 3- 4
	David Strathman	Northeastern	FR	D	21	0.19	2- 2- 4
	Vince Laise	Maine	SO	F	22	0.18	1- 3- 4
	Jacques Perreault	Northeastern	SO	D	23	0.17	1- 3- 4
	Chris Kane	Merrimack	SO	D	25	0.16	1- 3- 4
	Jay Anctil	Vermont	FR	F	26	0.15	1- 3- 4
	John Goebel	Merrimack	SO	F	30	0.13	3- 1- 4
	Barry Goers	UMass Lowell	FR	D	30	0.13	1- 3- 4
	Andrew Linard	Northeastern	SO	D	30	0.13	1- 3- 4
	Justin Bonitatibus	Merrimack	FR	F	32	0.12	2- 2- 4
	Martin Nolet	Massachusetts	FR	D	32	0.12	1- 3- 4
	Joe Loprieno	Merrimack	FR	D	32	0.12	1- 3- 4
	Thomas Morrow	Boston University	SR	D	34	0.12	2- 2- 4
	Denis Chisholm	Northeastern	SO	D	35	0.11	2- 2- 4
	Jim Driscoll	Northeastern	FR	D	35	0.11	1- 3- 4
	Nick Monroe	UMass Lowell	SO	F	36	0.11	2- 2- 4
	Matt Lombardi	Boston College	FR	F	37	0.11	1- 3- 4
	Eric Gryba	Boston University	FR	D	38	0.11	1- 3- 4
	Joe Charlebois	New Hampshire	SO	D	39	0.10	0- 4- 4
170	Hank Carisio	Merrimack	JR	F	8	0.38	3- 0- 3
	Art Femenella	Vermont	SR	D	13	0.23	1- 2- 3
	David de Kastrozza	Maine	FR	F	21	0.14	0- 3- 3
	Evan Stoflet	Vermont	SR	D	21	0.14	0- 3- 3
	Yale Lewis	Northeastern	SR	F	24	0.12	1- 2- 3
	John Mori	Providence	SO	F	24	0.12	0- 3- 3
	Brock Wilson	Merrimack	SO	D	25	0.12	1- 2- 3
	Slavomir Tomko	Vermont	JR	D	26	0.12	1- 2- 3
	Tom Collingham	Vermont	SR	F	29	0.10	1- 2- 3

	Marc Bastarche	Providence	JR D	31	0.10	0- 3- 3
	Zach Cohen	Boston University	FR F	33	0.09	1- 2- 3
	Mike Vaskivuo	Merrimack	FR F	33	0.09	1- 2- 3
	Ryan Sullivan	Merrimack	SR D	34	0.09	1- 2- 3
183	Zach Sill	Maine	FR F	6	0.33	1- 1- 2
	Patrick Watson	Merrimack	SO G	12	0.17	0- 2- 2
	David Burkholder	Merrimack	FR D	13	0.15	0- 2- 2
	Jordan Virtue	Massachusetts	SO F	16	0.12	0- 2- 2
	Zech Klann	Massachusetts	JR F	21	0.10	1- 1- 2
	Kyle Kuk	Vermont	SO D	23	0.09	1- 1- 2
	David Cavanagh	Providence	FR D	25	0.08	1- 1- 2
	Trevor Ludwig	Providence	JR D	26	0.08	0- 2- 2
	Mickey Rego	Merrimack	SO F	28	0.07	1- 1- 2
	Carmen Posteraro	Merrimack	JR F	29	0.07	2- 0- 2
	Dan Owens	Vermont	SR F	30	0.07	1- 1- 2
	Reese Wisnowski	Vermont	JR F	30	0.07	0- 2- 2
	Brandon Sadlowski	Merrimack	FR D	32	0.06	0- 2- 2
	Brad Thiessen	Northeastern	FR G	33	0.06	0- 2- 2
	Kevin Regan	New Hampshire	JR G	35	0.06	0- 2- 2
	Jon Quick	Massachusetts	SO G	37	0.05	1- 1- 2
	Tim Filangieri	Boston College	SO D	37	0.05	0- 2- 2
	Pat Gannon	Boston College	JR F	42	0.05	1- 1- 2
	Cory Schneider	Boston College	JR G	42	0.05	0- 2- 2
202	Tyler Czuba	Maine	FR F	3	0.33	0- 1- 1
	Aaron Moore	Northeastern	SR F	4	0.25	0- 1- 1
	Jonathan Higgins	Vermont	FR F	9	0.11	1- 0- 1
	Kelly Sullivan	UMass Lowell	JR D	10	0.10	1- 0- 1
	Brad Cooper	Providence	SO F	10	0.10	0- 1- 1
	Steve Smolinsky	Boston University	SO F	12	0.08	1- 0- 1
	Jordan Hart	Merrimack	JR D	12	0.08	1- 0- 1
	Tony Morrone	Maine	FR F	12	0.08	0- 1- 1
	Jake Pence	UMass Lowell	SR D	14	0.07	0- 1- 1
	Kevin Kielt	Boston University	JR D	18	0.06	0- 1- 1
	Brian Boulay	Merrimack	SR D	20	0.05	0- 1- 1
	Andy Corran	Vermont	SR F	22	0.05	0- 1- 1
	Bryan Plaszcz	Maine	SO D	29	0.03	1- 0- 1
	Topher Bevis	Massachusetts	SO D	29	0.03	0- 1- 1
	Ben Bishop	Maine	SO G	34	0.03	0- 1- 1
	John Wessbecker	Massachusetts	SO D	38	0.03	1- 0- 1

GOALS AGAINST AVERAGE:

				MINUTES	GA	GAA
1	Joe Fallon	Vermont	JR	1996:59:00	62	1.86
2	John Curry	Boston University	SR	2154:20:00	72	2.01
3	Kevin Regan	New Hampshire	JR	2065:55:00	71	2.06
4	Ben Bishop	Maine	SO	1906:40:00	68	2.14
5	Cory Schneider	Boston College	JR	2516:33:00	90	2.15
6	Jon Quick	Massachusetts	SO	2223:38:00	80	2.16
7	Brad Thiessen	Northeastern	FR	1985:06:00	82	2.48
8	Tyler Sims	Providence	JR	1649:52:00	76	2.76
9	Carter Hutton	UMass Lowell	FR	1096:41:00	52	2.84
10	Jim Healey	Merrimack	SR	1126:18:00	56	2.98
11	Patrick Watson	Merrimack	SO	684:53:00	36	3.15

Minimum 33% of Team Minutes Played

SAVE PERCENTAGE:

				SAVES	GA	PCT
1	Kevin Regan	New Hampshire	JR	1025	71	0.935
2	Jon Quick	Massachusetts	SO	1046	80	0.929
3	John Curry	Boston University	SR	928	72	0.928
4	Cory Schneider	Boston College	JR	1111	90	0.925
5	Ben Bishop	Maine	SO	819	68	0.923
6	Brad Thiessen	Northeastern	FR	957	82	0.921
7	Joe Fallon	Vermont	JR	714	62	0.92
8	Jim Healey	Merrimack	SR	509	56	0.901
9	Tyler Sims	Providence	JR	667	76	0.898
10	Carter Hutton	UMass Lowell	FR	418	52	0.889
11	Patrick Watson	Merrimack	SO	279	36	0.886

Minimum 33% of Team Minutes Played

WINNING PERCENTAGE:

				W- L- T	PCT
1	Kevin Regan	New Hampshire	JR	24- 9- 2	0.714
2	Cory Schneider	Boston College	JR	29-12- 1	0.702
3	Ben Bishop	Maine	SO	21- 9- 2	0.688
4	John Curry	Boston University	SR	17-10- 8	0.6
5	Jon Quick	Massachusetts	SO	19-12- 5	0.597
6	Joe Fallon	Vermont	JR	17-14- 3	0.544
7	Brad Thiessen	Northeastern	FR	11-17- 5	0.409
8	Carter Hutton	UMass Lowell	FR	3-10- 5	0.306
9	Tyler Sims	Providence	JR	7-19- 2	0.286
10	Patrick Watson	Merrimack	SO	2- 8- 1	0.227
11	Jim Healey	Merrimack	SR	1-16- 3	0.125

Minimum 33% of Team Minutes Played

Ivy League
228 Alexander Street
Princeton, New Jersey 08544
www.ivyleaguesports.com

Executive Director
Jeffrey H. Orleans
Phone: 609.258.6426
Fax: 609.258.1690
email: jorleans@princeton.edu

Senior Associate Director
Carolyn S. Campbell-McGovern
Phone: 609.258.6426
Fax: 609.258.1690
email: carolyn@princeton.edu

Associate Director
Chuck Yrigoyen III
Phone: 609.258.6426
Fax: 609.258.1690
email: yrigoyen@princeton.edu

Assistant Director
Brett Hoover

Public Information Senior Assistant
LaKesha Whitaker

Public Information Assistant
Eddy Lentz

Brown University
Cornell University
Dartmouth College
Harvard University
Princeton University
Yale University

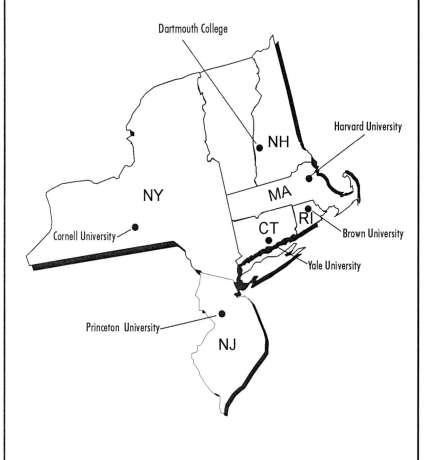

IVY LEAGUE
FINAL 2006-07 CONFERENCE STANDINGS

		Pts	GP	Record	Win%	GF-GA	GP	Record	Win%	GF-GA
1	Dartmouth	13	10	6- 3- 1	0.65	28- 23	33	18-12- 3	0.591	105- 93
	Yale	13	10	6- 3- 1	0.65	35- 26	31	11-17- 3	0.403	78- 98
3	Cornell	11	10	5- 4- 1	0.55	30- 30	31	14-13- 4	0.516	90- 78
4	Brown	8	10	3- 5- 2	0.4	27- 27	32	11-15- 6	0.438	96- 95
	Princeton	8	10	3- 5- 2	0.4	27- 32	34	15-16- 3	0.485	102-100
6	Harvard	7	10	3- 6- 1	0.35	26- 35	33	14-17- 2	0.455	88- 90

IVY LEAGUE REGULAR SEASON CHAMPIONS

1934 Dartmouth College
1935 Yale University
1936 Harvard University
1937 Harvard University
1938 Dartmouth College
1939 Dartmouth College
1940 Yale University
1941 Princeton University
1942 Dartmouth College
1943 Dartmouth College
1947 Dartmouth College
1948 Dartmouth College
1949 Dartmouth College
1950 Brown University
1951 Brown University
1952 Yale University
1953 Princeton University
1954 Harvard University
1955 Harvard University
1956 Harvard University
1957 Harvard University
1958 Harvard University
1959 Dartmouth College
1960 Dartmouth College
1961 Harvard University
1962 Harvard University
1963 Harvard University
1964 Dartmouth College
1965 Brown University
1966 Cornell University
1967 Cornell University
1968 Cornell University
1969 Cornell University
1970 Cornell University
1971 Cornell University
1972 Cornell University
1973 Cornell University
1974 Harvard University

1975 Harvard University
1976 Brown University
1977 Cornell University
1978 Cornell University
1979 Dartmouth College
1980 Dartmouth College
1981 Yale University
1982 Harvard University
1983 Harvard University
        Cornell University
1984 Harvard University
1985 Harvard University
        Cornell University
        Yale University
1986 Harvard University
1987 Harvard University
1988 Harvard University
1989 Harvard University
1990 Harvard University
1991 Brown University
1992 Yale University
1993 Harvard University
1994 Harvard University
1995 Brown University
1996 Cornell University
1997 Cornell University
1998 Yale University
1999 Princeton University
        Yale University
2000 Harvard Universiy
2001 Yale University
2002 Cornell University
2003 Cornell University
2004 Brown University
2005 Cornell University
2006 Harvard University
2007 Dartmouth College

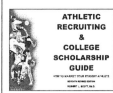

**Midwest Collegiate
Hockey Association**
1025 North Broadway
Milwaukee, Wisconsin 53202
www.mchahockey.com

President
Terry Brand
Office 715.359.6563
Cell 715.216.5700
Fax 715.355.9153
Email: tbrand@dce.k12.wi.us

Public Relations Director / Secretary
Chris Zills
Office 414.229.4593
Fax 414.229.6759
czills@uwm.edu

Referee Supervisor
Ed Zepeda
Office 651.578.3712
ed.zepeda@thomson.com

Adrian College *(2007/2008)*

Concordia University Wisconsin *(2007/2008)*

Finlandia University

Lake Forest College *(2009/2010)*

Lawrence University

Marian College of Fond du Lac

Milwaukee School of Engineering

University of Minnesota Crookston

Northland College

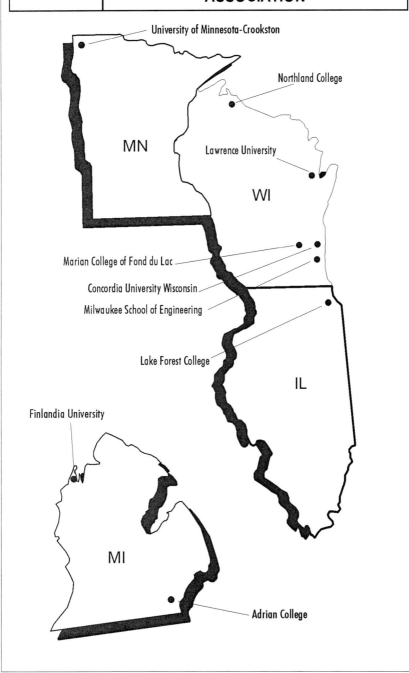

MCHA	**MIDWEST COLLEGIATE HOCKEY ASSOCIATION**

University of Minnesota-Crookston

Northland College

MN

Lawrence University

WI

Marian College of Fond du Lac

Concordia University Wisconsin

Milwaukee School of Engineering

Lake Forest College

IL

Finlandia University

MI

Adrian College

MIDWEST COLLEGIATE HOCKEY ASSOCIATION
FINAL 2006-07 CONFERENCE STANDINGS

		Pts	GP	Record	Win%	GF-GA	GP	Record	Win%	GF-GA
1	Milwaukee Engineering	34	20	16- 2- 2	0.850	89- 43	27	19- 6- 2	0.741	119- 71
2	Finlandia	30	20	15- 5- 0	0.750	106- 47	27	19- 8- 0	0.704	134- 76
3	Marian	26	20	12- 6- 2	0.650	83- 51	29	14-12- 3	0.534	114- 88
4	Lawrence	17	20	8-11- 1	0.425	60- 66	29	13-14- 2	0.483	87- 95
5	Minnesote-Crookston	12	20	5-13- 2	0.300	54- 93	26	7-16- 3	0.327	72-123
6	Northland	1	20	0-19- 1	0.025	29-121	27	0-26- 1	0.019	35-159

2007 MIDWEST COLLEGIATE HOCKEY ASSOCIATION PLAYOFFS

QUARTER FINALS *(2.23-24.07)*

Northland College	0	Marion College	9
Northland College	1	Marion College	7
University of Minnesota-Crookston	3	Lawrence University	5
University of Minnesota-Crookston	2	Lawrence University	2

SEMI FINALS *(3.03.07)*

Lawrence University	0	Milwaukee School of Engineering	4
Marion College	3	Finlandia College	6

THIRD PLACE *(3.04.07)*

Lawrence College	4	Marion College	2

CHAMPIONSHIP *(3.04.07)*

Finlandia College	4	Milwaukee School of Engineering	3

MIDWEST COLLEGIATE HOCKEY ASSOCIATION CHAMPIONS

	REGULAR		TOURNAMENT
1999	University of Findlay	1999	University of Findlay
2000	University of Minnesota-Crookston	2000	University of Minnesota-Crookston
2001	University of Minnesota-Crookston	2001	Marian College of Fond Du Lac
2002	Marian College of Fond Du Lac	2002	Marian College of Fond Du Lac
2003	University of Minnesota-Crookston	2003	University of Minnesota-Crookston
2004	Marian College of Fond Du Lac	2004	University of Minnesota-Crookston
2005	Milwaukee School of Engineering	2005	Milwaukee School of Engineering
2006	Milwaukee School of Engineering	2006	Milwaukee School of Engineering
2007	Milwaukee School of Engineering	2007	Finlandia College

				GP	PPG	G - A - P
1	Josh Paquette	Finlandia	JR F	27	1.70	21-25-46
2	Lee Swallow	Milwaukee S. E.	JR F	27	1.44	16-23-39
3	Ryan Sullivan	Finlandia	SO F	27	1.41	24-14-38
4	Blair Hanberg	Milwaukee S. E.	JR F	27	1.37	24-13-37
	Joe Beaudry	Finlandia	SO F	27	1.37	14-23-37
6	James Goodfellow	Marian	SO F	28	1.25	17-18-35
	Joe Searl	Lawrence	SR F	29	1.21	18-17-35
8	Brian Soik	Milwaukee S. E.	SR F	26	1.31	7-27-34
9	R.G. Flath	Milwaukee S. E.	SO F	27	1.22	19-14-33
10	Marc Marcotte	Finlandia	SO D	24	1.25	8-22-30
11	Nick Cinquegrani	Marian	FR F	26	1.12	14-15-29
12	Mike Parks	Finlandia	JR F	24	1.17	12-16-28
13	Teal Plaine	Minn-Crookston	JR F	26	1.04	12-15-27
	Marc Howe	Lawrence	FR F	29	0.93	15-12-27
15	Ryan Leadens	Minn-Crookston	SR F/D	26	1.00	10-16-26
	Michael Duta	Milwaukee S. E.	SR F	27	0.96	10-16-26
	Carl Bresser	Marian	JR F	28	0.93	15-11-26
18	Jason Woll	Milwaukee S. E.	SO D	25	0.92	6-17-23
	Matt Hann	Minn-Crookston	JR F	26	0.88	9-14-23
	Nick Jennette	Lawrence	SO F	29	0.79	8-15-23
21	Simon Labrosse-Gelinas	Milwaukee S. E.	SO F	26	0.85	6-16-22
	Keith Johnstone	Finlandia	SO F	27	0.81	10-12-22
23	Andrew Corvo	Marian	SO F	26	0.81	10-11-21
	Blake Miller	Finlandia	JR D	26	0.81	9-12-21
	Bill Griffore Jr.	Marian	SO F	29	0.72	11-10-21
26	Jacob Anderson	Milwaukee S. E.	SO F	26	0.77	5-15-20
27	Kalle Larsson	Lawrence	SR F	22	0.86	10- 9-19
28	Nick Bilpush	Milwaukee S. E.	SR F	27	0.67	12- 6-18
	Travis Hanson	Finlandia	JR F	27	0.67	8-10-18
	Jason Ford	Marian	FR F	28	0.64	3-15-18
	Billy Siers	Lawrence	FR F	29	0.62	9- 9-18
32	John Lombardi	Minn-Crookston	FR F	24	0.71	5-12-17
33	Lindsey Boulter	Northland	FR F	27	0.59	10- 6-16
	Jim Junker	Northland	SR F	27	0.59	8- 8-16
35	Jason Aldrich	Finlandia	JR F	27	0.56	6- 9-15
	Tyler Fletcher	Marian	FR F	27	0.56	6- 9-15
	Josh Peterson	Lawrence	JR D	27	0.56	3-12-15
38	Brian Ferguson	Minn-Crookston	FR F	25	0.56	9- 5-14
	Corey Blake	Finlandia	SO F	27	0.52	1-13-14
	Brett Fox	Marian	SR D	29	0.48	4-10-14
	Nick Henkemeyer	Marian	FR D	29	0.48	2-12-14
42	Evan Thornton	Lawrence	SR F	27	0.48	6- 7-13
	Gregory Copeland	Marian	SO D	27	0.48	1-12-13
	Jeffrey Wills	Marian	SO D	28	0.46	3-10-13
45	Brent Groenke	Minn-Crookston	JR D	24	0.50	6- 6-12
	Aaron LaFave	Lawrence	SO F	28	0.43	2-10-12
47	Joe Welgos	Finlandia	SR F	20	0.55	5- 6-11
	Josh McAndrew	Marian	SO F	28	0.39	4- 7-11
	Ryan Hitchcock	Marian	FR F	29	0.38	4- 7-11
50	Travis Van Dyn Hoven	Marian	JR F	18	0.56	5- 5-10
	Michael Jantzi	Milwaukee S. E.	FR D	20	0.50	3- 7-10
	Ryan Tucker	Minn-Crookston	JR D	26	0.38	1- 9-10
	Kyle Jones	Marian	SO D	27	0.37	4- 6-10
54	Ross Rouleau	Finlandia	FR D	14	0.64	0- 9- 9
	Matt Marchel	Minn-Crookston	FR D	19	0.47	3- 6- 9
	Mike Ackley	Lawrence	SO D	19	0.47	1- 8- 9
	Matt Waclawik	Minn-Crookston	FR F	23	0.39	5- 4- 9
	Fred Kooser	Minn-Crookston	FR F	25	0.36	3- 6- 9

	Ken Walters	Milwaukee S. E.	JR	D	26	0.35	3- 6- 9
	David Olynyk	Lawrence	SR	F	29	0.31	2- 7- 9
61	Derek Onkalo	Finlandia	SR	F	25	0.32	3- 5- 8
	Brandon VanAcker	Finlandia	FR	F	27	0.30	3- 5- 8
	Matt Tanneberg	Northland	FR	D	27	0.30	2- 6- 8
64	Ross Chawansky	Milwaukee S. E.	JR	D	21	0.33	0- 7- 7
	Kasey Kreuter	Finlandia	FR	D	24	0.29	5- 2- 7
	Andy Finco	Northland	FR	F	26	0.27	1- 6- 7
	Kyle Rasmussen	Marian	SO	F	28	0.25	4- 3- 7
	Austin Montgomery	Lawrence	JR	D	28	0.25	2- 5- 7
69	Chad Kenyon	Milwaukee S. E.	FR	F	19	0.32	2- 4- 6
	Reid Crawford	Milwaukee S. E.	FR	F	20	0.30	3- 3- 6
	Peter Stafford	Lawrence	SO	D	22	0.27	0- 6- 6
	Josh Spiegel	Northland	FR	F	23	0.26	4- 2- 6
	Brett Saari	Minn-Crookston	SO	F	24	0.25	2- 4- 6
	Ryan Hunt	Northland	JR	F	27	0.22	0- 6- 6
75	Taurean White	Northland	FR	D	13	0.38	2- 3- 5
	Charles Zieserl	Lawrence	FR	D	13	0.38	0- 5- 5
	Billy Schill	Marian	SO	F	19	0.26	3- 2- 5
	Jason Yolo	Milwaukee S. E.	SO	D	24	0.21	0- 5- 5
	Steve O'Hern	Northland	JR	D/F	27	0.19	1- 4- 5
	Blake Royle	Lawrence	SO	D	28	0.18	1- 4- 5
81	Collin Perry	Minn-Crookston	FR	F	11	0.36	2- 2- 4
	Ross Oestreich	Marian	SO	F	13	0.31	1- 3- 4
	Jesse Jacobs	Lawrence	SO	F	14	0.29	2- 2- 4
	Brad VanTassel	Finlandia	JR	D	18	0.22	0- 4- 4
	Jacob Osland	Minn-Crookston	SO	F/D	20	0.20	1- 3- 4
	David Yolo	Milwaukee S. E.	SR	D	23	0.17	1- 3- 4
	Masa Takahashi	Lawrence	FR	F	25	0.16	4- 0- 4
	Jon Sacks	Lawrence	FR	F	26	0.15	1- 3- 4
	Matt Lindgren	Finlandia	SO	D	27	0.15	2- 2- 4
	Alex Ehler	Northland	FR	F	27	0.15	2- 2- 4
	Brian Zwawa	Northland	FR	D	27	0.15	2- 2- 4
92	Scott Ross	Marian	SO	D	9	0.33	0- 3- 3
	Chris Lawson	Lawrence	SO	F	21	0.14	0- 3- 3
	Neil Wallace	Lawrence	JR	F	22	0.14	1- 2- 3
	Mike Marquette	Milwaukee S. E.	SO	D/F	23	0.13	0- 3- 3
	Michael Herbert	Marian	FR	F	24	0.12	3- 0- 3
	Matt Fastelin	Milwaukee S. E.	JR	F	24	0.12	2- 1- 3
	Kyle Sponholtz	Minn-Crookston	JR	D	24	0.12	0- 3- 3
	Eric DeCaires	Northland	JR	D	27	0.11	1- 2- 3
100	CJ Fisher	Finlandia	JR	F	7	0.29	0- 2- 2
	Donovan Haugstad	Minn-Crookston	FR	F	10	0.20	2- 0- 2
	Matt Krueger	Finlandia	FR	F	11	0.18	2- 0- 2
	Chris Sculley	Minn-Crookston	FR	F	11	0.18	0- 2- 2
	Joe Juntilla	Finlandia	SR	G	13	0.15	0- 2- 2
	Clark Dingeman	Minn-Crookston	FR	D	20	0.10	1- 1- 2
	Bryan Solander	Finlandia	FR	D	21	0.10	0- 2- 2
	Thomas Anick	Minn-Crookston	FR	F	22	0.09	0- 2- 2
	Adam Brand	Lawrence	SO	D	24	0.08	2- 0- 2
	Bo Storozuk	Northland	FR	G	26	0.08	0- 2- 2
	Joe Belanger	Northland	FR	D/F	27	0.07	1- 1- 2
111	Jonathan Stover	Milwaukee S. E.	FR	D	2	0.50	0- 1- 1
	Jack Aide	Marian	JR	F	5	0.20	0- 1- 1
	Travis Pederson	Minn-Crookston	SO	F	10	0.10	1- 0- 1
	Ted Thompson Jr.	Marian	JR	D	12	0.08	0- 1- 1
	Jason Jadczak	Marian	SO	G	13	0.08	0- 1- 1
	Lukas Alberer	Finlandia	JR	G	14	0.07	0- 1- 1
	Ted Greeley	Lawrence	SO	D	16	0.06	0- 1- 1
	Mitch Tallent	Finlandia	JR	F	17	0.06	1- 0- 1

Paul Haviland	Milwaukee S. E.	FR	D	17	0.06	0- 1- 1
Mike Stevens	Northland	JR	F	18	0.06	0- 1- 1
Peter Jerome	Minn-Crookston	FR	F	21	0.05	0- 1- 1
Steve Zutz	Minn-Crookston	SR	F	24	0.04	0- 1- 1
Pat Sierocinski	Northland	FR	F	26	0.04	0- 1- 1
Mike Tatavosian	Northland	JR	F	27	0.04	1- 0- 1

GOALS AGAINST AVERAGE:

				MINUTES	GA	GAA
1	Cullen Caldwell	Marian	FR	1002:54:00	41	2.45
2	Lukas Alberer	Finlandia	JR	843:48:00	35	2.49
3	Matt Burzon	Milwaukee S. E.	SR	1122:03:00	53	2.83
4	Joe Juntilla	Finlandia	SR	781:00:00	40	3.07
5	Andrew Isaac	Lawrence	SR	1325:06:00	70	3.17
6	Kyle Knudsen	Minn-Crookston	SR	758:04:00	48	3.8
7	Jason Jadczak	Marian	SO	621:13:00	40	3.86
8	Bo Storozuk	Northland	FR	1453:02:00	135	5.57

Minimum 33% of Team Minutes Played

SAVE PERCENTAGE:

				SAVES	GA	PCT
1	Cullen Caldwell	Marian	FR	445	41	0.916
2	Andrew Isaac	Lawrence	SR	672	70	0.906
3	Matt Burzon	Milwaukee S. E.	SR	482	53	0.901
4	Lukas Alberer	Finlandia	JR	310	35	0.899
5	Bo Storozuk	Northland	FR	1091	135	0.89
6	Jason Jadczak	Marian	SO	300	40	0.882
7	Joe Juntilla	Finlandia	SR	294	40	0.88
8	Kyle Knudsen	Minn-Crookston	SR	351	48	0.88

Minimum 33% of Team Minutes Played

WINNING PERCENTAGE:

				W- L- T	PCT
1	Lukas Alberer	Finlandia	JR	11- 3- 0	0.786
2	Matt Burzon	Milwaukee S. E.	SR	13- 3- 2	0.778
3	Cullen Caldwell	Marian	FR	9- 5- 2	0.625
4	Joe Juntilla	Finlandia	SR	8- 5- 0	0.615
5	Andrew Isaac	Lawrence	SR	12-10- 1	0.543
6	Kyle Knudsen	Minn-Crookston	SR	6- 5- 1	0.542
7	Jason Jadczak	Marian	SO	3- 7- 1	0.318
8	Bo Storozuk	Northland	FR	0-25- 1	0.019

Minimum 33% of Team Minutes Played

Minnesota Intercollegiate Athletic Conference
475 Cleveland Avenue N., Ste. 307
St. Paul, MN 55104
www.miac-online.org

Executive Director
Dan McKane
Phone: 651.644.3964
Fax: 651.647.6422
Email: dpmckane@miac-online.org

Assistant to the Executive Director
Matt Ten Haken
Phone: 651.644.3965
Fax: 651.647.6422
E-mail: mtenhaken@miac-online.org

Assistant Director
Kelly Anderson
Phone: 651.246.5957
E-mail: kdiercks@miac-online.org

Augsburg College

Bethel University

Concordia College

Gustavus Adolphus College

Hamline University

St. John's University

St. Mary's College of Minnesota

St. Olaf College

University of St. Thomas

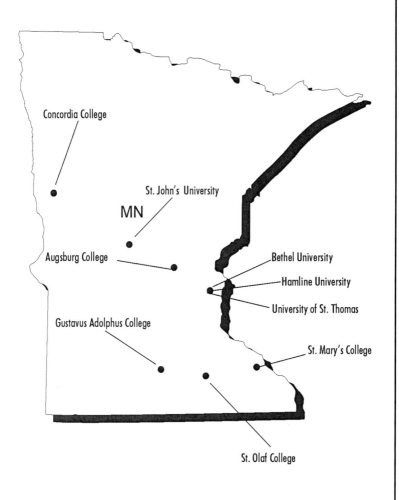

MINNESOTA INTERCOLLEGIATE ATHLETIC CONFERENCE

FINAL 2006-07 CONFERENCE STANDINGS

		Pts	GP	Record	Win%	GF-GA	GP	Record	Win%	GF-GA
1	Bethel	25	16	12- 3- 1	0.781	69- 35	29	18-10- 1	0.638	112- 82
2	St. Thomas	24	16	12- 4- 0	0.750	76- 46	27	17-10- 0	0.630	107- 82
3	Augsburg	22	16	9- 3- 4	0.688	59- 42	26	12-10- 4	0.538	85- 75
4	St. Olaf	20	16	9- 5- 2	0.625	50- 45	27	11-14- 2	0.444	70- 80
5	Gustavus Adolphus	19	16	9- 6- 1	0.594	51- 49	26	11-13- 2	0.462	85- 92
6	St. John's	13	16	6- 9- 1	0.406	45- 49	25	9-14- 2	0.400	67- 77
7	St. Mary's	9	16	4-11- 1	0.281	46- 54	25	7-17- 1	0.300	74- 96
8	Concordia	6	16	3-13- 0	0.188	40- 76	25	7-18- 0	0.280	70-117
	Hamline	6	16	3-13- 0	0.188	39- 79	25	7-18- 0	0.280	71-123

2007 MINNESOTA INTERCOLLEGIATE ATHLETIC CONFERENCE PLAYOFFS

PLAY-IN ROUND *(2.27.07)*

Gustavus Adolphus College   1   St. Olaf College   3

SEMI FINALS *(3.01.07)*

Augsburg College   1   University of St. Thomas   3

St. Olaf College   1   Bethel University   5

CHAMPIONSHIP *(3.03.07)*

University of St. Thomas   3   Bethel College   5

MINNESOTA INTERCOLLEGIATE ATHLETIC CONFERENCE CHAMPIONS

1923	University of St. Thomas	1964	St. Mary's College
	Hamline College	1965	St. Mary's College
	Macalester College	1966	Gustavus Adolphus College
1924	No Title (World War I)	1967	Gustavus Adolphus College
1925	No Title (World War I)	1968	Gustavus Adolphus College
1926	No Title (World War I)	1699	Gustavus Adolphus College
1927	No Title (World War I)	1970	Gustavus Adolphus College
1928	Augsburg College	1971	Gustavus Adolphus College
1929	St. Mary's College	1972	Gustavus Adolphus College
1930	Macalester College	1973	Gustavus Adolphus College
1931	Macalester College	1974	University of St. Thomas
1932	Hamline College	1975	Gustavus Adolphus College
	Macalester College	1976	Gustavus Adolphus College
1933	Macalester College	1977	Gustavus Adolphus College
1934	University of St. Thomas		Augsburg College
1935	St. John's College	1978	Augsburg College
1936	Macalester College	1979	Augsburg College
1937	Macalester College	1980	Augsburg College
1938	University of St. Thomas	1981	Augsburg College
	St. Olaf College		Concordia College
1939	St. Olaf College	1982	Augsburg College
	Macalester College	1983	University of St. Thomas
1940	University of St. Thomas	1984	Gustavus Adolphus College
1941	University of St. Thomas	1985	University of St. Thomas
1942	University of St. Thomas	1986	University of St. Thomas
1943	No Title (World War II)	1987	Concordia College
1944	No Title (World War II)	1988	St. Mary's College
1945	No Title (World War II)	1989	University of St. Thomas
1946	No Title (World War II)	1990	University of St. Thomas
1947	University of St. Thomas	1991	University of St. Thomas
1948	Hamline College	1992	University of St. Thomas
1949	University of St. Thomas	1993	University of St. Thomas
1950	Macalester College		Gustavus Adolphus College
	St. John's College	1994	University of St. Thomas
1951	Macalester College	1995	St. Mary's College
	University of St. Thomas	1996	St. John's College
1952	University of St. Thomas	1997	St. John's College
1953	University of St. Thomas	1998	Augsburg College
	University of Minnesota-Duluth	1999	University of St. Thomas
1954	University of Minnesota-Duluth	2000	Concordia College
1955	University of St. Thomas	2001	St. John's College
1956	University of Minnesota-Duluth	2002	University of St. Thomas
1957	University of Minnesota-Duluth	2003	St. John's College
1958	University of Minnesota-Duluth	2004	St. John's College
1959	University of Minnesota-Duluth	2005	St. John's University
1960	University of Minnesota-Duluth	2006	University of St. Thomas
1961	University of Minnesota-Duluth	2007	Bethel College
1962	Macalester College		
1963	Macalester College		

#	Name	Team			GP	PPG	G - A - P
1	Nick Pernula	St. Thomas	JR	F	27	1.74	25-22-47
2	Kevin Rollwagen	St. Thomas	SR	F	27	1.63	20-24-44
3	Aaron Johnson	Augsburg	SR	F	26	1.62	15-27-42
4	Nick Harris	St. Thomas	SR	F	26	1.58	16-25-41
5	Critter Nagurski	Augsburg	SR	F	26	1.54	17-23-40
6	Dustin Fulton	Hamline	SO	F	25	1.36	13-21-34
7	Nick Miller	Bethel	SO	F	29	1.00	10-19-29
8	Eric Bigham	Gustavus Adolphus	FR	F	25	1.08	11-16-27
	Anthony Bohn	St. Mary's	FR	F	25	1.08	8-19-27
10	Alec Holen	Concordia	SO	F	20	1.30	13-13-26
11	Steve Festler	Hamline	SO	F	25	1.00	14-11-25
	Mike Hosfield	Gustavus Adolphus	SR	F	26	0.96	7-18-25
	Jeff Balvin	Bethel	JR	F	29	0.86	7-18-25
14	Ryan Clukey	Concordia	SO	F	24	0.96	8-15-23
	Joe Long	Hamline	SO	F	25	0.92	13-10-23
	Jon Keseley	Gustavus Adolphus	SR	D	26	0.88	11-12-23
	Steve Eastman	Bethel	SR	D/F	29	0.79	9-14-23
18	Adam Gill	St. Mary's	JR	F	25	0.88	13- 9-22
	Steven Jensen	Gustavus Adolphus	SR	F	26	0.85	7-15-22
	Nate Ryan	St. Thomas	JR	F	27	0.81	8-14-22
21	Benoit Duhamel	Bethel	JR	F	25	0.84	8-13-21
	A.J. Hau	Augsburg	FR	F	26	0.81	10-11-21
	Ben Ollila	Gustavus Adolphus	JR	F	26	0.81	8-13-21
	Dylan Mueller	St. Olaf	SO	F	26	0.81	8-13-21
	Brad Peterson	Bethel	SO	F	29	0.72	9-12-21
26	Tony Janssen	Concordia	FR	F	25	0.80	8-12-20
	Greg May	Augsburg	SR	F	26	0.77	11- 9-20
	Kent Bostrom	Bethel	SO	F	29	0.69	9-11-20
	Jon Kramer	Bethel	SR	F	29	0.69	8-12-20
	Dan Bonne	Bethel	JR	F	29	0.69	8-12-20
31	Justin Wild	St. John's	SR	F	24	0.79	9-10-19
	Knut Bitustoeyl	Concordia	FR	F	25	0.76	9-10-19
	Chris Johnson	Augsburg	FR	F	26	0.73	8-11-19
34	David Gross	St. Mary's	JR	F	25	0.72	9- 9-18
	Matt Staehely	St. Mary's	FR	F	25	0.72	9- 9-18
36	Tim Ornell	Gustavus Adolphus	JR	F	22	0.77	10- 7-17
	Joe Welch	Gustavus Adolphus	FR	F	22	0.77	7-10-17
	Andy Roberts	St. Mary's	SO	F	25	0.68	5-12-17
	Jeff Budish	St. Olaf	JR	F	26	0.65	8- 9-17
	Ryan Van Bockel	St. Thomas	SR	D	27	0.63	1-16-17
41	Mark Buchholz	Concordia	SR	D	25	0.64	4-12-16
	John Paulson	St. Olaf	JR	D	27	0.59	8- 8-16
43	Cory Johnson	Concordia	SO	F	20	0.75	4-11-15
	Blake Williams	St. John's	SR	F	22	0.68	3-12-15
	Jesse Polk	St. Mary's	JR	F	25	0.60	10- 5-15
	Neal Carlson	Bethel	SR	D	25	0.60	5-10-15
	Ryan Hoehn	St. Thomas	JR	F	27	0.56	7- 8-15
48	Jake Hipp	St. John's	SO	F	20	0.70	7- 7-14
	John Egge	St. Olaf	SR	F	22	0.64	5- 9-14
	Tom Freeman	St. John's	JR	F	24	0.58	6- 8-14
	Nick Stalock	St. Olaf	SO	F	25	0.56	8- 6-14
	Kyle Kurr	Hamline	FR	F	25	0.56	5- 9-14
	Pat Eagles	St. John's	JR	F	25	0.56	4-10-14
	Matt Hall	Bethel	JR	F	27	0.52	6- 8-14
	Ryan Adams	Bethel	SR	F	29	0.48	7- 7-14
	Bill Menozzi	Bethel	JR	D	29	0.48	3-11-14
57	Patrick Dynan	Bethel	FR	F	19	0.68	7- 6-13
	Blaine Gamst	Concordia	FR	F	25	0.52	5- 8-13

	Cory Krogen	Hamline	FR	D	25	0.52	1-12-13
	Chad Georgell	Augsburg	SR	D	26	0.50	1-12-13
61	Tom Knutson	St. Thomas	SO	F	23	0.52	2-10-12
	Pat Connelly	St. John's	SO	F	25	0.48	9- 3-12
	Kevin Eidsmo	St. Mary's	JR	D	25	0.48	1-11-12
	Brett Way	Augsburg	SO	F	26	0.46	6- 6-12
	Niko Suoraniemi	Gustavus Adolphus	JR	D	26	0.46	3- 9-12
	Casey Dynan	St. Olaf	SO	F	27	0.44	5- 7-12
67	Lee Joos	Hamline	FR	F	24	0.46	6- 5-11
	Sami Idris	Gustavus Adolphus	JR	F	24	0.46	5- 6-11
	Andy Ockuly	St. Olaf	JR	F	25	0.44	6- 5-11
	Shawn Bakke	Augsburg	SR	F	26	0.42	4- 7-11
	Brent Kettelkamp	Bethel	SO	D	27	0.41	5- 6-11
72	Andy Panchenko	St. Thomas	JR	F	21	0.48	6- 4-10
	Ian Ross	St. John's	SR	F	22	0.45	7- 3-10
	Joachim Flaten	Concordia	FR	F	25	0.40	4- 6-10
	Alex Coles	St. Thomas	FR	F	25	0.40	3- 7-10
76	Mike Christensen	St. Mary's	FR	F	20	0.45	6- 3- 9
	Justin Hanna	Hamline	SO	D	22	0.41	1- 8- 9
	Matt Wocken	St. John's	SR	D	24	0.38	3- 6- 9
	Mike MacMillan	St. Olaf	JR	F	24	0.38	2- 7- 9
	Todd Alexander	St. Thomas	SO	D	27	0.33	4- 5- 9
	John Kovacs	Bethel	SO	D	28	0.32	2- 7- 9
82	Andrew Birkholz	Hamline	SO	F	10	0.80	3- 5- 8
	Joel Stacklie	St. John's	SO	F	18	0.44	5- 3- 8
	Matt Buckley	Hamline	SO	F	20	0.40	5- 3- 8
	Alex Arnason	St. Thomas	FR	F	20	0.40	4- 4- 8
	Cody Mosbeck	Gustavus Adolphus	FR	D	25	0.32	2- 6- 8
	Cullum Buetow-Staples	St. Mary's	SR	F	25	0.32	2- 6- 8
	A.J. Woodward	St. Mary's	FR	D	25	0.32	2- 6- 8
	Jeff Miller	St. Mary's	FR	D	25	0.32	1- 7- 8
	John Arundel	Gustavus Adolphus	SR	F	26	0.31	6- 2- 8
	Nick Nelson	St. Thomas	JR	F	26	0.31	5- 3- 8
92	Clayton Rehm	St. John's	SO	D	18	0.39	0- 7- 7
	Danny Carlson	Augsburg	JR	F	21	0.33	2- 5- 7
	Rory Dynan	Bethel	FR	F	22	0.32	3- 4- 7
	Andrew Edwards	St. Thomas	SR	D	25	0.28	1- 6- 7
96	Sean Lofgren	Concordia	SO	F	18	0.33	3- 3- 6
	Matt Kaiser	St. Thomas	JR	F	19	0.32	0- 6- 6
	Mitch Mudra	St. Olaf	SR	D	20	0.30	1- 5- 6
	Jordan Swan	St. John's	JR	F	21	0.29	1- 5- 6
	Eric Dahl	St. Mary's	FR	F	22	0.27	1- 5- 6
	Justin Green	St. Olaf	JR	F	23	0.26	5- 1- 6
	Ben Umhoefer	St. Olaf	FR	F	23	0.26	4- 2- 6
	Ben Kenyon	St. Mary's	FR	F	23	0.26	0- 6- 6
	Jim Erickson	Hamline	SO	F	24	0.25	2- 4- 6
	Sam Windsor	St. Olaf	SO	D	24	0.25	2- 4- 6
	Jason Weigel	St. John's	JR	F	25	0.24	4- 2- 6
	Tom Doyle	Augsburg	SR	F	26	0.23	3- 3- 6
	A.J. Panchenko	St. Thomas	SO	D	26	0.23	2- 4- 6
109	Kevin Kratz	Concordia	SO	F	12	0.42	3- 2- 5
	Michael McDonough	Hamline	SO	F	22	0.23	3- 2- 5
	Carl Babich	Concordia	SO	D/F	22	0.23	2- 3- 5
	Casey Olson	Concordia	FR	D	23	0.22	0- 5- 5
	Shawn Goos	Concordia	FR	F	24	0.21	1- 4- 5
	Nate Meinz	St. John's	JR	D	24	0.21	1- 4- 5
115	Karl Gilbert	St. John's	FR	F	12	0.33	1- 3- 4
	Lance Wheeler	St. John's	SO	D	14	0.29	0- 4- 4
	Gabriel Harren	St. John's	FR	F	15	0.27	3- 1- 4
	Nate Peasley	Bethel	SR	D	15	0.27	2- 2- 4

	Name	School						
	Karl Reinke	St. Mary's	SO	F	18	0.22	2- 2- 4
	Mike Carr	Gustavus Adolphus	SO	F	20	0.20	0- 4- 4
	Dustin Postell	Hamline	FR	D	22	0.18	1- 3- 4
	Jay Phillips	Gustavus Adolphus	SR	D	23	0.17	2- 2- 4
	Kevin Broten	Bethel	SO	F	24	0.17	1- 3- 4
	Kyle Dynan	Bethel	FR	D	24	0.17	1- 3- 4
	Chris Babich	Concordia	SO	D	24	0.17	1- 3- 4
	Ben Bradbury	Augsburg	SO	D	25	0.16	2- 2- 4
	James Leathers	Gustavus Adolphus	FR	F	25	0.16	2- 2- 4
	Dan Leopold	Augsburg	JR	D	26	0.15	2- 2- 4
	Kellen Chamblee	Augsburg	SO	F	26	0.15	1- 3- 4
130	Dan Perry	Concordia	SR	F	5	0.60	1- 2- 3
	Roger Trousdale	St. Olaf	SO	F	10	0.30	0- 3- 3
	Scott Paul	St. John's	SO	F	14	0.21	2- 1- 3
	Barret Simons	St. Olaf	SO	D	15	0.20	1- 2- 3
	Joe McEaney	St. Thomas	FR	F	15	0.20	1- 2- 3
	Kyle Hilmershausen	St. Olaf	SR	F	17	0.18	1- 2- 3
	Brett Sands	Concordia	FR	F	18	0.17	1- 2- 3
	Tony Palma	Gustavus Adolphus	FR	D	18	0.17	0- 3- 3
	Tom Hartman	St. John's	SR	D	18	0.17	0- 3- 3
	Sam Lundquist	Hamline	FR	D	19	0.16	0- 3- 3
	Bill Leier	St. Mary's	FR	D	19	0.16	0- 3- 3
	Patrick Fogerty	Augsburg	SO	D	20	0.15	1- 2- 3
	Adam Fleishman	St. Mary's	SR	F	21	0.14	2- 1- 3
	Matthew Andres	Gustavus Adolphus	FR	F	21	0.14	1- 2- 3
	Jacob Smith	Augsburg	JR	F	21	0.14	0- 3- 3
	Jimmy VanAsch	Hamline	FR	D	22	0.14	1- 2- 3
	Adam Campbell	Concordia	FR	F	23	0.13	2- 1- 3
	Spencer Campion	Gustavus Adolphus	FR	D	24	0.12	0- 3- 3
	Thomas Erickson	Augsburg	SR	F	26	0.12	2- 1- 3
	David Adams	St. Olaf	FR	D	26	0.12	1- 2- 3
	Garrett Gruenke	St. Thomas	JR	D	26	0.12	0- 3- 3
151	Joe Mayer	St. Mary's	FR	F	4	0.50	1- 1- 2
	Jake Bergquist	Hamline	FR	F	5	0.40	1- 1- 2
	Tyler Neu	Concordia	JR	F	6	0.33	0- 2- 2
	Andrew Birkholz	St. Olaf	SO	F	6	0.33	0- 2- 2
	Morgan Sheperd	St. Mary's	FR	F	7	0.29	1- 1- 2
	Nick Carlson	St. Mary's	FR	D	8	0.25	0- 2- 2
	Deven VanHouse	St. Mary's	SO	F	9	0.22	1- 1- 2
	Josh Brodeen	Bethel	FR	F	10	0.20	2- 0- 2
	Brett Sobolik	St. John's	SO	F	12	0.17	2- 0- 2
	Kyle Rohlfs	Gustavus Adolphus	JR	F	13	0.15	2- 0- 2
	Matt LaBombard	St. Olaf	FR	F	14	0.14	2- 0- 2
	John Jacques	St. Thomas	FR	D	14	0.14	0- 2- 2
	Bryan Osmondson	St. Olaf	FR	F	15	0.13	1- 1- 2
	Kyle Henkemeyer	St. John's	FR	F	15	0.13	0- 2- 2
	Alex Gruetzmacher	Hamline	FR	F	16	0.12	0- 2- 2
	Chris Murray	St. John's	FR	F	17	0.12	0- 2- 2
	Luke Chilson	Hamline	SO	F	20	0.10	0- 2- 2
	Cole Scattarelli	Hamline	FR	D	21	0.10	0- 2- 2
	Tony Clafton	St. Mary's	FR	D	22	0.09	0- 2- 2
	Dustin Mercado	St. John's	SR	D	23	0.09	0- 2- 2
	Devin Firl	St. Mary's	JR	D	23	0.09	0- 2- 2
	Andrew Gastineau	St. Olaf	SR	D	24	0.08	0- 2- 2
	Tim Lawson	Augsburg	JR	F	26	0.08	0- 2- 2
	Ryan Hampson	St. Olaf	SO	D	26	0.08	0- 2- 2
175	Sam Dorr	St. John's	JR	D	2	0.50	0- 1- 1
	Kevin Mahoney	St. Thomas	FR	F	3	0.33	1- 0- 1
	Wes Jirovec	St. Thomas	FR	F	5	0.20	1- 0- 1
	Mike Persson	Concordia	FR	G	7	0.14	0- 1- 1

Josh Gaw	Gustavus Adolphus	SR	F	7	0.14	0- 1- 1
Chris Kopelke	Augsburg	FR	D	10	0.10	0- 1- 1
Hampus Gunnarsson	Gustavus Adolphus	FR	D	11	0.09	1- 0- 1
Will Smith	St. Olaf	SO	F	11	0.09	1- 0- 1
Tyler Antony	Gustavus Adolphus	FR	F	12	0.08	0- 1- 1
Paul Solberg	St. Thomas	SO	D	14	0.07	0- 1- 1
Jack Madryga	Hamline	SO	D	15	0.07	1- 0- 1
Brett Kistner	St. Olaf	JR	F	15	0.07	1- 0- 1
Andy Murray	Concordia	SO	F	15	0.07	0- 1- 1
Tony Webber	Concordia	SO	F	16	0.06	0- 1- 1
Sean Bryant	St. Thomas	SO	F	18	0.06	0- 1- 1
Ian Bing	Augsburg	SR	D	19	0.05	0- 1- 1
Matt Cosmos	Concordia	SO	F	20	0.05	1- 0- 1
Kirby Markowsky	Concordia	JR	D	23	0.04	0- 1- 1
Matt Zilles	Hamline	SO	D	24	0.04	1- 0- 1

GOALS AGAINST AVERAGE:

				MINUTES	GA	GAA
1	Aaron Damjanovich	Bethel	FR	1242:37:00	53	2.56
2	Andy Kent	Augsburg	SO	1334:34:00	60	2.7
3	Jeff Wilde	St. Olaf	SR	1330:56:00	61	2.75
4	Cameron Voss	St. Thomas	FR	798:09:00	37	2.78
5	Vince Wheeler	St. John's	SO	1161:33:00	56	2.89
6	Treye Kettwick	St. Thomas	SR	695:54:00	36	3.1
7	Kevin Johnson	Gustavus Adolphus	SO	1319:54:00	75	3.41
8	Dan Smith	St. Mary's	JR	1257:07:00	72	3.44
9	Jeremy Boniface	Concordia	SO	1025:46:00	75	4.39
10	Matt Wanvig	Hamline	FR	1324:01:00	105	4.764

Minimum 33% of Team Minutes Played

SAVE PERCENTAGE:

				SAVES	GA	PCT
1	Aaron Damjanovich	Bethel	FR	556	53	0.913
2	Jeff Wilde	St. Olaf	SR	568	61	0.903
3	Dan Smith	St. Mary's	JR	640	72	0.899
4	Andy Kent	Augsburg	SO	530	60	0.898
5	Vince Wheeler	St. John's	SO	454	56	0.89
6	Cameron Voss	St. Thomas	FR	296	37	0.889
7	Jeremy Boniface	Concordia	SO	532	75	0.876
8	Treye Kettwick	St. Thomas	SR	255	36	0.876
9	Matt Wanvig	Hamline	FR	694	105	0.869
10	Kevin Johnson	Gustavus Adolphus	SO	446	75	0.856

Minimum 33% of Team Minutes Played

WINNING PERCENTAGE:

				W- L- T	PCT
1	Aaron Damjanovich	Bethel	FR	14- 6- 1	0.69
2	Treye Kettwick	St. Thomas	SR	8- 4- 0	0.667
3	Cameron Voss	St. Thomas	FR	8- 5- 0	0.615
4	Jeff Wilde	St. Olaf	SR	11- 9- 2	0.545
	Andy Kent	Augsburg	SO	10- 8- 4	0.545
6	Kevin Johnson	Gustavus Adolphus	SO	11-10- 1	0.523
7	Vince Wheeler	St. John's	SO	7-10- 2	0.421
8	Matt Wanvig	Hamline	FR	7-15- 0	0.318
9	Dan Smith	St. Mary's	JR	6-14- 0	0.3
10	Jeremy Boniface	Concordia	SO	5-13- 0	0.278

Minimum 33% of Team Minutes Played

OPPORTUNITIES IN HOCKEY SEMINAR

Since 1990 The Hockey Guides have been the ultimate reference for hockey players, parents, counselors, educational consultants, coaches and administrators as they investigate college hockey opportunities by providing valuable resource information, support and seminars.

Now bring this proven educational program to your association, league, team or school by scheduling an Opportunities In Hockey seminar at your location. Our program is designed to prepare student-athletes academically, athletically and mentally for college hockey and the recruiting process. This seminar will provide valuable information to assist your players and their parents evaluate their options and make informed decisions in the college investigation and selection process.

For additional information, or to schedule a seminar, please contact Tom Keegan at The Hockey Guides.

For further information please contact:
The Hockey Guides
PO Box 1050 • Flagler Beach, FL 32136
386.439.2250
Email agp@flaglernet.com

New England Small College Athletic Conference
100 Venture Way, Box 13
Hadley, MA 01035
www.nescac.com

Executive Director
Andrea Savage
Phone: 413.587.2105
Fax: 413.587.2167

Assistant Director for Conference Operations
Dan Fisher
Phone: 413.587.2105
Fax: 413.587.2167

Amherst College

Bowdoin College

Colby College

Connecticut College

Hamilton College

Middlebury College

Trinity College

Tufts University

Wesleyan University

Williams College

ME

Colby College

Middlebury College

Bowdoin College

VT

NH

Hamilton College

NY

Trinity College

Wesleyan University

CT

Connecticut College

Amherst College

Tufts University

MA

Williams College

NEW ENGLAND SMALL COLLEGE ATHLETIC CONFERENCE

FINAL 2006-07 CONFERENCE STANDINGS

		Pts	GP	Record	Win%	GF-GA	GP	Record	Win%	GF-GA
1	Bowdoin	24	19	11- 6- 2	0.632	73- 53	26	16- 7- 3	0.673	111- 68
	Middlebury	24	19	11- 6- 2	0.632	64- 46	31	20- 8- 3	0.694	112- 71
3	Colby	23	19	11- 7- 1	0.605	76- 56	25	14- 9- 2	0.600	106- 70
4	Wesleyan	22	19	9- 6- 4	0.579	56- 48	24	11- 8- 5	0.562	72- 64
5	Amherst	21	19	10- 8- 1	0.553	71- 71	25	14-10- 1	0.580	93- 86
6	Conn. College	19	19	9- 9- 1	0.500	59- 56	25	10-13- 2	0.440	69- 81
7	Williams	18	19	8- 9- 2	0.474	53- 58	24	8-14- 2	0.375	61- 85
8	Trinity	15	19	6-10- 3	0.395	67- 61	25	8-13- 4	0.400	86- 83
9	Hamilton	13	19	6-12- 1	0.342	57- 76	24	7-16- 1	0.312	68- 99
10	Tufts	6	19	3-16- 0	0.158	53- 99	24	6-18- 0	0.250	71-119

2007 NEW ENGLAND SMALL COLLEGE ATHLETIC CONFERENCE PLAYOFFS

QUARTER FINALS (2.24.07)

Trinity College	3	Bowdoin College	7
Amherst College	2	Wesleyan University	0
Connecticut College	1	Colby College	5
Williams College	1	Middlebury College	5

SEMI FINALS (3.3.07)

Amherst College	3	Bowdoin College	6
Colby College	3	Middlebury College	4

CHAMPIONSHIP (3.04.07)

Middlebury College	4	Bowdoin College	2

NEW ENGLAND SMALL COLLEGE ATHLETIC CONFERENCE CHAMPIONS

REGULAR

2000	Middlebury College
2001	Middlebury College
2002	Middlebury College
2003	Trinity College
2004	Middlebury College
2005	Trinity College
2006	Middlebury College
2007	Bowdoin College
	Middlebury College

#	Name	School			GP	PPG	G - A - P
1	Greg Osborne	Colby	SR	F	25	1.64	21-20-41
2	Arthur Fritch	Colby	JR	D	25	1.48	12-25-37
3	Will Bennett	Wesleyan	SR	F	24	1.46	11-24-35
	Joel Covelli	Amherst	SO	F	25	1.40	11-24-35
5	Josh Reber	Colby	JR	F	25	1.36	9-25-34
	Mickey Gilchrist	Middlebury	JR	F	31	1.10	19-15-34
7	T.J. Kelley	Colby	JR	F	23	1.35	15-16-31
8	Rob Campbell	Conn. College	JR	F	25	1.16	11-18-29
9	Joe Rothwell	Colby	JR	D	25	1.12	9-19-28
10	John Halverson	Trinity	SR	D	25	1.08	12-15-27
	Tom Maldonado	Middlebury	JR	D	31	0.87	3-24-27
12	Sean Ellis	Amherst	SR	F	23	1.13	11-15-26
13	David Layne	Wesleyan	FR	F	24	1.04	13-12-25
	Ross Gimbel	Tufts	JR	F	24	1.04	12-13-25
15	John Sales	Middlebury	SR	F	29	0.83	9-15-24
16	Greg McCarthy	Tufts	SO	F	22	1.05	9-14-23
	Kyle Schoppel	Amherst	JR	F	24	0.96	10-13-23
18	Patrick Rutherford	Colby	SR	F	25	0.88	9-13-22
	Jeff Landers	Amherst	SO	D	25	0.88	5-17-22
	Tim McVaugh	Bowdoin	SR	D/F	26	0.85	9-13-22
21	Ryan Blossom	Bowdoin	FR	F	25	0.84	11-10-21
	Colin MacCormick	Bowdoin	FR	F	25	0.84	8-13-21
23	Joe Milo	Tufts	SO	F	19	1.05	10-10-20
	Ryan Howarth	Conn. College	FR	F	23	0.87	13- 7-20
	Colin Hughes	Bowdoin	JR	D	25	0.80	8-12-20
	Mike Corbelle	Bowdoin	FR	D	26	0.77	12- 8-20
27	Jamie McKenna	Middlebury	SO	F	23	0.83	6-13-19
	Casey Deak	Hamilton	SR	F	24	0.79	8-11-19
	Ryan Chrenek	Colby	JR	D	25	0.76	7-12-19
	Matt Smith	Bowdoin	SO	D	25	0.76	6-13-19
	Greg McConnell	Bowdoin	SR	F	25	0.76	5-14-19
32	Greg O'Connell	Tufts	JR	F	17	1.06	4-14-18
	Kurt Hertzog	Tufts	JR	F	22	0.82	6-12-18
	Travis Blood	Hamilton	SO	F	23	0.78	7-11-18
	Taylor Evans	Wesleyan	SR	F	24	0.75	4-14-18
	Mike Westerman	Bowdoin	JR	F	25	0.72	8-10-18
37	Trevor Bradley	Conn. College	FR	F	18	0.94	5-12-17
	Bryan Ciborowski	Bowdoin	SR	F	19	0.89	8- 9-17
	Kyle Roulston	Hamilton	SO	D	24	0.71	4-13-17
	Chris Powers	Trinity	SO	D	25	0.68	10- 7-17
	Robbie Tesar	Conn. College	SO	F	25	0.68	8- 9-17
	Brandon Zangel	Amherst	SR	D	25	0.68	5-12-17
	Brett Shirreffs	Middlebury	SR	D	27	0.63	9- 8-17
44	Doug Wilson	Tufts	FR	D	23	0.70	6-10-16
	William Maheras	Trinity	SR	F	25	0.64	6-10-16
	Evgeny Saidachev	Middlebury	SR	F	29	0.55	5-11-16
47	John Gordon	Hamilton	SR	D	19	0.79	4-11-15
	Brandon Jackmuff	Williams	JR	F	20	0.75	11- 4-15
	Naoto Hamashima	Trinity	FR	F	21	0.71	7- 8-15
	Chris Lorenc	Hamilton	FR	F	23	0.65	6- 9-15
	Tom Price	Trinity	SO	F	24	0.62	9- 6-15
	Kevin Colwell	Williams	SR	F	24	0.62	5-10-15
	Brendan Powers	Amherst	SO	F	25	0.60	8- 7-15
54	Jerome Wallace	Hamilton	FR	F	23	0.61	9- 5-14
	Jake Davis	Hamilton	SO	F	23	0.61	7- 7-14
	Leland Fidler	Bowdoin	FR	F	23	0.61	6- 8-14
	Andrew Decristoforo	Hamilton	JR	F	24	0.58	9- 5-14
	Jack Baer	Amherst	FR	F	24	0.58	4-10-14

	Name	School	Yr	Pos	GP	Avg	G-A-Pts
	Gregg Adamo	Amherst	JR	F	25	0.56	6- 8-14
	Rylan Burns	Amherst	SO	D	25	0.56	5- 9-14
	Michael McIntosh	Amherst	JR	F/D	25	0.56	3-11-14
	Sean Driscoll	Conn. College	FR	F	25	0.56	3-11-14
	John Sullivan	Middlebury	FR	F	27	0.52	8- 6-14
	Scott Bartlett	Middlebury	JR	F	31	0.45	7- 7-14
65	John Carter	Trinity	FR	F	16	0.81	4- 9-13
	James Gadon	Bowdoin	SR	F	21	0.62	2-11-13
	Riley Hicks	Trinity	SO	F	22	0.59	5- 8-13
	Dallas Bossort	Wesleyan	SO	D	22	0.59	5- 8-13
	J.J. Evans	Wesleyan	SO	F	23	0.57	6- 7-13
	Owen Holm	Williams	FR	F	23	0.57	5- 8-13
	Darwin Hunt	Middlebury	SR	F	28	0.46	7- 6-13
72	Jeff Beck	Wesleyan	FR	F	13	0.92	6- 6-12
	Daniel Maturi	Trinity	JR	F	14	0.86	7- 5-12
	Sam Robinson	Wesleyan	FR	F	21	0.57	4- 8-12
	Eric LaFreniere	Middlebury	SR	F	23	0.52	4- 8-12
	Alex Smigelski	Williams	FR	F	24	0.50	7- 5-12
	Richard Hollstein	Trinity	FR	D	24	0.50	6- 6-12
	Andrew Schremp	Amherst	JR	F	24	0.50	3- 9-12
	Brett Moore	Conn. College	FR	F	24	0.50	3- 9-12
	Ted Vickers	Amherst	FR	F	24	0.50	2-10-12
	Samuel Driver	Middlebury	JR	F	25	0.48	9- 3-12
	Mitch Dillon	Bowdoin	FR	F	25	0.48	7- 5-12
	Matt Strickland	Colby	FR	D	25	0.48	4- 8-12
84	Ryan Hendrickson	Wesleyan	SR	F	24	0.46	6- 5-11
	Brett Haraguchi	Williams	SO	F	24	0.46	6- 5-11
	Mike Collins	Bowdoin	SO	F	24	0.46	5- 6-11
	Mike Butler	Colby	JR	F	25	0.44	4- 7-11
	Jake Henry	Conn. College	SR	D	25	0.44	4- 7-11
89	Ross Grubin	Trinity	JR	D	13	0.77	2- 8-10
	Ryan Masucci	Trinity	SO	F	16	0.62	2- 8-10
	Pat McGarry	Hamilton	SR	D	21	0.48	2- 8-10
	Steve Bruch	Williams	JR	F/D	24	0.42	4- 6-10
	Greg Schultz	Williams	JR	F	24	0.42	4- 6-10
	Sebastien Belanger	Bowdoin	JR	F	24	0.42	3- 7-10
	Brian Warner	Conn. College	SO	D	25	0.40	2- 8-10
96	Robert MacIntyre	Middlebury	JR	D	16	0.56	3- 6- 9
	Brian Bailey	Tufts	SR	F	20	0.45	3- 6- 9
	Mike Policinski	Colby	FR	F	22	0.41	5- 4- 9
	Matt Lentini	Bowdoin	SO	F	22	0.41	4- 5- 9
	Brenton Stafford	Wesleyan	JR	D	22	0.41	2- 7- 9
	Colin Greenhalgh	Williams	SR	F	22	0.41	0- 9- 9
	Matt Dreiheim	Williams	SO	F	24	0.38	2- 7- 9
	Ryan Joyce	Conn. College	FR	D	24	0.38	1- 8- 9
	Joe Cappellano	Tufts	JR	D	24	0.38	1- 8- 9
	Will Collins	Amherst	SO	F	25	0.36	5- 4- 9
106	Brian Liamero	Conn. College	SO	F	16	0.50	6- 2- 8
	Olufemi Amurawaiye	Amherst	SO	F	22	0.36	6- 2- 8
	Jeoffrey Jarnot	Colby	FR	D	22	0.36	1- 7- 8
	Simon Dionne	Trinity	SR	F	22	0.36	1- 7- 8
	Steve Lunau	Williams	SR	F	24	0.33	3- 5- 8
111	John Murphy	Tufts	SR	D	14	0.50	4- 3- 7
	Woody Redpath	Wesleyan	FR	F	16	0.44	6- 1- 7
	Cory Korchin	Tufts	FR	F	16	0.44	4- 3- 7
	Casey Ftorek	Middlebury	JR	F	17	0.41	3- 4- 7
	Evan Crosby	Tufts	FR	F	20	0.35	4- 3- 7
	Will Reycraft	Bowdoin	JR	D	21	0.33	1- 6- 7
	Christopher Fahey	Williams	SO	D	21	0.33	1- 6- 7
	Eric Simmons	Colby	FR	F	23	0.30	3- 4- 7

	Matthew Rafuse	Trinity	SR	F	24	0.29	5- 2- 7
	Scott Burns	Wesleyan	SO	D	24	0.29	3- 4- 7
	Ed Klein	Wesleyan	JR	D	24	0.29	1- 6- 7
	Walt Wright	Conn. College	JR	D	24	0.29	0- 7- 7
123	Keith Nelson	Amherst	FR	F	10	0.60	0- 6- 6
	Michael Mortimer	Trinity	FR	D	12	0.50	0- 6- 6
	Josh Rich	Trinity	SO	F	13	0.46	2- 4- 6
	Charlie Townsend	Middlebury	FR	F	14	0.43	4- 2- 6
	Michael Belliveau	Colby	FR	F	18	0.33	4- 2- 6
	Richie Fuld	Middlebury	SR	F	18	0.33	1- 5- 6
	Jared Leslie	Hamilton	SO	D	19	0.32	1- 5- 6
	Andrew Lepore	Williams	FR	F	20	0.30	2- 4- 6
	Chris Diozzi	Trinity	SO	D	21	0.29	1- 5- 6
	Greg Camarco	Trinity	SR	D	24	0.25	2- 4- 6
	Mason Graddock	Middlebury	SO	F	30	0.20	3- 3- 6
134	Ryan Crapser	Trinity	FR	D	14	0.36	1- 4- 5
	Zachary Wissman	Trinity	FR	F	14	0.36	1- 4- 5
	Alex Shklyarevsky	Wesleyan	JR	F	14	0.36	1- 4- 5
	Griffin Biedron	Amherst	SO	D	16	0.31	2- 3- 5
	Jim Nolan	Hamilton	SR	F	18	0.28	1- 4- 5
	Shane Mandes	Middlebury	FR	F	19	0.26	0- 5- 5
	Greg Valenski	Colby	SO	F	20	0.25	1- 4- 5
	Ian Drummond	Middlebury	SO	D	21	0.24	2- 3- 5
	Phil Clark	Tufts	SO	D	21	0.24	2- 3- 5
	Chris DeBaere	Williams	SO	F	22	0.23	3- 2- 5
	Nate Miller	Hamilton	JR	F	24	0.21	3- 2- 5
	Matt McCarthy	Williams	SR	D	24	0.21	1- 4- 5
	Mike White	Colby	FR	D	25	0.20	0- 5- 5
147	Kyle Koziara	Middlebury	SO	D	6	0.67	4- 0- 4
	Octavian Jordan	Williams	SO	F	15	0.27	3- 1- 4
	Matthew Crum	Trinity	JR	F	16	0.25	2- 2- 4
	Adam Marino	Colby	JR	F	17	0.24	0- 4- 4
	Mike Fitoussi	Tufts	FR	F	18	0.22	1- 3- 4
	Matt Dalton	Tufts	SR	F	21	0.19	2- 2- 4
	Joe Rosano	Tufts	FR	F	21	0.19	1- 3- 4
	Brian Gallagher	Conn. College	JR	F	22	0.18	3- 1- 4
	Jason Miller	Conn. College	SR	F	22	0.18	1- 3- 4
	Myles Neumann	Tufts	FR	D	22	0.18	0- 4- 4
	Trevor Calamel	Amherst	SR	D	24	0.17	3- 1- 4
	David Ramsay	Williams	SO	D	24	0.17	3- 1- 4
	Patrick Collins	Conn. College	SO	F	25	0.16	2- 2- 4
	Chris Talbert	Colby	SO	D	25	0.16	0- 4- 4
	David Ransom	Bowdoin	JR	F	26	0.15	3- 1- 4
162	Steven Thompson	Bowdoin	JR	D	6	0.50	2- 1- 3
	Jeff Cutter	Bowdoin	SO	F	8	0.38	1- 2- 3
	Mike Kelly	Conn. College	FR	F	9	0.33	1- 2- 3
	Mack Cummins	Middlebury	SO	D	10	0.30	1- 2- 3
	Ryan Zemel	Wesleyan	FR	F	15	0.20	0- 3- 3
	Brian O'Malley	Hamilton	FR	F	16	0.19	2- 1- 3
	Justin Gaines	Middlebury	JR	D	16	0.19	2- 1- 3
	Brian Erensen	Wesleyan	JR	F	16	0.19	1- 2- 3
	Jonathan Kestner	Tufts	JR	F/D	18	0.17	0- 3- 3
	Andrew Stevenson	Amherst	FR	D	19	0.16	2- 1- 3
	Kevin Armstrong	Wesleyan	JR	F	20	0.15	1- 2- 3
	Shawn Donaher	Trinity	SO	D	21	0.14	1- 2- 3
	Peter Corbett	Tufts	SO	D	22	0.14	1- 2- 3
	Jed McDonald	Middlebury	JR	D	27	0.11	1- 2- 3
	Jack Kinder	Middlebury	SO	D	29	0.10	1- 2- 3
177	Brian Dew	Wesleyan	SO	F	5	0.40	1- 1- 2
	Thomas Wenstrom	Trinity	JR	D	5	0.40	0- 2- 2

	Duncan Smith	Bowdoin	JR	D	6	0.33	2- 0- 2
	Avi Meyers	Conn. College	SO	D	7	0.29	2- 0- 2
	Derek Chase	Trinity	SO	F	7	0.29	0- 2- 2
	Ben Kirtland	Tufts	FR	F/D	12	0.17	0- 2- 2
	Matt Ryder	Tufts	FR	D	13	0.15	1- 1- 2
	David Antonelli	Tufts	FR	F	16	0.12	0- 2- 2
	Ryan Seavy	Middlebury	FR	D	17	0.12	1- 1- 2
	Brian Fry	Bowdoin	FR	D	17	0.12	0- 2- 2
	Chris Lynn	Conn. College	SR	F	18	0.11	2- 0- 2
	Marc Trostle	Hamilton	FR	F	18	0.11	2- 0- 2
	Mike Dorsey	Wesleyan	JR	F	18	0.11	0- 2- 2
	William Burns	Trinity	SO	D	20	0.10	0- 2- 2
	Jared Crittenden	Colby	FR	F	21	0.10	1- 1- 2
	Jon Peros	Hamilton	JR	D	22	0.09	1- 1- 2
	Ben Eischen	Conn. College	SO	D	24	0.08	1- 1- 2
194	Shane Farrell	Bowdoin	SO	F	1	1.00	0- 1- 1
	Matt Mesi	Hamilton	JR	F	2	0.50	0- 1- 1
	Jocko DeCarolis	Middlebury	SR	F	3	0.33	0- 1- 1
	Erik Lund	Amherst	SR	F	5	0.20	1- 0- 1
	Chris Graceffa	Wesleyan	SR	F	5	0.20	1- 0- 1
	Mike Barbera	Wesleyan	SR	D	5	0.20	0- 1- 1
	Dave Scardella	Wesleyan	SR	G	5	0.20	0- 1- 1
	Bo Armstrong	Hamilton	SO	F	6	0.17	0- 1- 1
	Todd Davis	Hamilton	FR	F	7	0.14	1- 0- 1
	Anthony Christiano	Wesleyan	FR	D	8	0.12	0- 1- 1
	Richard Leahy	Bowdoin	JR	D	9	0.11	0- 1- 1
	Jared Melillo	Tufts	SO	F	9	0.11	0- 1- 1
	Vaclav Tomicek	Hamilton	FR	F	10	0.10	1- 0- 1
	Shane Lennox	Amherst	SO	D	11	0.09	0- 1- 1
	Peter Gustavson	Hamilton	FR	F	11	0.09	0- 1- 1
	Shawn Keefe	Conn. College	SO	D	12	0.08	1- 0- 1
	Zach Miller	Williams	FR	F	12	0.08	0- 1- 1
	Kevin Plant	Conn. College	SO	F	16	0.06	0- 1- 1
	David Norton	Conn. College	SO	D	16	0.06	0- 1- 1
	Doug Raeder	Middlebury	SO	G	16	0.06	0- 1- 1
	Evan Seely	Williams	FR	D	17	0.06	0- 1- 1
	Andrew Delorey	Tufts	SO	F	18	0.06	0- 1- 1
	Brent Winship	Wesleyan	SO	D	18	0.06	0- 1- 1
	James Kalec	Tufts	JR	G	19	0.05	0- 1- 1
	Matt Ahern	Colby	SO	F	21	0.05	1- 0- 1
	Rob Gannon	Hamilton	FR	D	22	0.05	0- 1- 1
	Will Bruce	Williams	JR	F	23	0.04	1- 0- 1
	David Murison	Trinity	FR	G	23	0.04	0- 1- 1
	Rob Stevenson	Amherst	JR	D	24	0.04	1- 0- 1
	Ben Grandjean	Colby	SR	G	25	0.04	0- 1- 1

GOALS AGAINST AVERAGE:

				MINUTES	GA	GAA
1	Mike Palladino	Wesleyan	SO	1158:30:00	41	2.12
2	Doug Raeder	Middlebury	SO	891:06:00	33	2.22
3	Ross Cherry	Middlebury	JR	989:13:00	38	2.3
4	Ben Grandjean	Colby	SR	1482:12:00	64	2.59
5	Greg Parker	Conn. College	FR	1020:42:00	46	2.7
6	Chris Rossi	Bowdoin	FR	886:51:00	41	2.77
7	David Murison	Trinity	FR	1331:11:00	72	3.25
8	Marc Pulde	Williams	FR	687:44:00	38	3.32
9	Josh Fillman	Amherst	SR	1152:47:00	67	3.49
10	Rick Redmond	Williams	SO	753:26:00	45	3.58
11	Matt Crowson	Hamilton	SO	823:59:00	53	3.86
12	Ian Stearns	Hamilton	FR	527:17:00	39	4.44
13	James Kalec	Tufts	JR	939:35:00	73	4.66
14	Issa Azat	Tufts	JR	494:48:00	42	5.09

Minimum 33% of Team Minutes Played

SAVE PERCENTAGE:

				SAVES	GA	PCT
1	Mike Palladino	Wesleyan	SO	469	41	0.92
2	Greg Parker	Conn. College	FR	501	46	0.916
3	Ben Grandjean	Colby	SR	677	64	0.914
4	Doug Raeder	Middlebury	SO	319	33	0.906
5	Marc Pulde	Williams	FR	350	38	0.902
6	Ross Cherry	Middlebury	JR	337	38	0.899
7	Chris Rossi	Bowdoin	FR	357	41	0.897
8	Rick Redmond	Williams	SO	391	45	0.897
9	Josh Fillman	Amherst	SR	559	67	0.893
10	David Murison	Trinity	FR	585	72	0.89
11	Matt Crowson	Hamilton	SO	395	53	0.882
12	Ian Stearns	Hamilton	FR	286	39	0.88
13	James Kalec	Tufts	JR	520	73	0.877
14	Issa Azat	Tufts	JR	287	42	0.872

Minimum 33% of Team Minutes Played

WINNING PERCENTAGE:

				W- L- T	PCT
1	Doug Raeder	Middlebury	SO	13- 3- 0	0.812
2	Chris Rossi	Bowdoin	FR	11- 4- 0	0.733
3	Ben Grandjean	Colby	SR	14- 8- 2	0.625
4	Mike Palladino	Wesleyan	SO	10- 6- 4	0.6
5	Josh Fillman	Amherst	SR	11- 8- 1	0.575
6	Ross Cherry	Middlebury	JR	7- 5- 3	0.567
7	Greg Parker	Conn. College	FR	8- 7- 2	0.529
8	Matt Crowson	Hamilton	SO	5- 8- 1	0.393
9	David Murison	Trinity	FR	7-12- 4	0.391
10	Marc Pulde	Williams	FR	5- 8- 0	0.385
11	Issa Azat	Tufts	JR	3- 5- 0	0.375
12	Rick Redmond	Williams	SO	3- 6- 2	0.364
13	James Kalec	Tufts	JR	3-13- 0	0.188
14	Ian Stearns	Hamilton	FR	1- 8- 0	0.111

Minimum 33% of Team Minutes Played

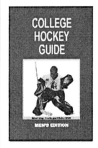
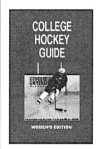

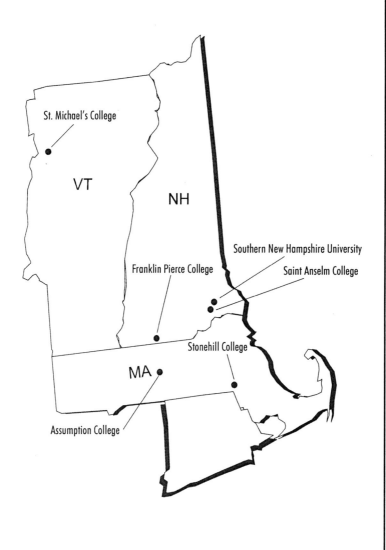

NORTHEAST-10 CONFERENCE
FINAL 2006-07 CONFERENCE STANDINGS

		Pts	GP	Record	Win%	GF-GA	GP	Record	Win%	GF-GA
1	Saint Anselm	8	5	4- 1- 0	0.800	32- 9	28	13-12- 3	0.518	99- 81
2	Stonehill	7	5	3- 1- 1	0.700	16- 14	27	14-12- 1	0.537	114-104
3	Saint Michael's	6	5	3- 2- 0	0.600	24- 18	26	6-20- 0	0.231	72-122
	Southern N.H.	6	5	3- 2- 0	0.600	19- 16	27	12-14- 1	0.463	99-121
5	Franklin Pierce	2	5	1- 4- 0	0.200	13- 31	24	5-17- 2	0.250	66-130
6	Assumption	1	5	0- 4- 1	0.100	9- 25	27	7-18- 2	0.296	77-134

2007 NORTHEAST-10 CONFERENCE PLAYOFFS

QUARTER FINALS (2.24.07)

Assumption College	4	Saint Michael's College	2
Franklin Pierce College	2	Southern New Hampshire Univ.	4

SEMI FINALS (2.28.07)

Southern New Hampshire Univ.	3	Saint Anselm College	4
Assumption College	2	Stonehill College	6

CHAMPIONSHIP SERIES (3.03-04.07)

Stonehill College	5	Saint Anselm College	9
Stonehill College	5	Saint Anselm College	3

NORTHEAST 10 CHAMPIONS

<u>REGULAR</u>   <u>TOURNAMENT</u>

2004	Saint Anselm College			
2005	Saint Anselm College	2005	Saint Anselm College
2006	Southern New Hampshire University	2006	Saint Anselm College
	Saint Anselm College			
2007	Saint Anselm College	2007	Stonehill College

					GP	PPG	G - A - P
1	Brandon Hammermeister	Southern N.H.	JR	F	27	1.74	21-26-47
2	Brendan O'Brien	Stonehill	SO	F	23	1.96	12-33-45
3	Matt Curran	Stonehill	JR	F	26	1.69	30-14-44
	Dominic DiMarzo	Southern N.H.	JR	F	27	1.63	23-21-44
5	Jared Silver	Saint Michael's	SR	F	22	1.27	15-13-28
6	Mike Foley	Saint Anselm	JR	F	26	1.00	13-13-26
7	Ryan Mero	Saint Michael's	SO	F	19	1.32	10-15-25
	Joseph Fields	Franklin Pierce	JR	F	22	1.14	6-19-25
	Pat Forshner	Saint Anselm	JR	F	27	0.93	11-14-25
	James Florentino	Stonehill	SO	D	27	0.93	7-18-25
11	Atte Uola	Assumption	FR	F	25	0.96	13-11-24
	Jim Trahon	Assumption	JR	F	27	0.89	5-19-24
	Colin Fitzpatrick	Saint Anselm	JR	F	28	0.86	9-15-24
14	Brian DelSavio	Franklin Pierce	SR	F	23	1.00	14- 9-23
	Pete Roundy	Stonehill	FR	F	27	0.85	6-17-23
16	Ethan Porter	Southern N.H.	SR	F	24	0.92	4-18-22
17	John Burns	Saint Michael's	SO	D	24	0.88	1-20-21
18	Chuck Matthews	Franklin Pierce	SR	F	23	0.83	5-14-19
	Brett Smith	Saint Anselm	SR	D	28	0.68	6-13-19
20	Dan Surette	Assumption	SR	D	24	0.75	5-13-18
	Paul Reissfelder	Stonehill	SO	F	27	0.67	7-11-18
22	Anthony Zanetti	Stonehill	JR	F	26	0.65	5-12-17
	Brian Hartigan	Saint Anselm	SO	D	28	0.61	2-15-17
24	John Durkin	Stonehill	JR	F	19	0.84	7- 9-16
	Matt Hall	Saint Michael's	JR	D/F	26	0.62	8- 8-16
	Nick Sacca	Saint Anselm	SR	F	28	0.57	7- 9-16
27	Derek Evjenth	Saint Anselm	SR	F	24	0.62	8- 7-15
	Billy Ninteau	Stonehill	SO	D	26	0.58	5-10-15
	Matt Paget	Assumption	JR	F	27	0.56	6- 9-15
	Danny Ohlson	Saint Anselm	SR	F	27	0.56	5-10-15
31	Brian Davis	Stonehill	JR	F	19	0.74	6- 8-14
	Dave Carroll	Southern N.H.	SO	D	21	0.67	3-11-14
	Derek Girouard	Saint Michael's	SR	F	25	0.56	8- 6-14
	Frank Amato	Stonehill	SO	F	26	0.54	7- 7-14
35	Luke McDonough	Assumption	JR	F	20	0.65	6- 7-13
	Shane Masotta	Saint Anselm	JR	D	22	0.59	2-11-13
	John Routhier	Assumption	JR	F	24	0.54	6- 7-13
	Sean Staid	Assumption	SO	F	25	0.52	6- 7-13
	Frank Bova	Assumption	SO	F	26	0.50	6- 7-13
40	Chris Rogers	Stonehill	FR	F	20	0.60	5- 7-12
	Ryan DiBartolomeo	Southern N.H.	FR	F	21	0.57	5- 7-12
	Jeff Kasper	Franklin Pierce	SO	F	24	0.50	6- 6-12
	Kent Honeyman	Southern N.H.	FR	D	24	0.50	4- 8-12
	Chris Gunn	Southern N.H.	JR	F	27	0.44	8- 4-12
	Chase Feole	Stonehill	JR	F	27	0.44	7- 5-12
46	Erik Caron	Saint Michael's	JR	F	19	0.58	4- 7-11
	Coursen Schneider	Franklin Pierce	SO	F	22	0.50	5- 6-11
	Ben Reynolds	Franklin Pierce	JR	F	22	0.50	2- 9-11
	Kyle Bousquet	Southern N.H.	SR	D	23	0.48	1-10-11
	John Frey	Southern N.H.	FR	F	24	0.46	4- 7-11
	Mike Rust	Assumption	JR	F	26	0.42	6- 5-11
	Mike Curtis	Saint Anselm	SR	F	27	0.41	5- 6-11
53	Joe McCarthy	Franklin Pierce	FR	F	23	0.43	4- 6-10
	Chet Riley	Southern N.H.	SR	F	24	0.42	3- 7-10
	Andrew Gartman	Saint Anselm	SR	F	25	0.40	6- 4-10
	Joshua Douglas	Southern N.H.	JR	F	27	0.37	6- 4-10
	Seth Goodrich	Saint Anselm	FR	D	27	0.37	2- 8-10
	Evan Spencer	Stonehill	SR	D	27	0.37	2- 8-10

	Rob Carpenter	Stonehill	JR	F	27	0.37	2- 8-10
60	Matt Sayer	Southern N.H.	FR	F	6	1.50	4- 5- 9
	Tom Kerwin	Saint Anselm	SO	F	20	0.45	5- 4- 9
	Chris Genovese	Assumption	SO	D	22	0.41	3- 6- 9
	Kyle Kruse	Franklin Pierce	FR	D	24	0.38	3- 6- 9
	Mike Nunziato	Saint Anselm	SO	D	25	0.36	4- 5- 9
	James Capulli	Assumption	FR	F	25	0.36	1- 8- 9
	Matt Farley	Southern N.H.	FR	F	26	0.35	6- 3- 9
	Chris Healey	Saint Michael's	SO	F	26	0.35	4- 5- 9
68	Ken Burlage	Southern N.H.	SR	D	21	0.38	1- 7- 8
	Joe Fernald	Saint Anselm	SO	F	25	0.32	3- 5- 8
	Patrick Ciummo	Assumption	JR	F	26	0.31	5- 3- 8
	Jonathan Silver	Saint Michael's	FR	F	26	0.31	1- 7- 8
72	Matt Grazioso	Saint Anselm	JR	F	15	0.47	3- 4- 7
	Casey Goodell	Franklin Pierce	FR	F	17	0.41	5- 2- 7
	Jean-Maxime Legare	Saint Michael's	FR	F	22	0.32	4- 3- 7
	Zachary Cantin	Stonehill	FR	F	23	0.30	3- 4- 7
	David Vorozilchak	Saint Michael's	FR	D	26	0.27	0- 7- 7
	Brian Dobler	Saint Anselm	SR	D	27	0.26	3- 4- 7
78	Tim Dancey	Saint Michael's	JR	F	12	0.50	5- 1- 6
	Randy Morin	Assumption	JR	D	20	0.30	2- 4- 6
	Peter Wilson	Franklin Pierce	JR	F	21	0.29	4- 2- 6
	Matt Whitney	Franklin Pierce	SO	F	23	0.26	3- 3- 6
	Evan Williams	Southern N.H.	JR	F	23	0.26	2- 4- 6
	Mike Ciardullo	Saint Michael's	SR	F	26	0.23	4- 2- 6
	Andrick Deppmeyer	Saint Michael's	JR	D	26	0.23	1- 5- 6
85	Ed Kus	Franklin Pierce	SO	D	15	0.33	1- 4- 5
	Dan Anctil	Saint Michael's	JR	F	20	0.25	1- 4- 5
	Phil Demers	Assumption	JR	D	23	0.22	1- 4- 5
	James Killeen	Stonehill	SO	D	26	0.19	0- 5- 5
89	Chris O'Brien	Saint Anselm	JR	F	4	1.00	1- 3- 4
	Chris MacPhee	Saint Anselm	FR	F	10	0.40	2- 2- 4
	Nick Stevenson	Southern N.H.	FR	D	12	0.33	0- 4- 4
	Alex Higgins	Saint Michael's	FR	F	19	0.21	3- 1- 4
	Stephen Murphy	Franklin Pierce	FR	D	19	0.21	0- 4- 4
	Patrick McGuirk	Saint Michael's	FR	F	20	0.20	1- 3- 4
	Rob Perretta	Franklin Pierce	SO	D	22	0.18	3- 1- 4
	Josh Goodman	Southern N.H.	JR	D	24	0.17	1- 3- 4
	Thomas Ohlson	Southern N.H.	FR	F	24	0.17	1- 3- 4
	Andy DiMasi	Saint Michael's	SR	D	26	0.15	0- 4- 4
	Frank Cavaliere	Stonehill	SO	D	27	0.15	2- 2- 4
100	Michael Sabo	Southern N.H.	JR	F	8	0.38	1- 2- 3
	Tyler Cleary	Assumption	FR	F	16	0.19	1- 2- 3
	Dominic Cavallaro	Southern N.H.	SR	D	16	0.19	0- 3- 3
	Tim Dupuis	Assumption	FR	D	22	0.14	1- 2- 3
	Jeff Harris	Saint Michael's	SR	F	23	0.13	2- 1- 3
	Ryan Strayer	Franklin Pierce	JR	F	24	0.12	2- 1- 3
	Jon Retelle	Assumption	FR	D	25	0.12	1- 2- 3
	Bryan Dodge	Saint Michael's	SO	D	26	0.12	0- 3- 3
	Tim Ivers	Saint Anselm	FR	D	27	0.11	1- 2- 3
109	Steve Wardynski	Southern N.H.	JR	F/D	3	0.67	0- 2- 2
	Josh Lupinek	Franklin Pierce	SO	D	5	0.40	2- 0- 2
	Brett Bilodeau	Franklin Pierce	SR	F	7	0.29	1- 1- 2
	Mike St. Lawrence	Assumption	FR	F	11	0.18	1- 1- 2
	C.J. Demmons	Franklin Pierce	SR	F	11	0.18	0- 2- 2
	Corey Glynn	Stonehill	FR	D	15	0.13	0- 2- 2
	Derek Whitney	Assumption	FR	D	21	0.10	0- 2- 2
	Pat Keenan	Assumption	FR	D	25	0.08	1- 1- 2
	Andrew Goduco	Southern N.H.	JR	F	26	0.08	1- 1- 2
118	James Wood	Assumption	JR	F	6	0.17	1- 0- 1

Andrew Woodford	Saint Anselm	SO D	6	0.17	0- 1- 1
Mike Cafferty	Stonehill	SO F	7	0.14	1- 0- 1
Mark Lodge	Southern N.H.	FR D	8	0.12	0- 1- 1
Shane Murphy	Franklin Pierce	SO F	9	0.11	0- 1- 1
Ben Gunn	Saint Anselm	SO F	9	0.11	0- 1- 1
Brian Hopper	Saint Michael's	SO D	9	0.11	0- 1- 1
Carmine Vetrano	Southern N.H.	FR G	9	0.11	0- 1- 1
Mike Daraio	Stonehill	FR F	9	0.11	0- 1- 1
Derek Jackson	Saint Michael's	SR G	11	0.09	0- 1- 1
Steven Della Calce	Franklin Pierce	FR F	12	0.08	0- 1- 1
Phil LaCasse	Southern N.H.	FR D	13	0.08	0- 1- 1
John Sommers	Stonehill	SO F	13	0.08	0- 1- 1
Kevin Corley	Saint Anselm	SR D	16	0.06	1- 0- 1
Trevor Clark	Franklin Pierce	JR F	21	0.05	0- 1- 1
Mike Anderson	Franklin Pierce	SR D	23	0.04	0- 1- 1

GOALS AGAINST AVERAGE:

				MINUTES	GA	GAA
1	Jason Zuck	Saint Anselm	FR	1055:33:00	40	2.27
2	Jason Rafuse	Saint Anselm	SR	573:13:00	32	3.35
3	Josh Green	Stonehill	SR	753:46:00	46	3.66
4	Matt Gorman	Stonehill	SR	870:21:00	55	3.79
5	Matt Courchesne	Southern N.H.	SO	1337:48:00	90	4.04
6	Derek Jackson	Saint Michael's	SR	590:42:00	40	4.06
7	Jamie DiGiulio	Assumption	FR	1003:00:00	71	4.25
8	Spencer Utman	Franklin Pierce	JR	975:53:00	78	4.8
9	Erik Smith	Saint Michael's	SR	797:44:00	64	4.81

Minimum 33% of Team Minutes Played

SAVE PERCENTAGE:

				SAVES	GA	PCT
1	Jason Zuck	Saint Anselm	FR	427	40	0.914
2	Jamie DiGiulio	Assumption	FR	581	71	0.891
3	Jason Rafuse	Saint Anselm	SR	247	32	0.885
4	Derek Jackson	Saint Michael's	SR	304	40	0.884
5	Matt Gorman	Stonehill	SR	416	55	0.883
6	Josh Green	Stonehill	SR	345	46	0.882
7	Matt Courchesne	Southern N.H.	SO	614	90	0.872
8	Spencer Utman	Franklin Pierce	JR	526	78	0.871
9	Erik Smith	Saint Michael's	SR	428	64	0.87

Minimum 33% of Team Minutes Played

WINNING PERCENTAGE:

				W-L-T	PCT
1	Josh Green	Stonehill	SR	8- 3- 1	0.708
2	Jason Zuck	Saint Anselm	FR	10- 5- 2	0.647
3	Matt Courchesne	Southern N.H.	SO	11-13- 0	0.458
4	Matt Gorman	Stonehill	SR	6- 9- 0	0.4
5	Derek Jackson	Saint Michael's	SR	4- 7- 0	0.364
6	Jamie DiGiulio	Assumption	FR	5-11- 1	0.324
7	Jason Rafuse	Saint Anselm	SR	3- 7- 1	0.318
8	Spencer Utman	Franklin Pierce	JR	4-11- 2	0.294
9	Erik Smith	Saint Michael's	SR	2-11- 0	0.154

Minimum 33% of Team Minutes Played

Northern Collegiate
Hockey Association

www.nchahockey.org

President
Bill Kronschnabel
Phone: 651.222.5000
email: wkronsch@kkblawfirm.com

Sports Information Director
Layne Pitt
Phone: 715.232.2275
Fax: 715.232.1684
email: pittl@uwstout.edu

Supervisor of Officials
Ed Zepeda
Phone: 651.578.3712
Fax: 651.603.3216
email: ed.zepeda@thomson.com

Lake Forest College *(thru 2008/2009)*

St. Norbert College

College of St. Scholastica

University of Wisconsin Eau Claire

University of Wisconsin River Falls

University of Wisconsin Stevens Point

University of Wisconsin Stout

University of Wisconsin Superior

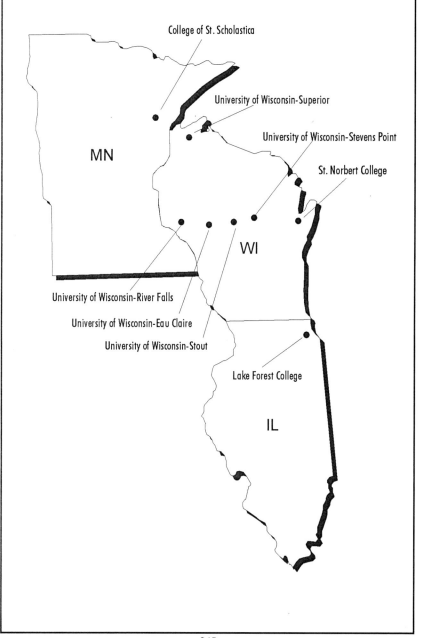

NCHA

NORTHERN COLLEGIATE HOCKEY ASSOCIATION

College of St. Scholastica

University of Wisconsin-Superior

University of Wisconsin-Stevens Point

St. Norbert College

MN

WI

University of Wisconsin-River Falls

University of Wisconsin-Eau Claire

University of Wisconsin-Stout

Lake Forest College

IL

NORTHERN COLLEGIATE HOCKEY ASSOCIATION
FINAL 2006-07 CONFERENCE STANDINGS

		Pts	GP	Record	Win%	GF-GA	GP	Record	Win%	GF-GA
1	Wisconsin-River Falls	21	14	10- 3- 1	0.750	45- 31	29	21- 6- 2	0.759	110- 65
	St. Norbert	21	14	10- 3- 1	0.750	55- 32	31	25- 4- 2	0.839	136- 56
	Wisconsin-Stout	21	14	10- 3- 1	0.750	49- 34	28	21- 5- 2	0.786	106- 65
4	Wisconsin-Superior	19	14	9- 4- 1	0.679	48- 35	27	20- 6- 1	0.759	109- 63
5	St. Scholastica	13	14	6- 7- 1	0.464	45- 45	29	15-12- 2	0.552	88- 80
6	Wisconsin-Stevens Pt.	7	14	3-10- 1	0.250	41- 61	27	7-18- 2	0.296	83-118
	Wisconsin-Eau Claire	7	14	2- 9- 3	0.250	30- 46	27	9-14- 4	0.407	74- 81
8	Lake Forest	3	14	0-11- 3	0.107	26- 55	27	3-21- 3	0.167	62-118

2007 NORTHERN COLLEGIATE HOCKEY ASSOCIATION PLAYOFFS

FIRST ROUND (2.16-17.07)
(Best of Three Series)

St. Scholastica College	2	University of Wisconsin Superior	1
University of Wisconsin Eau Claire	0	St. Norbert College	2
Lake Forest College	0	University of Wisconsin River Falls	2
University of Wisconsin Stevens Point	0	University of Wisconsin Stout	2

SEMI FINALS (2.24.07)

University of Wisconsin-Stout	1	St. Norbert College	4
College of St. Scholastica	2	University of Wisconsin River Falls	1

CHAMPIONSHIP (3.03.07)

College of St. Scholastica	0	St. Norbert College	3

NORTHERN COLLEGIATE HOCKEY ASSOCIATION CHAMPIONS

	REGULAR	TOURNAMENT
1982	Bemidji State University	
1983	Bemidji State University	
1984	Bemidji State University	
1985	Bemidji State University	
1986	Mankato State University	Bemidji State University
	Bemidji State Univesity	
1987	Mankato State University	Bemidji State University
	Bemidji State University	
1988	University of Wisconsin River Falls	University of Wisconsin River Falls
1989	University of Wisconsin Stevens Point	University of Wisconsin Stevens Point
1990	University of Wisconsin Stevens Point	University of Wisconsin Stevens Point
1991	Mankato State University	University of Wisconsin Stevens Point
	Bemidji State University	
1992	University of Wisconsin Stevens Point	University of Wisconsin Stevens Point
1993	University of Wisconsin Stevens Point	University of Wisconsin Stevens Point
1994	University of Wisconsin Superior	University of Wisconsin Superior
1995	Bemidji State University	Bemidji State University
1996	University of Wisconsin River Falls	University of Wisconsin River Falls
1997	St. Norbert College	University of Wisconsin Superior
1998	St. Norbert College	St. Norbert College
1999	St. Norbert College	St. Norbert College
2000	University of Wisconsin Stevens Point	University of Wisconsin Superior
2001	University of Wisconsin Superior	University of Wisconsin Superior
2002	St. Norbert College	University of Wisconsin Superior
2003	St. Norbert College	St. Norbert College
2004	St. Norbert College	St. Norbert College
2005	St. Norbert College	St. Norbert College
2006	St. Norbert College	University of Wisconsin Superior
2007	University of Wisconsin River Falls	St. Norbert College
	St. Norbert College	
	University of Wisconsin Stout	

#	Name	Team	Yr	Pos	GP	PPG	G - A - P
1	Tyler Dahl	Wis-River Falls	JR	F	29	1.79	12-40-52
2	Marc Belanger	St. Norbert	JR	F	30	1.37	21-20-41
3	Jeff Hazelwood	St. Norbert	SO	F	30	1.33	17-23-40
4	Scott Motz	Wis-Stout	FR	F	28	1.29	18-18-36
5	Derek Hansberry	Wis-River Falls	SO	F	29	1.21	21-14-35
6	Andy Wiesner	Wis-Stout	SR	F	28	1.18	15-18-33
7	Braden Desmet	Wis-Superior	FR	F	23	1.39	14-18-32
8	Matt Boyd	St. Norbert	FR	F	30	1.03	10-21-31
9	Chris Berry	Wis-Superior	FR	F	27	1.11	16-14-30
10	Sean Fish	Wis-Stevens Pt.	SO	F	27	1.04	13-15-28
	Tyler Canal	Lake Forest	SR	F	27	1.04	9-19-28
	Andrew Derton	St. Norbert	SR	D	27	1.04	7-21-28
	Derek Hanson	Wis-Stout	FR	F	28	1	12-16-28
	Pat Borgestad	Wis-River Falls	JR	F	29	0.97	16-12-28
	Shane Wheeler	St. Norbert	FR	F	31	0.9	8-20-28
16	Corey Stark	Wis-Superior	FR	F	26	1.04	17-10-27
	Sean Garrity	Wis-Eau Claire	JR	F	26	1.04	13-14-27
	Steven Sleep	St. Norbert	SO	F	31	0.87	11-16-27
19	A.J. Tucker	St. Scholastica	SO	F	29	0.9	10-16-26
	Troy Boisjoli	St. Norbert	SR	F	31	0.84	17- 9-26
21	Nate Rein	Wis-Superior	SO	F	25	1	10-15-25
22	Greg Peterson	Wis-Eau Claire	SO	D	27	0.89	7-17-24
	Jim Henkemeyer	Wis-River Falls	JR	D	28	0.86	8-16-24
24	Josh Calleja	Wis-Stevens Pt.	FR	F	25	0.92	7-16-23
25	Jesse Vesel	Wis-Eau Claire	SO	F	27	0.81	4-18-22
	Lonny Forrester	St. Norbert	SR	F	30	0.73	7-15-22
27	Tyler Kostiuk	Wis-River Falls	SR	F	29	0.72	9-12-21
28	Pat Lee	Wis-Stevens Pt.	FR	F	13	1.54	11- 9-20
	Brian Lee	Lake Forest	JR	F	26	0.77	10-10-20
	Dustin Norman	Wis-River Falls	SO	F	27	0.74	10-10-20
	Ryan Petersen	St. Norbert	SO	F	30	0.67	13- 7-20
32	Myles Palliser	Wis-Superior	SR	F	25	0.76	7-12-19
	Jake Nelson	St. Scholastica	SO	F	28	0.68	8-11-19
34	Brett Beckfeld	Wis-Stevens Pt.	SO	F	25	0.72	10- 8-18
	Jake Erickson	Wis-Stout	JR	F	28	0.64	7-11-18
	Luke Schroeder	Wis-Stout	JR	F	28	0.64	6-12-18
37	Andrew Johnson	Wis-Eau Claire	SO	F	27	0.63	10- 7-17
	Bobby Kuehl	Wis-Stout	FR	D	27	0.63	3-14-17
	Joey Hughes	St. Scholastica	SO	F	28	0.61	6-11-17
	Andrew Stearns	Wis-Stout	SR	F	28	0.61	5-12-17
41	Derek Paige	Wis-Superior	JR	D	22	0.73	2-14-16
	Chris Wilson	Lake Forest	SO	F	25	0.64	6-10-16
	Joey Martini	St. Scholastica	SO	F	26	0.62	9- 7-16
	Paul Henderson	Wis-Stout	FR	F/D	28	0.57	9- 7-16
	Mitch Kerns	Wis-River Falls	FR	F	28	0.57	6-10-16
	Matt Mlynarczyk	Wis-Stout	SR	F	28	0.57	6-10-16
	Kurtis Peterson	St. Norbert	SR	F	30	0.53	9- 7-16
48	Seth Reda	Wis-Superior	SO	F	26	0.58	6- 9-15
	Trevor Geiger	St. Scholastica	SO	F	28	0.54	6- 9-15
	Wade Harstad	Wis-River Falls	JR	F	29	0.52	5-10-15
	Kelly Reynolds	St. Scholastica	SO	D	29	0.52	3-12-15
52	Rolf Ulvin	Wis-Stevens Pt.	SR	F	19	0.74	5- 9-14
	Jim Jensen	Wis-River Falls	JR	D	23	0.61	4-10-14
	Aaron Berman	Wis-Superior	SO	D	25	0.56	3-11-14
	Matt Stendahl	Wis-Stevens Pt.	SO	F	26	0.54	4-10-14
56	Mike Kneeland	Lake Forest	SO	F	14	0.93	7- 6-13
	Kyle Luschinski	St. Scholastica	SO	F	23	0.57	5- 8-13
	Corey Lennartson	Wis-Superior	SR	F	26	0.5	8- 5-13

	Nick Zebro	Wis-Stevens Pt.	SR	F	27	0.48	6- 7-13
60	Ben Hendrick	Wis-Eau Claire	SO	F	24	0.5	8- 4-12
	Jack Wolgemuth	Wis-Stout	SO	D	25	0.48	2-10-12
	Peter Morrison	Lake Forest	SO	F	27	0.44	4- 8-12
	Jordan McIntyre	Wis-River Falls	FR	F	28	0.43	4- 8-12
64	Russel Law	Wis-Stevens Pt.	SO	F	24	0.46	6- 5-11
	Nick Klaren	Wis-Stout	SO	D	24	0.46	5- 6-11
	Steve Dus	Wis-Eau Claire	SR	F	25	0.44	4- 7-11
	Matt Saler	St. Scholastica	SO	F	26	0.42	4- 7-11
	Matt Oke	Lake Forest	SO	D	26	0.42	2- 9-11
	Trevor Bayda	St. Norbert	SR	F	26	0.42	2- 9-11
70	Andrew MacKenzie	Wis-Superior	SO	F	21	0.48	6- 4-10
	Greg Ihnken	Lake Forest	SR	F	21	0.48	3- 7-10
	Matt Stengl	St. Scholastica	SO	F	22	0.45	8- 2-10
	Shawn Bartlette	St. Scholastica	JR	F	26	0.38	4- 6-10
74	Adam Tobias	Lake Forest	JR	F	10	0.9	4- 5- 9
	Sheldon Wing	St. Norbert	SR	D	11	0.82	2- 7- 9
	David Moncur	Wis-Superior	SO	D	11	0.82	2- 7- 9
	Rob Turnville	Wis-Superior	SO	F	11	0.82	2- 7- 9
	Cory Mozak	Wis-Stout	SO	F	19	0.47	5- 4- 9
	Jordan Baird	St. Scholastica	FR	D	21	0.43	4- 5- 9
	Dan Francis	Wis-Stevens Pt.	SR	F	25	0.36	5- 4- 9
	Aaron Spotts	St. Scholastica	FR	F	26	0.35	3- 6- 9
	Jared Sailer	Wis-River Falls	SR	F	27	0.33	5- 4- 9
	Kyle Garner	Wis-Eau Claire	SR	D	27	0.33	1- 8- 9
	Jon Skoog	St. Norbert	SO	D	29	0.31	0- 9- 9
85	Dan Fina	Wis-Eau Claire	SO	F	15	0.53	5- 3- 8
	Jameson Lundquist	St. Scholastica	FR	F	20	0.4	4- 4- 8
	Matt Lamirande	Wis-Superior	FR	F	21	0.38	3- 5- 8
	Brett Coburn	Wis-Stevens Pt.	SR	F	23	0.35	3- 5- 8
	Jordan Chong	St. Scholastica	FR	F	24	0.33	5- 3- 8
	Brian Bina	Wis-Superior	FR	D	26	0.31	2- 6- 8
	Dave Coleman	Wis-Eau Claire	SR	F	27	0.3	6- 2- 8
	Justin Taylor	Lake Forest	FR	F	27	0.3	3- 5- 8
	Adam Setten	Wis-Stevens Pt.	SR	D	27	0.3	0- 8- 8
94	Peter Fylling	St. Norbert	FR	F	15	0.47	3- 4- 7
	Evan Byers	Wis-Eau Claire	SO	D	19	0.37	3- 4- 7
	Sam Tikka	St. Norbert	FR	D	19	0.37	1- 6- 7
	Lance Malark	Wis-River Falls	SO	F	19	0.37	1- 6- 7
	James Switzer	St. Norbert	SR	F	26	0.27	2- 5- 7
	Jeff Herman	Wis-Superior	SO	D	26	0.27	1- 6- 7
	Tyler Gow	St. Norbert	SR	D	27	0.26	0- 7- 7
	Scott Honkola	St. Scholastica	SR	D	28	0.25	0- 7- 7
102	Art Clark	Wis-Superior	FR	F	8	0.75	1- 5- 6
	Kris Boyce	St. Scholastica	FR	F	10	0.6	3- 3- 6
	Reed Lally	Wis-Stevens Pt.	FR	F	21	0.29	2- 4- 6
	Tyler Allen	St. Norbert	FR	F	21	0.29	1- 5- 6
	Tom Upton	Wis-Stevens Pt.	FR	D	23	0.26	0- 6- 6
	Adam Boche	Wis-Stout	SR	D	27	0.22	3- 3- 6
	Todd Wynia	Wis-Stout	JR	D	27	0.22	2- 4- 6
	Cory Baldwin	Wis-River Falls	FR	F	29	0.21	3- 3- 6
110	Joey Nigro	St. Scholastica	FR	F	7	0.71	1- 4- 5
	Mark Stockdale	Wis-Eau Claire	FR	F	8	0.62	3- 2- 5
	Brad Herman	St. Norbert	FR	F	14	0.36	0- 5- 5
	Ross Johnson	Wis-Stevens Pt.	SO	F	15	0.33	4- 1- 5
	Brooks Lockwood	Wis-Eau Claire	SR	F	19	0.26	1- 4- 5
	Scott Hellquist	Wis-Stout	SR	D	20	0.25	1- 4- 5
	Andy Sternberg	Wis-Stout	FR	F	21	0.24	2- 3- 5
	Dane Bushey	Wis-Superior	FR	F	24	0.21	0- 5- 5
	Shane Auger	St. Scholastica	SO	D	26	0.19	1- 4- 5

	Sam Bauler	Wis-Eau Claire	SO	F	27	0.19	2- 3- 5
	Chris Robinson	Wis-River Falls	SO	D	29	0.17	2- 3- 5
121	Joel Gaulrapp	Wis-Superior	FR	F	8	0.5	3- 1- 4
	Jeff Wheeler	Wis-Stout	SO	F	12	0.33	2- 2- 4
	Christopher Blackmon	St. Scholastica	FR	F	13	0.31	3- 1- 4
	Andy Cankar	Wis-Stevens Pt.	SO	F	17	0.24	2- 2- 4
	Mike Schneider	Wis-Eau Claire	SO	F	18	0.22	2- 2- 4
	Tyler Trudell	Wis-Eau Claire	FR	D	23	0.17	2- 2- 4
	Sean Pettinger	Wis-River Falls	FR	D	23	0.17	1- 3- 4
	Neil Sauter	St. Scholastica	FR	D	26	0.15	1- 3- 4
	Joe Papineau	Lake Forest	SO	D	27	0.15	2- 2- 4
	BJ Garczynski	Wis-Stout	SR	D	27	0.15	0- 4- 4
131	Shane McCormick	St. Norbert	JR	F	11	0.27	3- 0- 3
	Eric Bausano	Wis-Superior	SO	F	11	0.27	1- 2- 3
	Jason Usher	Wis-River Falls	JR	D	13	0.23	1- 2- 3
	Ryan Kuntz	Wis-Superior	SO	F	15	0.2	1- 2- 3
	Joe Bluhm	Wis-Superior	FR	F	17	0.18	2- 1- 3
	Rob Mueller	Wis-Stout	SO	F	18	0.17	2- 1- 3
	Chris Thiess	Lake Forest	FR	F	20	0.15	2- 1- 3
	Adam Love	Lake Forest	FR	F	24	0.12	1- 2- 3
	Blake O'Keefe	Lake Forest	JR	F	25	0.12	2- 1- 3
	Graham Melbourne	Lake Forest	SR	D	26	0.12	2- 1- 3
	Nicholas Kuqali	Wis-Eau Claire	FR	D	26	0.12	1- 2- 3
	Chris Meagher	St. Scholastica	FR	D	26	0.12	0- 3- 3
	Dustin Cosgrove	Wis-Superior	JR	D	27	0.11	1- 2- 3
	Jason Nopper	St. Norbert	FR	D	28	0.11	1- 2- 3
145	Jamie Lazorko	Wis-Superior	JR	D	5	0.4	1- 1- 2
	Chris Conway	Wis-Stevens Pt.	FR	F	9	0.22	1- 1- 2
	Tom Flikeid	Wis-River Falls	SO	F	11	0.18	1- 1- 2
	Dustin Dubas	St. Norbert	FR	D	12	0.17	0- 2- 2
	Nick Ghidina	Lake Forest	FR	D	13	0.15	1- 1- 2
	Michael Epp	St. Scholastica	SR	D	13	0.15	0- 2- 2
	Jake Gullickson	Wis-Stout	FR	D/F	14	0.14	1- 1- 2
	Karl Larsen	Wis-Stevens Pt.	SO	D	16	0.12	0- 2- 2
	Josh Seifert	Wis-Superior	FR	D	16	0.12	0- 2- 2
	Nick Bydal	Wis-Stevens Pt.	SO	D	20	0.1	0- 2- 2
	Taylor Guay	Wis-Stevens Pt.	SO	F	22	0.09	1- 1- 2
	Kevin Russette	Lake Forest	JR	D	26	0.08	1- 1- 2
	Matt Schoepflin	Lake Forest	SO	F	27	0.07	1- 1- 2
	AJ Bucchino	Wis-River Falls	SO	G	29	0.07	0- 2- 2
159	Chris Rampone	St. Norbert	JR	F	3	0.33	1- 0- 1
	Matt Buha	Wis-Stevens Pt.	SO	F	4	0.25	0- 1- 1
	T.J. Warkentin	Wis-River Falls	FR	F	5	0.2	0- 1- 1
	Skylar Christoffersen	Wis-River Falls	FR	F	5	0.2	0- 1- 1
	Scott Sikkink	Wis-Stout	JR	F	5	0.2	0- 1- 1
	Steve Bounds	St. Scholastica	SO	G	6	0.17	0- 1- 1
	Jeremiah Weber	Wis-Eau Claire	JR	F	6	0.17	0- 1- 1
	Chris Rashotte	Lake Forest	FR	F	7	0.14	1- 0- 1
	Tom Vernelli	Wis-Stevens Pt.	JR	F	9	0.11	1- 0- 1
	Ben Bosworth	Wis-Eau Claire	SO	F	9	0.11	0- 1- 1
	Kyle Crable	Wis-Stout	JR	F	9	0.11	0- 1- 1
	Anthony Casmano	Wis-Superior	FR	F	9	0.11	0- 1- 1
	Joe Krahn	Wis-Eau Claire	FR	F	11	0.09	1- 0- 1
	Jeff Gagnon	St. Scholastica	FR	F	11	0.09	0- 1- 1
	Joe Adams	Wis-River Falls	JR	F	12	0.08	1- 0- 1
	Devin Underwood	Wis-River Falls	SO	F	12	0.08	0- 1- 1
	Matt Forsyth	Lake Forest	SR	F	13	0.08	0- 1- 1
	Kevin Knapp	Wis-Eau Claire	SR	D	14	0.07	0- 1- 1
	Tyler Weigel	Wis-Eau Claire	FR	F	14	0.07	0- 1- 1
	Petter Andersson	Lake Forest	FR	D	15	0.07	0- 1- 1

Nate Sorenson	Wis-Stevens Pt.	JR	D	16	0.06	1- 0- 1
Mikael Virta	St. Norbert	SR	D	16	0.06	0- 1- 1
Will Stoner	Lake Forest	FR	F	17	0.06	1- 0- 1
Shane Foster	Wis-Stevens Pt.	SO	F	17	0.06	1- 0- 1
Chad Beiswenger	Wis-Superior	SO	G	21	0.05	0- 1- 1
Dan Lohr	Wis-Eau Claire	SR	D	23	0.04	0- 1- 1
Peter Bracker	Wis-Eau Claire	SO	F	24	0.04	1- 0- 1
Anthony Noreen	Wis-Stevens Pt.	SR	D	26	0.04	0- 1- 1
Josh Meyers	Wis-River Falls	SO	D	29	0.03	0- 1- 1

GOALS AGAINST AVERAGE:

				MINUTES	GA	GAA
1	Kyle Jones	St. Norbert	SO	1767:54:00	52	1.76
2	AJ Bucchino	Wis-River Falls	FR	1095:39:00	38	2.08
3	Matthew Bonelly	Wis-Superior	SR	1161:14:00	43	2.22
4	Tyler Johnson	St. Scholastica	SO	560:26:00	24	2.57
5	Steve Bounds	St. Scholastica	FR	1064:11:00	49	2.76
6	Brandon Kohuch	Lake Forest	FR	871:29:00	41	2.82
7	Marcus Paulson	Wis-Stevens Pt.	FR	1272:49:00	61	2.88
8	Scott Campbell	Lake Forest	FR	806:49:00	40	2.97
9	Matt Koenig	Wis-Stout	FR	750:31:00	38	3.04
10	Mike Stone	Wis-Stout	SO	920:12:00	49	3.19
11	Steffan Braunlich	Wis-Eau Claire	SR	1355:00:00	79	3.5

Minimum 33% of Team Minutes Played

SAVE PERCENTAGE:

				SAVES	GA	PCT
1	AJ Bucchino	Wis-River Falls	FR	570	38	0.938
2	Brandon Kohuch	Lake Forest	FR	506	41	0.925
3	Scott Campbell	Lake Forest	FR	485	40	0.924
4	Kyle Jones	St. Norbert	SO	589	52	0.919
5	Matthew Bonelly	Wis-Superior	SR	472	43	0.917
6	Mike Stone	Wis-Stout	SO	491	49	0.909
7	Steve Bounds	St. Scholastica	FR	463	49	0.904
8	Steffan Braunlich	Wis-Eau Claire	SR	691	79	0.897
9	Matt Koenig	Wis-Stout	FR	331	38	0.897
10	Tyler Johnson	St. Scholastica	SO	201	24	0.893
11	Marcus Paulson	Wis-Stevens Pt.	FR	508	61	0.893

Minimum 33% of Team Minutes Played

WINNING PERCENTAGE:

				W- L- T	PCT
1	Kyle Jones	St. Norbert	SO	24- 4- 2	0.833
2	Matthew Bonelly	Wis-Superior	SR	13- 5- 2	0.7
3	Tyler Johnson	St. Scholastica	SO	6- 3- 0	0.667
4	Brandon Kohuch	Lake Forest	FR	9- 5- 0	0.643
5	AJ Bucchino	Wis-River Falls	FR	10- 5- 3	0.639
6	Mike Stone	Wis-Stout	SO	9- 7- 0	0.562
7	Steve Bounds	St. Scholastica	FR	9- 7- 2	0.556
8	Marcus Paulson	Wis-Stevens Pt.	FR	10- 8- 3	0.548
9	Matt Koenig	Wis-Stout	FR	6- 6- 0	0.5
10	Scott Campbell	Lake Forest	FR	6- 8- 0	0.429
11	Steffan Braunlich	Wis-Eau Claire	SR	2-19- 2	0.13

Minimum 33% of Team Minutes Played

Junior Hockey Guide

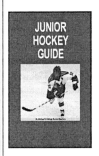

The **Junior Hockey Guide** provides US Major Junior, Tier 1, Junior A, B and C league and team contacts and Canadian Junior A & B league and team contacts. The Guide is an excellent resource for prospective players as they investigate a variety of junior hockey opportunities. Learn which leagues and teams have the best record of success in placing players in college hockey programs. The **Junior Hockey Guide** is the definitive reference work for junior hockey.

To Order by Phone Call:
800.255.1050

www.hockeybookstore.com

To order by Mail
Send Check or Money Order in the amount of $45.95 U.S. to:
Athletic Guide Publishing
PO Box 1050
Flagler Beach, FL 32136
386.439.2250

Prep School Hockey Guide

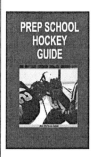

The **Prep School Hockey Guide** covers the investigation and selection of a prep school, including admission, tuition, acceptance and financial aid information; admission and hockey contacts for leading prep schools in the U.S. and Canada.

To Order by Phone Call:
800.255.1050

www.hockeybookstore.com

To order by Mail
Send Check or Money Order in the amount of $42.95 U.S. to:
Athletic Guide Publishing
PO Box 1050
Flagler Beach, FL 32136
386.439.2250

**State University of New York
Athletic Conference**
State University of New York - Fredonia
Fredonia, New York 14063
www.sunyac.com/icehockey

**Commissioner
Dr. Patrick R. Damore**
Office: 716.673.3105
Fax: 716.673.3135
sunyac@fredonia.edu

**Publicist
John Czarnecki**
Office: 716.673.3105
Fax: 716.673.3135
sunyac.pub@fredonia.edu

SUNY - Brockport

SUNY - Buffalo State

SUNY - Cortland

SUNY - Fredonia

SUNY - Geneseo

SUNY - Morrisville

SUNY - Oswego

SUNY - Plattsburgh

SUNY - Potsdam

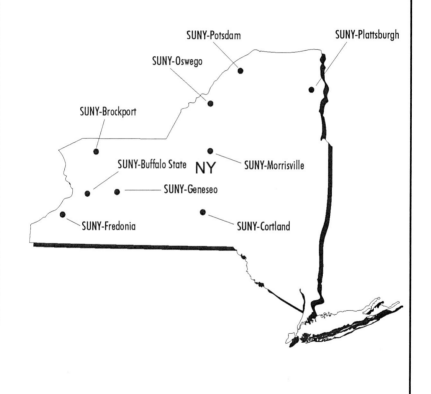

| SUNYAC | STATE UNIVERSITY OF NEW YORK ATHLETIC CONFERENCE |

STATE UNIVERSITY OF NEW YORK
ATHLETIC CONFERENCE
FINAL 2006-07 CONFERENCE STANDINGS

		Pts	GP	Record	Win%	GF-GA	GP	Record	Win%	GF-GA
1	Oswego	24	14	11- 1- 2	0.857	64- 28	29	23- 3- 3	0.845	139- 56
2	Geneseo	20	14	10- 4- 0	0.714	52- 30	26	16-10- 0	0.615	99- 86
3	Plattsburgh	16	14	6- 4- 4	0.571	61- 40	28	14- 8- 6	0.607	129- 76
4	Buffalo State	13	14	6- 7- 1	0.464	45- 46	26	12-12- 2	0.500	90- 86
5	Fredonia	12	14	5- 7- 2	0.429	39- 48	29	15-10- 4	0.586	106- 93
6	Brockport	11	14	3- 6- 5	0.393	39- 54	26	7-12- 7	0.404	67-100
7	Cortland	9	14	3- 8- 3	0.321	41- 62	25	8-14- 3	0.380	71-102
8	Potsdam	7	14	3-10- 1	0.250	42- 75	25	5-19- 1	0.220	68-130

2007 STATE UNIVERSITY OF NEW YORK ATHLETIC CONFERENCE PLAYOFFS

QUARTER FINALS (2.20.07)

SUNY - Fredonia	2	SUNY - Buffalo State	1
SUNY - Brockport	2	SUNY - Plattsburgh	9

SEMI FINALS (2.24.07)

SUNY - Plattsburgh	8	SUNY - Geneseo	2
SUNY - Fredonia	3	SUNY - Oswego	2

CHAMPIONSHIP (3.03.07)
(Best of Three Series)

SUNY - Fredonia	6	SUNY - Plattsburgh	4

STATE UNIVERSITY OF NEW YORK
ATHLETIC CONFERENCE TOURNAMENT CHAMPIONS

TOURNAMENT

Year	Champion	Year	Champion
1978	SUNY Plattsburgh	1993	SUNY Plattsburgh
1979	SUNY Plattsburgh	1994	SUNY Fredonia
1980	SUNY Oswego	1995	SUNY Fredonia
1981	SUNY Oswego	1996	SUNY Potsdam
1982	SUNY Oswego	1997	SUNY Plattsburgh
	SUNY Plattsburgh	1998	SUNY Plattsburgh
1983	SUNY Plattsburgh	1999	SUNY Plattsburgh
1984	SUNY Oswego	2000	SUNY Plattsburgh
1985	SUNY Plattsburgh	2001	SUNY Plattsburgh
1986	SUNY Geneseo	2002	SUNY Plattsburgh
1987	SUNY Plattsburgh	2003	SUNY Oswego
1988	SUNY Plattsburgh	2004	SUNY Plattsburgh
1989	SUNY Oswego	2005	SUNY Geneseo
1990	SUNY Plattsburgh	2006	SUNY Geneseo
1991	SUNY Oswego	2007	SUNY Fredonia
1992	SUNY Plattsburgh		

SUNYAC LEAGUE SCORING (OVERALL):

					GP	PPG	G - A - P
1	Mitch Stephens	Geneseo	SR	F	26	2.12	10-45-55
	Brendan McLaughlin	Oswego	SO	F	29	1.90	24-31-55
3	Neal Sheehan	Fredonia	JR	F	29	1.59	22-24-46
4	Ryan Ellis	Oswego	SO	F	26	1.62	16-26-42
5	Jason Hill	Buffalo State	SO	F	23	1.70	14-25-39
6	Barry McLaughlin	Cortland	JR	F	25	1.52	23-15-38
7	Ryan Busby	Plattsburgh	SR	F	27	1.30	14-21-35
	Pier-Luc Belanger	Plattsburgh	FR	F	28	1.25	16-19-35
	Peter Magagna	Oswego	SO	F	28	1.25	11-24-35
10	Mike MacDonald	Geneseo	SR	F	26	1.27	14-19-33
11	Kevin Galan	Plattsburgh	SO	F	27	1.11	13-17-30
12	Nick Rolls	Plattsburgh	SO	D	28	1.00	5-23-28
	Kyle Bozoian	Fredonia	SR	F	29	0.97	14-14-28
14	Garren Reisweber	Oswego	SO	F	24	1.12	15-12-27
	D'Arcy Thomas	Buffalo State	FR	F	25	1.08	14-13-27
	Riley Hill	Plattsburgh	SO	F	25	1.08	11-16-27
17	C.J. Thompson	Oswego	JR	F	29	0.90	14-12-26
	Steve Albert	Fredonia	JR	D	29	0.90	3-23-26
19	Ryan McCarthy	Potsdam	SR	F	22	1.14	14-11-25
	Nick Catanzaro	Cortland	SO	F	24	1.04	8-17-25
	Mike DeMarco	Buffalo State	SR	F	25	1.00	5-20-25
	Colin Sarfeh	Fredonia	SO	D	28	0.89	5-20-25
23	Luke Beck	Potsdam	FR	F	24	1.00	7-17-24
	Trent Cassan	Geneseo	JR	F	25	0.96	16- 8-24
	Connor Treacy	Potsdam	FR	F	25	0.96	13-11-24
	Ryan Woodward	Oswego	SR	F	29	0.83	9-15-24
27	Mike Thomson	Plattsburgh	SO	F	25	0.92	9-14-23
	Mathieu Cyr	Geneseo	JR	F	26	0.88	12-11-23
	Scott Bradley	Fredonia	SR	F	27	0.85	5-18-23
30	Gerard Heinz	Cortland	FR	D	24	0.92	5-17-22
	Buddy Anderson	Cortland	SR	F	25	0.88	5-17-22
	Bryan Goudy	Fredonia	SO	F	28	0.79	10-12-22
33	Adam Gebara	Potsdam	SR	F	25	0.84	8-13-21
	Ryan Koresky	Oswego	SR	D	25	0.84	3-18-21
	Chris Koras	Brockport	JR	F	26	0.81	2-19-21
	Kraig Kuzma	Fredonia	SR	F	29	0.72	9-12-21
37	Matt McKeown	Fredonia	FR	F	22	0.91	11- 9-20
	Shawn Dennis	Plattsburgh	SO	F	23	0.87	8-12-20
	Tony DiNunzio	Oswego	JR	F	29	0.69	8-12-20
40	Joey Wilson	Plattsburgh	FR	F	26	0.73	14- 5-19
41	Johnny Duco	Buffalo State	JR	F	23	0.78	5-13-18
	Casey Smith	Plattsburgh	SO	D	25	0.72	6-12-18
	Tyson Terry	Geneseo	SR	F	25	0.72	4-14-18
	Gordon Pritchard	Brockport	JR	F	26	0.69	12- 6-18
45	Chris Kestell	Geneseo	SO	D	26	0.65	8- 9-17
	Anthony Leccese	Brockport	SR	D	26	0.65	4-13-17
	Rich Zalewski	Oswego	SO	D	28	0.61	7-10-17
48	Andrew Willock	Plattsburgh	FR	F	22	0.73	3-13-16
	Shane Remenda	Plattsburgh	SR	F	24	0.67	7- 9-16
	Pat Lemay	Potsdam	JR	F	25	0.64	5-11-16
	Sebastian Panetta	Geneseo	FR	F	26	0.62	9- 7-16
	Matt Whitehead	Oswego	SO	F	26	0.62	8- 8-16
53	Paul Michael Rivest	Buffalo State	FR	F	26	0.58	6- 9-15
	Cody Cole	Buffalo State	SO	D	26	0.58	5-10-15
	Steve Sankey	Geneseo	JR	D	26	0.58	4-11-15
56	Tom Breslin	Plattsburgh	FR	D	25	0.56	1-13-14
	Ward Smith	Plattsburgh	FR	D	26	0.54	3-11-14
	Neil Musselwhite	Oswego	FR	F	28	0.50	8- 6-14

59	Justin Merritt	Buffalo State	FR	D	24	0.54	3-10-13
	Aaron Boyer	Brockport	SO	F	25	0.52	6- 7-13
61	Jeff Mok	Buffalo State	JR	D	15	0.80	5- 7-12
	Phil Farrow	Plattsburgh	FR	F	20	0.60	4- 8-12
	Jeff Zatorski	Potsdam	FR	D	23	0.52	4- 8-12
	Steve Seedhouse	Brockport	JR	F	26	0.46	7- 5-12
	Richard Curtis	Buffalo State	SO	F	26	0.46	5- 7-12
66	Frank Rizzo	Cortland	FR	F	15	0.73	6- 5-11
	Mark Lozzi	Oswego	SO	F	17	0.65	1-10-11
	Vince Tarantino	Potsdam	SR	D	20	0.55	5- 6-11
	Zach Dehm	Cortland	JR	F	22	0.50	7- 4-11
	Nik Bibic	Potsdam	JR	D	23	0.48	2- 9-11
	Sean O'Malley	Brockport	FR	F	24	0.46	6- 5-11
	C.J. Tozzo	Plattsburgh	JR	F	24	0.46	2- 9-11
	Matt Pfalzer	Fredonia	FR	D	24	0.46	1-10-11
	Brad Dormiedy	Oswego	FR	F	25	0.44	6- 5-11
	Greg Schwind	Brockport	JR	F	25	0.44	3- 8-11
	Francois Gagnon	Oswego	SO	D	27	0.41	2- 9-11
77	Joe Curry	Buffalo State	SO	F	21	0.48	6- 4-10
	Shareef Labreche	Buffalo State	FR	F	21	0.48	6- 4-10
	Pat Capella	Fredonia	FR	F	21	0.48	4- 6-10
	Steve Cornelissen	Potsdam	FR	D	23	0.43	2- 8-10
	Mark Schwamberger	Geneseo	SR	F	25	0.40	4- 6-10
	Derrell Levy	Oswego	SO	F	27	0.37	1- 9-10
	Joe Muli	Fredonia	SR	F	28	0.36	7- 3-10
84	Brett Bestwick	Geneseo	SR	F	11	0.82	3- 6- 9
	Dennis Sicard	Buffalo State	FR	F	14	0.64	3- 6- 9
	Nick Shackford	Cortland	FR	F	16	0.56	4- 5- 9
	Dan Brown	Geneseo	FR	F	22	0.41	3- 6- 9
	Wil Barlow	Fredonia	SR	F	23	0.39	4- 5- 9
	Casey Balog	Geneseo	SO	F	24	0.38	5- 4- 9
	T.J. Cooper	Plattsburgh	JR	F	25	0.36	7- 2- 9
	Travis Whitehead	Buffalo State	SO	F	26	0.35	3- 6- 9
	Tyler Lyon	Oswego	FR	D	27	0.33	3- 6- 9
93	Lucas Schott	Brockport	FR	F	18	0.44	2- 6- 8
	Jason Dolgy	Brockport	JR	F	22	0.36	5- 3- 8
	Chris Brown	Brockport	JR	D	26	0.31	5- 3- 8
	Don Jaeger	Fredonia	SR	D	26	0.31	2- 6- 8
	Adam Haberman	Fredonia	JR	F	28	0.29	4- 4- 8
98	Ryan Watts	Potsdam	JR	F	19	0.37	1- 6- 7
	Mike Egan	Cortland	SO	D	22	0.32	2- 5- 7
	Rick Janco	Plattsburgh	JR	D	25	0.28	1- 6- 7
	Phil Rose	Geneseo	FR	F	26	0.27	4- 3- 7
102	Tyler Soehner	Buffalo State	FR	D	10	0.60	1- 5- 6
	Rick Varone	Oswego	SO	F	22	0.27	1- 5- 6
	Jesse Adair	Buffalo State	FR	D	24	0.25	3- 3- 6
	Blake Rielly	Brockport	SO	F	24	0.25	2- 4- 6
	Warren Sly	Potsdam	JR	D	24	0.25	0- 6- 6
	Matt Nichols	Cortland	JR	F	25	0.24	4- 2- 6
108	Mike Fiume	Buffalo State	JR	F	8	0.62	1- 4- 5
	Lance Smith	Potsdam	JR	D	18	0.28	1- 4- 5
	Peter Deloria	Cortland	SR	D	23	0.22	0- 5- 5
	Kyle McCutcheon	Oswego	SO	F	23	0.22	0- 5- 5
	Mike Luzarraga	Buffalo State	FR	F	25	0.20	1- 4- 5
	AJ Maio	Brockport	SR	F	26	0.19	4- 1- 5
	Mike Gershon	Brockport	SO	D	26	0.19	1- 4- 5
115	Mike Ansell	Buffalo State	JR	D	13	0.31	2- 2- 4
	Trevor Gilligan	Oswego	SR	F	16	0.25	2- 2- 4
	Eric Greene	Plattsburgh	FR	D	16	0.25	2- 2- 4
	Tyler Laws	Oswego	SO	D	16	0.25	0- 4- 4

	Tony Marinello	Brockport	JR	F	17	0.24	2- 2- 4
	James Muscatello	Fredonia	FR	F	21	0.19	1- 3- 4
	Tim Crowley	Brockport	SO	F	23	0.17	1- 3- 4
	Ryan LaShomb	Cortland	SR	F	24	0.17	2- 2- 4
	John Gleason	Brockport	JR	D	25	0.16	2- 2- 4
	Richard Boyce	Fredonia	SO	F	25	0.16	1- 3- 4
	Niles Moore	Cortland	FR	F	25	0.16	0- 4- 4
126	Evan DiValentino	Fredonia	JR	D	5	0.60	0- 3- 3
	Jordan Stevenson	Plattsburgh	FR	F	8	0.38	1- 2- 3
	Paul Gagnon	Buffalo State	JR	F	15	0.20	1- 2- 3
	Geoff Schweikhard	Brockport	JR	F	16	0.19	2- 1- 3
	Andrew Dissanayake	Fredonia	FR	F	17	0.18	1- 2- 3
	Jeff Aonso	Fredonia	FR	F	17	0.18	1- 2- 3
	Casey Hubbard	Cortland	SO	D	21	0.14	0- 3- 3
	Mike Novak	Oswego	SO	D	21	0.14	0- 3- 3
	Matt Goslant	Cortland	JR	F	22	0.14	1- 2- 3
	Ricky Gates	Brockport	JR	F	23	0.13	0- 3- 3
	Jeff MacPhee	Geneseo	FR	D	23	0.13	0- 3- 3
137	Ryan Silveira	Plattsburgh	FR	F	6	0.33	1- 1- 2
	Dave McNab	Brockport	SO	F	8	0.25	0- 2- 2
	Craig Carlyle	Brockport	SO	D	12	0.17	1- 1- 2
	Andrew Rebus	Geneseo	FR	D	12	0.17	1- 1- 2
	Chris Corso	Cortland	SO	F	14	0.14	1- 1- 2
	Jason Gorrie	Plattsburgh	FR	F	15	0.13	1- 1- 2
	Mike Knapp	Potsdam	JR	F	15	0.13	1- 1- 2
	Josh Gilson	Potsdam	SO	F	17	0.12	2- 0- 2
	Shawn O'Donoghue	Buffalo State	SO	F	17	0.12	0- 2- 2
	Clay Lewis	Buffalo State	SR	D	17	0.12	0- 2- 2
	Mike Baccaro	Plattsburgh	JR	F	19	0.11	0- 2- 2
	John Southwick	Potsdam	SO	D	20	0.10	1- 1- 2
	Sean Brackin	Potsdam	JR	F	21	0.10	1- 1- 2
	Patrick Palmisano	Cortland	FR	F	21	0.10	0- 2- 2
	Justin Kocent	Cortland	SO	F	22	0.09	2- 0- 2
	Ryan Trimble	Potsdam	SR	D	22	0.09	1- 1- 2
	Frank Soscia	Fredonia	FR	D	22	0.09	0- 2- 2
	Jeff Sylvester	Fredonia	SO	D	23	0.09	1- 1- 2
	Steve Jordan	Geneseo	SR	D	24	0.08	0- 2- 2
	Jon Sandos	Cortland	SR	D	25	0.08	0- 2- 2
157	Chris Hyk	Oswego	SO	G	4	0.25	0- 1- 1
	Kelly Stokley	Geneseo	FR	F	7	0.14	1- 0- 1
	Justin Bodine	Cortland	JR	F	7	0.14	0- 1- 1
	Dave Dobrinsky	Geneseo	FR	F	9	0.11	0- 1- 1
	Corey LaRoche	Cortland	SO	F	10	0.10	0- 1- 1
	Mike Bush	Fredonia	FR	F	11	0.09	0- 1- 1
	Connor King	Buffalo State	FR	F	12	0.08	0- 1- 1
	Ryan Burke	Plattsburgh	SO	D	12	0.08	0- 1- 1
	Greg Van't Hof	Brockport	JR	G	13	0.08	0- 1- 1
	Mike Friel	Cortland	FR	F	15	0.07	1- 0- 1
	Steve Wowchuk	Brockport	JR	D	15	0.07	0- 1- 1
	Ryan Ramage	Buffalo State	FR	D	16	0.06	1- 0- 1
	Sean Hayden	Geneseo	SO	D	18	0.06	1- 0- 1
	Ram Sidhu	Geneseo	JR	F	18	0.06	0- 1- 1
	Dan Quartucio	Potsdam	SR	F	21	0.05	0- 1- 1
	Derek Jokic	Geneseo	JR	G	23	0.04	0- 1- 1
	Brandon French	Geneseo	SO	F	25	0.04	0- 1- 1

GOALS AGAINST AVERAGE:

				MINUTES	GA	GAA
1	Ryan Scott	Oswego	JR	1534:36:00	51	1.99
2	Karl Helgesson	Plattsburgh	JR	581:33:00	22	2.27
3	Chris Molinaro	Plattsburgh	SO	1104:21:00	50	2.72
4	Derek Jokic	Geneseo	JR	1318:25:00	68	3.09
5	Pat Street	Fredonia	FR	1122:29:00	60	3.21
6	Sean Sheehan	Buffalo State	SR	1370:20:00	74	3.24
7	Ben Binga	Cortland	FR	1285:20:00	75	3.5
8	Todd Sheridan	Brockport	FR	871:14:00	51	3.51
9	Greg Van't Hof	Brockport	JR	688:49:00	43	3.75
10	Rob Barnhardt	Potsdam	JR	696:53:00	55	4.74
11	Vince Cuccaro	Potsdam	SR	762:03:00	66	5.2

Minimum 33% of Team Minutes Played

SAVE PERCENTAGE:

				SAVES	GA	PCT
1	Ryan Scott	Oswego	JR	597	51	0.921
2	Pat Street	Fredonia	FR	590	60	0.908
3	Derek Jokic	Geneseo	JR	652	68	0.906
4	Ben Binga	Cortland	FR	704	75	0.904
5	Karl Helgesson	Plattsburgh	JR	201	22	0.901
6	Chris Molinaro	Plattsburgh	SO	452	50	0.9
7	Sean Sheehan	Buffalo State	SR	667	74	0.9
8	Rob Barnhardt	Potsdam	JR	435	55	0.888
9	Greg Van't Hof	Brockport	JR	321	43	0.882
10	Todd Sheridan	Brockport	FR	379	51	0.881
11	Vince Cuccaro	Potsdam	SR	389	66	0.855

Minimum 33% of Team Minutes Played

WINNING PERCENTAGE:

				W- L- T	PCT
1	Ryan Scott	Oswego	JR	19- 3- 3	0.82
2	Chris Molinaro	Plattsburgh	SO	10- 5- 4	0.632
3	Derek Jokic	Geneseo	JR	13- 9- 0	0.591
4	Karl Helgesson	Plattsburgh	JR	4- 3- 2	0.556
5	Sean Sheehan	Buffalo State	SR	10-11- 2	0.478
6	Todd Sheridan	Brockport	FR	4- 5- 4	0.462
7	Pat Street	Fredonia	FR	6- 8- 4	0.444
8	Ben Binga	Cortland	FR	7-12- 3	0.386
9	Greg Van't Hof	Brockport	JR	3- 7- 3	0.346
10	Vince Cuccaro	Potsdam	SR	3-11- 1	0.233
11	Rob Barnhardt	Potsdam	JR	2- 8- 0	0.2

Minimum 33% of Team Minutes Played

Western Collegiate Hockey Association

559 D'Onofrio Drive, Suite 103
Madison, WI 53719-2096
www.wcha.com

Commissioner
Bruce M. McLeod
Office: 303.871.4223
Fax: 303.871.4770
email: bmcleod@du.edu

Assistant Commissioner
of Operations
Carol LaBelle-Ehrhardt
Office: 303.871.4223
Fax: 303.871.4770
email: clabelle@du.edu

Associate Commissioner
for Public Relations
Doug Spencer
Office: 608.829.0100
Fax: 608.829.0200
email: dspencer@mailbag.com

Assistant to the Commissioner
Jeff Sauer
email: coachjsauer@juno.com

Supervisor of Officials
Greg Shepherd
Office: 303.451.9995
Fax: 303.451.9995
Cell: 303.478.3696
Pager: 612.539.6423
email: g.shepherd@mailstation.com

University of Alaska Anchorage
Colorado College
University of Denver
Michigan Technological University
Minnesota State University Mankato
University of Minnesota Duluth
University of Minnesota Twin Cities
University of North Dakota
St. Cloud State University
University of Wisconsin Madison

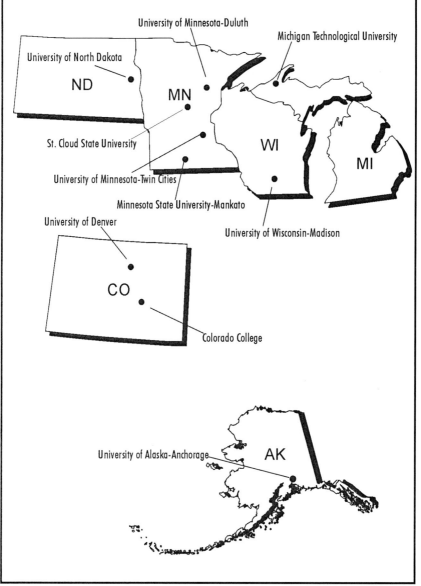

University of Minnesota-Duluth

Michigan Technological University

University of North Dakota

ND

MN

St. Cloud State University

WI

MI

University of Minnesota-Twin Cities

Minnesota State University-Mankato

University of Denver

University of Wisconsin-Madison

CO

Colorado College

University of Alaska-Anchorage

AK

WESTERN COLLEGIATE HOCKEY ASSOCIATION
FINAL 2006-07 CONFERENCE STANDINGS

		Pts	GP	Record	Win%	GF-GA	GP	Record	Win%	GF-GA
1	Minnesota Twin Cities	39	28	18- 7- 3	0.696	91- 67	44	31-10- 3	0.739	161-101
2	St. Cloud State	35	28	14- 7- 7	0.625	89- 70	40	22-11- 7	0.638	127- 99
3	North Dakota	31	28	13-10- 5	0.554	93- 75	43	24-14- 5	0.616	153-116
4	Denver	30	28	13-11- 4	0.536	73- 73	40	21-15- 4	0.575	107- 95
5	Colorado College	29	28	13-12- 3	0.518	79- 74	39	18-17- 4	0.513	111- 98
6	Michigan Tech	27	28	11-12- 5	0.482	69- 64	40	18-17- 5	0.512	90- 87
	Wisconsin	27	28	12-13- 3	0.482	59- 53	41	19-18- 4	0.512	93- 83
8	Minnesota State	25	28	10-13- 5	0.446	81- 99	38	13-19- 6	0.421	106-132
9	Minnesota Duluth	20	28	8-16- 4	0.357	64- 84	39	13-21- 5	0.397	103-121
10	Alaska Anchorage	17	28	8-19- 1	0.304	62-101	37	13-21- 3	0.392	90-124

2007 WESTERN COLLEGIATE HOCKEY ASSOCIATION PLAYOFFS

FIRST ROUND *(3.09.07 - 3.11.07)*
(Best of Three Series)

University of Minnesota Duluth	1	St. Cloud State University	2
University of Alaska Anchorage	1	University of Minnesota Twin Cities	2
Michigan Tech University	2	Colorado College	1
University of Wisconsin	2	Denver University	0
Minnesota State University	0	University of North Dakota	2

QUARTER FINAL *(3.15.07)*

University of Wisconsin	4	Michigan Tech University	0

SEMI FINALS *(3.16.07)*

University of North Dakota	6	St. Cloud State University	2
University of Wisconsin	2	University of Minnesota Twin Cities	4

THIRD PLACE GAME *(3.17.07)*

University of Wisconsin	4	St. Cloud State University	3

BROADMOOR TROPHY CHAMPIONSHIP *(3.17.07)*

University of North Dakota	2	University of Minnesota Twin Cities	3

WESTERN COLLEGIATE HOCKEY ASSOCIATION CHAMPIONS

	REGULAR	TOURNAMENT
1952	Colorado College	
1953	University of Minnesota Twin Cities	
1954	University of Minnesota Twin Cities	
1955	Colorado College	
1956	University of Michigan Ann Arbor	
1957	Colorado College	
1958	University of North Dakota	
1960	University of Denver	
1961	University of Denver	
1962	Michigan Technological University	
1963	University of Denver	
1964	University of Denver	
1965	Michigan Technological University	
1966	Michigan Technological University	
1967	University of North Dakota	
1968	University of Denver	
1969	Michigan Technological University	
1970	University of Minnesota Twin Cities	
1971	Michigan Technological University	
1972	University of Denver	
1973	University of Denver	
1974	Michigan Technological University	
1975	University of Minnesota Twin Cities	
1976	Michigan Technological University	
1977	University of Wisconsin	
1978	University of Denver	
1979	University of North Dakota	
1980	University of North Dakota	
1981	University of Minnesota Twin Cities	
1982	University of North Dakota	
1983	University of Minnesota Twin Cities	
1984	University of Minnesota Duluth	University of Minnesota Duluth
1985	University of Minnesota Duluth	University of Minnesota Duluth
1986	University of Denver	University of Denver
1987	University of North Dakota	University of North Dakota
1988	University of Minnesota Twin Cities	University of Wisconsin
1989	University of Minnesota Twin Cities	Northern Michigan University
1990	University of Wisconsin	University of Wisconsin
1991	Northern Michigan University	Northern Michigan University
1992	University of Minnesota Twin Cities	Northern Michigan University
1993	University of Minnesota Duluth	University of Minnesota Twin Cities
1994	Colorado College	University of Minnesota Twin Cities
1995	Colorado College	University of Wisconsin
1996	Colorado College	University of Minnesota Twin Cities
1997	University of North Dakota	University of North Dakota
	University of Minnesota Twin Cities	
1998	University of North Dakota	University of Wisconsin
1999	University of North Dakota	University of Denver
2000	University of Wisconsin	University of North Dakota
2001	University of North Dakota	St. Cloud State University
2002	University of Denver	University of Denver
2003	Colorado College	University of Minnesota Twin Cities
2004	University of North Dakota	University of Minnesota Twin Cities
2005	University of Denver	University of Denver
	Colorado College	
2006	University of Minnesota Twin Cities	University of North Dakota
2007	University of Minnesota Twin Cities	University of Minnesota Twin Cities

					GP	PPG	G - A - P
1	Ryan Duncan	North Dakota	SO	F	43	1.33	31-26-57
2	T.J. Oshie	North Dakota	SO	F	43	1.21	17-35-52
3	Jonathan Toews	North Dakota	SO	F	34	1.35	18-28-46
	Mason Raymond	Minnesota Duluth	SO	F	39	1.18	14-32-46
	Andreas Nodl	St. Cloud State	FR	F	40	1.15	18-28-46
6	Andrew Gordon	St. Cloud State	JR	F	40	1.12	22-23-45
7	Jay Barriball	Minnesota	FR	F	44	0.98	20-23-43
8	Kyle Okposo	Minnesota	FR	F	40	1.00	19-21-40
	Brock Trotter	Denver	FR	F	40	1.00	16-24-40
10	Travis Morin	Minnesota State	SR	F	38	1.03	17-22-39
	Ryan Lasch	St. Cloud State	FR	F	40	0.97	16-23-39
	Mike Vannelli	Minnesota	SR	D	44	0.89	10-29-39
	Alex Goligoski	Minnesota	JR	D	44	0.89	9-30-39
14	Blake Wheeler	Minnesota	SO	F	44	0.86	18-20-38
15	Ryan Dingle	Denver	JR	F	40	0.93	22-15-37
16	Rhett Rakhshani	Denver	FR	F	40	0.90	10-26-36
17	Tyler Ruegsegger	Denver	FR	F	40	0.85	15-19-34
18	Jimmy Kilpatrick	Colorado College	JR	F	37	0.86	7-25-32
	Nate Dey	St. Cloud State	JR	F	40	0.80	10-22-32
	Robbie Bina	North Dakota	JR	D	43	0.74	10-22-32
21	Justin Bourne	Alaska Anchorage	SR	F	37	0.84	10-21-31
	Chad Rau	Colorado College	SO	F	39	0.79	14-17-31
	Matt Niskanen	Minnesota Duluth	SO	D	39	0.79	9-22-31
	Taylor Chorney	North Dakota	SO	D	39	0.79	8-23-31
	Ben Gordon	Minnesota	JR	F	42	0.74	12-19-31
26	Peter Rouleau	Michigan Tech	JR	F	40	0.75	7-23-30
	Chris Porter	North Dakota	SR	F	43	0.70	13-17-30
28	Steve Wagner	Minnesota State	JR	D	38	0.76	6-23-29
	Andrew Joudrey	Wisconsin	SR	F	40	0.72	9-20-29
30	Joel Hanson	Minnesota State	JR	F	38	0.74	15-13-28
	Bryan McGregor	Minnesota Duluth	SR	F	39	0.72	16-12-28
32	Jon Kalinski	Minnesota State	SO	F	37	0.73	17-10-27
	MacGregor Sharp	Minnesota Duluth	SO	F	38	0.71	11-16-27
	Chris Butler	Denver	SO	D	39	0.69	10-17-27
35	Bill Sweatt	Colorado College	FR	F	30	0.87	9-17-26
	Brian Lee	North Dakota	SO	D	38	0.68	2-24-26
	Dan Kronick	St. Cloud State	SR	F	40	0.65	14-12-26
38	Jake Dowell	Wisconsin	SR	F	41	0.61	19- 6-25
39	Paul Crowder	Alaska Anchorage	FR	F	37	0.65	11-13-24
	Josh Meyers	Minnesota Duluth	SO	D	37	0.65	11-13-24
	Lee Sweatt	Colorado College	SR	D	37	0.65	9-15-24
	Tyler Shelast	Michigan Tech	JR	F	38	0.63	15- 9-24
	Justin Fletcher	St. Cloud State	SR	D	38	0.63	6-18-24
	Scott McCulloch	Colorado College	JR	F	39	0.62	18- 6-24
	Matt Stephenson	St. Cloud State	JR	D	40	0.60	2-22-24
	Ryan Stoa	Minnesota	SO	F	41	0.59	12-12-24
	Michael Davies	Wisconsin	FR	F	41	0.59	11-13-24
	Brad Miller	North Dakota	SO	F	41	0.59	10-14-24
	Erik Johnson	Minnesota	FR	D	41	0.59	4-20-24
50	John Swanson	St. Cloud State	SO	F	34	0.68	9-14-23
	Ross Carlson	Wisconsin	SR	F	34	0.68	5-18-23
52	Tyler Hirsch	Minnesota	SR	F	15	1.47	4-18-22
53	Lars Helminen	Michigan Tech	SR	D	40	0.53	2-19-21
54	Josh Lunden	Alaska Anchorage	FR	F	31	0.65	11- 9-20
	Chad Anderson	Alaska Anchorage	SR	D	34	0.59	7-13-20
	Jay Beagle	Alaska Anchorage	SO	F	36	0.56	10-10-20
	Mike Carman	Minnesota	FR	F	41	0.49	9-11-20
58	Mick Berge	Minnesota State	SO	F	30	0.63	12- 7-19

	Name	School	Yr	Pos	GP	Avg	G-A-Pts
	Merit Waldrop	Alaska Anchorage	JR	F	35	0.54	5-14-19
	Brandon Polich	Colorado College	SR	F	36	0.53	4-15-19
	Jimmy Kerr	Michigan Tech	JR	F	39	0.49	10- 9-19
	Geoff Kinrade	Michigan Tech	SO	D	40	0.47	5-14-19
	Tony Lucia	Minnesota	FR	F	43	0.44	7-12-19
	Chay Genoway	North Dakota	FR	F/D	43	0.44	5-14-19
65	Jack Skille	Wisconsin	SO	F	26	0.69	8-10-18
	Jamie McBain	Wisconsin	FR	D	36	0.50	3-15-18
67	Evan Kaufmann	Minnesota	JR	F	32	0.53	11- 6-17
	Kevin Clark	Alaska Anchorage	FR	F	35	0.49	8- 9-17
	Brian Connelly	Colorado College	FR	D	35	0.49	2-15-17
	Patrick Mullen	Denver	SO	F	37	0.46	5-12-17
	Matt Watkins	North Dakota	SO	F	38	0.45	6-11-17
	Geoff Paukovich	Denver	JR	F	39	0.44	8- 9-17
	Malcolm Gwilliam	Michigan Tech	SO	F	40	0.42	9- 8-17
	Ben Street	Wisconsin	SO	F	41	0.41	10- 7-17
75	Andreas Vlassopoulos	Colorado College	FR	F	24	0.67	5-11-16
	Braydon Cox	Colorado College	SR	F	38	0.42	7- 9-16
	Michael Gergen	Minnesota Duluth	SO	F	39	0.41	5-11-16
78	Alex Gagne	Michigan Tech	FR	F	34	0.44	5-10-15
	Kael Mouillierat	Minnesota State	FR	F	37	0.41	8- 7-15
	Jack Hillen	Colorado College	JR	D	38	0.39	7- 8-15
	Tyler Skworchinski	Michigan Tech	SR	F	40	0.38	8- 7-15
	Jim O'Brien	Minnesota	FR	F	43	0.35	7- 8-15
	Derek Peltier	Minnesota	JR	D	44	0.34	4-11-15
84	Mike Curry	Minnesota Duluth	JR	F	36	0.39	3-11-14
	Trevor Bruess	Minnesota State	FR	F	37	0.38	3-11-14
86	Kyle Klubertanz	Wisconsin	JR	D	34	0.38	1-12-13
	Adrian Veideman	Denver	SR	F	36	0.36	3-10-13
	Peter Cartwright	Alaska Anchorage	JR	F	37	0.35	5- 8-13
	Keith Seabrook	Denver	FR	D	37	0.35	2-11-13
	Jerad Stewart	Minnesota State	FR	F	38	0.34	5- 8-13
	Scott Thauwald	Colorado College	JR	F	39	0.33	7- 6-13
	Matthew Ford	Wisconsin	JR	F	39	0.33	7- 6-13
	Brian Gifford	Denver	FR	F	40	0.33	3-10-13
	Ryan Flynn	Minnesota	FR	F	43	0.30	5- 8-13
95	Nick Kemp	Minnesota Duluth	SO	F	32	0.38	4- 8-12
	Tom Gorowsky	Wisconsin	SO	F	33	0.36	5- 7-12
	Zach Harrison	Minnesota State	FR	F	36	0.33	3- 9-12
	Rylan Kaip	North Dakota	JR	F	38	0.32	5- 7-12
	Mike Howe	Minnesota	JR	F	39	0.31	5- 7-12
	Nate Raduns	St. Cloud State	SR	F	40	0.30	6- 6-12
101	Geoff Irwin	Minnesota State	FR	F	30	0.37	3- 8-11
	Aaron Brocklehurst	St. Cloud State	JR	D/F	32	0.34	5- 6-11
	Mark Smith	Alaska Anchorage	SR	D	36	0.31	5- 6-11
	Kurtis Kisio	Minnesota State	SR	F	37	0.30	4- 7-11
	Erik Fabian	North Dakota	SR	F	39	0.28	5- 6-11
	Casey Borer	St. Cloud State	SR	D	40	0.28	2- 9-11
	Andrew Kozek	North Dakota	SO	F	41	0.27	5- 6-11
108	Mike Testwuide	Colorado College	FR	F	29	0.34	8- 2-10
	Ryan Bunger	Michigan Tech	FR	F	29	0.34	5- 5-10
	Derek Patrosso	Colorado College	JR	F	30	0.33	3- 7-10
	Nils Backstrom	Alaska Anchorage	FR	D	33	0.30	1- 9-10
	Addison DeBoer	Colorado College	FR	F	35	0.29	5- 5-10
	Ryan Geris	Minnesota Duluth	SR	D	36	0.28	1- 9-10
	Drew Akins	Minnesota Duluth	FR	F	38	0.26	7- 3-10
	Jordan Fulton	Minnesota Duluth	FR	F	38	0.26	3- 7-10
	Ryan Angelow	Michigan Tech	SO	F	39	0.26	5- 5-10
	Darcy Zajac	North Dakota	FR	F	41	0.24	8- 2-10
	Davis Drewiske	Wisconsin	JR	D	41	0.24	4- 6-10

119	Ryan Martens	North Dakota	SO	F	20	0.45	3- 6- 9
	James Gaulrapp	Minnesota State	FR	F	24	0.38	4- 5- 9
	Phil Axtell	Michigan Tech	FR	F	27	0.33	2- 7- 9
	Matt McKnight	Minnesota Duluth	JR	F	29	0.31	4- 5- 9
	Gary Houseman	St. Cloud State	SR	F	35	0.26	5- 4- 9
	Nick Lowe	Alaska Anchorage	SR	F/D	36	0.25	3- 6- 9
	Luke Beaverson	Alaska Anchorage	JR	D	37	0.24	5- 4- 9
	Matt Hartman	St. Cloud State	JR	F	37	0.24	4- 5- 9
	Mat Robinson	Alaska Anchorage	SO	D	37	0.24	2- 7- 9
	Cody Lampl	Colorado College	SO	D/F	37	0.24	2- 7- 9
	Chris VandeVelde	North Dakota	FR	F	38	0.24	3- 6- 9
	Jordan Foote	Michigan Tech	JR	F	39	0.23	2- 7- 9
131	Charlie Kronschnabel	Alaska Anchorage	SR	F	22	0.36	2- 6- 8
	Justin St. Louis	Michigan Tech	SO	F	28	0.29	6- 2- 8
	Brian Schack	Minnesota	FR	D	28	0.29	1- 7- 8
	Nick Canzanello	Minnesota State	FR	D	31	0.26	1- 7- 8
	Matt Greer	Minnesota Duluth	SO	F	32	0.25	4- 4- 8
	Justin Bostrom	Minnesota	SO	F	34	0.24	4- 4- 8
	Andrew Carroll	Minnesota Duluth	SO	F	36	0.22	3- 5- 8
	Grant Clafton	St. Cloud State	SR	F/D	39	0.21	2- 6- 8
139	Jake Wilkens	Michigan Tech	JR	D	31	0.23	2- 5- 7
	Garrett Raboin	St. Cloud State	FR	D	38	0.18	0- 7- 7
	Andrew Thomas	Denver	JR	D	40	0.17	2- 5- 7
	Joe Finley	North Dakota	SO	D	41	0.17	1- 6- 7
143	J.D. Corbin	Denver	SR	F	10	0.60	2- 4- 6
	R.J. Anderson	Minnesota	SO	D	32	0.19	0- 6- 6
	Brian Kilburg	Minnesota State	SO	D	33	0.18	0- 6- 6
	Blake Geoffrion	Wisconsin	FR	F	36	0.17	2- 4- 6
	Blake Friesen	Minnesota State	SO	D	36	0.17	1- 5- 6
	Jeff McFarland	Minnesota Duluth	SR	F	38	0.16	4- 2- 6
	Andy Brandt	Wisconsin	SR	F	40	0.15	3- 3- 6
	Jeff Likens	Wisconsin	SR	D	40	0.15	1- 5- 6
151	Lucas Fransen	Minnesota State	SR	D	19	0.26	2- 3- 5
	Tom May	Denver	JR	F	21	0.24	1- 4- 5
	Kevin Huck	Minnesota State	SO	F	22	0.23	2- 3- 5
	Drew Dobson	Michigan Tech	FR	D	23	0.22	1- 4- 5
	Blair Tassone	Alaska Anchorage	JR	F	24	0.21	3- 2- 5
	Marty Mjelleli	St. Cloud State	JR	F	25	0.20	3- 2- 5
	John Schwarz	Michigan Tech	SO	D	29	0.17	0- 5- 5
	Michael Olson	St. Cloud State	SO	F	31	0.16	2- 3- 5
	Alex Lord	Michigan Tech	SO	F	33	0.15	2- 3- 5
	Ryan Helgason	Denver	SR	F	36	0.14	3- 2- 5
	Chris Tarkir	Alaska Anchorage	JR	F	36	0.14	1- 4- 5
	Brandon Straub	Colorado College	SR	D	36	0.14	1- 4- 5
	Mike Batovanja	Michigan Tech	SR	F	37	0.14	2- 3- 5
	Travis Gawryletz	Minnesota Duluth	JR	D	37	0.14	0- 5- 5
	Joe Piskula	Wisconsin	JR	D	38	0.13	1- 4- 5
	Michael Handza	Denver	SR	F	39	0.13	1- 4- 5
	Kyle Radke	North Dakota	JR	D	41	0.12	2- 3- 5
	David Fischer	Minnesota	FR	D	42	0.12	0- 5- 5
169	Shane Lovdahl	Alaska Anchorage	SO	D	18	0.22	0- 4- 4
	T.J. Fast	Denver	SO	D	19	0.21	0- 4- 4
	Kris Fredheim	Colorado College	FR	D	23	0.17	1- 3- 4
	Alex Stalock	Minnesota Duluth	FR	G	23	0.17	0- 4- 4
	Jason Wiley	Minnesota State	FR	F	25	0.16	1- 3- 4
	James Brannigan	Colorado College	JR	F	30	0.13	0- 4- 4
	Josh Engel	Wisconsin	JR	D	30	0.13	0- 4- 4
	R.J. Linder	Minnesota State	JR	D	32	0.12	1- 3- 4
	Chad Brownlee	Minnesota State	SR	D	34	0.12	0- 4- 4
	Eli Vlaisavljevich	Michigan Tech	FR	D	36	0.11	1- 3- 4

	Steven Cook	Denver	SR	F	38	0.11	1- 3- 4
180	Scott Foyt	North Dakota	SR	D/F	8	0.38	1- 2- 3
	Mitch Ryan	Minnesota Duluth	FR	F	10	0.30	1- 2- 3
	Trevor Hunt	Alaska Anchorage	FR	D	15	0.20	0- 3- 3
	John Mitchell	Wisconsin	FR	F	18	0.17	1- 2- 3
	Brandon Vossberg	Denver	FR	F	21	0.14	2- 1- 3
	Jason Garrison	Minnesota Duluth	SO	D	21	0.14	1- 2- 3
	Nate Prosser	Colorado College	FR	D	21	0.14	0- 3- 3
	Jay Cascalenda	Minnesota Duluth	SO	D	24	0.12	1- 2- 3
	David Carlisle	St. Cloud State	SO	D	25	0.12	0- 3- 3
	Adam Corrin	Alaska Anchorage	SO	F	27	0.11	1- 2- 3
	Ben Grotting	Wisconsin	FR	F	32	0.09	2- 1- 3
	Aaron Bendickson	Wisconsin	FR	F	34	0.09	0- 3- 3
	Bobby Goepfert	St. Cloud State	SR	G	35	0.09	0- 3- 3
	J.P. Testwuide	Denver	SO	D	37	0.08	0- 3- 3
	Mark Malekoff	Michigan Tech	JR	D	39	0.08	0- 3- 3
	Matt Olinger	Wisconsin	SR	D	41	0.07	0- 3- 3
	Zach Jones	North Dakota	SO	D	42	0.07	0- 3- 3
197	Michael Forney	North Dakota	FR	F	16	0.12	0- 2- 2
	Andy Bohmbach	Wisconsin	FR	F	17	0.12	1- 1- 2
	Ryan Peckskamp	St. Cloud State	FR	F	19	0.11	0- 2- 2
	Brian McMillin	Colorado College	FR	F	22	0.09	1- 1- 2
	Logan Gorsalitz	Minnesota Duluth	FR	F	22	0.09	0- 2- 2
	Jared Tuton	Alaska Anchorage	FR	F/D	36	0.06	0- 2- 2
	Jake Gannon	Colorado College	SO	D	37	0.05	1- 1- 2
	Philippe Lamoureux	North Dakota	JR	G	37	0.05	0- 2- 2
205	Craig Gaudet	St. Cloud State	FR	D	4	0.25	1- 0- 1
	Hunter Bishop	North Dakota	FR	F	4	0.25	0- 1- 1
	John Kivisto	Michigan Tech	FR	D/F	6	0.17	0- 1- 1
	Ryan Gunderson	Minnesota State	FR	F	6	0.17	0- 1- 1
	Drew O'Connell	Colorado College	SO	G	8	0.12	0- 1- 1
	Zach Blom	Denver	SR	D	10	0.10	1- 0- 1
	Derek Kitti	Michigan Tech	SO	F	10	0.10	1- 0- 1
	Chase Ryan	Minnesota Duluth	FR	D	10	0.10	0- 1- 1
	Ken Selby	Alaska Anchorage	FR	F	12	0.08	0- 1- 1
	Jon Olthuis	Alaska Anchorage	FR	G	14	0.07	0- 1- 1
	Dan Tormey	Minnesota State	SO	G	14	0.07	0- 1- 1
	Jon Ammerman	St. Cloud State	FR	D	14	0.07	0- 1- 1
	A.J. Gale	St. Cloud State	FR	F	18	0.06	0- 1- 1
	Matt Tyree	Minnesota State	JR	F	25	0.04	1- 0- 1
	Mike Zacharias	Minnesota State	SO	G	25	0.04	0- 1- 1
	Nathan Lawson	Alaska Anchorage	JR	G	27	0.04	0- 1- 1
	Cody Brookwell	Denver	FR	D	30	0.03	0- 1- 1
	Trent Palm	Minnesota Duluth	FR	D	32	0.03	1- 0- 1
	Matt Zaba	Colorado College	SR	G	33	0.03	0- 1- 1
	Brian Elliott	Wisconsin	SR	G	36	0.03	0- 1- 1

GOALS AGAINST AVERAGE:

				MINUTES	GA	GAA
1	Michael-Lee Teslak	Michigan Tech	SO	1258:33:00	42	2
2	Brian Elliott	Wisconsin	SR	2053:16:00	72	2.1
3	Kellen Briggs	Minnesota	SR	1518:37:00	54	2.13
4	Josh Johnson	Minnesota Duluth	SR	1065:06:00	38	2.14
5	Rob Nolan	Michigan Tech	SO	1170:05:00	44	2.26
6	Bobby Goepfert	St. Cloud State	SR	2148:30:00	82	2.29
7	Peter Mannino	Denver	JR	1020:46:00	39	2.29
8	Glenn Fisher	Denver	SR	1393:34:00	54	2.32
9	Jeff Frazee	Minnesota	SO	1148:13:00	45	2.35
10	Matt Zaba	Colorado College	SR	1907:46:00	76	2.39
11	Philippe Lamoureux	North Dakota	JR	2183:49:00	88	2.42
12	Nathan Lawson	Alaska Anchorage	JR	1522:48:00	77	3.03
13	Mike Zacharias	Minnesota State	SO	1427:59:00	73	3.07
14	Alex Stalock	Minnesota Duluth	FR	1363:30:00	76	3.34

Minimum 33% of Team Minutes Played

SAVE PERCENTAGE:

				SAVES	GA	PCT
1	Bobby Goepfert	St. Cloud State	SR	1004	82	0.924
2	Brian Elliott	Wisconsin	SR	867	72	0.923
3	Josh Johnson	Minnesota Duluth	SR	452	38	0.922
4	Glenn Fisher	Denver	SR	612	54	0.919
5	Peter Mannino	Denver	JR	441	39	0.919
6	Kellen Briggs	Minnesota	SR	600	54	0.917
7	Matt Zaba	Colorado College	SR	839	76	0.917
8	Michael-Lee Teslak	Michigan Tech	SO	459	42	0.916
9	Philippe Lamoureux	North Dakota	JR	919	88	0.913
10	Rob Nolan	Michigan Tech	SO	446	44	0.91
11	Jeff Frazee	Minnesota	SO	417	45	0.903
12	Nathan Lawson	Alaska Anchorage	JR	644	77	0.893
13	Mike Zacharias	Minnesota State	SO	605	73	0.892
14	Alex Stalock	Minnesota Duluth	FR	560	76	0.881

Minimum 33% of Team Minutes Played

WINNING PERCENTAGE:

				W- L- T	PCT
1	Jeff Frazee	Minnesota	SO	14- 3- 1	0.806
2	Kellen Briggs	Minnesota	SR	17- 7- 2	0.692
3	Philippe Lamoureux	North Dakota	JR	21-12- 4	0.622
4	Bobby Goepfert	St. Cloud State	SR	17-10- 7	0.603
5	Glenn Fisher	Denver	SR	13- 9- 2	0.583
6	Michael-Lee Teslak	Michigan Tech	SO	11- 8- 3	0.568
7	Peter Mannino	Denver	JR	8- 6- 2	0.562
8	Matt Zaba	Colorado College	SR	15-13- 4	0.531
9	Josh Johnson	Minnesota Duluth	SR	8- 7- 2	0.529
10	Mike Zacharias	Minnesota State	SO	10- 9- 6	0.52
11	Brian Elliott	Wisconsin	SR	15-17- 2	0.471
12	Rob Nolan	Michigan Tech	SO	7- 9- 2	0.444
13	Nathan Lawson	Alaska Anchorage	JR	10-15- 2	0.407
14	Alex Stalock	Minnesota Duluth	FR	5-14- 3	0.295

Minimum 33% of Team Minutes Played

INDEENDENTS

Becker College
SUNY - Morrisville

DIVISION 3 INDEPENDENTS
FINAL 2006-07 OVERALL STANDINGS

		Pts	GP	Record	Win%	GF-GA	GP	Record	Win%	GF-GA
1	Becker						22	2-18- 2	0.136	55-111
	Morrisville						17	7-10- 0	0.412	50- 72
	Scranton						0	0- 0- 0	——	0- 0

Colleges

COLLEGE TEAM PAGE LAYOUT

The College Hockey Guide Men's Edition provides background information on the rostered players including players by class, country of origin and last competitive team, as well as the league or level of play. Throughout the team pages we have used the following abbreviations:

YB - Year of Birth   **GR** - Graduation Year   **Ht/Wt** - Height/Weight   **P** - Position

ACCHL	Atlantic Coast Collegiate Hockey League
ACHA	American Collegiate Hockey Association
AHL	Atlantic Hockey Association
AJHL	Alberta Junior Hockey League
AtJHL	Atlantic Junior Hockey League
AWHL	America West Hockey League
BCHL	British Columbia Junior Hockey League
CapJHL	Capital Junior Hockey League
CCHA	Central Collegiate Hockey Association
CEGEP	Canadian Junior College
CEHL	Continental Elite Hockey League
CHA	College Hockey America
CJHA	Continental Junior Hockey Association
CJHL	Central Junior Hockey League
CSHL	Central States Junior Hockey League
ECAC	Eastern College Athletic Conference
ECAC-E	Eastern College Athletic Conference-East
ECAC-NE	Eastern College Athletic Conference-Northeast
ECAC-W	Eastern College Athletic Conference-West
EJHL	Eastern Junior Hockey League
EmJHL	Empire Junior Hockey League
EOJHL	Eastern Ontario Junior Hockey League
FEL	Finnish Elite League
FJL	Finnish Junior League
GHJHL	Golden Horseshoe Junior Hockey League
HEA	Hockey East Association
HJHL	Heritage Junior Hockey League
HS	High School
IJHL	Interstate Junior Hockey League
Ind Jr	Independent Junior Teams
KIJHL	Kootenay International Junior Hockey League
KJHL	Keystone Junior Hockey League
LHJAAAQ	Quebec Junior Hockey League
MAAC	Metro Atlantic Athletic Conference
ManJHL	Manitoba Junior Hockey League
MarJHL	Maritime Junior Hockey League
MCHA	Midwest Collegiate Hockey Association
MIAC	Minnesota Intercollegiate Athletic Conference
MJHL	Metropolitan Junior Hockey League
MnJHL	Minnesota Junior Hockey League
MonJHL	Montreal Junior Hockey League
MWHL	Midwestern Junior Hockey League
MWJHL	Mid-West Junior Hockey League
NAHL	North American Junior Hockey League
NCAA	National Collegiate Athletic Association
NCHA	Northern Collegiate Hockey Association

NEAJHL	Northeastern Alberta Junior Hockey League
NEJDL	New England Junior Development League
NEPSAC	New England Prep School Athletic Council
NESCAC	New England Small College Athletic Conference
NJCAA	National Junior College Athletic Association
NJHL	North West Junior Hockey League
NWJHL	Northwest Junior Hockey League
NOJHL	Northern Ontario Junior Hockey League
NPJHL	Northern Pacific Junior Hockey League
NSJBHL	Nova Scotia Junior Hockey League
NSkJHL	North Saskatchewan Junior Hockey League
OPJHL	Ontario Provincial Junior Hockey League
PIJHL	Pacific International Junior Hockey League
PS	Prep School
QJAHL	Quebec Junior AAA Hockey League
SEL	Swedish Elite League
SIJHL	Superior International Junior Hockey League
SJHL	Saskatchewan Junior Hockey League
SSkJHL	South Saskatchewan Junior Junior Hockey League
StJJHL	St. John's Junior Hockey League
SUNYAC	State University of New York Athletic Conference
TBJHL	Thunder Bay Junior Hockey League
USHL	United States Junior Hockey League
U. S. Team	U. S. National Development Team
VIJHL	Vancouver Island Junior Hockey League
WOJHL	Western Ontario Junior Hockey League
WSHL	Western States Junior Hockey League

ADRIAN COLLEGE

Division 3

HOCKEY STAFF

HOCKEY STAFF

HEAD COACH
Ron Fogarty *(Colgate '95)*

ASSISTANT COACHES
Brian Burke

HOCKEY OFFICE
Adrian College Hockey Office
110 S. Madison Street
Adrian, MI 49221
O 517.264.3838
rfogarty@adrian.edu

HOCKEY MEDIA CONTACT
Nate Jorgensen - Sports Info Director
Adrian College Hockey Office
110 S. Madison Street
Adrian, MI 49221
O 517.264.3280 / F 517.264.3810
njorgensen@adrian.edu

HOCKEY RINK
Arrington Ice Arena (On Campus)

Size 200' x 85', Capacity 700

ATHLETIC DIRECTOR
Mike Duffy - Athletic Director
Adrian College
110 S. Madison Street
Adrian, MI 49221
O 517.264.3997
mduffy@adrian.edu

CHARGERS PLAYERS

Player	YB GR Ht/Wt	P	Hometown/Last Team

Adrian College
begins play in
MCHA in 2007/2008

ROSTER ANALYSIS (SCHOLARSHIPS - 0)

Class	Country	Last Team		
Fr	USA	US JR A	CDN JR A	ACHA
So	Canada	US JR B	CDN JR B	NJCAA
Jr	Europe	US PS	CDN PS	NCAA
Sr	Asia	US HS	CDN HS	USNDT
Gr	Other	US Midget	CDN Midget	Other

ADMISSIONS, ENROLLMENT & CAMPUS INFORMATION

Founded 1859	Average acceptance rate - 85 %	Carolyn Quinlan - Director of Admissions
Private, small city campus	Freshman financial aid - 85 %	Adrian College
465 men / 550 women	Early decision application deadline - N/A	110 S. Madison Street
Tuition, room & board - $ 27 K	Regular application deadline - Rolling	Adrian, MI 49221
Avg ACT - 22	Financial aid deadline - Rolling	O 800.877.2246

UNIVERSITY OF ALABAMA-HUNTSVILLE

Division 1

HOCKEY STAFF

HEAD COACH
Danton Cole *(Michigan State '89)*

ASSISTANT COACHES
Dennis Williams *(Bowling Green '01)*
Lance West *(Alabama-Huntsville '97)*
John McCabe *(Alabama-Huntsville '98)*

HOCKEY OFFICE
University of Alabama-Huntsville
205 Spragins Hall
Huntsville, AL 35899
O 256.824.2198/ F 256.824.7306
coled@email.uah.edu

HOCKEY MEDIA CONTACT
Jamie Gilliam - Sports Info Director
University of Alabama-Huntsville
205 Spragins Hall
Huntsville, AL 35899
O 256.824.2201/ F 256.824.6947
gilliaj@email.uah.edu

HOCKEY RINK
Von Braun Arena (Off Campus)
700 Monroe Street
Huntsville, AL 35801
Size 200' x 85', Capacity 6,800
O 256.551.2388

ATHLETIC DIRECTOR
Jim Harris - Athletic Director
University of Alabama-Huntsville
205 Spragins Hall
Huntsville, AL 35899
O 256.824.6144/ F 256.824.7306
harrisj@email.uah.edu

CHARGERS PLAYERS

Player	YB	GR	Ht/Wt	P	Hometown/Last Team
Shaun Arvai	82	07	5'10"/170	D	W Lorne,ON/Petrolia Jets (WOJHL)
Brennan Barker	85	10	6' 0"/195	D	Long Sault,ON/Penticton Vees (BCHL)
Steve Canter	83	07	6' 0"/190	F	St. Louis,MO/Billings Bulls (NAHL)
Derek Conter	83	08	6' 2"/205	F	Toronto,ON/Wichita Falls Rustlers (AWHL)
Jordan Erickson	84	09	6' 0"/180	F	Ft McNeill,BC/Spruce Grove Saints (AJHL)
Joe Federoff	84	09	6' 2"/205	F	Pittsburgh,PA/Robert Morris (CHA)
Kevin Galerno	84	09	5' 7"/160	F	Kitchener,ON/Kitchener Dutchmen (MWJHL)
Tyler Hilbert	84	08	5' 9"/185	F	Okotoks,AB/Olds Grizzlys (AJHL)
Scott Kalinchuk	84	09	6' 1"/195	D	Sylvan Lk,AB/Canmore Eagles (AJHL)
AJ Larivee	83	07	6' 1"/205	D	Dublin,ON/St. Mary's Lincolns (WOJHL)
Troy Maney	82	07	6' 2"/200	D	Huntsville,AL/Capital Centre Pride (NAHL)
Brett McConnachie	85	07	5'10"/185	F	Ajax,ON/Wexford Raiders (OPJHL)
Matt Montes	83	08	6' 0"/195	D	Forest Pk,IL/Springfield Blues (NAHL)
Kevin Morrison	86	10	6' 0"/190	F	Mississauga,ON/Milton Icehawks (OPJHL)
Josh Murray	84	09	5'11"/190	F	Terrace,BC/Williams Lake Timberwolves (BCHL)
Marc Narduzzi	82	08	6' 2"/190	G	Vancouver,BC/Surrey Eagles (BCHL)
Davide Nicoletti	86	10	6' 3"/210	D	Toronto,ON/Springfield Blues (NAHL)
David Nimmo	82	07	6' 3"/200	F	St. Albert,AB/Melfort Mustangs (SJHL)
Brandon Roshko	85	10	5' 9"/180	D	Hamilton,ON/Aurora Tigers (OPJHL)
Dominik Rozman	83	07	5'11"/190	F	Wallaceburg,ON/Sarnia Blast (WOJHL)
Mike Salekin	85	08	6' 0"/185	D	Castlegar,BC/Merritt Centennials (BCHL)
Grant Selinger	83	07	5'11"/180	F	Regina,SK/Surrey Eagles (BCHL)
Matt Sweazey	84	09	6' 4"/195	F	Toronto,ON/Georgetown Raiders (OPJHL)
Cale Tanaka	86	10	5' 9"/180	F	Stouffville,ON/Aurora Tigers (OPJHL)
Tom Train	85	10	6' 0"/190	F	Hurst,TX/Texas Tornado (NAHL)

ROSTER ANALYSIS (SCHOLARSHIPS - 14)

Class		Country		Last Team			
Fr	6	USA	5	US JR A	6	CDN JR A	14	ACHA
So	6	Canada	20	US JR B		CDN JR B	4	NJCAA
Jr	5	Europe		US PS		CDN PS		NCAA 1
Sr	8	Asia		US HS		CDN HS		USNDT
Gr		Other		US Midget		CDN Midget		Other

ADMISSIONS, ENROLLMENT & CAMPUS INFORMATION

Founded 1950
Public, suburban campus
2,767 men / 2,358 women
Tuition, room & board - $ 10 K / $ 15 K
Avg SAT - 1,164/ Avg ACT - 25

Average acceptance rate - 89 %
Freshman financial aid - 52 %
Early decision application deadline - N/A
Regular application deadline - Aug 15
Financial aid deadline - Apr 1

Director of Admissions
University of Alabama-Huntsville
University Center - Office of Admissions
Huntsville, AL 35899
O 256.890.6070/ F 256.824.6841

www.uahchargers.com

UNIVERSITY OF ALASKA - ANCHORAGE

Anchorage

WESTERN COLLEGIATE HOCKEY ASSOCIATION

Division 1

HOCKEY STAFF

HEAD COACH
Dave Shyiak *(Northern Michigan '93)*

ASSISTANT COACHES
Campbell Blair *(Maine '91)*
Damon Whitten *(Michigan State '01)*
Brian Kraft *(Alaska Anchorage '93)*

HOCKEY OFFICE
University of Alaska Anchorage
3211 Providence Drive
Anchorage, AK 99508
O 907.786.1227 / F 907.786.6116
andps@uaa.alaska.edu

HOCKEY MEDIA CONTACT
Tad Dunham - Hockey Info Director
University of Alaska Anchorage
3211 Providence Drive
Anchorage, AK 99508
O 907.786.4625 / F 907.563.4565
td@uaa.alaska.edu

HOCKEY RINK
Sullivan Arena (On Campus)
1600 Gambell Street
Anchorage, AK 99501
Size 200' x 100', Capacity 6,406
O 907.279.2071

ATHLETIC DIRECTOR
Steve Cobb - Athletic Director
University of Alaska Anchorage
3211 Providence Drive
Anchorage, AK 99508
O 907.786.1225 / F 907.786.1142
ansrc@uaa.alaska.edu

SEAWOLVES PLAYERS

Player	YB	GR	Ht/Wt	P	Hometown/Last Team
Chad Anderson	82	07	6' 3"/215	D	Chisago City,MN/Tri-City Storm (USHL)
Nils Backstrom	86	10	6' 1"/200	D	Stocksund,Sweden/Djurgardens (SEL)
Jay Beagle	85	09	6' 3"/200	F	Calgary,AB/Calgary Royals (AJHL)
Luke Beaverson	84	08	6' 5"/210	D	Vadnais Hts,MN/Green Bay Gamblers (USHL)
Ryan Berry	85	10	6' 0"/185	D	Edmonton,AB/Spruce Grove Saints (AJHL)
Justin Bourne	82	07	6' 1"/185	F	Kelowna,BC/Vernon Vipers (BCHL)
Peter Cartwright	84	08	6' 1"/190	F	Anchorage,AK/Williams Lake Timberwolves (BCHL)
Kevin Clark	87	10	5' 8"/160	F	Winnipeg,MB/Winnipeg South Blues (ManJHL)
Adam Corrin	85	09	6' 1"/195	F	Winnipeg,MB/Winnipeg South Blues (ManJHL)
Paul Crowder	85	10	6' 3"/205	F	Victoria,BC/Burnaby Express (BCHL)
Trevor Hunt	86	10	5'10"/195	D	Maple Ridge,BC/Chilliwack Chiefs (BCHL)
Charlie Kronschnabel	83	07	6' 4"/195	F	Mendota Hts,MN/Omaha Lancers (USHL)
Nathan Lawson	83	08	6' 1"/175	G	Calgary,AB/Olds Grizzlys (AJHL)
Shane Lovdahl	84	09	5'11"/210	D	Anchorage,AK/Cedar Rapids RoughRiders (USHL)
Nick Lowe	83	07	5'11"/195	F	Surrey,BC/Surrey Eagles (BCHL)
Josh Lunden	86	10	6' 2"/195	F	Pt Coquitlam,BC/Chilliwack Chiefs (BCHL)
Jon Olthuis	85	10	6' 3"/195	G	Neerlandia,AB/Chilliwack Chiefs (BCHL)
Mat Robinson	86	09	5'10"/160	D	Calgary,AB/Calgary Royals (AJHL)
Mike Rosett	84	09	6' 1"/180	G	Anchorage,AK/Princeton Posse (KIJHL)
Ken Selby	86	10	6' 1"/185	F	Winnipeg,MB/Dauphin Kings (ManJHL)
Mark Smith	83	07	6' 0"/180	D	Edmonton,AB/Sherwood Park Crusaders (AJHL)
Chris Tarkir	84	08	6' 2"/190	F	Fresno,CA/Chilliwack Chiefs (BCHL)
Blair Tassone	83	08	6' 0"/195	F	Castlegar,BC/Victoria Salsa (BCHL)
Jared Tuton	85	10	6' 1"/190	F/D	Whitehorse,YT/Merritt Centennials (BCHL)
Merit Waldrop	83	08	5'10"/175	F	Anchorage,AK/Texarkana Bandits (NAHL)

ROSTER ANALYSIS (SCHOLARSHIPS - 18)

Class		Country		Last Team				
Fr	9	USA	8	US JR A	5	CDN JR A	18	ACHA
So	5	Canada	16	US JR B		CDN JR B	1	NJCAA
Jr	6	Europe	1	US PS		CDN PS		NCAA
Sr	5	Asia		US HS		CDN HS		USNDT
Gr		Other		US Midget		CDN Midget		EU	1

ADMISSIONS, ENROLLMENT & CAMPUS INFORMATION

Founded 1954
Public, urban campus
3,944 men / 5,917 women
Tuition, room & board - $ 10 K /$ 17 K
Avg SAT - 1,015 / Avg ACT - 21

Average acceptance rate - 81 %
Freshman financial aid - 66 %
Early decision application deadline - N/A
Regular application deadline - Aug 1
Financial aid deadline - Apr 1

Linda Berg Smith - Enrollment
Univ. of Alaska Anchorage - ADM 158
3211 Providence Drive
Anchorage, AK 99508
O 907.786.1480 / F 907.786.4888

www.uaa.alaska.edu

www.goseawolves.com

UNIVERSITY OF ALASKA - FAIRBANKS

Division 1

HOCKEY STAFF

HEAD COACH
Doc DelCastillo *(St. Cloud State '92)*

ASSISTANT COACHES
Wade Klippenstein *(Alaska-Fairbanks '93)*
Dallas Ferguson *(Alaska-Fairbanks '96)*
Preston McKay *(Alaska-Fairbanks '05)*

HOCKEY OFFICE
University of Alaska-Fairbanks
PO Box 757440
211 Patty Center
Fairbanks, AK 99775
O 907.474.6899/ F 907.474.5162
doc.delcastillo@uaf.edu

HOCKEY MEDIA CONTACT
Jamie Schanback - Hockey Info Director
University of Alaska-Fairbanks
PO Box 757440
211 Patty Center
Fairbanks, AK 99775-7440
O 907.474.6805/ F 907.474.5162
fnjms4@uaf.edu

HOCKEY RINK
Carlson Center (On Campus)
2010 2nd Avenue
Fairbanks, AK 99701
Size 200' x 100', Capacity 4,324
O 907.451.9878

ATHLETIC DIRECTOR
Forrest Karr - Interim Athletic Director
University of Alaska-Fairbanks
PO Box 757440
211 Patty Center
Fairbanks, AK 99775-7440
O 907.474.6812/ F 907.474.5162
forrest.karr@uaf.edu

NANOOKS PLAYERS

Player	YB	GR	Ht/Wt	P	Hometown/Last Team
Justin Binab	84	09	5'11"/190	F	Victoria,BC/Langley Hornets (BCHL)
Lucas Burnett	82	07	6' 2"/224	F	Rossland,BC/Trail Smoke Eaters (BCHL)
Darcy Campbell	84	08	5'11"/175	D	Airdrie,AB/Olds Grizzlys (AJHL)
TJ Campbell	83	08	6' 0"/185	D	Ft McMurray,AB/Fort McMurray Oil Barons (AJHL)
Tyler Eckford	85	09	6' 3"/215	D	Langley,BC/Surrey Eagles (BCHL)
Jordan Emmerson	82	07	6' 4"/220	F	Abbotsford,BC/Merritt Centennials (BCHL)
Nathan Fornataro	83	07	6' 1"/195	D	Calgary,AB/Calgary Royals (AJHL)
Curtis Fraser	82	07	6' 2"/190	F	Surrey,BC/Vernon Vipers (BCHL)
Brandon Gawryletz	83	08	6' 0"/195	D	Trail,BC/Trail Smoke Eaters (BCHL)
Zach Geiszler	84	09	6' 0"/195	D	Tigard,OR/Williams Lake Timberwolves (BCHL)
Kyle Greentree	83	08	6' 3"/200	F	Victoria,BC/Victoria Salsa (BCHL)
Trevor Hyatt	85	09	5' 9"/185	F	Anchorage,AK/Estevan Bruins (SJHL)
Chad Johnson	86	09	6' 2"/175	G	Calgary,AB/Brooks Bandits (AJHL)
Kyle Jones	84	09	5'10"/180	F	Airdrie,AB/Trail Smoke Eaters (BCHL)
Brandon Knelsen	87	10	5'11"/190	F	Three Hills,AB/Drumheller Dragons (AJHL)
Dion Knelsen	89	10	5' 9"/180	F	Three Hills,AB/Drumheller Dragons (AJHL)
Erik Largen	86	10	5'11"/185	G	Fairbanks,AK/Southern Minnesota Express (NAHL)
Aaron Lee	85	08	6' 0"/180	F	Calgary,AB/Sherwood Park Crusaders (AJHL)
Jeff Lee	88	10	6' 2"/210	F	Calgary,AB/Sherwood Park Crusaders (AJHL)
Dustin Molle	85	10	6' 2"/215	D	Anchorage,AK/Alaska Anchorage (WCHA)
Ryan Muspratt	84	08	6' 0"/190	F	Calgary,AB/Camrose Kodiaks (AJHL)
Adam Naglich	84	09	6' 1"/185	F	Las Vegas,NV/Victoria Salsa (BCHL)
Jordan Pernarowski	86	10	6' 1"/195	D	Dauphin,MB/Dauphin Kings (ManJHL)
Wylie Rogers	85	08	5'10"/160	G	Fairbanks,AK/Victoria Salsa (BCHL)
Cody Rymut	85	10	6' 1"/195	F	Bonnyville,AB/Chilliwack Chiefs (BCHL)
Steve Vanoosten	85	09	6' 1"/195	D	Langley,BC/Williams Lake Timberwolves (BCHL)
Braden Walls	85	09	6' 2"/205	F	Calgary,AB/Drayton Valley Thunder (AJHL)

ROSTER ANALYSIS (SCHOLARSHIPS - 18)

Class		Country		Last Team				
Fr	7	USA	6	US JR A	1	CDN JR A	25	ACHA
So	9	Canada	21	US JR B		CDN JR B		NJCAA
Jr	7	Europe		US PS		CDN PS		NCAA 1
Sr	4	Asia		US HS		CDN HS		USNDT
Gr		Other		US Midget		CDN Midget		Other

ADMISSIONS, ENROLLMENT & CAMPUS INFORMATION

Founded 1917
Public, Suburban campus
2,349 men / 2,444 women
Tuition, room & board - $ 9 K / $ 16 K
Avg SAT - 1,050 / Avg ACT - 22

Average acceptance rate - 91 %
Freshman financial aid - 68 %
Early decision application deadline - N/A
Regular application deadline - Aug 1
Financial aid deadline - Jul 1

Ann Tremarello - Admissions Director
University of Alaska-Fairbanks
P. O. Box 757440
Fairbanks, AK 99775-7440
O 907.474.6244/ F 907.474.5379

www.uaf.edu

www.uafhockey.com

AMERICAN INTERNATIONAL COLLEGE

Division 1

HOCKEY STAFF

HEAD COACH
Gary Wright *(Vermont '76)*

ASSISTANT COACHES
Eric Lang *(AIC '98)*
Trevor Large *(Ferris State '04)*

HOCKEY OFFICE
American International College
1000 State Street, Box 4B
Springfield, MA 01109
O 413.205.3522 / F 413.205.3916
gary.wright@aic.edu

HOCKEY MEDIA CONTACT
Greg Royce - Sports Info Director
American International College
1000 State Street, Box 4B
Springfield, MA 01109
O 413.205.3572 / F 413.205.3571
sid@acad.aic.edu

HOCKEY RINK
Olympia Ice Center (Off Campus)
125 Capital Drive
Springfield, MA 01109
Size 200' x 85', Capacity 1,200
O 413.747.6544

ATHLETIC DIRECTOR
Robert Burke - Athletic Director
American International College
1000 State Street, Box 4B
Springfield, MA 01109-3189
O 413.205.3532 / F 413.731.5710
burkeath@aol.com

YELLOW JACKETS PLAYERS

Player	YB	GR	Ht/Wt	P	Hometown/Last Team
Chris Bolognino	83	08	6' 0"/220	D	Carol Stream,IL/Springfield Blues (NAHL)
Denis Budai	86	09	6' 0"/190	F	Subotica,Yugoslavia/Albany (NEPSAC)
Chris Campanale		10	6' 0"/190	F	Chester Spgs,PA/Green Mountain Glades (EJHL)
Frankie DeAngelis		10	5'10"/185	D	Woodbridge,ON/Georgetown Raiders (OPJHL)
Ben Ellsworth	84	07	6' 3"/200	F	Saranac Lk,NY/Northfield Mount Hermon (NEPSAC)
Tom Fenton	84	09	6' 0"/180	G	Sarnia,ON/Milton Icehawks (OPJHL)
Mike Field	83	08	5'10"/180	F	Marquette,MI/Helena Bighorns (NAHL)
Josh Froese		10	5'10"/180	F	Winkler,MB/Winkler Flyers (ManJHL)
Mark Fuqua	83	07	5'11"/175	F	Shelby Twnsp,MI/Sarnia Blast (WOJHL)
Greg Genovese	85	08	6' 2"/205	F	Hingham,MA/Pomfret (NEPSAC)
Andy Gevorkyan		10	5' 9"/180	F	Glendale,CA/Santa Fe Roadrunners (NAHL)
Brent Griffin	84	08	6' 0"/185	D	Leyden,MA/Northfield Mount Hermon (NEPSAC)
Eric Griffin	84	09	6' 2"/190	D	Magnolia,TX/Helena Bighorns (NAHL)
Jay Holladay		10	6' 2"/200	D	Virginia Bch,VA/Helena Bighorns (NAHL)
Bryan Jurynec	83	08	5'11"/190	F	Orland Pk,IL/Springfield Blues (NAHL)
Jeason Lecours	84	07	5'11"/175	F	Sherbrooke,QC/Gilmour (PS)
Jeremy Leroux	82	07	5'10"/170	F	Lunenburg,ON/Cornwall Colts (CJHL)
Mike McMillan		10	5' 8"/160	F	Sault Ste. Marie,ON/Soo Thunderbirds (NOJHL)
Mark Pavli	84	08	6' 0"/180	F	Sarnia,ON/Petrolia Jets (WOJHL)
Chad Richardson	84	09	5'10"/190	F	Regina,SK/Melfort Mustangs (SJHL)
Coby Robinson	84	09	6' 4"/185	G	Stevenson Rch,CA/New England Huskies (EJHL)
Keith Rodger	84	09	6' 0"/190	D	Parshall,CO/Helena Bighorns (NAHL)
Neil Sullivan	84	07	5'10"/160	F	Buffalo,NY/Bishop Timon (PS)
Jereme Tendler	83	08	6' 2"/185	F	Viceroy,SK/Weyburn Red Wings (SJHL)
Matt Tourville	82	07	5' 9"/175	G	Sandwich,MA/Green Mountain Glades (EJHL)
David Turco	85	09	5' 9"/175	F	Sault Ste. Marie,ON/Cambridge Winterhawks (MWJHL)
Matt Woodard	85	09	6' 0"/195	D	St. Louis Pk,MN/Helena Bighorns (NAHL)
Dean Yakura		10	5'11"/185	F	W Vancouver,BC/Dauphin Kings (ManJHL)

ROSTER ANALYSIS (SCHOLARSHIPS - 8)

Class		Country		Last Team				
Fr	7	USA	16	US JR A	8	CDN JR A	8	ACHA
So	8	Canada	11	US JR B	3	CDN JR B	3	NJCAA
Jr	7	Europe	1	US PS	6	CDN PS		NCAA
Sr	6	Asia		US HS		CDN HS		USNDT
Gr		Other		US Midget		CDN Midget		Other

ADMISSIONS, ENROLLMENT & CAMPUS INFORMATION

Founded 1885	Average acceptance rate - 85 %	Peter Miller - Admissions Director
Private, urban campus	Freshman financial aid - 84 %	American International College
589 men / 638 women	Early decision application deadline - N/A	1000 State Street - Box 4B
Tuition, room & board - $ 29 K	Regular application deadline - N/A	Springfield, MA 01109
Avg SAT - 980	Financial aid deadline - May 1	O 413.205.3201 / F 413.205.3943

AMHERST COLLEGE

Division 3

HOCKEY STAFF

HEAD COACH
Jack Arena *(Amherst '83)*

ASSISTANT COACH
Darren Reaume *(Amherst '02)*

HOCKEY OFFICE
Amherst College - Box 2230
PO Box 5000
Amherst, MA 01002-5000
O 413.542.7950 / F 413.542.2026
jaarena@amherst.edu

HOCKEY MEDIA CONTACT
Tanner Lipsett - Interim Sports Info Dir.
Amherst College - Box 2202
PO Box 5000
Amherst, MA 01002-5000
O 413.542.2390 / F 413.542.2527
tdlipsett@amherst.edu

HOCKEY RINK
Orr Rink (On Campus)
Route 116
Amherst, MA 01002
Size 200' x 85', Capacity 800
O 413.542.7950

ATHLETIC DIRECTOR
David Hixon - Interim Athletic Director
Amherst College - Alumni Gym
PO Box 5000
Amherst, MA 01002-5000
O 413.542.2069 / F 413.542.2026
ddhixon@amherst.edu

LORD JEFFS PLAYERS

Player	YB	GR	Ht/Wt	P	Hometown/Last Team
Gregg Adamo	85	08	6'0"/195	F	Manalapan,NJ/Green Mountain Glades (EJHL)
Olufemi Amurawaiye	86	09	6'1"/190	F	Whitby,ON/Holderness (NEPSAC)
Jack Baer	88	10	5'10"/165	F	Edina,MN/St. Thomas (PS)
Griffin Biedron	84	09	6'1"/215	D	Chelsea,MI/Capital District Selects (EJHL)
Ryland Burns	84	09	6'1"/200	D	Mill Bay,BC/Merritt Centennials (BCHL)
Trevor Calamel	83	07	6'2"/190	D	Lockport,NY/Capital Centre Pride (NAHL)
Will Collins	87	09	5'11"/160	F	Edina,MN/Edina (HS)
Joel Covelli	84	09	5'7"/165	F	Carlisle,ON/Colby (NESCAC)
Sean Ellis	83	07	5'10"/165	F	Springfield,MA/New England Coyotes (EJHL)
Josh Fillman	83	07	6'1"/205	G	Charlestown,MA/Nobles (NEPSAC)
Jeff Landers	86	09	6'0"/205	D	Hanover,MA/Deerfield (NEPSAC)
Shane Lennox	84	09	6'5"/215	D	N Vancouver,BC/New Jersey Hitmen (EJHL)
Erik Lund	84	07	5'9"/170	F	Edina,MN/Edina (HS)
Sean Lynch		09	5'10"/175	G	Winooski,VT/Bishop Brady (PS)
Michael McIntosh	83	08	5'8"/175	D	Soldotna,AK/Thornhill Islanders (OPJHL)
Keith Nelson	87	10	5'11"/180	F	Manalapan,NJ/Milton (NEPSAC)
Sean Patterson	87	10	6'5"/215	D	Lake Worth,FL/Westminster (NEPSAC)
Brendan Powers	86	09	6'0"/205	F	Walpole,MA/Roxbury Latin (NEPSAC)
Kyle Schoppel	84	08	5'10"/185	F	Cambridge,ON/Kitchener Dutchmen (MWJHL)
Andrew Schremp	85	08	5'7"/175	F	Denver,CO/Blake (PS)
AJ Scola	86	09	5'11"/180	G	Holden,MA/Phillips Exeter (NEPSAC)
Andrew Stevenson	86	10	5'10"/190	D	Newton,MA/Walpole Stars (EJHL)
Rob Stevenson	83	08	6'0"/190	D	Newton,MA/Walpole Stars (EJHL)
Ted Vickers	85	10	6'2"/205	D	Chilliwack,BC/Quesnel Millionaires (BCHL)
Brandon Zangel	84	07	6'1"/205	D	Highlands Rch,CO/Hotchkiss (NEPSAC)

ROSTER ANALYSIS (SCHOLARSHIPS - 0)

Class		Country		Last Team					
Fr	5	USA	19	US JR A	1	CDN JR A	3	ACHA	
So	10	Canada	6	US JR B	6	CDN JR B	1	NJCAA	
Jr	5	Europe		US PS	11	CDN PS		NCAA	1
Sr	5	Asia		US HS	2	CDN HS		USNDT	
Gr		Other		US Midget		CDN Midget		Other	

ADMISSIONS, ENROLLMENT & CAMPUS INFORMATION

Founded 1821
Private, Suburban campus
868 men / 770 women
Tuition, room & board - $ 42 K
Avg SAT - 1,455 / Avg ACT - 32

Average acceptance rate - 21 %
Freshman financial aid - 100 %
Early decision application deadline - Nov 15
Regular application deadline - Dec 31
Financial aid deadline - Feb 15

Katie Fretwell - Admissions Director
Amherst College - Box 2231
P. O. Box 5000
Amherst, MA 01002-5000
O 413.542.2328 / F 413.542.2040

UNIVERSITY OF ARIZONA

INDEPENDENT

EST. 1991
ACHA

Division 1

HOCKEY STAFF

HEAD COACH
Leo Golembiewski *(Benedictine '71)*

ASSISTANT COACHES
Dave Dougall
Tim Vlcek

WEBMASTER COORDINATOR
Gary Gould
uaicecats@aol.com

HOCKEY OFFICE
Arizona Icecats
2521 North Calle Noche
Tucson, AZ 85749
O 520.749.5530/ F 520.749.5530
coachlbg@worldnet.att.net

HOCKEY MEDIA CONTACT
John Dadante - Public Relations
Icecat Hockey Inc.
8987 E Tanque Verde, # 246
Tucson, AZ 85749
johnniedee@earthlink.net

HOCKEY RINK
Tucson Convention Center (Off Campus)
260 South Church Avenue
Tucson, AZ 85701
O 520.791.4101
Size 200' x 85', Capacity 6,850

ATHLETIC DIRECTOR
Jim Livengood
The University of Arizona
McKale Center
Tucson, AZ 87521
O 520.621.2200

ICECATS PLAYERS

Player	YB	GR	Ht/Wt	P	Hometown/Last Team
Nick Boddy	84	09	6' 2"/195	G	Bozeman,MT/Tri-City (NPJHL)
Devon Brady	86	08	6' 0"/195	D	Colorado Springs,CO/Hamline (MIAC)
Barett Buckowich	86	10	5' 9"/180	F	Lake Forest,IL/Lake Forest (HS)
Austin Capobianco	86	10	6' 2"/200	D	Branford,CT/Boston Harbor Wolves (EJHL)
Zach Cherney	87	10	5'11"/185	D	New York,NY/Salisbury (NEPSAC)
Matt Conover	84	09	6' 1"/180	F	East Amherst,NY/Bay City Bombers (WSHL)
Zack Davis	86	09	5' 7"/160	F	Piedmont,CA/California Gold Rush (Midget AA)
Joe Del Rossi	87	09	5'10"/165	F	Las Vegas,NV/West Chester Quakers (Midget AA)
Clay Desmond	87	09	6' 0"/155	F	Tucson,AZ/Salpointe Catholic (PS)
Matt Disney	84	09	6' 2"/205	F	Richland,MI/SUNY-Morrisville (NJCAA)
Luke Edwall	85	08	6' 4"/195	G	Minnetonka,MN/St. Louis Park (HS)
John Hansen	86	09	6' 0"/190	F	Fairfield,CT/Fairfield (PS)
Sean Hayes	88	10	5'11"/175	G	Newington,CT/Newington (HS)
Craig Irwin	85	08	5' 9"/175	F	Poughkeepsie,NY/Bay City Bombers (WSHL)
Eric Kowalek	84	07	5'10"/175	D	Shavertown,PA/Wyoming (PS)
Dan Kozak	87	09	5' 8"/155	F	St Johnsbury,VT/National Sports (PS)
Evan Marro	85	07	6' 5"/195	D	Albertson,NY/Nassau (NJCAA)
Scott Marshall	85	08	5' 9"/175	F	The Woodlands,TX/Bay City Bombers (WSHL)
Bryan Meagher	84	07	6' 0"/185	F	Hopkins,MN/Hopkins (HS)
Cody Morin	84	09	6' 1"/175	F	Phoenix,AZ/Phoenix (WSHL)
Robbie Nowinski	84	09	5'11"/180	F	Haslett,MI/Bay City Bombers (WSHL)
Keith Patterson	86	10	6' 0"/190	F	Phoenix,AZ/Phoenix Polar Bears (WSHL)
Brandon Robinson	87	09	6' 0"/175	F	La Mesa,CA/San Diego (WSHL)
Zach Samson	87	10	6' 3"/220	D	Long Grove,IL/Governor's (NEPSAC)
Richard Scardina	88	10	5'10"/155	F	Burr Ridge,IL/Hinsdale Central (HS)
Max Sliwinski	84	08	6' 0"/180	D	Hanover,NH/Laconia Leafs (AtJHL)
Zack Stommen	84	09	5'10"/165	D	Kalamazoo,MI/Bay City Bombers (WSHL)
Kevin West	85	09	5'11"/185	D	Breckenridge,CO/New England (EJHL)

ROSTER ANALYSIS (SCHOLARSHIPS - 0)

Class		Country		Last Team					
Fr	7	USA	28	US JR A		CDN JR A		ACHA	
So	13	Canada		US JR B	12	CDN JR B		NJCAA	2
Jr	5	Europe		US PS	6	CDN PS		NCAA	1
Sr	3	Asia		US HS	5	CDN HS		USNDT	
Gr		Other		US Midget	2	CDN Midget		Other	

ADMISSIONS, ENROLLMENT & CAMPUS INFORMATION

Founded 1885
Public, urban campus
12,812 men / 15,041 women
Tuition, room & board - $ 13 K/$ 22 K
Avg SAT - 1,110 / Avg ACT - 24

Average acceptance rate - 83 %
Freshman financial aid - 66 %
Early decision application deadline - N/A
Regular application deadline - Apr 1
Financial aid deadline - Mar 1

Lori Goldman - Admissions Director
University of Arizona
Nugent Building
Tucson, AZ 85721
O 520.621.3237/ 520.621.7783

www.arizona.edu

www.uaicecats.com

ASSUMPTION COLLEGE

Division 2

<table>
<tr><td colspan="2">

HOCKEY STAFF
</td><td colspan="5">

ICE DOGS PLAYERS
</td></tr>
</table>

HEAD COACH
Kevin Zifcak *(Bowdoin '97)*

ASSISTANT COACHES
Bob Harris *(Boston State '68)*
Brian Payne *(Lake Forest '94)*

HOCKEY OFFICE
Buffone Rink
284 Lake Avenue
Worcester, MA 01609-1296
O 508.767.7179 / F 508.798.2568
ihockey@assumption.edu

HOCKEY MEDIA CONTACT
Steve Morris - Sports Info Director
500 Salisbury Street
Worcester, MA 01609-1296
O 508.767.7240 / F 508.798.2568
merc@assumption.edu

HOCKEY RINK
Buffone Rink (Off Campus)
284 Lake Avenue
Worcester, MA 01604
Size 180' x 85', Capacity 1,200
O 508.755.0582

ATHLETIC DIRECTOR
Ted Paulauskas - Athletic Director
Assumption College
500 Salisbury Street
Worcester, MA 01609-1296
O 508.767.7279 / F 508.798.2568

Player	YB	GR	Ht/Wt	P	Hometown/Last Team
Frank Bova	86	09	5'6"/160	F	Princeton,MA/Wachusett (HS)
Riordan Cannata	88	10	6'0"/165	D	Charlestown,MA/Malden (PS)
James Capulli	87	10	5'11"/185	F	Hampstead,NH/Williston Northampton (NEPSAC)
Chris Charlton	87	09	5'10"/185	F	Melrose,MA/Melrose (HS)
Ron Cincotta	86	09	5'9"/170	F	Waltham,MA/Tilton (NEPSAC)
Patrick Ciummo	84	08	5'8"/160	F	Harrisville,RI/Winchendon (NEPSAC)
Tyler Cleary	87	10	6'0"/165	F	Newington,CT/Connecticut Clippers (MJHL)
Phil Demers	86	08	6'1"/200	D	Rutland,MA/St. John's (PS)
Jamie DiGiulio	87	10	5'8"/165	G	Peabody,MA/Tilton (NEPSAC)
Tim Dupuis	88	10	6'0"/185	D	W Suffield,CT/New England Falcons (EJHL)
Nick Fusco	87	10	5'10"/180	F	Saugus,MA/Bridgton (NEPSAC)
Chris Genovese	85	09	5'11"/210	D	Woburn,MA/Governor's (NEPSAC)
Pat Keenan	88	10	5'10"/185	D	Candia,NH/New Hampshire Monarchs (EJHL)
Luke McDonough	85	08	5'9"/170	F	Norfolk,MA/Mount St. Charles (PS)
Casey McNally	87	09	5'10"/160	G	Lunenburg,MA/New England Renegades (EJHL)
Randy Morin	85	08	6'0"/190	D	Auburn,ME/Portland Pirates (MJHL)
Matt Paget	84	08	5'10"/180	F	Hingham,MA/Winchendon (NEPSAC)
David Pinkham	87	09	6'1"/165	F	Malden,MA/Arlington (PS)
Jon Retelle	87	10	5'10"/185	D	Monmouth,ME/Portland Pirates (MJHL)
John Routhier	85	08	5'9"/165	F	Malden,MA/Winchendon (NEPSAC)
Mike Rust	84	08	5'10"/180	F	Swanzey,NH/Cushing (NEPSAC)
Mike St. Lawrence	87	10	5'9"/165	F	Holyoke,MA/Springfield Pics (IJHL)
Sean Staid	84	09	5'10"/160	F	Peabody,MA/Northfield Mount Hermon (NEPSAC)
Dan Surette	85	07	5'10"/175	D	Woburn,MA/Woburn (HS)
Jim Trahon	83	08	5'8"/180	F	Needham,MA/Bridgewater Bandits (EJHL)
Atte Uola	86	10	5'11"/175	F	Turku,Finland/Holderness (NEPSAC)
Derek Whitney	86	10	6'5"/220	D	Scituate,MA/Bridgewater Bandits (EJHL)
James Wood	86	08	5'8"/155	F	Hamden,CT/Hamden (HS)

ROSTER ANALYSIS (SCHOLARSHIPS - 0)

Class		Country		Last Team			
Fr	11	USA	27	US JR A		CDN JR A	ACHA
So	7	Canada		US JR B	9	CDN JR B	NJCAA
Jr	9	Europe	1	US PS	15	CDN PS	NCAA
Sr	1	Asia		US HS	4	CDN HS	USNDT
Gr		Other		US Midget		CDN Midget	Other

ADMISSIONS, ENROLLMENT & CAMPUS INFORMATION

Founded 1904	Average acceptance rate - 69 %	Mary Bresnahan - Admissions Director
Private, suburban campus	Freshman financial aid - 70 %	Assumption College
931 men / 1,233 women	Early decision application deadline - Nov 1	500 Salisbury Street
Tuition, room & board $ 34 K	Regular application deadline - Feb 15	Worcester, MA 01609-1296
Avg SAT - 1,085 / Avg ACT - 22	Financial aid deadline - Feb 1	O 888.882.7786 / F 508.799.4412

www.assumption.edu   www.assumptiongreyhounds.com

This is Where Winning Teams Have Winning Dreams

At Courtyard by Marriott, up to 4 team members or fans can enjoy a spacious guest room, free HBO and ESPN, a swimming pool, whirlpool, exercise room, guest laundry, and dependable Courtyard service, for a very nice price. And everyone will enjoy our comfortable restaurant, featuring a delicious breakfast buffet. Team up with Courtyard the next time you travel!

Boston Westborough   Boston Marlborough

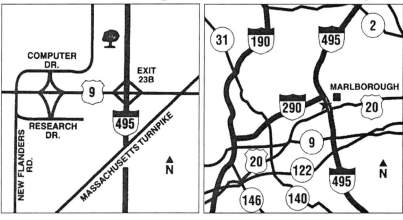

WESTBOROUGH, MASSACHUSETTS
3 Technology Drive • Westborough, MA 01581
(508) 836-4800 • Fax (508) 870-5577
800-321-2211

MARLBOROUGH, MASSACHUSETTS
75 Felton Street • Marlborough, MA 01752
(508) 480-0015 • Fax (508) 485-2242
800-321-2211

AUGSBURG COLLEGE

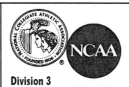

Division 3

HOCKEY STAFF

HEAD COACH
Chris Brown *(Wisconsin-River Falls '94)*

ASSISTANT COACHES
Mike LaValle *(Lakewood)*
Mike Burkhardt *(Augsburg '81)*
Bruce Johnson *(Augsburg '68)*
Chris Lepper *(St. Cloud State '93)*

HOCKEY OFFICE
Augsburg College - Melby Hall
2211 Riverside Avenue South
Minneapolis, MN 55454
O 612.330.1301 / F 612.330.1372
brownc3@augsburg.edu

HOCKEY MEDIA CONTACT
Don Stoner - Sports Info Director
Augsburg College - Sports Info Office
2211 Riverside Ave, Campus Box #145
Minneapolis, MN 55454
O 612.330.1677 / F 612.330.1780
stoner@augsburg.edu

HOCKEY RINK
Augsburg Arena (On Campus)
2323 Riverside Avenue
Minneapolis, MN 55454
Size 200' x 85', Capacity 800
O 612.330.1251

ATHLETIC DIRECTOR
Paul Grauer - Athletic Director
Augsburg College
2211 Riverside Avenue South
Minneapolis, MN 55454
O 612.330.1243 / F 612.330.1372
grauerp@augsburg.edu

AUGGIES PLAYERS

Player	YB	GR	Ht/Wt	P	Hometown/Last Team
Shawn Bakke	82	07	5'10"/195	F	New Hope,MN/Robert Morris (CHA)
Ian Bing	85	07	6' 2"/205	D	Cannon Fls,MN/Farmington (HS)
Ben Bradbury		09	5'11"/190	D	Winnipeg,MB/Guelph (CIAU)
Danny Carlson	83	08	5' 6"/175	F	Roseville,MN/Roseville (HS)
Kellen Chamblee	85	09	6' 2"/195	F	Falcon Hts,MN/Soo Indians (NAHL)
Tom Doyle	85	07	5'10"/170	F	St. Paul,MN/Como Park (HS)
Tony Eden	88	10	6' 1"/195	F	Vancouver,BC/St. George's (NEPSAC)
Thomas Erickson		07		F	Lakeville,MN/Apple Valley (HS)
Patrick Fogerty	87	09	6' 0"/185	D	Forest Lk,MN/Forest Lake (HS)
Justin Gauthier	86	09	6' 0"/175	D	Cupertino,CA/Cupertino (HS)
Chad Georgell		07	6' 1"/210	D	North Pole,AK/Wisconsin River Falls (NCHA)
AJ Hau	86	10	6' 0"/190	F	Ft Collins,CO/Fairbanks Ice Dogs (NAHL)
Adam Hendel	85	08	6' 0"/175	G	Red Wing,MN/Fairbanks Ice Dogs (NAHL)
Michael Henrichsen	86	08	6' 3"/175	G	Bothell,WA/Bothell (HS)
Aaron Johnson	82	07	5' 8"/170	F	Plymouth,MN/Armstrong (HS)
Chris Johnson	85	10	5'11"/175	F	Verona,WI/Fairbanks Ice Dogs (NAHL)
Andy Kent	84	09	5' 9"/175	G	Lakeville,MN/Twin Cities Northern Lights (MnJHL)
Chris Kopelke	88	10	5'11"/185	D	Shoreview,MN/Mounds View (HS)
Tim Lawson	84	08	5'11"/170	F	Monument,CO/Lewis-Palmer (HS)
Dan Leopold	85	08	6' 0"/175	D	Afton,MN/Stillwater (HS)
Greg May	85	07	5' 8"/160	F	Burnsville,MN/Burnsville (HS)
Trevor McCormick	85	08	5'10"/180	F	Mankato,MN/Mankato West (HS)
Ian McDougall	85	10	6' 0"/195	F	Mission Viejo,CA/Capistrano Valley (HS)
Critter Nagurski	83	07	6' 2"/205	F	Int'l Falls,MN/International Falls (HS)
Josh Ramberg	87	10	6' 1"/195	F	Fargo,ND/Fargo South (HS)
Jacob Smith	83	08	6' 0"/190	F	Hermantown,MN/St. Scholastica (MIAC)
Brett Way	84	09	6' 4"/210	F	Grand Ledge,MI/Hawkesbury Hawks (CJHL)

ROSTER ANALYSIS (SCHOLARSHIPS - 0)

Class		Country		Last Team					
Fr	6	USA	25	US JR A	4	CDN JR A	1	ACHA	
So	6	Canada	2	US JR B	1	CDN JR B		NJCAA	
Jr	7	Europe		US PS	1	CDN PS		NCAA	3
Sr	8	Asia		US HS	16	CDN HS		USNDT	
Gr		Other		US Midget		CDN Midget		CIAU	1

ADMISSIONS, ENROLLMENT & CAMPUS INFORMATION

Founded 1869	Average acceptance rate - 79 %	Sally Daniels - Admissions Director
Private, urban campus	Freshman financial aid - 81 %	Augsburg College Admissions Office
1,306 men / 1,414 women	Early decision application deadline - N/A	211 Riverside Avenue South
Tuition, room & board - $ 28 K	Regular application deadline - May 1	Minneapolis, MN 55454
Avg SAT - 1,100 / Avg ACT - 23	Financial aid deadline - April 15	O 800.788.5678 / F 612.330.1590

www.augsburg.edu   www.augsburg.edu/athletics

BABSON COLLEGE

H O C K E Y
EAST

Division 3

HOCKEY STAFF

HEAD COACH
Jamie Rice *(Babson '90)*

ASSISTANT COACHES
Jason Smith *(Salem State '98)*
Ed Kesell

HOCKEY OFFICE
Babson College
Webster Center
Babson Park, MA 02457
O 781.239.5981 / F 781.239.6070
jrice@babson.edu

HOCKEY MEDIA CONTACT
Chris Buck - Sports Info Director
Babson College
Webster Center
Babson Park, MA 02457-0901
O 781.239.4553 / F 781.239.5218
cbuck@babson.edu

HOCKEY RINK
Babson Skating Center (On Campus)
150 Great Plain Avenue
Wellesley, MA 02181
Size 200' x 85', Capacity 1,000
O 781.239.6058

ATHLETIC DIRECTOR
Judy Blinstrub - Interim Athletic Director
Babson College
Webster Center
Babson Park, MA 02457-0901
O 781.239.4418 / F 781.239.5218
blinstrub@babson.edu

BEAVERS PLAYERS

Player	YB	GR	Ht/Wt	P	Hometown/Last Team
JT Balben		09	5'8"/155	F	Wayland,MA/Belmont Hill (NEPSAC)
Brad Baldelli		09	5'7"/165	F	Northboro,MA/Salisbury (NEPSAC)
Ed Baran		08	5'9"/185	D	Danbury,CT/Brunswick (NEPSAC)
Matt Baron		08	5'10"/185	D	DeWitt,NY/Syracuse Stars (OPJHL)
Taylor Bergeron		10	5'9"/170	F	Milton,VT/St. Paul's (NEPSAC)
Greg Boxer		07	5'9"/165	G	Bernardsville,NJ/Loomis Chaffee (NEPSAC)
Liam Chatterton		10	6'0"/190	D	Staten Island,NY/St. George's (NEPSAC)
Gabriel Chenard-Poirier		10	6'1"/205	D	St. Augustin,QC/Grande Prairie Storm (AJHL)
Alex DiPietro		09	5'11"/180	D	Winthrop,MA/Apple Core (EJHL)
Ryan Farrell		07	6'0"/200	F	E Islip,NY/Capital Centre Pride (NAHL)
Shane Farrell		10	5'11"/195	F	W Warwick,RI/New Hampshire Monarchs (EJHL)
Casey Fazekas		10	5'10"/190	D	Montreal,QC/Westminster (NEPSAC)
Ryan Ferguson		08	5'8"/160	F	Sydney,NS/St. George's (NEPSAC)
John Geverd		08	6'0"/205	F	Hooksett,NH/New Hampshire Monarchs (EJHL)
Ian Goodwin		10	5'9"/165	D	Cooper City,FL/Canterbury (NEPSAC)
Matt Harrington		09	5'10"/180	F	Hanover,MA/Thayer (NEPSAC)
Nick Jones		09	6'2"/215	D	Melrose,MA/New England Falcons (EJHL)
Tom Maregni		08	5'10"/185	F	Ashland,MA/St. Sebastian's (NEPSAC)
Pat McCarthy		09	6'0"/190	D	Warwick,RI/Milton (NEPSAC)
Pat McLaughlin		09	5'10"/170	F	Berlin,MA/Cushing (NEPSAC)
Mike McMahon		10	5'10"/170	D	Wilmington,MA/Phillips Exeter (NEPSAC)
Ryan Moses		10	5'11"/185	G	Beford,NY/Hotchkiss (NEPSAC)
Skylar Nipps		09	6'1"/190	G	Orlando,FL/St. Paul's (NEPSAC)
Chris Sabo		10	5'10"/180	F	Wellesley,MA/Valley Warriors (EJHL)
Jason Schneider		10	5'10"/170	F	Littleton,MA/Lawrence (NEPSAC)
Nate Smith		08	5'11"/185	F	Madrid,NY/Holderness (NEPSAC)
Mike Venit		08	5'8"/180	F	Ridley Park,PA/Bay State Breakers (EJHL)

ROSTER ANALYSIS (SCHOLARSHIPS - 0)

Class		Country		Last Team					
Fr	11	USA	26	US JR A	1	CDN JR A	2	ACHA	
So	8	Canada	2	US JR B	6	CDN JR B		NJCAA	
Jr	7	Europe		US PS	19	CDN PS		NCAA	4
Sr	2	Asia		US HS		CDN HS		USNDT	
Gr		Other		US Midget		CDN Midget		Other	

ADMISSIONS, ENROLLMENT & CAMPUS INFORMATION

Founded 1919	Average acceptance rate - 37 %	Charles Nolan - Admissions Director
Private, suburban campus	Freshman financial aid - 98 %	Babson College - Admissions
1,018 men / 679 women	Early decision application deadline - Nov 15	231 Forest Street
Tuition, room & board - $ 42 K	Regular application deadline - Jan 15	Babson Park, MA 02457-0310
Avg SAT - 1,245 / Avg ACT - 27	Financial aid deadline - Feb 15	O 781.239.5522 / F 781.239.4135

www.babson.edu www3.babson.edu/athletics/

BECKER COLLEGE

INDEPENDENT	

Division 3

HOCKEY STAFF

HEAD COACH
Steve Hoar *(Boston College '76)*

ASSISTANT COACH
John Coughlin *(AIC '69)*

HOCKEY OFFICE
Becker College
61 Sever Street / PO Box 15071
Worcester, MA 01615-0071
O 508.791.9241 x464/ F 508.892.8131
steve.hoar@beckercollege.edu

HOCKEY MEDIA CONTACT
Bettiann Michalik - Sports Info Director
Becker College
61 Sever Street / PO Box 15071
Worcester, MA 01615-0071
O 508.791.9241 x477/ F 508.892.8131
bmichalik@beckercollege.edu

HOCKEY RINK
Buffone Arena (Off Campus)
Worcester, MA
Size 200' x 85'
Horgan Arena (Off Campus)
Auburn, MA
Size 200' x 85'

ATHLETIC DIRECTOR
Craig Barnett
Becker College
61 Sever Street / POB 15071
Worcester, MA 01615-0071
O 508.791.9241 x464/ F 508.892.8131
craig.barnett@beckercollege.edu

HAWKS PLAYERS

Player	YB GR Ht/Wt	P	Hometown/Last Team
Robert Adler	10 6'0"/165	D	Winthrop,MA/Arlington (PS)
Dan Bailey	10 5'11"/180	F	Colchester,CT/Norwich Ice Breakers (AEHL)
Justin Benedict	10 5'10"/170	F	Deansboro,NY/Northwood (PS)
Chris Benoit	07 6'2"/190	D	Dummerston,VT/Springfield Pics (IJHL)
Garrett Blair	10 5'9"/165	F	Antrim,NH/Exeter Seawolves (AEHL)
John Blair	10 5'9"/180	D	Antrim,NH/Exeter Seawolves (AEHL)
John Blomgren	10 6'3"/190	D	W Haven,CT/Notre Dame-West Haven (PS)
Mike Caprio	10 5'9"/175	F	Valencia,CA/Northern Michigan Black Bears (NOJHL)
Jim Ceglarek	10 6'1"/200	D	Chicago,IL/Northern Michigan Black Bears (NOJHL)
Jack Collins	10 5'8"/170	F	Lisle,IL/Naperville North (HS)
Derek Collwell	10 6'0"/185	G	Dover,NH/Exeter Seawolves (AEHL)
Joe Dorney	10 5'10"/180	D	Williamsburg,PA/Hudson Valley Eagles (MJHL)
Keith Dube	10 5'10"/175	F	Monson,MA/Springfield Pics (IJHL)
Chris Erdman	10 5'11"/175	F	Cumming,GA/Boston Bulldogs (AtJHL)
Andrew Ford	10 6'1"/185	D	Cherry Hill,NJ/Green Mountain Glades (EJHL)
Brian Gonsalves	10 5'9"/165	F	Milford,CT/Connecticut Clippers (MJHL)
Sean Hayes	10 5'8"/165	F	Burlington,VT/Green Mountain Glades (EJHL)
Jared Kersner	10 5'8"/175	F	Rockville,MD/New Jersey Rockets (MJHL)
John McCarthy	10 5'8"/150	F	Ridgefield,CT/Northwood (PS)
Brandon Melikian	10 5'9"/150	G	Wilbraham,MA/Springfield Pics (IJHL)
Joey Meyer	10 5'11"/165	F	E Concord,NY/St. Francis (PS)
Rick Odria	10 6'2"/180	G	Coral Spgs,FL/Exeter Seawolves (AEHL)
Anthony Oliveria	10 5'9"/170	G	Stratham,NH/New Hampshire Monarchs (EJHL)
Matt Oster	10 5'11"/195	F	Stillwater,MN/Twin Cities Northern Lights (MnJHL)
Phil Pinkham	10 5'8"/150	F	Buxton,ME/New Hampshire Monarchs (EJHL)
Justin Rada	10 5'6"/160	F	Spotsylvania,VA/Green Mountain Glades (EJHL)
Chris Reilly	09 5'10"/180	F/D	Lexington,MA/Johnson & Wales (ECAC NE)
Andrew Scampoli	09 5'11"/200	D	Islip,NY/Hudson Valley Eagles (MJHL)
Derek Stabile	10 5'11"/190	F	Sault Ste. Marie,MI/N Michigan Black Bears (NOJHL)
Kevin Switek	10 6'1"/185	F	Philadelphia,PA/Hudson Valley Eagles (MJHL)
Kevin Sychowski	10 6'0"/165	F	Chicago,IL/Loyola (PS)
Nate Towse	10 5'11"/175	D	Westfield,MA/Springfield Pics (IJHL)

ROSTER ANALYSIS (SCHOLARSHIPS - 0)

Class		Country		Last Team				
Fr	29	USA	32	US JR A		CDN JR A	3	ACHA
So	2	Canada		US JR B	21	CDN JR B		NJCAA
Jr		Europe		US PS	6	CDN PS		NCAA
Sr	1	Asia		US HS	1	CDN HS		USNDT
Gr		Other		US Midget		CDN Midget		Other

ADMISSIONS, ENROLLMENT & CAMPUS INFORMATION

Founded 1784	Average acceptance rate - 80 %	Admissions Director
Private, suburban campus	Freshman financial aid - 75 %	Becker College - Admissions
480 men / 720 women	Early decision application deadline - n/a	61 Sever Street / POB 15071
Tuition, room & board - $ 27 K	Regular application deadline - Rolling	Worcester, MA 01615-0071
Avg SAT - 1,600	Financial aid deadline - March 1	O 877.523.2537/ F 508.890.1500

www.beckercollege.edu   www.beckercollege.edu/studentlife/athletics.htm

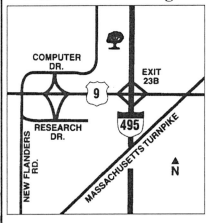
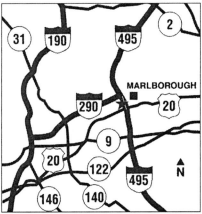

BEMIDJI STATE UNIVERSITY

Division 1

HOCKEY STAFF

HEAD COACH
Tom Serratore *(Bemidji State '87)*

ASSISTANT COACHES
Bert Gilling *(Minnesota-Duluth '99)*
Ted Belisle *(Bemidji State '01)*
Ryan McKelvie *(Minnesota State '06)*

HOCKEY OFFICE
Bemidji State University - Athletic Dept.
1500 Birchmont Drive NE - PE 217, Box 29
Bemidji, MN 56601-2699
O 218.755.2879/F 218.755.3898
tserratore@bemidjistate.edu

HOCKEY MEDIA CONTACT
Andy Bartlett - Hockey Info Director
Bemidji State University - Athletic Dept.
1500 Birchmont Drive NE - PE 203, Box 29
Bemidji, MN 56601-2699
O 218.755.4603/ F 218.755.3898
jbartlett@bemidjistate.edu

HOCKEY RINK
Glas Fieldhouse (On Campus)
1500 Birchmont Drive NE
Bemidji, MN 56601-2699
Size 200' x 85', Capacity 2,358
O 218.755.3700

ATHLETIC DIRECTOR
Dr. Rick Goeb - Athletic Director
Bemidji State University - Athletic Dept.
1500 Birchmont Drive NE - PE 200, Box 29
Bemidji, MN 56601-2699
O 218.755.4022/ F 218.755.3898
rgoeb@bemidjistate.edu

BEAVERS PLAYERS

Player	YB	GR	Ht/Wt	P	Hometown/Last Team
Orlando Alamano	83	08	5'10"/165	G	Fresno,CA/Swan Valley Stampeders (ManJHL)
Matt Allen	84	09	6'0"/195	F	New Westminster,BC/Victoria Salsa (BCHL)
Jake Bluhm	83	08	5'11"/190	F	Red Wing,MN/Fairbanks Ice Dogs (NAHL)
Cody Bostock	84	09	5'11"/200	F	Salmon Arm,BC/Vernon Vipers (BCHL)
Matt Climie	83	08	6'3"/185	G	Leduc,AB/Truro Bearcats (MarJHL)
Dave Deterding	83	08	6'1"/205	F	Alexandria,MN/Sioux City Musketeers (USHL)
Luke Erickson	82	07	5'9"/160	F	Roseau,MN/Topeka Scarecrows (USHL)
Matt Francis	85	08	5'9"/185	F	Surrey,BC/St. Cloud (WCHA)
Kyle Hardwick	86	10	5'11"/190	D	Warroad,MN/Lincoln Stars (USHL)
Shane Holman	84	07	5'11"/160	F/D	Hibbing,MN/Fargo-Moorhead Jets (NAHL)
Blaine Jarvis	84	08	6'0"/200	F	Gladstone,MB/Salmon Arm Silverbacks (BCHL)
Tyler Lehrke	86	10	5'8"/175	F	Park Rapids,MN/Green Bay Gamblers (USHL)
Brandon Marino	86	09	5'9"/185	F	Riverside,CA/Helena Bighorns (NAHL)
Chris McKelvie	85	10	6'1"/190	F	New Brighton,MN/Bozeman Icedogs (NAHL)
Graham McManamin	85	10	5'10"/205	D	Anchorage,AK/Bozeman Icedogs (NAHL)
Ryan Miller	84	07	5'8"/180	F	Fergus Fls,MN/Topeka Scarecrows (USHL)
Joey Moggach	85	10	5'7"/165	F	Brandon,MB/Dauphin Kings (ManJHL)
Chris Peluso	86	10	5'10"/185	D	Wadena,MN/Sioux Falls Stampede (USHL)
Matt Pope	82	08	6'1"/180	F	Langley,BC/Langley Hornets (BCHL)
Garrett Roth	82	07	5'11"/165	F	Cary,IL/Bismarck Bobcats (NAHL)
Nathan Schwartzbauer	82	07	6'4"/215	D	Wasilla,AK/Sioux City Musketeers (USHL)
Tyler Scofield	84	09	5'8"/150	F	Prince George,BC/OCN Blizzard (ManJHL)
Layne Sedevie	83	07	5'10"/180	G	Bismarck,ND/Topeka Scarecrows (USHL)
Rob Sirianni	83	07	5'11"/175	F	Edmonton,AB/Bonnyville Pontiacs (AJHL)
John Vadnais	86	10	6'0"/195	D	Stillwater,MN/Des Moines Buccaneers (USHL)
Riley Weselowski	85	08	6'0"/190	D	Pilot Mound,MB/Neepawa Natives (ManJHL)
Travis Winter	84	09	6'1"/185	F	St. Cloud,MN/Indiana Ice (USHL)

ROSTER ANALYSIS (SCHOLARSHIPS - 14)

Class		Country		Last Team					
Fr	7	USA	17	US JR A	16	CDN JR A	10	ACHA	
So	5	Canada	10	US JR B		CDN JR B		NJCAA	
Jr	8	Europe	3	US PS		CDN PS		NCAA	1
Sr	7	Asia		US HS		CDN HS		USNDT	
Gr		Other		US Midget		CDN Midget		Other	

ADMISSIONS, ENROLLMENT & CAMPUS INFORMATION

Founded 1919	Average acceptance rate - 73 %	Paul Muller - Admissions Director
Public, small town campus	Freshman financial aid - 75 %	Bemidji State University Admissions
2,328 men / 2,194 women	Early decision application deadline - N/A	1500 Birchmont Drive NE
Tuition, room & board $ 12 K/ $ 18 K	Regular application deadline - rolling	Bemidji, MN 56601-2699
Avg ACT - 22	Financial aid deadline - May 15	O 218.755.2040 / F 218.755.3074

info.bemidjistate.edu info.bemidjistate.edu/sports

BENTLEY COLLEGE

Division 1

HOCKEY STAFF

HEAD COACH
Ryan Soderquist *(Bentley '00)*

ASSISTANT COACH
Mark White *(New Hampshire '01)*
Charlie Carkin *(Mass-Boston '92)*

HOCKEY OFFICE
Bentley College
175 Forest Street
Waltham, MA 02452-4705
O 781.891.2492/ F 781.891.2648
rsoderquist@bentley.edu

HOCKEY MEDIA CONTACT
Dick Lipe - Sports Info Director
Bentley College
175 Forest Street
Waltham, MA 02452-4705
O 781.891.2334/ F 781.891.2648
rlipe@bentley.edu

HOCKEY RINK
Ryan Arena (Off Campus)
1 Paramount Place
Watertown, MA 02172
Size 200' x 85', Capacity 1,200
O 617.972.6468

ATHLETIC DIRECTOR
Bob DeFelice - Athletic Director
Bentley College
175 Forest Street
Waltham, MA 02452-4705
O 781.891.2256/ F 781.891.2282
rdefelice@bentley.edu

FALCONS PLAYERS

Player	YB	GR	Ht/Wt	P	Hometown/Last Team
Jay Bletzer	85	08	6' 0"/180	D	Medfield,MA/Walpole Stars (EJHL)
Anthony Canzoneri	85	09	5'10"/180	F	Homer Glen,IL/Youngstown Phantoms (NAHL)
Joe Cucci	85	08	5'11"/185	D	Glen Ridge,NJ/Avon (NEPSAC)
Nick DeCroo	86	10	6' 3"/220	F	Sarver,PA/Junior Bruins (EJHL)
Tom Dickhudt	84	09	5'11"/190	F	Woodbury,MN/Fargo-Moorhead Jets (NAHL)
Andrew Goberstein	85	09	5'11"/185	F	Northbrook,IL/Santa Fe Roadrunners (NAHL)
Jeff Gumaer	84	09	5' 9"/175	F	St. Louis,MO/Springfield Blues (NAHL)
Blake Hamilton	86	10	5'10"/180	F	Edmonton,AB/Spruce Grove Saints (AJHL)
Brendan Harrison	85	10	5' 9"/175	F	Scituate,MA/Walpole Stars (EJHL)
John Hooks	82	07	6' 1"/215	F	Brown Mills,NJ/Springfield Blues (NAHL)
Ray Jean	84	09	5' 9"/185	G	Randolph,ME/Maine (HEA)
Jaye Judd	83	08	6' 2"/210	D	Brandon,MB/Salmon Arm Silverbacks (BCHL)
Jason Kearney	84	09	5' 7"/175	G	Gibsonia,PA/Soo Indians (NAHL)
Justin Kemmerer	86	10	6' 2"/180	D	Hershey,PA/Pomfret (NEPSAC)
Mark Menzione	85	10	5'10"/175	F	Darien,IL/Mahoning Valley Phantoms (NAHL)
Nick Moise	84	09	6' 3"/190	G	E Walpole,MA/Bay State Breakers (EJHL)
Anders Olson	85	10	6' 3"/200	F	Edina,MN/Williams Lake Timberwolves (BCHL)
Kane Osmars	85	10	5'10"/180	F	Kanata,ON/Kanata Stallions (CJHL)
Anthony Pellarin	83	08	6' 0"/205	F	N Merrick,NY/Texas Tornado (NAHL)
Pat Percella	85	10	6' 0"/200	F	Bayonne,NJ/Boston University (HEA)
Bobby Preece	85	10	6' 2"/205	D	Bonita Spgs,FL/Fargo-Moorhead Jets (NAHL)
Dain Prewitt	84	09	5'11"/190	F	Westminster,CO/Fargo-Moorhead Jets (NAHL)
Casey Russell	84	09	6' 1"/210	D	Orange,CT/Junior Bruins (EJHL)
Paul Scalici	84	09	5' 9"/185	F	Bingham Farms,MI/Toledo IceDiggers (NAHL)
Nick Vitale	87	10	6'0"/180	G	Peabody,MA/Brewster (NEPSAC)
Jesse Williams	86	10	5' 9"/185	D	Webster,NY/Valley Warriors (EJHL)
Mark Zarbo	86	10	6' 0"/190	D	Grand Island,NY/Capital District Selects (EJHL)
Marc Zwickey	83	08	5'10"/180	F	Basel,Switzerland/Clarkson (ECAC)

ROSTER ANALYSIS (SCHOLARSHIPS - 11)

Class		Country		Last Team					
Fr	11	USA	24	US JR A	11	CDN JR A	4	ACHA	
So	11	Canada	3	US JR B		CDN JR B	7	NJCAA	
Jr	5	Europe	1	US PS	3	CDN PS		NCAA	3
Sr	1	Asia		US HS		CDN HS		USNDT	
Gr		Other		US Midget		CDN Midget		Other	

ADMISSIONS, ENROLLMENT & CAMPUS INFORMATION

Founded 1917
Private, suburban campus
Tuition, room & board - $ 31 K
2,592 men / 1,658 women
Avg SAT - 1,200 / Avg ACT - 25

Average acceptance rate - 45 %
Freshman financial aid - 90 %
Early decision application deadline - Nov 15
Regular application deadline - Feb 1
Financial aid deadline - Feb 1

Joann McKenna - Admissions Director
Bentley College
175 Forest Street
Waltham, MA 02452
O 781.891.2244/ F 781.891.3414

www.bentley.edu   www.bentley.edu/athletics

BETHEL UNIVERSITY

Division 3

HOCKEY STAFF	ROYALS PLAYERS

HOCKEY STAFF

HEAD COACH
Joel Johnson *(Bethel '92)*

ASSISTANT COACHES
Chris Carroll *(Bethel '04)*
Matt Millar *(Bethel '05)*
Brian Saintey *(Bethel)*
Dan Roby

HOCKEY OFFICE
Bethel University
3900 Bethel Drive
St. Paul, MN 55112
O 651.638.6471 / F 651.635.8645
joel-johnson@bethel.edu

HOCKEY MEDIA CONTACT
Dan Berglund - Sports Info Director
Bethel University
3900 Bethel Drive
St. Paul, MN 55112
O 651.635.8537 / F 651.635.8645
daniel-berglund@bethel.edu

HOCKEY RINK
Columbia Arena (Off Campus)
7011 University Avenue
Fridley, MN 55304
Size 200' x 85 ', Capacity 1,500
O 651.571.6701

ATHLETIC DIRECTOR
Bob Bjorklund - Athletic Director
Bethel University
3900 Bethel Drive
St. Paul, MN 55112
O 651.638.6395 / F 651.638.6001
robert-bjorklund@bethel.edu

ROYALS PLAYERS

Player	YB	GR	Ht/Wt	P	Hometown/Last Team
Eric Adams	09		6' 4"/195	F	Litchfield,MN/Northern Lights (MnJHL)
Ryan Adams	07		6' 0"/180	F	Litchfield,MN/Northern Lights (MnJHL)
Jeff Balvin	08		6' 0"/185	F	Maple Gr,MN/Topeka Scarecrows (USHL)
Dan Bonne	08		5'10"/185	F	White Bear Lk,MN/White Bear Lake (HS)
Kent Bostrom	09		5'11"/170	F	Vadnais Hgts,MN/Sioux City Musketeers (USHL)
Ben Boycott	10		6' 1"/170	G	Kenai,AK/Anchorage Northstars (Midget AAA)
Josh Brodeen	10		5'11"/180	F	Warroad,MN/Lincoln Stars (USHL)
Kevin Broten	09		5'10"/190	F	Roseau,MN/Roseau (HS)
Neal Carlson	07		5'10"/175	D	Roseville,MN/Roseville (HS)
Aaron Damjanovich	10		5'11"/165	G	Coleraine,MN/Billings Bulls (NAHL)
Benoit Duhamel	08		5'11"/175	F	Drummondville,QC
Kyle Dynam	10		5'11"/170	D	Maple Plain,MN/Orono (HS)
Patrick Dynam	10		5'11"/195	F	Maple Plain,MN/North Iowa Outlaws (NAHL)
Rory Dynam	10		5' 9"/185	F	Maple Plain,MN/Central Texas Blackhawks (NAHL)
Steve Eastman	07		5'11"/185	D/F	Edina,MN/Quinnipiac (ECAC)
Matt Hall	08		5'10"/170	F	Brooklyn Pk,MN/St. Thomas (MIAC)
Don Hochbrunn	09		5'10"/180	D	Circle Pines,MN/Centennial (HS)
Kenny Holvig	07		6' 3"/190	F	New City,NY/Hudson Valley (NJCAA)
Ben Jorgenson	07		6' 0"/180	F	Little Falls,MN/Little Falls (HS)
Brent Kettelkamp	09		6' 0"/195	D	Richfield,MN/Breck (PS)
Tyler Kettelkamp	07		6' 1"/175	D	Richfield,MN/Breck (PS)
Patrick Kiely	10		6' 0"/175	G	Muskegon,MI/Reeths-Puffer (HS)
John Kovacs	09		6' 0"/205	D	White Bear Lk,MN/Fargo-Moorhead Jets (NAHL)
Jonathan Kramer	07		5'11"/190	F	St. Paul,MN/Como Park (HS)
Bill Menozzi	08		6' 4"/215	D	Lakeville,MN/Robert Morris (CHA)
Nick Miller	09		6' 3"/220	F	Coon Rpds,MN/Topeka Scarecrows (USHL)
Christian Ostigaard	10		5'11"/170	F	Byers,CO/St. Paul Lakers (MnJHL)
Nate Peasley	07		6' 0"/185	D	N St. Paul,MN/North St. Paul (HS)
Brad Peterson	09		6' 0"/210	F	Bloomington,MN/Des Moines Buccaneers (USHL)
Dustin Thompson	07		5'10"/150	G	Lino Lakes,MN/Centennial (HS)

ROSTER ANALYSIS (SCHOLARSHIPS - 0)

Class		Country		Last Team				
Fr	8	USA	29	US JR A	9	CDN JR A	ACHA	
So	8	Canada	1	US JR B	3	CDN JR B	NJCAA	1
Jr	5	Europe		US PS	2	CDN PS	NCAA	3
Sr	9	Asia		US HS	10	CDN HS	USNDT	
Gr		Other		US Midget	1	CDN Midget	Other	1

ADMISSIONS, ENROLLMENT & CAMPUS INFORMATION

Founded 1887	Average acceptance rate - 86 %	John C. Lassen - Admissions Director
Private, urban campus	Freshman financial aid - 82 %	Bethel University
1,298 men / 1,721 women	Early decision application deadline - Dec 1	3900 Bethel Drive
Tuition, room & board $ 29 K	Regular application deadline - Mar 1	St. Paul, MN 55112
Avg SAT - 1,170 / Avg ACT - 24	Financial aid deadline - Apr 15	O 651.638.6242 / F 651.635.1490

www.bethel.edu   cas.bethel.edu/athletics/

BOSTON COLLEGE

Division 1

HOCKEY STAFF

HEAD COACH
Jerry York *(Boston College '67)*

ASSOCIATE HEAD COACH
Mike Cavanaugh *(Bowdoin '90)*

ASSISTANT COACHES
Jim Logue *(Boston College '61)*
Greg Brown *(Boston College '90)*

HOCKEY OFFICE
Boston College - Conte Forum
140 Commonwealth Avenue
Chestnut Hill, MA 02467
O 617.552.3028/ F 617.552.0029
yorkje@bc.edu

HOCKEY MEDIA CONTACT
Tim Clark - Hockey Info Director
Boston College
321 Conte Forum - SID Office
Chestnut Hill, MA 02467
O 617.552.8841/ F 617.552.4903
clarktb@bc.edu

HOCKEY RINK
Kelley Rink (On Campus)
2599 Beacon Street
Chestnut Hill, MA 02467
Size 200' x 87', Capacity 7,884
O 617.552.4747

ATHLETIC DIRECTOR
Gene DeFilippo - Athletic Director
Boston College - Conte Forum
Chestnut Hill, MA 02467
O 617.552.4681
eugene.difilippo.2@bc.edu

EAGLES PLAYERS

Player	YB	GR	Ht/Wt	P	Hometown/Last Team
Joe Adams	84	08	5'10"/175	F	Wayzata,MN/New Hampshire Monarchs (EJHL)
Anthony Aiello	86	09	6'1"/195	D	Braintree,MA/Thayer (NEPSAC)
Dan Bertram	87	08	5'11"/175	F	Calgary,AB/Camrose Kodiaks (AJHL)
Brian Boyle	84	07	6'7"/220	F	Hingham,MA/St. Sebastian's (NEPSAC)
Brock Bradford	87	09	5'10"/170	F	Burnaby,BC/Omaha Lancers (USHL)
Mike Brennan	86	08	5'11"/190	D	Smithtown,NY/USNDT (NAHL)
Joseph Ehiorobo	86	10	5'11"/190	F	Farmingdale,ME/Lawrence (NEPSAC)
Benn Ferriero	87	09	5'11"/185	F	Essex,MA/Governor's (NEPSAC)
Tim Filangieri	87	09	6'2"/195	D	Islip Terr,NY/Waterloo Blackhawks (USHL)
Pat Gannon	84	08	5'7"/155	F	Arlington,MA/Junior Bruins (EJHL)
Nathan Gerbe	87	09	5'6"/160	F	Oxford,MI/USNDT (NAHL)
Justin Greene	84	07	5'10"/185	D	Plymouth,MA/Boston College (PS)
Matt Greene	85	08	5'8"/175	F	Plymouth,MA/Boston College (PS)
Corey Griffin	86	10	6'1"/195	F	Hingham,MA/Taft (NEPSAC)
Kyle Kucharski	87	09	6'3"/200	F	Saugus,MA/Andover (NEPSAC)
Tim Kunes	87	09	6'1"/180	D	Huntington,NY/New England Falcons (EJHL)
Matt Lombardi	87	10	5'11"/185	F	Milton,MA/Governor's (NEPSAC)
Brett Motherwell	86	09	5'11"/195	D	St. Charles,IL/Omaha Lancers (USHL)
Brian O'Hanley	84	08	5'11"/190	D	Quincy,MA/Salisbury (NEPSAC)
Andrew Orpik	86	09	6'2"/200	F	E Amherst,NY/Thayer (NEPSAC)
Joe Pearce	82	07	6'4"/205	G	Brick,NJ/Chicago Steel (USHL)
Matt Price	88	10	5'10"/185	F	Milton,OH/Milton Icehawks (OPJHL)
Adam Reasoner	84	09	6'2"/200	G	Honeoye Fls,NY/Bay State Breakers (EJHL)
Joe Rooney	85	07	5'10"/175	F	Canton,MA/Walpole Stars (EJHL)
Cory Schneider	86	08	6'2"/195	G	Marblehead,PA/Andover (NEPSAC)
Ben Smith	88	10	5'11"/195	F	Avon,CT/Westminster (NEPSAC)
Carl Sneep	87	10	6'3"/205	D	Nisswa,MN/Brainerd (HS)

ROSTER ANALYSIS (SCHOLARSHIPS - 18)

Class		Country		Last Team					
Fr	6	USA	25	US JR A	4	CDN JR A	2	ACHA	
So	10	Canada	2	US JR B	5	CDN JR B		NJCAA	
Jr	7	Europe		US PS	13	CDN PS		NCAA	
Sr	4	Asia		US HS	1	CDN HS		USNDT	2
Gr		Other		US Midget		CDN Midget		Other	

ADMISSIONS, ENROLLMENT & CAMPUS INFORMATION

Founded 1863	Average acceptance rate - 32 %	Undergraduate Amissions Office
Private, suburban campus	Freshman financial aid - 100 %	Boston College
4,258 men / 4,801 women	Early decision application deadline - N/A	Devlin Hall # 208
Tuition, room & board -$ 40 K	Regular application deadline - Jan 2	Chestnut Hill, MA 02167
Avg SAT - 1,325	Financial aid deadline - Feb 1	O 617.552.3100/ F 617.552.0798

www.bc.edu   www.bceagles.com

BOSTON UNIVERSITY

Division 1

HOCKEY STAFF

HEAD COACH
Jack Parker *(Boston University '68)*

ASSOCIATE HEAD COACH
David Quinn *(Boston University '88)*

ASSISTANT COACHES
Mike Bavis *(Boston University '93)*
Mike Geragosian *(Mass. Lowell '75)*

HOCKEY OFFICE
Boston University Hockey Office
285 Babcock Street
Boston, MA 02215
O 617.353.4639 / F 617.353.4321
hockey@bu.edu

HOCKEY MEDIA CONTACT
Christy Jeffries - Hockey Info Director
Boston University
285 Babcock Street
Boston, MA 02215
O 617.353.2163 / F 617.353.5286
jeffries@bu.edu

HOCKEY RINK
Agganis Arena (On Campus)
285 Babcock Street
Boston, MA 02215
Size 200' x 90', Capacity 6,300
O 617.353.5286

ATHLETIC DIRECTOR
Mike Lynch - Athletic Director
Boston University
285 Babcock Street
Boston, MA 02215
O 617.353.1905

TERRIERS PLAYERS

Player	YB	GR	Ht/Wt	P	Hometown/Last Team
Brett Bennett	88	10	6' 1"/185	G	Williamsville,NY/USNDT (NAHL)
Zach Cohen	87	10	6' 3"/195	F	Schaumburg,IL/Tri-City Storm (USHL)
John Curry	84	07	5'11"/185	G	Shorewood,MN/Taft (NEPSAC)
Bryan Ewing	85	08	5'10"/160	F	Plymouth,MA/Cushing (NEPSAC)
Karson Gillespie	83	08	5'11"/175	G	Mankota,SK/Bonnyville Pontiacs (AJHL)
Matt Gilroy	84	09	6' 2"/190	F	N Bellmore,NY/Walpole Stars (EJHL)
Eric Gryba	88	10	6' 3"/215	D	Saskatoon,SK/Green Bay Gamblers (USHL)
Chris Higgins	86	09	5'11"/165	F	Lynnfield,MA/New Hampshire Monarchs (EJHL)
Kevin Kielt	84	08	6' 0"/190	D	Brick,NJ/New Hampshire Monarchs (EJHL)
Jason Lawrence	87	09	5'10"/180	F	Saugus,MA/USNDT (NAHL)
Peter MacArthur	85	08	5'10"/180	F	Clifton Pk,NY/Waterloo Blackhawks (USHL)
John McCarthy	86	09	6' 1"/195	F	Andover,MA/Des Moines Buccaneers (USHL)
Dan McGoff	86	08	6' 1"/200	D	Winchester,MA/Nobles (NEPSAC)
Brian McGuirk	85	08	5'11"/200	F	Danvers,MA/Governor's (NEPSAC)
Ryan Monaghan	85	08	6' 3"/205	D	Wilmette,IL/Northfield Mount Hermon (USHL)
Thomas Morrow	83	07	6' 6"/210	D	Afton,MN/Des Moines Buccaneers (USHL)
Luke Popko	88	10	5'10"/200	F	Skillman,NJ/USNDT (NAHL)
Kenny Roche	84	07	6' 0"/190	F	S Boston,MA/St. Sebastian's (NEPSAC)
Craig Sanders	84	08	6' 1"/185	F	Wellesley,MA/Merrimack (HEA)
Kevin Schaeffer	84	07	6' 1"/190	D	S Huntington,NY/Apple Core (EJHL)
Steve Smolinsky	86	09	5'10"/165	F	Plymouth,MA/Salisbury (NEPSAC)
Brian Strait	88	10	6' 1"/200	D	Waltham,MA/USNDT (NAHL)
Sean Sullivan	84	07	6' 0"/190	D	Braintree,MA/St. Sebastian's (NEPSAC)
Eric Thomassian	83	07	5'11"/180	F	Rye,NY/Deerfield (NEPSAC)
Ryan Weston	84	08	6' 2"/200	F	Henniker,NH/New England Coyotes (EJHL)
Brandon Yip	85	09	6' 1"/185	F	Maple Ridge,BC/Coquitlam Express (BCHL)

ROSTER ANALYSIS (SCHOLARSHIPS - 18)

Class		Country		Last Team				
Fr	5	USA	23	US JR A	5	CDN JR A	2	ACHA
So	6	Canada	3	US JR B	5	CDN JR B		NJCAA
Jr	9	Europe		US PS	9	CDN PS		NCAA 1
Sr	6	Asia		US HS		CDN HS		USNDT 4
Gr		Other		US Midget		CDN Midget		Other

ADMISSIONS, ENROLLMENT & CAMPUS INFORMATION

Founded 1839
Private, urban campus
6,222 men / 9,731 women
Tuition, room & board $ 43 K
Avg SAT - 1,305 / Avg ACT - 28

Average acceptance rate - 55 %
Freshman financial aid - 1 %
Early decision application deadline - Nov 1
Regular application deadline - Jan 1
Financial aid deadline - Feb 15

Thomas M. Rajala - Admissions Director
Boston University
881 Commonwealth Avenue
Boston, MA 02215
O 617.353.2300 / F 617.353.9695

web.bu.edu

www.bu.edu/athletics/

BOWDOIN COLLEGE

Division 3

HOCKEY STAFF

HEAD COACH
Terry Meagher *(Boston University '76)*

ASSISTANT COACH
Bill Riley *(Colby '99)*

HOCKEY OFFICE
Bowdoin College - Athletic Department
Brunswick, ME 04011-9903
O 207.725.3328 / F 207.725.3019
tmeagher@bowdoin.edu

HOCKEY MEDIA CONTACT
James P. Caton - Sports Info Director
Bowdoin College - Communications
Brunswick, ME 04011
O 207.725.3254 / F 207.725.3033
jcaton@bowdoin.edu

HOCKEY RINK
Dayton Arena (On Campus)
Haarpswell Road & Bath Road
Brunswick, ME 04011
Size 200' x 85', Capacity 2,713
O 207.725.3332

ATHLETIC DIRECTOR
Jeff Ward - Athletic Director
Bowdoin College - Athletic Department
Brunswick, ME 04011
O 207.725.3016 / F 207.725.3019
jward2@bowdoin.edu

POLAR BEARS PLAYERS

Player	YB	GR	Ht/Wt	P	Hometown/Last Team
Sebastien Belanger	08		5'10"/180	F	Deauville,ON/Upper Canada (PS)
Ryan Blossom	10		6'1"/195	F	Concord,NH/St. Paul's (NEPSAC)
Matt Bruch	10		5'7"/165	F	Toronto,ON/St. Michael's (PS)
Bryan Ciborowski	07		6'0"/195	F	W Springfield,MA/Deerfield (NEPSAC)
Mike Collins	09		6'0"/200	F	Wheaton,IL/Deerfield (NEPSAC)
Alden Cook	08		5'11"/195	F	Stanhope,PE/Kent (NEPSAC)
Mike Corbelle	10		6'0"/180	D	Byfield,MA/Pingree (NEPSAC)
Jeff Cutter	09		5'9"/170	F	Medfield,MA/Medfield (HS)
Paul DeCoster	08		6'0"/210	G	Averill Park,NY/Averill Park (HS)
Mitch Dillon	10		6'3"/215	F	Aurora,ON/Cardinal Carter (HS)
Jake Edwards	10		6'2"/210	D	S Freeport,ME/Andover (NEPSAC)
Leland Fidler	10		6'1"/180	F	Waltham,MA/B B & N (NEPSAC)
Brian Fry	10		6'1"/210	D	Colorado Spgs,CO/Hotchkiss (NEPSAC)
James Gadon	07		5'10"/200	F	Toronto,ON/St. Michael's (PS)
Ian Hanley	07		6'1"/190	F	Pembroke,MA/B B & N (NEPSAC)
Colin Hughes	08		6'2"/205	F	Charlottetown,PE/Lawrenceville (PS)
Richard Leahy	08		6'1"/200	D	Larchmont,NY/Millbrook (NEPSAC)
Matt Lentini	09		5'9"/165	F	Belmont,MA/Deerfield (NEPSAC)
Colin MacCormick	10		6'0"/205	F	Bedford,NS/Allen (HS)
Greg McConnell	07		6'2"/215	F	Charlottetown,PE/Kent (NEPSAC)
Tim McVaugh	07		6'3"/210	D/F	Hamilton,NY/Hamilton (HS)
David Ransom	08		6'0"/185	F	New Britain,PA/Lawrenceville (PS)
Will Reycraft	08		5'11"/190	D	Pelham Mnr,NY/Taft (NEPSAC)
Chris Rossi	10		5'10"/155	G	Barrington,RI/LaSalle (PS)
Duncan Smith	08		5'10"/175	D	Kentville,NS/Westminster (NEPSAC)
Matt Smith	09		5'11"/195	F	Yarmouth,ME/Taft (NEPSAC)
Nick Smith	09		5'10"/180	G	Dover-Foxcroft,ME/St. Paul's (NEPSAC)
Peter Smith	07		6'2"/220	F	S Hamilton,NB/Andover (NEPSAC)
Steven Thompson	08		5'11"/180	D	Mamaroneck,NY/Mamaroneck (HS)
Mike Westerman	08		6'2"/195	F	Ann Arbor,MI/Ann Arbor Pioneer (HS)

ROSTER ANALYSIS (SCHOLARSHIPS - 0)

Class		Country		Last Team				
Fr	9	USA	20	US JR A		CDN JR A		ACHA
So	5	Canada	10	US JR B		CDN JR B		NJCAA
Jr	10	Europe		US PS	20	CDN PS	4	NCAA
Sr	6	Asia		US HS	5	CDN HS	1	USNDT
Gr		Other		US Midget		CDN Midget		Other

ADMISSIONS, ENROLLMENT & CAMPUS INFORMATION

Founded 1794
Private, rural campus
832 men / 832 women
Tuition, room & board - $ 41 K
Avg SAT - 1,375

Average acceptance rate - 24 %
Freshman financial aid - 100 %
Early decision application deadline - Nov 15
Regular application deadline - Jan 1
Financial aid deadline - Feb 15

James Miller - Dean of Admissions
Bowdoin College - Admissions
Brunswick, ME 04011
O (207)725-3100 / F (207)725-3101

www.bowdoin.edu

www.bowdoin.edu/athletics/

BOWLING GREEN STATE UNIVERSITY

Division 1

HOCKEY STAFF

HEAD COACH
Scott Paluch *(Bowling Green '91)*

ASSISTANT COACHES
Doug Schueller *(Bowling Green '01)*

HOCKEY OFFICE
Bowling Green State University
Ice Arena - Hockey Office
Bowling Green, OH 43403
O 419.372.2964 / F 419.372.9800
spaluch@bgsu.edu

HOCKEY MEDIA CONTACT
JD Campbell - Athletic Communications
Bowling Green State University
Athletic Department
201 Perry Stadium East
Bowling Green, OH 43403-0030
O 419.372.7075 / F 419.372.6015
jdcampb@bgsu.edu

HOCKEY RINK
BGSU Ice Arena (On Campus)
Mercer Road
Bowling Green, OH 43403
Size 200' x 85', Capacity 5,000
O 419.372.2069

ATHLETIC DIRECTOR
Paul Krebs - Athletic Director
Bowling Green State University
Athletic Department
Perry Stadium East
Bowling Green, OH 43403
O 419.372.2401
pkrebs@bgnet.bgsu.edu

FALCONS PLAYERS

Player	YB	GR	Ht/Wt	P	Hometown/Last Team
Brian Bales	85	09	5'10"/190	F	Anchorage,AK/Sioux City Musketeers (USHL)
Josh Boyd	86	10	5'6"/155	F	Columbus,OH/Portage Terriers (ManJHL)
Jeremy Bronson	83	07	5'11"/185	D	Bowling Green,OH/Compuware Ambassadors (NAHL)
Tommy Dee	85	10	5'11"/180	F	Maple Gr,MN/Bismarck Bobcats (NAHL)
Jon Erickson	83	08	6'3"/200	F	Eden Pr,MN/St. Louis Heartland (USHL)
Ben Geelan	84	08	6'1"/190	F	Buffalo,MN/Chicago Steel (NAHL)
Phil Greer	85	10	5'11"/200	G	Franklin,MA/Santa Fe Roadrunners (NAHL)
Michael Hodgson	84	08	5'10"/185	D	Surfside,CA/Sioux City Musketeers (USHL)
Ryan Hohl	85	10	5'9"/185	F	Northville,MI/Sioux City Musketeers (USHL)
Kai Kantola	87	10	6'1"/175	F	Raleigh,NC/Fargo-Moorhead Jets (NAHL)
Jonathan Matsumoto	86	08	6'0"/185	F	Orleans,ON/Cumberland Grads (CJHL)
Tim Maxwell	84	09	5'11"/165	D	Sherwood Pk,AB/Maine (HEA)
John Mazzei	84	08	5'9"/170	F	Kelowna,BC/Williams Lake Timberwolves (BCHL)
Todd McIlrath	86	10	5'8"/180	F	Northville,MI/Indiana Ice (USHL)
Rich Meloche	85	07	5'11"/185	F	Oakville,ON/Milton Merchants (OPJHL)
Brett Molnar	86	10	5'10"/180	F	Sylvania,OH/Markham Waxers (OPJHL)
Brian Moore	85	10	5'11"/205	D	Carmel,IN/Bozeman Icedogs (NAHL)
Mike Nesdill	84	08	6'2"/185	D	Phoenix,AZ/Lincoln Stars (USHL)
Eddie Neville	85	10	5'10"/180	G	Greene,NY/Green Bay Gamblers (USHL)
Kyle Page	87	10	5'10"/185	D	Wixom,MI/Indiana Ice (USHL)
James Perkin	87	10	5'8"/170	F	Calgary,AB/Lincoln Stars (USHL)
Thomas Petruska	86	10	5'11"/200	F	Presov,Slovakia/Cleveland Barons (NAHL)
Jon Ralph	84	09	6'0"/170	D	Chesterfield,NJ/Chicago Steel (USHL)
Kevin Schmidt	86	09	6'1"/185	D	Markham,ON/St. Michael's (PS)
Russ Sinkewich	85	09	6'3"/200	D	Westlake,OH/Cornwall Colts (CJHL)
Jimmy Spratt	85	09	6'1"/175	G	Chesterfield,MI/Sioux City Musketeers (USHL)
Brandon Svendson	85	09	5'11"/170	F	Roseville,MN/Cedar Rapids RoughRiders (USHL)
James Unger	85	07	6'2"/190	F	Garfield Hgts,OH/Topeka Scarecrows (USHL)
Derek Whitmore	84	08	5'11"/185	F	Rochester,NY/Lincoln Stars (USHL)

ROSTER ANALYSIS (SCHOLARSHIPS - 18)

Class		Country		Last Team					
Fr	12	USA	22	US JR A	21	CDN JR A	6	ACHA	
So	7	Canada	6	US JR B		CDN JR B		NJCAA	
Jr	7	Europe	1	US PS	1	CDN PS	1	NCAA	1
Sr	3	Asia		US HS		CDN HS		USNDT	
Gr		Other		US Midget		CDN Midget		Other	

ADMISSIONS, ENROLLMENT & CAMPUS INFORMATION

Founded 1910	Average acceptance rate - 90 %	Gary Swegan - Admissions Director
Public, rural campus	Freshman financial aid - 72 %	Bowling Green State Univ. - Admissions
6,720 men / 8,908 women	Early decision application deadline - N/A	110 McFall Center
Tuition, room & board - $16 K /$23 K	Regular application deadline - Feb 1	Bowling Green, OH 43403
Avg SAT - 1,023 / Avg ACT - 22	Financial aid deadline - N/A	O 419.372.2086 / F 419.372.6955

www.bgsu.edu

bgsufalcons.collegesports.com

BROWN UNIVERSITY

Division 1

HOCKEY STAFF

HEAD COACH
Roger Grillo (Maine '86)

ASSISTANT COACHES
Danny Brooks (Brandon '93)
Mark Workman (St. Scholastica '93)
Tony Ciresi (Rhode Island '79)

HOCKEY OFFICE
Brown University - Meehan Auditorium
PO Box 1847
Providence, RI 02912
O 401.863.1915 / F 401.863.3409
roger_grillo@brown.edu

HOCKEY MEDIA CONTACT
Jeanne Carhart - Hockey Info Director
Brown University
PO Box 1932
Providence, RI 02912
O 401.863.1094 / F 401.863.1436
jeanne_carhart@brown.edu

HOCKEY RINK
Meehan Auditorium (On Campus)
235 Hope Street
Providence, RI 02912
Size 200' x 85', Capacity 2,495
O 401.863.3507

ATHLETIC DIRECTOR
Michael Goldberger - Athletic Director
Brown University
Providence, RI 02912
O 401.863.2972 / F 401.863.1436
michael_goldberger@brown.edu

BEARS PLAYERS

Player	YB	GR	Ht/Wt	P	Hometown/Last Team
Paul Baier	85	08	6' 4"/225	D	N Kingston,RI/Deerfield (NEPSAC)
Sean Dersch	84	07	5'10"/185	F	Edmonton,AB/Sherwood Park Crusaders (AJHL)
Tristan Favro	87	10	5'10"/185	G	Westfield,NJ/Apple Core (EJHL)
Ryan Garbutt	85	09	6'0"/190	F	Winnipeg,MB/Winnipeg South Blues (ManJHL)
Sean Hurley	83	08	6' 3"/210	D	Rutland,VT/Chicago Steel (USHL)
Brian Ihnacak	85	07	6'0"/195	F	Toronto,ON/St. Michael's (PS)
Todd Johnson	85	08	6' 4"/215	F	Riverside,CT/Taft (NEPSAC)
Sean McMonagle	88	10	6' 1"/195	F	Oakville,ON/Hamilton Red Wings (OPJHL)
Brian McNary	86	08	5'11"/185	F	Edmonton,AB/St. Albert Saints (AJHL)
Sean Muncy	85	09	6'0"/185	F	Chesterfield,MO/Waterloo Blackhawks (USHL)
Matt Palmer	84	09	5'11"/195	D	Anchorage,AK/Billings Bulls (NAHL)
Jordan Pietrus	85	10	5'11"/180	F	Vermillion,AB/Cedar Rapids RoughRiders (USHL)
Chris Poli	85	08	6' 1"/210	F	Medfield,MA/Nobles (NEPSAC)
Jeff Prough	86	08	5'10"/170	F	Farmington,MI/Sioux Falls Stampede (USHL)
David Robertson	85	08	6'1"/195	D	Saunderstown,RI/Omaha Lancers (USHL)
Dan Rosen	87	10	5'11"/175	G	Syosset,NY/Green Bay Gamblers (USHL)
Antonin Roux	82	07	6' 2"/200	F	Danville,QC/Pembroke Lumber Kings (CJHL)
Jeremy Russell	87	10	6' 1"/200	D	St. Albert,AB/Drayton Valley Thunder (AJHL)
Mark Sibbald	84	09	6'0"/185	F	Ridgeway,ON/Vernon Vipers (BCHL)
Eric Slais	85	09	6' 2"/190	F	Fenton,MO/Chicago Steel (USHL)
Mike Stuart	87	09	6' 6"/230	F	Rome,NY/Indiana Ice (USHL)
Hunter Thunell	87	10	6' 3"/200	D	Walpole,MA/Andover (NEPSAC)
Devin Timberlake	85	10	6' 2"/195	F	Pt Alberni,BC/Alberni Valley Bulldogs (BCHL)
Scott VanderLinden	86	10	6' 1"/205	D	Antigonish,NS/Notre Dame (PS)
Matt Vokes	85	09	6' 1"/190	F	Auburn,MA/Cedar Rapids RoughRiders (USHL)
Aaron Volpatti	85	10	6' 1"/195	F	Revelstoke,BC/Vernon Vipers (BCHL)

ROSTER ANALYSIS (SCHOLARSHIPS - 0)

Class		Country		Last Team					
Fr	8	USA	14	US JR A	10	CDN JR A	9	ACHA	
So	7	Canada	12	US JR B	1	CDN JR B		NJCAA	
Jr	7	Europe		US PS	4	CDN PS	2	NCAA	
Sr	4	Asia		US HS		CDN HS		USNDT	
Gr		Other		US Midget		CDN Midget		Other	

ADMISSIONS, ENROLLMENT & CAMPUS INFORMATION

Founded 1764
Private, urban campus
2,771 men / 3,001 women
Tuition, room & board - $ 41 K
Avg SAT - 1,415 / Avg ACT - 30

Average acceptance rate - 17 %
Freshman financial aid - NA %
Early decision application deadline - Nov 1
Regular application deadline - Jan 1
Financial aid deadline - Jan 1

Mike Goldberger - Admissions Director
Brown University
Providence, RI 02912
O 401.863.2378 / F 401.863.9300

www.brown.edu   www.brownbears.com

CANISIUS COLLEGE

Division 1

GOLDEN ICE GRIFFS PLAYERS

Player	YB	GR	Ht/Wt	P	Hometown/Last Team
Vincent Amigone		10	6'1"/180	F	Williamsville,NY/Capital District Selects (EJHL)
Chris Angelo	84	07	5'9"/170	F	Depew,NY/Depew Saints (Midget AA)
Greg Brown	84	08	6'0"/215	F	E Amherst,NY/Welland Cougars (GHJHL)
Max Buetow	82	07	6'5"/200	G	Denver,CO/Springfield Spirit (NAHL)
Kyle Bushee	85	08	5'11"/180	D	Ostego,MI/Des Moines Buccaneers (USHL)
Spencer Churchill	85	09	6'0"/175	F	Brantford,ON/Burlington Cougars (OPJHL)
David Cianfrini	85	10	6'0"/205	D	Dundas,ON/Thorold Blackhawks (GHJHL)
Joey Coccimiglio	84	07	6'0"/190	F	Sault Ste. Marie,ON/Soo Thunderbirds (NOJHL)
Michael Cohen	85	07	5'11"/190	F	Williamsville,NY/Berkshire (NEPSAC)
Scott Follett	85	08	6'0"/175	D	Hamilton,NY/Trinity-Pawling (NEPSAC)
Chris Forsman	86	10	5'10"/175	F	Powell Rvr,BC/Powell River Kings (BCHL)
Jaymie Harrington	81	07	6'3"/200	D	W Boylston,MA/Iona (MAAC)
Josh Heidinger	85	10	5'11"/180	F	Buffalo,NY/Bozeman Icedogs (NAHL)
Carl Hudson	86	10	6'1"/210	D	Smooth Rock Fls,ON/Hawkesbury Hawks (CJHL)
Billy Irish-Baker	83	07	5'11"/185	F	Clarence,NY/Chicago Freeze (NAHL)
David Kasch	83	07	6'4"/205	F	Sault Ste. Marie,ON/Soo Indians (NAHL)
Joel Kitchen	83	08	6'1"/190	F	Orillia,ON/Aurora Tigers (OPJHL)
Ryan Klusendorf	85	09	5'11"/175	F	Peoria,IL/Springfield Blues (NAHL)
Kevin Kozlowski	85	09	5'9"/155	D	Lockport,NY/Abitibi Ekimos (NOJHL)
Andrew Loewen	85	10	6'0"/200	G	Winnipeg,MB/Winnipeg South Blues (ManJHL)
Bryce Luker	85	08	6'3"/200	F	Rigaud,QC/Burnaby Express (BCHL)
Peter MacDougal	85	10	6'0"/175	F	Lumsden,SK/Weyburn Red Wings (SJHL)
Bret Norris	82	07	6'0"/190	F	Snowmass,CO/Toledo IceDiggers (NAHL)
John Patera	86	09	6'0"/200	D	Edina,MN/Blake (PS)
Jason Weeks	85	10	5'10"/200	F	Seattle,WA/Texarkana Bandits (NAHL)

ROSTER ANALYSIS (SCHOLARSHIPS - 11)

Class		Country		Last Team					
Fr	8	USA	15	US JR A	8	CDN JR A	9	ACHA	
So	4	Canada	10	US JR B	1	CDN JR B	2	NJCAA	
Jr	5	Europe		US PS	3	CDN PS		NCAA	1
Sr	8	Asia		US HS		CDN HS		USNDT	
Gr		Other		US Midget	1	CDN Midget		Other	

CASTLETON STATE COLLEGE

HOCKEY
EAST

Division 3

HOCKEY STAFF

HEAD COACH
Alex Todd *(Union '01)*

ASSISTANT COACHES
Terry Moran
TJ Moran

HOCKEY OFFICE
Castleton State College Hockey Office
62 Alumni Drive
Castleton, VT 05735
O 802.468.6429
alex.todd@castleton.edu

HOCKEY MEDIA CONTACT
Jeff Weld - Sports Info Director
Castleton State College
Castleton, VT 05735
O 802.468.6052
jeff.weld@castleton.edu

HOCKEY RINK
Rutland Regional Fieldhouse
100 Diamond Run Place
Rutland, VT 05701
O 802.775.3100

ATHLETIC DIRECTOR
Deanna Tyson - Athletic Director
Castleton State College
Castleton, VT 05735
O 802.468.1365
deanna.tyson@castleton.edu

SPARTANS PLAYERS

Player	YB	GR	Ht/Wt	P	Hometown/Last Team
Jeff Alexander		10	6'0"/170	F/D	Gilbert,AZ/New England Huskies (EJHL)
Mike Anderson	85	09	6'0"/185	D	Oshkosh,WI/Grand Rapids Owls (CSHL)
Ryan Bartlett	84	09	5'10"/180	F	Brunswick,ME/Portland Pirates (AtJHL)
Jeff Beecher	08		5'5"/155	F	S Glens Falls,NY/Hudson Valley (NJCAA)
Kirk Bolduc		10	5'11"/215	F	Lewiston,ME/Cleveland Lumberjacks (CSHL)
Andy Brolsma		09	5'10"/175	F	Syracuse,NY/Buffalo Lightning (OPJHL)
Ross Carmichael	84	09	5'10"/210	F	Jacobstown,NJ/Tri-State Selects (EmJHL)
Steve Culbertson		10	5'11"/200	F	Bowling Green,OH/Alpena Icediggers (NAHL)
Eric Curtis		10	5'7"/170	F	Rockford,MI/Helena Bighorns (NAHL)
Brandon Heck	84	09	5'10"/190	F	Forrestburg,AB/Winkler Flyers (ManJHL)
Joe Huchko	85	07	5'9"/185	D	Congers,NY/SUNY Morrisville (NJCAA)
Jared Lavender	84	09	5'11"/180	D	Cleveland Hts,OH/Northern Michigan Black Bears (NOJHL)
Jeff Lazeren	85	09	6'0"/185	F	Marquette,MI/Grand Rapids Owls (CSHL)
Matthew Link	07		5'11"/170	D	Clifton Pk,NY/SUNY Oswego (ACHA)
Chris Manemeit	08		6'0"/185	F	Durham,CT/Connecticut Wolves (NAHL)
Travis Martell	83	08	6'5"/225	D	Kelowna,BC/Minot State Bottineau (NJCAA)
Rich McKenna	83	07	5'9"/185	D/F	Monroe,NY/Hudson Valley Eagles (MJHL)
Craig Richardson		09	6'2"/195	D	Muskegon,MI/Soo Indians (NAHL)
Evan Romeo		10	5'10"/190	F/D	Kanata,ON/Smiths Falls Bears (CJHL)
Jay Seals	84	09	5'11"/205	G	Alma,MI/Port Colborne Sailors (GHJHL)
Steve Smiddy		10	5'8"/165	F	Grand Rpds,MI/Helena Bighorns (NAHL)
Tom Smith	86	09	5'11"/180	F	Audobon,NJ/Valley Forge Minutemen (MJHL)
Brent Swanson		10	5'8"/170	F	Ames,IA/Quad City Express (CSHL)
Jeff Swanson	85	09	5'8"/165	G	Grand Haven,MI/Tecumseh Chiefs (WOJHL)
Nick Westcott		10	6'1"/195	D	Kanata,ON/Ottawa Senators (NAHL)
Blake White		10	6'0"/190	G	Rockford,MI/Buffalo Lightning (OPJHL)
Tyler White	08		5'9"/175	F	Bennington,VT/Albany River Rats

ROSTER ANALYSIS (SCHOLARSHIPS - 0)

Class		Country		Last Team					
Fr	9	USA	23	US JR A	5	CDN JR A	6	ACHA	1
So	11	Canada	4	US JR B	10	CDN JR B	2	NJCAA	3
Jr	4	Europe		US PS		CDN PS		NCAA	
Sr	3	Asia		US HS		CDN HS		USNDT	
Gr		Other		US Midget		CDN Midget		Other	

ADMISSIONS, ENROLLMENT & CAMPUS INFORMATION

Founded 1787
Public, rural campus
766 men / 974 women
Tuition, room & board $14 K / $21 K
Avg SAT - 955 / Avg - 19

Average acceptance rate - 83 %
Freshman financial aid - 78 %
Early decision application deadline - N/A
Regular application deadline - rolling
Finanical aid deadline - Feb 15

Admissions Office
Wright House
Castleton State College
Castleton,VT 05735
800.639.8521

www.castleton.edu

www.castleton.edu/athletics/index.htm

CLARKSON UNIVERSITY

"Golden Knights"

Division 1

HOCKEY STAFF

HEAD COACH
George Roll *(Bowling Green '86)*

ASSOCIATE HEAD COACH
Greg Drechsel *(Colgate '88)*

ASSISTANT COACH
Jean-Francois Houle *(Clarkson '97)*

HOCKEY OFFICE
Clarkson University
PO Box 5830
Potsdam, NY 13699-5830
O 315.268.3874/ F 315.268.7613
groll@clarkson.edu

HOCKEY MEDIA CONTACT
Gary Mikel - Hockey Info Director
Clarkson University
106 Alumni Gym
PO Box 5830
Potsdam, NY 13699-5830
O 315.268.6673/ F 315.268.7613
mikelg@clarkson.edu

HOCKEY RINK
Cheel Center (On Campus)
8 Clarkson Avenue
Potsdam, NY 13699
Size 200' x 85', Capacity 3,000
O 315.268.6688

ATHLETIC DIRECTOR
Steve Yianoukos - Athletic Director
Clarkson University
PO Box 5830
Potsdam, NY 13699-5830
O 315.268.6622/ F 315.268.7613
stevey@clarkson.edu

GOLDEN KNIGHTS PLAYERS

Player	YB	GR	Ht/Wt	P	Hometown/Last Team
Mike Arciero	85	08	6' 1"/210	F	Avon,CT/Avon (NEPSAC)
Matt Beca	86	10	5'10"/180	F	Mississauga,ON/Wexford Raiders (OPJHL)
Adam Bellows	87	09	6' 3"/185	D	Lancaster,NY/Nichols (PS)
David Cayer	83	08	5'10"/175	F	Longueuil,QC/Longueuil Francais (QJAHL)
Grant Clitsome	85	08	5'11"/200	D	Gloucester,ON/Nepean Raiders (CJHL)
Jeremiah Crowe	86	10	5'11"/170	D	Kenmore,NY/Markham Waxers (OPJHL)
Matt Curley	83	07	6' 0"/180	D	Madrid,NY/Hawkesbury Hawks (CJHL)
Chris D'Alvise	86	09	5'11"/165	F	Mississauga,ON/Wexford Raiders (OPJHL)
Nick Dodge	86	08	5'10"/175	F	Oakville,ON/Oakville Blades (OPJHL)
Michael Grenzy	84	07	6' 3"/200	D	Lockport,NY/Chicago Steel (USHL)
Shea Guthrie	87	09	6' 0"/190	F	Carleton Pl,ON/St. George's (NEPSAC)
Max Kolu	83	07	6' 0"/185	F	Tuky,Finland/TPS (FEL)
David Leggio	84	08	6' 0"/185	G	Buffalo,NY/Capital District Selects (EJHL)
Tim Marks	85	10	6' 2"/220	F	Brownville,NY/Nepean Raiders (OPJHL)
Jon Marshall	86	09	6' 2"/210	F	Victor,NY/Wexford Raiders (OPJHL)
Tyrell Mason	86	09	6' 2"/180	D	Dawson Cr,BC/Salmon Arm Silverbacks (BCHL)
Kyle McNulty	82	07	5'10"/180	G	Wakefield,RI/Junior Bruins (EJHL)
Philippe Paquet	87	09	6' 3"/200	D	St. Augustin,QC/Salisbury (NEPSAC)
Brodie Rutherglen	82	07	5' 8"/165	F	Trail,BC/Merritt Centennials (BCHL)
Matt Smith	88	10	6' 0"/205	G	Mississauga,ON/Mississauga Chargers (OPJHL)
Mike Sullivan	84	07	6' 1"/185	F	Stouffville,ON/Stouffville Spirit (OPJHL)
Dan Tuttle	85	09	5'10"/185	F	Augusta,ME/Portland Pirates (MJHL)
Shawn Weller	86	08	6' 1"/190	F	S Glens Falls,NY/Capital District Selects (EJHL)
Mike Willemsen	86	09	6' 0"/205	F	Stittsville,ON/Cumberland Grads (CJHL)
Steve Zalewski	86	08	6' 0"/185	F	New Hartford,NY/Northwood (PS)

ROSTER ANALYSIS (SCHOLARSHIPS - 18)

Class		Country		Last Team					
Fr	4	USA	12	US JR A	1	CDN JR A	14	ACHA	
So	8	Canada	12	US JR B	4	CDN JR B		NJCAA	
Jr	7	Europe	1	US PS	5	CDN PS		NCAA	
Sr	6	Asia		US HS		CDN HS		USNDT	
Gr		Other		US Midget		CDN Midget		EU	1

ADMISSIONS, ENROLLMENT & CAMPUS INFORMATION

Founded 1896	Average acceptance rate - 86 %	Brian T. Grant - Admissions Director
Private, rural campus	Freshman financial aid - 96 %	Clarkson University - Holcroft House
2,119 men / 598 women	Early decision application deadline - Dec 1	Potsdam, NY 13699
Tuition, room & board - $ 36 K	Regular application deadline - Feb 1	O 315.268.6479/ F 315.268.7647
Avg SAT - 1,190/Avg ACT - 26	Financial aid deadline - Mar 1	

www.clarkson.edu

www.clarksonathletics.com

COLBY COLLEGE

Division 3

HOCKEY STAFF

HEAD COACH
Jim Tortorella *(Maine '81)*

ASSISTANT COACHES
Matt Dennehy *(Saint Anselm '02)*

HOCKEY OFFICE
Colby College - Alfond Athletic Center
4900 Mayflower Hill Drive
Waterville, ME 04901-8840
O 207.859.4913 / F 207.859.4965
jtortor@colby.edu

HOCKEY MEDIA CONTACT
Bill Sodoma - Sports Info Director
4900 Mayflower Hill Drive
Waterville, ME 04901-8849
O 207.859.4940 / F 207.859.4902
wcsodoma@colby.edu

HOCKEY RINK
Alfond Arena (On Campus)
4900 Mayflower Drive
Waterville, ME 04901
Size 200' x 85', Capacity 2,200
O 207.872.3420

ATHLETIC DIRECTOR
Marcella Zalot - Athletic Director
Colby College - Athletic Department
4900 Mayflower Hill Drive
Waterville, ME 04901-8849
O 207.859.4904 / F 207.872.3420
mkzalot@colby.edu

WHITE MULES PLAYERS

Player	YB	GR Ht/Wt	P	Hometown/Last Team
Matt Ahern	09	5' 9"/190	F	Melrose,MA/Governor's (NEPSAC)
Michael Belliveau	10	5' 7"/175	F	Bridgewater,NS/Upper Canada (PS)
Mike Butler	08	5'10"/170	F	Saint John,NB/Deerfield (NEPSAC)
Ryan Chrenek	08	6' 0"/185	D	Grande Prairie,AB/Grande Prairie Storm (AJHL)
Jared Crittenden	10	5'11"/175	F	Fairport,NY/Seguin Bruins (OPJHL)
Mike DiMaggio	09	5'10"/180	F	Sudbury,MA/Worcester (NEPSAC)
Dean Feole	09	5' 6"/165	G	Windham,NH/St. John's (PS)
Arthur Fritch	08	6' 3"/200	D	S Boston,MA/St. Sebastian's (NEPSAC)
Ben Grandjean	07	5'10"/170	G	Waterford,CT/Canterbury (NEPSAC)
Jeoffrey Jarnot	10	5'11"/195	D	Concord,NH/New Hampshire Monarchs (EJHL)
TJ Kelley	08	5'10"/180	F	Ridgefield,CT/Taft (NEPSAC)
Adam Marino	08	5'10"/170	F	Lexington,MA/Nobles (NEPSAC)
Greg Osborne	07	5'11"/175	F	Stoughton,MA/Pomfret (NEPSAC)
Mike Policinski	10	6' 4"/190	F	Shorewood,MN/Blake (PS)
Josh Reber	08	5' 9"/165	F	Edina,MN/Taft (NEPSAC)
Joe Rothwell	08	6' 4"/210	D	Unionville,ON/Markham Waxers (OPJHL)
Patrick Rutherford	07	5' 8"/160	F	Truro,NS/St. Paul's (NEPSAC)
Tom Scott	10	5'11"/185	D	Middlebury,VT/Middlesex (NEPSAC)
Eric Simmons	10	6' 2"/220	F	Cheektowaga,NY/Buffalo Sabres (OPJHL)
Brett Souza	10	6' 1"/165	D	Bethesda,MD/Northwood (PS)
Matt Strickland	10	5'11"/195	D	Leduc,AB/Fort McMurray Oil Barons (AJHL)
Chris Talbert	09	6' 0"/180	D	Hinesburg,VT/Holderness (NEPSAC)
Jared Tepper	10	5' 9"/155	G	Monroe Twnsp,NJ/New Jersey Titans (ContHA)
Greg Valenski	09	5' 7"/170	F	Massapequa Pk,NY/St. Paul's (NEPSAC)
Mike White	10	5'10"/180	D	Miller Pl,NY/Apple Core (EJHL)

ROSTER ANALYSIS (SCHOLARSHIPS - 0)

Class		Country		Last Team				
Fr	10	USA	19	US JR A		CDN JR A	5	ACHA
So	5	Canada	6	US JR B	3	CDN JR B		NJCAA
Jr	7	Europe		US PS	16	CDN PS	1	NCAA
Sr	3	Asia		US HS		CDN HS		USNDT
Gr		Other		US Midget		CDN Midget		Other

ADMISSIONS, ENROLLMENT & CAMPUS INFORMATION

Founded 1813
Private, rural campus
783 men / 1,037 women
Tuition, room & board - $ 42 K
Avg SAT - 1,355 / Avg ACT - 30

Acceptance rate - 37 %
Freshman financial aid - 100 %
Early decision application deadline - Nov 15
Regular application deadline - Jan 1
Financial aid deadline - Feb 1

Parker Beverage - Admissions Director
Colby College
4800 Mayflower Hill Drive
Waterville, ME 04901-8841
O 207.872.3168 / F 207.872.3474

www.colby.edu   www.colby.edu/athletics/

COLGATE UNIVERSITY

Division 1

HOCKEY STAFF

HEAD COACH
Don Vaughan *(St. Lawrence '84)*

ASSISTANT COACH
Andrew Dickson *(Colgate '93)*
Brad Dexter *(Colgate '96)*

HOCKEY OFFICE
Colgate University - Hockey Office
Reid Athletic Center
Hamilton, NY 13346-1398
O 315.228.7572/ F 315.228.7925
dvaughan@mail.colgate.edu

HOCKEY MEDIA CONTACT
Michele Kelley - Hockey Info Director
Colgate University
13 Oak Drive
Hamilton, NY 13346-1398
O 315.228.7860/ F 315.228.7977
mkelley@mail.colgate.edu

HOCKEY RINK
Starr Rink (On Campus)
13 Oak Drive
Hamilton, NY 13346
Size 200' x 85', Capacity 2,246
O 315.824.2310

ATHLETIC DIRECTOR
David Roach - Athletic Director
Colgate University
13 Oak Drive
Hamilton, NY 13346-1398
O 315.228.7611/ F 315.228.7008
droach@mail.colgate.edu

RED RAIDERS PLAYERS

Player	YB	GR	Ht/Wt	P	Hometown/Last Team
Mark Anderson	86	09	5'11"/180	D	Hastings,NE/Shattuck-St. Mary's (PS)
Peter Bogdanich	85	09	5'11"/205	F	Burnaby,BC/Chilliwack Chiefs (BCHL)
Tyler Burton	85	08	5' 9"/180	F	Langley,BC/Chilliwack Chiefs (BCHL)
Mike Campaner	83	07	5' 8"/170	D	Thunder Bay,ON/Gloucester Rangers (CJHL)
Ben Camper	84	08	6' 3"/200	F	Rocky River,OH/Bay State Breakers (EJHL)
Sean Carty	87	10	6' 5"/235	F	Glen Ellyn,IL/Taft (NEPSAC)
Ethan Cox	87	10	5'10"/180	F	Richmond,BC/Powell River Kings (BCHL)
Joe DeBello	86	09	6' 0"/195	D	Oswego,IL/Avon (NEPSAC)
Mark Dekanich	86	08	6' 2"/190	G	N Vancouver,BC/Coquitlam Express (BCHL)
Jason Fredricks	87	09	6' 2"/200	F	Eagle Rvr,WI/Shattuck-St. Mary's (PS)
Marc Fulton	83	07	6' 1"/200	F	Vancouver,BC/Williams Lake Timberwolves (BCHL)
Dustin Gillanders	84	07	6' 2"/215	F	Kyle,SK/North Battleford North Stars (SJHL)
Alex Greig	83	07	6' 5"/195	D	Pickering,ON/Georgetown Raiders (OPJHL)
Liam Huculak	83	07	6' 5"/195	F	Lethbridge,AB/Penticton Panthers (BCHL)
Justin Kowalkoski	86	08	5'10"/165	G	Young America,MN/Blake (PS)
Charles Long	86	10	6' 0"/185	G	Cleveland,OH/Brockville Braves (CJHL)
David McIntyre	87	10	6' 0"/185	F	Pefferlaw,ON/Newmarket Hurricanes (OPJHL)
Tom Riley	86	09	5'10"/185	F	Nepean,ON/Brockville Braves (CJHL)
David Sloane	85	09	6' 4"/205	D	Ambler,PA/Brockville Braves (CJHL)
Nick St. Pierre	85	09	6' 0"/185	D	St. Etienne,QC/Hawkesbury Hawks (CJHL)
Matt Torti	84	08	6' 5"/210	D	Oxford,MA/Boston Bulldogs (AtJHL)
Mike Werner	86	08	5'10"/175	F	Niagara-on-the-Lake,ON/National Sports (PS)
Jason Williams	86	10	5'10"/195	F	Plattsburgh,NY/New Hampshire Monarchs (EJHL)
Jesse Winchester	83	08	6' 1"/200	F	Long Sault,ON/Cornwall Colts (CJHL)

ROSTER ANALYSIS (SCHOLARSHIPS - 18)

Class		Country		Last Team				
Fr	5	USA	9	US JR A		CDN JR A	15	ACHA
So	7	Canada	15	US JR B	3	CDN JR B		NJCAA
Jr	7	Europe		US PS	6	CDN PS		NCAA
Sr	5	Asia		US HS		CDN HS		USNDT
Gr		Other		US Midget		CDN Midget		Other

ADMISSIONS, ENROLLMENT & CAMPUS INFORMATION

Founded 1819	Average acceptance rate - 33 %	Gary L. Ross - Admissions Director
Private, rural campus	Freshman financial aid - 100 %	Colgate University
1,288 men / 1,512 women	Early decision application deadline - Nov 15	13 Oak Drive
Tuition, room & board - $ 40 K	Regular application deadline - Jan 15	Hamilton, NY 13346-1398
Avg SAT - 1,350 / Avg ACT - 30	Financial aid deadline - Feb 1	O 315.228.7606/ F 315.228.7798

www.colgate.edu www.gocolgateraiders.com

COLORADO COLLEGE

Division 1

HOCKEY STAFF

HEAD COACH
Scott Owens *(Colorado College '79)*

ASSISTANT COACHES
Joe Bonnett *(Western Michigan '93)*
Norm Bazin *(Massachusetts-Lowell '94)*
Brad DeFauw *(North Dakota '00)*

HOCKEY OFFICE
Colorado College
14 East Cache la Poudre Street
Colorado Springs, CO 80903-3298
O 719.389.6480/ F 719.389.6873
sowens@coloradocollege.edu

HOCKEY MEDIA CONTACT
Dave Moross - Hockey Info Director
Colorado College
14 East Cache la Poudre Street
Colorado Springs, CO 80903-3298
O 719.389.6755/ F 719.389.6256
dmoross@coloradocollege.edu

HOCKEY RINK
Colorado Spgs World Arena (Off Campus)
30 West Cache la Poudre Street
Colorado Springs, CO 80903
Size 200' x 100', Capacity 7,343
O 719.576.2626

ATHLETIC DIRECTOR
Julie Soriero - Athletic Director
Colorado College
14 East Cache La Poudre Street
Colorado Springs, CO 80903-3298
O 719.389.6475/ F 719.389.6873
jsoriero@coloradocollege.edu

TIGERS PLAYERS

Player	YB	GR	Ht/Wt	P	Hometown/Last Team
James Brannigan	84	08	5'10"/175	F	Brooklyn,NY/Cedar Rapids RoughRiders (USHL)
Brian Connelly	86	10	5' 9"/165	D	Bloomington,MN/Tri-City Storm (USHL)
Braydon Cox	83	07	5' 9"/185	F	Sherwood Pk,AB/Sherwood Park Crusaders (AJHL)
Addison DeBoer	88	10	5'11"/180	F	Spring Lake Pk,MN/Spring Lake Park (HS)
Kris Fredheim	87	10	6' 2"/180	D	Campbell Rvr,BC/Notre Dame (PS)
Jake Gannon	87	09	6' 1"/195	D	Roselle,IL/Sioux City Musketeers (USHL)
Jack Hillen	86	08	5'10"/175	D	Minnetonka,MN/Tri-City Storm (USHL)
Chris Kawano	85	07	5' 9"/155	G	Aurora,CO/Dallas Stars (Midget AAA)
Jimmy Kilpatrick	85	08	5'11"/180	F	New Prague,MN/Green Bay Gamblers (USHL)
Cody Lampl	86	09	5'10"/160	D	Ketchum,ID/Chicago Steel (USHL)
Scott McCulloch	86	08	6' 1"/200	F	Lacombe,AB/Grande Prairie Storm (AJHL)
Brian McMillin	88	10	6' 2"/200	F	Roseau,MN/Roseau (HS)
Drew O'Connell	87	09	6' 0"/175	G	Anchorage,AK/Waterloo Blackhawks (USHL)
Matt Overman	87	10	5' 2"/175	F	Bloomington,MN/Sioux Falls Stampede (USHL)
Derek Patrosso	84	08	6' 1"/195	F	Northville,MI/Danville Wings (USHL)
Brandon Polich	82	07	5' 8"/160	F	Osseo,MN/Sioux City Musketeers (USHL)
Nate Prosser	86	10	6' 2"/200	D	Elk River,MN/Sioux Falls Stampede (USHL)
Dan Quilco	86	10	5' 9"/160	F	Thousand Oaks,CA/Trail Smoke Eaters (BCHL)
Chad Rau	87	09	5'11"/185	F	Eden Pr,MN/Des Moines Buccaneers (USHL)
Brandon Straub	83	07	6' 4"/220	D	Colorado Spgs,CO/Findlay (CHA)
Billy Sweatt	88	10	6' 0"/185	F	Elburn,IL/USNDT (NAHL)
Lee Sweatt	85	07	5' 9"/180	D	Elburn,IL/Chicago Steel (USHL)
Mike Testwuide	87	10	6' 3"/220	F	Vail,CO/Waterloo Blackhawks (USHL)
Scott Thauwald	84	07	5'11"/185	F	Rochester,MN/Mayo (HS)
Andreas Vlassopoulos	87	10	6' 0"/180	F	Los Angeles,CA/USNDT (NAHL)
Matt Zaba	83	07	6' 1"/175	G	Yorktown,SK/Vernon Vipers (BCHL)

ROSTER ANALYSIS (SCHOLARSHIPS - 18)

Class		Country		Last Team					
Fr	10	USA	22	US JR A	14	CDN JR A	4	ACHA	
So	4	Canada	4	US JR B		CDN JR B		NJCAA	
Jr	5	Europe		US PS		CDN PS	1	NCAA	1
Sr	7	Asia		US HS	3	CDN HS		USNDT	2
Gr		Other		US Midget	1	CDN Midget		Other	

ADMISSIONS, ENROLLMENT & CAMPUS INFORMATION

Founded 1874
Private,urban campus
917 men / 1,077 women
Tuition, room & board - $ 39 K
Avg SAT - 1,265/ Avg ACT - 28

Average acceptance rate - 44 %
Freshman financial aid - 97 %
Early decision application deadline - N/A
Regular application deadline - Jan 15
Financial aid deadline - Feb 15

Mark Hatch - Admissions Director
Colorado College
14 East Cache La Poudre Street
Colorado Springs, CO 80903-3298
O 719.389.6344/ F 719.389.6816

CONCORDIA COLLEGE

Division 3

HOCKEY STAFF

HEAD COACH
Steve Baumgartner *(Concordia '82)*

ASSISTANT COACH
Tim Laurila

HOCKEY OFFICE
Concordia College
901 South 8th Street
Moorhead, MN 56562
O 218.299.4166 / F 218.299.4189
baumgart@cord.edu

HOCKEY MEDIA CONTACT
Jim Cella - Sports Info Director
Concordia College
901 South 8th Street
Moorhead, MN 56562
O 218.299.3194 / F 218.299.4189
sid@cord.edu

HOCKEY RINK
Moorhead Sports Arena (Off Campus)
324 24th Street South
Moorhead, MN 56560
Size 200' x 85', Capacity 3,150
O 218.299.5354

ATHLETIC DIRECTOR
Dr. Larry Papenfuss - Athletic Director
Concordia College
901 South 8th Street
Moorhead, MN 56562
O 218.299.4434
papenfus@cord.edu

COBBERS PLAYERS

Player	YB	GR	Ht/Wt	P	Hometown/Last Team
Carl Babich	09		6' 0"/165	D/F	Eveleth,MN/Eveleth-Gilbert (HS)
Chris Babich	09		6' 0"/165	D	Eveleth,MN/Eveleth-Gilbert (HS)
Knut Bitustoeyl	10		5'11"/185	F	Asker,Norway/Frisk Asker Tigers (NEL)
Jeremy Boniface	09		6' 1"/180	F	Goderich,ON/Mount Forest (HS)
Mark Buchholz	07		6' 2"/185	D	Moorhead,MN/Topeka Scarecrows (USHL)
Adam Campbell	10		5'10"/175	F	Fargo,ND/Fargo South (HS)
Ryan Clukey	09		5'10"/175	F	Moorhead,MN/Moorhead (HS)
Matt Cosmos	09		6' 0"/215	F	Middlebury,CT/Massachusetts Boston (ECAC East)
Joachim Flaten	10		6' 0"/200	F	Baerum,Norway/Frisk Asker Tigers (NEL)
Blaine Gamst	10		5'11"/205	F	Willow River,MN/Dubuque Thunderbirds (MnJHL)
Shawn Goos	10		5'11"/165	F	Fergus Fls,MN/Fergus Falls (HS)
Guy Grivas	09		5'11"/200	F	Southlake,TX/Humboldt Broncos (SJHL)
Josh Hand	08		6' 2"/205	G	Temple,PA/Thunder Bay (SIJHL)
Alec Holen	09		5' 9"/170	F	Thief River Fls,MN/Fargo-Moorhead Jets (NAHL)
Tony Janssen	10		5'11"/185	F	Superior,WI/Fairbanks Ice Dogs (NAHL)
Cory Johnson	09		5' 8"/185	F	Moorhead,MN/Moorhead (HS)
Kevin Kratz	09		5'11"/185	F	Farmington,MN/Farmington (HS)
Sean Lofgren	09		5'10"/185	F	Moorhead,MN/Moorhead (HS)
Kirby Markowsky	08		6' 3"/215	D	Wakaw,SK/Minot State Bottineau (NJCAA)
Andy Murray	09		5'11"/185	F	Staples,MN/Dubuque Thunderbirds (MnJHL)
Tyler Neu	08		6' 1"/180	F	Wadena,MN/Wadena-Deer Creek (HS)
Casey Olson	10		6' 0"/210	F	Rock Springs,WY/Hartford Wolfpack (AtJHL)
Dan Perry	07		6' 5"/235	F	Fergus Fls,MN/Fergus Falls (HS)
Mike Persson	10		6' 0"/190	G	Regina,SK/Fort Worth Texans (WSHL)
Brett Sands	10		6' 0"/175	F	Cypress,TX/Dubuque Thunderbirds (MnJHL)
Tony Webber	09		5' 4"/140	F	Farmington,MN/Farmington (HS)
Paul Westmark	09		6' 1"/185	D	Appleton,WI/Appleton (HS)

ROSTER ANALYSIS (SCHOLARSHIPS - 0)

Class		Country		Last Team					
Fr	9	USA	22	US JR A	3	CDN JR A	2	ACHA	
So	13	Canada	3	US JR B	5	CDN JR B		NJCAA	1
Jr	3	Europe	2	US PS		CDN PS		NCAA	1
Sr	2	Asia		US HS	12	CDN HS	1	USNDT	
Gr		Other		US Midget		CDN Midget		NEL	2

ADMISSIONS, ENROLLMENT & CAMPUS INFORMATION

Founded 1891	Average acceptance rate - 85 %	Lee E. Johnson - Admissions Director
Private, urban campus	Freshman financial aid - 95 %	Concordia College
1,017 men / 1,731 women	Early decision application deadline - N/A	901 South 8th Street
Tuition, room & board - $ 23 K	Regular application deadline - rolling	Moorhead, MN 56562
Avg SAT - 1,160 / Avg ACT - 24	Financial aid deadline - Apr 15	O 218.299.3004 / F 218.299.3947

www.cord.edu   www.cord.edu/dept/sports/

CONCORDIA UNIVERSITY WISCONSIN

  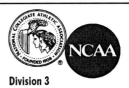

Division 3

HOCKEY STAFF	CHARGERS PLAYERS

HEAD COACH
Tony Hrkac *(North Dakota)*

ASSISTANT COACHES

HOCKEY OFFICE
Concordia University Hockey Office
LU 108 C
12800 N. Lake Shore Drive
Mequon, WI 53097-2402
O 262.243.4355 / 262.243.4475
tony.hrkac@cuw.edu

HOCKEY MEDIA CONTACT
Rick Riehl - Associate AD / SID
Concordia University Wisconsin
FH 106 B
12800 N. Lake Shore Drive
Mequon, WI 53097-2402
O 262.243.4544

HOCKEY RINK
Ozaukee Ice Center (Off Campus)
5505 W. Pioneer Road
Cedarburg, WI 53012
Size 200' x 85', Capacity 800 & 1,400

ATHLETIC DIRECTOR
Dr. Rob Barnhill - Athletic Director
Concordia University Wisconsin
FH 106 D
12800 N. Lake Shore Drive
Mequon, WI 53097-2402
O 262.243.4404

Player   YB GR Ht/Wt   P   Hometown/Last Team

Concordia University Wisconsin
begins play in
MCHA in 2007/2008

ROSTER ANALYSIS (SCHOLARSHIPS - 0)

Class	Country	Last Team		
Fr	USA	US JR A	CDN JR A	ACHA
So	Canada	US JR B	CDN JR B	NJCAA
Jr	Europe	US PS	CDN PS	NCAA
Sr	Asia	US HS	CDN HS	USNDT
Gr	Other	US Midget	CDN Midget	Other

ADMISSIONS, ENROLLMENT & CAMPUS INFORMATION

Founded 1881	Average acceptance rate - 85 %	Joe Koepel - Dir. of Enrollment Services
Private, lakefront, small town campus	Freshman financial aid - 100 %	Concordia University Wisconsin
700 men / 900 women	Early decision application deadline - N/A	12800 N. Lake Shore Drive
Tuition, room & board - $ 25 K	Regular application deadline - Rolling	Mequon, WI 53097-2402
Avg SAT - 1,035 / Avg ACT - 23	Financial aid deadline - Rolling	O 800.877.2246

CONNECTICUT COLLEGE

Division 3

HOCKEY STAFF

HEAD COACH
Jim Ward *(SUNY-Geneseo '85)*

ASSISTANT COACHES
Nick Vealitzek *(Conn. College '04)*

HOCKEY OFFICE
Connecticut College
Department of Athletics
270 Mohegan Avenue
New London, CT 06320
O 860.439.5237 / F 860.439.2516
jbwar2@conncoll.edu

HOCKEY MEDIA CONTACT
Will Tomasian - Sports Info Director
Connecticut College - Box 5343
270 Mohegan Drive
New London, CT 06320-4196
O 860.439.2501 / F 860.439.5119
wgtom@conncoll.edu

HOCKEY RINK
Dayton Arena (On Campus)
270 Mohegan Avenue
New London, CT 06320
Size 200' x 85', Capacity 750
O 860.439.2575

ATHLETIC DIRECTOR
Fran Shields - Athletic Director
Connecticut College
270 Mohegan Drive
New London, CT 06320-4196
O 860.439.2570 / F 860.439.2516
fjshi@conncoll.edu

CAMELS PLAYERS

Player	YB	GR	Ht/Wt	P	Hometown/Last Team
Dan Beauregard	09		5' 9"/170	G	Medfield,MA/Thayer (NEPSAC)
Trevor Bradley	10		6' 1"/190	F	W Hartford,CT/Avon (NEPSAC)
Rob Campbell	08		5'10"/185	F	Reading,MA/Proctor (NEPSAC)
Patrick Collins	09		5' 8"/160	F	Rutland,VT/Phillips Exeter (NEPSAC)
Mike Delaney	09		6' 0"/195	F	Stamford,CT/Pomfret (NEPSAC)
Sean Driscoll	10		6' 0"/180	F	Peabody,MA/Pomfret (NEPSAC)
Colin Edge	10		5' 9"/165	G	Katonah,NY/Holderness (NEPSAC)
Ben Eischen	09		6' 1"/195	D	Brookfield,NH/Hill (PS)
Ryan Feldhoff	08		6' 1"/210	D	Quincy,MA/Thayer (NEPSAC)
Brian Gallagher	08		6' 2"/210	F	Davidsonville,MD/Governor's (NEPSAC)
Matt Gluck	07		6' 3"/210	G	Morganville,NJ/Lawrenceville (PS)
Jake Henry	07		6' 1"/185	D	Winchester,MA/Winchester (HS)
Ryan Howarth	10		6' 2"/190	F	Grand Blanc,MI/Syracuse Stars (EJHL)
Ryan Joyce	10		5'10"/195	D	Dorchester,MA/Pomfret (NEPSAC)
Shawn Keefe	09		6' 0"/170	D	Waltham,MA/Waltham (HS)
Mike Kelly	10		5'11"/175	F	Duxbury,MA/Phillips Exeter (NEPSAC)
Chris Lynn	07		6' 0"/195	F	New Canaan,CT/Rhode Island (ACHA)
Avi Meyers	09		5' 9"/185	D	Maple Glen,PA/Hartford Wolfpack (AtJHL)
Jason Miller	07		5' 7"/160	F	Winnetka,IL/Lawrenceville (PS)
Brett Moore	10		5'10"/200	F	Medfield,MA/Lawrenceville (PS)
Brendan Moses	09		5'10"/175	F	Medfield,MA/St. Sebastian's (NEPSAC)
David Norton	09		6' 0"/190	D	Marlborough,MA/Lake Forest (NCHA)
Greg Parker	10		5'10"/170	G	Trenton,ON/Groton (NEPSAC)
Kevin Plant	09		5'10"/180	F	Carver,MA/Lawrence (NEPSAC)
Robbie Tesar	09		5' 9"/170	F	Lake Bluff,IL/Avon (NEPSAC)
Bryan Warner	09		5'10"/190	D	Waltham,MA/Avon (NEPSAC)
Walt Wright	08		5'10"/175	D	Plymouth Meeting,PA/Lawrence (NEPSAC)

ROSTER ANALYSIS (SCHOLARSHIPS - 0)

Class		Country		Last Team				
Fr	8	USA	26	US JR A		CDN JR A	ACHA	1
So	11	Canada	1	US JR B	2	CDN JR B	NJCAA	
Jr	4	Europe		US PS	21	CDN PS	NCAA	1
Sr	4	Asia		US HS	2	CDN HS	USNDT	
Gr		Other		US Midget		CDN Midget	Other	

ADMISSIONS, ENROLLMENT & CAMPUS INFORMATION

Founded 1911
Private, suburban campus
718 men / 1,078 women
Tuition, room & board - $ 42 K
Avg SAT - 1,325 / ACT - 27

Average acceptance rate - 34 %
Freshman financial aid - 100 %
Early decision application deadline - Nov 15
Regular application deadline - Jan 1
Financial aid deadline - Jan 15

Martha Merrill - Admissions Director
Connecticut College
270 Mohegan Drive
New London, CT 06320
O 860.439.2200 / F 860.439.4301

www.conncoll.edu

www.conncoll.edu/athletics/

UNIVERSITY OF CONNECTICUT

Division 1

HOCKEY STAFF

HEAD COACH
Bruce Marshall *(Connecticut '85)*

ASSISTANT COACHES
Glenn Stewart *(New Hampshire '94)*
Matt Plante *(Quinnipiac '02)*
Brett Soucy *(Central Conn. State '93)*

HOCKEY OFFICE
University of Connecticut - Athletics
2111 Hillside Road, Unit 3078
Storrs, CT 06269-3078
O 860.486.3072 / F 860.486.6783
bruce.marshall@uconn.edu

HOCKEY MEDIA CONTACT
Mike Enright - Associate AD Comm.
University of Connecticut - Athletics
Harry A. Gampel Pavillion
2095 Hillside Road
Storrs, CT 06269-3078
O 860.486.3531 / F 860.486.5085
mike.enright@uconn.edu

HOCKEY RINK
UCONN Ice Rink (On Campus)
Stadium Road
Storrs, CT 06269
Size 200' x 85', Capacity 2,000
O 860.486.5654

ATHLETIC DIRECTOR
Jeffrey Hathaway - Athletic Director
University of Connecticut - Athletics
2111 Hillside Road
Storrs, CT 06269-3078
O 860.486.2725 / F 860.486.3300

HUSKIES PLAYERS

Player	YB	GR	Ht/Wt	P	Hometown/Last Team
Jon Anderson	84	09	6' 0"/185	G	Vadnais Hts,MN/Billings Bulls (NAHL)
BJ Bayers	85	09	5' 9"/175	F	St. Louis Pk,MN/Santa Fe Roadrunners (NAHL)
Brian Burns	82	07	6' 0"/180	F	Binghamton,NY/Omaha Lancers (USHL)
Michael Coppola	85	10	5' 8"/185	F	Old Brookville,NY/New York Bobcats (AtJHL)
William Crum	83	07	6' 2"/205	D	Hampden,MA/New England Coyotes (EJHL)
Eric Dahlberg	85	09	5'10"/195	D	Duluth,MN/Santa Fe Roadrunners (NAHL)
Beau Erickson	85	10	6' 0"/170	G	Hinton,IA/Sioux City Musketeers (USHL)
Sean Erickson	84	09	6' 0"/175	D	Eden Pr,MN/Springfield Spirit (NAHL)
Ryan Hawkins	84	09	5' 9"/170	F	Eden Pr,MN/Alexandria Blizzard (NAHL)
Frederic Jean	86	10	5' 8"/175	F	Gatineau,QC/St. Jerome Panthers (QJAHL)
Chris Johnson	85	10	5'11"/180	D	Brooklyn Pk,MN/Alexandria Blizzard (NAHL)
Alec Kirschner	86	10	5'10"/180	F	Dix Hills,NY/New Jersey Hitmen (EJHL)
Cole Koidahl	83	07	5' 8"/165	F	Minneapolis,MN/Iona (MAAC)
Nick Marean	82	07	6' 1"/210	D	Waukee,IA/Danville Wings (USHL)
Scott McDougall	84	07	6' 1"/195	F	Mansfield,MA/Walpole Stars (EJHL)
Chris Myhro	85	09	5'10"/175	F	Mound Westonka,MN/Fargo-Moorhead Jets (NAHL)
Chris Ochoa	85	10	5' 8"/170	F	Santa Monica,CA/Wichita Falls Wildcats (NAHL)
Brendan Olinyk	86	10	6' 1"/180	D	Wisconsin Rpds,WI/Fairbanks Ice Dogs (NAHL)
Michael Olmstead	86	10	6' 0"/185	D	E Lansing,MI/Texas Tornado (NAHL)
Jarrett Scarpaci	84	07	5' 8"/165	F	Billerica,MA/Junior Bruins (EJHL)
Matt Scherer	82	07	6' 0"/195	F	Seattle,WA/Tri-City Storm (USHL)
Nick Schneider	84	09	5' 9"/170	D/F	Maplewood,MN/Bismarck Bobcats (NAHL)
Charles Solberg	84	08	5'11"/195	F	Barrington,IL/Springfield Blues (NAHL)
Eric St. Arnauld	81	07	6' 2"/165	F	Marquette,MI/Bozeman Icedogs (NAHL)
Trevor Stewart	82	07	5'10"/175	F	Elk River,MN/Waterloo Blackhawks (USHL)
John Stockler	84	08	5'11"/170	F	Princeton,MN/Valley Warriors (EJHL)
Scott Tomes	84	07	5'11"/170	G	Windham,NH/Valley Warriors (EJHL)

ROSTER ANALYSIS (SCHOLARSHIPS - 11*)

Class		Country		Last Team				
Fr	8	USA	26	US JR A	18	CDN JR A	1	ACHA
So	7	Canada	1	US JR B	7	CDN JR B		NJCAA
Jr	2	Europe		US PS		CDN PS		NCAA	1
Sr	10	Asia		US HS		CDN HS		USNDT
Gr		Other		US Midget		CDN Midget		Other

ADMISSIONS, ENROLLMENT & CAMPUS INFORMATION

Founded 1881
Public, rural campus
8,393 men / women
Tuition, room & board - $ 16 K /$ 29 K
Avg SAT - 1,325 / Avg ACT - 25

Average acceptance rate - 50 %
Freshman financial aid - 71 %
Early decision application deadline - N/A
Regular application deadline - Feb 1
Financial aid deadline - Mar 1

James D. Morales - Admissions Director
University of Connecticut - Admissions
2131 Hillside Road
Storrs, CT 06269-3078
O 860.486.3137 / F 860.486.1476

www.uconn.edu

www.uconnhuskies.com/sports

- 407 -

CORNELL UNIVERSITY

Division 1

HOCKEY STAFF

HEAD COACH
Mike Schafer *(Cornell '86)*

ASSISTANT COACHES
Brent Brekke *(Western Michigan '94)*
Scott Garrow *(Western Michigan '91)*

HOCKEY OFFICE
Cornell University
Teagle Hall
Ithaca, NY 14853-6501
O 607.255.6674/ F 607.254.5351
mcs14@cornell.edu

HOCKEY MEDIA CONTACT
Eric Lawrence - Hockey Info Director
Cornell University - Teagle Hall
Ithaca, NY 14853-6501
O 607.255.5627/ F 607.255.9791
etl8@cornell.edu

HOCKEY RINK
James Lynah Rink (On Campus)
Campus Drive
Ithaca, NY 14850
Size 200' x 85', Capacity 3,836
O 607.255.3533

ATHLETIC DIRECTOR
Andy Noel - Athletic Director
Cornell University
Teagle Hall
Ithaca, NY 14853-6501
O 607.255.7265/ F 607.255.9791
jan16@cornell.edu

BIG RED PLAYERS

Player	YB	GR	Ht/Wt	P	Hometown/Last Team
Cam Abbott	83	06	6'0"/190	F	Sarnia,ON/Sarnia (WOJHL)
Evan Barlow	85	09	5'9"/170	F	Strathmore,AB/Salmon Arm Silverbacks (BCHL)
Byron Bitz	84	07	6'4"/200	F	Corman Pk,SK/Nanaimo Clippers (BCHL)
Mitch Carefoot	85	07	6'1"/210	F	Dauphin,MB/Salmon Arm Silverbacks (BCHL)
Matt Connors	86	09	6'1"/200	F	Buffalo,NY/Apple Core (EJHL)
Taylor Davenport	85	09	5'10"/190	D	Okotoks,AB/Drayton Valley Thunder (AJHL)
Troy Davenport		09	6'1"/175	G	Inver Grove Hts,MN/Des Moines Buccaneers (USHL)
Dan DiLeo	84	09	5'11"/175	G	St. Louis,MO/Wichita Falls Wildcats (NAHL)
Chris Fontas		08	6'2"/210	F	Nashua,NH/Massachusetts Lowell (HEA)
Blake Gallagher		10	5'7"/175	F	Dartmouth,NS/Notre Dame (PS)
Dan Glover	83	07	6'3"/200	D	Delburne,AB/Camrose Kodiaks (AJHL)
Colin Greening		10	6'2"/210	F	St. John's,NF/Nanaimo Clippers (BCHL)
Matt Hedge		07	6'0"/180	D	Ithaca,NY/Ithaca (HS)
Michael Kennedy	86	09	6'2"/195	F	Dorchester,ON/St. Thomas Stars (WOJHL)
Ryan Kindret	85	09	6'2"/200	F	Winnipeg,MB/Quesnel Millionaires (BCHL)
Doug Krantz	83	08	6'3"/195	D	Marysville,BC/Alberni Valley Bulldogs (BCHL)
Justin Krueger		10	6'3"/205	D	Davos,Switzerland/Penticton Vees (BCHL)
Mark McCutcheon	84	07	6'1"/185	F	Pittsford,NY/New England Coyotes (EJHL)
Kevin McLeod		07	6'3"/220	D	Calgary,AB/Calgary Canucks (AJHL)
Justin Milo		10	5'8"/180	F	Eden Pr,MN/Lincoln Stars (USHL)
Tyler Mugford	85	09	6'1"/190	F	Prince Albert,SK/Nanaimo Clippers (BCHL)
Brendon Nash		10	6'3"/205	D	Kamloops,BC/Salmon Arm Silverbacks (BCHL)
Tony Romano		10	5'11"/185	F	Smithtown,NY/New York Bobcats (AtJHL)
Evan Salmela	83	07	6'0"/185	D	Whitefish Bay,WI/Chicago Freeze (NAHL)
Raymond Sawada	85	08	6'2"/195	F	Richmond,BC/Nanaimo Clippers (BCHL)
Joe Scali		10	6'0"/190	F	Coquitlam,BC/Alberni Valley Bulldogs (BCHL)
Topher Scott	85	08	5'6"/160	F	Buffalo Gr,IL/Chicago Freeze (NAHL)
Ben Scrivens		10	6'2"/180	G	Spruce Gr,AB/Spruce Grove Saints (AJHL)
Jared Seminoff	86	09	5'10"/195	D	Nelson,BC/Nanaimo Clippers (BCHL)

ROSTER ANALYSIS (SCHOLARSHIPS - 0)

Class		Country		Last Team					
Fr	8	USA	10	US JR A	5	CDN JR A	16	ACHA	
So	9	Canada	18	US JR B	3	CDN JR B	2	NJCAA	
Jr	4	Europe	1	US PS		CDN PS	1	NCAA	1
Sr	8	Asia		US HS	1	CDN HS		USNDT	
Gr		Other		US Midget		CDN Midget		Other	

ADMISSIONS, ENROLLMENT & CAMPUS INFORMATION

Founded 1865	Average acceptance rate - 29 %	Wendy Schaerer - Admissions Director
Private, urban campus	Five year graduation rate - 100 %	Cornell University
6,924 men / 6,653 women	Early decision application deadline - Nov 1	410 Thurston Avenue
Tuition,room & board - $ 41 K	Regular application deadline - Jan 1	Ithaca, NY 14850
Avg SAT - 1,390 / Avg ACT - 30	Financial aid deadline - Feb 11	O 607.255.5241 / F 607.255.0659

CURRY COLLEGE

Division 3

HOCKEY STAFF

HEAD COACH
Robert Davies *(Boston University '82)*

ASSISTANT COACHES
Bob Roche *(Brown '92)*
Tom MacDonald *(Salem State '94)*

HOCKEY OFFICE
Curry College
1071 Blue Hill Avenue
Milton, MA 02186
O 617.333.2224/ F 617.333.2027
rdavies@curry.edu

HOCKEY MEDIA CONTACT
Ken Golner - Sports Info Director
Curry College
1071 Blue Hill Avenue
Milton, MA 02186
O 617.333.2324/ F 617.333.2027
kgolner@curry.edu

HOCKEY RINK
Max Ulin Memorial Rink (Off Campus)
111 Unquity Road
Milton, MA 02186
Size 200' x 85', Capacity 1,500
O 617.696.9869

ATHLETIC DIRECTOR
Steve Nelson - Athletic Director
Curry College
1071 Blue Hill Avenue
Milton, MA 02186
O 617.333.2109/ F 617.333.2027
snelson@curry.edu

COLONELS PLAYERS

Player	YB	GR	Ht/Wt	P	Hometown/Last Team
Andrew Broughton	09		5' 9"/185	F	Plymouth,MA/Texarkana Bandits (NAHL)
George Cademartori	07		5' 9"/155	F	Warrenville,IL/Springfield Blues (NAHL)
Tucker Callen	10		5' 6"/160	F	Annadale,NJ/Oswego Admirals (OPJHL)
Zachary Cardella	10		6' 2"/200	G	Spokane,WA/Trail Smoke Eaters (BCHL)
Mark Cerretani	10		5' 9"/185	F	N Andover,MA/Boston Bulldogs (AtJHL)
Eddie Chlanda	08		6' 1"/205	F	Central Islip,NY/Lebanon Valley (ECAC West)
Ross Enmark	10		5'11"/170	F	Shelby Twnsp,MI/Alpena Icedogs (NAHL)
Geoffrey Ferreira	07		5'11"/175	D/F	Wilmington,MA/Boston Harbor Wolves (EJHL)
Dave Gault	10		5' 8"/150	F	St. Clair Shores,MI/Wasilla Spirit (NAHL)
Patrick Haley	09		5' 9"/165	F	Shelburne,VT/Green Mountain Glades (EJHL)
Thomas Harrison	10		5'10"/190	D	Springfield,VA/Capital District Selects (EJHL)
Ricky Helmbrecht	10		5'11"/180	D	Mora,MN/Cleveland Barons (NAHL)
Jeremy Hmura	09		5'10"/180	F	New Lenox,IL/Coburn Colts (OPJHL)
Louis Hoey	09		5' 9"/175	F	Doylestown,PA/Springfield Spirit (NAHL)
Steve Kelleher	07		5' 7"/185	F	Rockland,MA/Massachusetts Boston (ECAC East)
Andrew Lisi	10		5'10"/185	G	Warwick,RI/Trinity-Pawling (NEPSAC)
Justin Liut	09		6' 1"/230	F	Birmingham,MI/Bowling Green (CCHA)
Bill McCreary	07		5'10"/175	F	Howell,MI/Providence (HEA)
Edmund McDonough	10		5' 7"/160	G	Dedham,MA/Boston Harbor Wolves (NAHL)
Steven Murphy	10		5'10"/170	F	Anchorage,AK/Wasilla Spirit (NAHL)
James Pentecost	09		6' 0"/180	F	Marquette,MN/Soo Indians (NAHL)
Donald Rankin	10		5'10"/190	D	Inverness,IL/Springfield Blues (NAHL)
Nathaniel Robie	08		6' 0"/190	D	Weymouth,MA/Proctor (NEPSAC)
Robert Sequeira	07		5'11"/200	D	Providence,RI/Boston Harbor Wolves (NAHL)
Jarrett Sousa	09		5'11"/180	D	Providence,RI/Merrimack (HEA)
Trevor Spiridi	08		5' 8"/175	F	Cranston,RI/Northwood (PS)
Sean Sylvester	10		6' 0"/180	F	Randolph,NJ/Salisbury (NEPSAC)
Jason Tarbell	09		6' 2"/205	D	Manchester,NH/New Hampshire Monarchs (EJHL)
Eric Tetzlaff	09		5' 9"/185	F	Westlake,OH/Bay State Breakers (EJHL)
Jonathan Whitham	08		5'11"/220	D	Fitchburg,MA/Lowell Loch Monsters (EJHL)

ROSTER ANALYSIS (SCHOLARSHIPS - 0)

Class		Country		Last Team					
Fr	12	USA	30	US JR A	9	CDN JR A	3	ACHA	
So	9	Canada		US JR B	9	CDN JR B		NJCAA	
Jr	4	Europe		US PS	4	CDN PS		NCAA	5
Sr	5	Asia		US HS		CDN HS		USNDT	
Gr		Other		US Midget		CDN Midget		Other	

ADMISSIONS, ENROLLMENT & CAMPUS INFORMATION

Founded 1879
Private, urban campus
1,164 men / 1,300 women
Tuition, room & board - $ 33 K
Avg SAT - 990

Average acceptance rate - 74 %
Freshman financial aid - %
Early decision application deadline - Dec 1
Regular appplication deadline - Apr 1
Financial aid deadline - Mar 1

Michael Poll - Admissions Director
Curry College
1071 Blue Hill Avenue
Milton, MA 02186
O 617.333.2210/ F 617.333.6860

www.curry.edu | www.curry.edu/athletics/

DARTMOUTH COLLEGE

Division 1

HOCKEY STAFF

HEAD COACH
Bob Gaudet *(Dartmouth '81)*

ASSISTANT COACHES
Dave Peters *(Boston College '82)*
Brendan Whittet *(Brown '94)*
Ed Walsh *(Salem State '83)*

HOCKEY OFFICE
Dartmouth College
6083 Alumni Gym
Hanover, NH 03755-3512
O 603.646.2469/ F 603.646.3348
robert.gaudet@dartmouth.edu

HOCKEY MEDIA CONTACT
Heather Croze - Hockey Info Director
Dartmouth College
6083 Alumni Gym
Hanover, NH 03755-3512
O 603.646.9340/ F 603.646.1286
heather.croze@dartmouth.edu

HOCKEY RINK
Thompson Arena (On Campus)
South Park Street
Hanover, NH 03755
Size 200' x 90', Capacity 4,500
O 603.646.2468

ATHLETIC DIRECTOR
Josie Harper - Athletic Director
Dartmouth College
6083 Alumni Gym
Hanover, NH 03755-3512
O 603.646.2465/ F 603.646.3348
josie.harper@dartmouth.edu

BIG GREEN PLAYERS

Player	YB	GR	Ht/Wt	P	Hometown/Last Team
Ryan Bellows	87	09	6' 0"/175	F	St. Catharines,ON/Thorold Blackhawks (GHJHL)
Will Boardman	85	08	6' 3"/190	D	Brattleboro,VT/Deerfield (NEPSAC)
Peter Boldt	87	10	6' 1"/190	D	Greenwich,CT/Sodertalje (SEL)
Mike Devine	85	08	5'11"/185	G	Orchard Pk,NY/Buffalo Lightning (OPJHL)
TJ Galiardi	88	10	6' 2"/180	F	Calgary,AB/Calgary Royals (AJHL)
Joe Gaudet	87	10	6' 2"/200	F	Hanover,NH/New Hampshire Monarchs (EJHL)
John Gibson	85	09	6' 3"/195	D	Okotoks,AB/Calgary Royals (AJHL)
Josh Gillam	88	10	6' 0"/180	F	Peterborough,ON/Peterborough Stars (OPJHL)
Tanner Glass	83	07	6' 0"/200	F	Craven,SK/Nanaimo Clippers (BCHL)
Dan Goulding	86	09	5'11"/185	G	Toronto,ON/Bowmanville Eagles (OPJHL)
Jon Grecu	86	08	6' 1"/175	F	Calgary,AB/Calgary Canucks (AJHL)
Joe Grossman	85	10	5'11"/175	G	Toronto,ON/Bowmanville Eagles (OPJHL)
Brandon Harrington	85	09	6' 1"/190	F	Rochester,MN/Sioux Falls Stampede (USHL)
Mike Hartwick	83	07	6' 3"/220	D	Bedford,NH/Boston Bulldogs (AtJHL)
Chris Johnson	86	09	6' 0"/180	D	Duluth,MN/Springfield Blues (NAHL)
Nick Johnson	85	08	6' 2"/190	F	Calgary,AB/St. Albert Saints (AJHL)
David Jones	84	08	6' 3"/220	F	N Vancouver,BC/Coquitlam Express (BCHL)
Grant Lewis	85	07	6' 3"/190	D	Upper St. Clair,PA/Pittsburgh Forge (NAHL)
Ben Lovejoy	84	07	6' 2"/210	D	Canaan,NH/Boston College (HEA)
Kevin McCarthy	87	10	6' 2"/220	D	Stoneham,MA/Phillips Exeter (NEPSAC)
Rob Pritchard	84	09	5'10"/180	F	Burnaby,BC/Prince George Spruce Kings (BCHL)
Connor Shields	84	09	6' 0"/180	F	Edmonton,AB/Bonnyville Pontiacs (AJHL)
Dan Shribman	84	07	5' 9"/180	F	Swampscott,MA/Deerfield (NEPSAC)
Rob Smith	87	10	6' 3"/195	F	Brooks,AB/Calgary Canucks (AJHL)
Kevin Swallow	86	09	6' 0"/180	F	Stanwood,MI/Chicago Steel (USHL)
Harry Taylor	87	10	6' 3"/210	D	Toronto,ON/St. Michael's (PS)
JT Wyman	86	08	6' 2"/175	F	Shorewood,MN/Blake (PS)

ROSTER ANALYSIS (SCHOLARSHIPS - 0)

Class		Country		Last Team					
Fr	8	USA	13	US JR A	4	CDN JR A	13	ACHA	
So	8	Canada	14	US JR B	2	CDN JR B	1	NJCAA	
Jr	6	Europe		US PS	4	CDN PS	1	NCAA	1
Sr	5	Asia		US HS		CDN HS		USNDT	
Gr		Other		US Midget		CDN Midget		SEL	1

ADMISSIONS, ENROLLMENT & CAMPUS INFORMATION

Founded 1769	Average acceptance rate - 19 %	Karl Furstenberg - Admissions Director
Private, rural campus	Freshman financial aid - 100 %	Dartmouth College
1,958 men / 2,038 women	Early decision application deadline - Nov 1	McNutt 6016
Tuition, room & board - $ 40 K	Regular application deadline - Jan 1	Hanover, NH 03755-3512
Avg SAT - 1,455/ Avg ACT - 31	Financial aid deadline - Feb 1	O 603.646.2875/ F 603.646.1216

www.dartmouth.edu | www.dartmouth.edu/athletics

UNIVERSITY OF DENVER

Division 1

HOCKEY STAFF

HEAD COACH
George Gwozdecky *(Wisconsin '78)*

ASSISTANT COACHES
Steve Miller *(St. Mary's '88)*
Derek Lalonde *(SUNY Cortland '95)*
David Tenzer *(New York University '84)*
Matt Laatsch *(Denver '04)*

HOCKEY OFFICE
University of Denver
2201 East Asbury Avenue, Room 4216
Denver, CO 80208-0320
O 303.871.3397 / F 303.871.3890
ggwozdec@du.edu

HOCKEY MEDIA CONTACT
Erich Bacher - Hockey Info Director
University of Denver
2201 East Asbury Avenue, Room 4672
Denver, CO 80208-0320
O 303.871.2390 / F 303.871.3890
ebacher@du.edu

HOCKEY RINK
Magness Arena (On Campus)
2199 South University Drive
Denver, CO 80208
Size 200' x 85', Capacity 6,026
O 303.871.3922

ATHLETIC DIRECTOR
Peg Bradley-Doppes - Athletic Director
University of Denver
2201 East Asbury Avenue, Room 4676
Denver, CO 80208-0320
O 303.871.4048 / F 303.871.3890
mhall2@du.edu

PIONEERS PLAYERS

Player	YB	GR	Ht/Wt	P	Hometown/Last Team
Zach Blom	83	08	6'0"/185	D	Englewood,CO/Wichita Falls (NAHL)
Cody Brookwell	86	10	6'4"/215	D	Calgary,AB/Williams Lake Timberwolves (BCHL)
Chris Butler	86	09	6'1"/185	D	St. Louis,MO/Sioux City Musketeers (USHL)
Steven Cook	84	07	6'1"/190	F	Anchorage,AK/Omaha Lancers (USHL)
JD Corbin	85	07	5'10"/185	F	Littleton,CO/USNDT (NAHL)
Ryan Dingle	84	08	5'10"/190	F	Steamboat Spgs,CO/Tri-City Storm (USHL)
TJ Fast	87	09	6'0"/185	D	Calgary,AB/Camrose Kodiaks (AJHL)
Glenn Fisher	83	07	6'1"/190	G	Edmonton,AB/Fort Saskatchewan Traders (AJHL)
Brian Gifford	85	10	6'2"/195	F	Moorhead,MN/Indiana Ice (USHL)
Matt Glasser	87	10	5'10"/180	F	Calgary,AB/Fort McMurray Oil Barons (AJHL)
Michael Handza	83	07	6'1"/210	F	Glenshaw,PA/Pittsburgh Forge (NAHL)
Ryan Helgason	84	07	6'0"/195	F	Woodbury,MN/Fairbanks Ice Dogs (NAHL)
Danny King	82	07	5'10"/170	G	Colorado Spgs,CO/Huntsville Muskota Otters (OPJHL)
Peter Mannino	84	08	6'0"/200	G	Farmington Hls,MI/Tri-City Storm (USHL)
Julian Marcuzzi	87	09	5'10"/205	D	N Vancouver,BC/Salmon Arm Silverbacks (BCHL)
Tom May	85	08	6'3"/215	F	Eagan,MN/Des Moines Buccaneers (USHL)
Patrick Mullen	86	09	5'10"/170	F	Pittsburgh,PA/Sioux Falls Stampede (USHL)
Geoff Paukovich	86	08	6'4"/220	F	Englewood,CO/USNDT (NAHL)
Rhett Rakhshani	88	10	5'10"/170	F	Huntington Bch,CA/USNDT (NAHL)
Tyler Ruegsegger	88	10	5'11"/180	F	Lakewood,CO/Shattuck-St. Mary's (PS)
Keith Seabrook	88	10	6'0"/200	D	Delta,BC/Burnaby Express (BCHL)
JP Testwuide	84	09	6'0"/210	D	Vail,CO/Waterloo Blackhawks (USHL)
Andrew Thomas	85	08	6'2"/220	D	Bow,NH/Waterloo Blackhawks (USHL)
Brock Trotter	87	09	5'10"/170	D	Brandon,MB/Lincoln Stars (USHL)
Adrian Veideman	83	07	6'2"/190	F	Sicamous,BC/Salmon Arm Silverbacks (BCHL)
Brandon Vossberg	85	10	6'2"/205	F	St. Paul,MN/Santa Fe Roadrunners (NAHL)

ROSTER ANALYSIS (SCHOLARSHIPS - 18)

Class		Country		Last Team				
Fr	7	USA	18	US JR A	14	CDN JR A	8	ACHA
So	6	Canada	8	US JR B		CDN JR B		NJCAA
Jr	6	Europe		US PS	1	CDN PS		NCAA
Sr	7	Asia		US HS		CDN HS		USNDT 3
Gr		Other		US Midget		CDN Midget		Other

ADMISSIONS, ENROLLMENT & CAMPUS INFORMATION

Founded 1864
Private, suburban campus
2,229 men / 2,414 women
Tuition, room & board - $ 36 K
Avg SAT - 1,145 / Avg ACT - 25

Average acceptance rate - 87 %
Freshman financial aid - 75 %
Early decision application deadline - N/A
Regular application deadline - Jan 15
Financial aid deadline - Feb 15

Roger Campbell - Admissions Director
University of Denver - MRB # 107
2201 East Asbury Avenue
Denver, CO 80208-0320
O 800.525.9495 / F 303.871.3301

www.du.edu

www.denverpioneers.collegesports.com

DUKE UNIVERSITY

Division 2

HOCKEY STAFF

HEAD COACH
Brent Selman *(Wilfrid Laurier '95)*

ASSISTANT COACHES
Rob Preston
Curtis Atkinson
Dr. Ron Olson

HOCKEY OFFICE
1325 Harvard Parkway, # 108
Garner, NC 27529
brentselman@hotmail.com

HOCKEY MEDIA CONTACT
Josh Wirth - League Representative
joshua.wirth@duke.edu

HOCKEY RINK
Triangle Sportsplex (Off Campus)
One Dan Kidd Drive
Hillsborough, NC 27278
Size 200' x 85', Capacity 1,200
O 919.644.8222 / F 919.644.2120

HOCKEY DIRECTOR
Drew Evans - Team President
andrew.evans@duke.edu

HOCKEY MANAGER
Matt Crawford - Hockey Manager
itiahp@yahoo.com

BLUE DEVILS PLAYERS

Player	YB	GR	Ht/Wt	P	Hometown/Last Team
Christopher Baker	10		5' 8"/160	F	Skillman, NJ
Andrew Barbour	07		6' 3"/180	G	Fairfax,VA/Williston (NEPSAC)
Jay Butler	09		6' 0"/175	F	Centerville, MA
Ryan Eick	08		6' 6"/215	D	Moristown,NJ/Delbarton (PS)
Peter Elkins-Williams	07		6' 0"/185	F	Chapel Hill,NC/Durham (PS)
Judd Fastenberg	08		5'10"/160	F	Jericho,NY
Kevin Ford	07		5' 8"/155	D	Rancho Palos Verdes,CA/Bay Harbor
Trevor Foskett	09		5'10"/175	D	Ardmore,PA
Steven Galanis	10		5'11"/205	G	Glenview,IL
Khaled Hassan		G		D	Durham,NC
Kevin Hatala	09		6' 1"/195	D	Cazenovia,NY
Ben Hu	10		5' 7"/160	F	Winterville, NC
Slater Hurst	10		5'11"/165	F	Milton, MA
Brandon Jenkins	08		6' 0"/160	F	McLean,VA
Issey Kato	08		5'11"/160	D	Evanston,IL/Roxbury Latin (PS)
Wilson Korel		G		6' 3"/180	F	Portland,ME
Brian Lake	09		5' 8"/175	F	Glencoe,IL
Daniel Larrea	08		5' 9"/160	F	Houston,TX
Mike Lehrhoff	09		5'10"/190	F	Morristown,NJ
Aaron Lerner	09		6' 1"/185	D	Bethesda,MD
Jeremiah Liao	07		6' 1"/150	F	West Windsor,NJ/Lawrenceville (PS)
Bert Maidment	07		5' 8"/175	F	Overland Park,KS/KC (Midget AA)
Matt McLeod	09		6' 2"/170	D	St. Albert.AB
Elderidge Nichols	10			G	Westhampton,NJ
Marc Perez	10		5' 9"/170	F	Harrison City, PA
Daniel Phan	08		5' 9"/162	D	Bedminster,NJ
Alex Putterman	07		5' 9"/180	F	Oyster Bay Cove,NY/Syosset (HS)
Jason Rehlaender	10			D	Greenwich, CT
Emily Sherman	10		5' 8"/140	F	Winnetka, IL
Kimberly Silenzi	10		5' 4"/140	F	Northlake, IL
Jared Smith	09		6' 0"/175	F	Lake Forest,IL
Yu Tanebe	09		5' 9"/160	F	Thornhill, ON
Ryan Tolkin	08		5'11"/175	F	Jericho,NY
Ben Tyson	07		5'10"/175	F	Milwaukee,WI/University (PS)
Jack Wilkinson	10			D	Dover,MA

ROSTER ANALYSIS (SCHOLARSHIPS - 0)

Class	Country	Last Team			
Fr	USA	US JR A	CDN JR A	ACHA	
So	Canada	US JR B	CDN JR B	NJCAA	
Jr	Europe	US PS	CDN PS	NCAA	
Sr	Asia	US HS	CDN HS	USNDT	
Gr	Other	US Midget	CDN Midget	Other	

ADMISSIONS, ENROLLMENT & CAMPUS INFORMATION

Founded 1838
Private, suburban campus
3,176 men / 2,931 women
Tuition, room & board $ 42 K
Avg SAT - 1,380 / Avg ACT - 30

Average acceptance rate - 23 %
Freshman financial aid - 100 %
Early decision application deadline - Nov 1
Regular application deadline - Jan 2
Financial aid deadline - Feb 1

Christoph Guttentag - Admissions Dir.
Duke University
2138 Campus Drive, Box 90586
Durham, NC 27706-0586
O 919.684.3214 / F 919.681.8941

www.duke.edu   www.dukehockey.com

EASTERN MICHIGAN UNIVERSITY

Division 1

HOCKEY STAFF

HEAD COACH
Paul Fassbender *(Eastern Michigan '98)*

ASSISTANT COACH
Lance Pierce *(Eastern Michigan '00)*

HOCKEY OFFICE
Paul Fassbender
714 Carver
Ypsilanti, MI 48198-3002
O 734.480.1085/ F 734.480.1085
paulfassbender@emuhockey.com

GENERAL MANAGER
Chris Wilk

HOCKEY RINK
Ann Arbor Ice Cube
2121 Oak Valley Drive
Ann Arbor, MI 48103
200' x 85'/ Capacity 1,800
O 734.213.1600

PUBLIC RELATIONS DIRECTOR
Robert Stumpmier

EAGLES PLAYERS

Player	YB	GR	Ht/Wt	P	Hometown/Last Team
Tom Burke	85	09	5'11"/175	D	Brownstown,MI/Taylor Wild (Midget AA)
Josh Cabaniss	85	09	6' 0"/180	F	Oconomowac,WI/Twin Bridges Lightning (Midget AA)
Adam Cole	86	09	6' 1"/210	D	Monroe,MI/Michigan Ice Dogs (CSHL)
Ryan Connolly	85	09	6' 0"/165	F	Gibraltar,MI/Woodhaven (HS)
Craig Drdek	85	07	5'10"/160	F	Brooklyn,OH/Brooklyn (HS)
Lucas Hartman	88	10	6' 2"/170	D	Milan,MI/Saline (HS)
Matt Hattie	86	10	6' 0"/185	F	Dexter,MI/Washtenaw (HS)
Dustin Henning	84	10	6' 0"/195	D	Oklahoma City,OK/Nichols (ECAC)
Steve Jacobs	84	07	6' 1"/220	D	Plymouth,MI/Plymouth Salem (HS)
AJ Jensen	85	09	5'10"/195	D	Trenton,MI/Toledo Cherokee (CSHL)
Jeremy Kaleniecki	86	09	5' 8"/165	G	Addison Twsp,MI/Traverse City North Stars (NAHL)
Steve Kardel	86	08	6' 1"/170	F	Canton,MI/Motown Hitmen (Midget AAA)
Brad Kerch	87	10	5'11"/170	F	Ann Arbor,MI/Saline (HS)
Kelly Koester	82	07	5' 8"/160	F	Temperance,MI/Toledo Cherokee (CSHL)
Brian Markowicz	82	07	6' 1"/195	G	Novi,MI/Western Michigan (ACHA)
Bobby Mayes	82	07	6' 2"/220	F	Monroe,MI/Toledo Cherokee (CSHL)
Joakim Nilsson	84	10	6' 0"/205	F	Ann Arbor,MI/Davenport (HS)
Josh Nummerdor	87	10	5'10"/175	F	Saline,MI/Saline (HS)
Daniel Olgren	85	07	6' 1"/195	F	Trenton,MI/Trenton (HS)
Matt Opyd	84	08	5' 8"/155	F	Oak Forest,IL/Toledo Cherokee (CSHL)
Greg Pellegrin	85	09	5'11"/205	F	Howell,MI/Michigan Stars (Jr. A)
PJ Pinkerton	84	08	5'11"/175	D	Oklahoma City,OK/Connecticut Whalers (IJHL)
Derek Porter	84	09	6' 2"/195	F	Bozeman,MT/Nichols (ECAC)
Sean Preston	87	10	6' 0"/190	D	Riverview,MI/Riverview (HS)
Joseph Rutherford	85	09	6' 0"/190	G	Ann Arbor,MI/Metro Jets (CSHL)
Jeff Snook	88	10	6' 3"/185	F	Highland,MI/Milford (HS)
Kevin Steffer	87	09	5'10"/200	D	Sterling Heights,MI/St. Clair Shores (HS)

ROSTER ANALYSIS (SCHOLARSHIPS - 0)

Class		Country		Last Team					
Fr	8	USA	27	US JR A	2	CDN JR A		ACHA	1
So	10	Canada		US JR B	7	CDN JR B		NJCAA	
Jr	3	Europe		US PS		CDN PS		NCAA	2
Sr	6	Asia		US HS	12	CDN HS		USNDT	
Gr		Other		US Midget	3	CDN Midget		Other	

ADMISSIONS, ENROLLMENT & CAMPUS INFORMATION

Founded 1849
Public, urban campus
10,721 men / 7,764 women
Tuition, room & board $ 12 K / $ 22 K
Avg SAT - 1,010 / Avg ACT - 21

Average acceptance rate - 78 %
Freshman financial aid - 59 %
Early decision application deadline - N/A
Regular application deadline - Feb 15
Financial aid deadline - Mar 15

Judy Tatem - Admissions Director
Eastern Michigan University
400 Pierce Hall
Ypsilanti, MI 48197
O 734.487.3060 / F 734.487.6559

ELMIRA COLLEGE

HOCKEY WEST

Division 3

HOCKEY STAFF

HEAD COACH
Tim Ceglarski *(Boston College '87)*

ASSISTANT COACH
Aaron Saul *(Elmira '98)*
Greg Moore *(Elmira '92)*

HOCKEY OFFICE
Elmira College
One Park Place
Elmira, NY 14901
O 607.735.1970 / F 607.735.1717
tceglarski@elmira.edu

HOCKEY MEDIA CONTACT
Matt Donohue - Sports Info Director
Elmira College
One Park Place
Elmira, NY 1491
O 607.735.1976 / F 607.735.1717
mdonohue@elmira.edu

HOCKEY RINK
Murray Athletic Center (Off Campus)
Route 14
Horseheads, NY 14845
Size 200' x 85', Capacity 4,000
O 607.739.8786

ATHLETIC DIRECTOR
Patricia Thompson - Athletic Director
Elmira College
One Park Place
Elmira, NY 14901
O 607.735.1730 / F 607.735.1717
pthompson@elmira.edu

SOARING EAGLES PLAYERS

Player	YB	GR	Ht/Wt	P	Hometown/Last Team
Ryan Arnone	08		6'0"/190	F	Colchester,CT/Norwich Ice Breakers (AEHL)
Andrew Bedford	08		6'1"/175	F	Mississauga,ON/Mississauga Chargers (OPJHL)
Kyle Branson	09		5'10"/175	D	Whitby,ON/Bowmanville Eagles (OPJHL)
Raphael Cundari	08		6'0"/195	G	Sault Ste. Marie,ON/Bay State Breakers (EJHL)
Nicolas Dumoulin	09		5'11"/195	D	Prevost,QC/St. Jerome Panthers (QJAHL)
Kevin Fitzpatrick	09		5'8"/165	F	E Amherst,NY/Loomis Chaffee (NEPSAC)
Scott Gamble	10		6'1"/205	D	Toronto,ON/North York Rangers (OPJHL)
Justin Joy	07		5'8"/190	F	Norfolk,NY/SUNY Plattsburgh (SUNYAC)
Nick Kiella	07		6'1"/185	F	Traverse City,MI/Danville Wings (USHL)
Noel Lortie	10		6'2"/200	F	North Bay,ON/Toronto Thunderbirds (OPJHL)
Rick Lynch	07		5'9"/180	D	W Seneca,NY/Buffalo Lightning (OPJHL)
Rusty Masters	10		6'0"/185	F	Grafton,ON/Port Hope Predators (OPJHL)
Dave McKenna	09		5'9"/175	F	Toronto,ON/North York Rangers (OPJHL)
Albert Mitchell	09		5'4"/140	F	Davidson,MI/Green Mountain Glades (EJHL)
Greg Moore	10		5'10"/195	D	Chateauguay,QC/Vaudreuil Mustangs (QJAHL)
Adam Nicholas	10		6'0"/210	D	Springvale,ME/Valley Warriors (EJHL)
Darin Pandovski	10		5'11"/190	F	Toronto,ON/North York Rangers (OPJHL)
Darcy Pettie	07		6'0"/205	F	Kingston,ON/Kingston Voyageurs (OPJHL)
Michael Richard	08		5'9"/220	F	LaSalle,QC/Gloucester Rangers (CJHL)
Derrick Ryan	09		5'10"/180	F	Fournier,ON/Ottawa Senators (CJHL)
Stefan Schoen	09		5'10"/175	F	Arth,Switzerland/Thornhill Rattlers (OPJHL)
Russell Smith	08		6'4"/230	F/D	Annapolis,MD/Lowell Loch Monsters (EJHL)
Robert Toomey	10		5'7"/175	D	Woodbridge,ON/Toronto Thunderbirds (OPJHL)
Casey Tuttle	10		6'0"/185	G	Chelsea,ME/Portland Pirates (AtJHL)
Jan Velich	10		6'4"/200	F	Pardubice,Czech Republic/Wexford Raiders (OPJHL)

ROSTER ANALYSIS (SCHOLARSHIPS - 0)

Class		Country		Last Team				
Fr	9	USA	9	US JR A	1	CDN JR A	16	ACHA
So	7	Canada	14	US JR B	6	CDN JR B		NJCAA
Jr	5	Europe	2	US PS	1	CDN PS		NCAA 1
Sr	4	Asia		US HS		CDN HS		USNDT
Gr		Other		US Midget		CDN Midget		EU

ADMISSIONS, ENROLLMENT & CAMPUS INFORMATION

Founded 1855	Acceptance rate - 67 %	William Neal - Admissions Director
Private, urban campus	Freshman financial aid - 82 %	Elmira College
405 men / 1,043 women	Early decision application deadline - Nov 15	Hamilton Hall
Tuition, room & board - $ 37 K	Regular application deadline - Feb 1	Elmira, NY 14901
Avg SAT - 1,140 / Avg ACT - 21	Financial aid deadline - Feb 1	O 607.735.1800 / F 607.735.1701

www.elmira.edu · www.elmira.edu/Athletics/

FERRIS STATE UNIVERSITY

Division 1

HOCKEY STAFF

HEAD COACH
Bob Daniels *(Michigan State '82)*

ASSOCIATE HEAD COACH
Drew Famulak *(Wisc.-Stevens Pt. '90)*

ASSISTANT COACH
Mark Kaufman *(Michigan State '84)*
Dave Cencer *(Franciscan '03)*

HOCKEY OFFICE
Ferris State University
Ewigleban Ice Arena
210 Sports Drive
Big Rapids, MI 49307-2741
O 231.591.2884/ F 231.591.2883
danielsb@ferris.edu

HOCKEY MEDIA CONTACT
Joe Gorby - Hockey Info Director
Ferris State University
West 025, 330 Oak Street
Big Rapids, MI 49307-2031
O 231.591.2336/ F 231.591.3775
gorbyj@ferris.edu

HOCKEY RINK
Ewigleben Ice Arena (On Campus)
210 Sports Drive
Big Rapids, MI 49307
Size 200' x 85', Capacity 2,493
O 231.591.2397

ATHLETIC DIRECTOR
Tom Kirinovic - Athletic Director
Ferris State University
210 Sports Drive
Big Rapids, MI 49307-2741
O 231.591.2863/ F 231.591.2869
kirinovt@ferris.edu

BULLDOGS PLAYERS

Player	YB	GR	Ht/Wt	P	Hometown/Last Team
Jordan Barber	87	10	6' 2"/190	G	Caledonia,MI/Grand Rapids Owls (CSHL)
Mark Bomersback	82	07	5' 9"/180	F	Rochester,AB/Canmore Eagles (AJHL)
Evan Case	86	09	6' 1"/175	D	Grosse Pt Woods,MI/Youngstown Phantoms (NAHL)
Matt Case	86	10	6' 0"/190	D	Plymouth,MN/Green Bay Gamblers (USHL)
Cody Chupp	85	10	6' 0"/195	F	Big Rapids,MI/Waterloo Blackhawks (USHL)
Brendan Connolly	85	09	5' 6"/160	F	Canmore,AB/Brooks Bandits (AJHL)
Corey Couturier	85	09	6' 0"/180	F	Traverse City,MI/Green Bay Gamblers (USHL)
JT Dahlinger	85	09	6' 1"/175	F	Grosse Pt Park,MI/Chatham Maroons (WOJHL)
Matt Frank	83	08	6' 0"/185	F	Billings,MT/Bozeman Icedogs (NAHL)
Casey Haines	86	10	5'10"/180	F	Indiana,PA/Texarkana Bandits (NAHL)
Jim Jorgensen	85	08	5'11"/185	D	Sault Ste. Marie,MI/Soo Indians (NAHL)
Justin Lewandowski	85	09	5' 9"/180	F	Naperville,IL/Chicago Steel (USHL)
Aaron Lewicki	87	10	6' 0"/205	F	Livonia,MI/Texarkana Bandits (NAHL)
Derek MacIntyre	85	08	6' 2"/185	G	Stanwood,MI/Soo Indians (NAHL)
Adam Miller	84	08	6' 0"/180	F	Livonia,MI/Des Moines Buccaneers (USHL)
Mitch O'Keefe	84	09	6' 2"/230	G	Almonte,ON/Hawkesbury Hawks (CJHL)
Zac Pearson	84	07	5' 9"/180	F	White Lake,MI/Cedar Rapids RoughRiders (USHL)
Dan Riedel	85	09	5' 9"/180	F	Rochester Hls,MI/Lincoln Stars (USHL)
Blair Riley	85	10	6' 0"/222	F	Kamloops,BC/Nanaimo Clippers (BCHL)
Jeremy Scherlinck	82	07	6' 4"/195	D	Grosse Pt,MI/Capital Centre Pride (NAHL)
Alex Spezia	85	08	5'10"/190	D	Farmington Hls,MI/Chicago Steel (USHL)
Joe VanCulin	82	07	5'10"/165	D	Monticello,MN/Wichita Falls (AWHL)
Matt Verdone	83	07	6' 0"/200	F	Summerstown,ON/Cornwall Colts (CJHL)
Eric Vesely	82	07	5'11"/180	F	Woodstock,IL/Topeka Scarecrows (USHL)
Adam Welch	83	08	6' 0"/190	D	Hastings,MN/Wichita Falls (NAHL)
Chris Zarb	83	09	6' 4"/200	D	Waterford,MI/Tri-City Storm (USHL)

ROSTER ANALYSIS (SCHOLARSHIPS - 18)

Class		Country		Last Team			
Fr	6	USA	21	US JR A	19	CDN JR A	6	ACHA
So	8	Canada	5	US JR B		CDN JR B	1	NJCAA
Jr	6	Europe		US PS		CDN PS		NCAA
Sr	6	Asia		US HS		CDN HS		USNDT
Gr		Other		US Midget		CDN Midget		Other

ADMISSIONS, ENROLLMENT & CAMPUS INFORMATION

Founded 1884
Public, rural campus
5,768 men / 4,532 women
Tuition, room & board - $ 14 K
Avg ACT - 20

Average acceptance rate - 49 %
Freshman financial aid - 75 %
Early decision application deadline - N/A
Regular application deadline - N/A
Financial aid deadline - Mar 15

Don Mullins - Interim Admissions Director
Ferris State University
420 Oak Street PRK 101
Big Rapids, MI 49307-2020
O 231.591.2100/ F 231.591.2978

www.ferris.edu

www.ferris.edu/htmls/sports

FINLANDIA UNIVERSITY

Division 3

HOCKEY STAFF

HEAD COACH
Joe Burcar

ASSISTANT COACHES
Brian Hannon
Ross Rinkinen *(Finlandia '04)*
Jason Moilanen *(Michigan Tech)*

HOCKEY OFFICE
Finlandia University Men's Hockey Office
601 Quincy Street
Hancock, MI 49930
O 906.487.7316/ F 906.487.7525
joe.burcar@finlandia.edu

HOCKEY MEDIA CONTACT
Victoria Huenink - Sports Info Director
601 Quincy Street
Hancock, MI 49930
O 906.487.7388
victoria.huenink@finlandia.edu

HOCKEY RINK
Houghton County Ice Arena (Off Campus)
1500 Birch Street
Houghton, MI
Size 200' x 85', Capacity 1,200
O 906.487.7214

ATHLETIC DIRECTOR
Chris Salani - Athletic Director
601 Quincy Street
Hancock, MI 49930
O 906.487.7378/ F 906.487.7525
chris.salani@finlandia.edu

LIONS PLAYERS

Player	YB GR Ht/Wt	P	Hometown/Last Team
Lukas Alberer	08 6'2"/185	G	Poertscach,Austria/EC Tarco (AEL)
Jason Aldrich	08 5'6"/175	F	Hancock,MI/Central Texas Blackhawks (NAHL)
Joe Beaudry	09 5'8"/180	F	Marquette,MI/Soo Indians (NAHL)
Corey Blake	09 5'11"/185	F	Marquette,MI/Marquette Electricians (Midget AAA)
Rob DeVaun	09 6'2"/195	G	Rockford,MI/Ojibwa Eagles (Midget AAA)
CJ Fisher	08 5'9"/170	F	Yakima,WA/Tri-City Titans (Midget AAA)
Travis Hanson	08 6'1"/210	F	Bark River,MI/Escanaba (HS)
Keith Johnstone	09 6'0"/195	F	Marquette,MI/Helena Bighorns (NAHL)
Joe Juntilla	07 5'9"/165	G	Calumet,MI/Calumet (HS)
Kevin Korte	09 6'2"/200	D	Kennewick,WA/Tri-City Titans (Midget AAA)
Matt Lindgren	09 6'0"/205	D	Port Huron,MI/St. Clair (OCAA)
Marc Marcotte	09 5'8"/185	D	Baraga,MI/Utica (ECAC West)
Blake Miller	08 6'3"/205	D	Hancock,MI/Valencia Vipers (WSHL)
Derek Onkalo	07 5'9"/175	F	Chassell,MI/Northwest Wisconsin Knights (MnJHL)
Josh Paquette	08 6'0"/185	F	Marquette,MI/Helena Bighorns (NAHL)
Mike Parks	08 5'10"/165	F	Marquette,MI/Bozeman Icedogs (NAHL)
Jon Redfield	10 6'2"/205	D	Cohasset,MN/Silver Bay (HS)
Bryan Solander	10 6'3"/205	D	Marquette,MI/Marquette Electricians (Midget AAA)
Ryan Sullivan	09 5'8"/170	F	Marquette,MI/Helena Bighorns (NAHL)
Luke Taintor	10 5'9"/155	F	Silver Bay,MN/Silver Bay (HS)
Mitch Tallent	08 5'11"/195	F	Garland,TX/Columbus Stars
Brandon VanAcker	10 5'8"/160	F	Lincoln Pk,MI/Helena Bighorns (NAHL)
Brad VanTassel	08 5'11"/195	D	Houghton,MI/Texarkana Bandits (NAHL)
Joe Welgos	07 6'2"/195	F	Darien,IL/Hinsdale South (HS)

ROSTER ANALYSIS (SCHOLARSHIPS - 0)

Class		Country		Last Team				
Fr	4	USA	23	US JR A	8	CDN JR A	ACHA	
So	8	Canada		US JR B	3	CDN JR B	NJCAA	
Jr	9	Europe	1	US PS		CDN PS	NCAA	1
Sr	3	Asia		US HS	5	CDN HS	USNDT	
Gr		Other		US Midget	5	CDN Midget	Other	2

ADMISSIONS, ENROLLMENT & CAMPUS INFORMATION

Founded 1896
Private, rural campus
207 men / 297 women
Tuition, room & board $ 22 K
Avg SAT - N/A

Average acceptance rate - 95 %
Freshman financial aid - 80 %
Early decision application deadline - N/A
Regular application deadline - Aug 20
Finanical aid deadline - Aug 1

Ben Larson - Admissions Director
Finladia University
601 Quincy Street
Fitchburg, MA 01420-2697
O 487.7274/ F 906.487.7383

FITCHBURG STATE COLLEGE

HOCKEY
NORTHEAST

Division 3

HOCKEY STAFF

HEAD COACH
Dean Fuller *(Fitchburg State '78)*

ASSOCIATE HEAD COACH
Malcom MacPherson *(Keene State '75)*

ASSISTANT COACHES
Steve Lowney *(Fitchburg State '94)*
Vincent Giambrocco *(Maine)*

HOCKEY OFFICE
Fitchburg State College
160 Pearl Street
Fitchburg, MA 01420-2697
O 978.665.4691 / F 978.665.3710
fullerd47474@yahoo.com

HOCKEY MEDIA CONTACT
Rusty Eggen - Sports Info Director
Fitchburg State College
160 Pearl Street
Fitchburg, MA 01420-2697
O 978.665.3343 / F 978.665.4310
reggen@fsc.edu

HOCKEY RINK
George Wallace Civic Center (Off Campus)
1000 John Fitch Highway
Fitchburg, MA 01420
Size 200' x 85', Capacity 1,800
PB 978.348.1712

ATHLETIC DIRECTOR
Sue Lauder - Athletic Director
Fitchburg State College
160 Pearl Street
Fitchburg, MA 01420-2697
O 978.665.3314 / F 978.665.3710
slauder@fsc.edu

FALCONS PLAYERS

Player	YB	GR	Ht/Wt	P	Hometown/Last Team
Matt Arsenault	09		5' 7"/185	F	Gardner,MA/Gardner (HS)
Wayne Bonkowski	09		5' 9"/180	D	Onsted,MI/Boston Blackhawks (IJHL)
Christopher Brecken	10		5' 6"/155	D	Hudson,MA/Hudson (HS)
Steve Carkin	07		6' 4"/245	D	Fitchburg,MA/Junior Bruins (EJHL)
Ron Carlucci	10		5' 9"/170	F	Stamford,CT/New Jersey Hitmen (EJHL)
John Coutts	09		5' 9"/160	F	Milford,CT/Kent (NEPSAC)
Patrick Dolan	09		6' 2"/220	D	St. Louis,MO/St. Louis Blues (CSHL)
Mike Dryer	07		6' 2"/205	F	Rockland,MA/Bay State Breakers (EJHL)
Chris Fraterrigo	08		5' 9"/180	F	Laguna Hills,CA/Bay City Bombers (WSHL)
Ross Goff	08		5'11"/195	D	Seattle,WA/Fernie Ghostriders (NAHL)
Michael Goulet	08		6' 0"/200	F	Blackstone,MA/SUNY Canton (NJCAA)
Chris Guyer	10		5'10"/150	G	Northborough,MA/Mass Maple Leafs (Jr B)
Andrew Hutton	10		6' 0"/180	F	Brewster,MA/Boston Harbor Wolves (EJHL)
Bob Kaloustian	09		5' 6"/180	D	Marlborough,MA/Suffolk (ECAC)
Dave Kaloustian	07		5' 9"/180	D	Marlborough,MA/Marlboro (HS)
Chadd Larkowski	08		6' 0"/190	F	St. Louis,MO/St. Louis Blues (CSHL)
Mike LaRoche	07		6' 0"/195	F	Townsend,MA/St. Bernard's (PS)
Jason Ledo	07		5'10"/185	D	Somerset,MA/Somerset (HS)
Greg Mailloux	07		6' 0"/195	F	Gardner,MA/Gardner (HS)
Eric Mayhew	08		6' 0"/220	D	Littleton,CO/Traverse City Enforcers (CEHL)
Devan McConnell	07		5' 9"/160	G	Lake Stevens,WA/St. Louis Blues (CSHL)
Ryan Moore	07		5' 7"/180	F	Randolph,MA/Curry (ECAC NE)
Brandon Rieth	09		6' 2"/190	F	Farmington Hls,MI/Boston Blackhawks (IJHL)
Shawn Riggins	10		5' 8"/140	G	Gardner,MA/Hoosac (NEPSAC)
Stephen Schofield	07		6' 2"/200	F	Sherman Oaks,CA/Bay State Breakers (EJHL)
Aaron Tiernan	09		6' 1"/220	D	Anchorage,AK/Central Texas Marshals (NAHL)
Ryan Tierney	08		5' 7"/165	F	Newburyport,MA/Brewster (NEPSAC)
Matt Welch	10		5' 6"/150	G	Burlington,VT/Full Stride Flyers (EmJHL)

ROSTER ANALYSIS (SCHOLARSHIPS - 0)

Class		Country		Last Team					
Fr	6	USA	28	US JR A	1	CDN JR A		ACHA	
So	7	Canada		US JR B	15	CDN JR B		NJCAA	1
Jr	6	Europe		US PS	4	CDN PS		NCAA	2
Sr	9	Asia		US HS	5	CDN HS		USNDT	
Gr		Other		US Midget		CDN Midget		Other	

ADMISSIONS, ENROLLMENT & CAMPUS INFORMATION

Founded 1894
Public, urban campus
1,512 men / 1,775 women
Tuition, room & board - $11 K / $17 K
Avg SAT - 1,010

Average acceptance rate - 68 %
Freshman financial aid - 99 %
Early decision application deadline - N/A
Regular application deadline - rolling
Financial aid deadline - Mar 1

Robert McGann - Admissions Director
Fitchburg State College
160 Pearl Street
Fitchburg, MA 01420-2697
O 978.665.3144 / F 978.665.4540

FRAMINGHAM STATE COLLEGE

HOCKEY STAFF

RAMS PLAYERS

HEAD COACH
Chris Heaney *(Norwich '90)*

ASSISTANT COACHES
Dan Richard *(Framingham State '04)*
Casey Reasonover *(Curry '05)*

HOCKEY OFFICE
Framingham State College
100 State Street
Framingham, MA 01701-9101
O 508.620.1220x4424 / F 508.626.4069
icehockey@frc.mass.edu

HOCKEY MEDIA CONTACT
Kathy Lynch - Sports Info Director
Framingham State College
100 State Street
Framingham, MA 01701-9101
O 508.626.4612 / F 508.626.4069
klynch@frc.mass.edu

HOCKEY RINK
Loring Arena (Off Campus)
Fountain Street
Framingham, MA 01702-3066
Size 200' x 85', Capacity 2,200
O 508.620.4876

ATHLETIC DIRECTOR
Tom Kelley - Athletic Director
Framingham State College
100 State Street
Framingham, MA 01701-9101
O 508.626.4614 / F 508.626.4612
tomk@frc.mass.edu

Player	YB	GR	Ht/Wt	P	Hometown/Last Team
Jason Akstin	85	08	6' 0"/200	F	Bridgewater,MA/Bridgewater Bandits (EJHL)
Sean Boudreau	86	09	6' 2"/190	F	Arlington,MA/Arlington (PS)
Stephen Butler	85	08	6' 0"/175	F	Dorchester,MA/Archbishop Williams (PS)
Gabriel Capozzi	10		6' 0"/190	F	Fair Lawn,NJ/Fair Lawn (HS)
Brett Casavant	10		6' 1"/160	F	Gardner,MA/Gardner (HS)
Ben Colby	84	07	5'11"/180	D	Newbury,MA/Triton (HS)
Stephan Davis	10		5'11"/180	D	Lafayette,CA/Dawson Creek Canucks (NWJHL)
Neil Donahue	86	09	5'10"/165	F	Medway,MA/Medway (HS)
Patrick Donovan	84	08	6' 4"/215	D	Sudbury,MA/Marian (PS)
Stephen Ficaro	10		5'10"/180	D	Manchester,NH/Kents Hill (NEPSAC)
Chris Gianatassio	86	08	5'10"/175	F	Everett,MA/Southern Maine (ECAC East)
Nicholas Glum	85	08	5' 9"/185	F	Bellingham,MA/Suffolk (ECAC NE)
Colin Goodwin	10		5'11"/185	D	Marblehead,MA/Hartford Wolfpack (AtJHL)
Kyle Hallett	86	09	6' 1"/185	F	Rocky Hill,CT/Connecticut Clippers (MJHL)
Joseph Hurley	10		6' 1"/180	F	Charleston,MA/Winchendon (NEPSAC)
Andrew Joce	10		5' 8"/130	G	Milford,MA/Marlborough (HS)
Trevor Johnson	10		5' 9"/150	F	Anchorage,AK/Eugene Generals (NPJHL)
Jonathan Lamken	86	08	5'11"/165	F	Wareham,MA/Wareham (HS)
Sean Maguire	86	09	5'10"/180	F	Plymouth,MA/Plymouth South (HS)
Joseph Mulvey	10		6' 0"/200	F	Marlborough,MA/Marlborough (HS)
Oliver Myer	84	09	6' 2"/180	F	Montpelier,VT/Connecticut Lazers (Midget)
Tim Richard		08	5' 5"/150	F	Leominster,MA/Leominster (HS)
Scott Rivers	10		6' 0"/180	D	Boxford,MA/Winchendon (NEPSAC)
Patrick Sampson	85	08	6' 0"/155	G	Braintree,MA/Braintree (HS)
Jeremy Schmidt	10		5' 7"/170	F	Huffman,TX/Kingwood Mustangs ()Midget)
Thomas Smith	10		5' 8"/135	G	Gilbertsville,PA/St. Thomas More (PS)
Ryan Sullivan	10		6' 0"/180	D	Atlanta,GA/Green Mountain Glades (EJHL)
David Trantin		09	5'11"/205	D	Odenton,MD/Fitchburg State (ECAC NE)
Matthew Trusz		09	6' 2"/220	G	Ludlow,MA/Hartford Wolfpack (AtJHL)
Joshua Williams	10		5' 9"/170	D	Upper Marlboro,MD/Washington Nationals (MJHL)

ROSTER ANALYSIS (SCHOLARSHIPS - 0)

Class		Country		Last Team					
Fr	14	USA	30	US JR A		CDN JR A		ACHA	
So	7	Canada		US JR B	8	CDN JR B		NJCAA	
Jr	8	Europe		US PS	6	CDN PS		NCAA	3
Sr	1	Asia		US HS	11	CDN HS		USNDT	
Gr		Other		US Midget	2	CDN Midget		Other	

ADMISSIONS, ENROLLMENT & CAMPUS INFORMATION

Founded 1839
Public, suburban campus
1,147 men / 2,329 women
Tuition, room & board - $11 K / $17 K
Avg SAT - 1,040

Average acceptance rate - 62 %
Freshman financial aid - 93 %
Early decision application deadline - N/A
Regular application deadline - May 15
Financial aid deadline - Feb 15

Dr. Philip Dooher - Admissions Director
Framingham State College
100 State Street
Framingham, MA 01701-9101
O 508.626.4500 / F 508.626.4592

www.framingham.edu

www.framingham.edu/Athletics/

FRANKLIN PIERCE COLLEGE

Division 2

HOCKEY STAFF

HEAD COACH
Scott Loiseau *(Franklin Pierce '02)*

ASSISTANT COACHES
Ryan Carney *(W New England '97)*
Pete McLaughlin *(Harvard '96)*

HOCKEY OFFICE
Franklin Pierce College Hockey Office
College Road
PO Box 60
Rindge, NH 03461
O 603.899.4367 / F 603.899.4328
loiseau@fpc.edu

HOCKEY MEDIA CONTACT
Doug Monson - Sports Info Director
Franklin Pierce College
College Road
PO Box 60
Rindge, NH 03461-0060
O 603.899.4222 / F 603.899.4372
monsond@fpc.edu

HOCKEY RINK
Clark Community Center (Off Campus)
155 Central Street
Winchendon, MA 01475
Size 200' x 85', Capacity 500
O 978.297.0102

ATHLETIC DIRECTOR
Bruce Kirsh - Athletic Director
College Road
PO Box 60
Rindge, NH 03461-0060
O 603.899.4080 / F 603.899.6448
kirshb@fpc.edu

RAVENS PLAYERS

Player	YB	GR	Ht/Wt	P	Hometown/Last Team
Mike Anderson	82	07	6'1"/200	D	Keene,NH/Laconia Leafs (AtJHL)
Brian Bator	87	09	5'9"/145	F	Erie,PA/Pittsburgh Penguins
Brett Bilodeau	84	07	5'8"/170	F	Skowhegan,ME/Hebron (NEPSAC)
Jie Blauner		10	/	G	Brattleboro,VT/Salem Ice Dogs (EmJHL)
John Bodie		10	/	D	Hanover,MA/Hanover (HS)
Styles Bridges	83	07	6'1"/185	F	Canton,NY/SUNY Canton (NJCAA)
Trevor Clark	86	08	6'0"/155	F	Randolph,MA/Randolph (HS)
Steven Della-Calce		10	/	F	New Jersey,NJ/New Jersey Dynamo
Brian DelSavio	85	07	6'1"/185	F	Orangeburg,NY/Pearl River (HS)
CJ Demmons	83	07	6'0"/195	F	Wolfeboro,NH/Kimball Union (NEPSAC)
Joseph Fields	84	08	6'0"/145	F	Lansdale,PA/Green Mountain Glades (EJHL)
Casey Goodell		10	/	F	Laconia,NH/Laconia Leafs (AtJHL)
Jeff Kasper	86	09	5'11"/170	F	S Boston,MA/Catholic Memorial (PS)
Kyle Kruse		10	/	D	Bourne,MA/Bourne (HS)
Ed Kus		09	/	D	Webster,MA/Norwich Ice Breakers (AEHL)
Phil LaBreck		10	/	F	Laconia,NH/Laconia Leafs (AtJHL)
Brad Leighton	83	07	5'8"/145	F	Cumberland,ME/East Coast Rangers (IJHL)
Josh Lupinek		09	6'0"/170	D	E Haddam,CT/Hartford Wolfpack (AtJHL)
Chuck Matthews	84	07	5'9"/175	F	Needham,MA/Bridgton (NEPSAC)
Joe McCarthy		10	/	F	Boston,MA/Boston Blackhawks (IJHL)
Steve Moore	86	08	6'2"/170	G	Londonderry,NH/American International (AHL)
Shane Murphy		09	/	F	Tolland,CT/Gunnery (NEPSAC)
Steven Murphy		10	5'11"/200	F	Boston,MA/Boston Blackhawks (IJHL)
Rob Perretta	85	09	5'10"/160	D	Staten Island,NY/Brockville Tikis (EOJHL)
Ben Reynolds	84	08	5'10"/185	F	Wallingford,PA/Green Mountain Glades (EJHL)
Jason Sabo		10	/	D	S Windsor,CT/Hebron (NEPSAC)
Courson Schneider	86	09	/	F	New York,NY/Avon (NEPSAC)
Jay Stempniak		09	/	F	RI/Johnson & Wales (ECAC NE)
Ryan Strayer	85	08	5'8"/155	F	Murfeesboro,TN/New England Coyotes (EJHL)
Jon Tuttle		10	/	G	Concord,NH/Concord (HS)
Spencer Utman		08	/	G	Canton,NY/SUNY Canton (NJCAA)
Matt Whitney	84	09	6'0"/175	F	Plymouth,BC/Hartford Wolfpack (AtJHL)
Peter Wilson		08	5'9"/155	F	Marshfield,MA/Marshfield (HS)

ROSTER ANALYSIS (SCHOLARSHIPS - 0)

Class		Country		Last Team					
Fr	10	USA	32	US JR A		CDN JR A		ACHA	
So	9	Canada	1	US JR B	13	CDN JR B	1	NJCAA	2
Jr	7	Europe		US PS	7	CDN PS		NCAA	2
Sr	7	Asia		US HS	6	CDN HS		USNDT	
Gr		Other		US Midget		CDN Midget		Other	2

ADMISSIONS, ENROLLMENT & CAMPUS INFORMATION

Founded 1962	Acceptance rate - 77 %	Lucy C. Shonk - Admissions Director
Private, rural campus	Freshman financial aid - 66 %	College Road - POB 60
793 men / 793 women	Early decision app deadline - N/A	Rindge, NH 03461-0060
Tuition, room & board $ 32 K	Regular app deadline - rolling	O 603.899.4054 / F 603.899.4372
Avg SAT - 990	Financial aid deadline - Mar 1	O 800.437.0048

GEORGE MASON UNIVERSITY

Division 2

HOCKEY STAFF

HEAD COACH
Craig MacDonald

ASSISTANT COACHES
Jeff Lange

HOCKEY OFFICE
O 703.297.2184
craiga5@hotmail.com

HOCKEY MEDIA CONTACT
Adam Wilkinson
awilkin1@gmu.edu

HOCKEY RINK
Fairfax Ice Arena
3779 Pickett Road
Fairfax, VA 22031
O 703.323.1132

HOCKEY PRESIDENT
Paul Balcerzak - Team President
O 703.244.7798
hockeyplaya61@yahoo.com

PLAYERS

Player	YB GR Ht/Wt	P	Hometown/Last Team

Roster Not Available

ROSTER ANALYSIS (SCHOLARSHIPS - 0)

Class	Country	Last Team		
Fr	USA	US JR A	CDN JR A	ACHA
So	Canada	US JR B	CDN JR B	NJCAA
Jr	Europe	US PS	CDN PS	NCAA
Sr	Asia	US HS	CDN HS	USNDT
Gr	Other	US Midget	CDN Midget	Other

ADMISSIONS, ENROLLMENT & CAMPUS INFORMATION

Founded 1972
Public, suburban campus
7,600 men / 9,288 women
Tuition, room & board $ 12 K / $ 25 K
Avg SAT - 1095 / Avg ACT - 23

Average acceptance rate - 69 %
Freshman financial aid - 68 %
Early decision application deadline - N/A
Regular application deadline - Jan 15
Finanical aid deadline - Mar 1

Andrew Flagel - Admissions Director
George Mason University
4400 University Drive, MSN 3A4
Fairfax, VA 22030
O 703.993.2400 / F 703.993.2392

www.gmu.edu

www.gmuhockey.net

GEORGETOWN UNIVERSITY

Division 2

HOCKEY STAFF

HEAD COACH
John Kokidko

ASSISTANT COACHES
Doug Stewart
Brad Card

HOCKEY OFFICE
John Kokidko
O 202.438.2267
georgetownhockey@gmail.com

HOCKEY MEDIA CONTACT
John Stebbins
Club Sports - Ice Hockey
316 Leavey Center
Georgetown University
Washington DC 20057
O 603.759.8107
georgetownhockey@gmail.com

HOCKEY RINK
Cabin John Rink
10610 Westlake Drive
Rockville, MD 20852
O 301.365.0585

CLUB PRESIDENT
Conor Hickton
O 412.977.2844
georgetownhockey@gmail.com

John Stebbins
O 603.759.8107
georgetownhockey@gmail.com

PLAYERS

Player	YB	GR	Ht/Wt	P	Hometown/Last Team
Peter Black	09		6'0"/190	F	Bethesda,MD/Georgetown (PS)
Anthony Campa	09		5'9"/151	D	Minneapolis,MN/Park (HS)
Rick Cella	08		6'1"/182	D	Long Valley,NJ/Colgate (ACHA)
Andrew Dorin	10		6'0"/200	F	
Eric Estey	08		5'10"/170	D	Toronto,ON/Upper Canada (PS)
Devon Falvey	07		6'1"/173	F	Pelham,NY/Iona (PS)
Dave Glynn	08		6'0"/165	F	Stoughton,MA/Phillips Exeter (NEPSAC)
Gregory Graham	10		5'7"/167	G	Downingtown,PA/Downingtown (HS)
Conor Hickton	08		6'2"/170	F	Pittsburgh,PA
Jackson Holahan	09		6'3"/175	D	East Haddam,CT/Choate (NEPSAC)
Luke Holden	07		5'10"/180	F	Cape Elizabeth,ME/Tufts (NESCAC)
Joe Horgan	10		5'10"/160	F	Lansvale,PA/LaSalle College (HS)
Chris Jordan	09		5'11"/220	F	Greenville,DE/Archmere (PS)
Vincent Ko	10		5'9"/155	F	Rockville,MD/Richard Montgomery (HS)
Gian Kull	07		6'1"/225	G	Zurich,Switzerland/Swiss Liga
Dan Lechner	10		5'10"/165	F	Rockville,MD/Gonzaga (PS)
Hugh Manahan	09		6'1"/185	D	Skillman,NJ/Lawrenceville (PS)
George McGinniss	09		6'0"/190	D	New Canaan,CT/New Canaan (HS)
Ryan Murphy	09		6'1"/180	D	Clifton Park,NY/Shenendehowa (HS)
Tim Noonan	09		6'0"/170	F	Rochester,NH/Berwick (NEPSAC)
George Razook	07		5'8"/170	D	Rye,NY/Tufts (NESCAC)
John Reppucci	08		5'10"/200	F	Newburyport,MA/Exeter (NEPSAC)
John Stebbins	07		5'11"/200	D	Portsmouth,NH/Exeter (NEPSAC)
Brendan Surma	09		6'0"/180	D	Pittsburgh,PA/Pittsburgh (USAH)
Charlie Walsh	10		6'0"/195	D	Cheshire,CT/Xavier (HS)
Adam Willner	09		5'7"/165	F	Upper Montclair,NJ/Deerfield (NEPSAC)

ROSTER ANALYSIS (SCHOLARSHIPS - 0)

Class	Country	Last Team		
Fr	USA	US JR A	CDN JR A	ACHA
So	Canada	US JR B	CDN JR B	NJCAA
Jr	Europe	US PS	CDN PS	NCAA
Sr	Asia	US HS	CDN HS	USNDT
Gr	Other	US Midget	CDN Midget	Other

ADMISSIONS, ENROLLMENT & CAMPUS INFORMATION

Founded 1879
Private, urban campus
2,764 men / 3,578 women
Tuition, room & board $ 44 K
Avg SAT - 1375 / Avg ACT - 25

Average acceptance rate - 22 %
Freshman financial aid - 100 %
Early decision application deadline - N/A
Regular application deadline - Jan 10
Financial aid deadline - Feb 1

Charles Deacon - Admissions Director
Georgetown University
103 White-Gravenor, Box 571002
Washington, DC 20057-1002
O 202.687.3600 / F 202.687.5084

GUSTAVUS ADOLPHUS COLLEGE

Division 3

HOCKEY STAFF

HEAD COACH
Brett Petersen *(Denver '92)*

ASSISTANT COACH
Mike Deschneau *(Gustavus '01)*

HOCKEY OFFICE
Gustavus Adolphus - Lund Center
800 West College Avenue
St. Peter, MN 56082
O 507.933.7615 / F 507.933.8412
bpeters4@gustavus.edu

HOCKEY MEDIA CONTACT
Tim Kennedy - Sports Info Director
Gustavus Adolphus - Lund Center
800 West College Avenue
St. Peter, MN 56082
O 507.933.7647 / F 507.933.8412
timgasid@gustavus.edu

HOCKEY RINK
Lund Center Arena (On Campus)
800 West College Avenue
St. Peter, MN 56082
Size 200' x 85', Capacity 2,200
O 507.933.7666

ATHLETIC DIRECTOR
Al Molde - Athletic Director
Gustavus Adolphus - Athletic Dept.
800 West College Avenue
St. Peter, MN 56082-1498
O 507.933.7622 / F 507.933.8412
amolde@gustavus.edu

GOLDEN GUSTIES PLAYERS

Player	YB	GR	Ht/Wt	P	Hometown/Last Team
Jared Ackmann	10		5' 9"/150	F	Buffalo,MN/Buffalo (HS)
Matthew Andres	10		5'10"/175	F	Edina,MN/Benilde-St. Margaret's (PS)
Tyler Antony	10		5'11"/170	F	Buffalo,MN/Buffalo (HS)
John Arundel	07		6' 2"/210	F	Eden Pr,MN/Minnetonka (HS)
Eric Bigham	10		6' 5"/210	F	Robbinsdale,MN/Santa Fe Roadrunners (NAHL)
Spencer Campion	10		6' 0"/200	D	Plymouth,MN/Benilde-St. Margaret's (PS)
Mike Carr	09		5' 9"/150	F	Mahtomedi,MN/Mahtomedi (HS)
Nate Fischer	10		5' 8"/160	G	St. Paul,MN/Johnson (HS)
Mac Garceau	10		6' 0"/180	D	White Bear Lk,MN/Hill-Murray (PS)
Josh Gaw	07		5' 6"/190	F	Burr Ridge,IL/Brookfield Central (HS)
Hampus Gunnarsson	10		6' 3"/190	D	Ljungby,Sweden/Troja-Ljungby (SEL)
Mike Hosfield	07		6' 0"/175	F	Golden Vly,MN/Armstrong (HS)
Sami Idris	08		5'10"/200	F	Gothenburg,MN/Burgarden (SEL)
Steven Jensen	07		5'10"/175	F	Kentwood,MI/Green Mountain Glades (EJHL)
Kevin Johnson	09		5'11"/170	G	Wayzata,MN/Wayzata (HS)
Jon Keseley	07		5'11"/160	D/F	St. Louis Pk,MN/St. Louis Park (HS)
James Leathers	10		5'10"/185	F	Savage,MN/Blake (PS)
Tomas Liskutin	09		6' 0"/185	D	Riverside,CA/Shattuck-St. Mary's (PS)
Jared Martz	08		5'10"/160	D	Mahtomedi,MN/Mahtomedi (HS)
Cody Mosbeck	10		5'10"/195	D	Emo,ON/North Iowa Outlaws (NAHL)
Ben Ollila	08		5' 8"/155	F	Lino Lakes,MN/Centennial (HS)
Tim Ornell	08		5'10"/170	F	Lino Lakes,MN/Centennial (HS)
Tony Palma	10		6' 0"/205	D	Lino Lakes,MN/Centennial (HS)
John Paszkiewicz	09		5'11"/160	G	Richfield,MN/Richfield (HS)
Jay Phillips	07		5'11"/175	D	Bemidji,MN/Borderland Thunder (SIJHL)
Joel Rindelaub	09		6' 3"/200	G	St. Cloud,MN/St. Cloud Cathedral (PS)
Kyle Rohlfs	08		5'11"/200	F	Fergus Fls,MN/Fergus Falls (HS)
Niko Suoraniemi	08		5' 9"/185	D	Angelholm,Sweden/Rogle B.K. (SEL)

ROSTER ANALYSIS (SCHOLARSHIPS - 0)

Class		Country		Last Team				
Fr	12	USA	26	US JR A	3	CDN JR A	1	ACHA
So	5	Canada	1	US JR B	1	CDN JR B		NJCAA
Jr	6	Europe	2	US PS	6	CDN PS		NCAA
Sr	6	Asia		US HS	15	CDN HS		USNDT
Gr		Other		US Midget		CDN Midget		SEL	3

ADMISSIONS, ENROLLMENT & CAMPUS INFORMATION

Founded 1862	Acceptance rate - 77 %	Mark Anderson - Admissions Director
Private, rural campus	Five year graduation rate - 88 %	Gustavus Adolphus - Admissions Dept.
1,048 men / 1,447 women	Early decision application deadline - N/A	800 West College Avenue
Tuition, room & board - $ 32 K	Regular application deadline - Apr 1	St. Peter, MN 56082-1498
Avg SAT - 1,190 / Avg ACT - 26	Financial aid deadline - Apr 15	O 507.933.7676 / F 507.933.6270

www.gustavus.edu | www.gustavus.edu/oncampus/athletics/

HAMILTON COLLEGE

Division 3

HOCKEY STAFF

HEAD COACH
Phil Grady *(Norwich '70)*

ASSISTANT COACHES
Dominick Davis *(Norwich '04)*
Ted Fauss *(Clarkson)*
Bill Fleet

HOCKEY OFFICE
Hamilton College - Athletic Department
198 College Hill Road
Clinton, NY 13323
O 315.859.4762 / F 315.859.4117
pgrady@hamilton.edu

HOCKEY MEDIA CONTACT
Jim Taylor - Sports Info Director
Hamilton College - Athletic Department
198 College Hill Road
Clinton, NY 13323
O 315.859.4685 / F 315.859.4117
jtaylor@hamilton.edu

HOCKEY RINK
Sage Rink (On Campus)
198 College Hill Road
Clinton, NY 13323
Size 185' x 85', Capacity 1,500
O 315.859.4675

ATHLETIC DIRECTOR
Dave Thompson - Athletic Director
Hamilton College
198 College Hill Road
Clinton, NY 13323
O 315.859.4114 / F 315.859.4117
dthompso@hamilton.edu

CONTINENTALS PLAYERS

Player	YB	GR	Ht/Wt	P	Hometown/Last Team
Bo Armstrong	09		6'0"/175	F	Dallas,TX/Hotchkiss (NEPSAC)
Harry Biggs	10		5'9"/160	F	W Newbury,MA/St. Mark's (NEPSAC)
Travis Blood	09		6'1"/200	F	Pepperell,MA/New England Huskies (EJHL)
Joe Buteau	08		6'2"/190	D	Burlington,VT/Tabor (NEPSAC)
Matt Crowson	09		6'2"/195	G	Kanata,ON/Berkshire (NEPSAC)
Jake Davis	09		5'11"/190	F	Dallas,TX/Taft (NEPSAC)
Todd Davis	10		6'1"/210	F	Wellesley,MA/St. Sebastian's (NEPSAC)
Casey Deak	07		5'9"/170	F	Bloomingdale,NJ/Bridgewater Bandits (EJHL)
Andrew Decristoforo	08		5'9"/170	F	Manotick,ON/SUNY Canton (NJCAA)
Paul Engelhardt	10		5'8"/175	F	Bay City,MI/Andover (NEPSAC)
Rob Gannon	10		6'0"/185	D	Saugus,MA/Northfield Mount Hermon (NEPSAC)
John Gordon	07		6'3"/220	D	Keene,ON/Lindsay Muskies (OPJHL)
Peter Gustavson	10		5'8"/175	F	Falmouth,ME/Pomfret (NEPSAC)
Chadd Hippensteel	10		5'11"/170	D	Barrington,NH/St. Mark's (NEPSAC)
Jared Leslie	09		5'11"/175	D	Markham,ON/St. Andrew's (PS)
Chris Lorenc	10		5'11"/185	F	Clifton,NJ/Wyoming (PS)
Pat McGarry	07		6'2"/210	D	Kennett Sq,PA/Boston Bulldogs (AtJHL)
Matt Mesi	08		6'0"/180	F	Orchard Pk,NY/Buffalo Lightning (OPJHL)
Andrew Miller	10		5'11"/165	G	Moorestown,NJ/Choate (NEPSAC)
Nate Miller	08		5'9"/200	F	Chesterland,OH/Thornhill Islanders (OPJHL)
Jim Nolan	07		6'0"/180	F	Lynnfield,MA/Northfield Mount Hermon (NEPSAC)
Brian O'Malley	10		6'0"/195	F	Oak Brook,IL/Northfield Mount Hermon (NEPSAC)
Kevin Osborne	09		5'7"/180	D	Peabody,MA/Pomfret (NEPSAC)
Jonathon Peros	08		5'10"/180	D	Falmouth,MA/St. Paul's (NEPSAC)
Kyle Roulston	09		6'0"/190	D	Markdale,ON/Pickering Panthers (OPJHL)
Ian Stearns	10		5'10"/160	G	Fitchburg,MA/Milton (NEPSAC)
Vaclav Tomicek	10		5'11"/175	F	Liberec,Czech Republic/Wyoming (PS)
Marc Trostle	10		5'10"/165	F	Bethlehem,PA/Kent (NEPSAC)
Jerome Wallace	10		6'0"/200	F	Libertyville,IL/Taft (NEPSAC)

ROSTER ANALYSIS (SCHOLARSHIPS - 0)

Class		Country		Last Team					
Fr	13	USA	23	US JR A		CDN JR A	4	ACHA	
So	7	Canada	5	US JR B	3	CDN JR B		NJCAA	1
Jr	5	Europe	1	US PS	20	CDN PS	1	NCAA	
Sr	4	Asia		US HS		CDN HS		USNDT	
Gr		Other		US Midget		CDN Midget		Other	

ADMISSIONS, ENROLLMENT & CAMPUS INFORMATION

Founded 1793	Average acceptance rate - 34 %	Richard Fuller - Admissions Director
Private, rural campus	Freshman financial aid - 99 %	Hamilton College - Root House
846 men / 916 women	Early decision application deadline - Nov 15	Clinton, NY 13323
Tuition, room & board - $ 43 K	Regular application deadline - Jan 1	O 315.859.4421 / F 315.859.4457
Avg SAT - 1,340	Financial aid deadline - Feb 1	O 800.843.2655

HAMLINE UNIVERSITY

M.I.A.C.
Minnesota Intercollegiate Athletic Conference

NCAA
Division 3

HOCKEY STAFF

HEAD COACH
Scott Bell *(Minnesota)*

ASSISTANT COACH
Jay Moser *(Minnesota)*
Tom Ostroot *(Idaho State)*

HOCKEY OFFICE
Hamline University - Athletic Department
1536 Hewitt Avenue
St. Paul, MN 55104-1284
O 651.523.2243/ F 651.523.2390
sbell01@hamline.edu

HOCKEY MEDIA CONTACT
Troy Mallat - Sports Info Director
Hamline University - Athletic Department
1536 Hewitt Avenue
St. Paul, MN 55104-1284
O 651.523.2786/ F 651.523.2390
tmallat01@hamline.edu

HOCKEY RINK
Fairgrounds Coliseum (Off Campus)
1265 Snelling Avenue North
St. Paul, MN 55108
Size 200' x 85', Capacity 6,000
O 612.643.6350

ATHLETIC DIRECTOR
Dan O'Brien - Athletic Director
Hamline University - Athletic Department
1536 Hewitt Avenue
St. Paul, MN 55104-1284
O 651.523.2326/ F 651.523.3075
dobrien@hamline.edu

FIGHTING PIPERS PLAYERS

Player	YB	GR	Ht/Wt	P	Hometown/Last Team
Luke Bierman	10		5'7"/170	F	Chaska,MN/St. Paul Lakers (MnJHL)
Matt Buckley	09		6'1"/210	F	Brooklyn Pk,MN/Des Moines Buccaneers (USHL)
Luke Chilson	09		5'9"/160	F	Rice Lake,WI/Rice Lake (HS)
Jim Erickson	09		6'1"/200	F	Brooklyn Pk,MN/Des Moines Buccaneers (USHL)
Steve Festler	09		5'8"/160	F	Little Falls,MN/Little Falls (HS)
Dustin Fulton	09		6'0"/170	F	Brooklyn Pk,MN/Bismarck Bobcats (NAHL)
Alex Gruetzmacher	10		5'9"/175	F	Richfield,MN/Richfield (HS)
Justin Hanna	09		5'8"/190	F	Little Canada,MN/Roseville (HS)
Lee Joos	10		6'1"/185	F	Eagan,MN/Alexandria Blizzard (NAHL)
Cory Krogen	09		6'1"/185	D	Marshall,MN/Marshall (HS)
Kyle Kurr	10		5'7"/165	F	Elk River,MN/Elk River (HS)
Joe Long	09		5'10"/180	F	Dayton,MN/Green Bay Gamblers (USHL)
Joe Lorentz	09		6'0"/185	F	Hastings,MN/Phoenix Polar Bears (WSHL)
Sami Lundquist	10		6'3"/200	D	Gillette,WY/Minnesota Owls (MnJHL)
Jack Madryga	09		5'9"/175	D	Burnsville,MN/Minnehaha (PS)
Ryan McCarthy	10		5'7"/165	F	Apple Valley,MN/Valley Forge Minutemen (MJHL)
Michael McDonough	09		5'8"/155	F	Burnsville,MN/Eastview (HS)
Dave Perri	08		5'10"/180	F	Plymouth,MN/Osseo (HS)
Todor Petkov	08		6'0"/180	G	Boucherville,QC/Streetsville Derbys (OPJHL)
Dustin Postell	10		6'1"/190	D	Wadena,MN/Alexandria Blizzard (NAHL)
Cole Scattarelli	10		5'11"/190	D	Elk River,MN/Green Mountain Glades (EJHL)
Sean Schneider	10		6'1"/190	G	Toms River,NJ/Toms River (HS)
Tom Stunyo	09		5'10"/175	F	Grand Rpds,MN/Grand Rapids (HS)
Kyle Turner	09		5'10"/170	D	Hudson,WI/Hudson (HS)
Jimmy VanAsch	10		6'1"/190	D	Blaine,MN/Fairbanks Ice Dogs (NAHL)
Matt Vanvig	10		6'2"/200	G	Brooklyn Pk,MN/Sante Fe Roadrunners (NAHL)
Matt Zilles	09		6'0"/155	D	Lake St. Croix Bch,MN/Stillwater (HS)

ROSTER ANALYSIS (SCHOLARSHIPS - 0)

Class		Country		Last Team				
Fr	12	USA	26	US JR A	8	CDN JR A	1	ACHA
So	13	Canada	1	US JR B	4	CDN JR B		NJCAA
Jr	2	Europe		US PS	1	CDN PS		NCAA
Sr		Asia		US HS	12	CDN HS		USNDT
Gr		Other		US Midget	1	CDN Midget		Other

ADMISSIONS, ENROLLMENT & CAMPUS INFORMATION

Founded 1854	Average acceptance rate - 78 %	Steven Bjork - Admissions Director
Private, urban campus	Freshman financial aid - 78 %	Hamline University - Admissions Dept.
699 men / 1,191 women	Early decision application deadline - N/A	1536 Hewitt Avenue
Tuition, room & board - $ 31 K	Regular application deadline - Rolling	St. Paul, MN 55104-1284
Avg SAT - 1,153/Avg ACT - 24	Financial aid deadline - Mar 1	O 651.523.2207/ F 651.523.2458

www.hamline.edu | www.hamline.edu/hamline_info/athletics/index.html

HARVARD UNIVERSITY

Division 1

HOCKEY STAFF

HEAD COACH
Ted Donato *(Harvard '91)*

ASSISTANT COACHES
Sean McCann *(Harvard '94)*
Bobby Jay *(Merrimack '88)*
Bruce Irving *(Cornell '85)*

HOCKEY OFFICE
Harvard University - Murr Center
65 North Harvard Street
Cambridge, MA 02163
O 617.495.2418/ F 617.495.3475
donato@fas.harvard.edu

HOCKEY MEDIA CONTACT
Cassie Lawton - Hockey Info Director
Harvard University
65 North Harvard Street
Cambridge, MA 02163
O 617.495.2206/ F 617.495.2130
lawton@fas.harvard.edu

HOCKEY RINK
Bright Hockey Center (On Campus)
79 North Harvard Street
Cambridge, MA 02138
Size 204' x 87', Capacity 2,850
O 617.495.3775

ATHLETIC DIRECTOR
Bob L. Scalise - Athletic Director
Harvard University - Murr Center
65 North Harvard Street
Cambridge, MA 02163
O 617.495.2204/ F 617.495.9950
scalise@fas.harvard.edu

THE CRIMSON PLAYERS

Player	YB	GR	Ht/Wt	P	Hometown/Last Team
Alex Biega	88	10	5'11"/205	D	Montreal,QC/Salisbury (NEPSAC)
Sam Bozoian	87	10	6'0"/185	F	St. Charles,MO/Choate (NEPSAC)
Brendan Byrne	83	07	5'9"/180	F	Milton,MA/Milton (NEPSAC)
Jack Christian	87	09	6'2"/225	D	Wilton,CT/Taft (NEPSAC)
Mike Coskren	84	09	5'8"/165	G	Walpole,MA/St. Sebastian's (NEPSAC)
Nick Coskren	86	09	5'11"/190	F	Walpole,MA/St. Sebastian's (NEPSAC)
Kevin Du	85	07	5'8"/175	F	Spruce Gr,AB/St. Albert Saints (AJHL)
Paul Dufault	84	08	5'9"/175	F	Shrewsbury,MA/St. John's (PS)
Jim Fraser	87	09	5'11"/185	F	Port Huron,MI/Port Huron
Bill Keenan	86	09	6'1"/180	F	New York,NY/Collegiate (PS)
Chris Kelley	84	08	6'2"/200	D	Winston-Salem,NC/Deerfield (NEPSAC)
David MacDonald	85	08	6'4"/210	D	Halifax,NS/St. Paul's (NEPSAC)
Tyler Magura	85	08	6'1"/195	F	Fargo,ND/Lincoln Stars (USHL)
Ryan Maki	85	07	6'3"/215	F	Shelby Tsp,MI/Port Huron
Steve Mandes	85	07	5'11"/185	F	Doylestown,PA/USNDT (NAHL)
JD McCabe	85	08	6'3"/200	D	Jamison,PA/Taft (NEPSAC)
Brian McCafferty	86	09	6'0"/205	D	Lexington,MA/Belmont Hill (NEPSAC)
Alex Meintel	85	08	5'9"/180	F	Yarmouth,ME/Taft (NEPSAC)
Chad Morin	88	10	6'0"/210	D	Auburn,NY/North
Jon Pelle	86	08	5'8"/160	F	W Islip,NY/New York (EJHL)
Dylan Reese	84	07	6'1"/205	D	Pittsburgh,PA/Pittsburgh Forge (NAHL)
Kyle Richter	86	10	6'1"/185	G	Calgary,AB/Springbank (HS)
John Riley	88	10	5'11"/175	G	Lake Forest,IL/Loyola (PS)
Doug Rogers	88	10	6'1"/195	F	Watertown,MA/St. Sebastian's (NEPSAC)
Steve Rolecek	86	09	5'10"/190	F	Bedford,NH/Andover (NEPSAC)
Nick Snow	85	09	6'4"/210	F	Ipswich,MA/St. Paul's (NEPSAC)
Ian Tallett	87	10	6'2"/200	D	St. Louis,MO/Ladue
Mike Taylor	86	08	5'11"/180	F	Maple Gr,MN/Holy Angels (PS)
Justin Tobe	84	07	6'0"/175	G	Northville,MI/Michigan State (CCHA)
Dave Watters	84	08	6'4"/205	D	Eden Pr,MN/Des Moines Buccaneers (USHL)

ROSTER ANALYSIS (SCHOLARSHIPS - 0)

Class		Country		Last Team					
Fr	7	USA	26	US JR A	3	CDN JR A	1	ACHA	
So	8	Canada	4	US JR B	1	CDN JR B		NJCAA	
Jr	9	Europe		US PS	18	CDN PS	1	NCAA	1
Sr	6	Asia		US HS		CDN HS		USNDT	1
Gr		Other		US Midget		CDN Midget		Other	4

ADMISSIONS, ENROLLMENT & CAMPUS INFORMATION

Founded 1636
Private, urban campus
3,281 men / 3,281 women
Tuition, room & board - $ 38 K
Avg SAT - 1,460 /Avg 33

Average acceptance rate - 11 %
Freshman financial aid - 100 %
Early decision application deadline - N/A
Regular application deadline - Jan 1
Financial aid deadline - N/A

Marlyn McGrath Lewis - Admissions Dir.
Harvard University - Byerly Hall
8 Garden Street
Cambridge, MA 02163
O 617.495.1551/ F 617.495.0500

www.harvard.edu

www.gocrimson.collegesports.com

- 425 -

HOBART COLLEGE

HOCKEY
WEST

Division 3

HOCKEY STAFF

HEAD COACH
Mark Taylor *(Elmira '85)*

ASSISTANT COACH
Phil Roy *(Clarkson '00)*

HOCKEY OFFICE
Hobart College
Bristol Gymnasium
Geneva, NY 14456-3397
O 315.781.3539 / F 315.781.3570
mtaylor@hws.edu

HOCKEY MEDIA CONTACT
Ken DeBolt - Sports Info Director
Hobart College
295 Pulteney Street
Geneva, NY 14456-3397
O 315.781.3538 / F 315.781.3400
debolt@hws.edu

HOCKEY RINK
Geneva Rec. Complex (Off Campus)
666 South Exchange Street
Geneva, NY 14456
Size 200' x 85', Capacity 500
O 315.789.2277

ATHLETIC DIRECTOR
Michael Hanna - Athletic Director
Hobart College - Bristol Gymnasium
Geneva, NY 14456-3397
O 315.781.3565 / F 315.781.3570
hanna@hws.edu

STATESMEN PLAYERS

Player	YB	GR	Ht/Wt	P	Hometown/Last Team
Ryan Adler	84	09	6' 0"/175	D	Piscataway,NJ/Boston Bulldogs (AtJHL)
Gregory Alberti	88	10	6' 0"/195	F	Bernardsville,NJ/New Jersey Devils
Blake Bonham	86	10	6' 2"/190	F	Toronto,ON/Newmarket Hurricanes (OPJHL)
Marc Borden	84	07	6' 0"/200	F	Glenview,IL/Governor's (NEPSAC)
Conor Bradley	84	07	6' 1"/200	F	W Hartford,CT/Hill (PS)
Andrew Brennan	85	09	5'10"/200	D	Milford,MA/Tabor (NEPSAC)
Edward Brzek	85	08	5' 4"/135	F	Duxbury,MA/St. Sebastian's (NEPSAC)
Bobby Cahill	85	10	5'10"/190	F	Farmington Hls,MI/Cornwall Colts (CJHL)
David Casey	87	10	5'10"/180	F	Midway,MA/B B & N (NEPSAC)
Brian Cibelli	85	08	5' 9"/160	F	Liverpool,NY/Syracuse Stars (OPJHL)
Kirk Golden	84	09	5'10"/170	F	Vail,CO/Cleveland Barons (NAHL)
Bryant Harris	85	09	6' 1"/190	D	Plainfield,NH/Walpole Stars (EJHL)
Shawn Houde	85	08	5'11"/170	F	Manchester,NH/Brewster (NEPSAC)
Steffan Kollevoll	86	10	6' 3"/215	F	Easton,PA/Vermont (NEPSAC)
Aleksey Koval	85	10	5'10"/190	F	Kiev,Ukraine/Albany (NEPSAC)
Aaron Laycock	83	07	6' 1"/215	F	Barrie,ON/Lowell Loch Monsters (EJHL)
Keith Longo	85	09	5'10"/175	G	Hopedale,MA/Central Texas Blackhawks (NAHL)
Mike Manos	82	07	5' 7"/150	D	N Andover,MA/Green Mountain Glades (EJHL)
Mike McCarthy	84	07	5' 8"/175	F	Medfield,MA/Boston Harbor Wolves (EJHL)
Jason Merritt	85	09	5'10"/180	F	Chapel Hill,NC/Holderness (NEPSAC)
Dan Miller	87	10	5'10"/180	D	Massena,NY/Smiths Falls Bears (CJHL)
Mike O'Brien	87	10	5'10"/180	D	Franklin Lks,NJ/Tabor (NEPSAC)
Dimitri Papaevagelou	85	08	5'11"/190	G	Windham,NH/New Hampshire Monarchs (EJHL)
Trevor Pieri	84	08	6' 2"/195	G	Needham,MA/Pomfret (NEPSAC)
Mike Polsonetti	84	07	6' 2"/175	D	Lynn,MA/Pomfret (NEPSAC)
Michael Pruchniewski	86	09	6' 4"/220	F	Westwood,MA/Walpole Stars (EJHL)
Adam Scott	83	07	5'11"/180	F	Manchester,MA/Valley Warriors (EJHL)
Michael Steiner	86	09	5' 8"/160	D	Shaker Hgts,OH/Bridgewater Bandits (EJHL)
Jonathan Swift	84	07	6' 1"/210	F	Andover,MA/Lawrence (NEPSAC)
Drew Wadsworth	86	10	6' 2"/180	D	Arlington,VA/Tabor (NEPSAC)

ROSTER ANALYSIS (SCHOLARSHIPS - 0)

Class		Country		Last Team					
Fr	9	USA	27	US JR A	2	CDN JR A	4	ACHA	
So	8	Canada	2	US JR B	9	CDN JR B		NJCAA	
Jr	5	Europe	1	US PS	14	CDN PS		NCAA	
Sr	8	Asia		US HS		CDN HS		USNDT	
Gr		Other		US Midget		CDN Midget		Other	1

ADMISSIONS, ENROLLMENT & CAMPUS INFORMATION

Founded 1822	Average acceptance rate - 63 %	Mara O'Laughlin - Admissions Director
Private, urban I campus	Freshman financial aid - 91 %	Hobart College - 639 South Main
858 men / 967 women	Early decision application deadline - Nov 15	Geneva, NY 14456-3397
Tuition, room & board - $ 39 K	Regular application deadline - Feb 1	O 315.781.3622 / F 315.781.3560
Avg SAT - 1,180	Financial aid deadline - Feb 1	O 800.245.0100

www.hws.edu
www.hws.edu/statesmen/

COLLEGE OF HOLY CROSS

Division 1

HOCKEY STAFF

HEAD COACH
Paul Pearl *(Holy Cross '89)*

ASSISTANT COACHES
Albie O'Connell *(Boston University '99)*
Brian Akashian *(Holy Cross '01)*
John Binkoski *(Mass.-Amherst '74)*

HOCKEY OFFICE
College of Holy Cross - Hockey Office
1 College Street
Worcester, MA 01610-2395
O 508.793.2326/ F 508.793.2229
ppearl@holycross.edu

HOCKEY MEDIA CONTACT
Jim Wrobel - Hockey Info Director
College of Holy Cross
1 College Street
Worcester, MA 01610-2395
O 508.793.2583/ F 508.793.2309
jwrobel@holycross.edu

HOCKEY RINK
Hart Recreation Center (On Campus)
1 College Street
Worcester, MA 01610
Size 200' x 85', Capacity 1,600
O 508.793.2329

ATHLETIC DIRECTOR
Richard M. Regan - Athletic Director
College of Holy Cross
1 College Street
Worcester, MA 01610-2395
O 508.793.2571/ F 508.793.2309
rregan@holycross.edu

CRUSADERS PLAYERS

Player	YB	GR	Ht/Wt	P	Hometown/Last Team
Matt Burke	85	08	6' 0"/190	D	Milton,MA/Milton (NEPSAC)
Tyler Chestnut	85	10	6' 1"/190	G	Faribault,MN/Pembroke Lumber Kings (CJHL)
Ian Dams	86	10	6' 0"/200	G	Manotick,ON/Nepean Raiders (CJHL)
Marty Dams	84	09	5'11"/190	D	Manotick,ON/Gloucester Rangers (CJHL)
Ryan Driscoll	87	10	5'10"/180	F	Dorchester,MA/Thayer (NEPSAC)
Tanner Fogarty	83	07	6' 1"/200	F	McMurray,PA/Taft (NEPSAC)
Rob Forshner	86	10	5' 9"/170	F	Sundre,AB/Victoria Salsa (BCHL)
Brent Franklin	84	08	6' 2"/205	D	Grosse Pt Farms,MI/Oakville Blades (OPJHL)
Brian Gabriel	83	08	6' 1"/190	D	Kenai,AK/Wichita Falls Rustlers (AWHL)
Rob Godfrey	82	07	5'11"/175	D	Thunder Bay,ON/Aurora Tigers (OPJHL)
Brian Kolb	84	08	5'11"/175	F	Sandwich,MA/Tabor (NEPSAC)
Jon Landry	84	07	6' 2"/190	D	Lexington,MA/Nobles (NEPSAC)
Charlie Lockwood	85	09	6' 0"/185	G	Breckenridge,CO/Bridgewater Bandits (EJHL)
Peter Lorinser	88	10	5' 9"/165	F	Marquette,MI/Marquette Electricians (Midget AAA)
Kai Magnussen	84	09	5'10"/190	F	Okotoks,AB/Weyburn Red Wings (SJHL)
Shane McAdam	87	09	6' 0"/200	D	Hamilton,ON/Hamilton Red Wings (OPJHL)
Bryce Nantes	84	08	5'11"/175	F	Calgary,AB/Yorkton Terriers (SJHL)
Sean Nappo	83	07	6' 0"/175	F	Northville,MI/Bismarck Bobcats (NAHL)
Frank O'Grady	84	07	5' 7"/160	D	Kimberly,BC/Helena Bighorns (NAHL)
Bill Pinel	88	10	6' 0"/180	D	Third Lake,IL/Lake Forest (PS)
Dale Reinhardt	86	08	5' 9"/170	F	Livingston,NJ/Delbarton (PS)
Brodie Sheahan	86	10	5'10"/170	F	Lethbridge,AB/Salmon Arm Silverbacks (BCHL)
James Sixsmith	84	07	5' 9"/160	F	Alexandria,VA/Canterbury (NEPSAC)
Cal St. Denis	84	08	6' 0"/180	F	Freelton,ON/Hamilton Red Wings (OPJHL)
Dewey Thomson	86	09	6' 0"/185	F	Northbridge,MA/St. Paul's (NEPSAC)
Chris Trovato	84	08	5'10"/170	F	N Attleboro,MA/Nobles (NEPSAC)
Jim Tselikis	84	08	5'10"/180	F	Cape Elizabeth,ME/New Hampshire Monarchs (EJHL)
Matt Werry	83	08	6' 0"/190	F	Regina,SK/Notre Dame (PS)

ROSTER ANALYSIS (SCHOLARSHIPS - 11*)

Class		Country		Last Team					
Fr	7	USA	17	US JR A	3	CDN JR A	11	ACHA	
So	5	Canada	11	US JR B	2	CDN JR B		NJCAA	
Jr	10	Europe		US PS	10	CDN PS	1	NCAA	
Sr	6	Asia		US HS		CDN HS		USNDT	
Gr		Other		US Midget	1	CDN Midget		Other	

ADMISSIONS, ENROLLMENT & CAMPUS INFORMATION

Founded 1843	Average acceptance rate - 44 %	Ann Bowe McDermott-Admissions Director
Private, urban campus	Freshman financial rate - 100 %	College of Holy Cross
1,223 men / 1,495 women	Early decision application deadline - Dec 15	1 College Street
Tuition, room & board - $ 42 K	Regular application deadline - Jan 15	Worcester, MA 01610-2395
Avg SAT - 1,255	Financial aid deadline - Feb 1	O 508.793.2243/ F 508.793.3888

www.holycross.edu www.goholycross.com

This is Where Winning Teams Have Winning Dreams

At Courtyard by Marriott, up to 4 team members or fans can enjoy a spacious guest room, free HBO and ESPN, a swimming pool, whirlpool, exercise room, guest laundry, and dependable Courtyard service, for a very nice price. And everyone will enjoy our comfortable restaurant, featuring a delicious breakfast buffet. Team up with Courtyard the next time you travel!

Boston Westborough   Boston Marlborough

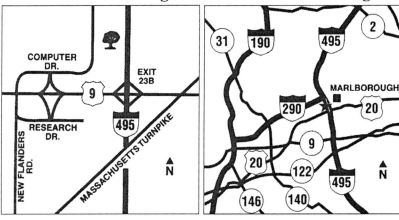

WESTBOROUGH, MASSACHUSETTS
3 Technology Drive • Westborough, MA 01581
(508) 836-4800 • Fax (508) 870-5577
800-321-2211

MARLBOROUGH, MASSACHUSETTS
75 Felton Street • Marlborough, MA 01752
(508) 480-0015 • Fax (508) 485-2242
800-321-2211

UNIVERSITY OF ILLINOIS - CHAMPAIGN

Division 1

HOCKEY STAFF

HEAD COACH
Chad Cassel *(Illinois '95)*

ASSISTANT COACHES
Darrin Trulock
Brett Duncan
Jim Rogers

HOCKEY OFFICE
Chad Cassel
305 West John
Champaign, IL 61820
O 217.369.4459 / F 217.333.1307
cassel@uiuc.edu

HOCKEY MEDIA CONTACT
Larry Kimball
510 East Scovill Street
Urbana, IL 61801
O 217.373.7226 / F 217.333.1307
H 217.328.6869
larrykimball99@hotmail.com

HOCKEY RINK
University of Illinois Ice Arena
406 East Amory
Champaign, IL 61820
O 217.333.2212 / F 217.333.1307
Size 200' x 115', Capacity 1,500

HOCKEY MANAGER
Travis Turngren - Dir. Hockey Operations

ILLINI PLAYERS

Player	YB	GR	Ht/Wt	P	Hometown/Last Team
Brad Bennett	85	08	5'11"/185	F	Palos Park,IL/Chicago Young Americans (Midget AAA)
Andy Betourne	86	09	5'11"/200	D	Hoffman Estates,IL/Barrington (HS)
Mike Burda	87	10	5'11"/165	G	Buffalo Grove,IL/Stevenson (HS)
Marshall Chubirka	84	07	5'11"/200	F	Crystal Lake,IL/Gilmour (PS)
Mike DeGeorge	84	07	5'8"/190	G	Wheeling,IL/Chicago Freeze (NAHL)
Mark Ergun	88	10	5'9"/145	F	Wood Dale,IL/Northwest Chargers (Midget AA)
Nick Fabbrini	85	08	5'11"/195	F	Forest Park,IL/Fenwick (HS)
Phil Gerber	83	07	5'10"/185	D	Highland Park,IL/Peoria Mustangs (CSHL)
Ricky Gomez	86	08	5'8"/175	D	Burr Ridge,IL/Chicago Flames (Midget AA)
Drew Heredia	86	10	6'0"/190	F	Wadsworth,IL/Chicago Mission (Midget AAA)
JJ Heredia	87	08	6'0"/160	F	Wadsworth,IL/Lake County Atoms (Midget AA)
Brad Hoelzer	87	10	6'0"/180	F	Batavia,IL/Waterloo Black Hawks (USHL)
Matt Jennings	88	10	6'1"/195	F	Chicago,IL/Chicago Steel (USHL)
Mike Kincaid	84	07	6'2"/210	F	Overland Park,KS/Kansas City Stars (Midget AA)
Johnny Liang	85	08	5'8"/170	F	Glenview,IL/Texarkana Bandits (NAHL)
Mike Mannina	84	09	5'9"/200	D	Schaumburg,IL/Springfield Junior Blues (NAHL)
Pat Mannina	86	09	5'10"/170	D	Schaumburg,IL/Springfield Junior Blues (NAHL)
Mark Myers	85	07	5'11"/185	D	Crystal Lake,IL/Crystal Lake Leafs (Midget AA)
Jason Nemeth	86	09	5'10"/175	F	Roanoke,TX/Chicago Mission (Midget AAA)
Alex Park	84	08	5'10"/180	F	Park Ridge,IL/Springfield Junior Blues (NAHL)
Jordan Pringle	87	09	6'0"/165	F	South Barrington,IL/Barrington (HS)
Joey Resch	86	08	5'6"/155	F	Las Vegas,NV/Shattuck-St. Mary's (PS)
Dave Schmitt	86	08	6'0"/210	D	Palatine,IL/Chicago Flames (Midget AA)
Alex Tauchen	84	07	6'0"/190	D	Villa Park,IL/Chicago Mission (Midget AAA)
Kevin Wicklin	86	08	5'10"/190	F	Chicago,IL/Chicago Young Americans (Midget AAA)

ROSTER ANALYSIS (SCHOLARSHIPS - 0)

Class		Country		Last Team				
Fr	5	USA	25	US JR A	7	CDN JR A		ACHA
So	5	Canada		US JR B	1	CDN JR B		NJCAA
Jr	9	Europe		US PS	4	CDN PS		NCAA
Sr	6	Asia		US HS	2	CDN HS		USNDT
Gr		Other		US Midget	11	CDN Midget		Other

ADMISSIONS, ENROLLMENT & CAMPUS INFORMATION

Founded 1868	Average acceptance rate - 68 %	Keith Marshall - Admissions Director
Public, urban campus	Freshman financial aid - 89 %	University of Illinois - Champaign
14,755 men / 14,176 women	Early decision application deadline - N/A	901 West Illinois
Tuition, room & board $ 15 K / $ 28 K	Regular application deadline - Jan 1	Urbana, IL 61801-3028
Avg SAT - 1,290 / Avg ACT - 28	Financial aid deadline - Mar 15	O 217.333.0302 / F 217.244.0903

www.uiuc.edu www.illinihockey.com

2007

COLLEGE / PREP SHOWCASE EVENTS

NATIONAL COLLEGIATE DEVELOPMENT CAMP
PRINCETON SPORTS CENTER
MONMOUTH JUNCTION, NEW JERSEY
JULY 15 - 22, 2007

NATIONAL PREP DEVELOPMENT CAMP
PRINCETON SPORTS CENTER
MONMOUTH JUNCTION, NEW JERSEY
JULY 15 - 22, 2007

PRE PREP SHOWCASE
SALEM ICENTER
SALEM, NEW HAMPSHIRE
AUGUST 2-5, 2007

HOCKEY NIGHT IN BOSTON - MIDWEST
ANN ARBOR ICE CUBE
ANN ARBOR, MICHIGAN
JUNE 21-23, 2007

HOCKEY NIGHT IN BOSTON - PACIFIC
GLACIAL GARDENS
LAKEWOOD, CALIFORNIA
JUNE 21-23, 2007

NATIONAL HOCKEY TRAINING
UNIVERSITY OF SOUTHERN MAINE
GORHAM, MAINE
JULY 2007

IOWA STATE UNIVERSITY

Division 1

HOCKEY STAFF

HEAD COACH
Dr. Alan J. Murdoch *(Iowa State)*

ASSISTANT COACHES
Chris Schmale
Marc Rogers
Joe Eisenman

HOCKEY OFFICE
Cyclone Hockey
B7A Industrial Education II
Iowa State University
Ames, IA 50011-3310
O 515.294.6164 / F 515.232.0307
C 515.290.0389
amurdoch@iastate.edu

HOCKEY MEDIA CONTACT
Shane Bast - Director of Marketing
sb1@iastate.edu

HOCKEY RINK
Iowa State Ice Arena (On Campus)
1507 Gateway Hills Park Drive
Ames, IA 50010
Size 200' x 85', Capacity 1,400
O 515.292.6835 / F 515.239.5355

HOCKEY DIRECTOR
Lisa Meshke - General Manager
lmeshke@iastate.edu

CYCLONES PLAYERS

Player	YB	GR	Ht/Wt	P	Hometown/Last Team
Bill Adolph		09	5'11"/185	F	St. Paul,MN/Wisconsin Mustangs (MnJHL)
Cody Aidala		10	5'9"/180	D	Davenport,IA/Valencia Vipers (WSHL)
Trent Baker		07	6'0"/200	G	Lincoln,RI/New England Coyotes (EJHL)
Derek Bol		10	6'4"/215	D	Lindenhurst,IL/Valencia Vipers (WSHL)
Jason Brown		07	5'7"/160	F	Waukee,IA/Des Moines (HS)
Josh Callander		10	6'2"/190	F	Mora,MN/Central Penn Panthers (MJHL)
Brent Cornelius		10	6'0"/170	D	Fairbanks,AK/Tri-City Storm (USHL)
Zach Hargis		08	6'4"/250	D	Madison,WI/Wisconsin-Eau Claire (NCHA)
Christian Johansson		08	5'10"/170	G	Goteborg,Sweden/Backen (SEL)
Brad Krueger		10	6'0"/185	F	Des Moines,IA/North Iowa Outlaws (NAHL)
Marc Lorence		10	6'3"/200	D	Ankeny,IA/North Iowa Outlaws (NAHL)
Peter Majkozak		10	5'10"/185	F	White Bear Lake,MN/Billings Bulls (NAHL)
Matt McLin		10	5'6"/225	D	Overland Pk,KS/Northwest Wisconsin Knights (MnJHL)
Geoff Miller		08	6'0"/195	G	Urbandale,IA/Des Moines (HS)
Adam Mueller		08	6'0"/200	D	Broomfield,CO/Wasilla Spirit (NAHL)
Mike Murtaugh		09	5'10"/195	F	Alexander,IA/Quad City Express (CSHL)
Shane Mytnik		09	5'10"/170	F	Bartlett,IL/Grand Rapids Owls (CSHL)
Roch Naert		10	6'1"/200	D	Urbandale,IA/Des Moines Buccaneers (USHL)
Aaron Neville		09	5'10"/200	F	Shakopee,MN/Holy Angels (PS)
Mike Paulsen		08	6'3"/215	F	Mason City,IA/Mason City (HS)
Jayson Peterson		08	6'0"/180	F	Bemidji,MN/Minnesota Ice Hawks (MnJHL)
Allen Raushel		08	6'2"/200	F	Cloquet,MN/Cloquet (HS)
Jeremy Stegall		08	6'3"/210	F	Joliet,IL/Banff (PS)
Rob Tauer		07	6'1"/225	F	Sleepy Eye,MN/Portland Pioneers (NPJHL)
Matt Verdoni		07	5'10"/175	D	Lindenhurst,IL/Chicago Force (CSHL)
Josh Westbrook		09	6'0"/185	D	Laramie,WY/Minnesota Ice Hawks (MnJHL)

ROSTER ANALYSIS (SCHOLARSHIPS - 0)

Class		Country		Last Team					
Fr	9	USA	25	US JR A	6	CDN JR A		ACHA	
So	5	Canada		US JR B	12	CDN JR B		NJCAA	
Jr	8	Europe	1	US PS	1	CDN PS	1	NCAA	1
Sr	4	Asia		US HS	4	CDN HS		USNDT	
Gr		Other		US Midget		CDN Midget		SEL	1

ADMISSIONS, ENROLLMENT & CAMPUS INFORMATION

Founded 1858
Public, small town campus
11,756 men / 9,237 women
Tuition, room & board $ 12 K / $ 22 K
Avg SAT 1,210 / Avg ACT - 25

Average acceptance rate - 90 %
Freshman financial aid - 83 %
Early decision application deadline - N/A
Regular application deadline - Aug 1
Financial aid deadline - Mar 1

Phil Caffrey - Admissions Director
Iowa State University
Alumni Hall #100
Ames, IA 50011-2011
O 515.294.1088 / F 515.294.1088

Iowa State University

Cyclone Hockey

- Iowa State combines outstanding academics with hard-hitting and exciting hockey competition to create opportunities for student-athletes.

- The Cyclones won the American Collegiate Hockey Association National Tournament in 1992.

- Iowa State University, which competes in the tough Central States Collegiate Hockey League, compliments its schedule against national and international opponents. Within the CSCHL, the Cyclones face the University of Michigan-Dearborn, The University of Illinois, Marquette University, Wisconsin-Whitewater, Eastern Michigan University and Purdue.

- The majority of ISU hockey games are played in the Ames/ISU Ice Arena, which also serves as the Cyclone's practice arena. Most home games are sell-outs

- Academically speaking, ISU is one of the most highly regarded institutions in North America. The school offers over 150 programs of study taught by an award winning collection of instructors, ISU's land grant campus is known for its landscape and beauty, and its student population in excess of 25,000 is considered friendly and diverse. Tuition is very reasonable when compared to other Midwestern Universities and private colleges.

For Further Information Contact
Al Murdoch
at 515.294.4980
or visit our website at www.iastate.edu/~hockey/

JOHNSON & WALES UNIVERSITY

HOCKEY
NORTHEAST

Division 3

HOCKEY STAFF

HEAD COACH
Erik Noack *(RIT '98)*

ASSISTANT COACHES
Kevin Conway *(Rhode Island Coll. '97)*
Garth Noack *(Johnson & Wales '04)*

HOCKEY OFFICE
Johnson & Wales University
8 Abbott Park Place
Providence, RI 02903
O 401.598.1636/ F 401.598.1465
enoack@jwu.edu

HOCKEY MEDIA CONTACT
Daniel Booth - Sports Info Director
Johnson & Wales University
8 Abbott Park Place
Providence, RI 02903
O 401.598.1632/ F 401.598.1465
daniel.booth@jwu.edu

HOCKEY RINK
Schneider Arena (Off Campus)
Huxley Avenue
Providence, RI 02918
Size 200' x 85', Capacity 3,030
O 401.865.2168

ATHLETIC DIRECTOR
John Parente - Athletic Director
Johnson & Wales University
8 Abbott Park Place
Providence, RI 02903
O 401.598.1604/ F 401.598.1465
john.parente@jwu.edu

WILDCATS PLAYERS

Player	YB	GR	Ht/Wt	P		Hometown/Last Team
Charlie Bacon	85	08	6' 0"/185	G		Hudson,MA/Salem Ice Dogs (EmJHL)
Tyler Bickford	84	09	6' 1"/200	D		Concord,NH/Laconia Leafs (AtJHL)
Colin Brophy	84	07	5'11"/170	D		Medford,NJ/Medford (Midget AAA)
Andrew Buchanan	86	09	5'10"/170	F		Harrisville,RI/Hill (PS)
Tim Campbell	87	10	6' 0"/195	G		Weymouth,MA/Weymouth (HS)
Zach Cobb	85	07	5'11"/180	F		Dover,NH/Dover (HS)
John Curley	85	07	6' 4"/205	D		Chalfont,PA/Philadelphia Flyers (MJHL)
Adam Frew	84	08	5'11"/170	F		Concord,NH/Laconia Leafs (AtJHL)
Brian Goetz	84	09	6' 3"/200	D		Marlton,NJ/New Jersey Jaguars (Midget A)
Dan Guariglio	87	09	5' 7"/170	F		Harwich,MA/Harwich (HS)
Broan Hazen	88	10	5'11"/190	G		Manchester,CT/Manchester (HS)
Craig Houlr	84	10	5' 9"/160	F		Burrillville,RI/Portland Pirates (AtJHL)
Ryan Jacobs	83	08	5'11"/175	F		Derby,VT/Laconia Leafs (AtJHL)
Jakub Kubrak	85	08	6' 1"/195	D		New York,NY/National Sports (PS)
John Madsen	86	10	6' 2"/210	D		Somers ,CT/New England Falcons (EJHL)
Kevin Marchesi	86	10	5' 9"/170	F	S	Portland,ME/New Hampshire Monarchs (EJHL)
Matt McGilvary	84	08	5'10"/180	F		Rochester,NH/Laconia Leafs (AtJHL)
DJ McNaughton	87	10	5'10"/190	F		Hollowell,ME/Portland Pirates (MJHL)
Brian Noiles	85	09	6' 0"/180	G		Burlington,MA/Boston Harbor Wolves (EJHL)
Dave Notartomaso	84	09	5'10"/180	F		Winchester,MA/Boston Harbor Wolves (EJHL)
Mike O'Malley	85	09	5'10"/185	D		Woonsocket,RI/Boston Harbor Wolves (EJHL)
Stephen Pfeiffer	86	10	5'10"/180	F		Queens,NY/Hartford Wolfpack (AtJHL)
Shane Poulin	86	10	6' 2"/200	D		Concord,NH/Northern Mass Cyclones (AtJHL)
Robert Rambone	85	09	6' 3"/205	F		Burrillville,RI/Kents Hill (NEPSAC)
Shawn Roach	85	08	5'11"/185	F		Grapevine,TX/Connecticut Whalers (IJHL)
Jeff Spencer	86	10	6' 2"/215	D		Brentwood,NH/Valley Warriors (EJHL)

ROSTER ANALYSIS (SCHOLARSHIPS - 0)

Class		Country		Last Team				
Fr	9	USA	26	US JR A		CDN JR A		ACHA
So	8	Canada		US JR B	17	CDN JR B		NJCAA
Jr	6	Europe		US PS	3	CDN PS		NCAA
Sr	3	Asia		US HS	4	CDN HS		USNDT
Gr		Other		US Midget	2	CDN Midget		Other

ADMISSIONS, ENROLLMENT & CAMPUS INFORMATION

Founded 1914
Private, urban campus
4,346 men / 4,900 women
Tuition, room & board - $ 29 K
Avg SAT - 970

Average acceptance rate - 76 %
Freshman financial aid - 66 %
Early decision application deadline - N/A
Regular application deadline - rolling
Financial aid deadline - N/A

Ken DiSaia - Admissions Director
Johnson & Wales University
8 Abbott Park Place
Providence, RI 02903-3703
O 401.598.2310/ F 401.598.2948

www.jwu.edu

www.jwu.edu/prov/athletics/

- 434 -

KENT STATE UNIVERSITY

EST. 1991

Division 1

HOCKEY STAFF	ICE FLASHES PLAYERS

HOCKEY STAFF

HEAD COACH
Curtis Carr

ASSISTANT COACH
Zac Desjardins
Jim Underwood

HOCKEY OFFICE
Curt Carr
PO Box 1013
Kent, OH 44240
O 330.221.3093
kenthockey@aol.com

HOCKEY MEDIA CONTACT

HOCKEY RINK
Kent State Ice Arena
Kent, OH 44242
O 330.672.2415
200' x 85' - Capacity 1,500

HOCKEY MANAGER
Christian Wilk - General Manager
O 330.221.4411
homestyle8@aol.com

ICE FLASHES PLAYERS

Player	YB GR Ht/Wt	P	Hometown/Last Team
Matt Androne	09 5'9"/150	F	North Olmsted,OH/SUNY-Brockport (SUNYAC)
Dave Bruder	10 6'0"/175	F	Parma,OH/Cleveland Lumberjacks (CSHL)
Kye Budziszewski	10 5'10"/165	D	Bethel Park,PA/Bethel Park (HS)
Jon Canniff	09 6'0"/195	F	Clarkston,MI/Rochester Americans (EmJHL)
Nick DiLorenzo	09 5'10"/180	D	Waterford,NY/Capitol District Selects (EJHL)
Kyle Everett	08 5'10"/170	D	Skaneateles Falls,NY/Broome (NJCAA)
Brian Gahagan	08 6'0"/165	D	Batavia,NY/Capitol District Selects (EJHL)
Greg Goldkind	08 6'0"/145	F	Olney,MD/Broome (NJCAA)
Ryan Gregory	10 5'9"/165	G	Novi,MI/Peoria Mustangs (CSHL)
Chris Hourigan	09 6'0"/190	F	Hudson,OH/Cleveland Lumberjacks (CSHL)
Rob MacInnes	08 5'9"/160	F	Indianapolis,IN/Indianapolis Checkers (Midget AA)
John Mihalik	07 6'0"/185	F	Strongsville,OH/Strongsville (HS)
Jon Moser	09 6'4"/190	D	Columbus,OH/Columbus Blue Jackets (CSHL)
TJ Murphy	10 5'10"/175	F	North Olmsted,OH/North Olmstead (HS)
Ryan Nawrocki	09 5'10"/175	F	Chicago,IL/Chicago Force (CSHL)
Mike Nelson	09 5'10"/175	F	Fredonia,NY/Wheatfield Blades (GHJHL))
Kyle Nova	09 5'9"/145	G	Whitby,ON/Ajax Axemen (OPJHL)
Jason O'Bannon	08 5'10"/185	F	North Royalton,OH/Cleveland Lumberjacks (CSHL)
Brad Puchmeyer	10 6'0"/175	D	Grafton,OH/Midview (HS)
Derek Purvis	08 6'2"/250	D	Pittsburgh,PA/Syracuse Crunch (OPJHL)
Jeff Reed	10 5'9"/155	G	CranberryTownship,PA/Willmar (HS)
Nick Robillard	09 6'0"/190	D	Rochester,NY/Rochester Americans (EmJHL)
Andrew Schmidt	08 5'10"/170	F	Independence,OH/Padua (PS)
Carl Seitz	10 6'2"/180	D	Niles,MI/Marian (PS)
Stu Smith	09 6'1"/200	F	Cincinnati,OH/Quad City Express (CSHL)
John Stefani	09 6'1"/230	F	Albany,NY/Capitol District Selects (EJHL)
Wolff Volet	08 6'0"/185	F	Houston,TX/Cleveland Lumberjacks (CSHL)
Kurt Voss-Hoynes	08 6'3"/205	D	Moreland Hills,OH/Thornhill Islanders (OPJHL)
Matt Widing	09 5'11"/175	F	Chagrin Falls,OH/Cleveland Lumberjacks (CSHL)

ROSTER ANALYSIS (SCHOLARSHIPS - 0)

Class		Country		Last Team					
Fr	7	USA	28	US JR A		CDN JR A	2	ACHA	
So	12	Canada	1	US JR B	16	CDN JR B		NJCAA	2
Jr	9	Europe		US PS	2	CDN PS		NCAA	1
Sr	1	Asia		US HS	5	CDN HS		USNDT	
Gr		Other		US Midget	1	CDN Midget		Other	

ADMISSIONS, ENROLLMENT & CAMPUS INFORMATION

Founded 1910
Public, suburban campus
6,912 men / 11,770 women
Tuition, room & board $ 14 K / $ 21 K
Avg SAT - 1,020 / Avg ACT - 22

Average acceptance rate - 92 %
Freshman financial aid - 55 %
Early decision application deadline - N/A
Regular application deadline - May 1
Financial aid deadline - Mar 1

Nancy DellaVecchia - Admissions Dir.
Kent State University
P.O. Box 5190
Kent, Ohio 44242-0001
O 330.672.2444 / F 330.672.2499

www.kent.edu

www.kentstatehockey.com

LAKE FOREST COLLEGE

Division 3

HOCKEY STAFF

HEAD COACH
Tony Fritz *(Wisconsin-Milwaukee)*

ASSISTANT COACHES
Chris Gallager *(Lake Forest '01)*
Ken Klein

HOCKEY OFFICE
Lake Forest College
Alumni Memorial Fieldhouse
555 North Sheridan Road
Lake Forest, IL 60045-2399
O 847.735.5294/ F 847.735.6290
fritz@lakeforest.edu

HOCKEY MEDIA CONTACT
Mike Wajerski - Sports Info Director
Lake Forest College
555 North Sheridan Road
Lake Forest, IL 60045-2399
O 847.735.6054/ F 847.735.6299
wajerski@lakeforest.edu

HOCKEY RINK
Alumni Fieldhouse (On Campus)
555 North Sheridan Road
Lake Forest, IL 60045-2399
Size 200' x 85', Capacity 1,000
O 847.735.6067

ATHLETIC DIRECTOR
Jackie Slaats - Athletic Director
Lake Forest College
Lake Forest, IL 60045-2399
O 847.735.5290/ F 847.735.6290
slaats@lakeforest.edu

FORESTERS PLAYERS

Player	YB GR Ht/Wt	P	Hometown/Last Team
Bobby Alderman	09 6'5"/190	F	Bellaire,TX/Northern Mass Cyclones (AtJHL)
Petter Anderson	10 6'0"/180	D	Nybro,Sweden/Springfield Blues (NAHL)
Jeff Birr	09 5'11"/185	F	Markdale,ON/Pickering Panthers (OPJHL)
Scott Campbell	09 6'3"/190	G	Bloomfield,ON/Elmira Sugar Kings (MWJHL)
Tyler Canal	07 5'8"/170	F	Thunder Bay,ON/Stratford Cullitons (MWJHL)
Matt Forsyth	07 6'7"/240	F	Calgary,AB/Calgary Royals (AJHL)
Stan Galkin	09 6'0"/195	D	Bellmore,NY/Gunnery (NEPSAC)
Nick Ghidina	10 5'10"/210	D	Pekin,IL/Wichita Falls Wildcats (NAHL)
Greg Ihnken	07 5'9"/200	F	Peoria,IL/Chicago Freeze (NAHL)
Chris Jackson	09 6'0"/185	D	Acworth,GA/Springfield Spirit (NAHL)
Mike Kneeland	09 5'11"/195	F	Calgary,AB/Calgary Royals (AJHL)
Brandon Kohuch	09 5'11"/175	G	Windsor,ON/Chatham Maroons (WOJHL)
Brian Lee	08 5'10"/195	F	Toronto,ON/Calgary Royals (AJHL)
Adam Love	10 5'11"/190	F	Durham,ON/Elmira Sugar Kings (MWJHL)
Graham Melbourne	07 6'1"/200	D	Belleville,ON/Trenton Sting (OPJHL)
Peter Morrison	09 6'0"/185	F	Roseville,MN/Roseville (HS)
Blake O'Keefe	08 6'0"/215	F	Almonte,ON/Gloucester Rangers (CJHL)
Matt Oke	09 6'1"/210	D	St. Lambert,QC/Nepean Raiders (CJHL)
Joe Papineau	09 6'0"/190	D	Stoney Pointe,ON/Kitchener Dutchmen (MWJHL)
Chris Rashotte	10 5'11"/185	F	Tweed,ON/Kanata Stallions (CJHL)
Kevin Russette	08 5'11"/190	D	Amherstburg,ON/Leamington Flyers (WOJHL)
Matt Schoepflin	09 5'11"/160	F	Arvada,CO/Culver (PS)
Will Stoner	10 5'10"/180	F	Kenosha,WI/Capital District Selects (EJHL)
Justin Taylor	10 6'1"/170	F	Guifer,CT/Walpole Stars (EJHL)
Chris Thiess	10 6'0"/195	F	Naperville,IL/Kingston Voyageurs (OPJHL)
Adam Tobias	08 5'10"/170	F	Rockford,IL/Robert Morris (CHA)
Chris Wilson	09 6'1"/185	F	Bloomfield Hls,MI/Cornwall Colts (CJHL)

ROSTER ANALYSIS (SCHOLARSHIPS - 0)

Class		Country		Last Team					
Fr	7	USA	12	US JR A	4	CDN JR A	10	ACHA	
So	12	Canada	14	US JR B	3	CDN JR B	6	NJCAA	
Jr	4	Europe	1	US PS	2	CDN PS		NCAA	1
Sr	4	Asia		US HS	1	CDN HS		USNDT	
Gr		Other		US Midget		CDN Midget		Other	

ADMISSIONS, ENROLLMENT & CAMPUS INFORMATION

Founded 1857
Private, suburban campus
531 men / 830 women
Tuition, room & board - $33 K
Avg SAT - 1,175/Avg ACT - 26

Average acceptance rate - 63 %
Freshman financial aid - 100 %
Early decision application deadline - Jan 1
Regular application deadline - Mar 1
Financial aid deadline - Mar 1

Bill Motzer - Admissions Director
Lake Forest College
555 North Sheridan Road
Lake Forest, IL 60045-2399
O 847.735.5000/ F 847.735.6271

www.lfc.edu   www.lakeforest.edu/foresters/

LAKE SUPERIOR STATE UNIVERSITY

Division 1

HOCKEY STAFF

HEAD COACH
Jim Roque *(Lake Superior State '87)*

ASSISTANT COACHES
Tim Christian *(Ferris State '95)*
Joe Shawhan *(Lake Superior State '87)*

HOCKEY OFFICE
Lake Superior State - Norris Center
650 West Easterday Avenue
Sault Sainte Marie, MI 49783-1699
O 906.635.2611 / F 906.635.2751
jroque@lssu.edu

HOCKEY MEDIA CONTACT
Linda Bouvet - Sports Info Director
Lake Superior State
650 West Easterday Avenue
Sault Sainte Marie, MI 49783-1699
O 906.635.2601 / F 906.635.2753
lbouvet@lssu.edu

HOCKEY RINK
Taffey Abel Ice Arena (On Campus)
650 West Easterday Avenue
Sault Sainte Marie, MI 49783-1699
Size 200' x 85', Capacity 4,000
O 906.635.2601

ATHLETIC DIRECTOR
Bill Crawford - Athletic Director
Lake Superior State - Norris Center
Sault Sainte Marie, MI 49783-1699
O 906.635.2878 / F 906.635.2753
bcrawford@lssu.edu

LAKERS PLAYERS

Player	YB	GR	Ht/Wt	P	Hometown/Last Team
Pat Aubry	85	10	6'1"/185	F	Ottawa,ON/Kanata Stallions (CJHL)
Ryan Baird	85	10	5'10"/175	D	Thunder Bay,ON/Fort William North Stars (SIJHL)
Barnabas Birkeland	83	07	6'0"/195	D	Buffalo,MN/Soo Thunderbirds (NOJHL)
Jason Blain	83	08	5'11"/200	F	Sault Ste. Marie,MI/Northeastern (HEA)
Trent Campbell	82	07	5'10"/195	F	Beauval,SK/La Ronge Ice Wolves (SJHL)
Mitch Edmondson	88	10	6'0"/175	G	Traverse City,MI/West (HS)
Dan Eves	86	08	6'2"/210	F	Lake Orion,MI/Texarkana Bandits (NAHL)
Michael George	85	10	6'1"/195	F	Battleford,SK/North Battleford North Stars (SJHL)
Marty Gurnoe	86	09	6'1"/200	D	Sault Ste. Marie,MI/Soo Indians (NAHL)
Justin Gutwald	83	08	6'0"/190	D	Grosse Pt,MI/Soo Indians (NAHL)
Simon Gysbers	87	10	6'4"/185	D	Richmond Hill,ON/Stouffville Spirit (OPJHL)
Pat Inglis	85	10	6'4"/215	G	Calgary,AB/Calgary (AJHL)
Jeff Jakaitis	83	07	5'10"/175	G	Rochester,MN/Waterloo Blackhawks (USHL)
Steven Kaunisto	86	10	5'11"/190	D	Sault Ste. Marie,MI/Cedar Rapids RoughRiders (USHL)
Matt Martello	87	10	6'0"/205	F	N York,ON/Vaughan Vipers (OPJHL)
Steven Olesky	86	09	6'0"/195	D	Chesterfield,MI/Traverse City North Stars (NAHL)
Dominic Osman	82	07	6'0"/200	F	Dearborn,MI/Soo Indians (NAHL)
Nathan Perkovich	85	10	6'5"/200	F	Canton,MI/Chicago Steel (USHL)
Jeffrey Rainville	84	07	5'11"/190	F	Blind River,ON/Soo Thunderbirds (NOJHL)
Troy Schwab	84	09	5'7"/200	F	Kindersly,SK/Kindersley Klippers (SJHL)
John Scrymgeour	86	10	6'1"/200	F	Pickering,ON/St. Michael's (PS)
Nik Sellers	86	10	5'10"/180	F	Plymouth,MI/Cedar Rapids RoughRiders (USHL)
Josh Sim	84	09	5'11"/190	F	Saskatoon,SK/Kindersley Klippers (SJHL)
Derek Smith	84	08	6'2"/200	D	Belleville,ON/Wellington Dukes (OPJHL)
Derek R. Smith	83	07	6'0"/210	F	Elmvale,ON/Estevan Bruins (SJHL)
Nathan Ward	81	07	6'0"/200	F	Edmonton,AB/Weyburn Red Wings (SJHL)
Matt Wheeler	85	09	6'2"/205	D	Arcola,SK/Weyburn Red Wings (SJHL)
Vince Wheeler	84	09	6'0"/185	G	Clearwater,MN/Bancroft Hawks (OPJHL)

ROSTER ANALYSIS (SCHOLARSHIPS - 18)

Class		Country		Last Team					
Fr	11	USA	13	US JR A	9	CDN JR A	16	ACHA	
So	6	Canada	15	US JR B		CDN JR B		NJCAA	
Jr	4	Europe		US PS		CDN PS	1	NCAA	1
Sr	7	Asia		US HS	1	CDN HS		USNDT	
Gr		Other		US Midget		CDN Midget		Other	

ADMISSIONS, ENROLLMENT & CAMPUS INFORMATION

Founded 1946
Public, small town campus
1,487 men / 1,266 women
Tuition, room & board - $13 K / $19 K
Avg SAT - 1,015 / Avg ACT - 21

Average acceptance rate - 85 %
Freshman financial aid - 78 %
Early decision application deadline - N/A
Regular application deadline - Aug 15
Financial aid deadline - Feb 21

Kevin Pollock - Admissions Director
Lake Superior State - Fletcher Center
Sault Sainte Marie, MI 49783-1699
O 906.635.2231 / F 906.635.2111

www.lssu.edu

lssulakers.collegesports.com/

LAWRENCE UNIVERSITY

Division 3

HOCKEY STAFF

HEAD COACH
Mike Szkodzinski *(St. Norbert '00)*

ASSISTANT COACHES
Scott Jewett *(St. Norbert '99)*
Ernie Thorp

HOCKEY OFFICE
Lawrence University - Development Ofc.
PO Box 599
Appleton, WI 54912-0599
O 920.832.7348 / F 920.832.7349
michael.w.szkodzinski@lawrence.edu

HOCKEY MEDIA CONTACT
Joe Vanden Acker - Sports Info Director
Lawrence University
Brokaw Hall #122
PO Box 599
Appleton, WI 54912-0599
O 920.832.6878 / F 920.832.6783
joseph.m.vandenacker@lawrence.edu

HOCKEY RINK
Appleton Family Ice Ctr. (Off Campus)
1717 East Witzke Boulevard
Appleton, WI 54911
Size 200' x 85', Capacity 500
O 920.830.7679

ATHLETIC DIRECTOR
Robert Beeman - Athletic Director
Lawrence University - Athletic Dept.
PO Box 599
Appleton, WI 54912-0559
O 920.832.7033 / F 920.832.7349
robert.l.beeman@lawrence.edu

VIKINGS PLAYERS

Player	YB	GR	Ht/Wt	P	Hometown/Last Team
Adam Brand	09		6' 1"/200	D	Antigo,WI/Bay State Breakers (EJHL)
Pat Greeley	10		6' 1"/175	G	Marquette,MI/Laconia Leafs (AtJHL)
Ted Greeley	09		6' 0"/180	D	Marquette,MI/Laconia Leafs (AtJHL)
Marc Howe	10		5'11"/185	F	Cedarburg,WI/Bozeman Icedogs (NAHL)
Andrew Isaac	07		5' 9"/170	G	Mississauga,ON/St. Michael's (PS)
Jesse Jacobs	09		5'11"/170	F	Pacifica,CA/San Jose Sharks (Midget AAA)
Nick Jennette	09		5' 7"/165	F	Grand Rpds,MI/Lansing Pride (Midget AAA)
Brian Kennihan	08		6' 1"/180	F	Valencia,PA/Butte Rough Riders (NPJHL)
Aaron LaFave	09		5'10"/185	F	Centerville,OH/Shattuck-St. Mary's (PS)
Kalle Larsson	07		6' 2"/205	D	Gothenburg,Sweden/Dayton Gems (CEHL)
Chris Lawson	09		6' 1"/195	F	Monument,CO/Pine Creek (HS)
Andrew Litchfield	09		6' 2"/160	G	Grayslake,IL/Barrington Red Wings (Midget AA)
Austin Montgomery	08		5'10"/180	D	Grand Rpds,MI/Grand Rapids Owls (CSHL)
David Olynyk	07		5'11"/185	F	Burlington,ON/Pearson (PS)
Josh Peterson	08		5'11"/185	D	Duluth,MN/Helena Bighorns (NAHL)
Blake Royle	09		5'10"/195	D	Burlington,ON/Full Stride Flyers (EmJHL)
Jon Sacks	10		5' 7"/175	F	Cherry Hill,NJ/Laconia Leafs (AtJHL)
Joe Searl	07		5' 8"/185	F	Fond du Lac,WI/Central Texas Blackhawks (NAHL)
Billy Siers	10		6' 2"/210	F	Mt Prospect,IL/Boston Bulldogs (AtJHL)
Peter Stafford	09		5'11"/195	D	Madison,WI/Green Mountain Glades (EJHL)
Masa Takahashi	10		5' 8"/180	F	Kanagawa,Japan/Shattuck-St. Mary's (PS)
Evan Thornton	07		6' 0"/170	F	Colorado Spgs,CO/Cheyenne Mountain (HS)
Pat Tuohy	08		6' 2"/190	D	Wrentham,MA/Rivers (NEPSAC)
Neil Wallace	08		6' 0"/180	F	Presque Isle,WI/Boston Blackhawks (IJHL)
Charles Zieserl	10		5'11"/210	D	Ashburnham,MA/Cushing (NEPSAC)

ROSTER ANALYSIS (SCHOLARSHIPS - 0)

Class		Country		Last Team				
Fr	6	USA	20	US JR A	3	CDN JR A		ACHA
So	9	Canada	3	US JR B	11	CDN JR B		NJCAA
Jr	5	Europe	1	US PS	4	CDN PS	2	NCAA
Sr	5	Asia	1	US HS	12	CDN HS		USNDT
Gr		Other		US Midget	3	CDN Midget		Other

ADMISSIONS, ENROLLMENT & CAMPUS INFORMATION

Founded 1847	Average acceptance rate - 66 %	Michael Thorp - Admissions Director
Private, urban campus	Freshman financial aid - 100 %	Lawrence University - Admissions Dept.
591 men / 753 women	Early decision application deadline - Nov 15	PO Box 599
Tuition, room & board - $ 34 K	Regular application deadline - Jan 15	Appleton, WI 54912-0559
Avg SAT - 1,255 / Avg ACT - 28	Financial aid deadline - Mar 15	O 920.832.6500 / F 920.832.6782

www.lawrence.edu

www.lawrence.edu/athletics/hockey

LEBANON VALLEY COLLEGE

WEST

Division 3

HOCKEY STAFF

HEAD COACH
Ted Russell *(New Hampshire)*

ASSISTANT COACHES
Mitch Lamoureaux
Tom Draper

HOCKEY OFFICE
Lebanon Valley College - Athletics Dept.
Lynch Hall 001-A
Annville, PA 17003-0501
O 717.867.6258 / F 717.867.6019
erussell@lvc.edu

HOCKEY MEDIA CONTACT
Braden Snyder - Sports Info Director
Lebanon Valley College
Laughlin 205
Annville, PA 17003-0501
O 717.867.6033 / F 717.867.6035
bsnyder@lvc.edu

HOCKEY RINK
Hersheypark Arena (Off Campus)
Hershey, PA
200' x 84', Capacity 7,225

ATHLETIC DIRECTOR
Kathy Tierney - Athletic Director
Lebanon Valley College
Arnold Sports Center
Annville, PA 17003-0501
O 717.867.6261 / F 717.867.6990
tierney@lvc.edu

FLYING DUTCHMEN PLAYERS

Player	YB	GR	Ht/Wt	P	Hometown/Last Team
Spiros Anastas	85	10	5'11"/200	F	Mississauga,ON/Huntsville Muskota Otters (OPJHL)
Alex Beatrice	83	07	5'11"/185	F	Randolph,NJ/Apple Valley (EJHL)
Matlock Bobechko	88	10	6'1"/185	D	Orangeville,ON/Orangeville Crushers (MWJHL)
Kelly Curl	86	09	5'10"/170	F	Mcleansville,NC/Hill (PS)
Eli Facchinei	86	09	6'4"/210	F	Atco,NJ/Gunnery (NEPSAC)
Jarred Frey	83	09	6'4"/200	F	Etters,PA/SUNY Fredonia (SUNYAC)
Scott Gartzke	86	10	5'8"/165	D	Camp Hill,PA/National Sports (PS)
Nick Harris	86	09	5'10"/150	F	Oakfield,NJ/Rochester Americans (EmJHL)
Justin Hastings		09	5'10"/185	D	Dauphin,PA/New York Bobcats (AtJHL)
Ryan Horgan	87	10	6'0"/185	D	Collegeville,PA/Gunnery (NEPSAC)
Bert Malloy	86	09	6'1"/180	D	Cheshire,CT/Hartford Wolfpack (AtJHL)
Ryan Merritt	84	07	6'3"/175	D	Whitesboro,NY/Lawrence (NEPSAC)
Casey Mignone	88	10	5'11"/160	F	Ramsey,NJ/Ramsey (HS)
Aaron Miller	87	10	5'11"/170	G	Toronto,ON/Huntsville Muskota Otters (OPJHL)
Andrew Murphy	85	09	6'2"/205	F	Auburn,MA/Avon (NEPSAC)
Andy Orsini	86	10	5'9"/165	F	Rochester,NY/South Grenville Rangers (EOJHL)
Rocky Romanella	87	10	5'9"/165	F	Cumming,GA/Gunnery (NEPSAC)
Pete Rossi	86	08	5'8"/190	F/D	Hamilton Sq,NJ/Princeton (NEPSAC)
Matt Rowe	84	09	5'11"/185	F	Newmarket,ON/Newmarket Hurricanes (OPJHL)
Anthony Scales	85	08	6'3"/205	D	Swarthmore,PA/Philadelphia Little Flyers (MJHL)
Rob Scales	83	08	6'3"/205	F	Swarthmore,PA/Borderland Thunder (SIJHL)
Kolja Schneider	83	08	6'2"/210	D	Oberursel,Germany/St. Scholastica (MIAC)
Pat Skehan	86	10	5'10"/175	F	York,PA/National Sports (PS)
EJ Smith	84	09	6'0"/195	D	Cranberry Twnsp,PA/Central Texas Marshals (NAHL)
Jeffrey Smith	84	07	5'11"/180	F	Fredericton,NB/Lake Forest (PS)
Kyle Smith	85	10	5'11"/190	F	Rochester,NY/Portland Pirates (AtJHL)
Ryan Tiburtini	84	07	5'9"/165	D	Ephrata,PA/Philadelphia Flyers (MJHL)
Sean Wilson	85	10	5'11"/180	D	Willoughby,OH/Portland Pirates (AtJHL)

ROSTER ANALYSIS (SCHOLARSHIPS - 0)

Class		Country		Last Team					
Fr	11	USA	22	US JR A	1	CDN JR A	4	ACHA	
So	9	Canada	5	US JR B	8	CDN JR B	2	NJCAA	
Jr	4	Europe	1	US PS	10	CDN PS		NCAA	2
Sr	4	Asia		US HS	1	CDN HS		USNDT	
Gr		Other		US Midget		CDN Midget		Other	

ADMISSIONS, ENROLLMENT & CAMPUS INFORMATION

Founded 1866
Private, rural campus
1,218 men / 451 women
Tuition, room & board $ 32 K
Avg SAT - 1,105 / Avg ACT - 23

Average acceptance rate - 73 %
Freshman financial aid - 87 %
Early decision application deadline - N/A
Regular application deadline - rolling
Financial aid deadline - Mar 1

Susan Sorisky - Admissions Director
Lebanon Valley College
101 North College Avenue
Annville, PA 17003-0501
O 717.867.6181 / F 717.867.6026

www.lvc.edu   www.lvc.edu/athletics/

LINDENWOOD UNIVERSITY

Division 1

HOCKEY STAFF

HEAD COACH
Derek Schaub

ASSISTANT COACHES
Mark Abney
Jeff Wear
Gregg Gevers

HOCKEY OFFICE
Lindenwood University
209 S. Kingshighway
St. Charles, MO 63301
O 636.949.4945 / F
dschaub@lindenwood.edu

HOCKEY MEDIA CONTACT

HOCKEY RINK
200' x 85' - Capacity 1,500

ATHLETIC DIRECTOR
John Creer
Lindenwood University
209 S. Kingshighway
St. Charles, MO 63301
O 639.949.4777 / F
jcreer@lindenwood.edu

LIONS PLAYERS

Player	YB GR Ht/Wt	P	Hometown/Last Team
Chris Abbott	10 6' 4"/205	G	North Delta,BC/Campbell River Storm (VIJHL)
Travis Bokina	08 5'10"/175	F	Milford,CT/New Jersey Hitmen (EJHL)
Ryan Bond	10 6' 0"/165	F	Northville,MI/Traverse City North Stars (NAHL)
Kyle Cook	08 6' 0"/205	D	Dorchester,ON/Del-Hi Travellers (OHA)
Matt Dennison	09 6' 0"/160	G	Chesterfield,MO/Marquette (HS)
Dave Easterbrook	07 6' 1"/190	F	Brampton,ON/Mississauga Chargers (OHA)
Gary Gardner	07 5'11"/190	F	Oakville,MO/Affton Americans (Midget AAA)
Tim Gardner	10 6' 0"/200	F	Oakville,MO/St. Louis Blues (CSHL)
Eric Gebhardt	10 5' 6"/160	F	St. Louis,MO/St. Louis Lightning (MnJHL)
Kyle Hagerman	08 6' 0"/170	D	Cleveland,OH/Cleveland Lumberjacks (CSHL)
Quinn Henry	08 6' 1"/200	F	Eddystone,MB/Naniamo Clippers (BCHL)
Joel Herr	08 6' 1"/195	D	Florissant,MO/Affton Americans (Midget AAA)
Nathan Hucker	07 5'10"/190	D	Florissant,MO/Nichols (ECAC)
Ken Jacobsmeyer	08 5'10"/185	F	St. Louis,MO/St. Louis Blues (CSHL)
Derek Janssen	08 5'10"/165	F	Eureka,MO/St. Louis Blues (CSHL)
Larry Kopecky	08 5' 8"/160	F	Fenton,MO/St. Louis Blues (CSHL)
Grahame Lippert	08 5'10"/180	G	Coquitlam,BC/Port Coquitlam (KIJHL)
Dan McNabb	07 6' 1"/190	F	Webster Groves,MO/Wisconsin-Stevens Point (NCHA)
Tony Miller	08 5'10"/220	D	Ballwin,MO/SUNY-Morrisville (NJCAA)
Bobby Prest	08 5'11"/185	F	St. Charles,MO/Northwest Wisconsin Knights (MnJHL)
Kyle Rickermann	08 5' 9"/180	D	Oakville,MO/St. Louis Blues (CSHL)
Adam Saito	07 6' 1"/185	F	Hazelwood,MO/St. Louis Amatuer Blues (Midget AAA)
Steve Schue	07 5'10"/170	F	Sheffield Village,OH/Cleveland Barons (NAHL)
Mark Skeels	08 6' 2"/200	F	Unionville,ON/Wexford Raiders (OPJHL)
Henri St. Arnault	09 5'10"/170	F	St. Paul,AB/Chilliwack Chiefs (BCHL)
Kevin Stephens	08 6' 0"/180	D	Ballwin,MO/Heartland Eagles (USHL)
Brett Wills	07 5' 9"/190	D	Coquitlam,BC/Port Coquitlam (KIJHL)

ROSTER ANALYSIS (SCHOLARSHIPS - 0)

Class		Country		Last Team					
Fr	4	USA	19	US JR A	3	CDN JR A	3	ACHA	
So	2	Canada	8	US JR B	9	CDN JR B	3	NJCAA	1
Jr	14	Europe		US PS		CDN PS		NCAA2	
Sr	7	Asia		US HS	1	CDN HS		USNDT	
Gr		Other		US Midget	3	CDN Midget	2	Other	

ADMISSIONS, ENROLLMENT & CAMPUS INFORMATION

Founded 1827	Average acceptance rate - 45 %	Admissions Director
Private, suburban campus	Freshman financial aid - %	Lindenwood University
2,000 men / 2,400 women	Early decision application deadline -	209 S. Kingshighway
Tuition, room & board $ 20 K	Regular application deadline - Rolling	St. Charles, MO 63301
Avg SAT - 1,020 / Avg ACT - 22	Financial aid deadline -	O 636.949.4949

www.lindenwood.edu   www.lindenwood.edu

UNIVERSITY OF MAINE

Division 1

HOCKEY STAFF

HEAD COACH
Tim Whitehead *(Hamilton '85)*

ASSOCIATE HEAD COACH
Guy Perron *(Maine '91)*

ASSISTANT COACHES
Grant Standbrook *(Minn. Duluth '61)*
Dan Kerluke *(Maine '01)*

HOCKEY OFFICE
University of Maine - Alfond Arena
Orono, ME 04469
O 207.581.1106 / F 207.581.1102
tim.whitehead@umit.maine.edu

HOCKEY MEDIA CONTACT
Brent Williamson - Hockey Info Director
University of Maine
5747 Memorial Gym
Orono, ME 04469-5747
O 207.581.4158 / F 207.581.3297
brent.williamson@umit.maine.edu

HOCKEY RINK
Alfond Sports Arena (On Campus)
5701 Alford Arena
Orono, ME 05569-5701
Size 200' x 85', Capacity 5,641
O 207.581.1106

ATHLETIC DIRECTOR
Blake James - Interim Athletic Director
University of Maine
5747 Memorial Gym
Orono, ME 04469
O 207.581.1052 / F 207.581.3297
blake.james@umit.maine.edu

BLACK BEARS PLAYERS

Player	YB	GR	Ht/Wt	P	Hometown/Last Team
Rob Bellamy	85	08	6'0"/195	F	Westfield,MA/New England (EJHL)
Ben Bishop	86	09	6'7"/220	G	Des Peres,MO/Texas Tornado (NAHL)
Brett Carriere	85	10	6'0"/200	D	Ottawa,ON/Northern Cyclones
Wes Clark	83	08	5'11"/185	F	Oakville,ON/Milton Icehawks (OPJHL)
Tyler Czuba	85	10	5'11"/200	F	Kelowna,BC/Swan Valley Stampeders (ManJHL)
Simon Danis-Pepin	88	09	6'7"/210	D	Vaudreuil-Dorion,QC/Gatineau (EOJHL)
David deKastrozza	86	10	6'3"/200	F	Toms River,NJ/Culver (PS)
Matt Duffy	86	09	6'2"/195	D	Windham,ME/New Hampshire Monarchs (EJHL)
Shane Foley	87	10	6'0"/180	G	Clinton,NY/Lawrenceville (PS)
Chris Hahn	85	09	5'9"/185	F	Ft Qu'Appelle,SK/Notre Dame (PS)
Mike Hamilton	83	07	6'0"/200	F	Victoria,BC/Merritt Centennials (BCHL)
Keenan Hopson	83	08	6'1"/190	F	Prince George,BC/Prince George Spruce Kings (BCHL)
Keith Johnson	84	07	5'11"/180	F	Windsor,CT/New England (EJHL)
Vince Laise	83	09	5'11"/165	F	Brampton,ON/Georgetown Raiders (OPJHL)
Michel Leveille	81	07	5'9"/180	F	Levis,QC/Nanaimo Clippers (BCHL)
Mike Lundin	84	07	6'2"/180	D	Apple Valley,MN/Apple Valley (HS)
Jeff Marshall	84	09	5'11"/190	F	Kyle,SK/La Ronge Ice Wolves (SJHL)
Tony Morrone	86	10	5'9"/205	F	W Palm Bch,FL/South Kent (NEPSAC)
Bryan Plaszcz	85	09	6'2"/205	D	Apple Valley,MN/Santa Fe Roadrunners (NAHL)
Teddy Purcell	85	10	6'3"/180	F	St. John's,NF/Cedar Rapids RoughRiders (USHL)
Travis Ramsey	83	08	6'4"/210	D	Lakewood,CA/Salmon Arm Silverbacks (BCHL)
Billy Ryan	83	08	6'1"/175	F	Milton,MA/Cushing (NEPSAC)
Brent Shepheard	83	07	6'0"/190	F	Shawnigan Lk,BC/Nanaimo Clippers (BCHL)
Zach Sill	88	10	6'0"/190	F	Colchester Cty,NS/Truro Bearcats (MarJHL)
Josh Soares	82	07	6'0"/195	F	Hamilton,ON/Hamilton Red Wings (OPJHL)
Bret Tyler	85	08	5'9"/185	D	Maynard,MA/Boston (EJHL)
Dave Wilson	85	10	6'1"/190	G	Caledon E,ON/Streetsville Derbys (OPJHL)

ROSTER ANALYSIS (SCHOLARSHIPS - 18)

Class		Country		Last Team					
Fr	8	USA	12	US JR A	3	CDN JR A	12	ACHA	
So	7	Canada	15	US JR B	4	CDN JR B	1	NJCAA	
Jr	6	Europe		US PS	4	CDN PS	1	NCAA	
Sr	6	Asia		US HS	1	CDN HS		USNDT	
Gr		Other		US Midget		CDN Midget	1	Other	

ADMISSIONS, ENROLLMENT & CAMPUS INFORMATION

Founded 1865	Average acceptance rate - 79 %	Jonathon H. Henry - Director of Admissions
Public, rural campus	Freshman financial aid - 82 %	University of Maine
4,366 men / 4,031 women	Early decision application deadline - N/A	Chadbourne Hall
Tuition, room & board - $ 14 / $ 23 K	Regular application deadline - rolling	Orono, ME 04469-5713
Avg SAT - 1,075 / Avg ACT - 23	Financial aid deadline - Mar 1	O 207.581.1561 / F 207.581.1213

MANHATTANVILLE COLLEGE

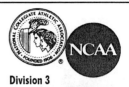

WEST

Division 3

VALIANTS PLAYERS

Player	YB	GR	Ht/Wt	P	Hometown/Last Team
Niklas Bernsston		10	5'10"/175	F	Goteborg,Sweden/Frolunda (SEL)
Vinny Ciardullo		09	5' 8"/165	F	Walden,NY/Canterbury (NEPSAC)
Jacob Cline		09	5' 9"/185	F	Covington,GA/Nichols (ECAC NE)
Joe Dicamillo		10	6' 0"/190	F	Rochester,NY/New Jersey Hitmen (EJHL)
Chris Galiotti	84	09	5'10"/180	D	Rochester,NY/Apple Valley (EJHL)
Andrew Gallant	82	07	6' 3"/200	G	Summerside,PE/OCN Blizzard (ManJHL)
Danny Genovese		10	5'11"/230	D	New York,NY/Chilliwack Chiefs (BCHL)
Scott Goheen	82	07	5'11"/185	F	Innisfil,ON/Aurora Tigers (OPJHL)
BJ Greaves	82	07	5' 7"/175	F	Nipigon,ON/Sioux City Musketeers (USHL)
Phil Hotarek		10	6' 1"/210	D	Foster City,CA/Port Hope Predators (OPJHL)
Zeke Hume	83	08	5'11"/200	D/F	Osoyoos,BC/Merritt Centennials (BCHL)
Mike Luzzi	86	09	5' 9"/185	F	Hamden,CT/Junior Bruins (EJHL)
Derek Lynden	85	09	5'10"/185	F	Pickering,ON/Pickering Panthers (OPJHL)
Troy Maleyko	83	07	5'10"/180	D	Belle River,ON/Quinnipiac (ECAC)
Arlen Marshall		10	5'10"/170	F	Quill Lake,SK/Humboldt Broncos (SJHL)
Brendan McIntyre	08		5' 9"/180	F	Ottawa,ON/Cumberland Grads (CJHL)
AJ Mikkelson		10	6' 2"/200	D	Chestermere,AB/Drumheller Dragons (AJHL)
Chris Mills	82	07	6' 0"/185	F	Calgary,AB/Penticton Panthers (BCHL)
Jason Murfitt	83	08	6' 2"/185	F	Ottawa,ON/Cumberland Grads (CJHL)
Craig Nooyan	08		6' 0"/200	D	Ottawa,ON/Brookfield
Matt Piezga		10	6' 0"/185	F	Chicago,IL/New Jersey Hitmen (EJHL)
Paul Reimer	84	08	6' 2"/170	G	Hamilton,ON/Flin Flon Bombers (SJHL)
Justin Rohr	82	07	5' 6"/175	F	Lloydminster,SK/La Ronge Ice Wolves (SJHL)
Matt Ruberto	08		6' 0"/200	D	Stoney Crk,ON/Canisius (AHL)
Mike Ruberto	08		6' 0"/195	F	Stoney Crk,ON/Canisius (AHL)
Jarret Rush		10	6' 5"/215	D	Pennington,NJ/Traverse City North Stars (NAHL)
Jens VaPouke		10	6' 1"/165	G	Maldegem,Belgium/Belgium National U-20
Sean Wadland		10	5' 9"/170	D	Andover,MA/Andover (NEPSAC)
Chris Wanchulak	83	08	6' 0"/190	D	Edson,AB/Camrose Kodiaks (AJHL)

HEAD COACH
Keith Levinthal *(Hobart '95)*

ASSISTANT HEAD COACH
Oly Hicks *(Victoria '93)*

ASSISTANT COACHES
Pat Boller *(SUNY-Potsdam '95)*
Dennis McNally *(Manhattanville '04)*

HOCKEY OFFICE
Manhattanville College
2900 Purchase Street
Purchase, NY 10577
O 914.323.7277/F 914.323.5130
levinthalk@mville.edu

HOCKEY MEDIA CONTACT
Michael LaPlaca - Sports Info Director
2900 Purchase Street
Purchase, NY 10577
O 914.323.7280/F 914.323.3180
laplacam@mville.edu

HOCKEY RINK
Playland Ice Casino (Off Campus)
Playland Parkway
Rye, NY 10580
Size 208' x 77', Capacity 1,400
O 914.323.5280

ATHLETIC DIRECTOR
Kevin Levinthal - Athletic Director
Manhattanville College
2900 Purchase Street
Purchase, NY 10577
O 914.323.7277/F 914.323.5130
levinthalk@mville.edu

ROSTER ANALYSIS (SCHOLARSHIPS - 0)

Class		Country		Last Team					
Fr	10	USA	10	US JR A	2	CDN JR A	14	ACHA	
So	5	Canada	17	US JR B	4	CDN JR B		NJCAA	
Jr	8	Europe	2	US PS	2	CDN PS		NCAA	4
Sr	6	Asia		US HS		CDN HS		USNDT	
Gr		Other		US Midget		CDN Midget		Other	3

ADMISSIONS, ENROLLMENT & CAMPUS INFORMATION

Founded 1841
Private, suburban campus
490 men / 1,042 women
Tuition, room & board $ 36 K
Avg SAT - 1,090 / Avg ACT - 24

Average acceptance rate - 57 %
Freshman financial aid - 80 %
Early decision application deadline - Dec 1
Regular application deadline - Mar 1
Financial aid deadline - Mar 1

Jose Flores - Admissions Director
Manhattanville College
2900 Purchase Street
Purchase, NY 10577
O 800.328.4553/F 914.694.1732

MARIAN COLLEGE OF FOND DU LAC

Division 3

<table>
<tr><th colspan="2">HOCKEY STAFF</th></tr>
</table>

HOCKEY STAFF

HEAD COACH
Jasen Wise *(St. Thomas)*

ASSISTANT COACHES
Jason Nordby
Jeff Worlton

HOCKEY OFFICE
Marian College of Fond du Lac
45 South National Avenue
Fond du Lac, WI 54935-4699
O 920.923.7667 / F 920.923.8134
jtwise@marioncollege.edu

HOCKEY MEDIA CONTACT
Mike Schoenborn - Sports Info Director
Marian College of Fond du Lac
45 South National Avenue
Fond du Lac, WI 54935-4699
O 920.923.8155 / F 920.923.8134
mtschoenborn73@marioncollege.edu

HOCKEY RINK
Blue Line Ice Center (Off Campus)
601 Martin Road
Fond du Lac, WI 54935
Size ' x ', Capacity 2,000
O 414.921.3317

ATHLETIC DIRECTOR
Doug Hammonds - Athletic Director
Marian College of Fond du Lac
45 South National Avenue
Fond du Lac, WI 54935-4699
O 920.923.7178 / F 920.923.8134
dhammonds@marioncollege.edu

SABRES PLAYERS

Player	YB	GR	Ht/Wt	P	Hometown/Last Team
Jack Aide	85	08	5'10"/165	F	Bismarck,ND/Minot State Bottineau (NJCAA)
Carl Bresser	83	08	6' 3"/195	F	Waupan,WI/Minnesota Ice Hawks (MnJHL)
Cullen Caldwell	86	10	5'11"/190	G	Calgary,AB/K&A Golden Hawks (SIJHL)
Nick Cinquegrani	86	10	6' 0"/185	F	Rolling Meadows,IL/Chicago Force (CSHL)
Gregory Copeland	84	09	6' 1"/200	D	Lloydminster,SK/Sherwood Park Crusaders (AJHL)
Andrew Corvo	84	09	6' 0"/195	F	Oak Park,IL/Peoria Mustangs (CSHL)
Dave DeSander	83	08	6' 1"/170	G	Saginaw,MI/Springfield Spirit (NAHL)
Andrew Fiore	84	09	6' 4"/220	D	Georgetown,ON/Youngstown Phantoms (NAHL)
Tyler Fletcher	85	10	6' 2"/195	F	Calgary,AB/Melville Millionaires (SJHL)
Jason Ford	85	10	5' 9"/190	F	Milford,MI/Valley Warriors (EJHL)
Brett Fox	82	07	5'10"/175	D	Detroit,MI/Billings Bulls (NAHL)
James Goodfellow	84	09	5' 8"/190	F	Naperville,IL/Chicago Force (CSHL)
Bill Griffore	84	09	5'10"/185	F	Milford,MI/Valley Warriors (EJHL)
Nick Henkemeyer	85	10	6' 4"/175	D	Prior Lake,MN/Twin Cities Northern Lights (MnJHL)
Michael Herbert	85	10	5' 8"/175	F	Naperville,IL/Northern Michigan Black Bears (NOJHL)
Ryan Hitchcock	87	10	6' 2"/190	F	Butte,MT/Wichita Falls Wildcats (NAHL)
Jason Jadczak	85	09	5' 9"/165	G	Des Plaines,IL/Chicago Force (CSHL)
Kyle Jones	84	09	5'11"/190	D	Sault Ste. Marie,ON/Soo Thunderbirds (NOJHL)
Josh McAndrew	84	09	5'10"/190	F	Atitokan,ON/Borderland Thunder (SIJHL)
Ross Oestreich	85	09	6' 2"/195	F	Waupaca,WI/Waupaca (HS)
Kyle Rasmussen	85	09	6' 0"/170	F	Altoona,WI/St. Paul Lakers (MnJHL)
Scott Ross	84	09	6' 0"/200	D	Rockford,IL/Chicago Force (CSHL)
Billy Schill	84	09	6' 2"/220	F	Sault Ste. Marie,ON/Blind River Beavers (NOJHL)
Alex Spies	86	09	5'11"/180	F	Forest Lk,MN/Hamline (MIAC)
Ted Thompson	83	08	6' 4"/200	D	Listowel,ON/Wisconsin Eau Claire (NCHA)
Jeffrey Wills	84	09	6' 0"/185	D	Davison,MI/Blind River Beavers (NOJHL)

ROSTER ANALYSIS (SCHOLARSHIPS - 0)

Class		Country		Last Team					
Fr	7	USA	18	US JR A	4	CDN JR A	8	ACHA	
So	14	Canada	8	US JR B	10	CDN JR B		NJCAA	1
Jr	4	Europe		US PS		CDN PS		NCAA	2
Sr	1	Asia		US HS	1	CDN HS		USNDT	
Gr		Other		US Midget		CDN Midget		Other	

ADMISSIONS, ENROLLMENT & CAMPUS INFORMATION

Founded 1936
Private, suburban campus
1,135 men / 464 women
Tuition, room & board - $ 26 K
Avg SAT - 995 / Avg ACT - 21

Acceptance rate - %
Freshman financial aid - %
Early decision application deadline - N/A
Regular application deadline - May 1
Financial aid deadline - Mar 1

Stacey Akey - Admissions Director
Marian College of Fond du Lac
45 South National Avenue
Fond du Lac, WI 54935-4699
O 920.923.7650 / F 920.923.8755

www.marioncollege.edu
www.marioncollege.edu/Athletics/

UNIV. OF MASSACHUSETTS-AMHERST

Division 1

HOCKEY STAFF

HEAD COACH
Don Cahoon *(Boston University '72)*

ASSISTANT COACHES
Len Quesnelle *(Princeton '88)*
Red Gendron *(New England '79)*
Jim Stewart *(Holy Cross '78)*

HOCKEY OFFICE
University of Massachusetts-Amherst
307 Mullins Center
Amherst, MA 01003
O 413.545.5175 / F 413.577.0542
dcahoon@admin.umass.edu

HOCKEY MEDIA CONTACT
Kimberly Gardner - Hockey Info Director
University of Massachusetts-Amherst
255 Boyden Building
Amherst, MA 01003
O 413.545.5292 / F 413.545.1556
kgardner@admin.umass.edu

HOCKEY RINK
Mullin Memorial Center (On Campus)
Commonwealth Avenue
Amherst, MA 01003
Size 200' x 95', Capacity 8,373
O 413.545.3001

ATHLETIC DIRECTOR
John McCutcheon - Athletic Director
University of Massachusetts-Amherst
Mullins Center #308
Amherst, MA 01003
O 413.545.9652 / F 413.545.1727
jmccutch@admin.umass.edu

MINUTEMEN PLAYERS

Player	YB	GR	Ht/Wt	P	Hometown/Last Team
Matt Anderson	82	07	5'11"/195	F	W Islip,NY/New England Coyotes (EJHL)
Alex Berry	86	09	6' 2"/215	F	Danvers,MA/Junior Bruins (EJHL)
Topher Bevis	86	09	6' 1"/205	D	Harvard,MA/Junior Bruins (EJHL)
Justin Braun	87	10	6' 1"/180	D	Vadnais Hgts,MN/Green Bay Gamblers (USHL)
Matt Burto	84	08	5'10"/195	F	Orange,CT/Junior Bruins (EJHL)
Chris Capraro	83	07	5' 7"/180	F	Medford,MA/Austin (PS)
Scott Crowder	85	09	5'11"/195	F	Nashua,NH/New Hampshire Monarchs (EJHL)
Sam D'Agostino	86	10	6' 0"/200	F	Medford,MA/Tri-City Storm (USHL)
Chris Davis	86	09	5'10"/190	F	Simsbury,CT/Avon (NEPSAC)
Patrick Dineen	83	08	6' 0"/190	F	Brooklyn,NY/Bentley (AHL)
PJ Fenton	86	08	5'11"/185	F	Longmeadow,MA/New England Coyotes (EJHL)
Jamie Gilbert	86	08	6' 2"/195	G	Lewiston,ME/Cornwall Colts (CJHL)
Dan Gordon	85	09	5'11"/180	F	Lynnfield,MA/New England Huskies (EJHL)
Kevin Jarman	85	07	6' 1"/210	F	Aurora,ON/Stouffville Spirit (OPJHL)
Kevin Kessler	85	10	6' 3"/215	D	Scarborough,ME/New Hampshire Monarchs (EJHL)
Zech Klann	83	08	6' 1"/190	F	Pottstown,PA/New Hampshire Monarchs (EJHL)
Michael Kostka	85	08	6' 2"/210	D	Ajax,ON/Aurora Tigers (OPJHL)
David Leaderer	86	08	5'11"/190	D	Rochester,NY/Junior Bruins (EJHL)
Kevin Maresco	86	09	6' 0"/195	F	Lynnfield,MA/Andover (NEPSAC)
Mark Matheson	84	07	6' 2"/205	D	Calgary,AB/Calgary Royals (AJHL)
Dan Meyers	85	10	6' 2"/215	G	Voorhees,NJ/Green Mountain Glades (EJHL)
Martin Nolet	86	10	6' 3"/205	D	Quebec City,QC/Champlain (QJAHL)
Will Ortiz	86	10	5' 9"/170	F	Framingham,MA/Salisbury (NEPSAC)
Jon Quick	86	09	6' 1"/200	G	Hampden,CT/Avon (NEPSAC)
Cory Quirk	86	09	5' 9"/180	F	Brockton,MA/Waterloo Blackhawks (USHL)
Jordan Virtue	84	09	6' 1"/200	F	Walpole,MA/Walpole Stars (EJHL)
Brett Watson	85	10	5'11"/170	F	Media,PA/Tri-City Storm (USHL)
John Wessbecker	86	09	6' 2"/195	D	Victoria,MN/Blake (PS)

ROSTER ANALYSIS (SCHOLARSHIPS - 18)

Class		Country		Last Team					
Fr	7	USA	24	US JR A	4	CDN JR A	5	ACHA	
So	10	Canada	4	US JR B	12	CDN JR B		NJCAA	
Jr	7	Europe		US PS	6	CDN PS		NCAA	1
Sr	4	Asia		US HS		CDN HS		USNDT	
Gr		Other		US Midget		CDN Midget		Other	

ADMISSIONS, ENROLLMENT & CAMPUS INFORMATION

Founded 1863	Average acceptance rate - 81 %	Joseph C. Marshall - Admissions Director
Public, suburban campus	Freshman financial aid - 83 %	University of Massachusetts-Amherst
9,373 men / 9,005 women	Early decision application deadline - N/A	Admissions Center
Tuition, room & board - $16 K/$25 K	Regular application deadline - Jan 15	Amherst, MA 01003
Avg SAT - 1,135	Financial aid deadline - Mar 1	O 413.545.0222 / F 413.545.4312

www.umass.edu

www.umassathletics.collegesports.com

UNIV. OF MASSACHUSETTS-BOSTON

HOCKEY EAST

NCAA
Division 3

HOCKEY STAFF

HEAD COACH
Peter Belisle *(UConn '95)*

ASSISTANT COACHES
Jerry Keefe *(Providence '00)*
Jeff Pellegrini

HOCKEY OFFICE
University of Massachusetts-Boston
100 Morrisey Boulevard
Boston, MA 02125-3393
O 617.287.7812
peter.belisle@umb.edu

HOCKEY MEDIA CONTACT
Alan Wickstrom - Sports Info Director
University of Massachusetts-Boston
100 Morrisey Boulevard
Boston, MA 02125
O 617.287.7815 / F 617.287.7840
alan.wickstrom@umb.edu

HOCKEY RINK
Clark Athletic Center (On Campus)
100 Morrissey Boulevard
Boston, MA 02125-3393
Size 200' x 85', Capacity 1,000
O 617.287.7815

ATHLETIC DIRECTOR
Pat Burns - Interim Athletic Director
University of Massachusetts-Boston
100 Morrisey Boulevard
Boston, MA 02125-3393
O 617.287.7808 / F 617.287.7840
pat.burns@umb.edu

BEACONS PLAYERS

Player	YB	GR	Ht/Wt	P	Hometown/Last Team
David Allen	87	10	6'2"/185	F/D	Londonderry,NH/Boston Harbor Wolves (EJHL)
Cody Austin	86	10	5'10"/175	F	Highland,MI/Billings Bulls (NAHL)
Aaron Burke	84	09	6'0"/215	F	Rowley,MA/Salem Ice Dogs (EmJHL)
Robert Carbone	86	09	5'9"/160	F	Bayside,NY/Suffolk PAL (MJHL)
Jake Carlson	85	10	5'6"/155	F	Hermantown,MN/Helena Bighorns (NAHL)
Wade Collins	86	09	5'11"/185	D	Corinth,NY/Utica (ECAC West)
Ryan Daust	85	10	6'3"/185	F	Marquette,MI/Wellington Dukes (OPJHL)
Jeff Diehl	85	10	6'1"/215	F	Grand Rpds,MI/Helena Bighorns (NAHL)
Ryan Donovan	85	10	6'0"/180	G	Rexford,NY/Hartford Wolfpack (AtJHL)
Hunter Dowd	84	08	5'9"/170	F	Brick,NJ/St. John Vianney (PS)
Peter Dundovich	85	10	6'2"/195	G	Philadelphia,PA/Philadelphia Flyers (MJHL)
Steve Ebbole	85	10	5'7"/180	D	Wheaton,IL/Helena Bighorns (NAHL)
Tyler English	87	09	5'9"/160	F	Cambridge,MA/Matignon (PS)
Marcus Fajardo	83	09	5'6"/165	F	New York,NY/LaSalle (PS)
Chris Flaherty	85	09	5'11"/170	F	S Boston,MA/Savio (PS)
Chris Gaffney	84	08	6'2"/220	F	Danvers,MA/Danvers (HS)
James Hall	86	09	5'8"/160	F/D	Middletown,NJ/New Jersey Titans (MJHL)
Drew Hursa	87	10	5'9"/175	D	Malden Br,NY/New York Bobcats (AtJHL)
Michael Jordan	85	10	5'9"/160	F	Pittsburgh,PA/Dubuque Thunderbirds (MnJHL)
Drew LaCombe	85	10	5'8"/160	F	Burlington,MA/Fort Worth Texans (WSHL)
Billy Langmaid	84	09	6'0"/200	D	Danvers,MA/Salem Ice Dogs (EmJHL)
Matthew Lopes	84	09	5'11"/190	G	Cape Cod,MA/Capital District Selects (EJHL)
Michael Muolo	87	09	6'1"/180	F	Stoneham,MA/Stoneham (HS)
Robert Schwartz	86	09	6'0"/200	D	Philadelphia,PA/Albany (NEPSAC)
Kyle Simpson	85	08	5'8"/185	F	Scituate,MA/Williston Northampton (NEPSAC)
Rich Stone	85	09	6'0"/170	F	Quincy,MA/North Quincy (HS)
Rick Tennyson	84	08	5'9"/175	F	Hingham,MA/Boston Harbor Wolves (EJHL)
Chris Testa	86	09	6'2"/210	G	Brooklyn,NY/Briarcliffe College (OCAA)
Andrew Ward	84	08	6'3"/175	D	Evanston,IL/Lowell Loch Monsters (EJHL)

ROSTER ANALYSIS (SCHOLARSHIPS - 0)

Class		Country		Last Team				
Fr	11	USA	29	US JR A	4	CDN JR A	1	ACHA
So	13	Canada		US JR B	13	CDN JR B		NJCAA	1
Jr	5	Europe		US PS	6	CDN PS		NCAA
Sr		Asia		US HS	3	CDN HS		USNDT
Gr		Other		US Midget		CDN Midget		Other	1

ADMISSIONS, ENROLLMENT & CAMPUS INFORMATION

Founded 1964
Public, urban campus
2,808 men / 4,041 women
Tuition (no housing) - $9 K / $19 K
Avg SAT - 985

Average acceptance rate - 53 %
Freshman financial aid - 86 %
Early decision application deadline - N/A
Regular application deadline - Mar 1
Financial aid deadline - Mar 1

Liliana Mickle - Director of Admissions
University of Massachusetts-Boston
100 Morrisey Boulevard
Boston, MA 02125-3393
O 617.287.6100 / F 617.287.6242

www.umb.edu

www.athletics.umb.edu/

UNIV. OF MASSACHUSETTS-DARTMOUTH

HOCKEY
NORTHEAST

Division 3

HOCKEY STAFF

HEAD COACH
Jonathan Rolli *(Salem State '73)*

ASSISTANT COACHES
Kenneth Gouveia
Shaun Tavares

HOCKEY OFFICE
University of Massachusetts-Dartmouth
Tripp Center 217
285 Old Westport Road
North Dartmouth, MA 02747-2300
O 508.999.8723 / F 508.999.8867
jrolli@umassd.edu

HOCKEY MEDIA CONTACT
Dave Geringer - Sports Info Director
University of Massachusetts-Dartmouth
Tripp Center 116
285 Old Westport Road
North Dartmouth, MA 02747-2300
O 508.990.9651 / F 508.999.8730
dgeringer@umassd.edu

HOCKEY RINK
Hetland Memorial Rink (Off Campus)
310 Hathaway Boulevard
New Bedford, MA 02740
Size 185' x 80', Capacity 1,500
O 508.999.9051

ATHLETIC DIRECTOR
Robert Mullen - Athletic Director
University of Massachusetts-Dartmouth
Tripp Center 212
285 Old Westport Road
North Dartmouth, MA 02747-2300
O 508.999.8722 / F 508.999.8867
rmullen@umassd.edu

CORSAIRS PLAYERS

Players	YB	GR	Ht/Wt	P	Hometown/Last Team
Matt Berard	87	10	5' 9"/170	F	Calgary,AB/Berkshire (NEPSAC)
Graeme Bourne	86	10	6' 4"/195	D	Redlands,CA/Campbell River Storm (VIJHL)
Chris Carpenter	85	10	6' 1"/185	D	Westford,MA/Berkshire (NEPSAC)
Paul Carr	84	07	5'11"/185	D	Springfield,MA/Springfield Cathedral (PS)
Billy Carroll	87	10	5'11"/165	F	Duxbury,MA/Bridgton (NEPSAC)
Tyler Crocker	86	08	5'11"/165	D	Wakefield,MA/Wakefield (HS)
Dave Doucette	85	09	6' 4"/200	D	Westford,MA/Kimball Union (NEPSAC)
Jonathan Finn	83	08	6' 0"/185	F/D	Warwick,RI/Boston Harbor Wolves (EJHL)
Jim Foley	85	07	6' 2"/175	F	Brockton,MA/Catholic Memorial (PS)
Paul Garabedian	85	08	6' 0"/175	F	Belmont,MA/Belmont (HS)
Jeff Grant	85	08	6' 0"/165	F	Burlington,MA/Austin (PS)
Jeff Green	85	09	6' 1"/200	G	Medway,MA/Valley Warriors (EJHL)
Francis Gunn	86	09	5'11"/180	F/D	Winthrop,MA/Berkshire (NEPSAC)
Ray Kirby	80	07	6' 0"/190	D	Fairhaven,MA/Salem State (ECAC East)
Alex Klimarchuk	87	10	5'11"/200	G	Saugus,MA/Saugus (HS)
Peter Lindner	85	07	6' 1"/195	F	Parlin,NJ/Christian Brothers (PS)
Bruce Maggio	84	08	5' 9"/180	G	Quincy,MA/North Quincy (HS)
Kyle McCullough	83	07	5'10"/175	F	Danvers,MA/Boston Blackhawks (IJHL)
Mike McNulty	84	08	6' 0"/185	D	Hingham,MA/Winchendon (NEPSAC)
Paul Moran	86	10	5'10"/175	D	Rockville Centre,NY/Boston Bulldogs (AtJHL)
Nick Paquin	86	09	5' 7"/175	D	Warwick,RI/Winchendon (NEPSAC)
Eric Quinlan	86	10	6' 0"/205	D	Saugus,MA/Avon (NEPSAC)
John Ripp	86	09	6' 0"/170	F	Bolton,CT/Connecticut (IJHL)
Matt Serino	87	10	5' 8"/155	F	Saugus,MA/Avon (NEPSAC)
Chris Shore	85	09	5' 9"/190	F	W Haven,CT/Winchendon (NEPSAC)
Mark Trahan	86	09	5' 8"/200	F	Chelmsford,MA/Chelmsford (HS)
Tyler Vrolyk	83	08	5'11"/175	F	Boylston,MA/New England Falcons (EJHL)
Pat Welch	85	10	6' 0"/195	F	Dorchester,MA/Pomfret (NEPSAC)

ROSTER ANALYSIS (SCHOLARSHIPS - 0)

Class		Country		Last Team					
Fr	9	USA	27	US JR A		CDN JR A		ACHA	
So	7	Canada	1	US JR B	6	CDN JR B	1	NJCAA	
Jr	7	Europe		US PS	15	CDN PS		NCAA	1
Sr	5	Asia		US HS	5	CDN HS		USNDT	
Gr		Other		US Midget		CDN Midget		Other	

ADMISSIONS, ENROLLMENT & CAMPUS INFORMATION

Founded 1895
Public, suburban campus
3,499 men / 3,361 women
Tuition, room & board - $ 16 K /$ 23 K
Avg SAT - 1,055 / Avg ACT - 21

Average acceptance rate - 68 %
Freshman financial aid - 86 %
Early decision application deadline - Nov 15
Regular application deadline - rolling
Financial aid deadline - Mar 1

Steve Briggs - Admissions Director
University of Massachusetts-Dartmouth
285 Old Westport Road
North Dartmouth, MA 02747-2300
O 508.999.8605 / F 508.999.8755

www.umassd.edu

www.umassd.edu/sports/

UNIV. OF MASSACHUSETTS-LOWELL

Division 1

HOCKEY STAFF

HEAD COACH
Blaise MacDonald *(RIT '85)*

ASSISTANT COACHES
Chris MacKenzie *(Niagara '00)*
Ken Rausch *(Boston University '95)*
Bob Ware *(Salem State '90)*

HOCKEY OFFICE
University of Massachusetts-Lowell
Tsongas Arena - Room 179
300 MLK Highway
Lowell, MA 01854
O 978.934.2339/ F 978.934.4986
hockey@uml.edu

HOCKEY MEDIA CONTACT
Chris O'Donnell - Sports Info Director
University of Massachusetts-Lowell
One University Drive
Lowell, MA 01854
O 978.934.2306/ F 978.934.2313
chris_odonnell@uml.edu

HOCKEY RINK
Tsongas Arena (Off Campus)
300 Arcand Drive
Lowell, MA 01852
Size 200' x 85', Capacity 6,496
O 978.934.4545

ATHLETIC DIRECTOR
Dana K. Skinner - Athletic Director
Univ. of Mass.-Lowell - Costello Gym
One University Avenue
Lowell, MA 01854
O 978.934.2310/ F 978.934.2313
dana_skinner@uml.edu

RIVER HAWKS PLAYERS

Player	YB	GR	Ht/Wt	P	Hometown/Last Team
Chris Auger	87	10	5'10"/170	F	Bellville,ON/Wellington Dukes (OPJHL)
Jason Bergeron	88	10	5' 8"/165	F	Ancaster,ON/Milton Icehawks (OPJHL)
JR Bria	82	07	5'11"/220	D	Monroe,CT/Colgate (ECAC)
Steve Capraro	86	10	5' 9"/195	D	Medford,MA/Avon (NEPSAC)
Jeremy Dehner	87	10	5' 8"/180	D	Madison,WI/Green Bay Gamblers (USHL)
Kory Falite	86	10	5'10"/175	F	Billerica,MA/Junior Bruins (EJHL)
Todd Fletcher	84	07	5'10"/165	F	Chelmsford,MA/Chelmsford (HS)
Rene Gauthier	82	07	5'10"/190	F	Tecumseh,ON/Chicago Steel (USHL)
Barry Goers	86	10	5' 9"/175	D	Ivyland,PA/Green Mountain Glades (EJHL)
Jeremy Hall	83	07	5'10"/180	F	Mays Landing,NJ/Danville Wings (USHL)
Nevin Hamilton	85	10	6' 2"/210	G	Ashland,MA/Junior Bruins (EJHL)
Ben Holmstrom	87	10	6' 1"/180	F	Colorado Spgs,CO/Sioux Falls Stampede (USHL)
Carter Hutton	85	10	6' 1"/185	G	Thunder Bay,ON/Fort William North Stars (SIJHL)
Cleve Kinley	84	07	6' 0"/190	D	Powell Rvr,BC/Powell River Kings (BCHL)
Jonathan Maniff	87	10	5'10"/175	F	Revere,MA/Walpole Stars (EJHL)
Vinny Monaco	86	09	5'11"/180	G	Andover,MA/New England Huskies (EJHL)
Nick Monroe	85	09	5' 9"/175	F	Groton,MA/New England Huskies (EJHL)
Jake Pence	83	07	6' 1"/190	D	Owatonna,MN/Junior Bruins (EJHL)
Mike Potacco	84	09	5'10"/185	F	Kinnelon,NJ/St. Michael's (PS)
Tommy Powers	85	10	6' 3"/205	D	Coral Spgs,FL/Cornwall Colts (CJHL)
Mark Roebothan	86	09	5'11"/200	F	St. John's,NF/Valley Warriors (EJHL)
Ian Schaser	85	10	5'11"/180	F	Eden Pr,MN/Bridgewater Bandits (EJHL)
Nick Schaus	86	10	5'11"/180	D	Orchard Pk,NY/Omaha Lancers (USHL)
Frank Stegnar	87	10	6' 4"/200	D	Toronto,ON/Brampton Capitals (OPJHL)
Kelly Sullivan	83	08	6' 0"/185	D	Beverly Hills,MI/Danville Wings (USHL)
Jason Tejchma	83	07	5'10"/180	F	Muskegon,MI/Danville Wings (USHL)
Paul Worthington	85	10	/	F	Langhorne,PA/Green Mountain Glades (EJHL)

ROSTER ANALYSIS (SCHOLARSHIPS - 18)

Class		Country		Last Team				
Fr	15	USA	20	US JR A	7	CDN JR A	6	ACHA
So	4	Canada	7	US JR B	10	CDN JR B		NJCAA
Jr	1	Europe		US PS	1	CDN PS	1	NCAA	1
Sr	7	Asia		US HS	1	CDN HS		USNDT
Gr		Other		US Midget		CDN Midget		Other

ADMISSIONS, ENROLLMENT & CAMPUS INFORMATION

Founded 1895	Average acceptance rate - 66 %	Lisa Johnson - Admissions Director
Public, urban campus	Freshman financial aid - 96 %	University of Massachusetts-Lowell
4,186 men / 2,157 women	Early decision application deadline - N/A	Dungan Hall, South Campus
Tuition, room & board - $ 15 K /$ 23 K	Regular application deadline - Jul 1	Lowell, MA 01854
Avg SAT - 1,090	Financial aid deadline - Mar 1	O 978.934.3931/ F 978.934.3086

www.uml.edu	www.goriverhawks.com/

MERCYHURST COLLEGE

Division 1

HOCKEY STAFF

HEAD COACH
Rick Gotkin *(SUNY-Brockport '82)*

ASSISTANT COACHES
John Rose *(New England '03)*
Bobby Ferraris *(St. Anselm '97)*

HOCKEY OFFICE
Mercyhurst College
501 East 38th Street
Erie, PA 16546
O 814.824.2542
rgotkin@mercyhurst.edu

HOCKEY MEDIA CONTACT
John Leisering - Sports Info Director
Mercyhurst College
501 East 38th Street
Erie, PA 16546
O 814.824.2525 / F 814.824.2591
jleiser@mercyhurst.edu

HOCKEY RINK
Mercyhurst Ice Center (On Campus)
East 38th Street
Erie, PA 16546
Size 200' x 85', Capacity 1,500
O 814.824.2167

ATHLETIC DIRECTOR
Pete Russo - Athletic Director
Mercyhurst College
501 East 38th Street
Erie, PA 16546
O 814.824.2226
prusso@mercyhurst.edu

LAKERS PLAYERS

Player	YB	GR	Ht/Wt	P	Hometown/Last Team
Kerry Bowman	84	08	5'11"/185	F	Leamington,ON/Surrey Eagles (BCHL)
Scott Champagne	83	07	5'11"/180	F	Cornwall,ON/Gloucester Rangers (CJHL)
Jamie Coghlan	84	08	6'2"/210	D	Toronto,ON/St. Michael's (PS)
Cody Collins	85	10	5'9"/195	F	Winfield,BC/Penticton Vees (BCHL)
Ben Cottreau	85	08	6'0"/200	F	Toronto,ON/Markham Waxers (OPJHL)
Cullen Eddy	88	10	6'0"/195	D	Hidden Vly,PA/Pittsburgh Penguins
Mike Ella	83	07	5'9"/190	F	Schomberg,ON/St. Michael's (PS)
Matt Fennell	86	10	6'0"/180	D	Melfort,SK/Melfort Mustangs (SJHL)
Derek Fisher	85	10	6'3"/200	D	Int'l Falls,MN/Seguin Bruins (OPJHL)
Mike Floyd	85	09	6'2"/200	F	Stratford,PE/Campbellton Tigers (MarJHL)
Kyle Gourgon	84	07	5'11"/190	F	Ottawa,ON/Chicago Freeze (NAHL)
Neil Graham	85	10	5'10"/180	F	Calgary,AB/Okotoks Oilers (AJHL)
Pat Henk	83	07	5'9"/175	D	Mentor,OH/Cleveland Barons (NAHL)
Denis Kirstein	83	07	6'0"/200	D	Bethel Park,PA/Pittsburgh Forge (NAHL)
Kirk Medernach	84	09	6'4"/215	D	Cudworth,SK/Weyburn Red Wings (SJHL)
Bobby Phillips	85	09	6'3"/210	D	Carmel,IN/Toledo IceDiggers (NAHL)
Matt Pierce	85	09	5'11"/180	F	Pakenham,ON/Kanata Stallions (CJHL)
Chris Risi	85	10	5'6"/170	F	Thorold,ON/Thorold Blackhawks (GHJHL)
Brett Robinson	85	09	5'11"/190	F	Alton,ON/Milton Icehawks (OPJHL)
Tyler Small	85	09	6'3"/175	G	Kincardine,ON/Owen Sound Greys (MWJHL)
Ryan Toomey	83	08	5'9"/180	F	Bolton,ON/Cornwall Colts (CJHL)
Chris Trafford	86	09	6'0"/195	F	Kinburn,ON/Kanata Stallions (CJHL)
Nick Vandenbeld	85	10	5'8"/175	F	Pt Coquitlam,BC/Melfort Mustangs (SJHL)
Jordan Wakefield	82	07	6'0"/175	G	Spruce Gr,AB/Grande Prairie Storm (AJHL)
Matt Warren	83	08	6'1"/180	F	Aylmer,QC/Pembroke Lumber Kings (CJHL)

ROSTER ANALYSIS (SCHOLARSHIPS - 11)

Class		Country		Last Team					
Fr	7	USA	5	US JR A	4	CDN JR A	16	ACHA	
So	7	Canada	20	US JR B	1	CDN JR B	2	NJCAA	
Jr	5	Europe		US PS		CDN PS	2	NCAA	
Sr	6	Asia		US HS		CDN HS		USNDT	
Gr		Other		US Midget		CDN Midget		Other	

ADMISSIONS, ENROLLMENT & CAMPUS INFORMATION

Founded 1926
Private, suburban campus
1,652 men / 2,103 women
Tuition, room & board - $ 28 K
Avg SAT - 1,080 / Avg ACT - 22

Average acceptance rate - 78 %
Freshman financial aid - 90 %
Early decision application deadline - N/A
Regular application deadline - rolling
Financial aid deadline - Mar 1

Robin Engel - Director of Admissions
Mercyhurst College
501 East 38th Street
Erie, PA 16546
O 814.824.2241 / F 814.824.2071

MERRIMACK COLLEGE

WARRIORS

Division 1

HOCKEY STAFF

HEAD COACH
Mark Dennehy *(Boston College '91)*

ASSISTANT COACHES
Martin Quarters
Darren Yopyk *(Princeton '00)*
Tom Welby *(Merrimack '01)*

HOCKEY OFFICE
Merrimack College - Volpe Complex
315 Turnpike Street
North Andover, MA 01845
O 978.837.5341 / F 978.837.5079
mark.dennehy@merrimack.edu

HOCKEY MEDIA CONTACT
Aaron Todd - Sports Info Director
Merrimack College
315 Turnpike Street
North Andover, MA 01845
O 978.837.5238 / F 978.837.5079
aaron.todd@merrimack.edu

HOCKEY RINK
Volpe Center (On Campus)
315 Turnpike Road
North Andover, MA 01845
Size 200' x 85', Capacity 3,617
O 508.837.5341

ATHLETIC DIRECTOR
Sean Frazier - Athletic Director
Merrimack College
South Peter Volpe Athletic Center
North Andover, MA 01845
O 978.837.5341 / F 978.837.5079

WARRIORS PLAYERS

Player	YB	GR	Ht/Wt	P	Hometown/Last Team
Mike Alexiou	85	07	6'2"/210	F	Pickering,ON/St. Michael's (PS)
Justin Bonitatibus	85	10	6'0"/190	F	Arlington,MA/Walpole Stars (EJHL)
Brian Boulay	84	07	6'1"/200	D	Auburn,MA/Des Moines Buccaneers (USHL)
Pat Bowen	85	10	6'0"/190	D	Marshfield,MA/New Hampshire Monarchs (EJHL)
Andre Brathwaite	85	10	6'2"/190	G	Kingston,ON/Chilliwack Chiefs (BCHL)
David Burkholder	87	10	5'11"/180	D	W Seneca,NY/Welland Canadians (GHJHL)
Matt Byrnes	82	07	5'9"/190	F	Lincoln,RI/Boston (EJHL)
Hank Carisio	83	08	6'2"/205	F	Cheshire,CT/Springfield (NAHL)
John Goebel	86	09	5'11"/175	F	Parma,OH/Cleveland Barons (NAHL)
Jordan Hart	83	08	6'2"/200	D	Huntington,NY/Cedar Rapids RoughRiders (USHL)
Jim Healey	83	07	6'1"/195	G	Holyrood,NF/Wexford Raiders (OPJHL)
Matt Jones	86	10	6'4"/205	F	Kentwood,MI/Sioux City Musketeers (USHL)
Chris Kane	85	09	6'1"/195	D	Irvine,CA/Sioux City Musketeers (USHL)
Pat Kimball	86	10	5'8"/170	F	Framingham,MA/Junior Bruins (EJHL)
Joe Loprieno	86	10	6'3"/205	D	Bloomingdale,IL/Chicago Steel (USHL)
Justin Mills	82	07	5'11"/200	F	Edgerton,AB/St. Albert Saints (AJHL)
Chris Nugent	86	09	6'1"/190	F	Dallas,TX/Green Bay Gamblers (USHL)
Derek Pallardy	83	08	5'10"/175	F	Chesterfield,MO/Springfield Blues (NAHL)
Carmen Posteraro		08	6'0"/175	F	Pittsburgh,PA/Bentley (AHL)
Mickey Rego	86	09	5'10"/170	F	Hudson,MA/Valley Warriors (EJHL)
Rob Ricci	84	09	5'9"/165	F	Brampton,ON/Cedar Rapids RoughRiders (USHL)
JC Robitaille	87	10	6'1"/195	F	Des Ruisseaux,QC/St. Jerome Panthers (QJAHL)
Brandon Sadlowski	86	10	6'0"/185	D	St. Paul,AB/Fort McMurray Oil Barons (AJHL)
Ryan Sullivan	85	07	6'2"/190	D	Toronto,ON/St. Michael's (PS)
Mike Vaskivuo	86	10	6'1"/185	F	Helsinki,Finland/South Kent (NEPSAC)
Patrick Watson	84	09	6'2"/180	G	Waltham,MA/Indiana Ice (USHL)
Brock Wilson	84	09	6'1"/210	D	St. Louis,MO/Brockville Braves (CJHL)

ROSTER ANALYSIS (SCHOLARSHIPS - 18)

Class		Country		Last Team					
Fr	10	USA	19	US JR A	11	CDN JR A	6	ACHA	
So	7	Canada	7	US JR B	5	CDN JR B	1	NJCAA	
Jr	4	Europe	1	US PS	1	CDN PS	2	NCAA	1
Sr	6	Asia		US HS		CDN HS		USNDT	
Gr		Other		US Midget		CDN Midget		Other	

ADMISSIONS, ENROLLMENT & CAMPUS INFORMATION

Founded 1947	Average acceptance rate - 64 %	Mary Lou Retelle - Admissions Director
Private, suburban campus	Freshman financial aid - 70 %	Merrimack College
1,161 men / 1,071 women	Early decision application - N/A	North Andover, MA 01845
Tuition, room & board - $ 35 K	Regular application deadline - Feb 1	O 978.837.5100/F 978.837.5133
Avg SAT - 1,095/Avg ACT - 24	Financial aid deadline - Feb 1	

MIAMI UNIVERSITY

Division 1

HOCKEY STAFF

HEAD COACH
Enrico Blasi *(Miami '94)*

ASSISTANT COACHES
Chris Bergeron *(Miami '93)*
Jeff Blashill *(Ferris State '98)*
Nick Petraglia *(Miami '04)*
Josh Fentonl *(Iowa State '01)*

HOCKEY OFFICE
Miami University
Goggin Ice Arena # 211
Oxford, OH 45056
O 513.529.9800 / F 513.529.9832
blasie@muohio.edu

HOCKEY MEDIA CONTACT
Jess Bechard - Hockey Info Director
Miami University - Millet Hall # 230
Oxford, OH 45056
O 513.529.1601 / F 513.529.8173
bechardja@muohio.edu

HOCKEY RINK
Goggin Ice Arena (On Campus)
Tallawanda Street & High Street
Oxford, OH 45056
Size 200' x 85', Capacity 2,200
O 513.529.1646

ATHLETIC DIRECTOR
Brad Bates - Athletic Director
Miami University - Millet Hall
Oxford, OH 45056
O 513.529.3113

RED HAWKS PLAYERS

Player	YB	GR	Ht/Wt	P	Hometown/Last Team
Matt Christie	85	07	5'10"/195	F	Ajax,ON/Aurora Tigers (OPJHL)
Joe Cooper	85	07	6'1"/190	F	Toronto,ON/St. Michael's (PS)
Nathan Davis	86	08	6'1"/190	F	Rocky River,OH/USNDT (NAHL)
Charlie Effinger	85	08	6'1"/180	G	Belleville,IL/St. Louis (USHL)
Raymond Eichenlaub	86	09	6'2"/200	D	Wilmette,IL/Cedar Rapids RoughRiders (USHL)
Charley Fetzer	85	08	6'1"/195	D	Chicago,IL/Youngstown Phantoms (NAHL)
Michael Findorff	84	09	6'6"/230	D	Colorado Spgs,CO/Indiana Ice (USHL)
Mitch Ganzak	84	08	5'11"/200	D	Redford,MI/Green Bay Gamblers (USHL)
Marty Guerin	82	07	5'10"/185	F	Lansing,MI/Des Moines Buccaneers (USHL)
Dane Hetland	87	10	6'0"/195	F	Bridgeville,PA/Bay State Breakers (EJHL)
Ryan Jones	84	08	6'0"/195	F	Chatham,ON/Chatham Maroons (WOJHL)
Brian Kaufman	84	09	6'4"/205	F	Shoreview,MN/Des Moines Buccaneers (USHL)
Alexandre Lacombe	86	09	5'11"/180	F	Orleans,ON/Gloucester Rangers (CJHL)
Bill Loupee	84	09	5'10"/175	F	Bloomfield,MI/Cedar Rapids RoughRiders (USHL)
Alec Martinez	87	09	6'1"/190	D	Rochester,MI/Cedar Rapids RoughRiders (USHL)
Justin Mercier	87	09	5'11"/180	F	Erie,PA/USNDT (NAHL)
Nino Musitelli	85	08	5'8"/180	F	Macomb,MI/Danville Wings (USHL)
Andy Nelson	82	07	5'11"/195	F	Superior,WI/Waterloo Blackhawks (USHL)
Jarod Palmer	86	10	6'0"/190	F	Fridley,MN/Tri-City Storm (USHL)
Brad Robbins	84	08	6'1"/200	D	W Bloomfield,MI/Danville Wings (USHL)
Kevin Roeder	86	09	5'9"/195	D	Glenview,IL/Chicago Steel (USHL)
Brandon Smith	86	10	6'0"/205	D	Pepper Pike,OH/Bridgewater Bandits (EJHL)
Geoff Smith	83	07	5'11"/180	F	Toronto,ON/Texas Tornado (NAHL)
Gary Steffes	87	10	6'1"/195	F	Grand Blanc,MI/Cedar Rapids RoughRiders (USHL)
Jon Whitacre	85	10	5'10"/200	G	Indianapolis,IN/Billings Bulls (NAHL)
Jeff Zatkoff	87	09	6'2"/160	G	Chesterfield,MI/Sioux City Musketeers (USHL)

ROSTER ANALYSIS (SCHOLARSHIPS - 18)

Class		Country		Last Team					
Fr	5	USA	21	US JR A	18	CDN JR A	2	ACHA	
So	9	Canada	5	US JR B	2	CDN JR B	1	NJCAA	
Jr	7	Europe		US PS		CDN PS	1	NCAA	
Sr	5	Asia		US HS		CDN HS		USNDT	2
Gr		Other		US Midget		CDN Midget		Other	

ADMISSIONS, ENROLLMENT & CAMPUS INFORMATION

Founded 1809
Public, rural campus
6,605 men / 8,406 women
Tuition, room & board $ 28 K
Avg SAT - 1,210 / Avg ACT - 27

Average acceptance rate - 71 %
Freshman financial aid - 70 %
Early decision deadline - Nov 1
Regular application deadline - Jan 31
Financial aid deadline - Feb 15

Michael Mills - Admissions Director
Miami University - Gloss Center
Oxford, OH 45056
O 513.529.2531 / F 513.529.1550

UNIVERSITY OF MICHIGAN-ANN ARBOR

Division 1

HOCKEY STAFF

HEAD COACH
Red Berenson *(Michigan '62)*

ASSOCIATE HEAD COACH
Mel Pearson *(Michigan Tech '81)*

ASSISTANT COACHES
Billy Powers *(Michigan '88)*
Stan Matwijiw

HOCKEY OFFICE
University of Michigan - Athletic Dept.
1000 South State Street, #3717
Ann Arbor, MI 48109-2201
O 734.647.1201 / F 734.647.7825
redbaron@umich.edu

HOCKEY MEDIA CONTACT
Matt Trevor - Hockey Info Director
University of Michigan - Sports Info
1000 South State Street, #2201
Ann Arbor, MI 48109-2201
O 734.763.4423 / F 734.647.1188

HOCKEY RINK
Yost Ice Arena (On Campus)
1000 South State Street
Ann Arbor, MI 48109
Size 200' x 85', Capacity 6,637
O 734.647.7916

ATHLETIC DIRECTOR
William Martin - Athletic Director
University of Michigan - Athletic Dept.
1000 South State Street, #2201
Ann Arbor, MI 48109-2201
O 734.647.2583 / F 734.764.3221
wcmartin@umich.edu

WOLVERINES PLAYERS

Player	YB	GR	Ht/Wt	P	Hometown/Last Team
Jason Bailey	87	09	6' 1"/210	F	Nepean,ON/USNDT (NAHL)
Anthony Ciraulo	85	10	5' 6"/175	F	Clinton Twp,MI/Mahoning Valley Phantoms (NAHL)
Andrew Cogliano	87	09	5'10"/185	F	Woodbridge,ON/St. Michael's (PS)
Tim Cook	84	07	6' 4"/220	D	Montclair,NJ/Omaha Lancers (USHL)
Jason Dest	84	07	5'11"/185	D	Fraser,MI/Omaha Lancers (USHL)
Eric Elmblad	86	10	6' 4"/195	D/F	St. Ignace,MI/Traverse City North Stars (NAHL)
Danny Fardig	86	09	5'11"/200	F	Ann Arbor,MI/USNDT (NAHL)
Chris Fragner	84	09	6' 1"/185	F	Ann Arbor,MI/Michigan (ACHA)
TJ Hensick	85	07	5'10"/190	F	Howell,MI/USNDT (NAHL)
Matt Hunwick	85	07	6' 0"/200	D	Roseville,MI/USNDT (NAHL)
Steve Jakiel	86	10	6' 4"/190	G	Santa Clarita,CA/Indiana Ice (USHL)
Jack Johnson	87	09	6' 1"/215	D	Ann Arbor,MI/USNDT (NAHL)
Steve Kampfer	88	10	5'11"/200	D	Jackson,MI/Sioux City Musketeers (USHL)
Chad Kolarik	86	08	5'10"/180	F	Abington,PA/USNDT (NAHL)
Brian Lebler	88	10	6' 2"/210	F	Penticton,BC/Penticton Panthers (BCHL)
Mike Mayhew	84	07	6' 0"/170	G	Owatonna,MN/Shattuck-St. Mary's (PS)
Tim Miller	87	09	6' 1"/190	F	Davisburg,MI/Omaha Lancers (USHL)
Mark Mitera	87	09	6' 3"/215	D	Livonia,MI/USNDT (NAHL)
Jon Montville	86	09	5'10"/195	D	Novi,MI/Michigan (ACHA)
Brandon Naurato	85	09	6' 0"/195	F	Livonia,MI/USNDT (NAHL)
Kevin Porter	86	08	5'11"/195	F	Northville,MI/USNDT (NAHL)
David Rohlfs	84	07	6' 3"/240	F	Northville,MI/Compuware (NAHL)
Billy Sauer	88	09	6' 2"/180	G	Walworth,NY/Chicago Steel (USHL)
Chris Summers	88	10	6' 2"/185	D	Milan,MI/USNDT (NAHL)
Travis Turnbull	86	09	6' 0"/195	F	Chesterfield,MO/Sioux City Musketeers (USHL)
Morgan Ward	82	07	6' 2"/205	F	W Redding,CT/US Military Academy (AHL)

ROSTER ANALYSIS (SCHOLARSHIPS - 18)

Class		Country	Last Team					
Fr	6	USA	23	US JR A	11	CDN JR A	1	ACHA	2
So	11	Canada	3	US JR B		CDN JR B		NJCAA	
Jr	2	Europe		US PS	1	CDN PS	1	NCAA	1
Sr	7	Asia		US HS		CDN HS		USNDT	9
Gr		Other		US Midget		CDN Midget		Other	

ADMISSIONS, ENROLLMENT & CAMPUS INFORMATION

Founded 1817
Public, urban campus
12,339 men / 12,339 women
Tuition, room & board - $ 17 K / $ 35 K
Avg SAT - 1,305 / Avg ACT - 28

Average acceptance rate - 32 %
Freshman financial aid - 90 %
Early decision application deadline - N/A
Regular application deadline - Feb 1
Financial aid deadline - Sep 30

Ted Spencer - Admissions Director
University of Michigan
1000 South State Street
Ann Arbor, MI 48109-2201
O 734.764.7433 / F 734.936.0740

UNIVERSITY OF MICHIGAN-DEARBORN

Division 1

HOCKEY STAFF

HEAD COACH
Dave Debol

ASSISTANT COACHES
Rich Gauthier
Derek Langlois

HOCKEY OFFICE
University of Mich.-Dearborn Fieldhouse
4901 Evergreen Road
Dearborn, MI 48128
O 313.593.3534 / F 313.593.5436
dcdeebs@aol.com

HOCKEY MEDIA CONTACT
Bryan Earl - Hockey Info Director
4901 Evergreen Road
Dearborn, MI 48128
O 313.593.5671 / F 313.593.5436
earlb@umich.edu

HOCKEY RINK
University of Michigan-Dearborn
Fieldhouse
4901 Evergreen Road
Dearborn, MI 48128
Size 200' X 85', Capacity 1,500

ATHLETIC DIRECTOR
Steve Rotta - Athletic Director
University of Michigan-Dearborn
Athletic Department
4901 Evergreen Road
Dearborn, MI 48128
O 313.593.5540 / F 313.593.5540

WOLVES PLAYERS

Player	YB GR Ht/Wt	P	Hometown/Last Team
Andrew Baron	5' 8"/180	F	Lincoln Park,MI/Mt. Carmel (PS)
Matthew Chromy	6' 6"/250	D	Crystal Lake,IL/Michigan Ice Dogs (CSHL)
Patrick Coldren	5'10"/185	F	Canton,MI/Catholic Central (PS)
Michael Crowley	6' 0"/185	F	Canton,MI/Michigan Stars (Jr. A)
Bryan Czajka	6' 1"/225	D	Brighton,MI/Brighton (HS)
Kahlin Dawson	6' 2"/190	F	Hamburg,MI/Pinckney (HS)
James Donovan	6' 2"/170	F	Brighton,MI/Brighton (HS)
Steve Galvan	6' 0"/180	F	Livonia,MI/Michigan Ice Dogs (CSHL)
Nick Hill	5' 7"/135	G	Livonia,MI/Canton Crush
Brian Hopper	6' 1"/165	D	Brownstown,MI/Carlson (HS)
Matthew Janiga	5' 9"/165	G	Dearborn,MI/Dearborn Unified (HS)
Joel Kuehn	6' 0"/180	F	Troy,MI/Cleveland Barons
Dan Lamonica	5' 7"/190	D	Livonia,MI/Stevenson (HS)
Mike Pangrazzi	5' 8"/145	D	Allen Park,MI/Gabriel Richard (HS)
Adam Pawloski	5' 9"/155	F	Dearborn,MI/Westland (HS)
Adam Perkins	5' 9"/150	F	Redford,MI/Dearborn Spiders
Steve Rademacher	5'10"/165	F	Dearborn Heights,MI/Compuware (Midget AAA)
Mike Ross	5' 5"/135	F	Ortonville,MI/Brandon (HS)
Marino Santi	5' 8"/185	D	Eastpointe,MI/Belle Tire (Midget AAA)
Walter Stepanenko	5'11"/185	F	St. Clair Shores,MI/St. Clair Shores (HS)
Adam Stoner	6' 1"/175	F	Livonia,MI/Stevenson (HS)
Joshua Thompson	5'10"/185	F	Waterford,MI/Michigan Ice Dogs (CSHL)
Kevin Thompson	5' 9"/160	F	Saline,MI/Saline (HS)
Jason Vella	5'11"/170	D	Livonia,MI/Stevenson (HS)
Bryan Walleman	5' 8"/155	F	St. Clair Shores,MI/St. Clair Shores (HS)
Shawn Wilson	5' 8"/160	F	Riverview,MI/Riverview (HS)
Stephen Yu	6' 2"/175	G	Garden City,MI/Wayne Wheels

ROSTER ANALYSIS (SCHOLARSHIPS - 0)

Class	Country		Last Team			
Fr	USA	27	US JR A	1	CDN JR A	ACHA
So	Canada		US JR B	3	CDN JR B	NJCAA
Jr	Europe		US PS	2	CDN PS	NCAA
Sr	Asia		US HS	15	CDN HS	USNDT
Gr	Other		US Midget	2	CDN Midget	Other 4

ADMISSIONS, ENROLLMENT & CAMPUS INFORMATION

Founded 1959
Public, suburban campus
3,124 men / 2,884 women
Tuition, (no housing) $ 7 K / $ 14 K
Avg ACT - 23

Average acceptance rate - 69 %
Freshman financial aid - 2 %
Early decision application deadline - N/A
Regular application deadline - rolling
Financial aid deadline - Apr 1

Gabrielle Williams - Admissions Director
University of Michigan-Dearborn
4901 Evergreen Road
Dearborn, MI 48128
O 313.593.5550 / F 313.436.9167

www.umd.umich.edu

www.umd.umich.edu/athletics/hockey/hockeyhome.html

MICHIGAN STATE UNIVERSITY

Division 1

HOCKEY STAFF

HEAD COACH
Rick Comley *(Lake Superior State '71)*

ASSISTANT COACHES
Tom Newton *(Bowling Green '80)*
Brian Renfrew *(Western Michigan '95)*
Rob Woodward *(Michigan State '00)*

HOCKEY OFFICE
Michigan State University
Munn Ice Arena
East Lansing, MI 48824-1047
O 517.355.1639 / F 517.432.1879
comley@ath.msu.edu

HOCKEY MEDIA CONTACT
Jamie Weir - Hockey Info Director
Michigan State University
222 Breslin Center
1 Birch Road
East Lansing, MI 48824
O 517.355.2271 / F 517.353.9636
jweir@ath.msu.edu

HOCKEY RINK
Munn Ice Arena (On Campus)
1 Chestnut Road
East Lansing, MI 48824
Size 200' x 85', Capacity 6,470
O 517.353.6359

ATHLETIC DIRECTOR
Ron Mason - Athletic Director
Michigan State University
220 Jenison Fieldhouse
East Lansing, MI 48824-1047
O 517.355.1623

SPARTANS PLAYERS

Player	YB	GR	Ht/Wt	P	Hometown/Last Team
Justin Abdelkader	87	09	6' 2"/205	F	Muskegon,MI/Cedar Rapids RoughRiders (USHL)
Tim Crowder	86	09	6' 3"/185	F	Victoria,BC/Surrey Eagles (BCHL)
Jeff Dunne	85	08	6' 0"/195	D	Grover,MO/Chicago Steel (USHL)
Brandon Gentile	87	09	6' 0"/195	D	Clarkston,MI/USNDT (NAHL)
Ethan Graham	82	07	6' 2"/195	D	Xenia,OH/Lincoln Stars (USHL)
Tyler Howells	83	07	5' 8"/185	D	Eden Pr,MN/Cedar Rapids RoughRiders (USHL)
Bobby Jarosz	87	10	6' 0"/175	G	Crystal Lk,IL/Cleveland Barons (NAHL)
Justin Johnston	86	10	6' 0"/175	D	Grosse Pt Woods,MI/Texarkana Bandits (NAHL)
Tim Kennedy	86	09	5'10"/175	F	Buffalo,NY/Sioux City Musketeers (USHL)
Kurt Kivisto	85	09	5' 8"/170	F	Milford,MI/Cleveland Barons (NAHL)
Chris Lawrence	82	07	5'10"/185	F	Havertown,PA/Pittsburgh Forge (NAHL)
Bryan Lerg	86	08	5'10"/175	F	Livonia,MI/USNDT (NAHL)
Jeff Lerg	86	09	5' 6"/155	G	Livonia,MI/Omaha Lancers (USHL)
Zak McClellan	83	08	6' 1"/195	F	Frankenmuth,MI/Bozeman Icedogs (NAHL)
Jim McKenzie	84	08	6' 2"/205	F	Woodbury,MN/Sioux Falls Stampede (USHL)
Steve Mnich	86	09	5' 8"/160	F	Northville,MI/Dallas Stars (Midget AAA)
Chris Mueller	86	08	5'11"/190	F	W Seneca,NY/Buffalo Saints (Midget AAA)
Mike Ratchuk	88	10	5'11"/180	D	Buffalo,NY/USNDT (NAHL)
Matt Schepke	85	09	5'11"/210	F	Warren,MI/Omaha Lancers (USHL)
Matt Shouneyia	85	09	5' 9"/180	D	Bloomfield Hls,MI/Cleveland Barons (NAHL)
Chris Snavely	82	07	5' 8"/175	D	Lancaster,PA/Cedar Rapids RoughRiders (USHL)
Jay Sprague	86	10	6' 3"/220	F	Georgetown,ON/Indiana Ice (USHL)
Dan Sturges	85	08	6' 0"/185	F	Verona,WI/Green Bay Gamblers (USHL)
Nick Sucharski	87	09	6' 2"/180	F	Toronto,ON/Wexford Raiders (OPJHL)
Ryan Turek	87	10	6' 0"/175	D/F	Northville,MI/Omaha Lancers (USHL)
Daniel Vukovic	86	08	6' 3"/235	D	N York,ON/St. Michael's (PS)
Brandon Warner	83	07	5'11"/170	D	Huntertown,IN/Pittsburgh Forge (NAHL)

ROSTER ANALYSIS (SCHOLARSHIPS - 18)

Class		Country		Last Team					
Fr	5	USA	24	US JR A	19	CDN JR A	2	ACHA	
So	10	Canada	3	US JR B		CDN JR B		NJCAA	
Jr	7	Europe		US PS		CDN PS	1	NCAA	
Sr	5	Asia		US HS		CDN HS		USNDT	3
Gr		Other		US Midget	2	CDN Midget		Other	

ADMISSIONS, ENROLLMENT & CAMPUS INFORMATION

Founded 1855
Public, suburban campus
15,798 men / 19,309 women
Tuition, room & board $ 13 K /$ 23 K
Avg SAT - 1,138 / Avg ACT - 25

Average aceptance rate - 79 %
Freshman financial aid - 79 %
Early decision application deadline - N/A
Regular application deadline - Aug 1
Financial aid deadline - Jun 30

Dr. Gordon E. Stanley - Admissions Director
Michigan State University - Admissions
250 Administration Building
East Lansing, MI 48824-1046
O 517.355.8332 / F 517.353.1647

www.msu.edu

msuspartans.collegesports.com

MICHIGAN TECHNOLOGICAL UNIV.

Division 1

HOCKEY STAFF

HEAD COACH
Jamie Russell *(Michigan Tech '89)*

ASSISTANT COACHES
Randy McKay *(Michigan Tech '88)*
Pat Mikesch *(Michigan Tech '96)*
Chris Tob *(Wisconsin '96)*

HOCKEY OFFICE
Michigan Technological University
1400 Townsend Drive - SDC
Houghton, MI 49931-1295
O 906.487.2104 / F 906.487.3430
jrussell@mtu.edu

HOCKEY MEDIA CONTACT
Jon Oman - Hockey Info Director
Michigan Technological University
1400 Townsend Drive - SDC # 233
Houghton, MI 49931-1295
O 906.487.2351 / F 906.487.3062
joman@mtu.edu

HOCKEY RINK
MacInnes Arena (On Campus)
MacInnes Drive
Houghton, MI 49931
Size 200' x 85', Capacity 4,200
O 906.487.2337

ATHLETIC DIRECTOR
Suzanne Sanregret - Athletic Director
Michigan Technological University
1400 Townsend Drive - SDC
Houghton, MI 49931-1295
O 906.487.2990 / F 906.487.3062
srsanreg@mtu.edu

HUSKIES PLAYERS

Player	YB	GR	Ht/Wt	P	Hometown/Last Team
Ryan Angelow	85	09	5'10"/175	F	Mississauga,ON/Oakville Blades (OPJHL)
Phil Axtell	82	10	6' 5"/240	F	New Windsor,MD/Cedar Rapids RoughRiders (USHL)
Mike Batovanja	82	07	5' 9"/175	F	Hinton,AB/Findlay (CHA)
Ryan Bunger	85	10	6' 1"/185	F	Sammamish,WA/Bozeman Icedogs (NAHL)
Drew Dobson	87	10	6' 0"/180	D	Palatine,IL/Waterloo Blackhawks (USHL)
Jordan Foote	85	08	6' 2"/180	F	Edmonton,AB/Nanaimo Clippers (BCHL)
Alex Gagne	85	09	6' 0"/190	F	Rock Forest,QC/Cowichan Valley Capitals (BCHL)
Malcolm Gwilliam	85	08	6' 1"/185	F	Kamloops,BC/Grande Prairie Storm (AJHL)
Kevin Hachey	84	08	5' 6"/150	G	Ontario,CA/Trail Smoke Eaters (BCHL)
Lars Helminen	85	07	5' 7"/195	D	Brighton,MN/Compuware Ambassadors (NAHL)
Jimmy Kerr	85	08	5'10"/190	F	Leduc,AB/Olds Grizzlys (AJHL)
Geoff Kinrade	85	09	5'10"/195	F	Nelson,BC/Cowichan Valley Capitals (BCHL)
Derek Kitti	85	09	6' 2"/200	F	Laurium,MI/Springfield (NAHL)
John Kivisto	86	10	5'10"/175	D/F	Milford,MI/Mahoning Valley Phantoms (NAHL)
Alex Lord	85	09	6' 1"/180	F	Magog,QC/Champlain (QJAHL)
Mark Malekoff	84	08	6' 2"/205	D	Grande Prairie,AB/Grande Prairie Storm (AJHL)
Rob Nolan	85	09	6' 0"/170	G	Sherwood Pk,AB/Fort McMurray Oil Barons (AJHL)
Peter Rouleau	83	08	5' 7"/165	F	Hancock,MI/Finlandia (MCHA)
John Schwarz	84	09	6' 3"/210	D	Calgary,AB/Fort McMurray Oil Barons (AJHL)
Tyler Shelast	84	08	6' 1"/195	F	Kamloops,BC/Powell River Kings (BCHL)
Tyler Skworchinski	82	07	6' 0"/190	F	Marathon,ON/Portage Terriers (ManJHL)
Justin St. Louis	85	09	6' 2"/190	F	Calgary,AB/Trail Smoke Eaters (BCHL)
Michael-Lee Teslak	85	09	6' 2"/175	G	Fernie,BC/Prince George Spruce Kings (BCHL)
Mike VanWagner	86	09	6' 3"/205	D	Traverse City,MI/Chicago Steel (USHL)
Eli Vlaisavljevich	85	10	5'11"/175	D	Shoreview,MN/Lincoln Stars (USHL)
Jake Wilkens	84	08	6' 1"/200	D	Eagle Rvr,AK/Vernon Vipers (BCHL)

ROSTER ANALYSIS (SCHOLARSHIPS - 18)

Class		Country		Last Team					
Fr	5	USA	11	US JR A	8	CDN JR A	16	ACHA	
So	10	Canada	15	US JR B		CDN JR B		NJCAA	
Jr	8	Europe		US PS		CDN PS		NCAA	2
Sr	3	Asia		US HS		CDN HS		USNDT	
Gr		Other		US Midget		CDN Midget		Other	

ADMISSIONS, ENROLLMENT & CAMPUS INFORMATION

Founded 1885	Average acceptance rate - 94 %	Nancy Rehling - Admissions Director
Public, rural campus	Freshman financial aid - 79 %	Michigan Technological University
4,498 men / 1,124 women	Early decision application deadline - N/A	1400 Townsend Drive
Tuition, room & board - $ 14 K / $ 16 K	Regular application deadline - rolling	Houghton, MI 49931-1295
Avg SAT - 1,210 / Avg ACT - 26	Financial aid deadline - Feb 21	O 906.487.2335 / F 906.487.2125

www.mtu.edu   michigantechhuskies.com

MIDDLEBURY COLLEGE

Division 3

HOCKEY STAFF

HEAD COACH
Bill Beaney *(New Hampshire '73)*

ASSISTANT COACH
John Dawson *(Middlebury '04)*

HOCKEY OFFICE
Middlebury College
Memorial Field House
Middlebury, VT 05753
O 802.443.5268/ F 802.443.2073
beaney@middlebury.edu

HOCKEY MEDIA CONTACT
Brad Nadeau - Sports Info Director
Middlebury College
Memorial Field House
Middlebury, VT 05753
O 802.443.5193/ F 802.443.2529
bnadeau@middlebury.edu

HOCKEY RINK
Chip Kenyon '85 Arena (On Campus)
Middlebury College
Middlebury, VT 05753
Size 200' x 95', Capacity 2,100
O 802.443.5000

ATHLETIC DIRECTOR
Russ Reilly - Athletic Director
Middlebury College
Memorial Field House
Middlebury, VT 05753
O 802.443.5253/ F 802.443.2124
reilly@middlebury.edu

PANTHERS PLAYERS

Player	YB	GR Ht/Wt	P	Hometown/Last Team
Scott Bartlett	08	5' 9"/165	F	Pittsford,NY/Deerfield (NEPSAC)
Ross Cherry	08	6' 1"/210	G	Basking Ridge,NJ/Delbarton (PS)
Mack Cummins	09	5'10"/185	D	SW Ranches,FL/St. Thomas Aquinas (PS)
Samuel Driver	08	6' 0"/175	F/D	St. Albans,VT/Taft (NEPSAC)
Ian Drummond	09	5'10"/185	D	Del Mar,CA/Phillips Exeter (NEPSAC)
Casey Ftorek	08	5' 9"/175	F	Wolfeboro,NH/Taft (NEPSAC)
Richie Fuld	07	6' 0"/190	F	Greenwich,CT/Brunswick (NEPSAC)
Justin Gaines	08	5'11"/180	F/D	Mequon,WI/Culver (PS)
Mickey Gilchrist	08	5' 9"/185	F	Ottawa,ON/Merivale (HS)
Mason Graddock	09	5' 7"/170	F	Stowe,VT/Stowe (HS)
Darwin Hunt	07	5'10"/190	F	Winnetka,IL/Deerfield (NEPSAC)
Max Kennedy	10	5' 8"/160	G	Cazenova,NY/Millbrook (NEPSAC)
Jack Kinder	09	5' 9"/165	D	Shaker Hgts,OH/Deerfield (NEPSAC)
Kyle Koziara	09	6' 5"/215	D	W Springfield,MA/Cushing (NEPSAC)
Eric LaFreniere	07	5' 9"/170	F	St. Anne,MB/Phillips Exeter (NEPSAC)
Robert MacIntyre	08	6' 0"/185	D	Calgary,AB/National Sports (PS)
Tom Maldonado	08	5' 8"/180	D	Bronx,NY/Taft (NEPSAC)
Shane Mandes	10	5' 9"/150	F	Doylestown,PA/Loomis Chaffee (NEPSAC)
Jed McDonald	08	6' 2"/200	D	Hingham,MA/Hingham (HS)
Jamie McKenna	09	5' 9"/170	F	Lake Placid,NY/Northwood (PS)
AJ Meyer	10	6' 0"/200	D	Westfield,NJ/Choate (NEPSAC)
Doug Raeder	09	6' 1"/175	G	Needham,MA/Longmeadow (HS)
Evgeny Saidachev	07	5'10"/165	F	Gig Harbor,WA/Culver (PS)
John Sales	07	6' 1"/185	D	Chatham,IL/Deerfield (NEPSAC)
Ryan Seavy	10	5' 9"/165	D	Denver,CO/East (HS)
Brett Shirreffs	07	6' 1"/205	D	Etna,NH/Hotchkiss (NEPSAC)
John Sullivan	10	5'10"/160	F	Delmar,NY/Albany (NEPSAC)
Charlie Townsend	10	6' 3"/205	F	Pennington,NJ/Taft (NEPSAC)

ROSTER ANALYSIS (SCHOLARSHIPS - 0)

Class		Country		Last Team				
Fr	6	USA	25	US JR A		CDN JR A		ACHA
So	7	Canada	3	US JR B		CDN JR B		NJCAA
Jr	9	Europe		US PS	23	CDN PS		NCAA
Sr	6	Asia		US HS	4	CDN HS	1	USNDT
Gr		Other		US Midget		CDN Midget		Other

ADMISSIONS, ENROLLMENT & CAMPUS INFORMATION

Founded 1800
Private, rural campus
1,155 men / 1,202 women
Tuition, room & board - $ 41 K
Avg SAT - 1,440 / Avg ACT - 30

Average acceptance rate - 26 %
Freshman financial aid - 100 %
Early decision application deadline - Dec 15
Regular application deadline - Jan 1
Financial aid deadline - Dec 31

John Hanson - Admissions Director
Middlebury College - Willard House
Middlebury, VT 05753
O 802.443.3000/ F 802.443.2065

MILWAUKEE SCHOOL OF ENGINEERING

Division 3

HOCKEY STAFF

HEAD COACH
Mark Ostapina *(Wisconsin '79)*

ASSISTANT COACHES
Mike Sullivan *(Wisconsin-Eau Claire)*
Josh Nickols *(MSOE '99)*
Andy Ostapina

HOCKEY OFFICE
Milwaukee School of Engineering
1025 North Broadway
Milwaukee, WI 53202
O 414.277.7565 / F 414.221.0610
ostapina@msoe.edu

HOCKEY MEDIA CONTACT
Brian Gibboney - Sports Info Director
1025 North Broadway
Milwaukee, WI 53202
O 414.277.2412 / F 414.221.0610
gibboney@msoe.edu

HOCKEY RINK
Kern Center (On Campus)
1245 N. Broadway
Milwaukee, WI
Size ' x ', Capacity
414.277.2672

ATHLETIC DIRECTOR
Dan Harris - Athletic Director
1025 North Broadway
Milwaukee, WI 53202
O 414.277.7230 / F 414.221.0610
harris@msoe.edu

RAIDERS PLAYERS

Player	YB	GR	Ht/Wt	P	Hometown/Last Team
Jacob Anderson	85	09	6' 0"/200	F	Toronto,ON/St. Michael's (PS)
Nick Bilpush	83	07	5'10"/180	F	Ellisville,MO/St. Louis Blues (CSHL)
Michael Bove	85	10	6' 0"/170	G	Cody,WY/Boston Harbor Wolves (EJHL)
Matt Burzon	85	07	5'11"/180	G	Lilse,VT/Holderness (NEPSAC)
Ross Chawansky	84	08	6' 2"/200	D	Waterford,MI/West Bloomfield (HS)
Reid Crawford	88	10	5'10"/175	F	Glendale,WI/Madison Capitals (Midget AAA)
Joe Dovalina	83	07	5'10"/185	G	Chicago,IL/Thornhill Rattlers (OPJHL)
Michael Duta	83	07	5' 9"/170	F	Seattle,WA/Seattle (NPJHL)
Matt Fastelin	85	08	5'10"/180	F	Hayward,WI/Hayward (HS)
RG Flath	84	09	5'11"/190	F	Salt Lake City,UT/Soo Indians (NAHL)
Blair Hanberg	83	08	6' 1"/200	F	Edmonds,WA/Helena Bighorns (NAHL)
Paul Haviland		10	6' 3"/205	D	Verona,WI/Madison Capitals (Midget AAA)
Michael Jantzi	85	10	6' 0"/215	D	E Amherst,NY/Fort Erie Meteors (GHJHL)
Nick King	85	09	5'10"/195	F	Snohomish,WA/California Wave (WSHL)
Simon Labrosse-Gelinas	82	09	6' 1"/195	F	Houston,TX/Thornhill Rattlers (OPJHL)
Matt Leitzan	86	09	6' 3"/200	F	Appleton,WI/Appleton West (HS)
Mike Marquette	85	09	5' 9"/170	D/F	Fairbanks,AK/Dubuque Thunderbirds (MnJHL)
Jared Moormeier	83	08	5'10"/180	D	Edmonds,WA/Edmonds (HS)
Josh Rudolph	84	07	6' 1"/185	G	Duluth,MN/Duluth Marshall (HS)
Brian Soik	84	07	6' 1"/190	F	Stevens Pt,WI/SPASH (HS)
Jonathan Stover	85	10	6' 0"/220	D	Corona,CA/Northwood (PS)
Lee Swallow	84	08	5'10"/185	F	Stanwood,MI/St. Michael's (PS)
Joseph Vargo	87	10	6' 0"/165	F	Glenview,IL/Glenbrook South (HS)
Kenneth Walters	85	08	6' 1"/195	D	Amery,WI/New Richmond (HS)
Jason Woll	84	09	6' 3"/215	D	Portland,OR/Bozeman Icedogs (NAHL)
David Yolo	84	07	6' 2"/190	D	Hartland,WI/Arrowhead (HS)
Jason Yolo	87	09	6' 2"/190	D	Hartland,WI/Arrowhead (HS)

ROSTER ANALYSIS (SCHOLARSHIPS - 0)

Class		Country		Last Team			
Fr	6	USA	26	US JR A	3	CDN JR A	2	ACHA
So	8	Canada	1	US JR B	5	CDN JR B	1	NJCAA
Jr	6	Europe		US PS	2	CDN PS	2	NCAA
Sr	7	Asia		US HS	10	CDN HS		USNDT
Gr		Other		US Midget	2	CDN Midget		Other

ADMISSIONS, ENROLLMENT & CAMPUS INFORMATION

Founded 1903
Private, urban campus
1,713 men / 376 women
Tuition, room & board - $ 30 K
Avg SAT - 1,215/Avg ACT - 31

Average acceptance rate - 63 %
Freshman financial aid - 68 %
Early decision application deadline - N/A
Regular application deadline - rolling
Financial aid deadline - Mar 15

Paul Borens - Admissions Director
Milwaukee School of Engineering
1025 North Broadway
Milwaukee, WI 53202-3109
O 414.277.7481 / F 414.277.7475

www.msoe.edu   www.msoe.edu/athletics/

UNIV. OF MINNESOTA-CROOKSTON

Division 3

HOCKEY STAFF

HEAD COACH
Gary Warren *(Minnesota-Duluth '77)*

ASSISTANT COACH
Dave Rolling *(Bemidji State '03)*

HOCKEY OFFICE
University of Minnesota-Crookston
Sports Center 151
Crookston, MN 56716
O 218.281.8428 / F 218.281.5223
gwarren@mail.crk.umn.edu

HOCKEY MEDIA CONTACT
Mitch Bakken - Sports Info Director
University of Minnesota-Crookston
Sports Center 139
Crookston, MN 56716
O 218.281.8414 / F 218.281.8430
sid@umcrookston.edu

HOCKEY RINK
Civic Arena (Off Campus)
220 East Roberts Street
Crookston, MN 56716
Size 'x', Capacity 2,713

ATHLETIC DIRECTOR
Stephanie Helgeson - Athletic Director
University of Minnesota-Crookston
Sports Center 141
Crookston, MN 56716
O 218.281.8422 / F 218.281.5223
helgeson@mail.crk.umn.edu

GOLDEN EAGLES PLAYERS

Player	YB	GR	Ht/Wt	P	Hometown/Last Team
Thomas Anick		10	6'1"/175	F	Grand Rapids,MN/Grand Rapids Jr Gold (HS)
Clark Dingeman		10	6'1"/180	D	Bismarck,ND/Bismarck Central (HS)
Brian Fergusson		10	6'0"/185	F	Lac du Bonnet,MB/Winkler Flyers (ManJHL)
Brent Groenke	86	08	5'9"/170	F	Morden,MB/Morden (PS)
Matt Hann	85	08	5'10"/175	F	Crookston,MN/Crookston Central (HS)
Jaden Isakson		08	5'9"/195	G	Bismarck,ND/Capital Thunder (WSHL)
Peter Jerome		10	5'9"/180	F	Devils Lake,ND/Cando (HS)
Jacob Karras		10	5'8"/220	F	Janesville,WI/Hudson Valley Eagles (MJHL)
Justin Klinkhammer	86	10	5'10"/165	G	Thief River Fls,MN/Lincoln (HS)
Kyle Knudsen	82	07	5'11"/175	F	Mead,WA/Minot State Bottineau (NJCAA)
Fred Kooser		10	5'8"/165	F	Omaha,NE/Quad City Express (CSHL)
Ryan Leadens	84	07	5'11"/170	F/D	S St. Paul,MN/South St. Paul (HS)
John Lombardi		10	6'2"/195	F	Apple Valley,MN/Fargo-Moorhead Jets (NAHL)
Matt Marchel		10	6'1"/180	D	Grand Forks,ND/Red River (HS)
Brett Miller	09		5'8"/160	F	Mayville,ND/Cando (HS)
Earl Nikula		10	5'10"/195	D	Silver Bay,MN/Minnesota Ice Hawks (MnJHL)
Jacob Osland	87	09	6'2"/180	F/D	Mayville,ND/Wayzata Jr Gold (HS)
Travis Pederson	86	09	5'10"/165	F	Cando,ND/Cando (HS)
Collin Perry		10	6'1"/195	F	Grand Forks,ND/Massachusetts (NCAA)
Teal Plaine	84	07	6'1"/180	F	Hallock,MN/Kittson Central (HS)
Jon Pritchard		09	6'0"/170	F	Kettering,OH/Hudson Valley (NJCAA)
Brett Saari		09	6'1"/220	F	Green Bay,WI/Hudson Valley Eagles (MJHL)
Brett Shelanski	83	07	6'0"/185	G	Bloomington,MN/Jefferson (HS)
Kyle Sponholtz	85	08	5'11"/205	D	Richland,WA/Minot State Bottineau (NJCAA)
Ryan Tucker	85	08	5'11"/200	D	Crookston,MN/Crookston Central (HS)
Matt Waclawik		10	5'11"/160	F	Fergus Fls,MN/Fergus Falls (HS)
Steve Zutz	85	07	5'8"/155	F	Red Lake Fls,MN/Red Lake Falls (HS)

ROSTER ANALYSIS (SCHOLARSHIPS - 0)

Class		Country		Last Team				
Fr	12	USA	25	US JR A	1	CDN JR A	1	ACHA
So	5	Canada	2	US JR B	5	CDN JR B		NJCAA	3
Jr	5	Europe		US PS		CDN PS	1	NCAA	1
Sr	5	Asia		US HS	15	CDN HS		USNDT
Gr		Other		US Midget		CDN Midget		Other

ADMISSIONS, ENROLLMENT & CAMPUS INFORMATION

Founded 1965
Public, rural campus
622 men / 530 women
Tuition, room & board $ 13 K
Avg SAT - 1,020 / Avg ACT - 21

Average acceptance rate - %
Freshman financial aid - 80 %
Early decision application deadline - N/A
Regular application deadline - Aug 15
Financial aid deadline - Mar 31

Russell L. Kreager
Director of Enrollment Managment
Minnesota-Crookston - 4 Hill Hall
Crookston, MN 56716
O 218.281.8569 / F 218.281.8050

www.crk.umn.edu   www.crk.umn.edu/people/athletics/

UNIVERSITY OF MINNESOTA-DULUTH

Division 1

HOCKEY STAFF

HEAD COACH
Scott Sandelin (North Dakota '87)

ASSISTANT COACHES
Lee Davidson (North Dakota '02)
Steve Rohlik (Wisconsin '90)
Bill Watson (Minnesota-Duluth '90)

HOCKEY OFFICE
University of Minnesota-Duluth
10 University Drive
Duluth, MN 55812-2496
O 218.726.8579 / F 218.726.6529
sandelin@d.umn.edu

HOCKEY MEDIA CONTACT
Bob Nygaard - Sports Info Director
University of Minnesota-Duluth
10 University Drive
Duluth, MN 55812
O 218.726.8191 / F 218.726.6529
bnygaard@d.umn.edu

HOCKEY RINK
Duluth Center (Off Campus)
350 Harbor Drive
Duluth, MN 55802
Size 190' x 85', Capacity 5,333
O 218.727.7939

ATHLETIC DIRECTOR
Bob Nielson - Athletic Director
University of Minnesota-Duluth
10 University Drive
Duluth, MN 55812-2496
O 218.726.8718 / F 218.726.6529
rnielson@d.umn.edu

BULLDOGS PLAYERS

Player	YB	GR	Ht/Wt	P	Hometown/Last Team
Drew Akins	85	10	5'11"/185	F	Excelsior,MN/Sioux Falls Stampede (USHL)
Andrew Carroll	85	09	5'11"/195	F	Shoreview,MN/Sioux Falls Stampede (USHL)
Jay Cascalenda	85	09	6'0"/185	D	St. Paul,MN/Indiana Ice (USHL)
Mike Curry	84	08	6'4"/205	F	Eagle Rvr,AK/Sioux City Musketeers (USHL)
Jordan Fulton	87	10	6'0"/195	F	Brooklyn Pk,MN/Breck (PS)
Jason Garrison	84	09	6'2"/205	D	White Rock,BC/Nanaimo Clippers (BCHL)
Travis Gawryletz	85	08	6'2"/200	D	Trail,BC/Trail Smoke Eaters (BCHL)
Michael Gergen	87	09	5'11"/190	F	Hastings,MN/Shattuck-St. Mary's (PS)
Ryan Geris	81	07	6'2"/195	D	Alexandria,MN/Sioux City Musketeers (USHL)
Logan Gorslitz	86	10	5'10"/175	F	Ft McMurray,AB/Camrose Kodiaks (AJHL)
Matt Greer	85	09	6'2"/200	F	Vadnais Hgts,MN/Des Moines Buccaneers (USHL)
Josh Johnson	84	07	6'0"/185	G	Cloquet,MN/Green Bay Gamblers (USHL)
Nick Kemp	86	09	6'1"/200	F	Hermantown,MN/Sioux City Musketeers (USHL)
Jeff McFarland	83	07	5'9"/175	D	Plymouth,MN/Lincoln Stars (USHL)
Bryan McGregor	84	07	6'0"/210	F	Niagara Fls,ON/Vernon Vipers (BCHL)
Matt McKnight	84	08	6'1"/195	F	Selkirk,AB/Camrose Kodiaks (AJHL)
Josh Meyers	85	09	6'3"/195	D	Alexandria,MN/Sioux City Musketeers (USHL)
Matt Niskanen	86	09	6'1"/195	D	Mountain Iron,MN/Buhl (HS)
Trent Palm	88	10	6'0"/195	D	Edina,MN/USNDT (NAHL)
Mason Raymond	85	09	6'0"/185	F	Cochrane,AB/Camrose Kodiaks (AJHL)
Chase Ryan	86	10	6'1"/200	D	Algonquin,IL/Des Moines Buccaneers (USHL)
Mitch Ryan	86	10	6'0"/200	F	Cloquet,MN/Waterloo Blackhawks (USHL)
MacGregor Sharp	85	09	6'1"/190	F	Red Deer,AB/Camrose Kodiaks (AJHL)
Alex Stalock	87	10	6'0"/185	G	St. Paul,MN/Cedar Rapids RoughRiders (USHL)
Nate Ziegelmann	82	07	5'9"/185	G	Grand Forks,ND/North Dakota (WCHA)

ROSTER ANALYSIS (SCHOLARSHIPS - 18)

Class		Country		Last Team					
Fr	7	USA	18	US JR A	13	CDN JR A	7	ACHA	
So	10	Canada	7	US JR B		CDN JR B		NJCAA	
Jr	3	Europe		US PS	2	CDN PS		NCAA	1
Sr	5	Asia		US HS	1	CDN HS		USNDT	1
Gr		Other		US Midget		CDN Midget		Other	

ADMISSIONS, ENROLLMENT & CAMPUS INFORMATION

Founded 1947
Public, urban campus
4,248 men / 4,602 women
Tuition, room & board - $14 K / $26 K
Avg ACT - 23

Average acceptance rate - 78 %
Freshman financial aid - 65 %
Early decision application deadline - N/A
Regular application deadline - Aug 1
Financial aid deadline - Mar 31

Beth Esselstrom - Admissions Director
University of Minnesota-Duluth
10 University Drive
Duluth, MN 55812-2496
O 218.726.7171 / F 218.726.6394

www.d.umn.edu · www.umdbulldogs.com/

UNIV. OF MINNESOTA-TWIN CITIES

Division 1

HOCKEY STAFF

HEAD COACH
Don Lucia *(Notre Dame '81)*

ASSISTANT COACHES
Mike Guentzel *(Minnesota '87)*
Robb Stauber *(Minnesota '89)*
John Hill *(Alaska Anchorage '88)*

HOCKEY OFFICE
University of Minnesota
121 Mariucci Arena
4 Oak Street Southeast
Minneapolis, MN 55455-2019
O 612.625.2886/ F 612.6256547
lucia004@umn.edu

HOCKEY MEDIA CONTACT
Kevin Kurtt - Hockey Info Director
University of Minn. - Bierman #208
516 15th Avenue Southeast
Minneapolis, MN 55455
O 612.625.4090/ F 612.625.0359
kurtt003@umn.edu

HOCKEY RINK
Mariucci Arena (On Campus)
1901 4th Street Southeast
Minneapolis, MN 55455
Size 200' x 100', Capacity 10,000
O 617.626.0844

ATHLETIC DIRECTOR
Joel Maturi - Athletic Director
University of Minnesota
516 15th Avenue Southeast
Minneapolis, MN 55455
O 612.625.4838/ F 612.625.7859
maturi@umn.edu

GOLDEN GOPHERS PLAYERS

Player	YB	GR	Ht/Wt	P	Hometown/Last Team
RJ Anderson	86	09	6' 0"/185	D	Lino Lakes,MN/Centennial (HS)
Jay Barriball	87	10	5' 9"/155	F	Prior Lake,MN/Sioux Falls Stampede (USHL)
Justin Bostrom	86	09	5' 9"/175	F	Vadnais Hgts,MN/Sioux City Musketeers (USHL)
Kellen Briggs	83	07	5'11"/190	G	Colorado Spgs,CO/Sioux Falls Stampede (USHL)
Mike Carman	88	10	6' 0"/175	F	Apple Valley,MN/USNDT (NAHL)
David Fischer	88	10	6' 3"/195	D	Apple Valley,MN/Apple Valley (HS)
Ryan Flynn	88	10	6' 3"/210	F	Lino Lakes,MN/USNDT (NAHL)
Jeff Frazee	87	09	6' 0"/200	G	Burnsville,MN/USNDT (NAHL)
Alex Goligoski	85	08	6' 0"/180	D	Grand Rpds,MN/Sioux Falls Stampede (USHL)
Ben Gordon	85	08	5'11"/165	F	Int'l Falls,MN/Lincoln Stars (USHL)
Nate Hagemo	86	08	5'11"/190	D	Edina,MN/USNDT (NAHL)
Tyler Hirsch	84	07	5' 9"/175	F	Bloomington,MN/Shattuck-St. Mary's (PS)
Mike Howe	84	08	5'11"/190	F	Oakdale,MN/Omaha Lancers (USHL)
Erik Johnson	88	10	6' 4"/222	D	Bloomington,MN/USNDT (NAHL)
Evan Kaufmann	84	08	5' 9"/170	F	Plymouth,MN/Omaha Lancers (USHL)
Tony Lucia	87	10	6' 0"/175	F	Plymouth,MN/Omaha Lancers (USHL)
Jim O'Brien	89	10	6' 2"/190	F	Maplewood,MN/USNDT (NAHL)
Kyle Okposo	88	10	6' 0"/200	F	St. Paul,MN/Des Moines Buccaneers (USHL)
Derek Peltier	85	08	6' 0"/190	D	Plymouth,MN/Cedar Rapids RoughRiders (USHL)
Tom Pohl	84	08	6' 1"/185	F	Red Wing,MN/Tri-City Storm (USHL)
Brian Schack	87	10	6' 2"/215	D	Lino Lakes,MN/Southern Minnesota Express (NAHL)
Brent Solei	84	08	5' 7"/150	G	Coon Rpds,MN/Fairbanks Ice Dogs (NAHL)
Ryan Stoa	87	09	6' 3"/215	F	Bloomington,MN/USNDT (NAHL)
Mike Vannelli	83	07	6' 2"/185	D	Mendota Hgts,MN/Sioux Falls Stampede (USHL)
Blake Wheeler	86	09	6' 4"/220	F	Plymouth,MN/Green Bay Gamblers (USHL)

ROSTER ANALYSIS (SCHOLARSHIPS - 18)

Class		Country		Last Team				
Fr	9	USA	25	US JR A	15	CDN JR A	ACHA	
So	5	Canada		US JR B		CDN JR B	NJCAA	
Jr	8	Europe		US PS	1	CDN PS	NCAA	
Sr	3	Asia		US HS	2	CDN HS	USNDT	7
Gr		Other		US Midget		CDN Midget	Other	

ADMISSIONS, ENROLLMENT & CAMPUS INFORMATION

Founded 1851
Public, urban campus
12,933 men / 15,807 women
Tuition, room & board - $ 16 K/ $ 27 K
Avg SAT - 1,220 / Avg ACT - 26

Average acceptance rate - 74 %
Freshman financial aid - 87 %
Early decision application deadline - N/A
Regular application deadline - rolling
Financial aid deadline - Jan 15

Wayne Sigler - Admissions Director
University of Minnesota
240 Williamson
Minneapolis, MN 55455-0213
O 612.625.2008/ F 612.626.1693

MINNESOTA STATE UNIV.-MANKATO

WESTERN COLLEGIATE HOCKEY ASSOCIATION

Division 1

HOCKEY STAFF

HEAD COACH
Troy Jutting *(Minnesota State '87)*

ASSISTANT COACHES
Darren Blue *(Minnesota State '96)*
Eric Means *(Minnesota '94)*
Des Christopher *(Minnesota State '98)*

HOCKEY OFFICE
Minnesota State Univ. Mankato - Athletics
PO Box 8400 / MSU Box 28
Mankato, MN 56002-8400
O 507.389.5196 / F 507.389.6378
troy.jutting@mnsu.edu

HOCKEY MEDIA CONTACT
Paul Allan - Sports Info Director
Minnesota State Univ. Mankato - Athletics
PO Box 8400 / MSU Box 28
Mankota, MN 56002-8400
O 507.389.2625 / F 507.389.1923
paul.allan@mnsu.edu

HOCKEY RINK
MSU Civic Center (Off Campus)
1 Civic Center Plaza
Mankato, MN 56001
Size 200' x 100', Capacity 4,832
O 507.389.3000

ATHLETIC DIRECTOR
Kevin Buisman - Athletic Director
Minnesota State Univ. Mankato - Athletics
PO Box 8400 / MSU Box 28
Mankato, MN 56002-8400
O 507.389.6111
kevin.buisman@mnsu.edu

MAVERICKS PLAYERS

Player	YB	GR	Ht/Wt	P	Hometown/Last Team
Mick Berge	85	09	5'10"/170	F	Oklahoma City,OK/Lincoln Stars (USHL)
Chad Brownlee	84	07	6' 2"/195	D	Kelowna,BC/Vernon Vipers (BCHL)
Trevor Bruess	86	10	6' 0"/200	F	Minneapolis,MN/Lincoln Stars (USHL)
Nick Canzanello	88	10	5'11"/175	D	Rochester,MN/Mayo (HS)
Chris Clark	82	07	5'10"/190	G	San Mateo,CA/Surrey Eagles (BCHL)
Lucas Fransen	82	07	6' 1"/185	D	Langley,BC/Langley Hornets (BCHL)
Blake Friesen	86	09	6' 2"/190	D	Excelsior,MN/Sioux Falls Stampede (USHL)
James Gaulrapp	85	10	6' 1"/195	F	Owatonna,MN/Southern Minnesota Express (NAHL)
Ryan Gunderson	86	10	6' 2"/195	F	Grant,MN/Tri-City Storm (USHL)
Joel Hanson	83	08	6' 2"/200	F	Elk River,MN/Waterloo Blackhawks (USHL)
Zach Harrison	87	10	5'11"/175	F	Flint,MI/Shattuck-St. Mary's (PS)
Kevin Huck	84	09	6' 0"/185	F	Eden Pr,MN/Wichita Falls (NAHL)
Geoff Irwin	85	10	5'11"/185	F	Victoria,BC/Burnaby Express (BCHL)
Jon Kalinski	87	09	6' 1"/175	F	Lacorey,AB/Bonnyville Pontiacs (AJHL)
Brian Kilburg	84	09	6' 3"/215	D	Mendota Hgts,MN/Tri-City Storm (USHL)
Kurtis Kisio	84	07	5'10"/170	F	Calgary,AB/Calgary Royals (AJHL)
RJ Linder	83	08	6' 2"/200	D	St. Cloud,MN/Portage Terriers (ManJHL)
Travis Morin	84	07	6' 2"/175	F	Brooklyn Pk,MN/Chicago Steel (USHL)
Kael Mouillierat	87	10	5'10"/170	F	Edmonton,AB/Drayton Valley Thunder (AJHL)
Jerad Stewart	87	10	5'11"/200	F	Hastings,MN/Hastings (HS)
Dan Tormey	85	09	6' 2"/195	G	Syracuse,NY/Cedar Rapids RoughRiders (USHL)
Matt Tyree	83	08	6' 1"/210	F	Spooner,WI/Bentley (AHL)
Steve Wagner	84	08	6' 2"/190	D	Grand Rpds,MN/Tri-City Storm (USHL)
Jason Wiley	85	10	6' 0"/200	F	Bloomington,MN/Southern Minnesota Express (NAHL)
Mike Zacharias	85	09	5'10"/175	G	Plymouth,MN/Tri-City Storm (USHL)

ROSTER ANALYSIS (SCHOLARSHIPS - 18)

Class		Country		Last Team				
Fr	9	USA	19	US JR A	13	CDN JR A	8	ACHA
So	7	Canada	6	US JR B		CDN JR B		NJCAA
Jr	4	Europe		US PS	1	CDN PS		NCAA	1
Sr	5	Asia		US HS	2	CDN HS		USNDT
Gr		Other		US Midget		CDN Midget		Other

ADMISSIONS, ENROLLMENT & CAMPUS INFORMATION

Founded 1868
Public, urban campus
5,338 men / 6,793 women
Tuition, room & board - $11 / $15 K
Avg ACT - N/A

Average acceptance rate - 90 %
Freshman financial aid - %
Early decision application deadline - N/A
Regular application deadline - rolling
Financial aid deadline - Mar 15

Walt Wolff - Admissions Director
Minnesota State Univ. Mankato - Adm.
PO Box 8400 / MSU Box 55
Mankato, MN 56001-8400
O 507.389.1822 / F 507.389.1511

www.mankato.msus.edu

www.msumavericks.com

UNIVERSITY OF NEBRASKA-OMAHA

Division 1

HOCKEY STAFF

HEAD COACH
Mike Kemp *(Gustavus Adolphus '75)*

ASSISTANT COACHES
Todd Jones *(North Dakota '96)*
Rob Facca *(Nebraska '02)*

HOCKEY OFFICE
University of Nebraska-Omaha
Saap Fieldhouse #25
6001 Dodge Street
Omaha, NE 68182
O 402.554.3629 / F 402.554.2555
mkemp@mail.unomaha.edu

HOCKEY MEDIA CONTACT
Mike Kros - Hockey Info Director
University of Nebraska-Omaha
Fieldhouse #12 - 60th and Dodge
Omaha, NE 68182
O 402.554.2140 / F 402.554.3694
mkros@unomaha.edu

HOCKEY RINK
Qwest Center Omaha (Off Campus)
455 North 10th Street
Omaha, NE 68102
Size 200' x 85', Capacity 14,700
O 402.341.1500

ATHLETIC DIRECTOR
David Herbster - Athletic Director
University of Nebraska-Omaha
Fieldhouse #7 - 60th and Dodge
Omaha, NE 68182
O 402.554.3389 / F 402.554.3694
dherbster@mail.unomaha.edu

MAVERICKS PLAYERS

Player	YB	GR	Ht/Wt	P	Hometown/Last Team
Eric Aarnio	83	08	5'10"/180	G	White Bear Lk,MN/Tri-City Storm (USHL)
Jeric Agosta	85	10	5'9"/175	F	Ruthwen,ON/Aurora Tigers (OPJHL)
Phil Angell	82	07	6'1"/200	D	Eagan,MN/Topeka Scarecrows (USHL)
Bill Bagron	82	08	5'9"/185	F	Eagle Rvr,AK/Chicago Steel (USHL)
Adam Bartholomay	83	09	5'11"/205	D	Agoura Hills,CA/Lincoln Stars (USHL)
Mark Bernier	85	10	5'11"/185	D	S St. Paul,MN/Tri-City Storm (USHL)
Dan Charleston	84	09	5'8"/180	F	Oak Forest,IL/Chicago Steel (USHL)
Eddie Del Grosso	85	10	5'11"/205	D	Las Vegas,NV/Indiana Ice (USHL)
Jeremie Dupont	88	10	6'2"/180	G	Richmond Hill,ON/Aurora Tigers (OPJHL)
Mike Eickman	83	07	5'11"/200	D	Grand Forks,ND/Lincoln Stars (USHL)
Nick Fanto	86	10	6'2"/200	F	Dearborn,MI/Omaha Lancers (USHL)
Bobby Henderson	82	07	5'11"/205	D	Langley,BC/Chilliwack Chiefs (BCHL)
Jerad Kaufmann	84	09	6'3"/190	G	Roseville,MN/Fairbanks Ice Dogs (NAHL)
Brent Kisio	82	07	5'10"/180	F	Calgary,AB/Vernon Vipers (BCHL)
Tomas Klempa	84	09	5'8"/170	F	Prestany,Slovakia/Indiana Ice (USHL)
Dan Knapp	82	07	6'1"/190	D	Hermantown,MN/Billings Bulls (NAHL)
JJ Koehler	85	10	5'6"/165	F	Colgate,WI/Lincoln Stars (USHL)
Mick Lawrence	83	08	5'10"/205	F	Pt Coquitlam,BC/Omaha Lancers (USHL)
Bryan Marshall	83	08	6'0"/170	F	Livonia,MI/Danville Wings (USHL)
Alex Nikiforuk	83	07	5'8"/170	F	Kelowna,BC/Salmon Arm Silverbacks (BCHL)
Scott Parse	84	07	6'1"/185	F	Portage,MI/Tri-City Storm (USHL)
JP Platisha	84	09	5'10"/190	F	Brainerd,MN/Tri-City Storm (USHL)
Brandon Scero	86	08	6'0"/190	F	Canton,MI/USNDT (NAHL)
Dan Swanson	85	10	5'9"/170	F	Menomonie,WI/Alexandria Blizzard (NAHL)
Juha Uotila	85	09	6'1"/185	D	Espoo,Finland/HIFK (FEL)
Chris Wilson	85	10	5'9"/170	F	Prince Albert,SK/Grande Prairie Storm (AJHL)

ROSTER ANALYSIS (SCHOLARSHIPS - 18)

Class		Country		Last Team				
Fr	7	USA	18	US JR A	18	CDN JR A	8	ACHA
So	8	Canada	10	US JR B		CDN JR B		NJCAA
Jr	9	Europe	2	US PS		CDN PS		NCAA	2
Sr	6	Asia		US HS		CDN HS		USNDT	1
Gr		Other		US Midget		CDN Midget		Other	1

ADMISSIONS, ENROLLMENT & CAMPUS INFORMATION

Founded 1908	Average acceptance rate - 87 %	Jolene Adams - Admissions Director
Public, suburban campus	Freshman financial aid - %	University of Nebraska-Omaha
4,722 men / 6,010 women	Early decision application deadline - N/A	60th and Dodge
Tuition, room & board - $10 K / $18 K	Regular application deadline - Aug 1	Omaha, NE 68182
Avg SAT - 1,090 / Avg ACT - 23	Financial aid deadline - Mar 1	O 402.544.2393 / F 402.554.3472

NEUMANN COLLEGE

HOCKEY
WEST

Division 3

<table>
<tr><td colspan="2">

HOCKEY STAFF

HEAD COACH

ASSISTANT COACHES
Steve Washkalavitch *(Neumann '03)*
Joe Dolan

HOCKEY OFFICE
Neumann College - Athletic Department
1 Neumann Drive
Aston, PA 19014-1298
O 610.361.5230/F 610.361.5238
@neumann.edu

HOCKEY MEDIA CONTACT
Leigh Matejkovic - Sports Info Director
1 Neumann Drive
Aston, PA 19014-1298
O 610.558.5639/F 610.558.5657
matejkol@neumann.edu

HOCKEY RINK
Ice Works (Off Campus)
701 West Duttons Mill Road
Aston, PA 19014
Size ' x ', Capacity 1,000
O 610.497.2200

ATHLETIC DIRECTOR
Chuck Sack - Athletic Director
Neumann College - Athletic Department
1 Neumann Drive
Aston, PA 19014-1298
O 610.558.5627/F 610.361.5238
sackc@neumann.edu

</td></tr>
</table>

KNIGHTS PLAYERS

Player	YB	GR	Ht/Wt	P	Hometown/Last Team
Dayne Bihn	83	08	5'10"/175	F	Toledo,OH/Toledo IceDiggers (NAHL)
Kyle Casey	84	09	5' 8"/165	F	Stratford,ON/Stratford Cullitons (MWJHL)
Jesse Cole	84	09	6' 2"/200	F	Stratford,ON/Stratford Cullitons (MWJHL)
Mike Collichio	85	08	5'11"/185	G	Rochester,NY/Syracuse Stars (EJHL)
Sean Cryer	83	08	5'11"/165	D	Brampton,ON/Pembroke Lumber Kings (CJHL)
Mike Demarchi	85	09	5'10"/170	F	Mississauga,ON/Milton Icehawks (OPJHL)
John Giacobbo	84	09	6' 0"/185	D	Deptford,NM/Philadelphia Little Flyers (MJHL)
Todd Gilmore	85	09	5'11"/180	F	Wasaga Bch,ON/Collingwood Blues (OPJHL)
Dave Gooch	85	10	5' 7"/185	D	Mantua,NJ/Borderland Thunder (SIJHL)
Mike Gooch	83	08	5' 9"/180	D	Mantu,NJ/OCN Blizzard (ManJHL)
Donavon Hall	84	09	6' 0"/190	F	Wishart,SK/Estevan Bruins (SJHL)
Mike Hedden	84	09	5' 9"/180	F	St. Catherines,ON/Thorold Blackhawks (GHJHL)
Ryan Heickert	84	09	5'11"/185	F	Oshawa,ON/Wexford Raiders (OPJHL)
Josh Jacobs	85	09	5' 9"/180	F	Innisfil,ON/Markham Waxers (OPJHL)
Jonathan Keating	85	10	5' 5"/170	G	Toronto,ON/Brampton Capitals (OPJHL)
Brett Leonhardt	82	09	6' 7"/195	G	Waterloo,ON/SUNY Oswego (SUNYAC)
Jeff Nuttal	83	08	5'11"/185	F	Campbell Rvr,BC/Humboldt Broncos (SJHL)
Charles Paterson	85	10	6' 0"/185	D	Navan,ON/Pembroke Lumber Kings (CJHL)
Tyler Rivers	81	10	6' 1"/200	D	Belleville,ON/SUNY Oswego (SUNYAC)
Keleigh Schrock	84	09	5'11"/180	F	Ft Wayne,IN/Toledo IceDiggers (NAHL)
Stewart Sjoberg	84	09	5'11"/175	F	Winnipeg,MB/Humboldt Broncos (SJHL)
Doug Slipacoff	84	09	6' 0"/190	D	Sarnia,ON/Tecumseh Chiefs (WOJHL)
Mike Stevens	85	10	5'10"/175	D	St. John's,NF/Yarmouth Mariners (MarJHL)
Erik Stoyanvich	84	09	6' 0"/170	F	London,ON/Stratford Cullitons (MWJHL)
Neil Trimm	83	08	6' 2"/190	F	Westmeath,ON/Pembroke Lumber Kings (CJHL)
Peter Vaisanen	84	09	6' 1"/190	F	Stouffville,ON/Newmarket Hurricanes (OPJHL)
Brock VanSlyke	84	09	6' 0"/200	D	Ingersol,ON/Stratford Cullitons (MWJHL)
Mark VanVliet	84	10	6' 0"/180	F	Dorchester,ON/Quinnipiac (ECAC)
Kyle Ward	85	10	6' 2"/225	F	Petawawa,ON/Pembroke Lumber Kings (CJHL)
Matt Ward	85	10	5' 8"/175	F	Kemptville,ON/Brockville Braves (CJHL)

ROSTER ANALYSIS (SCHOLARSHIPS - 0)

Class		Country		Last Team					
Fr	8	USA	6	US JR A	2	CDN JR A	17	ACHA	
So	16	Canada	24	US JR B	2	CDN JR B	6	NJCAA	
Jr	6	Europe		US PS		CDN PS		NCAA	3
Sr		Asia		US HS		CDN HS		USNDT	
Gr		Other		US Midget		CDN Midget		Other	

ADMISSIONS, ENROLLMENT & CAMPUS INFORMATION

Founded 1965	Average acceptance rate - 94 %	Scott Bogard - Admissions Director
Private, urban campus	Freshman financial aid - 65 %	Neumann College - Admissions Dept.
747 men / 1,450 women	Early decision application deadline - N/A	1 Neumann Drive
Tuition, room & board -$ 26 K	Regular application deadline - rolling	Aston, PA 19014-1298
Avg SAT - 875	Financial aid deadline - N/A	O 610.558.5616/F 610.558.5652

NEW ENGLAND COLLEGE

HOCKEY EAST

NCAA
Division 3

HOCKEY STAFF

HEAD COACH
Tom Carroll *(Wisconsin-Madison '83)*

ASSISTANT COACHES
Jim Hayes *(New England '75)*
Eddie Ardito *(New England '06)*

HOCKEY OFFICE
New England College - Athletic Dept.
24 Bridge Street, Box #17
Henniker, NH 03242-3296
O 603.428.2294 / F 603.428.6023
tcarroll@nec.edu

HOCKEY MEDIA CONTACT
Renee Hellert - Sports Info Director
New England College - Athletic Dept.
24 Bridge Street
Henniker, NH 03242-3296
O 603.428.2335 / F 603.428.6023
rhellert@nec.edu

HOCKEY RINK
Lee Clement Arena (On Campus)
29 Bridge Street
Henniker, NH 03242
Size 200' x 85', Capacity 1,100
O 603.428.7230

ATHLETIC DIRECTOR
Lori Runksmeier - Athletic Director
New England College
201 Clement Arena
Henniker, NH 03242-3309
O 603.428.2292 / F 603.428.6023
lrunksmei@nec.edu

PILGRIMS PLAYERS

Player	YB	GR	Ht/Wt	P	Hometown/Last Team
Jeff Armando	85	10	6'1"/180	F	Canton,MA/Walpole Express (AtJHL)
Ron Bala	85	10	6'2"/210	G	Milford,CT/Winchendon (NEPSAC)
Jon Bellonio	83	07	5'8"/180	F	Guilford,CT/South Kent (NEPSAC)
Viktor Berfelt	86	10	6'1"/190	D	Stockholm,Sweden/Hammarby (SEL)
Flip Bjork	86	10	6'1"/185	D	Stockholm,Sweden/Hammarby (SEL)
Robin Bjorkman	84	07	6'0"/185	D	Gothenburg,Sweden/Frolunda (SEL)
Bradley Bohlinger	85	10	5'11"/170	F	St. Clair Shores,MI/Queen City Cutthroats (NPJHL)
Nick Brzuchalski	85	10	6'1"/210	D	Forest Hill,MD/New England Huskies (EJHL)
Aaron Bujdos	83	08	5'9"/180	F	Lakewood,OH/Green Mountain Glades (EJHL)
Jason Butler	87	10	5'8"/175	F	W Hartford,CT/Hebron (NEPSAC)
Mike Carmody	83	08	5'11"/170	F	Falmouth,ME/New Hampshire Monarchs (EJHL)
Mark Ehl	85	10	6'0"/185	F	N Vancouver,BC/Powell River Kings (BCHL)
Evan Erdmann	83	08	5'11"/165	D/F	Columbus,IN/Markham Waxers (OPJHL)
Joe Garofalo	81	08	6'0"/190	D	Concord,NH/Norwich (ECAC East)
Jon Globke	85	10	6'4"/225	F/D	W Bloomfield,MI/Springfield Blues (NAHL)
Matt Gosselin	84	08	5'10"/190	D	Salem,NH/Elmira ()
Sean Gray	84	09	6'0"/185	D	Pickering,ON/Stouffville Spirit (OPJHL)
Dallas Hand	85	10	5'10"/175	F/D	Spruceview,AB/Okotoks Oilers (AJHL)
Connor King	85	10	5'8"/175	F	Brentwood,TN/Walpole Express (AtJHL)
Joe Loiselle	84	08	5'11"/185	F/D	Chepachet,RI/Bridgewater Bandits (EJHL)
Anders Lundholm	84	09	6'1"/170	F	Falun,Sweden/Nynashamn (SEL)
Anders Lusth	83	08	5'11"/180	F	Sandviken,Sweden/Massachusetts Amherst (HEA)
Matthew Lyon	85	10	6'2"/195	G	Langley,BC/Helena Bighorns (NAHL)
Pat Melillo	85	08	5'9"/190	F	Wallingford,CT/South Kent (NEPSAC)
Mike Mullen	83	08	6'0"/185	F	Pittsburgh,PA/Massachusetts Amherst (HEA)
Andrew Riddell	85	10	5'11"/190	D	Nanaimo,BC/Powell River Kings (BCHL)
Paul Ruta	84	07	5'10"/170	F	Pickering,ON/Pickering Panthers (OPJHL)
Jim Ryan	86	09	5'10"/230	G	Oak Forest,IL/Culver (PS)
Mickey Serra	83	08	5'8"/195	F	Coral Spgs,FL/Salem State (ECAC East)
Brian Shea	86	09	5'9"/185	F	Bow,NH/New Hampshire Monarchs (EJHL)
Branislav Srnka	84	08	6'0"/190	F	Banska Bystrica,Slovakia/Kents Hill (NEPSAC)
CJ Sullivan	85	09	5'9"/155	G	Danvers,MA/Bridgton (NEPSAC)
Trevor Turner	85	10	6'1"/175	D	Westbank,BC/Williams Lake Timberwolves (BCHL)
Ryan Yusishen	84	10	6'1"/230	G	St. Andrews,MB/Miramachi Timberwolves ()
Adam Zippin	87	10	5'10"/165	G	New Hartford,NY/Millbrook (NEPSAC)

ROSTER ANALYSIS (SCHOLARSHIPS - 0)

Class		Country		Last Team				
Fr	16	USA	21	US JR A	2	CDN JR A	7	ACHA
So	5	Canada	8	US JR B	8	CDN JR B	1	NJCAA
Jr	11	Europe	6	US PS	8	CDN PS		NCAA 4
Sr	3	Asia		US HS		CDN HS		USNDT
Gr		Other		US Midget		CDN Midget		Other 5

ADMISSIONS, ENROLLMENT & CAMPUS INFORMATION

Founded 1946
Private, rural campus
469 men / 450 women
Tuition, room & board - $ 31 K
Avg SAT - 930

Average acceptance rate - 83 %
Freshman financial aid - 81 %
Early decision application deadline - N/A
Regular application deadline - rolling
Financial aid deadline - Apr 1

Donald N. Parker - Admissions Director
New England College
26 Bridge Street
Henniker, NH 03242-3309
O 603.428.2223 / F 603.428.3155

UNIVERSITY OF NEW ENGLAND

Division 3

HOCKEY STAFF	NOR'EASTERS PLAYERS

HEAD COACH	Player YB GR Ht/Wt P Hometown/Last Team

ASSISTANT COACHES

HOCKEY OFFICE
University of New England
Athletic Office
11 Hills Beach Road
Biddeford, ME 04005
O 207.283.0171

University of New England begins play in 2010/2011

HOCKEY MEDIA CONTACT
Curt Smyth - Sports Info Director
University of New England
11 Hills Beach Road
Biddeford, ME 04005
O 207.602.2429
csmyth@une.edu

HOCKEY RINK
Biddeford Ice Arena (Off Campus)
Alfred Road, Route 111
Biddeford, ME 04005
Size 200' x 85', Capacity
O 207.283.0615
info@biddefordarena.com

ATHLETIC DIRECTOR
Kim Allen - Athletic Director
University of New England
11 Hills Beach Road
Biddeford, ME 04005
csmyth@une.edu

ROSTER ANALYSIS (SCHOLARSHIPS - 0)

Class	Country	Last Team		
Fr	USA	US JR A	CDN JR A	ACHA
So	Canada	US JR B	CDN JR B	NJCAA
Jr	Europe	US PS	CDN PS	NCAA
Sr	Asia	US HS	CDN HS	USNDT
Gr	Other	US Midget	CDN Midget	Other

ADMISSIONS, ENROLLMENT & CAMPUS INFORMATION

Founded 1831	Average acceptance rate - 90 %	Admissions Director
Private, coastal suburban campus	Freshman financial aid - 82 %	University of New England
400 men / 1,200 women	Early decision application deadline - N/A	11 Hills Beach Road
Tuition, room & board - $ 35 K	Regular application deadline - rolling	Biddeford, ME 04005
Avg SAT - 1,025	Financial aid deadline -	O 207.283.0170

www.une.edu	www.une.edu/athletics/

UNIVERSITY OF NEW HAMPSHIRE

Division 1

HOCKEY STAFF

HEAD COACH
Richard Umile *(New Hampshire '72)*

ASSOCIATE HEAD COACHES
Scott Borek *(Dartmouth '85)*
David Lassonde *(Providence '84)*

HOCKEY OFFICE
Univ. of New Hampshire - Field House
Durham, NH 03824
O 603.862.1161 / F 603.862.1741
rcu@unh.edu

HOCKEY MEDIA CONTACT
Pete Souris - Hockey Info Director
University of New Hampshire
Field House #151
145 Main Street
Durham, NH 03824
O 603.862.0730 / F 603.862.3839
pete.souris@unh.edu

HOCKEY RINK
Whittemore Center Arena (On Campus)
128 Main Street
Durham, NH 03824
Size 200' x 100', Capacity 6,501
O 603.862.0735

ATHLETIC DIRECTOR
Marty Scarano - Athletic Director
Univ. of New Hampshire - Field House
Durham, NH 03824
O 603.862.2013 / F 603.862.0159
marty.scarano@unh.edu

WILDCATS PLAYERS

Player	YB	GR	Ht/Wt	P	Hometown/Last Team
Bobby Butler	87	10	6'0"/180	F	Marlborough,MA/Junior Bruins (EJHL)
Joe Charlebois	86	09	6'1"/225	D	Potsdam,NY/Sioux City Musketeers (USHL)
Josh Ciocco	83	07	5'10"/185	F	Atco,NJ/Salmon Arm Silverbacks (BCHL)
Greg Collins	86	09	5'9"/170	F	Fairport,NY/Cedar Rapids RoughRiders (USHL)
Brad Flaishans	83	08	6'0"/180	D	Glendale,AZ/Texas Tornado (NAHL)
Matt Fornataro	85	08	6'0"/185	F	Calgary,AB/Waterloo Blackhawks (USHL)
Thomas Fortney	86	09	5'9"/170	F	Webster Gr,MO/Waterloo Blackhawks (USHL)
Brian Foster	87	10	6'2"/180	G	Pembroke,NH/Des Moines Buccaneers (USHL)
Jamie Fritsch	85	09	6'2"/200	D	Odenton,MD/New Hampshire Monarchs (EJHL)
Brett Hemingway	83	07	6'1"/195	F	Surrey,BC/Coquitlam Express (BCHL)
Kevin Kapstad	86	09	5'10"/185	D	Boxboro,MA/Governor's (NEPSAC)
Nick Krates	86	10	6'2"/195	D	Palos Park,IL/Omaha Lancers (USHL)
Peter LeBlanc	88	10	5'11"/190	F	Hamilton,ON/Hamilton Red Wings (OPJHL)
Kirk Manke	86	09	6'1"/200	G	Clifton Pk,NY/Capital District Selects (EJHL)
Jacob Micflikier	84	07	5'8"/180	F	Winnipeg,MB/Sioux Falls Stampede (USHL)
Chris Murray	84	07	6'2"/190	D	Dover,MA/Cushing (NEPSAC)
Jerry Pollastrone	86	09	5'10"/200	F	Revere,MA/Salisbury (NEPSAC)
Brian Pouliot	84	08	5'11"/185	F	Hooksett,NH/Cedar Rapids RoughRiders (USHL)
Mike Radja	85	08	6'0"/180	F	Yorkville,IL/Waterloo Blackhawks (USHL)
Kevin Regan	84	08	6'1"/190	G	S Boston,MA/Waterloo Blackhawks (USHL)
Dan Rossman	87	10	6'0"/185	F	Boxboro,MA/Valley Warriors (EJHL)
Trevor Smith	85	09	6'1"/190	F	N Vancouver,BC/Omaha Lancers (USHL)
Craig Switzer	84	08	6'1"/200	D	Peachland,BC/Salmon Arm Silverbacks (BCHL)
Alan Thompson	84	09	6'1"/190	F	Gilford,NH/Chicago Steel (USHL)
Shawn Vinz	82	07	6'0"/195	F	Mississauga,ON/Cedar Rapids RoughRiders (USHL)
John Webster	87	10	6'1"/210	D	Boxborough,MA/Acton-Boxborough (HS)

ROSTER ANALYSIS (SCHOLARSHIPS - 18)

Class		Country		Last Team				
Fr	6	USA	19	US JR A	14	CDN JR A	4	ACHA
So	9	Canada	7	US JR B	4	CDN JR B		NJCAA
Jr	6	Europe		US PS	3	CDN PS		NCAA
Sr	5	Asia		US HS	1	CDN HS		USNDT
Gr		Other		US Midget		CDN Midget		Other

ADMISSIONS, ENROLLMENT & CAMPUS INFORMATION

Founded 1866	Average acceptance rate - 68 %	Cecila J. Leslie - Admissions Director
Public, rural campus	Freshman financial aid - 83 %	University of New Hampshire
4,486 men / 6,456 women	Early decision applicaton deadline - N/A	Grant House
Tuition, room & board - $17 K / $28 K	Regular application deadline - Feb 1	Durham, NH 03824
Avg SAT - 1,120	Financial aid deadline - Mar 1	O 603.862.1360 / F 603.862.0077

web.unh.edu

www.unhwildcats.com

NIAGARA UNIVERSITY

Division 1

HOCKEY STAFF

HEAD COACH
Dave Burkholder *(RIT '83)*

ASSOCIATE COACH
Jerry Forton *(SUNY-Buffalo '86)*

ASSISTANT COACHES
Greg Gardner *(Niagara '00)*
Jeff Weber *(Colgate '90)*

HOCKEY OFFICE
Niagara University
Lewiston Road
Niagara University, NY 14109-2011
O 716.286.8239 / F 716.286.8785
db@niagara.edu

HOCKEY MEDIA CONTACT
Michele Schmidt - Sports Info Director
Niagara University
Lewiston Road
Niagara University, NY 14109-2011
O 716.286.8588 / F 716.286.8581
mdubert@niagara.edu

HOCKEY RINK
Dwyer Ice Arena (On Campus)
University Drive
Lewiston, NY 14106
Size 200' x 85', Capacity 1,600
O 716.286.8794

ATHLETIC DIRECTOR
Mike Hermann - Athletic Director
Niagara University
Lewiston Road
Niagara University, NY 14109-2011
O 716.286.8601 / F 716.286.8609
mjh@niagara.edu

PURPLE EAGLES PLAYERS

Player	YB	GR	Ht/Wt	P	Hometown/Last Team
Travis Anderson	84	08	6'1"/195	D	Coon Rpds,MN/Des Moines Buccaneers (USHL)
Ryan Annesley		10	5'10"/185	D	Ajax,ON/Pickering Panthers (OPJHL)
Allen Barton	84	07	6'0"/185	G	Spencerport,NY/Apple Core (EJHL)
Sean Bentivoglio	85	07	5'11"/190	F	Thorold,ON/Thorold Blackhawks (GHJHL)
Nate Bostic		10	5'11"/190	F	Holden,MA/New England Huskies (EJHL)
Jim Burichin		10	6'0"/185	D	Strongsville,OH/Bay State Breakers (EJHL)
Matt Caruana	85	08	6'0"/175	F	Orono,ON/Bowmanville Eagles (OPJHL)
Ted Cook	84	09	6'0"/205	F	Hogansburg,NY/Omaha Lancers (USHL)
Trevor Foster		10	6'1"/200	F	Clifton Pk,NY/Capital District Selects (EJHL)
Tyler Gotto		10	6'0"/195	D	Calgary,AB/Calgary Canucks (AJHL)
Blair Hennes		10		F	Thorsby,AB/Fort Saskatchewan Traders (AJHL)
Nick Jillson		10	6'1"/190	D	N Smithfield,RI/Walpole Stars (EJHL)
Cliff Ketchen	84	08	5'10"/170	F	Winnipeg,MB/Portage Terriers (ManJHL)
Scott Langdon	85	08	6'2"/195	D	Ancaster,ON/Hamilton Red Wings (OPJHL)
Tim Madsen	84	08	5'8"/170	F	Elk River,MN/Waterloo Blackhawks (MnJHL)
Egor Mironov		10	6'1"/200	F	Toronto,ON/St. Michael's (PS)
Scott Mollison	86	08	5'11"/175	G	Winnipeg,MB/Winnipeg South Blues (ManJHL)
Chris Moran		10	5'11"/180	F	Buffalo,NY/Omaha Lancers (USHL)
Chad Murray	82	07	5'9"/190	F	Vernon,BC/Vernon Vipers (BCHL)
Ryan Olidis		10	6'1"/195	F	Uxbridge,ON/Markham Waxers (OPJHL)
Pat Oliveto	84	07	6'2"/195	D	Rochester,NY/Apple Core (EJHL)
Juliano Pagliero	84	09	6'0"/195	G	Dalroy,AB/Estevan Bruins (SJHL)
Les Reaney	84	09	6'2"/220	F	Ceylon,SK/Williams Lake Timberwolves (BCHL)
Vince Rocco	87	09	5'10"/185	F	Woodbridge,ON/Vaughan Vipers (OPJHL)
Kyle Rogers	84	09	6'3"/210	F	Erie,PA/Buffalo Lightning (OPJHL)
Armando Scarlato	84	09	6'1"/220	D	Toronto,ON/Vaughan Vipers (OPJHL)
Tayler Simpson	85	08	5'8"/170	F	Ottawa,ON/St. Michael's (PS)
Dan Sullivan	87	09	5'11"/190	D	Scarborough,ON/Pickering Panthers (OPJHL)
Chevan Wilson		10	5'10"/175	F	St. Albert,AB/Fort McMurray Oil Barons (AJHL)

ROSTER ANALYSIS (SCHOLARSHIPS - 18)

Class		Country		Last Team				
Fr	11	USA	11	US JR A	3	CDN JR A	16	ACHA
So	7	Canada	18	US JR B	7	CDN JR B	1	NJCAA
Jr	7	Europe		US PS		CDN PS	2	NCAA
Sr	4	Asia		US HS		CDN HS		USNDT
Gr		Other		US Midget		CDN Midget		Other

ADMISSIONS, ENROLLMENT & CAMPUS INFORMATION

Founded 1856
Private, suburban campus
1,017 men / 1,808 women
Tuition, room & board - $ 29 K
Avg SAT - 1,050 / Avg ACT - 23

Average acceptance rate - 80 %
Freshman financial aid - 85 %
Early decision application deadline - N/A
Regular application deadline - Aug 1
Financial aid deadline - Feb 15

Mike Koropski - Admissions Director
Lewiston Road
Niagara University, NY 14109-2011
O 716.286.8700 / F 716.286.8710

www.niagara.edu www.purpleeagles.com/

NICHOLS COLLEGE

HOCKEY
NORTHEAST

Division 3

HOCKEY STAFF

HEAD COACH
Lou Izzi *(Providence '87)*

ASSISTANT COACH
Chris Davis *(Merrimack '96)*

HOCKEY OFFICE
Nichols College
Chalmers Field House
114 Center Road
PO Box 5000
Dudley, MA 01571-5000
O 508.213.2356 / F 508.213.2358
lrizzi@nichols.edu

HOCKEY MEDIA CONTACT
Stephanie Tunnera - Sports Info Director
Nichols College
Chalmers Field House
114 Center Road
PO Box 5000
Dudley, MA 01571
O 508.213.2352 / F 508.943.8250
stunnera@nichols.edu

HOCKEY RINK
Horgan Memorial Rink (Off Campus)
400 Oxford Street
North Auburn, MA 01501
Size 185' x 85', Capacity 1,500
O 508.832.5932

ATHLETIC DIRECTOR
Charlyn Robert - Athletic Director
Nichols College
Dudley, MA 01571
O 508.213.2368 / F 508.213.2384
robertca@nichols.edu

BISON PLAYERS

Player	YB	GR	Ht/Wt	P	Hometown/Last Team
Jason Arrighie	85	07	6' 0"/185	F	Cranston,RI/Johnson & Wales (ECAC NE)
Mark Baker	85	10	6' 3"/205	D	Tulsa,OK/Manitoulin Islanders (NOJHL)
Jeff Bieber	85	09	6' 2"/210	D	Littleton,CO/Cincinnati Cobras (CSHL)
Glenn Cacaro	84	09	6' 1"/190	D	Sioux Falls,SD/Cincinnati Cobras (CSHL)
Kyle Cook	85	09	5' 6"/175	F	Chino Hills,CA/Bay City Bombers (WSHL)
Zeke Costello	85	10	5' 9"/175	F	Shelby Tsp,MI/Traverse City North Stars (NAHL)
Eric Cremer	88	10	6' 2"/175	F	Chelsea,MI/Chelsea (HS)
Rocco Dabecco	85	09	5'11"/195	F	S Park,PA/New England Huskies (EJHL)
Keith Fink	85	09	5'10"/185	G	Easton,MD/Collingwood Blues (OPJHL)
Matt Gassman	85	10	5'10"/175	G	Littleton,CO/Helena Bighorns (NAHL)
Neal Gerber	85	10	5' 9"/165	F	Highland Pk,IL/Cincinnati Cobras (CSHL)
Ryan Gervais	85	09	5' 8"/180	F	Chicago,IL/Chicago Force (CSHL)
Corey Horner	80	07	6' 1"/205	F	S Bend,IN/Bay City Bombers (WSHL)
Colby Jones	85	10	6' 1"/185	D	Brockport,NY/Texarkana Bandits (NAHL)
Kris Kransky	85	10	6' 4"/220	F	Glendora,CA/Eugene Generals (NPJHL)
Zach Lindsay	83	07	6' 0"/195	F	Enfield,CT/Connecticut Whalers (IJHL)
Mark Malone	82	07	6' 4"/220	D	Pittsburgh,PA/Dubuque Thunderbirds (MnJHL)
Erik Miller	81	09	6' 1"/210	D	S Bend,IN/Cleveland Lumberjacks (CSHL)
Anthony Monte	84	09	5' 9"/175	F	Chicago,IL/Chicago Force (CSHL)
Chris Orlowsky	85	10	5' 9"/175	F	Monrovia,CA/Eugene Generals (NPJHL)
Cole Ruwe	85	09	6' 1"/210	D	Pekin,IL/Peoria Mustangs (CSHL)
Andrew Shieh	85	10	5' 9"/175	F	Burnaby,BC/Peoria Mustangs (CSHL)
Nick Unger	84	08	6' 1"/195	F	Brockport,NY/Buffalo Lightning (OPJHL)
Rich Walters	87	10	6' 1"/175	D	Gilbertsville,PA/Valley Forge Minutemen (MJHL)
Donny Wynia	85	10	5'11"/175	G	Minneapolis,MN/Wisconsin Mustangs (MnJHL)

ROSTER ANALYSIS (SCHOLARSHIPS - 0)

Class		Country		Last Team					
Fr	11	USA	24	US JRA	3	CDN JR A	2	ACHA	
So	9	Canada	1	US JR B	17	CDN JR B	1	NJCAA	
Jr	1	Europe		US PS		CDN PS		NCAA	1
Sr	4	Asia		US HS	1	CDN HS		USNDT	
Gr		Other		US Midget		CDN Midget		Other	

ADMISSIONS, ENROLLMENT & CAMPUS INFORMATION

Founded 1931	Average acceptance rate - 84 %	R. Joseph Bellavance - Admissions Director
Private, rural campus	Freshman financial aid - 70 %	Nichols College
1,004 men / 430 women	Early decision application deadline - N/A	PO Box 5000
Tuition, room & board - $ 29 K	Regular application deadline - rolling	Dudley, MA 01571
Avg SAT - 920	Financial aid deadline - Mar 1	O 508.943.2055 / F 508.943.9855

www.nichols.edu

www.nichols.edu/athletics/

UNIVERSITY OF NORTH CAROLINA

Division 2

HOCKEY STAFF

HEAD COACH
Dave Kurtz

HOCKEY OFFICE
Univ. of North Carolina at Chapel Hill
Campus Recreation
203 Woolen Gymnasium, CB #8605
Chapel Hill, NC 27599-8605
epyouth@earthlink.net

HOCKEY MEDIA CONTACT
Adam Arthur
webmaster@unchockey.com

HOCKEY RINK
Triangle Sportsplex (Off Campus)
One Dan Kidd Drive
Hillsborough, NC 27278
O 919.644.0339

HOCKEY PRESIDENT
Luke Ross
president@unchockey.com

HOCKEY MANAGER
Earl Anderson
O 919.403.1649
gm@unchockey.com

TARHEELS PLAYERS

Player	YB	GR	Ht/Wt	P	Hometown/Last Team
Kellet Atkinson					
Justin Blair	87		6' 2"/165	D	Kernersville,NC/East Forsyth (HS)
Phil Bowlby	85	07	6' 4"/205	F	Hamden,CT/Kent (NEPSAC)
Ray Brancato					
Tim Brunt					
Colin Connors					
Ian Cooley	87		6' 0"/195	D/F	Abington,PA/Abington (HS)
Matt Corey					
Jesse Freedman	84		5'10"/180	G	Cooper City,FL/Cooper City (HS)
Tyler Johnson	83		6' 0"/185	D	Greensboro,NC/Northwest Guiford (HS)
Curtis Large					
Jeff Millar	84	07	5' 8"/157	D	Regina,SK/Brewers
Colin Moore					
Benjamin Owens	87		6' 2"/180	D	Chapel Hill,NC/Chapel Hill (HS)
Andy Pavlina					
Peter Pavlina	85	08	5' 9"/185	D	Centerville,OH/Centerville (HS)
Mathieu Poirier	87		5'11"/145	F	Cary,NC/Raleigh Charter (HS)
Luke Russ	85	07	5'11"/170	F	Stanfield,NC/Charlotte (Midget)
Marc Weber	86	08	6' 0"/140	F	St. Louis,MO/Webster (Midget)
Jeff White					
Brian Willett					

ROSTER ANALYSIS (SCHOLARSHIPS - 0)

Class	Country	Last Team		
Fr	USA	US JR A	CDN JR A	ACHA
So	Canada	US JR B	CDN JR B	NJCAA
Jr	Europe	US PS	CDN PS	NCAA
Sr	Asia	US HS	CDN HS	USNDT
Gr	Other	US Midget	CDN Midget	Other

ADMISSIONS, ENROLLMENT & CAMPUS INFORMATION

Founded 1789
Public, suburban campus
6,747 men / 9,318 women
Tuition, room & board -$ 11 K / $ 24 K
Avg SAT - 1,290 / Avg ACT 28

Average acceptance rate - 36 %
Freshman financial aid - 100 %
Early decision application deadline - N/A
Regular application deadline - Jan 15
Financial aid deadline - Mar 1

Jereome A. Lucido - Admissions Director
Univ. of North Carolina-Chapel Hill
Chapel Hill, NC 27599-7000
O 919.966.3621 / F 919.962.3045
uadm@email.unc.edu

www.unc.edu

www.unchockey.com

NORTH CAROLINA STATE UNIVERSITY

Division 2

HOCKEY STAFF

HEAD COACH
Mike Young *(Plattsburgh State '89)*

ASSISTANT COACHES
Ben Bonnie
Mike Tefft *(NC State '99)*
Mark McElligott

HOCKEY OFFICE
5725 Thistleton Lane
Raleigh, NC 27606
O 919.378.3306

HOCKEY MEDIA CONTACT
Mandy McLin

HOCKEY RINK
The Reczone (Off Campus)
912 Hodges Street
Raleigh, NC
O 919.754.0441 / F 919.754.0444
www.reczone.net

HOCKEY DIRECTOR
Mike Young

WOLFPACK RETURNING PLAYERS

Player	YB	GR	Ht/Wt	P	Hometown/Last Team
Matt Adams	87	09	5'10"/180	F	Jamestown,NC/Greenville Growl
Jason Bartek	86	08	6'2"/200	F	Detroit,MI/Wayne State
Sean Burns	87	10	6'3"/195	F	Jamestown,NC/Hartford Jr Whalers
Robbie Caldwell	86	09	5'11"/195	F	Port Haven,MI/East Coast Eagles
John Carter	88	10	5'11"/195	D	Raleigh,NC/East Coast Eagles
Mike Cosentino	87	09	5'9"/150	F	Buffalo,NY/East Coast Eagles
Nick Cosentino	86	08	6'4"/215	D	Fayetteville,NC/Fayetteville Jr FireAntz
Andrew Demetros	86	09	5'9"/175	F	Cary,NC/Marlborough Flames
Ben Dombrowski	87	09	6'0"/185	D	Chicago,IL/Greensboro Stars
David Howard		10		F	
Jacob Johnson	88	10	5'11"/205	F	Dartmouth,MA/Mass Maple Leafs
Brett Koontz	84	07	6'4"/200	D	High Point,NC/East Coast Eagles
Chris Martucci	88	07	5'7"/175	D	Smithtown,NY/East Coast Eagles
Dan Masiulis	87	09	5'11"/160	F	Rochester,NY/Howard Huskies
Phil Mason	87	09	6'2"/200	D	Oakland,ME/Messalonskee Eagles
Matt Maw	87	10	5'9"/165	F	Bolton,ON/St Louis Lightning
Nick Olson	85	07	6'2"/220	F	Smithtown,NY/Richmond Royals
Nick Otte	87	10	6'0"/180	D	East Lyme,CT/East Lyme (HS)
Bobby Riehle	85	07	5'10"/175	D	Atlanta,GA/East Coast Eagles
Stephen Russell	86	10	5'11"/180	G	Raleigh,NC/Beaver Lodge Blades
Anthony Sandonato	88	10	6'10"/175	F	Roswell,GA/Atlanta Fire
Jeff Spontak		07		F	
Jason Traud	86	09	5'10"/175	G	Fuquay,NC/Raleigh Storm
Ed Tudrick	84	07	5'8"/180	F	Boston,MA/Lebanon Valley College
Ross Whitcher	87	09	5'10"/155	G	Cary,NC/East Coast Eagles
Wes White	86	10	6'1"/175	D	Raleigh,NC/Walpole Express

ROSTER ANALYSIS (SCHOLARSHIPS - 0)

Class	Country	Last Team		
Fr	USA	US JR A	CDN JR A	ACHA
So	Canada	US JR B	CDN JR B	NJCAA
Jr	Europe	US PS	CDN PS	NCAA
Sr	Asia	US HS	CDN HS	USNDT
Gr	Other	US Midget	CDN Midget	Other

ADMISSIONS, ENROLLMENT & CAMPUS INFORMATION

Founded 1887
Public, suburban campus
10,400 men / 7,500 women
Tuition, room & board -$ 8 K / $ 18
Avg SAT - 1,070 / Avg ACT - 25

Average acceptance rate - 66 %
Freshman financial aid - 72 %
Early decision application deadline - Nov 15
Regular application deadline - Feb 1
Financial aid deadline - Mar 1

Dr. George R. Dixon - Admissions Director
North Carolina State University
Box 7103, 112 Peele Hall
Raleigh, NC 27695-7103
O 919.515.2434 / F 919.515.5039

UNIVERSITY OF NORTH DAKOTA

WESTERN COLLEGIATE HOCKEY ASSOCIATION

Division 1

HOCKEY STAFF

HEAD COACH
Dave Hakstol *(North Dakota '96)*

ASSOCIATE HEAD COACH
Cary Eades *(North Dakota '84)*

ASSISTANT COACHES
Dane Jackson *(North Dakota '92)*
Scott Koberinski *(North Dakota)*

HOCKEY OFFICE
University of North Dakota
University Station - PO Box 9013
Grand Forks, ND 58202
O 701.777.3118/ F 701.777.2574
davehakstol@mail.und.nodak.edu

HOCKEY MEDIA CONTACT
Dan Benson - Hockey Info Director
University of North Dakota
University Station - PO Box 9013
Grand Forks, ND 58202-9013
O 701.777.2985/ F 701.777.4352
danbenson@mail.und.nodak.edu

HOCKEY RINK
Ralph Engelstad Arena (On Campus)
801 North Ralph Columbia
Grand Forks, ND 58203
Size 200' x 85', Capacity 11,407
O 703.777.3571

ATHLETIC DIRECTOR
Thomas Buning - Athletic Director
University of North Dakota
University Station - PO Box 9013
Grand Forks, ND 58202
O 701.777.2234/ F 701.777.2285
tombuning@mail.und.nodak.edu

FIGHTING SIOUX PLAYERS

Player	YB	GR	Ht/Wt	P	Hometown/Last Team
Robbie Bina	83	07	5' 8"/175	D	Grand Forks,ND/Lincoln Stars (USHL)
Hunter Bishop	87	10	6' 1"/190	F	Fairbanks,AK/Vernon Vipers (BCHL)
Taylor Chorney	87	09	6' 0"/190	D	Hastings,MN/Shattuck-St. Mary's (PS)
Ryan Duncan	85	09	5' 6"/160	F	Calgary,AB/Salmon Arm Silverbacks (BCHL)
Erik Fabian	83	07	6' 2"/205	F	Roseau,MN/Topeka Scarecrows (USHL)
Joe Finley	87	09	6' 7"/255	D	Edina,MN/Sioux Falls Stampede (USHL)
Michael Forney	88	10	6' 2"/195	F	Thief River Fls,MN/Lincoln (HS)
Scott Foyt	82	07	6' 1"/185	D	Andover,MN/Tri-City Storm (USHL)
Chay Genoway	86	10	5' 9"/170	D	Swan River,MB/Vernon Vipers (BCHL)
Anthony Grieco	88	10	6' 1"/190	G	Brampton,ON/Wellington Dukes (OPJHL)
Zach Jones	87	09	6' 0"/200	D	Lisle,IL/USNDT (NAHL)
Rylan Kaip	84	08	6' 1"/195	F	Wilcox,SK/Notre Dame (PS)
Andrew Kozek	86	09	5'11"/190	F	Sicamous,BC/Surrey Eagles (BCHL)
Philippe Lamoureux	84	08	5' 8"/155	G	Grand Forks,ND/Lincoln Stars (USHL)
Brian Lee	87	09	6' 3"/205	D	Moorhead,MN/Moorhead (HS)
Ryan Martens	85	09	6' 0"/195	F	Selkirk,MB/Quesnel Millionaires (BCHL)
Brad Miller	86	09	5'11"/170	F	Alpharetta,GA/Green Bay Gamblers (USHL)
TJ Oshie	86	09	6' 0"/190	F	Warroad,MN/Warroad (HS)
Chris Porter	84	07	6' 1"/200	F	Thunder Bay,ON/Lincoln Stars (USHL)
Kyle Radke	85	08	6' 0"/205	D	Bashaw,AB/Grande Prairie Storm (AJHL)
Jonathan Toews	88	09	6' 2"/205	F	Winnipeg,MB/Shattuck-St. Mary's (PS)
Chris VandeVelde	87	10	6' 2"/210	F	Moorhead,MN/Lincoln Stars (USHL)
Aaron Walski	84	09	5'11"/175	G	Fargo,ND/Bismarck Bobcats (NAHL)
Matt Watkins	86	09	5'10"/185	F	Aylesbury,SK/Vernon Vipers (BCHL)
Darcy Zajac	86	10	6' 0"/200	F	Winnipeg,MB/Salmon Arm Silverbacks (BCHL)

ROSTER ANALYSIS (SCHOLARSHIPS - 18)

Class		Country		Last Team					
Fr	6	USA	14	US JR A	9	CDN JR A	9	ACHA	
So	12	Canada	11	US JR B		CDN JR B		NJCAA	
Jr	3	Europe		US PS	2	CDN PS	1	NCAA	
Sr	4	Asia		US HS	3	CDN HS		USNDT	1
Gr		Other		US Midget		CDN Midget		Other	

ADMISSIONS, ENROLLMENT & CAMPUS INFORMATION

Founded 1883
Public, urban campus
5,676 men / 5,034 women
Tuition, room & board - $ 10 K/ $ 16 K
Avg SAT - 1,090 / Avg ACT - 23

Average acceptance rate - 69 %
Freshman financial aid - 83 %
Early decision application deadline - N/A
Regular application deadline - Jul 1
Financial aid deadline - Mar 15

Kenton Pauls - Enrollment Director
University of North Dakota
University Station - P. O. Box 9013
Grand Forks, ND 58202
O 701.777.4463/ F 701.777.2696

www.und.nodak.edu

www.fightingsioux.com

NORTHEASTERN UNIVERSITY

Division 1

HOCKEY STAFF

HEAD COACH
Greg Cronin *(Colby '86)*

ASSISTANT COACHES
Gene Reilly *(Elmira '86)*
Brendan Walsh *(Maine '00)*
Brendan Flynn *(Mass-Lowell '91)*

HOCKEY OFFICE
Northeastern University - Hockey
360 Huntington Avenue
Boston, MA 02115
O 617.373.2631 / F 617.373.8772
g.cronin@neu.edu

HOCKEY MEDIA CONTACT
Jack Grinold
Associate AD/Communications
Northeastern University - Sports Info
360 Huntington Avenue
Boston, MA 02115
O 617.373.2691 / F 617.373.3152
litchfield@gonu.com

HOCKEY RINK
Matthews Arena (On Campus)
238 South Botolph Street
Boston, MA 02115
Size 200' x 90', Capacity 6,000
O 617.373.5561

ATHLETIC DIRECTOR
Dave O'Brien - Athletic Director
Northeastern University
360 Huntington Avenue
Boston, MA 02115
O 617.373.7590 / F 617.373.8988
cy.white@neu.edu

HUSKIES PLAYERS

Player	YB	GR	Ht/Wt	P	Hometown/Last Team
Steve Birnstill	85	07	6' 2"/185	D	Commack,NY/Apple Core (EJHL)
John Brennan	85	07	6' 1"/200	F	Bryn Mawr,PA/Rhode Island (ACHA)
Denis Chisholm	86	09	5'11"/185	F	Fox Vly,SK/Notre Dame (PS)
Ryan Clauson	84	09	6' 6"/235	F	Hanover,NH/New England Huskies (EJHL)
Greg Costa	85	10	5' 7"/180	F	Crownsville,MD/Boston Bulldogs (AtJHL)
Chad Costello	86	10	5' 9"/175	F	Johnston,IA/Cedar Rapids RoughRiders (USHL)
Joe Cucci	86	10	5'11"/160	F	Melrose Pk,IL/Valley Warriors (EJHL)
Brian Deeth	85	07	5'11"/160	D	Gig Harbor,WA/Shattuck-St. Mary's (PS)
Chris Donovan	85	10	5' 8"/175	F	Fairfax Stn,VA/Junior Bruins (EJHL)
Jim Driscoll	85	10	5' 9"/185	D	Dedham,MA/Junior Bruins (EJHL)
Bryan Esner	83	07	5' 9"/165	F	Paradise Vly,AZ/Texas Tornado (NAHL)
Adam Geragosian	84	07	6' 0"/190	G	N Andover,MA/Boston Harbor Wolves (EJHL)
Ryan Ginand	86	09	5' 9"/165	F	Milford,MA/Junior Bruins (EJHL)
Randy Guzior	86	10	6' 1"/195	F	Lemont,IL/Chicago Steel (USHL)
Octavian Jordan	86	10	6' 3"/200	F	Waldwick,NJ/New England Huskies (EJHL)
Kyle Kraemer	85	10	5'10"/190	F	St. Louis,MO/Wichita Falls Wildcats (NAHL)
Yale Lewis	82	07	6' 2"/210	F	Carbondale,CO/Omaha Lancers (USHL)
Andrew Linard	84	09	6' 3"/195	F	Brighton,MI/Bay State Breakers (EJHL)
Louis Liotti	85	09	6' 1"/195	F	Westbury,NY/Sioux City Musketeers (USHL)
Dennis McCauley	85	09	6' 3"/205	F	Billerica,MA/Sioux City Musketeers (USHL)
Aaron Moore	85	07	6' 0"/195	F	Medfied,MA/Belmont Hill (NEPSAC)
Mike Morris	83	07	6' 0"/180	F	Briantree,MA/St. Sebastian's (NEPSAC)
Ray Ortiz	84	07	5'11"/190	F	Charlestown,MA/Belmont Hill (NEPSAC)
Jacques Perreault	85	09	6' 4"/215	D	Grosse Pt Farms,MI/Boston Bulldogs (AtJHL)
Rob Rassey	84	09	5'10"/175	F	Shelby Twnsp,MI/Youngstown Phantoms (NAHL)
Josh Robertson	84	08	6' 0"/195	F	Whitman,MA/Proctor (NEPSAC)
Jimmy Russo	85	08	6' 0"/175	F	S Weymouth,MA/Thayer (NEPSAC)
Joe Santilli	82	07	5' 9"/165	F	Westwood,MA/Walpole Stars (EJHL)
David Strathman	85	10	6' 2"/200	D	Tempe,AZ/Cedar Rapids RoughRiders (USHL)
Jake Thaler	84	09	6' 0"/195	F	S Burlington,VT/Cornwall Colts (CJHL)
Brad Thiessen	86	10	6' 0"/170	G	Aldergrove,BC/Merritt Centennials (BCHL)
Joe Vitale	85	09	5'11"/205	F	St. Louis,MO/Sioux Falls Stampede (USHL)

ROSTER ANALYSIS (SCHOLARSHIPS - 18)

Class		Country		Last Team					
Fr	10	USA	30	US JR A	10	CDN JR A	2	ACHA	1
So	10	Canada	2	US JR B	12	CDN JR B		NJCAA	
Jr	2	Europe		US PS	6	CDN PS	1	NCAA	
Sr	10	Asia		US HS		CDN HS		USNDT	
Gr		Other		US Midget		CDN Midget		Other	

ADMISSIONS, ENROLLMENT & CAMPUS INFORMATION

Founded 1898
Private, urban campus
7,017 men / 7,601 women
Tuition, room & board - $ 38 K
Avg SAT - 1,215 / Avg ACT - 26

Average acceptance rate - 42 %
Freshman financial aid - 68 %
Early decision application deadline - N/A
Regular application deadline - Feb 15
Financial aid deadline - Feb 15

Ronne A Patrick - Admissions Director
Northeastern University
360 Huntington Avenue
Boston, MA 02115
O 617.373.2200 / F 617.373.8780

NORTHERN MICHIGAN UNIVERSITY

Division 1

HOCKEY STAFF

HEAD COACH
Walt Kyle *(Northen Michigan '81)*

ASSISTANT COACHES
John Kyle *(Northern Michigan '81)*
John Olver *(Michigan '83)*

HOCKEY OFFICE
Northern Michigan University - Athletics
1401 Presque Isle Avenue
Marquette, MI 49855
O 906.227.1211/ F 906.227.2111
wkyle@nmu.edu

HOCKEY MEDIA CONTACT
David Faiella - Hockey Info Director
Northern Michigan University - Athletics
1401 Presque Isle Avenue
Marquette, MI 49855-5309
O 906.227.1013/ F 906.227.2492
dfaiella@nmu.edu

HOCKEY RINK
Berry Events Center (On Campus)
1401 Presque Isle Avenue
Marquette, MI 49855
Size 200' x 100', Capacity 3,902
O 906.228.8510

ATHLETIC DIRECTOR
Ken Godfrey - Athletic Director
Northern Michigan University - Athletics
Marquette, MI 49855
O 906.227.1826/ F 906.227.2492
kgodfrey@nmu.edu

WILDCATS PLAYERS

Player	YB	GR	Ht/Wt	P	Hometown/Last Team
Pat Bateman	82	07	6' 1"/195	F	Calgary,AB/Surrey Eagles (BCHL)
Matt Butcher	87	10	6' 2"/205	F	Bellingham,WA/Chilliwack Chiefs (BCHL)
Dusty Collins	85	07	6' 3"/195	F	Gilbert,AZ/USNDT (NAHL)
Blake Cosgrove	86	08	5'10"/190	D	Chilliwack,BC/Chilliwack Chiefs (BCHL)
Spencer Dillon	85	09	6' 4"/205	D	Santa Cruz,CA/Green Bay Gamblers (USHL)
Alan Dorich	86	10	6' 2"/205	D	Orland Pk,IL/Des Moines Buccaneers (USHL)
Tim Hartung	84	08	6' 0"/190	F	St. Paul,MN/Lone Star (NAHL)
Josh Hatinger	82	07	6' 0"/175	G	Negaunee,MI/Lansing (NAHL)
Ray Kaunisto	87	10	6' 4"/185	F	Sault Ste. Marie,MI/Cedar Rapids RoughRiders (USHL)
Jacques Lamoureux	86	10	6' 1"/185	F	Grand Forks,ND/Bismarck Bobcats (NAHL)
Rob Lehtinen	83	07	5'11"/175	D	Marquette,MI/Waterloo Blackhawks (USHL)
Mike Maltese	85	10	6' 3"/200	F	Eastpointe,MI/Mahoning Valley Phantoms (NAHL)
Bryant Marple	85	10	5'10"/175	F	Apple Valley,MN/Santa Fe Roadrunners (NAHL)
Matt Maunu	84	07	5'11"/175	D	Esko,MN/Waterloo Blackhawks (USHL)
Derek May	84	09	6'0"/185	D	White Rock,BC/Prince George Spruce Kings (BCHL)
Mick McCrimmon	86	10	5'10"/170	D	Brandon,MB/Lincoln Stars (USHL)
TJ Miller	86	10	6' 4"/210	D	Placetia,CA/Penticton Panthers (BCHL)
Darin Olver	85	07	6' 0"/170	F	Boise,ID/Chilliwack Chiefs (BCHL)
Mike Santorelli	85	08	6' 0"/190	F	Burnaby,BC/Vernon Vipers (BCHL)
Andrew Sarauer	84	08	6' 4"/205	F	Outlook,SK/Langley Hornets (BCHL)
Bobby Selden	85	07	6' 1"/200	D	Negaunee,MI/USNDT (NAHL)
Matt Siddall	84	08	6' 1"/210	F	N Vancouver,BC/Powell River Kings (BCHL)
Nathan Sigmund	86	09	5' 7"/150	F	San Diego,CA/Spruce Grove Saints (AJHL)
Nick Sirota	84	09	5'11"/190	F	Fox Lake,WI/Spruce Grove Saints (AJHL)
Brian Stewart	85	10	6' 4"/195	G	Burnaby,BC/Alberni Valley Bulldogs (BCHL)
Zach Tarkir	84	07	6' 1"/185	D	Fresno,CA/Chilliwack Chiefs (BCHL)
Bill Zaniboni	82	07	6' 1"/210	G	Plymouth,MA/Sault Ste. Marie (NAHL)

ROSTER ANALYSIS (SCHOLARSHIPS - 18)

Class		Country		Last Team					
Fr	9	USA	19	US JR A	12	CDN JR A	13	ACHA	
So	4	Canada	8	US JR B		CDN JR B		NJCAA	
Jr	5	Europe		US PS		CDN PS		NCAA	
Sr	9	Asia		US HS		CDN HS		USNDT	2
Gr		Other		US Midget		CDN Midget		Other	

ADMISSIONS, ENROLLMENT & CAMPUS INFORMATION

Founded 1899	Average acceptance rate - 83 %	Gerri Daniels - Admissions Director
Public, urban campus	Freshman financial aid - 76 %	Northern Michigan Univ. - Admissions
4,285 men / 4,833 women	Early decision application deadline - N/A	1401 Presque Isle Avenue, 304 Cohodas
Tuition, room & board - $ 12 K/ $ 15 K	Regular application deadline - rolling	Marquette, MI 49855
Avg ACT - 22	Financial aid deadline - Feb 20	O 906.227.2650/ F 906.227.1747

NORTHLAND COLLEGE

Division 3

HOCKEY STAFF

HEAD COACH
Steve Fabiilli *(Canisius '01)*

ASSISTANT COACHES
Aaron Wallace *(Northland '06)*
Winston Bother *(Northland '06)*
Ryan Becker *(Northland '05)*
Nate Dolentz *(Northland '06)*

HOCKEY OFFICE
Northland College
1411 Ellis Avenue
Ashland, WI 54806
O 715.682.1395 / F 715.682.1248
sfabilli@northland.edu

HOCKEY MEDIA CONTACT
Dan Roiger - Sports Info Director
Northland College
Ashland, WI 54806
O 715.682.1850
droiger@northland.edu

HOCKEY RINK
Bay Area Civic Ctr. Arena (Off Campus)
320 Fourth Avenue West
Ashland, WI 54806
Size ' x ', Capacity 1,000
O 715.682.2221

ATHLETIC DIRECTOR
Steve Wammer - Athletic Director
Northland College
Ashland, WI 54806
O 715.682.1244 / F 715.682.1248
swammer@northland.edu

LUMBERJACKS RETURNING PLAYERS

Player	YB	GR	Ht/Wt	P	Hometown/Last Team
Joe Belanger	86	10	5'8"/175	D/F	Ashland,WI/Wisconsin Mustangs (MnJHL)
Lindsey Boulter	85	10	5'11"/175	F	Uxbridge,ON/Seguin Bruins (OPJHL)
Corey Brenner	86	09	5'10"/160	G	Lanesborough,MA/Williston Northampton (NEPSAC)
Eric DeCaires	86	08	5'10"/205	D	Brownstown,MI/Woodhaven (HS)
Alex Ehler	88	10	6'0"/175	F	Park Rapids,MN/Park Rapids (HS)
Andy Finco	87	10	5'10"/175	F	Hibbing,MN/Hibbing (HS)
Adam Gorecki	86	10	5'8"/160	G	Arvada,CO/Laconia Leafs (AtJHL)
Justin Grant	81	07	6'1"/185	G	Burlington,IA/Thornhill Rattlers (OPJHL)
Ryan Hunt	86	08	5'8"/135	F	Brownstown,MI/Woodhaven (HS)
Jim Junker	85	07	5'8"/165	F	St. Paul,MN/Johnson (HS)
Steve O'Hern	85	08	5'10"/170	F	St. Paul,MN/St. Bernard's (PS)
Brandon Sachwitz	85	10	5'8"/185	F	Sterling,AK/St. Paul Lakers (MnJHL)
Pat Sierocinski	87	10	5'7"/150	F	Quakertown,PA/Hatfield Ice Dogs (Midget AA)
Josh Spiegel	88	10	5'10"/170	F	Wausau,WI/Wausau East (HS)
Mike Stevens	85	08	5'7"/155	F	Cadillac,MI/Cadillac (HS)
Bo Storozuk	85	10	5'10"/170	G	Swan Vly,MB/Swan Valley Stampeders (ManJHL)
Matt Tanneberg	88	10	6'0"/195	D	Kennewick,WA/Tri-City Titans (NPJHL)
Mike Tatavosian	83	08	5'7"/160	F	Irvine,CA/SUNY Canton (NJCAA)
Brian Zwawa	88	10	6'0"/195	D	Hamburg,NY/Buffalo Saints (Midget AAA)

ROSTER ANALYSIS (SCHOLARSHIPS - 0)

Class		Country		Last Team					
Fr	11	USA	17	US JR A		CDN JR A	3	ACHA	
So	1	Canada	2	US JR B	4	CDN JR B		NJCAA	1
Jr	5	Europe		US PS	2	CDN PS		NCAA	
Sr	2	Asia		US HS	7	CDN HS		USNDT	
Gr		Other		US Midget	2	CDN Midget		Other	

ADMISSIONS, ENROLLMENT & CAMPUS INFORMATION

Founded 1892	Average acceptance rate - 77 %	Eric A. Peterson - Admissions Director
Private, suburban campus	Freshman financial aid - 87 %	Northland College
272 men / 445 women	Early decision application deadline - N/A	Ashland, WI 54806-3999
Tuition, room & board - $ 26 K	Regular application deadline - rolling	O 715.682.1224 / F 715.682.1258
Avg SAT - 1,080 / Avg ACT - 24	Financial aid deadline - April 15	admit@wakefield.northland.edu
www.northland.edu	www.northland.edu/Northland/Athletics/	

NORWICH UNIVERSITY

HOCKEY
EAST

Division 3

HOCKEY STAFF

HEAD COACH
Mike McShane *(New Hampshire '71)*

ASSISTANT COACHES
Steve Mattson *(Norwich '77)*
Fred Coan *(Middlebury '77)*
Cory Gustafson *(Harvard '95)*

HOCKEY OFFICE
Norwich University
Andrews Hall
Northfield, VT 05663
O 802.485.2242 / F 802.485.2234
mmcshane@norwich.edu

HOCKEY MEDIA CONTACT
Scott Miller - Sports Info Director
Norwich University
Plumley Hall
Northfield, VT 05663
O 802.485.2160 / F 802.485.2161
smiller@norwich.edu

HOCKEY RINK
Kreitzberg Arena (On Campus)
58 Harmon Hill
Northfield, VT 05663
Size 200' x 90', Capacity 1,500
O 802.485.2253

ATHLETIC DIRECTOR
Tony Mariano - Athletic Director
Norwich University
Andrews Hall
Northfield, VT 05663
O 802.485.2232 / F 802.485.2234
tmariano@norwich.edu

CADETS PLAYERS

Player	YB	GR	Ht/Wt	P	Hometown/Last Team
Bryan Brunton		10	5'11"/185	D	Colorado Spgs,CO/Brooks Bandits (AJHL)
Rick Cleaver		08	5'11"/180	F	Vancouver,BC/Salmon Arm Silverbacks (BCHL)
James Duhamel		08	5'10"/170	F	Mississauga,ON/Mississauga Chargers (OPJHL)
DJ Fimiani		10	5'6"/150	F	Melrose ,MA/Walpole Stars (EJHL)
Adam Gaudreau		10	6'3"/210	D	Londonderry,NH/Tilton (NEPSAC)
Chance Gieni		09	6'0"/170	G	Saskatoon,SK/Notre Dame (PS)
Rob Harlow	85	09	5'7"/170	F	W Springfield,MA/Vermont (NEPSAC)
Matt Johnson		10	5'7"/170	F	Lynn,MA/Tilton (NEPSAC)
Nikita Kashirsky	85	09	6'0"/180	F	Moscow,Russia/Walpole Stars (EJHL)
Billy Kasper		10	5'9"/170	D	Worcester,MA/Junior Bruins (EJHL)
Ryan Klingensmith		10	5'10"/160	G	Morton,PA/Philadelphia Flyers (MJHL)
Jim Koehler	85	09	5'11"/190	F	Hooksett,NH/Boston Bulldogs (AtJHL)
Peter Langella	07		5'10"/185	D	Manchester,NH/Trinity (NESCAC)
Eric Lauriault	83	08	5'9"/180	F	Gatineau,QC/Valleyfield (QJAHL)
Jonathan Lechance	84	07	6'2"/190	D	Beauport,QC/Portland Pirates (AHL)
Noah Lucia		08	6'0"/180	D	Boston,MA/Boston Harbor Wolves (EJHL)
Eric Ouellette	84	08	6'0"/180	F	Valdor,QC/Valleyfield (QJAHL)
Rico Piatelli	86	09	5'9"/170	F	Danvers,MA/St. John's (PS)
Nick Quagliani		10	5'8"/155	F	W Haven,CT/Winchendon (NEPSAC)
Raphael Robitaille		08	5'10"/175	F	Cap-Rouse,QC/Notre Dame (PS)
Phil Sbrocchi		08	5'9"/180	D	Mississauga,ON/Georgetown Raiders (OPJHL)
Craig Serino		10	5'10"/180	D	Saugus,MA/Avon (NEPSAC)
Tyler Stitt		10	6'4"/190	D	Iroquois Fls,ON/Notre Dame (PS)
Eric Tallent		10	6'0"/185	F	Garland,TX/Weyburn Red Wings (SJHL)
Dana Thibault		08	5'9"/175	D	S Burlington,VT/Green Mountain Glades (EJHL)
David Thompson		10	5'11"/205	G	Wainwright,AB/Camrose Kodiaks (AJHL)
CJ Viso	84	09	5'10"/190	F	San Jose,CA/Notre Dame (PS)
Wendell Watson	84	09	5'9"/195	F	Holden,MA/Campbellton Tigers (MarJHL)
Justin Wissman	86	09	5'8"/170	D	Guilford,VT/Northfield Mount Hermon (NEPSAC)
Scott Wolf		10	5'8"/170	D	Loxahatchee,FL/South Kent (NEPSAC)

ROSTER ANALYSIS (SCHOLARSHIPS - 0)

Class		Country		Last Team					
Fr	12	USA	19	US JR A		CDN JR A	9	ACHA	
So	8	Canada	11	US JR B	8	CDN JR B		NJCAA	
Jr	8	Europe		US PS	9	CDN PS	3	NCAA	1
Sr	2	Asia		US HS		CDN HS		USNDT	
Gr		Other		US Midget		CDN Midget		Other	

ADMISSIONS, ENROLLMENT & CAMPUS INFORMATION

Founded 1819
Private, rural campus
1,440 men / 512 women
Tuition, room & board -$ 27 K
Avg SAT - 1,045 / Avg ACT - 22

Average acceptance rate - %
Freshman financial aid - %
Early decision application deadline - Nov 15
Regular application deadline - rolling
Financial aid deadline - Mar 1

Frank Griffis - Admissions Director
Norwich University - Roberts Hall
Northfield, VT 05663
O 802.485.2001 / F 802.485.2032
O 800.468.6679

www.norwich.edu
www.norwich.edu/athletics/index.html

UNIVERSITY OF NOTRE DAME

Division 1

HOCKEY STAFF

HEAD COACH
Jeff Jackson *(Michigan State '78)*

ASSOCIATE HEAD COACH
Paul Pooley *(Ohio State '84)*

ASSISTANT COACHES
Andy Slaggert *(Notre Dame '89)*
Mike McNeill *(Notre Dame '88)*

HOCKEY OFFICE
University of Notre Dame
Joyce Center
Notre Dame, IN 46556
O 574.631.3630 / F 574.631.4897
jackson.132@nd.edu

HOCKEY MEDIA CONTACT
Tim Connor - Hockey Information Dir.
University of Notre Dame
112 Joyce Center
Notre Dame, IN 46556-5678
O 574.631.7516 / F 574.631.7941
connor.21@nd.edu

HOCKEY RINK
Joyce Center (On Campus)
Juniper Road & Moose Krause Drive
Notre Dame, IN 46556
Size 200' x 85', Capacity 2,713
O 574.631.4899

ATHLETIC DIRECTOR
Kevin White
University of Notre Dame
Joyce Center
Notre Dame, IN 46556
O 574.631.6107 / F 574.631.8132

FIGHTING IRISH PLAYERS

Player	YB	GR	Ht/Wt	P	Hometown/Last Team
Noah Babin	84	07	6'0"/185	D	Palm Bch Gardens,FL/Green Bay Gamblers (USHL)
Michael Bartlett	85	07	6'0"/190	F	Morton Gr,IL/USNDT (NAHL)
Brett Blatchford	86	10	5'11"/190	D	Temperance,MI/Texas Tornado (NAHL)
David Brown	85	07	6'0"/185	G	Stoney Crk,ON/Hamilton Red Wings (OPJHL)
Stewart Carlin	85	10	5'11"/195	F/D	Jeannette,PA/Chicago Steel (USHL)
Erik Condra	86	09	5'11"/185	F	Livonia,MI/Lincoln Stars (USHL)
Brian D'Arcy	84	08	6'2"/205	D	Western Spgs,IL/Tri-City Storm (USHL)
Kevin Deeth	87	10	5'7"/160	F	Gig Harbor,WA/Green Bay Gamblers (USHL)
Christian Hanson	86	09	6'3"/205	F	Venetia,PA/Tri-City Storm (USHL)
TJ Jindra	82	07	5'11"/185	F	Faribault,MN/Omaha Lancers (USHL)
Dan Kissel	87	10	5'9"/165	F	Crestwood,IL/Chicago Steel (USHL)
Kyle Lawson	87	10	5'11"/205	D	New Hudson,MI/Tri-City Storm (USHL)
Christian Minella	85	10	6'1"/220	F	Aurora,CO/Sioux City Musketeers (USHL)
Wes O'Neill	86	07	6'4"/200	D	Essex,ON/Green Bay Gamblers (USHL)
Tom O'Brien	87	10	5'11"/190	G	Mokena,IL/Bridgewater Bandits (EJHL)
Jason Paige	84	07	6'0"/195	F	Saginaw,MI/Compuware Ambassadors (NAHL)
Jordan Pearce	86	09	6'1"/200	G	Anchorage,AK/Lincoln Stars (USHL)
Evan Rankin	86	08	6'1"/180	F	Portage,MI/Lincoln Stars (USHL)
Garrett Regan	85	09	5'11"/180	F	Hastings,MN/Waterloo Blackhawks (USHL)
Tom Sawatske	84	07	5'11"/190	D	Duluth,MN/Lincoln Stars (USHL)
Josh Sciba	85	07	5'11"/190	F	Westland,MI/USNDT (NAHL)
Brock Sheahan	84	08	5'11"/165	D	Lethbridge,AB/Crowsnest Pass (AJHL)
Ryan Thang	87	10	6'0"/190	F	Edina,MN/Omaha Lancers (USHL)
Mark VanGuilder	84	08	6'1"/185	F	Roseville,MN/Tri-City Storm (USHL)
Dan VeNard	85	08	6'0"/175	D	Vernon Hls,IL/Green Bay Gamblers (USHL)
Justin White	85	09	6'0"/185	F	Traverse City,MI/Sioux Falls Stampede (USHL)

ROSTER ANALYSIS (SCHOLARSHIPS - 18)

Class		Country		Last Team					
Fr	8	USA	23	US JR A	21	CDN JR A	2	ACHA	
So	5	Canada	3	US JR B	1	CDN JR B		NJCAA	
Jr	5	Europe		US PS		CDN PS		NCAA	
Sr	8	Asia		US HS		CDN HS		USNDT	2
Gr		Other		US Midget		CDN Midget		Other	

ADMISSIONS, ENROLLMENT & CAMPUS INFORMATION

Founded 1842	Average acceptance rate - 30 %	Daniel J. Saracino - Admissions Director
Private, suburban campus	Freshman financial aid - 100 %	University of Notre Dame
4,327 men / 3,995 women	Early decision application deadline - Nov 1	220 Main Building
Tuition, room & board - $ 37 K	Regular application deadline - Dec 31	Notre Dame, IN 46556
Avg SAT - 1,375 / Avg ACT - 62	Financial aid deadline - Feb 15	O 574.631.7505

OHIO UNIVERSITY

Division 1

HOCKEY STAFF

HEAD COACH
Dan Morris *(Ohio '97)*

ASSISTANT COACHES
Cody Loughlean
Mike Perino

HOCKEY OFFICE
205 Bird Arena
Athens, OH 45701
O 740.593.0251 / F 740.593.0777
O 740.707.1382
morrisd@ohio.edu

HOCKEY MEDIA CONTACT
Shane Bast - Media Director

HOCKEY RINK
Bird Arena
205 Bird Arena
Athens, OH 45701

HOCKEY MANAGER
Michelle Pendergast - General Manager
205 Bird Arena
Athens, OH 45701
O 470.593.4676 / F 740.593.0777
media@ohiobobcatshockey.com

Steven James - General Manager

BOBCATS PLAYERS

Player	YB	GR Ht/Wt	P	Hometown/Last Team
Justin Althof	07	5'10"/175	F	Erie,PA/Columbus Crush (CSHL)
Ryan Baksh	07	5' 9"/155	G	Kitchener,ON/Waterloo Siskins (MWJHL)
Dennis Belkin	07	5' 8"/170	F	Mayfield Heights,OH/Gilmour (PS)
Corey Bise	08	5' 6"/165	F	New Rochelle,NY/Northwood (PS)
Chris Carlson	10	5'10"/190	G	Williamsburg,VA/Helena Bighorns (NAHL)
Tom Ciaverilla	10	6' 0"/170	F	Novi,MI/Novi (HS)
Grady Clingan	09	6' 0"/180	F	Bethel Park,PA/Bethel Park (HS)
Derek DeFelice	09	5' 8"/160	G	McMurray,PA/Columbus Crush (CSHL)
Brandon Fackey	09	5' 9"/160	F	Hamilton,OH/New England College (ECAC East)
Justin Farmer	09	6' 0"/185	D	Mayfield Village,OH/Mayfield (HS)
Dave Fitzgerald	08	6' 0"/190	F	Pittsburgh,PA/Toledo Icediggers (NAHL)
Casey Fitzpatrick	07	5' 9"/165	F	Cleveland,OH/Lake Catholic (PS)
Jim Fuhs	08	5'10"/190	F	Pittsburgh,PA/Springfield Spirit (NAHL)
Brandon Hanley	07	6' 3"/215	F	Bethel Pk,PA/Bethel Park (HS)
Charles Harvey	10	5'11"/175	F	Columbus,OH/Hudson Valley Eagles (AJHL)
Gary Hupp	09	6' 1"/185	D	Anchorage,AK/Cleveland Barons (Midget AAA)
Jeff Jepson	08	5' 8"/155	F	Toledo,OH/Eastern Michigan (ACHA)
Clay LaBrosse	08	6' 3"/200	F	Pittsburgh,PA/Billings Bulls (NAHL)
Max Malone	08	6' 1"/180	D	Gibsonia,MI/Robert Morris (ACHA)
Paul Marshall	09	5'10"/170	G	Orland Park,IL/Chicago Young Americans (Midget AAA)
David Moyer	08	6' 2"/220	D	Meadville,PA/Meadville (HS)
Phil Oberlin	10	5'10"/175	F	Athens,OH/Cincinnati Cobras (CSHL)
Mike Peota	09	5' 9"/185	D	Lake Forest,IL/Chicago Force (CSHL)
JJ Plutt	09	5' 9"/170	F	Mentor,OH/Lake Catholic (PS)
Travis Preble	07	6' 2"/190	D	Salt Lake City,UT/Boston Bulldogs (AJHL)
Jim Roach	08	5' 9"/200	F	Mars,PA/Pennsylvania State (ACHA)
Brandon Steffek	08	6' 0"/190	F	Saginaw,MI/Heritage (HS)
Paul Warriner	07	5' 9"/180	F	Blenheim,ON/Chatham Maroons (WOJHL)
Ross Wimer	08	6' 0"/170	D	Carmel,IN/Couchiching Terriers (OPJHL)
John Yasak	07	6' 2"/200	D	Wheaton,IL/Darien Huskies (Midget AAA)

ROSTER ANALYSIS (SCHOLARSHIPS - 0)

Class		Country		Last Team					
Fr	4	USA	28	US JR A	4	CDN JR A	3	ACHA	3
So	8	Canada	2	US JR B	4	CDN JR B	2	NJCAA	
Jr	10	Europe		US PS	4	CDN PS		NCAA	1
Sr	8	Asia		US HS	6	CDN HS		USNDT	
Gr		Other		US Midget	3	CDN Midget		Other	

ADMISSIONS, ENROLLMENT & CAMPUS INFORMATION

www.ohio.edu   www.ohiobobcatshockey.com

OHIO STATE UNIVERSITY

Division 1

<table>
<tr><td colspan="2">

HOCKEY STAFF

</td><td colspan="5" align="center">

BUCKEYES PLAYERS

</td></tr>
</table>

Player	YB	GR	Ht/Wt	P	Hometown/Last Team
Bryce Anderson	82	07	6' 2"/195	F	Waterloo,IA/Des Moines Buccaneers (USHL)
Dave Barton	83	07	6' 2"/195	F	Calgary,AB/Calgary Canucks (AJHL)
Matt Beaudoin	84	07	5'11"/180	F	Rock Forest,QC/Cowichan Valley Capitals (BCHL)
Kenny Bernard	85	07	5'11"/210	F	Sarnia,ON/Sarnia Blast (WOJHL)
Nick Biondo	85	09	5' 9"/185	D	Cleveland,OH/Cleveland Barons (NAHL)
Sam Campbell	86	08	5'10"/170	F	Hamilton,ON/Hamilton Red Wings (OPJHL)
Sean Collins	83	07	6' 1"/205	D	Troy,MI/Sioux City Musketeers (USHL)
Jason DeSantis	86	08	5'11"/180	D	Oxford,MI/USNDT (NAHL)
John Dingle	84	08	6' 1"/210	F	Shaker Hgts,OH/Tri-City Storm (USHL)
Corey Elkins	85	09	6' 2"/200	F	W Bloomfield,MI/Sioux City Musketeers (USHL)
Nick Filion	88	10	5'11"/180	G	Cornwall,ON/Cornwall Colts (CJHL)
Tom Fritsche	86	08	5'11"/185	F	Parma,OH/USNDT (NAHL)
Tom Goebel	84	07	5' 7"/165	F	Parma,OH/Michigan State (CCHA)
Kyle Hood	84	08	5'11"/185	D	Osoyoos,BC/Cowichan Valley Capitals (BCHL)
Johann Kroll	84	08	6' 2"/195	D	Plymouth,MN/Sioux City Musketeers (USHL)
Phil Lauderdale	83	08	6' 1"/200	G	Greenwich,CT/New Hampshire Monarchs (EJHL)
Domenic Maiani	86	08	5'10"/175	F	Shelby Twnsp,MI/Sioux City Musketeers (USHL)
Matt McIlvane	85	08	6' 1"/200	F	Naperville,IL/Chicago Steel (USHL)
Kevin Montgomery	88	10	6' 1"/185	D	Rochester,NY/USNDT (NAHL)
Joseph Palmer	88	10	6' 1"/205	G	Utica,NY/USNDT (NAHL)
Zach Pelletier	84	08	6' 2"/220	F	China Village,ME/Boston Bulldogs (AtJHL)
Mathieu Picard	85	10	5'11"/175	F	St. Isidore,ON/Hawkesbury Hawks (CJHL)
Andrew Schembri	82	07	5' 6"/160	F	Mississauga,ON/Cornwall Colts (CJHL)
Tyson Strachan	84	07	6' 3"/210	D	Melfort,SK/Vernon Vipers (BCHL)
Matt Waddell	84	07	6' 1"/190	D	Armstrong,BC/Vernon Vipers (BCHL)

HEAD COACH
John Markell *(Bowling Green '79)*

ASSOCIATE HEAD COACH
Casey Jones *(Cornell '90)*

ASSISTANT COACHES
Jason Lammers *(SUNY-Geneseo '98)*
Shane Clifford

HOCKEY OFFICE
Ohio State University - Athletics
555 Arena Drive
Columbus, OH 43210
O 614.292.0820 / H 614.688.5857
markell.1@osu.edu

HOCKEY MEDIA CONTACT
Leann Parker - Hockey Info Director
Ohio State University - Athletics
St. John Arena, Room 124
410 Woody Hayes Drive
Columbus, OH 43210-1166
O 614.688.0294 / F 614.292.8547
parker.387@osu.edu

HOCKEY RINK
Value City Arena (On Campus)
Olentangy River Road & Lane Avenue
Columbus, OH 43210
Size 200' x 85', Capacity 17,500
O 614.688.5330

ATHLETIC DIRECTOR
Gene Smith - Athletic Director
Ohio State University - Athletics
St. John Arena, Room 235
410 Woody Hayes Drive
Columbus, OH 43210-1166
O 614.292.2477 / F 614.292.0506

ROSTER ANALYSIS (SCHOLARSHIPS - 18)

Class		Country		Last Team					
Fr	4	USA	15	US JR A	8	CDN JR A	9	ACHA	
So	2	Canada	10	US JR B	2	CDN JR B	1	NJCAA	
Jr	10	Europe		US PS		CDN PS		NCAA	1
Sr	9	Asia		US HS		CDN HS		USNDT	4
Gr		Other		US Midget		CDN Midget		Other	

ADMISSIONS, ENROLLMENT & CAMPUS INFORMATION

Founded 1870
Public, urban campus
18,770 men / 17,327 women
Tuition, room & board - $ 15 K / $ 25 K
Avg SAT - 1,180 / Avg ACT - 26

Average acceptance rate - 76 %
Freshman financial aid - 70 %
Early decision application deadline - N/A
Regular application deadline - Feb 1
Financial aid deadline - Mar 1

James J. Mager - Admissions Director
Ohio State University - Admissions Office
410 Woody Hayes Drive
Columbus, OH 43210-1200
O 614.292.3980 / F 614.292.4818

www.acs.ohio-state.edu

ohiostatebuckeyes.collegesports.com

Nittany Lion Ice Hockey

(For Advanced High School-Age Players)

Designed for students who are entering grades nine through twelve next fall and who plan to continue their participation in hockey beyond high school.

Camp Highlights

- Video analysis of team and individual play
- Power skating instruction and chalk talks on systems and tactics
- Officiated games Wednesday through Friday
- Lectures and handouts on college admissions, the differences in college programs, what coaches look for in players, what players should look for in college programs, academic preparation, and time management
- Copy of the College Hockey Guide, featuring up-to-date phone numbers and addresses of all college hockey coaches
- Flexibility, strength training, and conditioning programs as well as sports psychology and motivational techniques
- Full-time trainers on hand to help participants
- Goaltending (see "Goaltending Instruction" section)

Goaltending Instruction

- Additional on-ice instruction (goalies must wear throat protectors)
- Goalie instructors to provide specialized training on and off the ice
- Video analysis for each goalie
- Special goalie fees

Camp Acceptance

- Applications will be processed by position on a first-come, first-served basis until the session is filled.

Camp Dates

July 8–13 & August 5–10

Information

Penn State Sport Camps
The Pennsylvania State University
Multi-Sport Facility
University Park PA 16802
Phone: 814-865-0561
E-mail: SportCampInfo@outreach.psu.edu

PENNSYLVANIA STATE UNIVERSITY

INDEPENDENT

EST. 1991

Division 1

HOCKEY STAFF

HEAD COACH
Scott Balboni *(Providence '96)*

ASSISTANT COACHES
Matt Bertani *(Mercyhurst '99)*
John Segursky *(Penn State '89)*
Mo Stroemel *(Penn State)*
Dr. Ray Lombra

HOCKEY OFFICE
Penn State University - Hockey Office
123 East Area Locker Room
University Park, PA 16802
O 814.863.2037 / F 814.863.7906
spb9@psu.edu

HOCKEY MEDIA CONTACT
Marci Palmer - Information Director
Penn State University Hockey Office
123 East Area Locker Room
University Park, PA 16802
O 814.863.2037 / F 814.863.7906
mls3@psu.edu

HOCKEY RINK
Penn State Ice Pavilion (On Campus)
McKeen Road & Hastings Road
University Park, PA 16802
Size 200' x 85', Capacity 1,350
O 814.865.4102

ATHLETIC DIRECTOR
Tim Curley - Athletic Director
Penn State University
101 Bryce Jordan Center
University Park, PA 16802
O 814.865.1086
tmc3@psu.edu

NITTANY LIONS PLAYERS

Player	YB	GR	Ht/Wt	P	Hometown/Last Team
Frank Berry	86	09	6' 1"/190	F	Allentown,PA/Hill (PS)
Craig Brooks	86	09	5'10"/160	D	Douglas,MA/Mt. St. Charles (PS)
John Conte	86	10	6' 1"/195	D	Mahwah,NJ/New Jersey (EJHL)
Scott Dakan	85	09	6' 1"/175	D	Murrysville,PA/Chicago (CSHL)
Lukas DeLorenzo	85	09	5'11"/185	F	Export,PA/Cleveland (NAHL)
Mike Diethorn	86	09	5' 9"/175	F	Bethel Park,PA/Bethel Park (HS)
Dave Herel	86	10	6' 1"/210	F	Vestal,NY/Syracuse (EJHL)
Keith Jordan	84	08	6' 0"/195	D	State College,PA/Youngstown (NAHL)
Sean Kenney	84	08	6' 0"/205	F	Greensburg,PA/Billings (NAHL)
Matt Kirstein	88	10	6' 1"/195	F	Dublin,OH/Dublin Coffman (HS)
Chris Lepore	86	10	5'11"/190	D	Succasunna,NJ/New Jersey (EJHL)
Jason Lorenz	86	08	6' 2"/200	F	Pittsburgh,PA/Cleveland (Midget AAA)
Andrew Magulick	84	09	6' 2"/225	D	State College,PA/Syracuse (OPJHL)
Steve Marchi	87	09	5' 7"/170	F	Monroeville,PA/Pittsburgh (Midget AA)
Chris Matteo	84	07	5' 8"/170	G	Ringwood,NJ/New Jersey
Michael McMullen	83	07	6' 1"/205	F	Chester Springs,PA/Youngstown (NAHL)
Kyle Mills	86	09	6' 0"/185	D	Trumbull,CT/Canterbury (NEPSAC)
Aaron Myers	85	09	6' 2"/185	G	State College,PA/Penn State Altoona (ACHA)
Nate Obringer	86	08	5' 9"/180	F	Pittsburgh,PA/Washington & Jefferson (ACHA)
Mark Orlando	87	09	6' 1"/175	F	Havertown,PA/Haverford (HS)
Steve Peck	86	09	6' 2"/200	F	New Hartford,NY/New Hartford (HS)
Brandon Rubeo	84	09	5' 8"/170	F	McMurray,PA/Markham (OPJHL)
Matt Schwartz	86	08	5'11"/195	F	Venetia,PA/Bentley (AHA)
Nicholas Signet	85	09	6' 1"/195	G	Sewickley,PA/Mahoning Valley (CEHL)
Steve Thurston	86	09	6' 3"/200	D	Wallingford,CT/Fairfield (PS)
Brent Tranter	87	09	6' 0"/185	D	Cranberry Township,PA/Pittsburgh (EmJHL)
Jaime Zimmel	85	09	5' 9"/190	F	Lincroft,NJ/Green Mountain (EJHL)
Paul Zodtner	85	08	5'11"/185	F	Wayne,PA/Hill (PS)

ROSTER ANALYSIS (SCHOLARSHIPS - 0)

Class		Country		Last Team			
Fr	4	USA	28	US JR A	CDN JR A	ACHA	
So	16	Canada		US JR B	CDN JR B	NJCAA	
Jr	6	Europe		US PS	CDN PS	NCAA	
Sr	2	Asia		US HS	CDN HS	USNDT	
Gr		Other		US Midget	CDN Midget	Other	

ADMISSIONS, ENROLLMENT & CAMPUS INFORMATION

Founded 1855	Average acceptance rate - 58 %	Geoffrey Harford - Admissions Director
Public, small city campus	Freshman financial aid - 66 %	Penn State University
17,319 men / 16,639 women	Early decision application deadline - N/A	Shields 201
Tuition, room & board $ 18 K / $ 28 K	Regular application deadline - rolling	University Park, PA 16802
Avg - SAT 1,190	Financial aid deadline - Feb 15	O 814.863.0233 / F 814.863.7590

WE ARE...

Penn State was first chartered in 1855 when the faculty of four taught its first students, 11 of whom graduated in 1861. Classes were held in Old Main, which also served as a dormitory. A rebuilt Old Main now is the site of the offices of the University Administration, including Dr. Graham Spanier, who became Penn State's 16th president in September, 1995.

While Old Main was once all that existed of Penn State, today it sets in the middle of 4,767 acres that make up the University Park campus. Five-hundred-and-forty acres, which includes more than 12,000 trees, are devoted to classrooms and office buildings, residence halls and laboratories, with more than 700 buildings comprising the main campus.

From Old Main to Mount Nittany...from Pattee Library to the Creamery...from East Halls, West Halls, Nittany Suites, the Lion Shrine, the Palmer Museum of Art or the Bryce Jordan Center, Penn State's campus has a picture postcard look.

Penn State Rankings

18th Best Public University (U.S. News & World Report)
18th Best Value at State University (Kiplinger's)
A Best Value (Kaplan 2003)

College of Engineering #15- Aerospace Engineering #12
Chemical Engineering #15- Civil Engineering #11
Electrical Engineering #15- Industrial Engineering #4
Materials Sci. & Engr. #7- Mechanical Engineering #14
Nuclear Engineering #4- Petroleum Engineering #6
(US News & World Report, Graduate Rankings)

5th in NACDA (Sears) Cup
56 National NCAA Team Championships
18 Season and 7 Tournament Championships in Big Ten Play
Honor Roll for Athletic Departments
(US News & World Report)

PENN STATE!

www.psu.edu

UNIVERSITY OF PITTSBURGH

Division 1

HOCKEY STAFF

HEAD COACH
Tom Rieck

ASSISTANT COACH
John Rovnan

GENERAL MANAGER
Andy Mecs
O 412.716.3727
amecs@pitthockey.com

HOCKEY OFFICE
Pitt Ice Hockey
475 Salem Drive
Pittsburgh, PA 15243
O 412.716.3727

HOCKEY RINK
BladeRunners Ice - Harmarville (Off Campus)
66 Alpha Drive West
Pittsburgh, PA 15238
O 412.826.0800

PANTHERS PLAYERS

Player	YB	GR	Ht/Wt	P	Hometown/Last Team
Steven Adams	10		5'8"/160	D	Pittsburgh,PA/Pittsburgh Penguins (EmJHL)
Dale Arnold	09		5'5"/150	F	Bethel Pk,PA/BethelPark (HS)
Mark Barakat	08		5'10"/190	F	Montreal,QC/Millburn (HS)
Tomas Bednar	08		5'10"/160	F	N Wales,PA/Philadelphia Little Flyers (AtJHL)
Matt Boles	07		6'2"/200	D	Monroeville,PA/Gateway (HS)
Mike Clark	10		5'8"/145	F	Sarnia,ON/Moon (HS)
Joe Coleman	07		5'10"/175	D	Edinboro,PA/McClane (HS)
Matt Dzadovsky	07		5'9"/155	F	Pittsburgh,PA/Pitt-Johnstown (ACHA)
Max Gruin	09		6'2"/180	D	Hummelstown,PA/Hershey Bears (EmJHL)
Chas Hoffman	10		5'10"/150	D	Pittsburgh,PA/Baldwin (HS)
Matt Lazzaro	10		6'2"/200	F	McMurray,PA/Peters (HS)
Craig Lehocky	08		5'7"/135	F	Freedom,PA/Beaver County Badgers (MidgetAA)
Vince Luczak	07		5'10"/170	F	Pittsburgh,PA/North Catholic (PS)
Jake Mann	10		5'8"/160	F	Tenafly,NJ/Tenafly (HS)
Colin McCloskey	07		6'0"/170	G	Spencerport,NY/Spencerport (HS)
Bob Mirzabeigi	07		5'8"/165	F	Murraysville,PA/Franklin (HS)
Ed Nusser	09		5'10"/155	G	Pittsburgh,PA/North Jersey (AtJHL)
Sean O'Sullivan	10		5'11"/175	F	West Chester,PA/West Chester East (HS)
Matt Panek	09		5'11"/150	F	Buffalo,NY/Bishop Timon (PS)
Steve Quatchak	08		6'2"/175	F	Wexford,PA/North Alleghany (HS)
Tim Schaible	09		6'2"/185	D	Blue Bell,PA/LaSalle (PS)
Ryan Severyn	09		5'11"/155	F	Beaver,PA/Beaver County Badgers (MidgetAA)
BJ Tipton	08		6'0"/170	F	Butler,PA/Butler (HS)
Jeremy Wano	08		5'9"/160	D	Youngstown,PA/Latrobe (HS)

ROSTER ANALYSIS (SCHOLARSHIPS - 0)

Class		Country		Last Team				
Fr	6	USA	22	US JR A		CDN JR A	ACHA	1
So	6	Canada	2	US JR B	4	CDN JR B	NJCAA	
Jr	6	Europe		US PS	3	CDN PS	NCAA	
Sr	6	Asia		US HS	14	CDN HS	USNDT	
Gr		Other		US Midget	2	CDN Midget	Other	

ADMISSIONS, ENROLLMENT & CAMPUS INFORMATION

Founded 1787
Public, urban campus
8,172 men / 8,852 women
Tuition, room & board $ 19 K / $ 29 K
Avg SAT - 1255

Average acceptance rate - 53 %
Freshman financial aid - 76 %
Early decision application deadline - N/A
Regular application deadline - rolling
Financial aid deadline - Mar 1

Dr. Betsy A. Porter - Admissions Director
University of Pittsburgh
4227 Fifth Avenue, 1st Floor, Alumni Hall
Pittsburgh, PA 15260
O 412.624.7488 / F 412.648.8815

www.pitt.edu   www.pitthockey.com

PLYMOUTH STATE COLLEGE

HOCKEY NORTHEAST

Division 3

HOCKEY STAFF

HEAD COACH
Brett Tryder

ASSISTANT COACH
Craig Russell

HOCKEY OFFICE
Plymouth State College
PE Center, MSC #32
Plymouth, NH 03264-1600
O 603.535.2744 / F 603.535.2758
brtryder@plymouth.edu

HOCKEY MEDIA CONTACT
Kent Cherrington - Sports Info Director
Plymouth State College
P. O. Box 875
Plymouth, NH 03264
O 603.535.2477 / F 603.535.2868
kcherrington@plymouth.edu

HOCKEY RINK
Waterville Valley Ice Arena (Off Campus)
Route 49, Town Square
Waterville Valley, NH 03215
Size 200' x 85', Capacity 1,000
O 603.236.4813

ATHLETIC DIRECTOR
John Clark - Athletic Director
Plymouth State College
Holderness Road
Plymouth, NH 03264
O 603.535.2750 / F 603.535.2758
jpclark@plymouth.edu

PANTHERS PLAYERS

Player	YB	GR	Ht/Wt	P	Hometown/Last Team
Petter Adeberg		10	6'0"/190	F	Bromma,Sweden/Ska IK (SEL)
Kyle Allen		07	5'9"/165	F	Shrewsbury,MA/Shrewsbury (HS)
Derek Avakian		07	5'11"/195	F	Edgartown,MA/Martha's Vineyard (HS)
Matt Blonigen		08	5'10"/205	D	Newington,NH/Valley Warriors (EJHL)
Deni Bojadzic		08	5'11"/185	F	Gothenburg,Sweden/Molndal (SEL)
Chris Cadieux		08	5'10"/180	F	Nashua,NH/Salem Ice Dogs (EmJHL)
Chris Chambers		10	6'3"/190	F	Crofton,MD/Boston Harbor Wolves (EJHL)
Trevor Cherry		07	6'0"/165	G	Greenland,NH/Laconia Leafs (AtJHL)
Bill Dares		10	6'0"/200	D	Rockland,MA/Bay State Breakers (EJHL)
Bobby Dashner		08	6'2"/190	D	Hyde Park,MA/Winchendon (NEPSAC)
Gio DeGiocomo		10	6'4"/240	D	Plaistow,NH/Boston Bulldogs (AtJHL)
Brendan Fahy		07	5'6"/165	G	Plymouth,MA/Bridgton (NEPSAC)
Mick Fitzpatrick		10	6'0"/185	G	Lancaster,NY/Capital District Selects (EJHL)
Nate Gardner		07	5'9"/180	F	Manchester,NH/Connecticut Wolves (MJHL)
Pavel Gonzalez		09	5'10"/170	F	Stockholm,Sweden/Tyreso (SEL)
Mykul Haun		07	5'6"/160	F	Alameda,CA/Bridgewater Bandits (EJHL)
Goose LaCroix		08	5'8"/170	F	Moretown,VT/Green Mountain Glades (EJHL)
Topo LaCroix		08	5'7"/165	F	Moretown,VT/Green Mountain Glades (EJHL)
Jay Londer		07	5'8"/160	F	Philadelphia,PA/Laconia Leafs (AtJHL)
Steve Milley		07	6'2"/205	D	Sudbury,MA/Lincoln-Sudbury (HS)
Ryan Moreau		08	5'8"/175	F	Worcester,MA/Hoosac (NEPSAC)
Ryan Paglinco		10	5'10"/155	F	W Haven,CT/Hartford Wolfpack (AtJHL)
Rob Primeau		09	5'9"/165	F	E Greenwich,RI/Bishop Hendricken (PS)
Bryan Radomski		10	5'10"/145	D	W Hartford,CT/Connecticut Clippers (MJHL)
Pat Turcotte		09	5'10"/185	D	Goffstown,NH/Green Mountain Glades (EJHL)
Andy Weigand		10	5'9"/175	D	Burlington,VT/Burlington (HS)

ROSTER ANALYSIS (SCHOLARSHIPS - 0)

Class		Country		Last Team					
Fr	8	USA	23	US JR A		CDN JR A		ACHA	
So	3	Canada		US JR B	15	CDN JR B		NJCAA	
Jr	7	Europe	3	US PS	4	CDN PS		NCAA	
Sr	8	Asia		US HS	4	CDN HS		USNDT	
Gr		Other		US Midget		CDN Midget		Other	3

ADMISSIONS, ENROLLMENT & CAMPUS INFORMATION

Founded 1871	Average acceptance rate - 77 %	Gene Fahey - Admissions Director
Public, rural campus	Freshman financial aid - 61 %	Plymouth State College
2,009 men / 2,009 women	Early decision application deadline - N/A	17 High Street
Tuition, room & board - $13 K / $19 K	Regular application deadline - Apr 1	Plymouth, NH 03264-1595
Avg SAT - 960	Financial aid deadline - Mar 1	O 603.535.2237 / F 603.535.2714

www.plymouth.edu | www.plymouth.edu/athletic/

PRINCETON UNIVERSITY

Division 1

HOCKEY STAFF

HEAD COACH
Guy Gadowsky *(Colorado College '89)*

ASSISTANT COACHES
Keith Fisher *(St. Cloud State '00)*
John Riley *(UMass Boston '91)*

HOCKEY OFFICE
Princeton University
Baker Rink
PO Box 71
Princeton, NJ 08544 - 0071
O 609.258.6616/ F 609.258.6676
gadowsky@princeton.edu

HOCKEY MEDIA CONTACT
Yariv Amir - Hockey Info Director
Princeton University
9 Jadwin Gym
Faculty & Washington Roads
Princeton, NJ 08544-0071
O 609.258.5701/ F 609.258.2399
yamir@princeton.edu

HOCKEY RINK
Hobey Baker Rink (On Campus)
Faculty Road
Princeton, NJ 08540
Size 200' x 85', Capacity 2,092
O 609.258.1812

ATHLETIC DIRECTOR
Gary Walters - Athletic Director
Princeton University
110 West College
Princeton, NJ 08544
O 609.258.3535/ F 609.258.4477
walters@princeton.edu

TIGERS PLAYERS

Player	YB	GR	Ht/Wt	P	Hometown/Last Team
Dan Bartlett	86	10	5'10"/175	F	Portland,ME/New Hampshire Monarchs (EJHL)
Tyler Beachell	86	10	6'2"/190	F	Rosser,MB/Flin Flon Bombers (SJHL)
Max Cousins	83	07	6'0"/180	D	Calgary,AB/Yorkton Terriers (SJHL)
Kevin Crane	88	10	5'11"/175	D	Irvine,CA/Phillips Exeter (NEPSAC)
Cam French	86	10	6'3"/210	F	St. Albert,AB/Drayton Valley Thunder (AJHL)
Grant Goeckner-Zoeller	83	07	6'1"/210	F	Los Angeles,CA/Sioux City Musketeers (USHL)
Kyle Hagel	85	08	6'0"/205	D	Hamilton,ON/Hamilton Red Wings (OPJHL)
Lee Jubinville	85	09	5'10"/165	F	Edmonton,AB/Camrose Kodiaks (AJHL)
Kevin Kaiser	87	10	5'9"/175	F	Pelham,NH/St. Paul's (NEPSAC)
Zane Kalemba	85	10	5'11"/175	G	Saddle Brook,NJ/Flin Flon Bombers (SJHL)
Brandon Kushniruk	85	09	6'0"/190	F	Hudson Bay,SK/Nanaimo Clippers (BCHL)
Cam MacIntyre	85	10	6'1"/215	F	Sooke,BC/Salmon Arm Silverbacks (BCHL)
BJ Mackasey	83	07	5'10"/195	D	Beaconsfield,QC/Deerfield (NEPSAC)
Mark Magnowski	86	10	5'10"/175	F	Winnipeg,MB/Sioux Falls Stampede (USHL)
Daryl Marcoux	83	07	5'10"/185	D	Slave Lake,AB/Drayton Valley Thunder (AJHL)
Michael Moore	84	08	6'1"/190	D	Calgary,AB/Surrey Eagles (BCHL)
Jody Pederson	85	10	6'3"/200	D	Smithers,BC/Fort McMurray Oil Barons (AJHL)
Darroll Powe	85	07	5'11"/190	F	Kanata,ON/Kanata Stallions (CJHL)
Christian Read	85	07	6'0"/185	F	Skillman,NJ/Lawrenceville (PS)
Brad Schroeder	85	07	6'3"/195	D	Drake,SK/Humboldt Broncos (SJHL)
Keith Shattenkirk	85	08	6'0"/190	F	New Rochelle,NY/Taft (NEPSAC)
BJ Sklapsky	82	07	6'1"/190	G	Martensville,SK/Humboldt Broncos (SJHL)
Landis Stankievech	84	08	5'11"/180	F	Trochu,AB/Olds Grizzlys (AJHL)
Thomas Sychterz	87	09	6'1"/185	G	Lachine,QC/Lachine Maroons (QJAHL)
Brett Westgarth	82	07	6'2"/215	D	Amherstburg,ON/Chatham Maroons (WOJHL)
Kevin Westgarth	84	07	6'4"/235	F	Amherstburg,ON/Chatham Maroons (WOJHL)
Brett Wilson	85	09	6'0"/180	F	Calgary,AB/Calgary (AJHL)

ROSTER ANALYSIS (SCHOLARSHIPS - 0)

Class		Country		Last Team				
Fr	10	USA	7	US JR A	2	CDN JR A	17	ACHA
So	4	Canada	20	US JR B	1	CDN JR B	2	NJCAA
Jr	4	Europe		US PS	5	CDN PS		NCAA
Sr	9	Asia		US HS		CDN HS		USNDT
Gr		Other		US Midget		CDN Midget		Other

ADMISSIONS, ENROLLMENT & CAMPUS INFORMATION

Founded 1746
Private, suburban campus
2,479 men / 2,199 women
Tuition, room & board - $ 41 K
Avg SAT - 1,465

Average acceptance rate - 13 %
Freshman financial aid - 100 %
Early decision application deadline - Nov 1
Regular application deadline - Jan 2
Financial aid deadline - Feb 1

Fred A. Hargadon - Admissions Director
Princeton University - Box 430
P. O. Box 71
Princeton, NJ 08544-0430
O 609.258.3060/ F 609.258.6743

www.princeton.edu

www.goprincetontigers.collegesports.com

PROVIDENCE COLLEGE

Division 1

HOCKEY STAFF

HEAD COACH
Tim Army *(Providence '85)*

ASSISTANT COACHES
David Berard *(Providence '92)*
Stan Moore *(SUNY-Oswego '78)*
Jason Wilson *(Norwich '06)*

HOCKEY OFFICE
Providence College
Schneider Arena
Providence, RI 02918-0001
O 401.865.2551 / 401.865.2382
tarmy@providence.edu

HOCKEY MEDIA CONTACT
Jorge Rocha - Hockey Info Director
Providence College - Alumni Office
549 River Avenue
Providence, RI 02918-0001
O 401.865.2201 / F 401.865.2583
jrocha@providence.edu

HOCKEY RINK
Schneider Arena (On Campus)
Huxley Avenue
Providence, RI 02918
Size 200' x 85', Capacity 3,030
O 401.865.1414

ATHLETIC DIRECTOR
Robert Driscoll, Jr. - Athletic Director
Providence College - Alumni Hall
Providence, RI 02918-0001
O 401.865.2909
rdriscol@providence.edu

FRIARS PLAYERS

Player	YB	GR	Ht/Wt	P	Hometown/Last Team
Marc Bastarche	84	08	5'10"/185	D	Lynn,MA/New Hampshire Monarchs (EJHL)
Jamie Carroll	82	07	6'1"/200	F	Andover,CT/Cedar Rapids RoughRiders (USHL)
David Cavanagh	86	10	6'1"/205	D	Warwick,RI/Salisbury (NEPSAC)
John Cavanagh	87	10	5'9"/170	F	Warwick,RI/Salisbury (NEPSAC)
Greg Collins	86	10	5'11"/185	F	Hingham,MA/Salisbury (NEPSAC)
Brad Cooper	84	09	5'10"/175	F	Dallas,TX/Texas Tornado (NAHL)
Chris Eppich	86	10	5'10"/180	F	Surrey,BC/Chilliwack Chiefs (BCHL)
Mark Fayne	87	10	6'3"/220	D	Sagamore Bch,MA/Nobles (NEPSAC)
Bryan Horan	83	07	6'1"/185	F	Farmington,CT/Cedar Rapids RoughRiders (USHL)
Kyle Laughlin	84	09	5'11"/185	F	Gambrills,MD/Youngstown Phantoms (NAHL)
Trevor Ludwig	82	08	6'1"/200	D	Grapevine,TX/Texas Tornado (NAHL)
Chris Mannix	86	09	5'8"/190	G	Hubbardston,MA/Phillips Exeter (NEPSAC)
Nick Mazzolini	84	09	6'2"/210	F	Anchorage,AK/Texas Tornado (NAHL)
Colin McDonald	84	07	6'3"/190	F	Wethersfield,CT/New England (EJHL)
Austin Miller	85	09	5'10"/175	D	Dallas,TX/Texas Tornado (NAHL)
John Mori	86	09	6'1"/180	F	Westport,CT/Avon (NEPSAC)
Pierce Norton	85	09	6'2"/200	F	S Boston,MA/Thayer (NEPSAC)
Jon Rheault	82	08	5'10"/165	F	Deering,NH/New Hampshire Monarchs (EJHL)
Ryan Simpson	88	10	6'2"/200	G	Bow,NH/New Hampshire Monarchs (EJHL)
Tyler Sims	85	08	6'0"/180	G	Ft Worth,TX/Youngstown Phantoms (NAHL)
Dinos Stamoulis	83	07	6'0"/190	D	Carle Place,NY/Cedar Rapids RoughRiders (USHL)
Matt Taormina	86	09	5'11"/185	D	Washington Tsp,MI/Texarkana Bandits (NAHL)
Matt Tommasiello	85	10	5'9"/175	F	Cranston,RI/Bridgewater Bandits (EJHL)
Chase Watson	82	07	6'0"/195	F	Media,PA/Cedar Rapids RoughRiders (USHL)
Cody Wild	87	09	6'1"/185	D	N Providence,RI/Junior Bruins (EJHL)
Tony Zancanaro	82	07	5'6"/165	F	Trenton,MI/Springfield Blues (NAHL)

ROSTER ANALYSIS (SCHOLARSHIPS - 18)

Class		Country		Last Team				
Fr	7	USA	24	US JR A	12	CDN JR A	1	ACHA
So	9	Canada	2	US JR B	6	CDN JR B		NJCAA
Jr	4	Europe		US PS	7	CDN PS		NCAA
Sr	6	Asia		US HS		CDN HS		USNDT
Gr		Other		US Midget		CDN Midget		Other

ADMISSIONS, ENROLLMENT & CAMPUS INFORMATION

Founded 1917
Private, urban campus
1,939 men / 2,186 women
Tuition, room & board - $ 35 K
Avg SAT - 1,200 / Avg ACT - 25

Average acceptance rate - 54 %
Freshman financial aid - 88 %
Early decision application deadline - N/A
Regular application deadline - Jan 15
Financial aid deadline - Feb 1

Christopher P. Lydon - Admissions Director
Providence College - Admissions Office
549 River Avenue
Providence, RI 02918-0001
O 401.865.2535 / F 401.865.2826

web.providence.edu | www.friars.collegesports.com

QUINNIPIAC UNIVERSITY

Division 1

HOCKEY STAFF		BOBCATS PLAYERS				

HOCKEY STAFF

HEAD COACH
Rand Pecknold *(Connecticut '90)*

ASSISTANT COACHES
Ben Syer *(Western Ontario '98)*
Scott Robson *(Quinnipiac '98)*

HOCKEY OFFICE
Quinnipiac University
275 Mt. Carmel Avenue
Hamden, CT 06518-0569
O 203.582.5321 / F 203.281.8716
pecknold@quinnipiac.edu

HOCKEY MEDIA CONTACT
Michael Kobylanski - Sports Info Director
Quinnipiac University
275 Mt. Carmel Avenue
Hamden, CT 06518-0569
O 203.582.8625 / F 203.281.8716
michael.kobylanski@quinnipiac.edu

HOCKEY RINK
Northford Ice Pavilion (Off Campus)
24-30 Clintonville Road, Rte. 22
Northford, CT 06472
Size 200' x 85', Capacity 1,000

ATHLETIC DIRECTOR
Jack McDonald - Athletic Director
Quinnipiac University
Athletic Center
Hamden, CT 06518
O 203.582.8621 / F 203.582.3440
mcdonald@quinnipiac.edu

BOBCATS PLAYERS

Player	YB	GR	Ht/Wt	P	Hometown/Last Team
Mark Agnew	83	08	5' 9"/175	F	Hartney,MB/Fargo-Moorhead Jets (NAHL)
Mike Atkinson	85	10	5' 9"/165	F	Kinderhook,NY/Vermont (HEA)
Jamie Bates	85	08	6' 3"/195	F	Toronto,ON/Wexford Raiders (OPJHL)
Jean-Marc Beaudoin	85	10	5'10"/185	F	St. Paul,AB/Bonnyville Pontiacs (AJHL)
Michael Bordieri	84	07	6' 0"/155	F	Rocky Hill,CT/New England Coyotes (EJHL)
Reid Cashman	83	07	6' 1"/190	D	Red Wing,MN/Waterloo Blackhawks (USHL)
Dan Cullen	84	08	5'11"/170	G	Hamburg,NY/Binghamton Jr Senators (EmJHL)
John Doherty	84	07	6' 4"/235	D	Lynnfield,MA/New Hampshire (HEA)
Josh Duncan	86	10	5'11"/200	D	Rochester,MN/Victoria Salsa (BCHL)
Bud Fisher	87	09	5'11"/170	G	Peterborough,ON/Lindsay Muskies (OPJHL)
Dan Henningson	84	09	6' 1"/190	D	Edmonton,AB/Drayton Valley Thunder (AJHL)
Greg Holt	85	10	5' 9"/175	F	Mt Sinai,NY/New Hampshire Monarchs (EJHL)
Zach Kleiman	86	10	6' 3"/215	G	Saskatoon,SK/Milton Icehawks (OPJHL)
Eric Lampe	86	10	5'11"/170	f	Madison,WI/Chicago Steel (USHL)
Dan Lefort	86	08	5'10"/185	D	Ajax,ON/Wexford Raiders (OPJHL)
Brian Leitch	84	09	6' 3"/190	F	Coquitlam,BC/Merritt Centennials (BCHL)
Sami Liimatainen	87	10	5'11"/160	D	Riverside,IL/Chicago Steel (USHL)
David Marshall	85	09	5'11"/185	F	Buffalo,MN/Chicago Steel (USHL)
Andrew Meyer	85	09	6' 0"/185	D	Arnold,MO/Green Bay Gamblers (USHL)
Christopher Meyers	87	10	5' 8"/165	F	Eden Pr,MN/Sioux Falls Stampede (USHL)
Chris Myers	85	09	6' 0"/180	F	Wallaceburg,ON/Sarnia Blast (WOJHL)
Ben Nelson	83	08	5' 9"/195	F	Spokane,WA/Cowichan Valley Capitals (BCHL)
Mark Nelson	84	09	5'11"/185	F	Prince George,BC/Vernon Vipers (BCHL)
Matt Sorteberg	86	08	6' 1"/175	D	Anoka,MN/Anoka (HS)
Dan Travis	83	07	6' 3"/215	F	Wilton,NH/New Hampshire (HEA)
Peter Vetri		08	5'10"/175	G	Windham,NH/Massachusetts Lowell (HEA)
Brandon Wong	86	10	5'10"/175	F	Victoria,BC/Merritt Centennials (BCHL)
Jordan Zitoun	87	10	5'11"/195	D	Irving,TX/Wexford Raiders (OPJHL)

ROSTER ANALYSIS (SCHOLARSHIPS - 11)

Class		Country		Last Team					
Fr	10	USA	17	US JR A	7	CDN JR A	12	ACHA	
So	7	Canada	11	US JR B	3	CDN JR B	1	NJCAA	
Jr	7	Europe		US PS	1	CDN PS		NCAA	4
Sr	4	Asia		US HS		CDN HS		USNDT	
Gr		Other		US Midget		CDN Midget		Other	

ADMISSIONS, ENROLLMENT & CAMPUS INFORMATION

Founded 1929	Average acceptance rate - 55 %	Joan Mohr - Admissions Director
Private, suburban campus	Freshman financial aid - 64 %	Quinnipiac University
2,025 men / 3,304 women	Early decision application deadline - N/A	Hamden, CT 06518
Tuition, room & board - $ 35 K	Regular application deadline - Feb 1	O 203.582.8600 / F 203.582.8906
Avg SAT - 1,125 / Avg ACT - 24	Financial aid deadline - Mar 1	

www.quinnipiac.edu quinnipiacbobcats.collegesports.com

RENSSELAER POLYTECHNIC INSTITUTE

Division 1

HOCKEY STAFF

HEAD COACH
Seth Appert *(Ferris State '96)*

ASSISTANT COACHES
Jim Montgomery *(Maine '93)*
Shawn Kurluak *(Denver '99)*

HOCKEY OFFICE
RPI - Houston Field House
110 8th Street
Troy, NY 12180-3590
O 518.276.8534/ F 518.276.8669
appers@rpi.edu

HOCKEY MEDIA CONTACT
Kevin Beattie - Hockey Info Director
RPI - AS & RC Building
Troy, NY 12180-3590
O 518.276.2187/ F 518.276.2188
beattk@rpi.edu

HOCKEY RINK
Houston Fieldhouse (On Campus)
1900 Peoples Avenue
Troy, NY 12180
Size 200' x 85', Capacity 5,154
O 518.276.2661

ATHLETIC DIRECTOR
Ken Ralph - Athletic Director
RPI - AS & RC Building
Troy, NY 12180-3590
O 518.276.6702/ F 518.276.8997
ralphk@rpi.edu

ENGINEERS PLAYERS

Player	YB	GR	Ht/Wt	P	Hometown/Last Team
Jordan Alford	85	08	6'2"/180	G	Red Deer,AB/Canmore Eagles (AJHL)
Matt Angers-Goulet	86	09	5'11"/180	F	St. Augustin,QC/Notre Dame (PS)
Kevin Broad	82	07	6'0"/195	F	Humboldt,SK/Humboldt Broncos (SJHL)
Eric Burgdoerfer	88	10	6'2"/210	D	E Setauket,NY/Apple Core (EJHL)
Kurt Colling	85	09	6'0"/185	F	Ripley,ON/Vernon Vipers (BCHL)
Jordan Cyr	86	10	5'10"/185	F	Winnipeg,MB/Brockville Braves (CJHL)
Tyler Eaves	86	08	5'10"/190	F	Queensbury,NY/Shattuck-St. Mary's (PS)
Oren Eizenman	85	07	6'0"/175	F	Toronto,ON/Wexford Raiders (OPJHL)
Jason Fortino	87	10	6'0"/205	D	Stoney Crk,ON/Milton Icehawks (OPJHL)
Tommy Green	84	07	5'11"/165	F	Martensville,SK/Melfort Mustangs (SJHL)
Christian Jensen	86	10	6'3"/200	D	Watchung,NJ/Chicago Steel (USHL)
Paul Kerins	87	10	5'10"/175	F	Weston,ON/North York Rangers (OPJHL)
Reed Kipp	84	09	6'1"/200	D	Victoria,BC/Vernon Vipers (BCHL)
Seth Klerer	85	09	5'11"/175	F	Thornhill,ON/North York Rangers (OPJHL)
Mathias Lange	85	09	5'11"/180	G	Klagenfurt,Austria/Apple Core (EJHL)
Andrew Lord	85	08	6'3"/190	F	W Vancouver,BC/Vernon Vipers (BCHL)
Jake Luthi	82	07	6'0"/190	D	Palmer,AK/Sioux Falls Stampede (USHL)
Kirk MacDonald	83	07	6'2"/210	F	Victoria,BC/Victoria Salsa (BCHL)
Peter Merth	87	10	6'3"/225	D	New Westminster,BC/Burnaby Express (BCHL)
Jake Morissette	83	08	5'9"/180	F	Fruitvale,BC/Williams Lake Timberwolves (BCHL)
William Neubert	85	08	6'1"/180	D	Painted Post,NY/Capital District Selects (EJHL)
Jonathan Ornelas	86	08	5'9"/175	F	Mississauga,ON/Milton Icehawks (OPJHL)
Dan Peace	84	08	6'1"/185	F	Ann Arbor,MI/Toledo IceDiggers (NAHL)
Ryan Swanson	84	07	6'3"/210	D	Woodbury,MN/Soo Indians (NAHL)
Andrei Uryadov	86	09	6'1"/190	F	St. Petersburg,Russia/South Kent (NEPSAC)
Garrett Vassel	85	10	6'2"/195	F/D	Northampton,NY/Apple Core (EJHL)

ROSTER ANALYSIS (SCHOLARSHIPS - 18)

Class		Country		Last Team					
Fr	7	USA	8	US JR A	4	CDN JR A	15	ACHA	
So	6	Canada	16	US JR B	4	CDN JR B		NJCAA	
Jr	7	Europe	2	US PS	2	CDN PS	1	NCAA	
Sr	6	Asia		US HS		CDN HS		USNDT	
Gr		Other		US Midget		CDN Midget		Other	

ADMISSIONS, ENROLLMENT & CAMPUS INFORMATION

Founded 1824
Private, urban campus
4,000 men / 1,200 women
Tuition, room & board - $ 42 K
Avg SAT - 1,320/ Avg ACT - 27

Average acceptance rate - 75 %
Freshman financial aid - 94 %
Early decision application deadline - Nov 15
Regular application deadline - Jan 1
Financial aid deadline - Feb 15

Karen Long - Admissions Director
RPI - Admissions Building
110 8th Street
Troy, NY 12180-3590
O 518.276.6216/ F 518.276.4072

www.rpi.edu

www.rpi.edu/dept/athletics/

UNIVERSITY OF RHODE ISLAND

Division 1

HOCKEY STAFF

HEAD COACH
Joe Augustine

ASSISTANT COACHES
Christian Rigamonti
Paul Connell
Bobby Jackson

HOCKEY OFFICE
Rhode Island Men's Ice Hockey
3 Keaney Road, Suite 1
Kingston, RI 02881
401.874.9216
clubsports@uri.edu
jcoach55@aol.com

HOCKEY MEDIA CONTACT
Christian Rigamonti
O 401.241.6222 / F 401.588.5678
christian.rigamonti@t-mobile.com

HOCKEY RINK
Brad Boss Ice Arena
1 Keaney Road
Kingston, RI 02881
Size 200' x 85', Capacity 2,500
O 401.874.5480

ASS'T ATHLETIC DIRECTOR
Art Tuveson
O 401.874.5469

RAMS PLAYERS

Player	YB GR Ht/Wt	P	Hometown/Last Team
Sean Arthur	5'11"/165	D	Norwood,MA/Norwood (HS)
David Berard	6'4"/187	D	Stuart,FL/Pomfret (NEPSAC)
David Berardinelli	5'9"/174	F	Warwick,RI/Nichols (ECAC NE)
Jon Biliouris	6'2"/186	D	North Smithfield,RI/Baystate Breakers
Mike Bragger	5'10"/166	F	East Greenwich,RI/Tilton (NEPSAC)
Warren Byrne	6'1"/221	F	Penn Argyl,PA/Chicago Street
Ben Cuddy	5'9"/190	D	Cambridge,MA/Salem Ice Dogs
Mike Curran	5'9"/179	F	Devon,PA/Malvern (PS)
Derrek Douglas	5'11"/197	D	Battle Creek,MI/NJ Avalanche
Scott Eberenz	5'10"/183	F	Springfield,NJ/Lebanon Valley (ECAC West)
Anthony Feyock	6'1"/174	G	Johnstown,PA/Bishop McCort (PS)
Stephen Gaffney	5'8"/159	F	Warwick,RI/Loomis Chaffee (NEPSAC)
James Gaffney	5'8"/162	F	Warwick,RI/Loomis Chaffee (NEPSAC)
Mike Haggerty	6'0"/242	F	Danbury,CT/Sea Coast Kings
Ben Herring	6'0"/166	F	Sewickley,PA/Pittsburgh Hornets
Eric Hogberg	5'7"/215	F	Cranston,RI/LaSalle (PS)
Graham Johnson	6'1"/231	D	North Kingston,RI/Bridgewater Bandits
James Lang	6'1"/213	D	Warwick,RI/Loomis Chaffee (NEPSAC)
Mark Latter	5'8"/174	D	Westwood,MA/Pomfret (NEPSAC)
Matt Loftus	6'1"/182	F	Philadelphia,PA/LaSalle (PS)
Cory Manley	6'4"/231	F	Coventry,RI/Walpole Jr Stars
Ray Martin	5'10"/174	G	Warwick,RI/Neumann College
Bill McKiernan	6'3"/197	F	East Providence,RI/Bishop Hendricken (PS)
Rob Peterson	6'0"/170	D	Wilmington,MA/Canterbury (NEPSAC)
Cory Pinheiro	5'5"/165	F	Hope,RI/Bridgewater Bandits
Tyler Reinhardt	5'10"/205	D	Livingston,NJ/Canterbury (PS)
Anthony Rowella	5'7"/163	F	Ridgefield,CT/Skidmore College
Brian Smith	5'9"/158	F	Philadelphia,PA/Canterbury (NEPSAC)
Brendan Smith	6'2"/211	F	Fairhaven,NJ/Wexford Raiders
Ron Stenger	6'0"/223	G	Johnstown,PA/Duquesne (ACHA)
Matt Wodecki	5'8"/155	F	West Greenwich,RI/East Greenwich (HS)

ROSTER ANALYSIS (SCHOLARSHIPS - 0)

Class	Country	Last Team		
Fr	USA	US JR A	CDN JR A	ACHA
So	Canada	US JR B	CDN JR B	NJCAA
Jr	Europe	US PS	CDN PS	NCAA
Sr	Asia	US HS	CDN HS	USNDT
Gr	Other	US Midget	CDN Midget	Other

ADMISSIONS, ENROLLMENT & CAMPUS INFORMATION

Founded 1892
Public, rural campus
4,821 men / 6,136 women
Tuition, room & board - $15 K / $27 K
Avg SAT - 1,120

Average acceptance rate - 70 %
Freshman financial aid - 59 %
Early decision application deadline - N/A
Regular application deadline - Feb 1
Financial aid deadline - Mar 1

David Taggart - Dean of Admissions
University of Rhode Island
Kingston, RI 02881
O 401.874.7000 / F 401.874.5523
uriadmit@etal.uri.edu

www.urihockey.org

www.uri.edu/athletics/recservices/micehockey.html

ROBERT MORRIS COLLEGE

EAGLES HOCKEY

Robert Morris College

Division 1

HOCKEY STAFF

HEAD COACH
Mike Waldron

ASSISTANT COACH
Kevin High
Kelly Gee

HOCKEY OFFICE
O 847.963.8583/ F 847.963.8583
rmchockey@aol.com

HOCKEY MEDIA CONTACT
Lynn Wendlandt - Hockey Info Director

HOCKEY RINK
The Edge
735 East Jefferson
Bensenville, IL 60106
Capacity 1,100
O 630.766.8888

HOCKEY DIRECTOR
Tom Wendlandt - Dir. Hockey
Operations
109 North Wilke Road
Palatine, IL 60074
O 847.372.4745/ F 312.935.4544
tom.wendlandt@rmchockey.com

EAGLES PLAYERS

Player	YB	GR	Ht/Wt	P	Hometown/Last Team
Bobby Carlson	08		5'10"/175	F	Rockford,MI/Grand Rapids Owls (CSHL)
Mike Coomer	08		6'0"/180	D	Woodridge,IL/Traverse City Enforcers (CEHL)
Chris Goerdt			5'10"/180	F	Crystal Lake,IL/Motor City Chiefs (CSHL)
Mark Hammersmith			6'2"/225	D	Palatine,IL/Kent State (ACHA)
Ian Heinzen			6'1"/205	D	Sugar Land,TX/Motor City Chiefs (CSHL)
Peter Katowicz	07		5'9"/160	F	Downers Grove,IL/Downers Grove North (HS)
Nick Kostel			5'7"/165	F	West Chicago,IL/Cyclones (Midget AA)
Steve LaFrenier	08		5'5"/165	F	Addison,IL/Helena Bighorns (NAHL)
Kevin Lee			5'10"/180	F	Berrien Springs,MI/Motor City Chiefs (CSHL)
Adam Lesko			5'10"/170	D	Bartlett,IL/Bartlett (HS)
Derek Makula	08		6'2"/220	D	Garden City,MI/Metro Jets (CSHL)
Chris Malik	08		5'8"/170	F	Naperville,IL/Naperville Central (HS)
Aaron Merkle	07		5'11"/205	G	Flint,MI/Flint Generals (CSHL)
Ron Michalek			6'1"/185	G	West Chicago,IL/Motor City Chiefs (CSHL)
JC Moseley			5'11"/175	F	Hendersonville,TN/Team South
Mike Opyd			5'7"/160	F	Oak Forest,IL/Eastern Michigan (ACHA)
Micah Robbins			5'9"/190	G	Cheboygan,MI/Coeur d'Alene Colts (NPJHL)
Dan Solakiewicz			6'1"/165	F	Downers Grove,IL/Montine Catholic (PS)
Chris Tasic	08		5'7"/175	F	Tinley Park,IL/Helena Bighorns (NAHL)
Kyle Thistle	07		5'11"/195	D	Kingwood,TX/Flint Generals (CSHL)
Ryan Tomassoni	08		6'0"/165	D	Carol Stream,IL/Chicago Flames (Midget AA)
Mike Wolff	08		5'11"/210	F	Cicero,IL/Cleveland Barons (NAHL)
Marco Zenere			5'10"/175	F	Chicago,IL/Vikings (Midget AA)

ROSTER ANALYSIS (SCHOLARSHIPS - 0)

Class	Country		Last Team		
Fr	USA	23	US JR A	CDN JR A	ACHA
So	Canada		US JR B	CDN JR B	NJCAA
Jr	Europe		US PS	CDN PS	NCAA
Sr	Asia		US HS	CDN HS	USNDT
Gr	Other		US Midget	CDN Midget	Other

ADMISSIONS, ENROLLMENT & CAMPUS INFORMATION

Founded 1913	Average acceptance rate - 82 %	Candace Goodwin - Admissions Director
Private, urban campus	Freshman financial aid - 55 %	Robert Morris College
1,976 men / 3,225 women	Early decision application deadline - N/A	401 South State Street
Tuition, room & board - $ 21 K	Regular application deadline - rolling	Chicago, IL 60605
Avg SAT - / Avg ACT -	Financial aid deadline - N/A	O 800.762.5960/ F 312.935.6819

ROBERT MORRIS UNIVERSITY

Division 1

HOCKEY STAFF

HEAD COACH
Derek Schooley *(Western Michigan '94)*

ASSISTANT COACHES
Mike McCourt *(St. Lawrence '94)*
Matt Lindsay *(Williams '01)*

HOCKEY OFFICE
RMU Island Sports Center
7600 Grand Avenue
Pittsburgh, PA 15225
O 412.397.4477/ F 412.397.4488
schooley@rmu.edu

HOCKEY MEDIA CONTACT
Jim Duzyk, Jr. - Sports Info Director
Robert Morris University
Athletics Building 247
6001 University Boulevard
Moon Township, PA 15108
O 412.262.8314/ F 412.262.8557
duzyk@rmu.edu

HOCKEY RINK
RMU Island Sports Center
7600 Grand Avenue
Pittsburgh, PA 15225
Size 200' x 85', Capacity 1,000
O 412.262.3335/ F 412.269.4488

ATHLETIC DIRECTOR
Dr. Craig S. Coleman - Athletic Director
Robert Morris University
6001 University Boulevard
Moon Township,PA 15108
O 412.262.8295/ F 412.262.8557
colemanc@rmu.edu

COLONIALS PLAYERS

Player	YB	GR	Ht/Wt	P	Hometown/Last Team
Sean Berkstresser	86	08	6'0"/200	F	Apollo,PA/Pittsburgh Forge (NAHL)
Tom Biondich	83	08	5'10"/175	F	Int'l Falls,MN/Wichita Falls Rustlers (AWHL)
Logan Bittle	84	08	6'1"/200	F	Peoria,IL/Soo Indians (NAHL)
David Boguslawski	86	08	5'8"/180	F	Cottage Gr,MN/Tri-City Storm (USHL)
Andrew Bonello	86	08	5'8"/165	D	Brampton,ON/Milton Icehawks (OPJHL)
Christian Boucher	83	08	5'10"/180	G	Orleans,ON/Cumberland Grads (CJHL)
Parker Burgess	85	10	6'0"/200	F	Calgary,AB/Olds Grizzlys (AJHL)
Aaron Clarke	82	09	5'9"/175	F	Peterborough,ON/Niagara (CHA)
Doug Conley	83	07	5'11"/185	F	Amherst,NY/Tri-City Storm (USHL)
Dave Cowan	85	10	6'4"/205	D	Calgary,AB/Olds Grizzlys (AJHL)
Rob Cowan	86	08	6'4"/215	D	Calgary,AB/Olds Grizzlys (AJHL)
Ryan Cruthers	84	07	6'0"/175	F	Farmingdale,NY/US Military Academy (AHL)
Karac Davis	86	09	6'0"/170	G	Pittsburgh,PA/Shady Side (PS)
Kyle Frieday	87	10	5'7"/185	F	Burlington,ON/Oakville Blades (OPJHL)
Joel Gasper	83	08	6'2"/205	F	Crookston,MN/Billings Bulls (NAHL)
Jeff Gilbert	83	08	6'3"/200	D	Barrie,ON/Aurora Tigers (OPJHL)
Brett Hopfe	83	08	6'1"/205	F	Didsbury,AB/Olds Grizzlys (AJHL)
Chris Kaufman	83	08	6'2"/190	D	Gig Harbor,WA/Helena Bighorns (NAHL)
Chris Margott	84	09	5'10"/185	F	Thousand Oaks,CA/Bay State Breakers (EJHL)
Bryan Mills	83	07	6'0"/190	D	Oakville,ON/Niagara (CHA)
Jake Obermeyer	85	09	6'1"/180	D	Chanhassen,MN/Michigan Tech (WCHA)
Joey Olson	82	08	5'7"/180	F	Peoria,IL/Capital Centre Pride (NAHL)
Wes Russell	85	09	6'1"/190	G	Springfield,IL/Quinnipiac (ECAC)
Jake Sparks	83	08	5'10"/190	D	Evergreen,CO/Central Texas Blackhawks (NAHL)
Jason Towsley	86	09	5'11"/190	F	La Salle,ON/Leamington Flyers (WOJHL)
Eric Trax	86	08	6'1"/195	D	Finleyville,PA/Lone Star Calvary (NAHL)
Joe Tuset	82	07	6'0"/185	G	Eagan,MN/Northern Michigan (CCHA)
JC Velasquez	85	10	5'9"/185	F	Clarksen,MI/Green Bay Gamblers (USHL)
Tyler Webb	85	10	6'2"/200	F	Austin,TX/Fort McMurray Oil Barons (AJHL)

ROSTER ANALYSIS (SCHOLARSHIPS -8)

Class		Country		Last Team					
Fr	5	USA	18	US JR A	11	CDN JR A	9	ACHA	
So	6	Canada	11	US JR B	1	CDN JR B	1	NJCAA	
Jr	14	Europe		US PS	1	CDN PS		NCAA	6
Sr	4	Asia		US HS		CDN HS		USNDT	
Gr		Other		US Midget		CDN Midget		Other	

ADMISSIONS, ENROLLMENT & CAMPUS INFORMATION

Founded 1921
Private, suburban campus
2,235 men / 1,553 women
Tuition, room & board $ 23 K
Avg SAT - 1,010/Avg ACT - 20

Average acceptance rate - 84 %
Freshman financial aid - 74 %
Early decision application deadline - N/A
Regular application deadline - Dec 1
Financial aid deadline - Dec 1

Marianne Budziszewski-Admissions
Robert Morris University
6001 University Boulevard
Moon Township, PA 15108-1189
O 412.262.8206/ F 412.299.2425

ROCHESTER INST. OF TECHNOLOGY

Division 1

HOCKEY STAFF

HEAD COACH
Wayne Wilson *(Bowling Green '84)*

ASSISTANT COACHES
Brian Hills *(Bowling Green '83)*
Chris Palmer *(RIT '90)*
Mike Germaine *(SUNY-Cortland '94)*

HOCKEY OFFICE
Rochester Institute of Technology
51 Lomb Memorial Drive
Rochester, NY 14623-5603
O 585.475.5615/ F 585.475.5675
jwwatl@rit.edu

HOCKEY MEDIA CONTACT
Steve Jaynes - Sports Info Director
51 Lomb Memorial Drive
Rochester, NY 14623-5603
O 585.475.6154/ F 585.475.2617
skjsid@rit.edu

HOCKEY RINK
Ritter Memorial Arena (On Campus)
51 Lomb Memorial Drive
Rochester, NY 14623
Size 185' x 80', Capacity 2,100
O 585.475.6509

ATHLETIC DIRECTOR
Louis W. Spiotti Jr. - Athletic Director
Rochester Institute of Technology
51 Lomb Memorial Drive
Rochester, NY 14623-5603
O 585.475.2615/ F 585.475.5675
lxs4798@osfmail.rit.edu

TIGERS PLAYERS

Player	YB	GR	Ht/Wt	P	Hometown/Last Team
Brent Alexin	87	10	6' 2"/185	F	W Seneca,NY/Buffalo Sabres (OPJHL)
Stephen Burns	84	08	6' 0"/205	D	Newmarket,ON/Newmarket Hurricanes (OPJHL)
Steve Coon	86	10	6' 2"/195	D	Berne,NY/Capital District Selects (EJHL)
Matt Crowell	86	10	5'11"/175	F	Kelowna,BC/Williams Lake Timberwolves (BCHL)
Jared DeMichiel	85	10	6' 0"/185	G	Avon,CT/Chicago Steel (USHL)
Darrell Draper	83	08	6' 0"/205	F	Calgary,AB/Cowichan Valley Capitals (BCHL)
Tristan Fairbarn	82	07	5' 7"/160	F	Innisfil,ON/Newmarket Hurricanes (OPJHL)
Jocelyn Guimond	82	08	6' 0"/185	G	Quebec City,QC/Williams Lake Timberwolves (BCHL)
Brad Harris	82	07	6' 0"/190	F	Portage La Prairie,MB/Leamington Flyers (WOJHL)
Matt Harris	84	08	6' 1"/200	D	Toronto,ON/Ajax Axemen (OPJHL)
Justin Hofstetter	86	09	5'11"/195	D	Bright,ON/Cambridge Winterhawks (MWJHL)
Anton Kharin	85	10	5'11"/175	F	Twin Lake,MI/Bay State Breakers (EJHL)
Simon Lambert	83	08	6' 0"/170	F	Ste. Therese,QC/Cumberland Grads (CJHL)
Steven Matic	85	10	6' 0"/195	F	Burnaby,BC/Langley Hornets (BCHL)
Al Mazur		10	6' 0"/185	D	Burnaby,BC/Langley Hornets (BCHL)
Louis Menard	84	09	6' 1"/175	G	Chicoutimi,QC/Ottawa Senators (CJHL)
Jesse Newman	84	09	5'11"/175	F	Westbank,BC/Trail Smoke Eaters (BCHL)
Brent Patry	83	08	6' 1"/205	D	Ottawa,ON/Cumberland Grads (CJHL)
Steve Pinizzotto	84	09	6' 1"/185	F	Mississauga,ON/Oakville Blades (OPJHL)
Bobby Raymond	85	09	5'10"/185	D	Lucknow,ON/Owen Sound Greys (MWJHL)
Dan Ringwald	86	10	6' 1"/185	D	Oakville,ON/Oakville Blades (OPJHL)
Brennan Sarazin	84	09	5'10"/200	F	Nepean,ON/Nepean Raiders (CJHL)
Matt Smith	83	08	5'11"/190	F	Toronto,ON/Kitchener Dutchmen (MWJHL)
Rob Tarantino	83	07	5'10"/175	F	Toronto,ON/Oakville Blades (OPJHL)
Ricky Walton	83	08	5' 8"/185	F	Hamilton,ON/Hamilton Red Wings (OPJHL)

ROSTER ANALYSIS (SCHOLARSHIPS - 0)

Class		Country		Last Team				
Fr	8	USA	4	US JR A	1	CDN JR A	18	ACHA
So	6	Canada	21	US JR B	2	CDN JR B	4	NJCAA
Jr	8	Europe		US PS		CDN PS		NCAA
Sr	3	Asia		US HS		CDN HS		USNDT
Gr		Other		US Midget		CDN Midget		Other

ADMISSIONS, ENROLLMENT & CAMPUS INFORMATION

Founded 1829
Private, suburban campus
8,812 men / 2,938 women
Tuition, room & board - $ 33 K
Avg SAT - 1,210/ Avg ACT - 26

Average acceptance rate - 67 %
Freshman financial aid - 90 %
Early decision application deadline - Dec 1
Regular application deadline - Feb 1
Financial aid deadline - Mar 1

Daniel Shelly - Admissions Director
RIT - Bausch & Lomb Building
51 Lomb Memorial Drive
Rochester, NY 14623-5603
O 585.475.6631/ F 585.475.7424

www.rit.edu

www.ritathletics.com

RUTGERS UNIVERSITY

Division 1

HOCKEY STAFF

HEAD COACH
Mark DiGiovanni

ASSISTANT COACHES
Michael Stapleton *(So. New Hamp. '02)*
Jim Schwanda *(Lehigh '79)*
Kris Corso

HOCKEY OFFICE
22 Riverdale Avenue
Old Bridge, NJ 08857
O 609.947.3994
coach@rutgershockey.com
markd@rutgershockey.com

HOCKEY MEDIA CONTACT
Paul Presman, Manager/Media Relations

HOCKEY RINK
Princton Sports Center (Off Campus)
1000 Cornwall Road
South Brunswick, NJ
Size 200' x 85', Capacity 1,000
O 732.940.6800

HOCKEY DIRECTOR
Mark Stoddard
Rutgers College Recreation Services
Sonny Werblin Recreation Center
656 Barthelmew Road
Piscataway, NJ 08854
O 732.445.0462 / F 732.445.0472
mstoddar@rci.rutgers.edu

HOCKEY DIRECTOR
Andy Gojdycz - General Manager
andyg@rutgershockey.com

SCARLET KNIGHTS PLAYERS

Player	YB	GR	Ht/Wt	P	Hometown/Last Team
Jeff Chance	87	09	6'0"/180	F	Franklinville,NJ/Vineland (Midget AA)
Neil Cherry			6'0"/175	F	Basking Ridge,NJ/Delbarton (PS)
Mike Costa			5'10"/175	G	Beachwood,NJ/Toms River South (HS)
Mike DeRita			5'7"/135	F	West Collingswood Hts,NJ/Neuman (ECAC West)
Jon Donini			5'10"/160	G	Clifton,NJ/Clifton (HS)
Evan Ely	85	09	6'1"/230	D	Fair Haven,NJ/Elmira (ECAC West)
Brett Erdreich	84	09	5'8"/160	F	Monmouth Junction,NJ/Jersey Titans (MJHL)
Josh Esformes	87	09	5'9"/165	F	South Orange,NJ/St. Peter's (PS)
Frank Figarole	85	08	5'11"/155	G	Vineland,NJ/St. Augustine (PS)
Igor Gorovits			5'10"/165	F	Fair Lawn,NJ
Adam Huff			6'2"/205	G	Belford,NJ/Middletown North (HS)
Devin Jones	87	09	5'7"/160	F	Ocean Twp,NJ/Christian Brothers (PS)
Alex Kashmanian			5'8"/170	F	Bernards,NJ/Bernards (HS)
A.J. Kirschner	87	09	6'0"/200	F	Beverly,NJ/Holy Cross (HS)
Matt Lavit	87	09	6'2"/191	D	Vadnais Hts,MN/White Bear Lake (MnJHL)
Rory Levinson	86	09	6'3"/205	D	Voorhees,NJ/Jaguars (Midget AA)
Steve MacDonnell	85	08	6'0"/195	D	Mount Laurel,NJ/Brick (Midget AA)
Daniel Mazzucola	86	08	5'11"/195	F	Middletown,NJ/Middletown North (HS)
Eric Neilson			5'9"/140	F	Somerset,NJ/St.Joseph- Metuchen (PS)
Josh Owen	86	08	6'2"/225	D	New Haven,CT/Wilbur Cross (HS)
David Sarch	85	08	5'10"/230	D	Jersey City,NJ/William Paterson (ACHA)
Jack Schram	87	09	5'10"/170	F	Fort Wayne,IN/Ft. Wayne Komets (Midget AA)
Kyle Slickers			6'2"/185	F	Pine Beach,NJ/Toms River South (HS)
Max Stember-Young			6'0"/195	F	Plainsboro,NJ/West Windsor-Plainsboro (HS)
Lou Taranto	86	08	5'9"/165	F	Toms River,NJ/Toms River East (HS)
Matt Voit	85	08	6'0"/205	D	Mullica Hill,NJ/Philadelphia (Midget AAA)
Ryan Walter			6'0"/195	F	Succasunna,NJ/Delbarton (PS)

ROSTER ANALYSIS (SCHOLARSHIPS - 0)

Class	Country	Last Team		
Fr	USA	US JR A	CDN JR A	ACHA
So	Canada	US JR B	CDN JR B	NJCAA
Jr	Europe	US PS	CDN PS	NCAA
Sr	Asia	US HS	CDN HS	USNDT
Gr	Other	US Midget	CDN Midget	Other

ADMISSIONS, ENROLLMENT & CAMPUS INFORMATION

Founded 1776
Public, suburban campus
13,183 men / 13,183 women
Tuition, room & board $ 18 / $ 25 K
Average SAT 1,205

Average acceptance rate 61 %
Freshman financial aid 85 %
Early decision application deadline - N/A
Regular application deadline - rolling
Financial aid deadline - Mar 15

Office of Undergraduate Admissions
Rutgers University
65 Davidson Road - Room 202
Piscataway, NJ 08854
O 732.932.INFO

SACRED HEART UNIVERSITY

Division 1

HOCKEY STAFF

HEAD COACH
Shaun Hannah *(Cornell '94)*

ASSISTANT COACH
Lou Santini *(Iona '90)*

HOCKEY OFFICE
Sacred Heart University - Athletic Dept.
5151 Park Avenue
Fairfield, CT 06432
O 203.876.2480 / F 203.882.5941
hannahs@sacredheart.edu

HOCKEY MEDIA CONTACT
Gene Gumbs - Sports Info Director
Sacred Heart University - Athletic Dept.
5151 Park Avenue
Fairfield, CT 06432
O 203.396.8127 / F 203.371.7889
gumbsg@sacredheart.edu

HOCKEY RINK
Milford Ice Pavilion (Off Campus)
291 Bic Drive
Milford, CT 06460
Size 200' x 85', Capacity 1,000
O 203.371.7885

ATHLETIC DIRECTOR
C. Donald Cook - Athletic Director
Sacred Heart University - Athletic Dept.
5151 Park Avenue
Fairfield, CT 06432
O 203.365.7649 / F 203.365.7696
cookd@sacredheart.edu

PIONEERS PLAYERS

Player	YB	GR	Ht/Wt	P	Hometown/Last Team
Erik Boisvert	86	10	5'9"/175	F	Drummondville,QC/Notre Dame (PS)
Stefan Drew	85	09	5'11"/170	G	Dugald,MB/Portage Terriers (ManJHL)
Paul Ferraro	86	09	6'0"/200	D	Pleasantville,NY/Apple Core (EJHL)
Peter Ferraro	84	07	5'11"/180	F	Pleasantville,NY/Avon (NEPSAC)
Louis Gentile	83	07	5'10"/170	F	Beverly,MA/Valley Warriors (EJHL)
Eric Giosa	84	09	5'11"/190	F	Northville,MI/Toledo IceDiggers (NAHL)
Matt Gordon	87	10	6'2"/200	F	Lynnfield,MA/Belmont Hill (NEPSAC)
Dave Grimson	84	09	6'0"/180	D	Mozart,SK/Swan Valley Stampeders (ManJHL)
Frederic Harland	84	08	6'3"/210	D	Rosemere,QC/St. Eustache Gladiatuers (QJAHL)
Dave Jarman	86	10	5'11"/190	F	Toronto,ON/Georgetown Raiders (OPJHL)
Nick Johnson	86	10	5'11"/190	f	Windsor,CT/Springfield Falcons ()
Nick Kary	84	08	5'11"/195	F	Wetaskiwin,AB/Lloydminster Bobcats (AJHL)
Corey Laurysen	85	10	5'11"/195	D	Carp,ON/Brockville Braves (CJHL)
Scott Marchesi	83	08	6'2"/195	D	S. Portland,ME/New Hampshire Monarchs (EJHL)
Pierre-Luc O'Brien	82	07	5'9"/180	F	Nicolet,QC/Cowichan Valley Capitals (BCHL)
Alexandre Parent	84	08	5'11"/175	F	Boisbriand,QC/St. Eustache Gladiatuers (QJAHL)
Matt Richards	85	10	5'10"/180	F	Ridgefield,CT/Ridgefield (HS)
Gregg Rodriguez	85	10	6'3"/195	D	Saratoga,CA/Capital District Selects (EJHL)
Mike Rosata	85	10	5'10"/170	F	Needham,MA/New Hampshire Monarchs (EJHL)
Drew Sanders	83	07	5'8"/165	F	Modesto,CA/Great Falls Americans ()
David Smith	85	09	5'10"/190	F	Columbus,IN/Connecticut Wolves (MJHL)
Jason Smith	85	07	6'1"/180	G	St. Lambert,QC/Lennoxville Cougars (QJAHL)
Thomas Spencer	82	07	6'3"/210	F	Brentwood,NH/Valley Warriors (EJHL)
Bear Trapp	84	09	6'1"/185	F	Regina,SK/Estevan Bruins (SJHL)
Kyle Tyll	86	09	5'9"/190	F	Sandy Hook,CT/Trinity-Pawling (NEPSAC)
Charles Veilleux	83	07	5'8"/175	D	Quebec City,QC/Lennoxville Cougars (QJAHL)
Kalen Wright	83	07	6'2"/210	D	Candle Lake,SK/Melfort Mustangs (SJHL)

ROSTER ANALYSIS (SCHOLARSHIPS - 11)

Class		Country		Last Team				
Fr	8	USA	14	US JR A	1	CDN JR A	12	ACHA
So	7	Canada	13	US JR B	9	CDN JR B		NJCAA
Jr	4	Europe		US PS	3	CDN PS	1	NCAA
Sr	8	Asia		US HS	1	CDN HS		USNDT
Gr		Other		US Midget		CDN Midget		Other

ADMISSIONS, ENROLLMENT & CAMPUS INFORMATION

Founded 1963
Private, suburban campus
1,640 men / 2,360 women
Tuition, room & board - $ 32 K
Avg SAT - 1,060 / Avg ACT - 22

Average acceptance rate - 71 %
Freshman financial aid - 68 %
Early decision application deadline - Oct 1
Regular application deadline - rolling
Financial aid deadline - Feb 15

Karen N. Guastelle - Admissions Director
Sacred Heart University - Admissions Dept.
5151 Park Avenue
Fairfield, CT 06432-100
O 203.371.7880 / F 203.365.7607

ST. ANSELM COLLEGE

Division 2

HOCKEY STAFF

HEAD COACH
Ed Seney *(New England '81)*

ASSISTANT COACH
Michael Martiniello *(St. Anselm '02)*

HOCKEY OFFICE
Saint Anselm College - Alumni Hall
100 Saint Anselm Drive
Manchester, NH 03102-1323
O 603.222.4273/ F 603.641.7172
eseney@anselm.edu

HOCKEY MEDIA CONTACT
Ken Johnson, Jr. - Sports Info Director
Saint Anselm College
100 Saint Anselm Drive
Manchester, NH 03102-1323
O 603.641.7810/ F 603.641.7172
kejohnson@anselm.edu

HOCKEY RINK
Sullivan Arena (On Campus)
St. Anselm College
Rundlett Hill Road
Goffstown, NH 03102
Size ' x ', Capacity 1,700
O 603.222.4266

ATHLETIC DIRECTOR
Ed Cannon - Athletic Director
Saint Anselm College - Alumni Hall
100 Saint Anselm Drive
Manchester, NH 03102-1323
O 603.641.7800
ecannon@anselm.edu

HAWKS PLAYERS

Player	YB	GR	Ht/Wt	P	Hometown/Last Team
Mike Bourque	09		6'1"/180	F	Waltham,MA/Proctor (NEPSAC)
Kevin Corley	07		5'7"/175	D	Reading,MA/Reading (HS)
Mike Curtis	07		5'8"/160	F	Hanover,MA/Junior Bruins (EJHL)
Brian Dobler	07		5'9"/175	D	Jericho,NY/Apple Core (EmJHL)
Derek Evjenth	07		6'2"/190	F	Saratoga,CA/New Hampshire Monarchs (EJHL)
Joe Fernald	09		5'10"/190	F	Braintree,MA/Boston Bulldogs (AtJHL)
Colin Fitzpatrick	08		5'10"/170	F	Westwood,MA/Kimball Union (NEPSAC)
Mike Foley	08		5'11"/175	F	Medford,MA/Andover (NEPSAC)
Pat Forshner	08		5'7"/175	F	Natick,MA/Avon (NEPSAC)
Pat Gallagher	09		6'1"/175	G	Framingham,MA/Rivers (NEPSAC)
Andrew Gartman	07		6'1"/190	F	E Norwich,NY/Apple Core (EmJHL)
Seth Goodrich	10		5'11"/170	D	Salisbury,VT/Green Mountain Glades (EJHL)
Matt Grazioso	08		6'1"/175	F	Quincy,MA/Northfield Mount Hermon (NEPSAC)
Ben Gunn	09		5'11"/170	F	Vineyard Hvn,MA/Boston Bulldogs (AtJHL)
Brian Hartigan	09		5'11"/195	D	Saugus,MA/Salisbury (NEPSAC)
Tim Ivers	10		5'9"/165	D	Chelmsford,MA/Tilton (NEPSAC)
Tom Kerwin	09		6'0"/190	F	Whitman,MA/Boston Bulldogs (AtJHL)
Adam Lang	10		5'8"/175	D	Bow,NH/Bridgton (NEPSAC)
Chris MacPhee	10		6'4"/190	F	Windham,NH/New Hampshire Monarchs (EJHL)
Shane Masotta	08		5'8"/165	D	Woburn,MA/Tilton (NEPSAC)
Mike Nunziato	09		5'8"/165	D	Guilford,CT/Connecticut Wolves (MJHL)
Danny Ohlson	07		6'1"/190	F	York,ME/New Hampshire Monarchs (EJHL)
Jason Rafuse	07		6'1"/200	G	Nepean,ON/North Country (NJCAA)
Nick Sacca	07		5'9"/175	F	Arlington,MA/Proctor (NEPSAC)
Brett Smith	07		6'0"/175	D	Hudson,MA/Canterbury (NEPSAC)
Andrew Woodford	09		5'11"/180	D	Westford,MA/Valley Warriors (EJHL)
Bryan Wright	08		6'2"/195	G	Reading,MA/Bentley (AHL)
Nick Yeomelakis	10		5'8"/150	F	Wilmington,MA/Malden (PS)
Jason Zuck	10		6'1"/190	G	Clifton,NJ/New Jersey Hitmen (EJHL)

ROSTER ANALYSIS (SCHOLARSHIPS - 0)

Class		Country		Last Team					
Fr	6	USA	28	US JR A		CDN JR A		ACHA	
So	8	Canada	1	US JR B	13	CDN JR B		NJCAA	1
Jr	16	Europe		US PS	13	CDN PS		NCAA	1
Sr	9	Asia		US HS	1	CDN HS		USNDT	
Gr		Other		US Midget		CDN Midget		Other	

ADMISSIONS, ENROLLMENT & CAMPUS INFORMATION

Founded 1889
Private, suburban campus
882 men / 1,078 women
Tuition, room & board - $ 36 K
Avg SAT - 1,100

Average acceptance rate - 66 %
Freshman financial aid - 82 %
Early decision application deadline - Dec 1
Regular application deadline - rolling
Financial aid deadline - Mar 1

Don Healy - Admissions Director
Saint Anselm College - Alumni Hall
100 Saint Anselm Drive
Manchester, NH 03102-1323
O 603.641.7500/ F 603.641.7500

www.anselm.edu

www.anselm.edu/athletics/

ST. CLOUD STATE UNIVERSITY

Division 1

HOCKEY STAFF

HEAD COACH
Bob Motzko *(St. Cloud State '87)*

ASSISTANT COACHES
Fred Harbinson *(Wis.-Superior '95)*
Eric Rud *(Colorado College '97)*

HOCKEY OFFICE
St. Cloud State University
National Hockey Center
720 Fourth Avenue South
St. Cloud, MN 56301-4498
O 320.308.4806/ F 320.308.5119
rgmotzko@stcloudstate.edu

HOCKEY MEDIA CONTACT
Tom Nelson - Hockey Info Director
St. Cloud State University
Halenbeck Hall #259-1
720 Fourth Avenue South
St. Cloud, MN 56301-4498
O 320.308.5400/ F 320.255.2099
tcnelson@stcloudstate.edu

HOCKEY RINK
National Hockey Center (On Campus)
1204 4th Avenue South
St. Cloud, MN 56301
Size 200' x 100', Capacity 5,763
O 320.654.5227

ATHLETIC DIRECTOR
Dr. Morris Kurtz - Athletic Director
St. Cloud State University
720 Fourth Avenue South
St. Cloud, MN 56301
O 320.308.3102
mkurtz@stcloudstate.edu

HUSKIES PLAYERS

Player	YB	GR	Ht/Wt	P	Hometown/Last Team
Jonathan Ammerman	87	10	6' 0"/195	D	Moorhead,MN/Indiana Ice (USHL)
Chris Anderson	84	08	6' 3"/205	D	White Bear Lk,MN/Danville Wings (USHL)
Casey Borer	85	07	6' 2"/205	D	Brooklyn Pk,MN/USNDT (NAHL)
Aaron Brocklehurst	85	08	5'10"/195	D	Nanaimo,BC/Victoria Salsa (BCHL)
David Carlisle	84	09	5'10"/180	D	Wyoming,MN/Lincoln Stars (USHL)
Grant Clafton	83	07	5'11"/175	D	Grand Rpds,MN/Omaha Lancers (USHL)
Nate Dey	85	08	6' 1"/185	F	Maplewood,MN/Green Bay Gamblers (USHL)
Justin Fletcher	83	07	5'11"/180	D	Maryville,IL/Sioux City Musketeers (USHL)
AJ Gale	87	10	6' 0"/180	F	Nanaimo,BC/Nanaimo Clippers (BCHL)
Craig Gaudet	85	10	5'10"/190	D	Redvers,SK/Nanaimo Clippers (BCHL)
Bobby Goepfert	83	07	5'10"/170	G	Kings Park,NY/Providence (HEA)
Andrew Gordon	85	08	5'11"/190	F	Porters Lake,NS/Notre Dame (PS)
Matt Hartman	84	08	6' 1"/195	F	St. Cloud,MN/Sioux City Musketeers (USHL)
Gary Houseman	83	07	5'10"/170	F	Saskatoon,SK/Sioux City Musketeers (USHL)
Dan Kronick	84	07	6' 4"/215	F	Inver Gr Hgts,MN/Minnesota Duluth (WCHA)
Ryan Lasch	87	10	5' 9"/175	F	Lake Forest,CA/Pembroke Lumber Kings (CJHL)
Marty Mjelleli	83	08	6' 1"/205	F	Faribault,MN/Des Moines Buccaneers (USHL)
Andreas Nodi	87	10	6' 1"/200	F	Vienna,Austria/Sioux Falls Stampede (USHL)
BJ O'Brien	85	10	6' 0"/170	G	Lakeville,MN/Fargo-Moorhead Jets (NAHL)
Michael Olson	84	09	5'11"/185	F	Tisdale,SK/Nanaimo Clippers (BCHL)
Ryan Peckskamp	85	10	5'10"/170	F	Sauk Rapids,MN/Indiana Ice (USHL)
Garrett Raboin	85	10	5'10"/180	D	Detroit Lks,MN/Lincoln Stars (USHL)
Nate Raduns	84	07	6' 3"/200	F	Sauk Rapids,MN/Omaha Lancers (USHL)
Matt Stephenson	84	08	6' 2"/205	D	Midland,ON/Nepean Raiders (CJHL)
John Swanson	85	09	5'11"/165	F	St. Cloud,MN/Chicago Steel (USHL)
Jase Weslosky	88	10	6' 2"/175	G	St. Albert,AB/Sherwood Park Crusaders (AJHL)

ROSTER ANALYSIS (SCHOLARSHIPS - 18)

Class		Country		Last Team					
Fr	9	USA	17	US JR A	14	CDN JR A	7	ACHA	
So	3	Canada	8	US JR B		CDN JR B		NJCAA	
Jr	7	Europe	1	US PS		CDN PS	1	NCAA	2
Sr	7	Asia		US HS		CDN HS		USNDT	2
Gr		Other		US Midget		CDN Midget		Other	

ADMISSIONS, ENROLLMENT & CAMPUS INFORMATION

Founded 1869	Average acceptance rate - 74 %	Pat Krueger - Admissions Director
Public, urban campus	Freshman financial aid - 81 %	St. Cloud State University
5,904 men / 7,216 women	Early decision application deadline - N/A	720 Fourth Avenue South
Tuition, room & board - $11 K/ $16 K	Regular application deadline - Dec 15	St. Cloud, MN 56301-4498
Avg ACT - 22	Financial aid deadline - May 1	O 320.255.2244/ F 320.255.2243

www.stcloudstate.edu   www.stcloudstate.edu/athletics/

SAINT JOHN'S UNIVERSITY

Minnesota Intercollegiate Athletic Conference

Division 3

HOCKEY STAFF

HEAD COACH
John Harrington *(Minn-Duluth '79)*

ASSISTANT COACHES
Dave Stone *(St. Cloud State '95)*
Jason Johnson *(St. John's '95)*
Chris Howe *(St. John's '99)*

HOCKEY OFFICE
Saint John's University
Athletic Department
Collegeville, MN 56321-7727
O 320.363.2242 / F 320.363.3130
jharrington@csbsju.edu

HOCKEY MEDIA CONTACT
Celest Stang - Sports Info Director
Saint John's University
Athletic Department
Collegeville, MN 56321-7155
O 320.363.3127 / F 320.363.3446
cstang@csbsju.edu

HOCKEY RINK
National Hockey Center (Off Campus)
1204 4th Avenue, South
St. Cloud, MN 56301
Size 200' x 100', Capacity 5,763
O 320.255.3327

ATHLETIC DIRECTOR
Timothy Backous, OSB - Athletic Director
Saint John's University
PO Box 7277
Collegeville, MN 56321-7155
O 320.363.3707 / F 320.363.3130
tbackous@csbsju.edu

JOHNNIES PLAYERS

Player	YB	GR	Ht/Wt	P	Hometown/Last Team
Brian Baker	85	09	5'10"/175	F	Brooklyn Pk,MN/Alexandria Blizzard (NAHL)
Pat Connelly	86	09	5' 8"/175	F	Birchwood,MN/White Bear Lake (HS)
Andy Cook	87	09	6' 2"/175	G	Golden Vly,MN/Colby (NESCAC)
Sam Dor	85	08	6' 0"/185	D	Roseville,MN/Roseville (HS)
Pat Eagles	85	08	5' 8"/160	F	Falcon Hgts,MN/Wichita Falls (NAHL)
Tom Freeman		08	6' 1"/175	F	Eagan,MN/Eagan (HS)
Karl Gilbert	88	10	6' 3"/180	F	Hermantown,MN/Hermantown (HS)
Gabriel Harren	85	10	6' 2"/185	F	Warroad,MN/Billings Bulls (NAHL)
Tom Hartman	82	07	5'10"/180	D	Faribault,MN/Texas Tornado (NAHL)
Kyle Henkemeyer	87	10	6' 1"/175	F	Sauk Rapids,MN/Rice (HS)
Jake Hipp	85	09	5' 9"/175	F	Bismarck,ND/Bismarck Bobcats (NAHL)
Nate Meinz	85	08	6' 0"/190	D	St. Cloud,MN/St. Cloud Tech (HS)
Dustin Mercado	84	07	6' 3"/200	D	White Bear Lk,MN/White Bear Lake (HS)
Chris Murray	87	10	5'10"/160	F	Chanhassen,MN/Blake (PS)
Ben Noah	85	10	6' 1"/200	F	Detroit Lks,MN/Bismarck Bobcats (NAHL)
Jason Paul	88	10	5'10"/180	G	Duluth,MN/Marshall (HS)
Scott Paul	86	09	5'10"/175	F	Duluth,MN/Bismarck Bobcats (NAHL)
Clayton Rehm	84	09	5'10"/160	D	Park Rapids,MN/St. Thomas (MIAC)
Ian Ross		07	6' 2"/190	F	Hibbing,MN/Union (ECAC)
Brett Sobolik	85	09	5' 8"/180	F	Hallock,MN/Bismarck Bobcats (NAHL)
Joel Stacklie	87	09	6' 2"/185	F	Ham Lk,MN/Blaine (HS)
Jordan Swan	85	08	6' 0"/175	F	Brooklyn Pk,MN/Champlin Park (HS)
Stu VanEss	87	10	5'10"/185	G	Kewaskum,WI/Gilmour (PS)
Jason Weigel	84	08	6' 3"/225	F	Madison,WI/Des Moines Buccaneers (USHL)
Lance Wheeler	84	09	6' 0"/185	D	Clearwater,MN/Bancroft Hawks (OPJHL)
Vince Wheeler	84	09	6' 0"/185	G	Clearwater,MN/Lake Superior (CCHA)
Justin Wild	84	07	5'10"/175	F	Bloomington,MN/Jefferson (HS)
Blake Williams	83	07	6' 0"/200	F	Brooklyn Pk,MN/Chicago Steel (USHL)
Matt Wocken	84	07	5'10"/190	D	Sauk Rapids,MN/Sauk Rapids (HS)

ROSTER ANALYSIS (SCHOLARSHIPS - 0)

Class		Country		Last Team			
Fr	7	USA	29	US JR A	10	CDN JR A	1	ACHA	
So	10	Canada		US JR B		CDN JR B		NJCAA	
Jr	6	Europe		US PS	2	CDN PS		NCAA	4
Sr	6	Asia		US HS	12	CDN HS		USNDT	
Gr		Other		US Midget		CDN Midget		Other	

ADMISSIONS, ENROLLMENT & CAMPUS INFORMATION

Founded 1857	Average acceptance rate - 86 %	Mary Milbert - Admissions Director
Private, rural campus	Freshman financial aid - 96 %	Saint John's University
1,865 men	Early decision application deadline - N/A	Admissions Department
Tuition, room & board - $ 30 K	Regular application deadline - rolling	Collegeville, MN 56321-7155
Avg SAT - 1,190 / Avg ACT - 26	Financial aid deadline - Mar 15	O 320.363.2196 / F 320.363.3206

www.csbsju.edu

www.gojohnnies.com

ST. LAWRENCE UNIVERSITY

Division 1

HOCKEY STAFF

HEAD COACH
Joe Marsh *(New Hampshire '77)*

ASSOCIATE HEAD COACH
Chris Wells *(St. Lawrence '92)*

ASSISTANT COACHES
Bob Prier *(St. Lawrence '99)*
Mike Hurlbut *(St. Lawrence '89)*

HOCKEY OFFICE
St. Lawrence University
Augsbury P.E. Center
Canton, NY 13617
O 315.229.5881 / F 315.229.5805
jmarsh@stlawu.edu

HOCKEY MEDIA CONTACT
Wally Johnson - Sports Info Director
St. Lawrence University
Augsbury P.E. Center
Canton, NY 13617
O 315.229.5588 / F 315.229.5589
wjohnson@stlawu.edu

HOCKEY RINK
Appleton Arena (On Campus)
Miner Street & Leigh Street
Canton, NY 13617
Size 200' x 85', Capacity 2,600
O 315.229.9816

ATHLETIC DIRECTOR
Margie Strait - Athletic Director
St. Lawrence University
Park Street
Canton, NY 13617
O 315.229.5784 / F 315.229.5589
mstrait@stlawu.edu

SKATING SAINTS PLAYERS

Player	YB	GR	Ht/Wt	P	Hometown/Last Team
Drew Bagnall	83	07	6'3"/215	D	Oakbank,MB/North Battleford North Stars (SJHL)
Tom Bardis	86	10	5'9"/195	F	Alpharetta,GA/Cushing (NEPSAC)
Dan Couglin	86	09	5'9"/200	D	Winthrop,MA/B B & N (NEPSAC)
Jeremiah Cunningham	86	10	5'9"/170	F	Ashburn,VA/Salisbury (NEPSAC)
Alex Curran	87	10	6'2"/180	F	Perth-Andover,NB/Cushing (NEPSAC)
Kevin DeVergilio	86	09	5'10"/165	F	Sterling Hgts,MI/Bay State Breakers (EJHL)
Shawn Fensel	86	09	5'9"/200	D	Nepean,ON/Nepean Raiders (CJHL)
Sean Flanagan	86	10	5'11"/170	F	Canton,NY/Cornwall Colts (CJHL)
Matt Generous	85	09	6'3"/195	D	Cheshire,CT/New England (EJHL)
Charlie Giffin	86	08	6'1"/175	F	Oakville,ON/Oakville Blades (OPJHL)
Jordan Hack	83	08	5'11"/175	F	Stony Mtn,MB/Melville Millionaires (SJHL)
John Hallas	85	08	6'0"/170	G	Largo,FL/Tampa Bay Lightning (Midget AA)
Derek Heller	86	10	5'10"/185	D	Wilkie,SK/North Battleford North Stars (SJHL)
Brock McBride	86	09	5'10"/195	F	Cornwall,ON/Cornwall Colts (CJHL)
Mike McKenzie	86	10	6'0"/190	F	Whitby,ON/St. Michael's (PS)
Zach Miskovic	85	09	6'1"/185	D	River Forest,IL/Cedar Rapids RoughRiders (USHL)
Pat Muir	83	07	6'1"/210	F	Needham,MA/Nepean Raiders (CJHL)
Chris Oetting	85	09	6'2"/200	F	Katonah,NY/Westminster (NEPSAC)
Justin Pesony	83	08	5'11"/175	G	Lac LaBiche,AB/North Battleford North Stars (SJHL)
Alex Petizian	87	10	5'10"/175	G	Kirkland,QC/Northwood (PS)
Kyle Rank	82	07	6'1"/185	F	Elmira,ON/Elmira Sugar Kings (MWJHL)
Jared Ross	84	09	6'0"/185	D	Stony Island,NS/Nepean Raiders (CJHL)
Andrzej Sandrzyk	82	07	6'1"/175	F	Montreal,QC/Nepean Raiders (CJHL)
Chris Smith	85	09	5'11"/185	D	Lakeview,NY/Nichols (PS)
Max Taylor	83	07	5'10"/175	F	Ottawa,ON/Cumberland Grads (CJHL)
Kain Tisi	85	10	5'11"/180	G	Mississauga,ON/St. Michael's (PS)
Travis Vermeulen	87	10	5'6"/170	F	Centerville,MN/Sioux Falls Stampede (USHL)
Mark Wallman	84	08	5'11"/180	F	Souris,MB/OCN Blizzard (ManJHL)
Paul Wallman	85	08	5'11"/170	D	Souris,MB/OCN Blizzard (ManJHL)

ROSTER ANALYSIS (SCHOLARSHIPS - 18)

Class		Country		Last Team					
Fr	9	USA	12	US JR A	2	CDN JR A	14	ACHA	
So	9	Canada	17	US JR B	2	CDN JR B	1	NJCAA	
Jr	6	Europe		US PS	7	CDN PS	2	NCAA	
Sr	5	Asia		US HS		CDN HS		USNDT	
Gr		Other		US Midget	1	CDN Midget		Other	

ADMISSIONS, ENROLLMENT & CAMPUS INFORMATION

Founded 1856
Private, rural campus
1,009 men / 1,093 women
Tuition, room & board - $ 42 K
Avg SAT - 1,160 / Avg ACT - 25

Average acceptance rate - 61 %
Freshman financial aid - 93 %
Early decision application deadline - Nov 15
Regular application deadline - Feb 15
Financial aid deadline - Feb 15

Terry Cowdrey - Admissions Director
St. Lawrence University
Park Street
Canton, NY 13617
O 315.229.5261 / F 315.229.5818

www.stlawu.edu

web.stlawu.edu/sports/

SAINT LOUIS UNIVERSITY

Division 1

HOCKEY STAFF

HEAD COACH
John Bosch

ASSISTANT COACHES
Kevin McGlynn
Justin Stiehr
Alex Kuehling
Jeff Oakley
Mike McLaughlin

HOCKEY OFFICE
1555 Wooden Bridge Trail
Ballwin, MO 63021-8411
O 636.861.3248 / F 314.977.3555
sluhockey@juno.com

HOCKEY MEDIA CONTACT
Saint Louis University Hockey Club
221 North Grand Boulevard
St. Louis, MO 63103
jbosch@sluhockey.com

HOCKEY RINK
The Summit Center
O 636.537.4200
Capacity 2,000

BILLIKENS PLAYERS

Player	YB	GR	Ht/Wt	P	Hometown/Last Team
Sean Breneman			5' 7"/155	F	St. Charles,MO/Duquesne (PS)
Blake Busse			6' 2"/200	D	St. Louis,MO/DeSmet (PS)
Pat Clark			6' 0"/180	D	Winnetka,IL/New Trier (HS)
Skipper Clark		08	5' 7"/160	F	Toledo,OH/St. John's (PS)
Josh Daugherty		09	5'10"/180	F	Chatham,IL/Peoria Rivermen (Midget AAA)
Corry Daus			5' 9"/155	F	Gurnee,IL/Deerfield Falcons (Midget AAA)
David Gregory			5'11"/180	D	St. Louis,MO/St. Louis Amatuer Blues (Midget AAA)
Zach Han		07	5'10"/165	F	Liberty Township,OH/Cinncinati Cobras (CSHL)
Worthe Holt		09	6' 2"/190	D	Fischers,IN/Hamilton Southeastern (HS)
Will Hux		08	5'11"/175	F	Indianapolis,IN/Brebeuf (PS)
Geoff Kienzle		09	6' 6"/235	D	Fenton,MO/Twin Bridges Lightning (Midget AAA)
Luke Lamming			5'11"/175	F	Hawthorn Woods,IL/Metropolitan State College
Tomas Larkin			5' 9"/165	D	Plano,TX/Dallas Jesuit (PS)
Phil Lombardo			6' 0"/175	F	St. Louis,MO/Christian Brothers (PS)
Jim Matela		08	5' 5"/160	F	Hickory Hills,IL/Chicago Chill (Midget AAA)
Brandon Moran			5' 9"/170	F	St. Louis,MO/St. Louis Blues (CSHL)
Ted Parran		09	5' 9"/165	D	Shaker Heights,OH/St. Ignatius (PS)
Aleks Perrin			5'11"/175	F	Edina,MN/Benilde-St. Margarets (PS)
Justin Petruska			6' 0"/170	F	St. Louis,MO/Affton Americans (Midget AAA)
Joe Schaber			5'11"/180	D	Peoria,IL/Peoria Rivermen (Midget AAA)
Dane Schikedanz		09	5'11"/170	D	Fairview Heights,IL/Belleville East (HS)
Joe Siepka		08	5'11"/170	G	Tinley Park,IL/Chicago Mission (Midget AAA)
Andrew Smith			6' 1"/175	F	Dallas,TX/Dallas Jesuit (PS)
Trey Spiller			5'11"/170	G	St. Louis,MO/St. Louis Blues (CSHL)
Brendan Swearengin			6' 0"/165	G	Carrollton,TX/Dallas Jesuit (PS)
Rex Szyper		07	6' 1"/180	D	Grafton,WI/Marquette Jesuit (PS)
Rob Westervelt		09	6' 1"/225	F	Arnold,MO/Seckman (HS)
Kyle Whitehead			6' 1"/165	F	St. Charles,MO/Duquesne (PS)
Andrew Wiltz			6' 0"/180	F	Metairie,LA/Dallas Jesuit (PS)
Ryan Wood		09	5'10"/165	F	Libertyville,IL/Lake County Atoms (Midget AAA)

ROSTER ANALYSIS (SCHOLARSHIPS - 0)

Class	Country		Last Team				
Fr	USA	30	US JR A		CDN JR A		ACHA
So	Canada		US JR B	3	CDN JR B		NJCAA
Jr	Europe		US PS	14	CDN PS		NCAA
Sr	Asia		US HS	3	CDN HS		USNDT
Gr	Other		US Midget	9	CDN Midget		Other	1

ADMISSIONS, ENROLLMENT & CAMPUS INFORMATION

Founded 1818
Private, urban campus
2,840 men / 4,088 women
Tuition, room & board - $ 33 K
Avg SAT - 1,195 / Avg ACT - 26

Average acceptance rate - 80 %
Freshman financial aid - 63 %
Early decision application deadline - N/A
Regular application deadline - Dec 1
Financial aid deadline - Mar 1

Shani Lenore - Admissions Director
Saint Louis University
221 North Grand Boulevard
St. Louis, MO 63103-2097
O 314.977.2500 / F 314.977.7136

www.slu.edu

www.sluhockey.com

SAINT MARY'S UNIVERSITY

Division 3

HOCKEY STAFF

HEAD COACH
Don Olson *(Harvard)*

ASSISTANT COACHES
Lenny Hoffman *(Saint Mary's '04)*
J Reszka *(Saint Mary's '01)*

HOCKEY OFFICE
Saint Mary's College
700 Terrace Heights # 62
Winona, MN 55987
O 507.457.1578 / F 507.457.1633
dolson@smumn.edu

HOCKEY MEDIA CONTACT
Don Nadeau - Sports Info Director
Saint Mary's College
700 Terrace Heights # 36
Winona, MN 55987
O 507.457.1634 / F 507.457.6967
dnadeau@smumn.edu

HOCKEY RINK
St. Mary's Arena (On Campus)
700 Terrace Heights
Winona, MN 55987
Size 190' x 90', Capacity 800
O 507.457.1412

ATHLETIC DIRECTOR
Chris Kendall - Athletic Director
Saint Mary's College
700 Terrace Heights # 62
Winona, MN 55987-1399
O 507.457.1781 / F 507.457.6640
ckendall@smumn.edu

CARDINALS PLAYERS

Player	YB	GR	Ht/Wt	P	Hometown/Last Team
Nick Berra		07	5'8"/180	G	St. Louis,MO/Vianney Golden Griffins ()
Anthony Bohn		10	5'11"/175	F	Spring Hill,FL/Santa Fe Roadrunners (NAHL)
Luke Buetow		10	6'3"/210	D	Wheatridge,CO/Cleveland Barons (NAHL)
Cullum Buetow-Staples	07		6'1"/180	F	Arden Hills,MN/Danville Wings (USHL)
Nick Carlson		10	5'9"/155	D	Inver Gr Hgts,MN/Rosemont (HS)
Mike Christiansen		10	6'1"/180	F	Detroit Lks,MN/Minnesota Ice Hawks (MnJHL)
Tony Clafton		10	6'2"/155	D	Grand Rpds,MN/Grand Rapids (HS)
Eric Dahl		10	5'9"/165	F	St. Cloud,MN/Wasilla Spirit (NAHL)
Kevin Eidsmo		08	6'1"/185	D	Chanhassen,MN/St. Olaf (MIAC)
Zach Faust		10	5'9"/165	G	White Bear Lk,MN/White Bear Lake (HS)
Devin Firl		08	5'11"/175	D	Red Wing,MN/Red Wing (HS)
Adam Fleishman	07		5'9"/180	F	Vernon Hls,IL/Vernon Hills (HS)
Adam Gill		08	5'11"/175	F	Rochester,MN/Fairbanks Ice Dogs (NAHL)
David Gross		08	5'11"/170	F	Grasston,MN/Pine City (HS)
Gordie Johnson	09		5'9"/180	F	Minneapolis,MN/Minnesota Ice Hawks (MnJHL)
Ben Kenyon		10	5'9"/170	F	Sparta,WI/Hudson Valley Eagles (MJHL)
Graham Kuehner		08	5'10"/155	F	N Mankato,MN/Mankato West (HS)
Bill Leier		10	5'10"/185	D	Woodbury,MN/Hill-Murray (PS)
Joe Mayer		10	6'0"/195	F	Woodbury,MN/Woodbury (HS)
Jeff Miller		10	6'0"/195	D	Portage ,MI/Alpena Icediggers (NAHL)
Andy Nadeau	07		5'8"/145	G	Winona,MN/Winona (HS)
Jesse Polk		08	6'1"/165	F	Hastings,MN/Wichita Falls Wildcats (NAHL)
Ryan Radke		08	5'10"/165	D	Woodbury,MN/Woodbury (HS)
Karl Reinke	09		5'10"/165	F	Duluth,MN/Minnesota Ice Hawks (MnJHL)
Andy Roberts	09		6'3"/230	F	Rochester,MN/Wichita Falls Wildcats (NAHL)
Morgan Sheperd		10	6'1"/190	F	Brainerd,MN/Springfield Blues (NAHL)
Dan Smith		08	6'1"/180	G	Rochester,MN/Amherst (NESCAC)
Matt Staehely		10	6'1"/185	F	Shorewood,IL/Springfield Blues (NAHL)
Travis VanDynHoven	08		5'7"/175	F	River Falls,WI/Minnesota Ice Hawks (MnJHL)
Deven VanHouse	09		5'11"/190	F	Silver Bay,MN/Minnesota Ice Hawks (MnJHL)
AJ Woodward		10	5'11"/180	D	Lenexa,KS/Billings Bulls (NAHL)

ROSTER ANALYSIS (SCHOLARSHIPS - 0)

Class		Country		Last Team				
Fr	14	USA	31	US JR A	11	CDN JR A		ACHA
So	4	Canada		US JR B	6	CDN JR B		NJCAA
Jr	9	Europe		US PS	1	CDN PS		NCAA	2
Sr	4	Asia		US HS	10	CDN HS		USNDT
Gr		Other		US Midget		CDN Midget		Other	1

ADMISSIONS, ENROLLMENT & CAMPUS INFORMATION

Founded 1912
Private, urban campus
668 men / 923 women
Tuition,room & board - $ 26 K
Avg SAT - 1,013

Average acceptance rate - 77 %
Freshman financial aid - 75 %
Early decision application deadline - N/A
Regular application deadline - May 1
Financial aid deadline - Mar 15

Anthony Piscitiello - Admissions Director
Saint Mary's College - #2
700 Terrace Heights
Winona, MN 55987-1399
O 507.457.1700 / F 507.457.1722

www.smumn.edu   sports.smumn.edu/

ST. MICHAEL'S COLLEGE

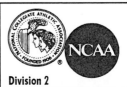

Division 2

HOCKEY STAFF

HEAD COACH
Chris Davidson *(St. Michael's '99)*

ASSISTANT COACHES
Christian Soucy *(Vermont '93)*

HOCKEY OFFICE
Saint Michael's College
Winooski Park
Colchester, VT 05439
O 802.654.2551 / F 802.654.2497
cdavidson@smcvt.edu

HOCKEY MEDIA CONTACT
Seth Cole - Sports Info Director
Saint Michael's College
Winooski Park
Colchester, VT 05439
O 802.654.2537 / F 802.654.2497
scole2@smcvt.edu

HOCKEY RINK
Cairns Arena (Off Campus)
Dorset Park
600 Swift Street
South Burlington, VT 05403
Size x , Capacity
O 802.658.5577

ATHLETIC DIRECTOR
Geri Knortz - Athletic Director
Saint Michael's College
Winooski Park
Colchester, VT 05439
O 802.654.2200 / F 802.654.2497
gknortz@smcvt.edu

ICE KNIGHTS PLAYERS

Player	YB	GR	Ht/Wt	P	Hometown/Last Team
Dan Anctil	07		5'11"/190	F	Rochester,NH/Valley Warriors (EJHL)
John Burns	08		6' 2"/200	D	Sandwich,MA/Connecticut, U of (AHL)
Erik Caron	08		5' 7"/175	F	Kanata,ON/Smiths Falls Bears (CJHL)
Mike Ciardullo	07		5' 8"/170	F	Walden,NY/Canterbury (NEPSAC)
Ryan Conroy	08		6' 2"/210	F	Carlsbad,CA/SUNY Buffalo State (SUNYAC)
Tim Dancey	08		6' 0"/190	F	Anaheim,CA/Berkshire (NEPSAC)
Andrick Deppmeyer	08		6' 0"/195	D	Claremont,NH/Bay State Breakers (EJHL)
Andy DiMasi	07		5'11"/170	D	Burlington,VT/Tilton (NEPSAC)
Bryan Dodge	09		6' 1"/190	D	Goffstown,NH/Governor's (NEPSAC)
Craig Gennings	10		5'10"/190	D	Wallingford,CT/South Kent (NEPSAC)
Derek Girouard	07		6' 0"/185	F	Metheun,MA/Central Catholic (PS)
Matt Hall	09		6' 0"/190	D/F	Scituate,MA/Bridgton (NEPSAC)
Jeff Harris	07		6' 1"/200	F	Clifton Pk,NY/Capital District Selects (EJHL)
Chris Healey	09		6' 1"/190	F	Salem,NH/New Hampshire Monarchs (EJHL)
Alex Higgins	10		5'11"/165	F	Phoenix,AZ/Kent (NEPSAC)
Brian Hopper	09		6' 0"/190	D	Trumbell,CT/Hartford Wolfpack (AtJHL)
Derek Jackson	07		6' 1"/185	G	Clifton,NY/Gunnery (NEPSAC)
Jean-Maxine Legare	10		6' 0"/190	F	St. Augustin,QC/Notre Dame (PS)
Chris Martin	09		6' 1"/200	F	E Longmeadow,MA/Loomis Chaffee (NEPSAC)
Patrick McGuirk	10		5'10"/170	F	Hingham,MA/Avon (NEPSAC)
Paul Nanicelli	10		5'10"/165	F	Walpole,MA/Xaverian (PS)
Jared Silver	07		5' 8"/165	F	Montreal,QC/Tabor (NEPSAC)
Jonathan Silver	10		5' 9"/165	F	Montreal,QC/Millbrook (NEPSAC)
Erik Smith	07		5'11"/170	G	Warwick,RI/Hill (PS)
Adam Sullivan	08		6' 4"/205	G	Winthrop,MA/Winthrop (HS)
David Vorozilchak	10		5' 9"/185	D	Summit,PA/Wyoming (PS)
Alex Watts	07		5' 8"/175	F	Cheshire,CT/Berkshire (NEPSAC)

ROSTER ANALYSIS (SCHOLARSHIPS - 0)

Class		Country		Last Team				
Fr	7	USA	23	US JR A		CDN JR A	1	ACHA	
So	5	Canada	4	US JR B	5	CDN JR B		NJCAA	
Jr	6	Europe		US PS	18	CDN PS	1	NCAA	2
Sr	9	Asia		US HS		CDN HS		USNDT	
Gr		Other		US Midget		CDN Midget		Other	

ADMISSIONS, ENROLLMENT & CAMPUS INFORMATION

Founded 1904	Average acceptance rate - 70 %	Jerry Flanagan - Admissions Director
Private, suburban campus	Freshman financial aid - 84 %	Saint Michael's College
888 men / 1,042 women	Early decision application deadline - N/A	One Winooski Park
Tuition, room & board - $ 34 K	Regular application deadline - Feb 1	Colchester, VT 05439
Avg SAT - 1,130 / Avg ACT - 23	Financial aid deadline - Mar 15	O 802.654.3000 / F 802.654.2906

www.smcvt.edu — www.smcvt.edu/athletics/

ST. NORBERT COLLEGE

Division 3

<table>
<tr><td colspan="2">

HOCKEY STAFF

HEAD COACH
Tim Coghlin *(Wisconsin-Stevens Pt '89)*

ASSISTANT COACHES
AJ Aitken *(Michigan Tech '00)*
Cory Borys *(St. Norbert '98)*
Ryan Wempe *(St. Norbert '02)*

HOCKEY OFFICE
St. Norbert College
Schuldes #119
100 Grant Street
DePere, WI 54115-2099
O 920.403.2025 / F 920.403.3128
tim.coghlin@snc.edu

HOCKEY MEDIA CONTACT
Dan Lukes - Sports Information Director
St. Norbert College
Schuldes #123
100 Grant Street
DePere, WI 54115-2099
O 920.403.3031 / F 920.403.3128
lukedr@mail.snc.edu

HOCKEY RINK
Cornerstone Center (Off Campus)
1640 Fernando Drive
Green Bay, WI 54304
Size 200' x 85', Capacity 1,876
O 920.983.7528

ATHLETIC DIRECTOR
Tim Bald - Athletic Director
St. Norbert College
Schuldes #117
100 Grant Street
DePere, WI 54115-2099
O 920.403.3986 / F 920.403.3128

</td></tr>
</table>

GREEN KNIGHTS PLAYERS

Player	YB GR Ht/Wt	P	Hometown/Last Team
Tyler Allen	10 5'11"/205	F	Midhurst,ON/Port Hope Predators (OPJHL)
Trevor Bayda	07 6' 0"/190	F	Saskatoon,SK/North Battleford North Stars (SJHL)
Marc Belanger	08 6' 1"/200	F	Nanaimo,BC/Penticton Panthers (BCHL)
Troy Boisjoli	07 5'11"/190	F	Glidden,SK/Kindersley Klippers (SJHL)
Matt Boyd	10 6' 0"/190	F	St. Albert,AB/Camrose Kodiaks (AJHL)
Pat Callahan	08 5'10"/175	F	St. Louis,MO/DeSmet (PS)
Andrew Derton	07 6' 0"/190	D	Powell Rvr,BC/Vernon Vipers (BCHL)
Dustin Dubas	10 5'11"/185	D	Rama,SK/La Ronge Ice Wolves (SJHL)
Lonny Forrester	07 5' 8"/165	F	Bromhead,SK/Estevan Bruins (SJHL)
Peter Fylling	10 6' 4"/205	F	Minot,ND/Bozeman Icedogs (NAHL)
Tyler Gow	07 6' 0"/195	D	Nanaimo,BC/Nanaimo Clippers (BCHL)
Jeff Hazelwood	09 6' 1"/185	F	Dublin,CA/Des Moines Buccaneers (USHL)
Brad Herman	10 6' 0"/185	F	Cranbrook,BC/Alberni Valley Bulldogs (BCHL)
Kyle Jones	08 6' 0"/200	G	N Delta,BC/Coquitlam Express (BCHL)
Kyle Kraemer	08 5'11"/180	G	Stillwater,MN/Stillwater (HS)
Elliot Krakora	09 6' 0"/180	G	Chandler,AZ/Chicago Cyclones (Midget AAA)
Jason Nopper	10 6' 1"/200	D	Calgary,AB/Drayton Valley Thunder (AJHL)
Ryan Petersen	09 5' 8"/175	F	N St. Paul,MN/Green Bay Gamblers (USHL)
Kurtis Peterson	07 5'10"/185	F	Midale,SK/Findlay (CHA)
Chris Rampone	08 6' 0"/210	F	Kelowna,BC/Fernie Ghostriders (NAHL)
Jon Skoog	09 6' 1"/195	D	Long Lake,MN/Fargo-Moorhead Jets (NAHL)
Steven Sleep	09 5' 9"/190	F	Thunder Bay,ON/Selkirk Steelers (ManJHL)
James Switzer	07 6' 0"/180	F	Peachland,BC/Nanaimo Clippers (BCHL)
Sam Tikka	10 6' 0"/185	D	Soldotna,AK/Fairbanks Ice Dogs (NAHL)
Mikael Virta	07 6' 3"/215	D	Bellingham,WA/Central Texas Blackhawks (NAHL)
Shane Wheeler	10 5' 4"/140	F	Eagle Rvr,AK/Fairbanks Ice Dogs (NAHL)
Sheldon Wing	07 6' 1"/195	D	Thunder Bay,ON/Melfort Mustangs (SJHL)

ROSTER ANALYSIS (SCHOLARSHIPS - 0)

Class		Country		Last Team			
Fr	8	USA	10	US JR A	8	CDN JR A	15	ACHA	
So	5	Canada	17	US JR B		CDN JR B		NJCAA	
Jr	5	Europe		US PS	1	CDN PS		NCAA	1
Sr	9	Asia		US HS	1	CDN HS		USNDT	
Gr		Other		US Midget	1	CDN Midget		Other	

ADMISSIONS, ENROLLMENT & CAMPUS INFORMATION

Founded 1898	Average acceptance rate - 84 %	Dan Meyer - Admissions Director
Private, suburban campus	Freshman financial aid - 88 %	St. Norbert College
848 men / 1,124 women	Early decision application deadline - Dec 1	100 Grant Street
Tuition, room & board - $ 29 K	Regular application deadline - rolling	DePere, WI 54115-2099
Avg ACT - 25	Financial aid deadline - Mar 1	O 920.403.3005 / F 920.403.4072

ST. OLAF COLLEGE

Division 3

LIONS / OLES PLAYERS

Player	YB	GR	Ht/Wt	P	Hometown/Last Team
David Adams	87	10	5'11"/170	D	Whychoff,NJ/Shattuck-St. Mary's (PS)
Andrew Birkholz	86	09	5' 8"/210	F	Maple Gr,MN/Breck (PS)
Jeff Budish	84	08	6' 1"/200	F	Edina,MN/Fargo-Moorhead Jets (NAHL)
Jake Busch	84	09	6' 0"/175	G	St. Louis,MO/Peoria Mustangs (CSHL)
Casey Dynan		09	5'11"/180	F	Orono,MN/Bismarck Bobcats (NAHL)
Brycen Eberwein	87	10	6' 0"/190	G	Grand Forks,ND/Shattuck-St. Mary's (PS)
John Egge	83	07	5'10"/175	F	Wisconsin Rpds,WI/Central Texas Blackhawks (NAHL)
Andrew Gastineau	83	07	6' 0"/190	D	Rochester,MN/Rochester (MnJHL)
Jason Gomez	86	09	6' 1"/200	F	Savage,MN/Central Texas Blackhawks (NAHL)
Justin Green	84	08	6' 3"/195	F	Shorewood,MN/Fort Francis (SIJHL)
Ryan Hampson	85	09	6' 2"/190	D	Chanhassen,MN/Bismarck Bobcats (NAHL)
Kyle Hilmershausen	84	07	6' 0"/185	F	Wausau,WI/Central Texas Blackhawks (NAHL)
Karl Hylie	88	10	6' 2"/200	D	Plymouth,MN/Breck (PS)
Thor Josefson	85	10	5' 9"/165	F	Bemidji,MN/Rochester (MnJHL)
Barrett Kennedy	86	09	6' 1"/185	D	Eagan,MN/Central Texas Blackhawks (NAHL)
Brett Kistner	83	08	6' 2"/190	F	Peoria,IL/Bozeman Icedogs (NAHL)
Matt LaBombard	87	10	6' 0"/175	F	Bloomington,MN/Jefferson (HS)
Tyler Lantz	84	09	6' 0"/185	G	Breckenridge,CO/Kootenai Colts (NPJHL)
Mike MacMillan	84	08	5' 9"/180	F	Buffalo,MN/Billings Bulls (NAHL)
Matt McDonald	84	09	6' 1"/200	F	Lakeville,MN/Bismarck Bobcats (NAHL)
Mitch Mudra	84	07	6' 0"/185	D	Edina,MN/Edina (HS)
Dylan Mueller	87	09	5' 9"/175	F	Plymouth,MN/Armstrong (HS)
Andy Ockuly	85	08	5' 9"/165	F	Hudson,MN/Dubuque Thunderbirds (MnJHL)
Matt Olson		10	5'10"/175	F	Ham Lk,MN/Blaine (HS)
Bryan Osmondson	87	10	6' 3"/195	F	Princeton,MN/Princeton (HS)
John Paulson	84	08	6' 4"/215	D	Eden Pr,MN/St. Louis (USHL)
Barret Simons	86	09	6' 1"/175	D	Wisconsin Rpds,WI/Team Wisconsin (Midget AAA)
Will Smith		09	6' 0"/175	F	Long Lake,MN/Orono (HS)
Nick Stalock	85	09	6' 1"/190	F	S St. Paul,MN/Santa Fe Roadrunners (NAHL)
Roger Trousdale		09	6' 0"/175	F	Rogers,MN/Buffalo (HS)
Ben Umhoefer	87	10	6' 2"/195	F	Marshfield,WI/Shattuck-St. Mary's (PS)
Jeff Wilde	83	07	5'11"/175	G	Watertown,SD/Bismarck Bobcats (NAHL)
Sam Windsor		09	5' 9"/175	D	Plymouth,MN/Minnesota (NAHL)

ROSTER ANALYSIS (SCHOLARSHIPS - 0)

Class		Country	Last Team					
Fr	8	USA	33	US JR A	14	CDN JR A	1	ACHA
So	14	Canada		US JR B	5	CDN JR B		NJCAA
Jr	6	Europe		US PS	5	CDN PS		NCAA
Sr	5	Asia		US HS	7	CDN HS		USNDT
Gr		Other		US Midget	1	CDN Midget		Other

COLLEGE OF SAINT SCHOLASTICA

Division 3

HOCKEY STAFF

HEAD COACH
Mark Wick *(St. Scholastica '85)*

ASSISTANT COACHES
Randy Barker *(UW-Superior '01)*
Brant Nicklin
Dave Reyelts *(St. Scholastica)*

HOCKEY OFFICE
St. Scholastica - Athletic Department
1200 Kenwood Avenue
Duluth, MN 55811-4199
O 218.723.6610 / F 218.723.5958
mwick2@css.edu

HOCKEY MEDIA CONTACT
Gregg Petcoff - Sports Info Director
St. Scholastica - SID Office
1200 Kenwood Avenue
Duluth, MN 55811-4199
O 218.723.6643 / F 218.723.5958
gpetcoff@css.edu

HOCKEY RINK
Mars-Lakeview Arena (Off Campus)
1201 Rice Lake Road
Duluth, MN 55811
Size 200' x 85', Capacity 1,200
O 218.722.4455

ATHLETIC DIRECTOR
Dr. Tony Barrett - Athletic Director
St. Scholastica - Athletic Department
1200 Kenwood Avenue
Duluth, MN 55811-4199
O 218.723.6721 / F 218.723.5958

SAINTS PLAYERS

Player	YB	GR	Ht/Wt	P	Hometown/Last Team
Shane Auger	84	09	5'10"/165	D	Russell,MB/Waywayseecappo (ManJHL)
Jordan Baird	85	10	5'11"/200	D	Port McNeill,BC/Victoria Salsa (BCHL)
Shawn Bartlette	08		6'1"/190	F	E Grand Forks,MN/Bismarck Bobcats (NAHL)
Christopher Blackmon	85	10	6'2"/215	F	Plano,TX/Chilliwack Chiefs (BCHL)
Steve Bounds	84	09	5'10"/175	G	Airdrie,AB/Powell River Kings (BCHL)
Kris Boyce	85	10	6'0"/175	F	Fruitvale,BC/Cowichan Valley Capitals (BCHL)
Jordan Chong	85	10	5'11"/175	F	N Vancouver,BC/Dryden Ice Dogs (SIJHL)
Nick Cuvelier	84	10	5'10"/185	F	Calgary,AB/Antigonish Bulldogs (ManJHL)
Michael Epp	07		6'3"/205	D	Winnipeg,MN/Melville Millionaires (SJHL)
Ben Fearing	86	10	6'3"/215	D	Coleraine,MN/Greenway (HS)
Jeff Gagnon	85	10	6'1"/210	F	Quesnel,BC/Victoria Salsa (BCHL)
Trevor Geiger	84	09	5'10"/185	F	Salmon Arm,BC/Salmon Arm Silverbacks (BCHL)
Scott Honkola	07		6'1"/200	D	Bismarck,ND/Bismarck Bobcats (NAHL)
Joey Hughes	84	09	5'11"/190	F	Melbourne,Australia/Cowichan Valley Capitals (BCHL)
Tyler Johnson	08		5'10"/170	G	E Grand Forks,MN/East Grand Forks (HS)
Jameson Lundquist	85	10	5'7"/155	F	Superior,WI/Fairbanks Ice Dogs (NAHL)
Kyle Luschinski	84	09	5'11"/170	F	Winnipeg,MB/Waywayseecappo (ManJHL)
Joey Martini	84	09	5'11"/190	F	Calgary,AB/Canmore Eagles (AJHL)
Chris Meagher	85	10	5'10"/175	D	Victoria,BC/Brooks Bandits (AJHL)
Jake Nelson	84	09	5'11"/195	F	Superior,WI/Minnesota (NAHL)
Joey Nigro	86	10	5'10"/190	F	Thunder Bay,ON/Fort William North Stars (SIJHL)
Kelly Reynolds	84	09	5'10"/185	D	Parksville,BC/Cowichan Valley Capitals (BCHL)
Matt Saler	84	09	5'10"/195	F	Minnedosa,MB/Powell River Kings (BCHL)
Neil Sauter	86	10	5'11"/185	D	Superior,WI/Lincoln Stars (USHL)
Aaron Spotts	85	10	6'1"/205	F	Spokane,WA/Cowichan Valley Capitals (BCHL)
Matt Stengl	85	09	6'0"/170	F	E Grand Forks,MN/Selkirk Steelers (ManJHL)
AJ Tucker	84	09	6'0"/195	F	Ft Frances,ON/Waywayseecappo (ManJHL)

ROSTER ANALYSIS (SCHOLARSHIPS - 0)

Class		Country		Last Team				
Fr	12	USA	11	US JR A	5	CDN JR A	20	ACHA
So	11	Canada	15	US JR B		CDN JR B		NJCAA
Jr	2	Europe		US PS		CDN PS		NCAA
Sr	2	Asia	1	US HS	2	CDN HS		USNDT
Gr		Other		US Midget		CDN Midget		Other

ADMISSIONS, ENROLLMENT & CAMPUS INFORMATION

Founded 1912
Private, suburban campus
589 men / 1,252 women
Tuition, room & board - $ 29 K
Avg SAT - 1,065 / Avg ACT - 24

Average acceptance rate - 89 %
Freshman financial aid - 83 %
Early decision application deadline - N/A
Regular application deadline - Jun 1
Financial aid deadline - Mar 15

Brian Dalton - Admissions Director
St. Scholastica - Admissions Office
1200 Kenwood Avenue
Duluth, MN 55811-4199
O 218.723.6046 / F 218.723.5991

www.css.edu   www.css.edu/depts/athletics/

UNIVERSITY OF ST. THOMAS

Minnesota Intercollegiate Athletic Conference

Division 3

HOCKEY STAFF

HEAD COACH
Terry Skrypek *(St. Mary's '70)*

ASSISTANT COACHES
Jeff Boeser *(St. Thomas '75)*
Eric Wenkus *(St. Thomas '02)*
Steve Aronson *(St. Thomas '00)*

HOCKEY OFFICE
University of St. Thomas - Mail #4041
2115 Summit Avenue
St. Paul, MN 55105-1096
O 651.962.5911 / F 651.962.5910
tpskrypek@stthomas.edu

HOCKEY MEDIA CONTACT
Gene McGivern - Sports Info Director
University of St. Thomas - Mail #5003
2115 Summit Avenue
St. Paul, MN 55105-1096
O 651.962.5903 / F 651.962.5910
ejmcgivern@stthomas.edu

HOCKEY RINK
St. Thomas Ice Arena (Off Campus)
920 Mendota Heights Road
Mendota Heights, MN 55120
Size 200' x 85', Capacity 1,000
O 651.209.6020

ATHLETIC DIRECTOR
Steve Fritz - Athletic Director
University of St. Thomas - Mail #5003
2115 Summit Avenue
St. Paul, MN 55105-1096
O 651.962.5901 / F 651.962.5910
sjfritz@stthomas.edu

TOMMIES PLAYERS

Player	YB	GR	Ht/Wt	P	Hometown/Last Team
Todd Alexander		09	5'11"/200	D	New Hope,MN/North Dakota (WCHA)
Alex Arnason		10	6'0"/185	F	Blaine,MN/Totino Grace (HS)
Sean Bryant	86	09	5'11"/185	F	Sartell,MN/Sartell (HS)
Alex Coles		10	6'0"/185	F	Apple Valley,MN/Apple Valley (HS)
Andrew Edwards	85	07	6'1"/200	D	Mounds View,MN/Mounds View (HS)
Garrett Gruenke	83	08	6'5"/210	D	Plymouth,MN/Benilde-St. Margaret's (PS)
Nick Harris	83	07	5'9"/170	F	Hastings,MN/Hastings (HS)
Ryan Hoehn	85	08	5'9"/170	F	Waseca,MN/Danville Wings (USHL)
John Jacques		10	6'0"/250	D	Duluth,MN/Duluth East (HS)
Wes Jirovec		10	6'4"/200	F	Stillwater,MN/St. Thomas (PS)
Matt Kaiser	86	08	5'11"/175	F	Bloomington,MN/Holy Angels (PS)
Craig Kaufman	86	08	6'2"/175	F	Shoreview,MN/Hill-Murray (PS)
Sam Kelly		10	6'0"/185	F	Mahtomedi,MN/Hill-Murray (HS)
Treye Kettwick	83	07	5'10"/175	G	DeWitt,IA/DeWitt (HS)
Tim Kleiman		10	6'0"/185	D	Duluth,MN/Marshall (HS)
Tom Knutson		09	6'2"/205	F	Duluth,MN/Wisconsin Superior (NCHA)
Ryan Kurtz		10	5'11"/165	F	Mendota Hgts,MN/Cretin-Derham (PS)
Matt Letourneau		10	5'11"/190	D	Duluth,MN/Marshall (HS)
Kevin Mahoney		10	6'1"/170	F	Duluth,MN/Marshall (HS)
Jake Maida	85	09	5'11"/175	G	Duluth,MN/East (HS)
Joe McEaney		10	5'7"/165	F	Woodbury,MN/Hill-Murray (HS)
Nick Nelson	83	08	5'10"/175	F	Duluth,MN/East (HS)
Kevin O'Leary	83	07	5'11"/200	F	Wisconsin Rpds,WI/Lincoln (HS)
AJ Panchenko	85	09	6'0"/195	D	Eagan,MN/Eastview (HS)
Andy Panchenko	83	08	5'9"/170	F	Eagan,MN/Eastview (HS)
Nick Pernula	84	08	5'9"/175	F	Osseo,MN/Osseo (HS)
Kevin Rollwagen	84	07	6'0"/180	F	Bloomington,MN/Holy Angels (PS)
Nate Ryan	84	08	5'11"/165	F	Apple Valley,MN/Wichita Falls Wildcats (NAHL)
Luke Salscheider	84	08	5'11"/175	D	St. Paul,MN/Cretin-Derham (PS)
Joe Schraeder		10	6'1"/160	G	E Stroudsberg,PA/Berkshire (NEPSAC)
Paul Solberg	85	09	6'1"/180	D	Osseo,MN/Osseo (HS)
Ryan VanBockel		07		D	Bloomington,MN/St. Thomas (PS)

ROSTER ANALYSIS (SCHOLARSHIPS - 0)

Class		Country		Last Team					
Fr	11	USA	32	US JR A	2	CDN JR A		ACHA	
So	6	Canada		US JR B		CDN JR B		NJCAA	
Jr	9	Europe		US PS	11	CDN PS		NCAA	2
Sr	6	Asia		US HS	17	CDN HS		USNDT	
Gr		Other		US Midget		CDN Midget		Other	

ADMISSIONS, ENROLLMENT & CAMPUS INFORMATION

Founded 1885	Average acceptance rate - 81 %	Marla Freiderichs - Admission Director
Private, urban campus	Freshman financial aid - 84 %	University of St. Thomas
2,460 men / 2,666 women	Early decision application deadline - N/A	2115 Summit Avenue
Tuition, room & board - $ 30 K	Regular application deadline - N/A	St. Paul, MN 55105-1096
Avg SAT - 1,160 / Avg ACT - 25	Financial aid deadline - Apr 1	O 651.962.6150 / F 651.962.6160

SALEM STATE COLLEGE

HOCKEY EAST

NCAA Division 3

HOCKEY STAFF

HEAD COACH
Bill O'Neill *(Boston University '79)*

ASSISTANT COACHES
Shawn McEachern
Alex Doren *(Quinnipiac '94)*
Paul Snell

HOCKEY OFFICE
Salem State College
O'Keefe Sports Center
225 Canal Street
Salem, MA 01970-4589
O 978.542.6575 / F 978.542.2926
william.oneill@salemstate.edu

HOCKEY MEDIA CONTACT
Tom C. Roundy -Sports Info Director
O'Keefe Sports Center, #306
225 Canal Street
Salem, MA 01970-4589
O 978.542.6549 / F 978.542.2926
thomas.roundy@salemstate.edu

HOCKEY RINK
Rockett Arena (On Campus)
O'Keefe Sports Center
225 Canal Street
Salem, MA 01970-4589
Size 200' x 85', Capacity 2,800
O 978.741.6560

ATHLETIC DIRECTOR
Tim P. Shea - Athletic Director
O'Keefe Center, #207
225 Canal Street
Salem, MA 01970-4589
O 978.542.6517 / F 978.542.2926
timothy.shea@salemstate.edu

VIKINGS PLAYERS

Player	YB	GR	Ht/Wt	P	Hometown/Last Team
Mark Bates	09		5'10"/190	F	Medford,MA/Massachusetts Boston (ECAC East)
Aaron Blades	10		5'10"/185	F	Chino,CA/Cushing (NEPSAC)
Jeff Chillson	09		5'11"/170	F	Enfield,CT/New England Falcons (EJHL)
Kevin Ciborowski	10		6'1"/195	F	W Springfield,MA/Springfield Pics (IJHL)
Troy Ciernia	09		6'1"/205	G	Eagan,MN/Melfort Mustangs (SJHL)
Matt Davis	10		6'2"/210	D	Wellesley,MA/Bridgewater Bandits (EJHL)
Joe Doherty	09		6'1"/205	D	Wellesley,MA/Assumption (NE10)
Zach Doyen	09		5'6"/155	F	Ortonville,MI/St. Mary's (PS)
Joshua Ex	10		5'10"/175	G	Flint,MI/Queen City Cutthroats (NPJHL)
Jonathan Fecteau	09		5'8"/175	D	St. Benuit Labre,QC/Campbellton Tigers (MarJHL)
Sean Ferguson	07		6'3"/205	F	Lynn,MA/Valley Warriors (EJHL)
Bill Glynn	09		5'10"/170	D	Pembroke,MA/Bay State Breakers (EJHL)
Ryan Hatch	09		6'0"/200	G	Medway,MA/Santa Fe Roadrunners (NAHL)
Dustin Hayes	10		6'0"/205	F	Danvers,MA/Danvers (HS)
Ryan Hayes	08		6'0"/220	F	Danvers,MA/Phillips Exeter (NEPSAC)
Kevin Hughes	10		6'2"/210	D	Natick,MA/Walpole Stars (EJHL)
Bryan McGrath	09		6'1"/195	F	S Boston,MA/Salem Ice Dogs (EmJHL)
Chris McInnis	10		5'8"/160	F	Waltham,MA/Walpole Stars (EJHL)
Damen Nisula	10		5'11"/195	F	Gardner,MA/Cushing (NEPSAC)
Brett Noll	10		6'2"/205	D	Sandwich,MA/Walpole Stars (EJHL)
Andrew O'Neill	07		5'10"/170	F	Salem,MA/Pingree (NEPSAC)
David Pazzaglia	09		6'0"/185	F	Oakdale,CT/Cornwall Colts (CJHL)
Jason Rexinis	10		5'11"/185	F	Lynn,MA/Tilton (NEPSAC)
Jeff Tellier	10		5'11"/195	F	Chicopee,MA/Springfield Pics (IJHL)
Luke Williams	07		6'2"/215	F	Lanesborough,MA/New England Coyotes (EJHL)

ROSTER ANALYSIS (SCHOLARSHIPS - 0)

Class		Country		Last Team					
Fr	11	USA	24	US JR A	1	CDN JR A	3	ACHA	
So	10	Canada	1	US JR B	12	CDN JR B		NJCAA	
Jr	1	Europe		US PS	6	CDN PS		NCAA	2
Sr	3	Asia		US HS	1	CDN HS		USNDT	
Gr		Other		US Midget		CDN Midget		Other	

ADMISSIONS, ENROLLMENT & CAMPUS INFORMATION

Founded 1854	Average acceptance rate - %	N. Bryant - Admissions Director
Public, suburban campus	Freshman financial aid - 73 %	Salem State College
2,193 men / 3,898 women	Early decision application deadline - N/A	352 Lafayette Street
Tuition, room & board $ 12 K / $ 18 K	Regular application deadline - rolling	Salem, MA 01970
Avg SAT - 945	Financial aid deadline - Apr 1	O 978.542.6200 / F 978.542.6893

www.salem.mass.edu | www.salemstate.edu/athletics/

SALVE REGINA UNIVERSITY

HOCKEY
NORTHEAST

Division 3

HOCKEY STAFF

HEAD COACH
Chris MacPherson *(Skidmore '96)*

ASSISTANT COACHES
Mike Monahan *(Skidmore '96)*
Rich Braun
Brian Torrello

HOCKEY OFFICE
Salve Regina University
100 Ochre Point Avenue
Newport, RI 02842-4192
O 401.341.2242/ F 401.341.2907
macpherc@salve.edu

HOCKEY MEDIA CONTACT
Ed Habershaw - Sports Info Director
Salve Regina University
Newport, RI 02842-4192
O 401.341.2271/ F 401.341.2907
habershe@salve.edu

HOCKEY RINK
Portsmouth Abbey (Off Campus)
285 Cory's Lane
Portsmouth, RI 02871
Size ' x ', Capacity
O 401.683.0621

ATHLETIC DIRECTOR
Del Malloy - Athletic Director
Salve Regina University
100 Ochre Point Avenue
Newport, RI 02842-4192
O 401.341.2268/ F 401.341.2960
malloyd@salve.edu

SEAHAWKS PLAYERS

Player	YB	GR	Ht/Wt	P	Hometown/Last Team
Patrick Bambury	10		6' 1"/185	F	Braintree,MA/Bridgewater Bandits (EJHL)
Nick Bartelloni	09		5'10"/180	D	Norfolk,MA/Worcester (NEPSAC)
Steve Belle-Isle	08		5'10"/160	G	Portsmouth,NH/Kents Hill (NEPSAC)
Eric Bouchard	10		6' 0"/180	F	Naples,ME/Portland Pirates (MJHL)
Nathaniel Burns	10		6' 4"/200	D	Sandwich,MA/Boston Harbor Wolves (IJHL)
Dan Carpentier	08		6' 1"/190	F	Auburn,ME/Portland Pirates (MJHL)
Ryan Comerford	09		5' 7"/145	G	Merrimack,NH/Worcester (NEPSAC)
Eric Davis	10		5'10"/215	D	Woburn,MA/Tilton (NEPSAC)
Ryan Doyle	07		5'10"/175	F	Lowell,MA/Lowell (HS)
Paul Forselius	10		6' 0"/210	D	Madison,CT/Springfield Blues (NAHL)
Brandon Goodnow	10		5'10"/185	F	Holden,MA/Worcester (NEPSAC)
Chase Goodrich	09		5'11"/175	G	Salisbury,VT/Bridgton (NEPSAC)
Bryan Goodwin	08		5'11"/185	D	Taunton,MA/Bridgewater Bandits (EJHL)
Travis Hampton	07		6' 0"/185	F	Billings,MT/Green Mountain Glades (EJHL)
Chris Hill	09		5'11"/180	F N	Chelmsford,MA/Green Mountain Glades (EJHL)
Mike Kravchuk	08		5'10"/155	D	Peabody,MA/Hebron (NEPSAC)
Mike Mallette	08		5' 7"/160	F	Chepachet,RI/Walpole Stars (EJHL)
Conor McCahill	09		6' 2"/200	F	Highlands Rch,CO/Fairbanks Ice Dogs (NAHL)
Brandt Nelson	08		6' 1"/180	D	Shelburne,VT/Kimball Union (NEPSAC)
Jake Noonan	08		5'11"/205	F	Arlington,MA/Green Mountain Glades (EJHL)
Jake Pickard	09		5' 9"/190	F	Wellfleet,MA/Tilton (NEPSAC)
Kyle Ratkey	10		5'10"/170	F	Carmel,IN/Culver (PS)
Richie Rice	08		5' 9"/165	F	Hampton Fls,NH/Valley Warriors (EJHL)
Bryn Sneddon	07		5'10"/165	F	Casper,WY/Valley Warriors (EJHL)
Zach Sufilka	09		5'10"/170	D	Lakewood,OH/Kimball Union (NEPSAC)
Tyler Trott	10		5'10"/160	F	Rehoboth,MA/Tilton (NEPSAC)

ROSTER ANALYSIS (SCHOLARSHIPS - 0)

Class		Country		Last Team				
Fr	8	USA	26	US JR A	2	CDN JR A		ACHA
So	7	Canada		US JR B	11	CDN JR B		NJCAA
Jr	8	Europe		US PS	12	CDN PS		NCAA
Sr	3	Asia		US HS	1	CDN HS		USNDT
Gr		Other		US Midget		CDN Midget		Other

ADMISSIONS, ENROLLMENT & CAMPUS INFORMATION

Founded 1934
Private, Urban campus
591 men / 1,448 women
Tuition, room & board - $ 34 K
Avg SAT - 1,075/Avg ACT - 24

Average acceptance rate - 56 %
Freshman financial aid - 68 %
Early decision application deadline - N/A
Regular application deadline - rolling
Financial aid deadline - Mar 1

Laura E. McPhie-Oliveira - Adm. Dir.
Salve Regina University
Newport, RI 02842-4192
O 401.341.2908/ F 401.848.2823

www.salve.edu

www.salve.edu/athletics/

UNIVERSITY OF SCRANTON

Division 3

HOCKEY STAFF

HEAD COACH
Bill Fitzgerald *(Boston College '69)*

ASSISTANT COACH
Don Tweedy

HOCKEY OFFICE
University of Scranton
209 Long Center
Scranton, PA 18510-4650
O 570.346.3300 / F 570.346.6106
fitzgeraldw2@scranton.edu

HOCKEY MEDIA CONTACT
Kevin Southard - Sports Info Director
University of Scranton - SID Office
208 Long Center
Scranton, PA 18510-4650
O 570.941.7571 / F 570.941.4223
southardk2@uofs.edu

HOCKEY RINK
Ice Box North (Off Campus)
Jenkins Township, PA
Size 200' x 85', Capacity 500
O 570.963.1020

ATHLETIC DIRECTOR
Toby Lovecchio - Athletic Director
University of Scranton - Athletic Dept.
210 Long Center
Scranton, PA 18510-4650
O 570.941.7440 / F 570.941.4223
lovecchiof2@scranton.edu

ROYALS PLAYERS

Player	YB	GR Ht/Wt	P	Hometown/Last Team
Joe Bonafede	07	6' 2"/185	D	Skaneateles, NY/Skaneateles (HS)
Chris Brearey	07	5'10"/195	F	Shaker Hgts, OH/St. Ignatius (PS)
Ryan Bruen	09	6' 0"/175	D	Morristown, NJ/Morristown (HS)
Tim Connolly	07	6' 2"/185	D	Skaneateles, NY/Skaneateles (HS)
Rich Fazio	07	5'10"/165	F	Scarsdale, NY/Scarsdale (HS)
Connor Field	10	5' 7"/180	D	Manalapan, NJ/St. John Vianney (PS)
Michael Fitzgerald	08	6' 2"/175	F	Scranton, PA/Scranton (PS)
Brian Flanagan	10	5'11"/180	F	Manchester Center, VT/Burr & Burton (PS)
John Forhecz	07	5' 8"/190	F	Old Tappan, NJ/Northern Valley (HS)
Philip Furtak	10	5' 8"/185	F	Philadelphia, PA/Father Judge (PS)
Scott Greene	10	6' 1"/185	D	Cedar Knolls, NJ/Whippany Park (HS)
Kevin Grunther	10	5'10"/180	F	Medford, NJ/Bishop Eustace (PS)
Dan Hertler	07	5'11"/165	D	Garden City, NJ/Garden City (HS)
Steven Kelley	08	5'10"/160	F	Freeport, NY/Kinnelon (HS)
Ryan Kleinschmidt	09	6' 0"/170	F	Valley Stream, NY/Kellenberg (HS)
Edmund Kocienda	10	6' 0"/180	F	Mineola, NY/Holy Trinity (PS)
Harry Lawall	08	5' 8"/165	F	Newtown, PA/Holy Ghost (PS)
Colin Lengyel	09	5'10"/165	G	Baltimore, MD/Mount St. Joseph (PS)
Jerry Malanga	10	6' 2"/210	F	Lavallette, NJ/Msgr. Donovan (PS)
Zac McAnally	08	6' 0"/190	D	Downington, PA/Bishop Shanahan (PS)
Patrick Nerney	10	5'10"/175	F	Ramsey, NJ/Ramsey (HS)
Mike Pace	09	5'11"/175	F	Branchburg, NY/St. Joseph's (PS)
Bobby Peckham	07	6' 1"/170	F	Dennisport, MA/Portsmouth Abbey (NEPSAC)
Joseph Previti	08	5' 5"/150	F	Hemstead, NY/Kellenberg (HS)
Dan Quinn	10	6' 1"/175	F	Marlboro, NJ/Marlboro (HS)
Chris Rji	10	5'10"/180	G	Belmar, NJ/Manasquan (HS)
Ted Rosenberg	09	5'11"/180	D	Philadelphia, PA/Springfield Township (HS)
David Skinner	07	6' 1"/175	G	Chatham, NJ/Chatham (HS)
Dan Stallone	07	5'11"/185	D	S Plainfield, NJ/St. Joseph's Metchuen (PS)
Paul Suggs	09	6' 2"/220	G	Chester, NJ/Mendham (HS)
Eric Teixeira	07	5' 7"/155	F	Avon, CT/Avon (HS)
Matt Torstrup	09	5'11"/175	F	Bridgewater, NJ/Hun (PS)

ROSTER ANALYSIS (SCHOLARSHIPS - 0)

Class		Country		Last Team			
Fr	10	USA	32	US JR A		CDN JR A	ACHA
So	7	Canada		US JR B		CDN JR B	NJCAA
Jr	5	Europe		US PS	15	CDN PS	NCAA
Sr	10	Asia		US HS	17	CDN HS	USNDT
Gr		Other		US Midget		CDN Midget	Other

ADMISSIONS, ENROLLMENT & CAMPUS INFORMATION

Founded 1888	Average acceptance rate - 75 %	Joseph M. Roback - Dean of Adm.
Private, urban campus	Freshman financial aid - 77 %	University of Scranton - St. Thomas Hall
1,672 men / 2,310 women	Early decision application deadline - N/A	800 Linden Street, 406
Tuition, room & board - $ 34 K	Regular application deadline - Mar 1	Scranton, PA 18510-4699
Avg SAT - 1,115 / Avg ACT - 23	Financial aid deadline - Feb 15	O 570.941.7540 / F 570.941.5928

matrix.scranton.edu   matrix.scranton.edu/athletics/at.shtml

SKIDMORE COLLEGE

HOCKEY
EAST

Division 3

HOCKEY STAFF

HEAD COACH
Neil Sinclair *(Middlebury '93)*

ASSISTANT COACHES
Jack Semler *(Vermont '68)*
Matt Vagvolgi *(Union '05)*

HOCKEY OFFICE
Skidmore College
Sports & Recreation #222
815 North Broadway
Saratoga Springs, NY 12866-1632
O 518.580.5374 / F 518.580.5365
nsinclai@skidmore.edu

HOCKEY MEDIA CONTACT
Bill Jones - Sports Info Director
Skidmore College
Sports & Recreation #205
815 North Broadway
Saratoga Springs, NY 12866-1632
O 518.580.5364 / F 518.580.5365
bjones@skidmore.edu

HOCKEY RINK
Saratoga Springs Ice Rink (Off Campus)
30 Weibel Avenue
Saratoga Springs, NY 12866
Size 200' x 100', Capacity 2,000
O 518.583.3744

ATHLETIC DIRECTOR
Gail Cummings-Danson - Athletic Dir.
Skidmore College
Sports & Recreation #216
815 North Broadway
Saratoga Springs, NY 12866-1632
O 518.580.5370
gcumming@skidmore.edu

THOROUGHBREDS PLAYERS

Player	YB GR Ht/Wt	P	Hometown/Last Team
Cam Clark	08 5' 5"/150	F	Indianapolis,IN/Park Tudor (PS)
Matt Czerkowicz	10 5'10"/185	F	Blackstone,MA/Kent (NEPSAC)
Tim Daley	10 5' 9"/170	F	Wilton,NY/Capital District Selects (EJHL)
DJ Delbuono	10 5' 8"/155	G	Westborough,MA/New England Huskies (EJHL)
Ernie Econimides	10 6' 0"/180	F	Buzzards Bay,MA/Tabor (NEPSAC)
Anthony Ferri	10 5' 8"/160	F	Jersey City,NJ/Loomis Chaffee (NEPSAC)
Joe Forstbauer	09 6' 2"/195	F	Briarcliff,NY/Rye (PS)
Mike Gibbons	09 5'10"/170	F	Braintree,MA/Xaverian (PS)
Teddy Gowan	09 6' 2"/220	F	Hamilton,NY/Westminster (NEPSAC)
Brady Greco	07 5'10"/175	D	Williamsville,NY/Westminster (NEPSAC)
Rob Hutchinson	07 5' 8"/150	F	Waterville,NY/Trinity-Pawling (NEPSAC)
Steve Keady	09 6' 2"/185	D	Canton,MA/Thayer (NEPSAC)
Eric Lampman	07 5'11"/170	F	Charlotte,VT/Lawrenceville (PS)
Ted Levine	08 5'11"/185	G	New York,NY/Westminster (NEPSAC)
Quinn MacNulty	07 6' 0"/200	D	Lynnfield,MA/St. John's (PS)
Trevor Marshall	08 6' 0"/225	D	Hingham,MA/Thayer (NEPSAC)
Steve Martorana	07 5'10"/170	D	Lakeland,FL/Loomis Chaffee (NEPSAC)
Phil McDavitt	09 5'11"/185	D	Duxbury,MA/Nobles (NEPSAC)
Taylor McKenna	07 6' 0"/195	F	Lake Placid,NY/Kent (NEPSAC)
Charlie Moroni	10 6' 0"/190	D	N Providence,RI/Loomis Chaffee (NEPSAC)
Morgan Nelson	08 5' 9"/170	F	Long Lake,MN/Orono (HS)
Joey Peller	09 5'11"/185	D	Canandaigua,NY/Williston Northampton (NEPSAC)
Nick Petrangelo	10 5'11"/185	D	Feeding Hills,MA/Loomis Chaffee (NEPSAC)
Jimmy Santacroce	10 5'10"/165	G	Lansdale,PA/Wyoming (PS)
Scott Schaub	07 5'11"/170	F	Pennington,NJ/Trinity-Pawling (NEPSAC)
Pat Tyman	09 6' 0"/195	F	W Suffield,CT/Loomis Chaffee (NEPSAC)
Matt Vredenburgh	09 6' 0"/190	F/D	Springfield,VT/New Jersey Hitmen (EJHL)
Chris Webb	10 5'10"/170	F	Holliston,MA/New England Huskies (EJHL)
Tim Welsh	09 6' 0"/180	D	Manchester Ctr,VT/Trinity-Pawling (NEPSAC)

ROSTER ANALYSIS (SCHOLARSHIPS - 0)

Class		Country		Last Team	
Fr	9	USA	29	US JR A	CDN JR A	ACHA
So	9	Canada		US JR B	4	CDN JR B	NJCAA
Jr	4	Europe		US PS	24	CDN PS	NCAA
Sr	7	Asia		US HS	1	CDN HS	USNDT
Gr		Other		US Midget		CDN Midget	Other

ADMISSIONS, ENROLLMENT & CAMPUS INFORMATION

Founded 1903	Average acceptance rate - 48 %	Mary Lou W. Bates - Director Admissions
Private, suburban campus	Freshman financial aid - 99 %	Skidmore College
1,122 men / 1,487 women	Early decision application deadline - Dec 1	815 North Broadway
Tuition, room & board - $ 40 K	Regular application deadline - Jan 15	Saratoga Springs, NY 12866-1632
Avg SAT - 1,200 / Avg ACT - 28	Financial aid deadline - Jan 15	O 518.580.5570 / F 518.580.5584

www.skidmore.edu

www2.skidmore.edu/athletics/index.cfm

UNIV. OF SOUTHERN CALIFORNIA

Division 2

HOCKEY STAFF

HEAD COACH
Mark Wilbur *(USC '85)*

ASSISTANT COACHES
Keith Rasmussen
Manny Ramirez *(USC '86)*

HOCKEY OFFICE
University of Southern California
Lyon University Center
Los Angeles, CA 90089-2500
O 310.849.9066/ F 310.544.4293
coach@uscicehockey.com

HOCKEY MANAGER
Jim Wilbur - Dir. of Hockey Operations
PO Box 1474
Lake Arrowhead, CA 92352
O 909.336.4304
jim.usc@verizon.net

HOCKEY RINK
Anaheim Ice (Off Campus)
300 West Lincoln Avenue
Anaheim, CA 92805
Size 200' x 100', Capacity - 1,800
O 714.535.7465

HOCKEY PRESIDENT
Rich Dyer - Team President
president@uscicehockey.com

TROJANS PLAYERS

Player	YB	GR Ht/Wt	P	Hometown/Last Team
Daylin Ackerman	09	5'11"/175	D	Woodland Hills,CA
Cory Adler	08	5'11"/190	F	Newport Beach,CA
Jonny Baron	09	6'0"/170	F	Los Angeles,CA
Jason Bush	10	6'0"/180	D	Redlands, CA
Matt Buttweiler	09	6'1"/210	G	Lakeville,MN
Matthew Carter-Tracy	07	5'10"/170	F	Darien,CT
Chris Dralla	07	6'1"/180	F	Los Altos,CA
Richard Dyer	07	5'11"/180	F	Simi Valley,CA
Ryan Farias	09	5'10"/185	F	Glendale,CA
Mark Farrish	07	6'0"/180	F	Marietta,GA
Jason Filantres	GR	5'8"/165	F	San Diego,CA
Joshua Frazier	10	5'10"/160	F	Alta Loma,CA
Mark Gangloff	07	6'0"/180	F	Buffalo,NY
Michael Gawlik	10	6'0"/185	D	Indianapolis,IN
Michael Joyce	10	5'7"/160	F	Mendota Heights,MN
Kevin Kliman	GR	6 3"/195	G	Toronto,ON
Mark Koechling	08	5'11"/175	F	Essex Fells,NJ
Matt Lewis	09	5'9"/160	D	San Diego,CA
Michael Mariani	GR	5'11"/185	F	Coral Springs,FL
Jake McKee	GR	6'0"/180	F	Bloomfield,NJ
Tyler McLinn	09	6'0"/180	F	Minneapolis,MN
Mickey Meyer	08	5'11"/160	G	Clinton,NY
Justin O'Neil	GR	5'9"/190	D	South Pasadena,CA
Brent Ozaki	09	5'11"/170	D	Poway,CA
Zach Porter	10	6'0"/185	D	Huntington Beach,CA
Bryan Price	08	6'4"/180	F	New Canaan,CT
Ryan Seals	07	6'2"/205	D	Valencia,CA
Shon Smith	07	5'9"/170	F	Sammamish,WA
Jonathan Stallsmith	09	5'11"/200	D	Hanover,NH

ROSTER ANALYSIS (SCHOLARSHIPS - 0)

Class	Country	Last Team		
Fr	USA	US JR A	CDN JR A	ACHA
So	Canada	US JR B	CDN JR B	NJCAA
Jr	Europe	US PS	CDN PS	NCAA
Sr	Asia	US HS	CDN HS	USNDT
Gr	Other	US Midget	CDN Midget	Other

ADMISSIONS, ENROLLMENT & CAMPUS INFORMATION

Founded 1880	Acceptance rate - 27 %	Laurel Tew - USC Office of Admission
Public urban campus	Freshman financial aid - 100 %	700 Childs Way
7,973 men / 8,298 women	Early decision application deadline - N/A	Los Angeles, CA 90089-0911
Tuition, room & board $ 40 K	Regular application deadline - Jan 10	O 213.740.1111/ F 213.740.6364
Avg SAT - 1,350 / Avg ACT - 29	Transfer application deadline - N/A	Financial Aid 213.740.2666

www.usc.edu   www.uscicehockey.com

UNIVERSITY OF SOUTHERN MAINE

H O C K E Y
EAST

Division 3

HOCKEY STAFF	HUSKIES PLAYERS

HOCKEY STAFF

HEAD COACH
Jeff Beaney *(New England '82)*

ASSISTANT COACHES
Brandon Cordua *(Southern Maine '05)*
Paul Evans

HOCKEY OFFICE
University of Southern Maine
37 College Avenue
Portland, ME 04102
O 207.780.5987 / F 207.780.5182
jbeaney@usm.maine.edu

HOCKEY MEDIA CONTACT
BL Elfring - Sports Info Director
Southern Maine - Hill Gymnasium
37 College Avenue
Gorham, ME 04038
O 207.780.5434 / F 207.780.5182
elfring@usm.maine.edu

HOCKEY RINK
USM Arena (On Campus)
37 College Avenue
Gorham, ME 04038
Size 200' x 100', Capacity 1,000
O 207.780.5991

ATHLETIC DIRECTOR
Albert Bean Jr. - Athletic Director
University of Southern Maine
37 College Avenue
Gorham, ME 04038
O 207.780.5588 / F 207.780.5182
albean@usm.maine.edu

HUSKIES PLAYERS

Player	YB	GR	Ht/Wt	P	Hometown/Last Team
David Beckles	07		6' 2"/200	G	Stamford,CT/SUNY Fredonia (SUNYAC)
Jake Berube	10		5'10"/175	F	Spotsylvania,PA/Boston Bulldogs (AtJHL)
Mark Carragher	07		5' 6"/160	F	Charlottetown,PE/Hoosac (NEPSAC)
Brad Flynn	10		5'10"/185	F	New Glasgow,NS/Weeks Crushers (MarJHL)
Tom Galiani	10		5' 7"/165	F	Lindenhurst,NY/Oswego Admirals (OPJHL)
Josh Giordani	09		5' 8"/160	F	Quincy,MA/Bridgton (NEPSAC)
Eric Graham	09		6' 3"/185	D	N Berwick,ME/Portland Pirates (MJHL)
Chris Helms	07		5' 6"/155	D	Sandwich,MA/Bridgton (NEPSAC)
Ryan Jean	10		5' 9"/195	D	Randolph,MA/Portland Pirates (MJHL)
Steve Jones	10		6' 5"/200	F	Portland,ME/Portland Pirates (MJHL)
Igor Karlov	10		6' 0"/190	F	Huntingdon Vly,PA/Boston Bulldogs (AtJHL)
Matt Lally	10		5' 9"/165	F	Natick,MA/Xaverian (PS)
Ben Loss	09		6' 1"/190	D	Wilmette,IL/Valley Warriors (EJHL)
Dane Marshall	08		5' 9"/185	D	Yarmouth,NS/Upper Canada (PS)
Tony Matt	10		5'10"/165	F	Newburyport,MA/Bridgton (NEPSAC)
Eric Morgani	09		6' 0"/185	D/F	Reading,MA/Bridgton (NEPSAC)
Tyler Ravlo	08		5'11"/190	G	Yarmouth,NS/Pembroke Lumber Kings (CJHL)
Aaron Runner	10		6' 0"/185	G	Alpharetta,GA/Boston Bulldogs (AtJHL)
Marc Santuccio	07		6' 1"/175	F	Gloucester,MA/Bridgton (NEPSAC)
Bobby Siers	07		6' 0"/185	F	Mt Prospect,IL/Hill (PS)
Jordan Skinner	10		6' 2"/205	D	London,ON/Milton Icehawks (OPJHL)
Steve Sloper	07		6' 2"/185	D	Concord,NH/Boston Bulldogs (AtJHL)
Kyle Smith	09		5'11"/180	F	Auburn,ME/Portland Pirates (MJHL)
Chris Sparkes	07		6' 4"/195	F	St. John's,NF/Bridgton (NEPSAC)
Mike Stevens	08		6' 2"/185	F	Dover,NH/Boston Bulldogs (AtJHL)
Ryan Sullivan	08		6' 2"/195	F	Newton,MA/Bridgton (NEPSAC)
Chris Travis	10		6' 0"/185	F	Scituate,MA/Bridgton (NEPSAC)
Brett Yancey	07		6' 1"/200	D	Natick,MA/Bridgton (NEPSAC)
Carmine Vetrano	10		6' 0"/185	G	Kings Pk,NY/Hudson Valley Eagles (MJHL)
Steve Wardynski	08		5'10"/180	F/D	Malden,MA/Malden (PS)
Evan Williams	08		5' 7"/175	F	Gilford,NH/Holderness (NEPSAC)

ROSTER ANALYSIS (SCHOLARSHIPS - 0)

Class		Country		Last Team					
Fr	12	USA	25	US JR A		CDN JR A	4	ACHA	
So	5	Canada	6	US JR B	11	CDN JR B		NJCAA	
Jr	6	Europe		US PS	14	CDN PS	1	NCAA	1
Sr	8	Asia		US HS		CDN HS		USNDT	
Gr		Other		US Midget		CDN Midget		Other	

ADMISSIONS, ENROLLMENT & CAMPUS INFORMATION

Founded 1878	Average acceptance rate - 75 %	David M. Parani - Admissions Director
Public, urban campus	Freshman financial aid - 71 %	University of Southern Maine
2,737 men / 4,105 women	Early decision application deadline - N/A	37 College Avenue
Tuition, room & board - $ 12 K / $ 20 K	Regular application deadline - Feb 15	Gorham, ME 04038-1088
Avg SAT - 1,040 / Avg ACT - 19	Financial aid deadline - Feb 15	O 207.780.5670 / F 207.780.5670

www.usm.maine.edu

www.usm.maine.edu/athletics/

SOUTHERN NEW HAMPSHIRE UNIV.

Division 2

<table>
<tr><td colspan="2">

HOCKEY STAFF

HEAD COACH
Ken Hutchins *(So. New Hampshire)*

ASSISTANT COACHES
Dave Dobrowski
John Nanof
Ross Smith

HOCKEY OFFICE
Southern New Hampshire University
Athletic Department
2500 North River Road
Manchester, NH 03106
O 603.645.9769 / F 603.645.9686
k.hutchins@snhu.edu

HOCKEY MEDIA CONTACT
Tom McDermott - Sports Info Director
So. New Hampshire Univ. - Athletics
2500 North River Road
Manchester, NH 03106
O 603.645.9638 / F 603.645.9686
t.mcdermott@snhu.edu

HOCKEY RINK
SNHU Ice Rink (On Campus)
25 North River Road
Manchester, NH 03106
Size ' x ', Capacity

ATHLETIC DIRECTOR
Chip Polak - Athletic Director
Southern New Hampshire University
2500 North River Road
Manchester, NH 03106-1045
O 603.645.9604 / F 603.645.9686
j.polak@snhu.edu

</td></tr>
</table>

PENMEN PLAYERS

Player	YB	GR	Ht/Wt	P	Hometown/Last Team
Kyle Bousquet	07		6'2"/220	D	E Longmeadow,MA/East Longmeadow (HS)
Ken Burlage	07		6'1"/180	D	Dover,NH/Bridgewater Bandits (EJHL)
Dave Carroll	09		5'9"/210	D	Arlington,MA/Bridgton (NEPSAC)
Dominic Cavallaro	07		6'1"/195	D	Revere,MA/Boston Blackhawks (EJHL)
Matt Courchesne	09		6'0"/180	G	Bow,NH/Exeter Seawolves (AEHL)
Ryan DiBartolomeo	10		5'9"/175	F	Leominster,MA/New England Huskies (EJHL)
Dominic DiMarzo	08		5'10"/185	F	E Boston,MA/Massachusetts Boston (ECAC East)
Joshua Douglas	08		5'9"/175	F	Mississauga,ON/Bridgton (NEPSAC)
Matt Farley	10		6'2"/200	F	Halifax,MA/Coyle & Cassidy (PS)
John Frey	10		5'9"/175	F	Westminster,CO/Cushing (NEPSAC)
Andrew Goduco	08		5'7"/165	F	Marlborough,MA/Marlborough (HS)
Josh Goodman	08		5'8"/175	D	Highland Hls,NY/Peterborough Bees (OPJHL)
Greg Gugumuck	09		6'0"/205	D	Malverne,NY/Full Stride Flyers (EmJHL)
Chris Gunn	08		6'0"/180	F	Wethersfield,CT/Hartford Wolfpack (AtJHL)
Brandon Hammermeister	08		5'11"/180	F	Calgary,AB/Fernie Ghostriders (NAHL)
Kent Honeyman	10		6'1"/190	D	Marietta,GA/Cushing (NEPSAC)
Phil LaCasse	10		6'2"/210	D	Concord,NH/Concord (HS)
Matt Lemay	08		6'0"/195	F	Biddeford,ME/Portland Pirates (MJHL)
Mark Lodge	10		5'9"/170	D	Alfred,ME/Laconia Leafs (AtJHL)
Thomas Ohlson	10		5'11"/190	F	York,ME/Bridgton (NEPSAC)
Ethan Porter	07		5'9"/180	F	Chino Hills,CA/Salem Ice Dogs (EmJHL)
Chet Riley	07		6'2"/175	F	Randolph,MA/Boston College (PS)
Michael Sabo	08		5'11"/165	F	S Windsor,CT/South Windsor (HS)
Matt Sayer	10		6'0"/190	F	Lowell,MA/New England Huskies (EJHL)
Jeff Steer	10		5'9"/165	G	Durham,NH/Proctor (NEPSAC)
Nick Stevenson	10		6'1"/200	D	Bridgewater,MA/Coyle & Cassidy (PS)
Carmine Vetrano	10		6'0"/185	G	Kings Pk,NY/Hudson Valley Eagles (MJHL)
Steve Wardynski	08		5'10"/180	F/D	Malden,MA/Malden (PS)
Evan Williams	08		5'7"/175	F	Gilford,NH/Holderness (NEPSAC)

ROSTER ANALYSIS (SCHOLARSHIPS - 0)

Class		Country		Last Team					
Fr	11	USA	27	US JR A	1	CDN JR A	1	ACHA	
So	3	Canada	2	US JR B	11	CDN JR B		NJCAA	
Jr	10	Europe		US PS	11	CDN PS		NCAA	1
Sr	5	Asia		US HS	4	CDN HS		USNDT	
Gr		Other		US Midget		CDN Midget		Other	

ADMISSIONS, ENROLLMENT & CAMPUS INFORMATION

Founded 1932	Average acceptance rate - 74 %	Brad Poznanski - Admissions Director
Private, suburban campus	Freshman financial aid - %	New Hampshire College
765 men / 936 women	Early decision application deadline - N/A	2500 North River Road
Tuition, room & board - $ 29 K	Regular application deadline - Mar 15	Manchester, NH 03106-1045
Avg SAT - 990	Financial aid deadline - Mar 15	O 603.645.9611 / F 603.645.9693

STONEHILL COLLEGE

NCAA

Division 2

<table>
<tr><td colspan="2">

HOCKEY STAFF

</td><td colspan="5">

SKYHAWKS PLAYERS

</td></tr>
</table>

Player	YB	GR	Ht/Wt	P	Hometown/Last Team
Frank Amato	85	09	6'1"/190	F	W Springfield,MA/Loomis Chaffee (NEPSAC)
Mike Cafferty	86	09	5'6"/160	F	Arlington,MA/Bridgton (NEPSAC)
Zachary Cantin	87	10	6'4"/255	F	Walpole,MA/Xaverian (PS)
Rob Carpenter	86	08	6'0"/195	F	Cohasset,MA/Cohasset (HS)
Frank Cavaliere	85	09	5'10"/215	D	Winthrop,MA/St. John's (PS)
Brendan Conners	86	10	5'11"/195	D	Lowell,MA/Xaverian (PS)
Matt Curran	85	08	5'10"/165	F	Scarborough,ME/North Yarmouth (PS)
Mike Daraio	88	10	5'8"/155	F	Harrison,NY/Harrison (HS)
Brian Davis	85	08	5'9"/165	F	Foxboro,MA/Foxboro (HS)
Joe Durkin	87	09	6'0"/195	D	Scituate,MA/Cohasset (HS)
John Durkin	85	08	5'8"/165	F	Scituate,MA/Pomfret (NEPSAC)
Chase Feole	85	08	5'8"/175	F	Windham,NH/Salem Ice Dogs (EmJHL)
James Florentino	87	09	6'2"/215	D	W Roxbury,MA/Xaverian (PS)
Corey Glynn	88	10	6'1"/200	D	Hamden,CT/Notre Dame (PS)
Matt Gorman	84	07	5'11"/170	G	Southboro,MA/St. John's (PS)
Josh Green	82	07	5'9"/155	G	Mendon,MA/Gunnery (NEPSAC)
James Killeen	85	09	5'10"/180	D	Derry,NH/Proctor (NEPSAC)
Billy Ninteau	85	09	6'3"/215	D	Litchfield,NH/Bishop Guertin (PS)
Brendan O'Brien	84	09	5'10"/185	F	Braintree,MA/Deerfield (NEPSAC)
Paul Reissfelder	86	09	6'1"/205	F	Plymouth,MA/Tilton (NEPSAC)
Chris Rogers	86	10	5'8"/170	F	Westford,MA/Pomfret (NEPSAC)
Pete Roundy	86	10	5'10"/170	F	Simsbury,CT/Kimball Union (NEPSAC)
John Sommers	86	09	5'11"/190	F	Manchester,CT/Kent (NEPSAC)
Evan Spencer	85	07	6'1"/205	D	Billerica,MA/Billerica (HS)
David Tanner	87	10	5'10"/180	G	Ipswich,MA/Austin (PS)
Anthony Zanetti	85	08	6'2"/190	F	Ludlow,MA/Springfield Cathedral (PS)

HEAD COACH
Scott Harlow *(Boston College '86)*

ASSISTANT COACHES
Mark Barry
Garry Hebert

HOCKEY OFFICE
Stonehill College
Athletic Office
North Easton, MA 02357
O 508.565.1598/F 508.565.1460
sharlow@stonehill.edu

HOCKEY MEDIA CONTACT
Jim Seavey - Sports Info Director
Stonehill College - Athletic Office
North Easton, MA 02357
O 508.565.1352/F 508.565.1504
jseavey@stonehill.edu

HOCKEY RINK
Bridgewater Ice Arena (Off Campus)
20 Bedford Park
Bridgewater, MA 02324
Size 200' x 85', Capacity 1,000

ATHLETIC DIRECTOR
Paula Sullivan - Athletic Director
Stonehill College
320 Washington Street
North Easton, MA 02357-5210
O 508.565.1391/F 508.565.1460
psullivan@stonehill.edu

ROSTER ANALYSIS (SCHOLARSHIPS - 0)

Class		Country		Last Team			
Fr	7	USA	26	US JR A		CDN JR A	ACHA
So	10	Canada		US JR B	1	CDN JR B	NJCAA
Jr	6	Europe		US PS	20	CDN PS	NCAA
Sr	3	Asia		US HS	5	CDN HS	USNDT
Gr		Other		US Midget		CDN Midget	Other

<table>
<tr><td colspan="3">

ADMISSIONS, ENROLLMENT & CAMPUS INFORMATION

</td></tr>
</table>

Founded 1948	Average acceptance rate - 57 %	Brian P. Murphy - Admissions Director
Private, suburban campus	Freshman financial aid - 82 %	Stonehill College
888 men / 1,513 women	Early decision application deadline - Nov 1	320 Washington Street
Tuition, room & board - $ 37 K	Regular application deadline - Jan 15	Easton, MA 02357-5210
Avg SAT - 1,180 / Avg ACT - 25	Financial aid deadline - Feb 1	O 508.565.1373/F 508.565.1545

www.stonehill.edu   www.stonehillskyhawks.com

SUFFOLK UNIVERSITY

Division 3

HOCKEY STAFF

HEAD COACH
Chris Glionna *(Suffolk '95)*

ASSISTANT COACHES
John Gilpatrick *(Suffolk '99)*
Greg Fowke *(Suffolk '93)*
Ken Frates *(Boston State '97)*

HOCKEY OFFICE
Suffolk University
41 Temple Street
Boston, MA 02114-4280
S 617.573.8379 / O 617.227.4935
cglionna@aol.com

HOCKEY MEDIA CONTACT
Brenda Laymance - Sports Info Director
Suffolk University
8 Ashburton Place
Beacon Hill
Boston, MA 02114-2770
O 617.573.8379 / F 617.227.4935
blaymanc@suffolk.edu

HOCKEY RINK
Brown Arena (Off Campus)
285 Babcock Street
Boston, MA 02215
Size 200' x 85', Capacity 3,684
O 617.573.8447

ATHLETIC DIRECTOR
James E. Nelson - Athletic Director
Suffolk University
41 Temple Street
Boston, MA 02114-4280
O 617.573.8379 / F 617.227.4935
jnelson@suffolk.edu

RAMS PLAYERS

Player	YB	GR	Ht/Wt	P	Hometown/Last Team
Kevin Adam		07	5'10"/195	G	Peabody,MA/Salem State (ECAC East)
Josh Barboza	84	08	6' 2"/195	D	New Bedford,MA/Bridgewater Bandits (EJHL)
Blaise Belfiore	86	09	5'11"/185	G	Brewster,NY/Philadelphia (AtJHL)
Sean Bertoni	84	07	5' 9"/175	G	Franklin,MA/Massachusetts Boston (ECAC East)
Joe Bonner	86	10	5' 7"/150	F	Londonderry,NH/Brewster (NEPSAC)
Andrew Christopher	85	09	6' 2"/185	D	Winchester,MA/Winchendon (NEPSAC)
Brian Collins	85	10	6' 0"/185	F	Hingham,MA/Tilton (NEPSAC)
Ryan Collins	85	09	5' 8"/165	F	Amesbury,MA/Laconia Leafs (AtJHL)
Dan Conklin		10	5'11"/185	F	Eaton Rapids,MI/Walpole Stars (EJHL)
Ryan Daly	86	10	5' 8"/160	F	Wayland,MA/Rivers (NEPSAC)
Nick Davis	85	10	6' 1"/205	D	Pittsburgh,PA/Northern Mass Cyclones (AtJHL)
John Delaney	84	07	5' 7"/160	F	Quincy,MA/Archbishop Williams (PS)
Joe Drago	87	10	5'11"/185	D	Waltham,MA/Boston Blackhawks (IJHL)
Carl Ellis	84	07	5' 8"/160	F	Gloucester,MA/Kimball Union (NEPSAC)
Bill Galvin	86	09	5'11"/190	F	Canton,MA/Hebron (NEPSAC)
Chris Galvin		10		F	Medford,MA/Medford (HS)
Bill Gilbert		10	5' 9"/160	G	Forestdale,MA/Bridgewater Bandits (EJHL)
Mark Grignon	85	09	5' 7"/145	G	Grosse Pt,MI/Hoosac (NEPSAC)
Sam Kessler	84	10	6' 1"/185	D	Dayton,OH/Boston Blackhawks (IJHL)
Jim Mellon	86	10	5'11"/180	F	Vail,CO/Laconia Leafs (AtJHL)
Mike Mondello	88	10	5' 8"/180	F	Revere,MA/St. Mary's (PS)
Trevor Moss	86	10	6' 3"/210	F	Eastham,MA/Williston Northampton (NEPSAC)
Bryan Myers	86	09	6' 3"/200	D	Rochester,NY/SUNY Morrisville (NJCAA)
Dan Pencinger	85	08	5' 9"/175	F	Randolph,NJ/Trinity-Pawling (NEPSAC)
Tim Recio	84	08	5'10"/180	D	Pittsburgh,PA/Massachusetts Boston (ECAC East)
Andrew Redvanly		08	5'11"/185	F	Hillsdale,NJ/New Jersey Avalanche (MJHL)
John Rocchio	85	09	5'10"/175	F	E Greenwich,RI/Bridgewater Bandits (EJHL)
Mitch Sabo		09	6' 2"/205	D	Bell Canyon,CA/Lawrence (MCHA)
Bryan Smusz		10		F	Daleville,MA/Laconia Leafs (AtJHL)
Mike Squillaciotti		08	5' 8"/185	D	Medford,MA/Minutemen Flames (IJHL)
Kyle Taylor	87	10	5'11"/195	D	Falmouth,MA/Vermont (NEPSAC)
Dave Vanderberg		10	5'11"/175	F	CA/St. George's (NEPSAC)
Scott Zanolli	85	09	5'10"/170	F	Tracy,CA/Boston Blackhawks (IJHL)

ROSTER ANALYSIS (SCHOLARSHIPS - 0)

Class		Country		Last Team				
Fr	15	USA	33	US JR A		CDN JR A		ACHA
So	9	Canada	1	US JR B	14	CDN JR B		NJCAA	1
Jr	5	Europe	1	US PS	13	CDN PS		NCAA	4
Sr	4	Asia		US HS	1	CDN HS		USNDT
Gr		Other		US Midget		CDN Midget		Other

ADMISSIONS, ENROLLMENT & CAMPUS INFORMATION

Founded 1906	Average acceptance rate - 85 %	Walter Caffey - Admissions Director
Private, urban campus	Freshman financial aid - 57 %	Suffolk University
1,740 men / 2,504 women	Early decision application deadline - N/A	41 Temple Street
Tuition, room & board - $ 34 K	Regular application deadline - Mar 1	Boston, MA 02108-2770
Avg SAT - 1,000 / Avg ACT - 20	Financial aid deadline - Mar 1	O 617.573.8460 / F 617.742.4291

www.suffolk.edu   www.suffolk.edu/athletics/

SUNY - BROCKPORT

Division 3

HOCKEY STAFF

HEAD COACH
Brian Dickinson *(N. Adams State '88)*

ASSISTANT COACH
Mark Digby *(SUNY-Brockport '05)*

HOCKEY OFFICE
SUNY-Brockport
Tuttle North Athletic Complex #B326
Brockport, NY 14420-2989
O 716.395.5351/ F 716.395.2160
bdickins@brockport.edu

HOCKEY MEDIA CONTACT
Kelly Vergin - Sports Info Director
SUNY-Brockport
Tuttle Building
Brockport, NY 14420-2989
O 716.395.2218/ F 716.395.2160
kvergin@brockport.edu

HOCKEY RINK
Tuttle North Ice Arena (On Campus)
New Campus Drive
Brockport, NY 14420
Size 185' x 85', Capacity 2,000
O 716.395.5351

ATHLETIC DIRECTOR
Linda J. Case - Athletic Director
SUNY-Brockport
Tuttle Building
Brockport, NY 14420-2989
O 716.395.5328/ F 716.395.2160
lcase@brockport.edu

GOLDEN EAGLES PLAYERS

Player	YB	GR	Ht/Wt	P	Hometown/Last Team
Aaron Boyer	84	09	6' 2"/190	F	Calgary,AB/Borderland Thunder (SIJHL)
Chris Brown	84	08	6' 1"/195	D	Toronto,ON/North York Rangers (OPJHL)
Craig Carlyle	84	09	5'11"/200	D	Winnipeg,MB/Aurora Tigers (OPJHL)
Tim Crowley	84	09	5'10"/170	F	Brasher Fls,NY/Cobourg Cougars (OPJHL)
Jason Dolgy	85	08	6' 1"/180	F	Montreal,QC/Williston Northampton (NEPSAC)
Richard Gates	83	08	5'10"/185	F	W Monroe,NY/Connecticut Wolves (MJHL)
Mike Gershon	84	09	5'10"/195	D	Sparta,NJ/St. Michael's (PS)
John Gleason	83	08	6' 3"/225	F	Soldotna,AK/Thornhill Majors ()
Chris Koras	83	08	6' 4"/220	F	Toronto,ON/Oakville Blades (OPJHL)
Anthony Lecesse	07		6' 1"/200	D	Rochester,NY/SUNY Plattsburgh (SUNYAC)
AJ Maio	81	07	5' 5"/185	F	Rochester,NY/Gates-Chili (HS)
Tony Marinello	85	08	5'11"/190	F	Clifton,NY/Capital District Selects (EJHL)
Sean O'Malley	10		5' 9"/165	F	Lakewood,OH/Syracuse Stars (EJHL)
Mark Pelligra	10		5' 4"/140	F	Webster,NY/Monroe (NJCAA)
Gordon Pritchard	83	08	5'10"/170	F	Yorktown,SK/Neepawa Natives (ManJHL)
BJ Quinto	84	09	6' 0"/195	F	King City,ON/Bramalea Blues (OPJHL)
Blake Rielly	84	09	5'10"/215	F	Newport Bch,CA/Surrey Eagles (BCHL)
Lucas Schott	10		5'10"/180	F	Erin,ON/North Bay Skyhawks (NOJHL)
Geoff Schweikhard	84	08	5'10"/155	F	Orchard Pk,NY/Buffalo Lightning (OPJHL)
Greg Schwind	84	08	5' 9"/180	F	Hilton,NY/Penn State (ACHA)
Steve Seedhouse	86	08	6' 0"/200	F	Whitting,ON/Bowmanville Eagles (OPJHL)
Todd Sheridan	10		6' 3"/205	G	Edison,NJ/Sarnia Blast (WOJHL)
Derek Spence	86	08	6' 1"/195	G	Kitchener,ON/Kitchener (Midget AAA)
Greg Van'tHof		08	6' 0"/170	G	Toronto,ON/Markham Waxers (OPJHL)
Steve Wowchuk	83	08	6' 2"/195	D	Merritt,BC/Campbell River Storm (VIJHL)

ROSTER ANALYSIS (SCHOLARSHIPS - 0)

Class		Country		Last Team					
Fr	4	USA	13	US JR A		CDN JR A	13	ACHA	1
So	6	Canada	12	US JR B	3	CDN JR B	2	NJCAA	1
Jr	13	Europe		US PS	1	CDN PS	1	NCAA	1
Sr	2	Asia		US HS	1	CDN HS		USNDT	
Gr		Other		US Midget		CDN Midget	1	Other	

ADMISSIONS, ENROLLMENT & CAMPUS INFORMATION

Founded 1867	Average acceptance rate - 50 %	J. Scott Atkinson - Admissions Director
Public, suburban campus	Freshman financial aid - 96 %	SUNY-Brockport
2,947 men / 3,907 women	Early decision application deadline - N/A	Rakov Center
Tuition, room & board - $13 K/ $19 K	Regular application deadline - Feb 1	Brockport, NY 14420-2997
Avg SAT - 1,060/ Avg ACT - 23	Financial aid deadline - Feb 15	O 585.395.2751/ F 585.395.5452

www.brockport.edu

www.brockport.edu/~athletics/

SUNY - BUFFALO STATE

Division 3

<table>
<tr><th colspan="2">HOCKEY STAFF</th></tr>
</table>

HOCKEY STAFF

HEAD COACH
Nick Carriere *(Niagara '01)*

ASSISTANT COACHES
Jason Greenway *(Findlay '02)*
Cory Mickey *(So. New Hampshire '05)*
Bob Janosz *(Canisius '98)*

HOCKEY OFFICE
SUNY - Buffalo State
Houston Gym
1300 Elmwood Avenue
Buffalo, NY 14222
O 716.878.3396 / F 716.878.6538
carrienr@buffalostate.edu

HOCKEY MEDIA CONTACT
Jeff Ventura - Sports Info Director
SUNY - Buffalo State
1300 Elmwood Avenue
Buffalo, NY 14222
O 716.878.6030 / F 716.878.6538
venturjm@buffalostate.edu

HOCKEY RINK
Buffalo State Ice Arena (On Campus)
1300 Elmwood Avenue
Buffalo, NY 14222
Size 200' x 85', Capacity 1,800
O 716.878.6030

ATHLETIC DIRECTOR
Jerry Boyes - Athletic Director
SUNY - Buffalo State
1300 Elmwood Avenue
Buffalo, NY 14222
O 716.878.6534 / F 716.878.3401
boyesjs@buffalostate.edu

BENGALS PLAYERS

Player	YB	GR	Ht/Wt	P	Hometown/Last Team
Jesse Adair	10		6'1"/185	D	Brampton,ON/Oakville Blades (OPJHL)
Mike Ansell	83	08	5'10"/190	D	Ashburn,VA/Fort Erie Meteors (GHJHL)
Cody Cole	84	09	5'10"/200	D	St. Catharines,ON/St. Catharines Falcons (GHJHL)
Joe Curry		09	5'10"/190	F	Indian River,ON/Port Colborne Sailors (GHJHL)
Richard Curtis	86	09	5'10"/170	F	Ottsville,PA/Philadelphia Little Flyers (MJHL)
Mike DeMarco	82	07	5'6"/150	F	Niagara Fls,NY/Fort Erie Meteors (GHJHL)
Johnny Duco		08	5'10"/180	F	Toronto,ON/SUNY Oswego (SUNYAC)
Mike Fiume		08	5'6"/185	F	King City,ON/Neumann (ECAC West)
Paul Gagnon	84	08	5'9"/185	F	Troy,MI/Binghamton Jr Senators (EmJHL)
Kyle Gunn-Taylor	10		5'9"/205	G	W Seneca,NY/Port Hope Predators (OPJHL)
Jason Hill	84	09	5'9"/175	F	Niagara Fls,NY/Welland Canadiens (GHJHL)
Dave Koch	10		5'7"/155	F	Hamburg,NY/St. Francis (PS)
Shareef Labreche	10		5'10"/185	F	Markham,ON/Markham Waxers (OPJHL)
Clay Lewis	07		6'4"/230	D	Boca Raton,FL/Cansius (AHL)
Mike Luzarraga	10		5'9"/175	F	Sugarland,TX/Walpole Express (AtJHL)
Justin Merritt	10		6'1"/190	D	Burlington,ON/Hamilton Red Wings (OPJHL)
Jeff Mok	83	08	5'11"/215	D	Richmond Hill,ON/North York Rangers (OPJHL)
Shawn O'Donoghue	83	09	6'0"/190	F	Carbondale,IL/Findlay Wolfpack (CEHL)
Ryan Ramage	10		6'0"/175	D	Ft Erie,ON/Brampton Capitals (OPJHL)
Paul-Michael Rivest	10		6'1"/175	F	Whitby,ON/Bowmanville Eagles (OPJHL)
David Roy	84	09	5'9"/165	F	Berlin,NH/Binghamton Jr Senators (EmJHL)
Sean Sheehan	82	07	6'3"/215	G	Mt Laurel,NJ/Abitibi Ekimos (NOJHL)
Dennis Sicard	10		5'11"/185	F	Cobourg,ON/Port Hope Predators (OPJHL)
Johnathan Sourwine	10		6'2"/190	G	Redwood,NY/Gananoque Islanders ()
D'Arcy Thomas	10		5'11"/210	F	Gatineau,QC/LaFleche Titans (QJAHL)
Travis Whitehead	09		6'1"/205	F	Cambridge,ON/Wisconsin Superior (NCHA)

ROSTER ANALYSIS (SCHOLARSHIPS - 0)

Class		Country		Last Team					
Fr	11	USA	13	US JR A		CDN JR A	10	ACHA	
So	7	Canada	13	US JR B	5	CDN JR B	5	NJCAA	4
Jr	5	Europe		US PS	1	CDN PS		NCAA	
Sr	3	Asia		US HS		CDN HS		USNDT	
Gr		Other		US Midget		CDN Midget		Other	

ADMISSIONS, ENROLLMENT & CAMPUS INFORMATION

Founded 1867
Public, suburban campus
9,105 men / 8,404 women
Tuition, room & board - $ 13 K / $ 20 K
Avg SAT - 1,160 / Avg ACT - 21

Average acceptance rate - 56 %
Freshman financial aid - 70 %
Early decision application deadline - Nov 15
Regular application deadline - Mar 1
Financial aid deadline - Mar 1

Lesa Loritts - Admissions Director
SUNY - Buffalo State
1300 Elmwood Avenue
Buffalo, NY 14222
O 716.878.4017 / F 716.878.6100

SUNY - CORTLAND

Division 3

HOCKEY STAFF

HEAD COACH
Joe Baldarotta *(Wi-Stevens Pt)*

ASSISTANT COACHES
Josh Murray *(SUNY-Oswego '94)*
Howie Thomas

HOCKEY OFFICE
SUNY-Cortland
Park Center
PO Box 2000
Cortland, NY 13045
O 607.753.4990/ F 607.753.4929
@cortland.edu

HOCKEY MEDIA CONTACT
Fran Elia - Sports Info Director
SUNY-Cortland
Park Center
PO Box 2000
Cortland, NY 13045
O 607.753.5673/ F 607.753.5789
eliaf@cortland.edu

HOCKEY RINK
Alumni Arena (On Campus)
SUNY-Cortland
Park Center
Cortland, NY 13045
Size 200' x 85', Capacity 2,500
O 607.753.5673

ATHLETIC DIRECTOR
Joan Sitterly - Athletic Director
SUNY-Cortland
Park Center
PO Box 2000
Cortland, NY 13045
O 607.753.4953/ F 607.753.4929
sitterly@cortland.edu

RED DRAGONS PLAYERS

Player	YB	GR	Ht/Wt	P	Hometown/Last Team
Buddy Anderson	82	07	5'10"/195	D	Washington Tsp,NJ/Bridgewater Bandits (EJHL)
Ben Binga	87	10	5' 8"/175	G	Rochester,NY/Syracuse Stars (OPJHL)
Justin Bodine	83	08	6' 4"/200	F	N Massapequa,NY/New England (ECAC East)
Jon Bova	86	08	5'10"/170	G	Camillus,NY/West Genesee (HS)
Brennan Briggs	85	08	5' 9"/155	F	Batavia,NY/Batavia (HS)
Nick Catanzaro	83	09	5' 7"/165	F	Buffalo,NY/Boston Harbor Wolves (EJHL)
Chris Corso	86	09	6' 2"/210	F	Oceanside,NY/Apple Core (EJHL)
Zach Dehm	85	08	5'11"/195	F	Trumbull,CT/Sacred Heart (AHL)
Peter Deloria	84	07	6' 1"/185	D	Saratoga Spgs,NY/Capital District Selects (EJHL)
Mike Egan	86	09	6' 5"/220	D	Smithtown,NY/Apple Core (EJHL)
Mike Friel	87	10	5'10"/170	F	Oswego,NY/Oswego Generals ()
Matt Goslant	84	08	6' 1"/185	F	Northfield,VT/SUNY Plattsburgh (SUNYAC)
Gerard Heinz	86	10	6' 0"/200	D	Kings Pk,NY/Apple Core (EJHL)
Brian Herlihy	83	07	5' 8"/150	F	Glens Fls,NY/Glens Falls (HS)
Casey Hubbard	85	09	6' 1"/185	D	Ronkonkoma,NY/New York Bobcats (AtJHL)
Taylor Indivero	87	09	5' 8"/155	D	Cicero,NY/Syracuse Stars (EJHL)
Justin Kocent	85	09	6' 0"/210	F	Batavia,NY/Rochester Americans (EmJHL)
Corey LaRoche	85	09	5' 9"/175	F	Bow,NH/Green Mountain Glades (EJHL)
Ryan LaShomb	84	07	6' 1"/170	F	Rush,NY/Aquinas (PS)
Tim Lloyd	87	09	6' 1"/200	D	Oswego,NY/Oswego (HS)
Jason Lojewski	83	07	5' 7"/155	G	Whitesboro,NY/Whitesboro (HS)
Barry McLaughlin	84	08	5' 7"/170	F	Bellport,NY/Bay State Breakers (EJHL)
Mike Mistretta	87	09	5'11"/170	G	Buffalo,NY/Northland (MCHA)
Niles Moore	86	10	5' 8"/200	F	Columbus,OH/Bay State Breakers (EJHL)
Matt Nichols	86	08	5' 9"/165	F	Potsdam,NY/Potsdam (HS)
Patrick Palmisano	85	10	6' 3"/195	F	Ann Arbor,MI/Bay State Breakers (EJHL)
John Perrotta	85	10	6' 0"/180	F	Middletown,NJ/New Jersey Hitmen (EJHL)
Robert Podlucky	84	09	5' 9"/195	D	Grand Island,NY/Buffalo Lightning (OPJHL)
Frank Rizzo	85	10	5' 9"/165	F	St. James,NY/New York Bobcats (AtJHL)
Jon Sandos	85	07	5' 6"/155	D	Oceanside,NY/Apple Core (EJHL)
Nick Shackford	85	10	5' 6"/160	F	Burke,VA/Bay State Breakers (EJHL)

ROSTER ANALYSIS (SCHOLARSHIPS - 0)

Class		Country		Last Team					
Fr	8	USA	31	US JR A		CDN JR A	2	ACHA	
So	10	Canada		US JR B	18	CDN JR B		NJCAA	
Jr	7	Europe		US PS	1	CDN PS		NCAA	4
Sr	6	Asia		US HS	6	CDN HS		USNDT	
Gr		Other		US Midget		CDN Midget		Other	

ADMISSIONS, ENROLLMENT & CAMPUS INFORMATION

Founded 1868
Public, urban campus
2,300 men / 3,300 women
Tuition, room & board - $ 13 K/ $ 19 K
Avg SAT - 1,075

Average acceptance rate - 47 %
Freshman financial aid - 75 %
Early decision application deadline - N/A
Regular application deadline - Mar 1
Financial aid deadline - Apr 1

Gradin Avery - Admissions Director
SUNY-Cortland
PO Box 2000
Cortland, NY 13045
O 607.753.4715/ F 607.753.5998

SUNY - FREDONIA

Division 3

HOCKEY STAFF

HEAD COACH
Jeff Meredith (SUNY-Brockport '82)

ASSISTANT COACH
Greg Heffernan (Concordia '94)

HOCKEY OFFICE
SUNY-Fredonia
51 Dods Hall
Fredonia, NY 14063-3111
O 716.673.3334 / F 716.673.3136
jeffrey.meredith@fredonia.edu

HOCKEY MEDIA CONTACT
Jerry Reilly - Sports Info Director
SUNY-Fredonia
112 Dods Hall
Fredonia, NY 14063-3111
O 716.673.3100 / F 716.673.3136
jerome.reilly@fredonia.edu

HOCKEY RINK
Steele Hall Arena (On Campus)
SUNY-Fredonia
Fredonia, NY 14063-3111
Size 195' x 78', Capacity 1,100
O 716.673.3233

ATHLETIC DIRECTOR
Greg Prechtl - Athletic Director
SUNY-Fredonia
116 Dods Hall
Fredonia, NY 14063-3111
O 716.673.3101 / F 716.673.3624
gregory.prechtl@fredonia.edu

BLUE DEVILS PLAYERS

Player	YB	GR	Ht/Wt	P	Hometown/Last Team
Steve Albert	84	08	6' 0"/180	D	Port Huron,MI/Sarnia Blast (WOJHL)
Kevin Amborski		10	5'10"/185	G	Bloomfield,NY/Burlington (OPJHL)
Jeff Aonso		10	5'10"/185	F	Toronto,ON/Milton Icehawks (OPJHL)
Wil Barlow	82	07	5' 9"/180	F	Oakville,ON/Oakville Blades (OPJHL)
Richard Boyce	84	09	6' 0"/180	F	Mississauga,ON/Brampton Capitals (OPJHL)
Kyle Bozoian	83	07	6' 1"/195	F	St. Charles,MO/Fairbanks Ice Dogs (NAHL)
Scott Bradley	82	07	5'10"/190	F	Belleville,ON/Conestoga (OCAA)
Mike Bush		10	5'10"/190	F	Ft Gratiot,MI/Petrolia Jets (WOJHL)
Pat Capella		10	5' 8"/155	F	Syracuse,NY/Gunnery (NEPSAC)
Craig Cole		10	6' 1"/205	D	E Islip,NY/Collingwood Blues (OPJHL)
Andrew Dissanayake		10	5' 9"/175	F	Ajax,ON/Pickering Panthers (OPJHL)
Evan DiValentino	83	08	5'11"/210	D	Burlington,ON/Oakville Blades (OPJHL)
Bryan Goudy	84	09	6' 2"/190	F	Port Huron,MI/Sarnia Blast (WOJHL)
Adam Haberman	83	08	6' 2"/210	F	Novi,MI/Sarnia Blast (WOJHL)
Kurt Hogard	84	09	6' 1"/210	D	Thunder Bay,ON/Borderland Thunder (SIJHL)
Don Jaeger	83	07	5'11"/190	D	Grosse Pt Woods,MI/Sarnia Blast (WOJHL)
Kraig Kuzma	82	07	6' 0"/210	F	Muskegon,MI/Capital Centre Pride (NAHL)
Joel Lenius		10	6' 0"/180	F	Markham,ON/Markham Waxers (OPJHL)
Matt McKeown		10		F	Niagara Fls,ON/Niagara Falls (GHJHL)
Joe Muli	82	07	5'11"/160	F	Sioux Lookout,ON/Chatham Maroons (WOJHL)
James Muscatello		10	6' 1"/205	D	Baldwinsville,NY/Northwood (PS)
Tyler Owens		10	5' 9"/170	G	Vernon,CT/Brockville Braves (CJHL)
Matt Pfalzer		10	5'10"/170	D	Getzville,NY/Nichols (PS)
Colin Sarfeh	85	09	5'11"/195	D	Laguna Niguel,CA/Northern Mich. Black Bears (NOJHL)
Tim Schoen		10	5' 9"/175	G	Whitesboro,NY/Walpole Stars (EJHL)
Neal Sheehan	83	08	5' 9"/170	F	Avon Lake,OH/Youngstown Phantoms (NAHL)
Frank Soscia		10	5' 8"/160	D	Richmond Hill,ON/Aurora Tigers (OPJHL)
Pat Street		10	6' 1"/190	G	Annapolis,MD/Gunnery (NEPSAC)
Jeff Sylvester	84	09	6' 1"/195	D	Windsor,ON/Stratford Cullitons (MWJHL)

ROSTER ANALYSIS (SCHOLARSHIPS - 0)

Class		Country		Last Team				
Fr	14	USA	17	US JR A	3	CDN JR A	12	ACHA
So	5	Canada	12	US JR B	1	CDN JR B	8	NJCAA
Jr	4	Europe		US PS	4	CDN PS		NCAA
Sr	6	Asia		US HS		CDN HS		USNDT
Gr		Other		US Midget		CDN Midget		Other	1

ADMISSIONS, ENROLLMENT & CAMPUS INFORMATION

Founded 1826
Public, rural campus
2,023 men / 2,911 women
Tuition, room & board - $ 13 K / $ 19 K
Avg SAT - 1,095 / Avg ACT - 24

Average acceptance rate - 55 %
Freshman financial aid - 67 %
Early decision application deadline - Nov 1
Regular application deadline - rolling
Financial aid deadline - Feb 1

J. Denis Bolton - Admissions Director
SUNY-Fredonia - Dods Hall
Fredonia, NY 14063-3111
O 716.673.3251 / F 716.673.3249

www.fredonia.edu   www.fredonia.edu/athletics/

SUNY - GENESEO

Division 3

HOCKEY STAFF

HEAD COACH
Chris Schultz *(SUNY-Geneseo '97)*

ASSISTANT COACHES
Chris Line *(Clarkson '03)*
Kris Heeres *(SUNY-Geneseo '06)*

HOCKEY OFFICE
SUNY-Geneseo
Wilson Ice Arena
Geneseo, NY 14454-1471
O 716.245.5356/ F 716.245.5347
schultz@geneseo.edu

HOCKEY MEDIA CONTACT
George Gagnier - Sports Info Director
SUNY-Geneseo
Alumni Fieldhouse
Geneseo, NY 14454-1471
O 716.245.5346/ F 716.245.5347
gagnier@geneseo.edu

HOCKEY RINK
Wilson Ice Arena (On Campus)
College Drive
Geneseo, NY 14654
Size 200' x 85', Capacity 3,500
O 716.245.5109

ATHLETIC DIRECTOR
Marilyn Moore - Athletic Director
SUNY-Geneseo
1 College Circle
Geneseo, NY 14454
O 716.245.5345/ F 716.245.5347
moorem@geneseo.edu

KNIGHTS PLAYERS

Player	YB	GR	Ht/Wt	P	Hometown/Last Team
Casey Balog	84	09	6' 2"/210	F	Brockport,NY/Bay State Breakers (EJHL)
Brett Bestwick	82	07	5' 7"/165	F	Nanaimo,BC/Nanaimo Clippers (BCHL)
Dan Brown	86	10	5'11"/200	F	Lancaster,NY/Capital District Selects (EJHL)
Trent Cassan	83	08	6' 1"/200	F	Medora,MB/Yorkton Terriers (SJHL)
Mathieu Cyr	85	08	5' 9"/155	F	New Maryland,NB/Hoosac (NEPSAC)
Denis Desjardins	86	09	5' 8"/165	F	Grand Fls,NB/Kent (NEPSAC)
Dave Dobrinsky	87	10	5' 9"/175	F	Oakville,ON/Bramalea Blues (OPJHL)
Brandon French	85	09	5' 8"/170	F	Ithaca,NY/Boston Harbor Wolves (EJHL)
Sean Hayden	86	09	6' 2"/195	D	Lockport,NY/Capital District Selects (EJHL)
Brett Huras	84	09	6' 1"/195	F	Waterloo,ON/St. Lawrence (ECAC)
Derek Jokic	85	08	5' 9"/185	G	Petersburg,ON/Kitchener Dutchmen (MWJHL)
Steve Jordan	82	07	5'11"/195	D	Coquitlam,BC/Prince George Spruce Kings (BCHL)
Chris Kestell	84	09	5'11"/200	D	Nelson,BC/Nanaimo Clippers (BCHL)
Mike MacDonald	84	07	5' 6"/150	F	New Glasgow,NS/Kent (NEPSAC)
Jeff MacPhee	85	10	6' 2"/200	D	Calgary,AB/Calgary Royals (AJHL)
Mike Morris	84	07	5'11"/170	D	Potsdam,NY/Kent (NEPSAC)
Sebastian Panetta	85	10	5'11"/185	F	Ottawa,ON/Nepean Raiders (CJHL)
Jeff Pasemko	84	09	6' 0"/170	G	Redwater,AB/Sherwood Park Crusaders (AJHL)
Andrew Rebus	85	10	6' 1"/200	D	Kelowna,BC/Victoria Salsa (BCHL)
Greg Richardson	85	10	6' 1"/175	G	Colton,NY/Ottawa Senators (CJHL)
Phil Rose	86	10	5'11"/170	F	Pittsford,NY/Valley Warriors (EJHL)
Steve Sankey	83	08	6' 2"/205	D	N Vancouver,BC/Merritt Centennials (BCHL)
Dave Schroeder	85	10	6' 6"/215	D	St. Charles,MO/Hartford Wolfpack (AtJHL)
Mark Schwamberger	84	07	6' 2"/220	F	Spencerport,NY/USNDT (NAHL)
Ram Sidhu	83	08	6' 1"/180	F	Pt Alberni,BC/Quesnel Millionaires (BCHL)
Mitch Stephens	82	07	6' 2"/165	F	Forrest,MB/Yorkton Terriers (SJHL)
Kelly Stokley	87	10	5'10"/180	F	Chatham,ON/Northwood (PS)
Tyson Terry	82	07	5'10"/200	F	Abbotsford,BC/Wisconsin Superior (NCHA)

ROSTER ANALYSIS (SCHOLARSHIPS - 0)

Class		Country		Last Team					
Fr	9	USA	9	US JR A		CDN JR A	13	ACHA	
So	7	Canada	19	US JR B	6	CDN JR B	1	NJCAA	
Jr	5	Europe		US PS	5	CDN PS		NCAA	2
Sr	7	Asia		US HS		CDN HS		USNDT	1
Gr		Other		US Midget		CDN Midget		Other	

ADMISSIONS, ENROLLMENT & CAMPUS INFORMATION

Founded 1871	Average acceptance rate - 44 %	Kris Shay - Admissions Director
Public, rural campus	Freshman financial aid - 78 %	SUNY-Geneseo
2,311 men / 3,064 women	Early decision application deadline - Nov 15	Erwin Building
Tuition, room & board - $13 K / $19 K	Regular application deadline - Jan 15	Geneseo, NY 14454-1471
Avg SAT - 1,270 / Avg ACT - 27	Financial aid deadline - Feb 15	O 585.245.5571/ F 585.245.5550

SUNY - MORRISVILLE

Division 3

HOCKEY STAFF

HEAD COACH
Earl Utter *(SUNY-Brockport '91)*

ASSISTANT COACH
Ryan Marvin *(SUNY-Brockport '06)*

HOCKEY OFFICE
IcePlex
SUNY-Morrisville
Madison Road
Morrisville, NY 13408
O 315.684.6488/ F 315.684.6672
utterel@morrisville.edu

HOCKEY MEDIA CONTACT
Brandy Wilcox - Sports Information Dir.
PO Box 901
Morrisville, NY 13408
O 315.684.6250/ F 315.684.6252
wilcoxbl@morrisville.edu

HOCKEY RINK
IcePlex
SUNY-Morrisville
Madison Road
Morrisville, NY 13408
O 315.684.6425 / F
Size 185' x 85', Capacity 1,000
Size 185' x 85', Capacity 100

ATHLETIC DIRECTOR
Greg Carroll - Athletic Director
PO Box 901
Morrisville, NY 13408
O 315.684.6072/ F 315.684.6252
carrolgm@morrisville.edu

MUSTANGS PLAYERS

Player	YB	GR Ht/Wt	P	Hometown/Last Team
Andrew Alarie	10	5' 8"/180	F	Carlisle,ON/Oshawa Legionaires (OPJHL)
Matt Bendall	09	6' 2"/215	F	Flint,MI/Rochester (EmJHL)
Christopher Cacace	08	5'11"/190	D	Cold Spring,NY/SUNY-Morrisville (NJCAA)
Dana Calderone	09	6' 3"/180	F	Bronx,NY/SUNY-Morrisville (NJCAA)
Nick Carelli	09	5'10"/175	F	Genelle,BC/SUNY-Morrisville (NJCAA)
Stefan Carnegie	10	5' 6"/160	F	Woodbridge,ON/Thornhill Rattlers (OPJHL)
Cody Casselman	10	6' 0"/190	D	Morrisburg,ON/Vaudreuil Mustangs (QJAHL)
Joakim Cedin	10	6' 0"/215	F	Spanga,Sweden/Puget Sound Tomahawks (NPJHL)
Matt Damskov	08	6' 2"/190	F	Spokane,WA/SUNY-Morrisville (NJCAA)
Timothy Dorak	09	6' 1"/185	D	Honeoye,NY/SUNY-Morrisville (NJCAA)
Samuel Forget	10	6' 2"/190	D	Saint-Eustache,QC/Port Hope Predators (OPJHL)
Brett Freese	08	5'11"/185	G	Geneseo,NY/SUNY-Morrisville (NJCAA)
Tyler Fulton	10	6' 2"/190	F	Highland Village,TX/Boston Harbor Wolves (EJHL)
Esteban Gonzalez	10	5' 7"/160	F	Little Falls,MN/Wheatfield Blades (GHJHL)
Andrew Green	08	6' 4"/230	D	Beamsville,ON/SUNY-Morrisville (NJCAA)
Joseph Herman	08	5' 6"/165	F	Congers,NY/SUNY-Morrisville (NJCAA)
Ryan Hirschfield	10	5' 7"/155	F	Cortland,NY/Cortland-Homer (NJCAA)
Tim Kamp	10	6' 0"/170	D	Racine,WI/Fort Worth Texans (WSHL)
Evan Kernohan	10	6' 0"/180	D	Minden,ON/Lindsay Muskies (OPJHL)
Travis Moore	10	6' 0"/185	G	Simcoe,ON/Bancroft Hawks (OPJHL)
Patrick Morss	09	6' 2"/210	F	Geneseo,NY/SUNY-Morrisville (NJCAA)
Steve Parsons	08	5' 9"/155	G	St. Louis,MO/SUNY-Morrisville (NJCAA)
Brent Quinn	10	5' 8"/170	F	Perth,ON/Perth Blue Wings (EOJHL)
CJ Schneider	10	6' 2"/220	D	Oaklyn,NJ/Thornhill Rattlers (OPJHL)
Shawn Smail	09	5' 7"/135	F	Winchester,ON/SUNY-Morrisville (NJCAA)
Corey Smith	09	5' 9"/170	D	N Chili,NY/SUNY-Morrisville (NJCAA)
Ryan Tetrault	10	5'10"/145	F	Burlington,VT/Burlington Cougars (OPJHL)
Cody Williams	07	6' 0"/190	G	Fairbault,MN/SUNY Cortland (SUNYAC)
Keith Williams	09	5'11"/175	F	Whitesboro,NY/SUNY-Morrisville (NJCAA)
Steven Williams	10	5'10"/175	D	Highland,NY/Cobourg Cougars (OPJHL)

ROSTER ANALYSIS (SCHOLARSHIPS - 0)

Class		Country		Last Team					
Fr	15	USA	19	US JR A		CDN JR A	9	ACHA	
So	8	Canada	11	US JR B	5	CDN JR B	1	NJCAA	13
Jr	6	Europe		US PS		CDN PS		NCAA	1
Sr	1	Asia		US HS	1	CDN HS		USNDT	
Gr		Other		US Midget		CDN Midget		Other	

ADMISSIONS, ENROLLMENT & CAMPUS INFORMATION

Founded 1908
Public, rural campus
1,800 men / 1,450 women
Tuition, room & board - $ 11.5 K
Avg SAT - 1,040 / Avg ACT -

Average acceptance rate - %
Freshman financial aid - 89 %
Early decision application deadline - n/a
Regular application deadline - rolling
Financial aid deadline - rolling

Admissions Director
SUNY-Morrisville
PO Box 901
Morrisville, NY 13408
O 800.258.0111/ F

SUNY - OSWEGO

Division 3

HOCKEY STAFF

HEAD COACH
Ed Gosek (SUNY-Oswego '83)

ASSISTANT COACHES
Glenn Sisman (SUNY-Oswego)
Pete Sears (SUNY-Oswego)

HOCKEY OFFICE
SUNY-Oswego
Laker Hall #202
Oswego, NY 13126
O 315.312.4145 / F 315.312.6397
egosek@oswego.edu

HOCKEY MEDIA CONTACT
Jeremy DaRin - Interim Sports Info Dir.
SUNY-Oswego
Laker Hall #202
Oswego, NY 13126
O 315.312.2488 / F 315.312.6397
darin@oswego.edu

HOCKEY RINK
Golden Romney Fieldhouse (On Campus)
SUNY-Oswego
Oswego, NY 13126
Size 200' x 95', Capacity 2,500
O 315.312.2403

ATHLETIC DIRECTOR
Timothy Hale - Athletic Director
SUNY-Oswego
Laker Hall #202
Oswego, NY 13126
O 315.312.2378 / F 315.312.6397
thale@oswego.edu

GREAT LAKERS PLAYERS

Player	YB	GR	Ht/Wt	P	Hometown/Last Team
Tony DiNunzio	08		5'11"/180	F	King City,ON/St. Michael's (PS)
Brad Dormiedy	10		6'0"/180	F	Ajax,ON/Bowmanville Eagles (OPJHL)
Ryan Ellis	09		6'0"/185	F	Georgetown,ON/Oakville Blades (OPJHL)
Francois Gagnon	09		6'1"/185	D	Beauport,QC/Portland Pirates (MJHL)
Trevor Gilligan	07		5'9"/175	F	Saranac Lk,NY/Northwood (PS)
Chris Hyk	09		6'0"/195	G	Hamilton,ON/Georgetown Raiders (OPJHL)
Jeffrey Johnstone	09		5'10"/190	F	Aurora,ON/Wexford Raiders (OPJHL)
Ryan Koresky	07		5'10"/185	D	Midhurst,ON/Cornwall Colts (CJHL)
Tyler Laws	09		6'0"/195	D	Ft Gratiot,MI/Bridgewater Bandits (EJHL)
Derrell Levy	09		5'10"/190	F	Markham,ON/Markham Waxers (OPJHL)
Mark Lozzi	09		6'0"/175	F	Richmond Hill,ON/St. Michael's (PS)
Tyler Lyon	10		6'0"/180	D	Foxboro,ON/Wellington Dukes (OPJHL)
Peter Magagna	09		5'9"/175	F	Orangeville,ON/Wellington Dukes (OPJHL)
Kyle McCutcheon	09		5'10"/185	F	Caledon E,ON/Brockville Braves (CJHL)
Brendan McLaughlin	09		5'7"/165	F	Brampton,ON/Brampton Capitals (OPJHL)
Neil Musselwhite	10		5'10"/180	F	Burlington,ON/Hamilton Red Wings (OPJHL)
Mike Novak	09		6'3"/205	D	Milton,ON/Wexford Raiders (OPJHL)
Garren Reisweber	09		5'10"/175	F	Williamsville,NY/Buffalo Lightning (OPJHL)
Ryan Scott	08		5'10"/195	G	Williamsville,NY/Abitibi Ekimos (NOJHL)
CJ Thompson	08		6'0"/190	F	Picton,ON/Wellington Dukes (OPJHL)
Rick Varone	09		5'8"/205	F	Woodbridge,ON/Newmarket Hurricanes (OPJHL)
Matt Whitehead	09		5'7"/160	F	Newmarket,ON/Newmarket Hurricanes (OPJHL)
Matt Wolf	08		5'11"/160	G	Cherry Vly,CA/Bay City Bombers (WSHL)
Ryan Woodward	07		5'11"/180	F	Picton,ON/Wellington Dukes (OPJHL)
Rich Zalewski	09		6'0"/205	D	New Hartford,NY/Gloucester Rangers (CJHL)

ROSTER ANALYSIS (SCHOLARSHIPS - 0)

Class		Country		Last Team				
Fr	3	USA	6	US JR A		CDN JR A	19	ACHA
So	15	Canada	19	US JR B	3	CDN JR B		NJCAA
Jr	4	Europe		US PS	1	CDN PS	2	NCAA
Sr	3	Asia		US HS		CDN HS		USNDT
Gr		Other		US Midget		CDN Midget		Other

ADMISSIONS, ENROLLMENT & CAMPUS INFORMATION

Founded 1861
Public, rural campus
2,986 men / 3,959 women
Tuition, room & board - $13 K / $20 K
Avg SAT - 1,100 / Avg ACT - 23

Average acceptance rate - 56 %
Freshman financial aid - 76 %
Early decision application deadline - Nov 15
Regular application deadline - Jan 15
Financial aid deadline - Apr 1

Joseph F. Grant, Jr. - Admissions Director
SUNY-Oswego
Culkin Hall #201
Oswego, NY 13126
O 315.312.2500 / F 315.312.3260

SUNY - PLATTSBURGH

Division 3

HOCKEY STAFF

HEAD COACH
Robert Emery *(Boston College '86)*

ASSISTANT COACHES
Steve Moffat *(SUNY-Plattsburgh '98)*
Jayson Barnhart *(SUNY-Plattsburgh '05)*
Gregg Fesette *(Kent State '93)*

HOCKEY OFFICE
SUNY-Plattsburgh
Memorial Hall
Plattsburgh, NY 12901-2697
O 518.564.3607 / F 518.564.3069
emeryrd@plattsburgh.edu

HOCKEY MEDIA CONTACT
Patrick Stewart - Sports Info Dir.
SUNY-Plattsburgh
Memorial Hall
Plattsburgh, NY 12901-2697
O 518.564.4148 / F 518.564.4132
micheebk@plattsburgh.edu

HOCKEY RINK
Stafford Ice Arena (Off Campus)
Rugers Street
Plattsburgh, NY 12901
Size 185' x 85', Capacity 3,500
O 518.564.3061

ATHLETIC DIRECTOR
Bruce Delventhal - Athletic Director
SUNY-Plattsburgh
101 Broad Street
Plattsburgh, NY 12901-2697
O 518.564.3140 / F 518.564.4155
delvenbw@plattsburgh.edu

CARDINALS PLAYERS

Player	YB	GR	Ht/Wt	P	Hometown/Last Team
Mike Baccaro	83	08	5' 7"/165	F	Rochester,NY/Couchiching Terriers (OPJHL)
Pier-Luc Belanger		10	6'0"/180	F	L'isle-Verte,QC/St. Lawrence (Midget AAA)
Tom Breslin		10	5'11"/185	D	Hampton,NH/New Hampshire Monarchs (EJHL)
Ryan Burke	84	09	5'9"/195	D	Southfield,MI/Chatham Maroons (WOJHL)
Ryan Busby	83	07	5' 6"/160	F	Gerogetown,ON/Georgetown Raiders (OPJHL)
TJ Cooper	84	08	5' 9"/190	F	Hamburg,NY/Buffalo Lightning (OPJHL)
Shawn Dennis		09	6'0"/175	F	Clinton Twnsp,MI/Niagara (CHA)
Jason Diamond		08	5'11"/185	D	Northridge,CA/Bismarck Bobcats (NAHL)
Phil Farrow		10	5'10"/160	F	Amherst,NS/Nepean Raiders (CJHL)
Kevin Galan	84	09	6' 1"/210	F	Salmon Arm,BC/Williams Lake Timberwolves (BCHL)
Jason Gorrie		10	5'10"/175	F	Etobicoke,ON/Streetsville Derbys (OPJHL)
Eric Greene		10	6' 1"/215	D	Cedar Knolls,NJ/Cobourg Cougars (OPJHL)
Karl Helgesson		08	6' 1"/175	G	Lerum,Sweden/Plymouth State (ECAC NE)
Riley Hill	87	09	5' 9"/180	F	Markham,ON/Markham Waxers (OPJHL)
Rick Janco	84	08	6' 1"/215	D	Mississauga,ON/St. Lawrence (ECAC)
Dave McNab	84	09	6' 0"/190	F	Hamilton,ON/Hamilton Red Wings (OPJHL)
Chris Molinaro	85	09	6' 2"/180	G	Nesconset,NY/New York Bobcats (AtJHL)
Shane Remenda	82	07	6' 0"/160	F	Grand Vly,ON/Georgetown Raiders (OPJHL)
Nick Rolls	84	09	6' 0"/195	D	Marysville,MI/Sarnia Blast (WOJHL)
Ryan Silveira		10	5' 9"/190	F	Brampton,ON/Streetsville Derbys (OPJHL)
Casey Smith	84	09	6' 0"/180	D	Rochester,NY/Capital District Selects (EJHL)
Ward Smith		10	6' 0"/185	D	Forest,ON/Sarnia Blast (WOJHL)
Jordan Stevenson		10	6' 1"/205	F	New Sarepta,AB/Weyburn Red Wings (SJHL)
Andy Stricker	84	09		G	St. George,UT/Fargo-Moorhead Jets (NAHL)
Mike Thomson	84	09	6' 0"/165	F	LaHabra Hghts,CA/Apple Core (EJHL)
CJ Tozzo	85	08	5' 9"/175	F	New Rochell,NY/Niagara (CHA)
Andrew Willcock		10	6' 0"/170	F	Mississauga,ON/Mississauga Chargers (OPJHL)
Joey Wilson		10	5'10"/175	F	Newmarket,ON/Newmarket Hurricanes (OPJHL)

ROSTER ANALYSIS (SCHOLARSHIPS - 0)

Class		Country		Last Team				
Fr	10	USA	13	US JR A	2	CDN JR A	14	ACHA
So	10	Canada	14	US JR B	4	CDN JR B	3	NJCAA
Jr	6	Europe	1	US PS		CDN PS		NCAA 4
Sr	2	Asia		US HS		CDN HS		USNDT
Gr		Other		US Midget		CDN Midget	1	Other

ADMISSIONS, ENROLLMENT & CAMPUS INFORMATION

Founded 1889
Public, urban campus
2,085 men / 3,128 women
Tuition, room & board - $12 K / $19 K
Avg SAT - 1,040 / Avg ACT - 22

Average acceptance rate - 60 %
Freshman financial aid - 85 %
Early decision application deadline - Nov 15
Regular application deadline - Aug 1
Financial aid deadline - Mar 1

Richard Higgins - Admissions Director
SUNY-Plattsburgh
Kehoe Building 10
Plattsburgh, NY 12901-2681
O 518.564.2040 / F 518.564.2045

www.plattsburgh.edu   www.cardinalhockey.net

SUNY - POTSDAM

Division 3

HOCKEY STAFF

HEAD COACH
Aaron Saul *(Elmira)*

ASSISTANT COACHES
Joe Munn *(SUNY-Potsdam '01)*
Bill Reid *(St. Lawrence '76)*

HOCKEY OFFICE
SUNY-Potsdam - Athletics
Maxcy Hall, P249
Potsdam, NY 13676-2316
O 315.267.2301 / F 315.267.2316
saulaa@potsdam.edu

HOCKEY MEDIA CONTACT
Boyd Jones - Hockey Info Director
SUNY-Potsdam - Athletics
Maxcy Hall
Potsdam, NY 13676-2294
O 315.267.2315 / F 315.267.2316
joneswb@potsdam.edu

HOCKEY RINK
Maxcy Hall (On Campus)
44 Pierrepont Avenue
Potsdam, NY 13676
Size 185' x 85', Capacity 4,000
O 315.264.2000

ATHLETIC DIRECTOR
James Zalacca - Athletic Director
SUNY-Potsdam - Athletics
Maxcy Hall
Potsdam, NY 13676
O 315.267.2314 / F 315.267.2316
zalaccja@potsdam.edu

BEARS PLAYERS

Player	YB	GR	Ht/Wt	P	Hometown/Last Team
Rob Barnhardt	08		6' 2"/180	G	Ft Erie,ON/Welland Cougars (GHJHL)
Luke Beck	10		5' 7"/200	F	Charlottetown,PE/Charlottetown Abbies (MarJHL)
Nik Bibic	08		6' 3"/220	D	Windsor,ON/Hamilton Red Wings (OPJHL)
Sean Brackin	08		5'10"/165	F	Whitby,ON/Bowmanville Eagles (OPJHL)
Dennis Colterman	07		5' 9"/180	D	Ajax,ON/Milton Merchants (OPJHL)
Steve Cornelissen	10		6' 0"/190	D	Courtice,ON/Bowmanville Eagles (OPJHL)
Vince Cuccaro	07		5' 8"/195	G	Ottawa,ON/Kanata Stallions (CJHL)
Mike Ehlers	09		5'10"/170	G	Orchard Pk,NY/St. Francis (PS)
Adam Gebara	07		5'11"/170	F	Ottawa,ON/Kanata Stallions (CJHL)
Josh Gilson	09		5' 8"/175	F	Canton,NY/Cornwall Colts (CJHL)
TJ Kenyon	08		6' 0"/200	D	Leesburg,VA/Elmira Jackals ()
Mike Knapp	08		5' 7"/170	F	Elmira,NY/Elmira (ECAC West)
Kyle Laurie	08		5' 9"/195	F	Canton,NY/SUNY Canton (NJCAA)
Pat Lemay	08		5' 9"/185	F	Orleans,ON/Smiths Falls Bears (CJHL)
Ryan McCarthy	07		5' 9"/175	F	Brampton,ON/Georgetown Raiders (OPJHL)
Dane Miron	09		6' 1"/195	F	Broken Arrow,OK/Springfield Spirit (NAHL)
Dan Quartucio	07		5'10"/180	F	Congers,NY/SUNY Morrisville (NJCAA)
Warren Sly	08		5' 9"/180	D	Collingwood,ON/Cambridge Winterhawks (MWJHL)
Lance Smith	08		6' 3"/195	D	Ft Covington,NY/Robert Morris (CHA)
John Southwick	09		6' 0"/215	D	Rouses Point,NY/Green Mountain Glades (EJHL)
Vince Tarantino	07		5' 9"/175	D	Oakville,ON/Wentworth (ECAC NE)
Loren Tennent	08		6' 0"/185	D	Bolton Ldg,NY/Plymouth State (ECAC NE)
Conner Treacy	10		5'11"/170	F	Markham,ON/Markham Waxers (OPJHL)
Ryan Trimble	07		6' 1"/205	D	Carleton Pl,ON/Lindsay Muskies (OPJHL)
Ryan Watts	08		6' 3"/200	F	Ottawa,ON/North Country (NJCAA)
Mitch West	10		6' 0"/205	F	Burlington,ON/Stoney Creek Warriors (GHJHL)
Jeff Zatorski	10		5'10"/210	D	Welland,ON/Mississauga Chargers (OPJHL)

ROSTER ANALYSIS (SCHOLARSHIPS - 0)

Class		Country		Last Team					
Fr	5	USA	10	US JR A	1	CDN JR A	13	ACHA	
So	4	Canada	17	US JR B	2	CDN JR B	3	NJCAA	3
Jr	11	Europe		US PS	1	CDN PS		NCAA	4
Sr	7	Asia		US HS		CDN HS		USNDT	
Gr		Other		US Midget		CDN Midget		Other	

ADMISSIONS, ENROLLMENT & CAMPUS INFORMATION

Founded 1816	Average acceptance rate - 72 %	Tom Nesbitt - Admissions Director
Public, rural campus	Freshman financial aid - 79 %	SUNY-Potsdam
1,566 men / 1,913 women	Early decision applicatin deadline - N/A	Potsdam Drive
Tuition, room & board - $13 K / $19 K	Regular application deadline - rolling	Potsdam, NY 13676
Avg SAT - 1,070 / Avg ACT - 23	Financial aid deadline - Mar 1	O 315.267.2180 / F 315.267.2163

www.potsdam.edu

www.potsdam.edu/sports/

TOWSON UNIVERSITY

Division 1

HOCKEY STAFF

HEAD COACH
Jaynen Rissling *(Mass-Amherst)*

ASSISTANT COACHES
Marshall Stevenson
Brett Kehler

HOCKEY OFFICE
Towson University Hockey
18206 Bunker Hill Road
Parkton, MD 21220-0922
O 410.343.0922 / F 775.719.5824
mstevenson@towson.edu

HOCKEY MANAGER
Tom Ranney Sr. - General Manager
Towson University
8000 York Road
Towson, MD 21252-0001

HOCKEY RINK
Mt. Pleasant Ice Arena (Off Campus)
6101 Hillen Road
Baltimore, MD 21239
Size 200' x 85', Capacity 1,000
O 410.444.1888

ATHLETIC DIRECTOR
Wayne Edwards - Athletic Director
Towson University
8000 York Road
Towson, MD 21252-0001
O 410.704.2758

TIGERS PLAYERS

Player	YB GR Ht/Wt	P	Hometown/Last Team
Kevin Baum	10 6'0"/160	F	Larchmont, NY
Daniel Coffey	09 6'0"/170	D	Middletown, MD
Darren Delullo	08 6'2"/220	G	Millersville, MD
Matthew Doyle	10 5'9"/160	F	West Chester, PA
Chris Duley	07 6'1"/185	F	New Market, MD
David Eden	10 6'0"/165	D	Pasadena, MD
Michael Emmet	10 5'8"/167	F	Yonkers, NY
Charlie Foulds	10 5'8"/185	D	College Point, NY
Brian Glass	09 6'2"/155	G	Erial, NJ
Keith Laxman	09 5'8"/165	F	Tuxedo, NY
James Marino	07 5'8"/185	F	Holbrook, NY
Jefferey Mekelburg	07 6'0"/215	G	Oakdale, NY
Scott Milli	07 5'10"/180	D	Olney, MD
Branden Murphy	10 5'9"/150	F	White Plains, MD
Ryan Parks	07 5'10"/185	F	Bowie, MD
Robert Plant	09 5'11"/175	F	Annapolis, MD
Dave Quader	07 5'8"/180	D	Gambrills, MD
Jonathan Scharff	10 5'10"/180	D	Neptune, NJ
Chad Sillery	07 6'3"/230	F	Gaithersburg, MD
John Trantin	09 6'1"/210	F	Odenton, MD
RJ Turnbull	07 5'10"/155	G	Hartsdale, NY
Christian Valvano	09 5'5"/150	F	Randolph, NJ
Robert Weir	10 5'11"/190	F	Brandywine, MD
Christopher Wetzel	09 5'9"/165	D	Frederick, MD
Jeremy Wolff	10 5'11"/160	F	Manalapan, NJ

ROSTER ANALYSIS (SCHOLARSHIPS - 0)

Class	Country	Last Team		
Fr	USA	US JR A	CDN JR A	ACHA
So	Canada	US JR B	CDN JR B	NJCAA
Jr	Europe	US PS	CDN PS	NCAA
Sr	Asia	US HS	CDN HS	USNDT
Gr	Other	US Midget	CDN Midget	Other

ADMISSIONS, ENROLLMENT & CAMPUS INFORMATION

Founded 1866
Public, suburban campus
4,633 men / 8,994 women
Tuition, room & board - $ 14 K / $ 23 K
Avg SAT - 855 / Avg ACT - 21

Average acceptance rate - 67 %
Freshman financial aid - 58 %
Early decision application deadline - N/A
Regular application deadline - Feb 15
Financial aid deadline - Mar 1

Louise Shulack - Admissions Director
Towson University
8000 York Road
Towson, MD 21252-0001
O 410.704.2113 / F 410.704.3030

www.towson.edu

www.towson.edu/icehockey

TRINITY COLLEGE

Division 3

HOCKEY STAFF

HEAD COACH
David Cataruzolo *(Bowdoin '98)*

ASSISTANT COACH
Paul Davidson *(Clarkson '69)*
David Breen *(Trinity '07)*

HOCKEY OFFICE
Trinity College
Ferris Athletic Center
300 Summit Street
Hartford, CT 06106-3100
O 860.297.5176 / F 860.297.2312
david.cataruzolo@trincoll.edu

HOCKEY MEDIA CONTACT
Dave Kingsley - Sports Info Director
Trinity College
79 Vernon Street
Hartford, CT 06106-3100
O 860.297.2137 / F 860.297.2312
david.kingsley@trincoll.edu

HOCKEY RINK
Kingswood Oxford Rink (Off Campus)
170 Kingswood Road
West Hartford, CT 06119
Size 200' X 80', Capacity 1,000
O 203.297.2137

ATHLETIC DIRECTOR
Richard Hazelton - Athletic Director
Trinity College
300 Summit Street
Hartford, CT 06106-3100
O 860.297.2055 / F 860.297.2312
richard.hazelton@trincoll.edu

BANTAMS PLAYERS

Player	YB	GR	Ht/Wt	P	Hometown/Last Team
Drew Barber	85	07	5'11"/180	G	Vestal,NY/South Kent (NEPSAC)
William Burns		09	6'3"/185	D	Livonia,MI/Green Mountain Glades (EJHL)
Greg Camarco		07	5'10"/175	D	S Windsor,CT/Choate (NEPSAC)
John Carter		10	6'2"/180	F	Mamaroneck,NY/Fox Lane ()
Derek Chase		09	5'10"/185	F	Sarasota,FL/Pomfret (NEPSAC)
Ryan Crosper		10	6'1"/190	D	Paxton,MA/Northfield Mount Hermon (NEPSAC)
Matthew Crum		08	6'1"/195	F	Clearwater,FL/Salisbury (NEPSAC)
Simon Dionne		07	5'10"/160	F	Montreal,QC/Choate (NEPSAC)
Chris Diozzi		09	5'9"/175	D	Belmont,MA/Walpole Stars (EJHL)
Shawn Donaher		09	6'0"/180	D	Lansdale,PA/Hill (PS)
Kent Graham		10	6'0"/185	D	Longmeadow,MA/Choate (NEPSAC)
Ross Grubin		08	5'9"/185	F	Newington,CT/South Kent (NEPSAC)
John Halverson		07	5'10"/170	F	Lexington,MA/Phillips Exeter (NEPSAC)
Naoto Hamashima		09	5'9"/170	F	Tokyo,Japan/Williston Northampton (NEPSAC)
Joseph Hanson		10	6'1"/175	G	Weymouth,MA/Middlesex (NEPSAC)
Riley Hicks		09	5'10"/200	F	Calgary,AB/Pomfret (NEPSAC)
Richard Hollstein		10	6'1"/185	F	Pembroke,MA/B B & N (NEPSAC)
William Maheras		07	5'10"/175	F	Milton,MA/Salisbury (NEPSAC)
Ryan Masucci		09	5'9"/165	F	Winthrop,MA/New Hampshire Monarchs (EJHL)
Daniel Maturi		08	6'0"/190	F	N Kingston,RI/Tabor (NEPSAC)
Michael Mortimer		10	5'9"/165	D	Spencer ,MA/Worcester (NEPSAC)
David Murison		10	6'2"/200	G	Woodstock,VT/Holderness (NEPSAC)
Chris Powers		09	6'1"/185	F	Lynnfield,MA/Northfield Mount Hermon (NEPSAC)
Adam Prescott		09	5'9"/170	G	Saco,ME/Portland Pirates (MJHL)
Tom Price		09	6'0"/175	F	Milton,MA/Phillips Exeter (NEPSAC)
Matthew Rafuse		07	5'11"/185	F	Lynn,MA/Pomfret (NEPSAC)
Josh Rich		09	5'11"/180	F	Palmyra,PA/Pomfret (NEPSAC)
Thomas Wenstrom		08	5'8"/170	D	Smithtown,NY/Valley Warriors (EJHL)
Zachary Wissman		10	5'9"/170	F	Guilford,VT/Northfield Mount Hermon (NEPSAC)

ROSTER ANALYSIS (SCHOLARSHIPS - 0)

Class		Country		Last Team			
Fr	8	USA	26	US JR A		CDN JR A	ACHA
So	11	Canada	2	US JR B	5	CDN JR B	NJCAA
Jr	4	Europe		US PS	23	CDN PS	NCAA
Sr	6	Asia	1	US HS		CDN HS	USNDT
Gr		Other		US Midget		CDN Midget	Other 1

ADMISSIONS, ENROLLMENT & CAMPUS INFORMATION

Founded 1823
Private, urban campus
1,053 men / 1,053 women
Tuition, room & board - $ 43 K
Avg SAT - 1,305 / Avg ACT - 27

Average acceptance rate - 40 %
Freshman financial aid - 100 %
Early decision application deadline - Nov 15
Regular application deadline - Jan 15
Financial aid deadline - Feb 1

Larry R. Dow - Admissions Director
Trinity College - Admissions Office
300 Summit Street
Hartford, CT 06106-3100
O 860.297.2180 / F 860.297.2287

www.trinncoll.edu   www.trincoll.edu/athletics/

TUFTS UNIVERSITY

Division 3

HOCKEY STAFF

HEAD COACH
Brian Murphy *(Tufts '95)*

ASSISTANT COACHES
Nick Mitropoulos *(Northeastern '82)*
John Burgess *(Norwich '92)*

HOCKEY OFFICE
Tufts University
Cousens Gym
161 College Avenue
Medford, MA 02155
O 617.627.5286 / F 617.627.3614
brian.murphy@tufts.edu

HOCKEY MEDIA CONTACT
Paul Sweeney - Sports Info Director
Tufts University
Cousens Gym
161 College Avenue
Medford, MA 02155
O 617.627.3586 / F 617.627.3516
paul.sweeney@tufts.edu

HOCKEY RINK
Malden Forum (Off Campus)
50 Holden Street
Malden, MA 02148
Size 200' x 85', Capacity 1,000
O 781.321.9554

ATHLETIC DIRECTOR
Bill Gehling - Athletic Director
Tufts University
Cousens Gym
Medford, MA 02155
O 617.627.3232 / F 617.627.3614
bill.gehling@tuft.edu

JUMBOS PLAYERS

Player	YB	GR	Ht/Wt	P	Hometown/Last Team
David Antonelli	87	10	5' 7"/165	F	Westwood,MA/Belmont Hill (NEPSAC)
Issa Azat	84	08	6' 1"/190	G	S Pasadena,CA/Berkshire (NEPSAC)
Brian Bailey	85	07	5' 8"/160	F	E Greenwich,RI/Mount St. Charles (PS)
Joe Cappellano	85	08	5' 9"/180	D	S Boston,MA/Nobles (NEPSAC)
Phil Clark	86	09	6' 0"/185	D	Norfolk,MA/Phillips Exeter (NEPSAC)
Peter Corbett	84	09	6' 0"/205	D	Winchester,MA/Winchester (HS)
Evan Crosby	87	10	5' 9"/180	F	Yarmouthport,MA/Phillips Exeter (NEPSAC)
Matt Dalton	83	07	6' 3"/225	F	Duxbury,MA/Nobles (NEPSAC)
Andrew Delorey	86	09	5'10"/175	F	Norwell,MA/Nobles (NEPSAC)
Mike Fitoussi	87	10	5' 8"/160	F	Great Neck,NY/Milton (NEPSAC)
Ross Gimbel	85	08	6' 2"/215	F	Ann Arbor,MI/Culver (PS)
Kurt Hertzog	85	08	5'10"/190	F	Long Beach,CA/Taft (NEPSAC)
James Kalec	85	08	6' 0"/185	G	E Amherst,NY/Fort Erie Meteors (GHJHL)
Jonathan Kestner	86	08	5' 9"/190	F/D	Chagrin Fls,OH/University (PS)
Ben Kirtland		10	5'11"/180	F/D	Lenexa,KS/Holderness (NEPSAC)
Cory Korchin	87	10	6' 1"/215	F	Fountain Vly,CA/Hotchkiss (NEPSAC)
Greg McCarthy	86	09	6' 1"/210	F	Medfield,MA/Boston Harbor Wolves (EJHL)
Jay McNamara	88	10	6' 1"/200	G	Weston,MA/St. Sebastian's (NEPSAC)
Jared Melillo	86	09	6' 0"/180	F	Medford,MA/Northfield Mount Hermon (NEPSAC)
Joe Milo	86	09	6' 1"/200	F	Woodbury,NY/New Hampshire Monarchs (EJHL)
John Murphy	85	07	5' 9"/165	D	Charlestown,MA/Belmont Hill (NEPSAC)
Myles Neumann	87	10	5'11"/185	D	Chester Spgs,PA/Hill (PS)
Greg O'Connell	84	08	6' 0"/190	F	Cohasset,MA/Belmont Hill (NEPSAC)
Joe Rosano	87	10	5' 9"/185	F	Cohasset,MA/Thayer (NEPSAC)
Matt Ryder	87	10	5'10"/200	D	Gates Mills,OH/University (PS)
Doug Wilson	86	10	6' 2"/200	D	Saratoga,CA/Valley Warriors (EJHL)

ROSTER ANALYSIS (SCHOLARSHIPS - 0)

Class		Country		Last Team					
Fr	10	USA	26	US JR A		CDN JR A		ACHA	
So	6	Canada		US JR B	3	CDN JR B	1	NJCAA	
Jr	7	Europe		US PS	21	CDN PS		NCAA	
Sr	3	Asia		US HS	1	CDN HS		USNDT	
Gr		Other		US Midget		CDN Midget		Other	

ADMISSIONS, ENROLLMENT & CAMPUS INFORMATION

Founded 1852	Average acceptance rate - 27 %	David Cuttino - Admissions Director
Private, suburban campus	Freshman financial aid - 100 %	Tufts University - Undergrad Office
2,444 men / 2,444 women	Early decision application deadline - Nov 15	Bendetson Hall
Tuition, room & board - $ 42 K	Regular application deadline - Jan 1	Medford, MA 02155
Avg SAT - 1,380 / Avg ACT - 30	Financial aid deadline - Feb 15	O 617.627.3170 / F 617.627.3860

www.tufts.edu

ase.tufts.edu/athletics/

UNION COLLEGE

Division 1

HOCKEY STAFF

HEAD COACH
Nate Leaman *(SUNY-Cortland '97)*

ASSISTANT COACHES
Rick Bennett *(Providence '90)*
Bill Riga *(Massachusetts-Lowell '96)*

HOCKEY OFFICE
Union College
Achilles Rink
Schenectady, NY 12308-2311
O 518.388.6570/ F 518.388.6323
leamann@union.edu

HOCKEY MEDIA CONTACT
Peter DiSanza - Hockey Info Director
Union College
Reamer Campus Center
807 Union Street
Schenectady, NY 12308-2311
O 518.388.6377/ F 518.388.6514
disanzap@union.edu

HOCKEY RINK
Achilles Rink (On Campus)
Alacander Lane
Schenectady, NY 12308-2311
Size 200' x 85', Capacity 2,504
O 518.388.6382

ATHLETIC DIRECTOR
Jim McLaughlin - Athletic Director
Union College
Alumni Gym
Schenectady, NY 12308
O 518.388.6284/ F 518.388.6695
mclaughj@union.edu

DUTCHMEN PLAYERS

Player	YB	GR	Ht/Wt	P	Hometown/Last Team
Michael Beynon	83	08	6' 3"/210	D	Nepean,ON/Nepean Raiders (CJHL)
Olivier Bouchard	84	07	6' 3"/205	D	Quebec,ON/Upper Canada (PS)
Sam Bowles	85	08	5'10"/190	F	Davidson,MD/Junior Bruins (EJHL)
Lane Caffaro	84	09	6' 1"/190	D	Slave Lake,AB/Fort McMurray Oil Barons (AJHL)
Jeff Christiansen	86	10	6' 2"/195	F	Elm Grove,WI/Billings Bulls (NAHL)
Matt Cook	86	09	5'11"/200	F	Belle Mead,NJ/Tabor (NEPSAC)
Josh Coyle	84	08	5'10"/180	F	Brooklyn,OH/New Hampshire Monarchs (EJHL)
Dustin DeGagne	85	10	6' 0"/180	D	Winnipeg,MB/Salmon Arm Silverbacks (BCHL)
Torren Delforte	84	08	5'11"/170	F	Shortsville,NY/Junior Bruins (EJHL)
Augie DiMarzo	85	09	5' 8"/150	F	W Haven,CT/Avon (NEPSAC)
Andrew Estey	86	10	6' 2"/190	F	Fredericton,NB/Alberni Valley Bulldogs (BCHL)
TJ Fox	84	09	6' 1"/200	F	Oswego,NY/Chicago Steel (USHL)
Mike Harr	87	09	5'11"/185	D	Norwood,MA/Junior Bruins (EJHL)
Jonathan Lareau	87	10	6' 1"/180	D	Plainville,MA/Junior Bruins (EJHL)
Brendan Milnamow	86	09	6' 3"/195	D	Wilton,CT/Taft (NEPSAC)
Justin Mrazek	85	08	6' 3"/190	G	Regina,SK/Estevan Bruins (SJHL)
Chris Potts	86	09	6' 0"/200	F	Phillipsburg,NJ/Tabor (NEPSAC)
Mike Schreiber	85	10	5'10"/170	D	Sherwood Pk,AB/Fort McMurray Oil Barons (AJHL)
Jake Schwan	83	08	5'11"/180	F	Clifton Pk,NY/Waterloo Blackhawks (MnJHL)
Tim Schwarz	86	10	6' 0"/200	D	Defreetsville,NY/Boston Bulldogs (AtJHL)
Jason Shaffer	86	10	5'10"/175	F	Arvada,CO/Trail Smoke Eaters (BCHL)
Rich Sillery	87	10	6' 3"/195	G	Hyattsville,MD/Gilmour (PS)
Sean Streich	82	07	5'11"/200	D	Kimberly,BC/Langley Hornets (BCHL)
Mario Valery-Trabucco	87	10	5'11"/180	F	Montreal,QC/Northwood (PS)
Mike Wakita	85	10	6' 2"/215	D	Kitimat,BC/Powell River Kings (BCHL)
Jason Walters	86	10	5'10"/180	F	Renfrew,ON/Pembroke Lumber Kings (CJHL)

ROSTER ANALYSIS (SCHOLARSHIPS - 0)

Class		Country		Last Team				
Fr	11	USA	15	US JR A	2	CDN JR A	10	ACHA
So	7	Canada	11	US JR B	7	CDN JR B		NJCAA
Jr	6	Europe		US PS	6	CDN PS	1	NCAA
Sr	2	Asia		US HS		CDN HS		USNDT
Gr		Other		US Midget		CDN Midget		Other

ADMISSIONS, ENROLLMENT & CAMPUS INFORMATION

Founded 1795	Average acceptance rate - 49 %	Daniel Lundquist - Admissions Director
Private, suburban campus	Freshman financial aid - 100 %	Union College - Becker Hall
1,201 men / 943 women	Early decision application deadline - Nov 15	Schenectady, NY 12308-2311
Tuition, room & board - $ 43 K	Regular application deadline - Jan 15	O 518.388.6112/ F 518.388.6986
Avg SAT - 1,250	Financial aid deadline - Feb 1	

UNITED STATES AIR FORCE ACADEMY

Division 1

HOCKEY STAFF

HEAD COACH
Frank Serratore *(Bemidji State '82)*

ASSISTANT COACHES
Lt. Andy Berg *(Air Force '03)*
Mike Corbett *(Denver '96)*

HOCKEY OFFICE
HQ USAFA/AHO
U.S. Air Force Academy, CO 80840-5461
O 719.333.3954/ F 719.333.7570
frank.serratore@usafa.af.mil

HOCKEY MEDIA CONTACT
Dave Toller - Hockey Info Director
HQ USAFA/AHSI; 2169 Field House Dr.
U.S. Air Force Academy, CO 80840-9500
O 719.333.3478/ F 719.333.3798
dave.toller@usafa.af.mil

HOCKEY RINK
Cadet Ice Arena (On Campus)
2169 Field House Drive
Colorado Springs, CO 80840-9500
Size 200' x 85', Capacity 2,502
O 719.472.1301

ATHLETIC DIRECTOR
Hans Mueh - Athletic Director
Department of Athletics (AH)
HQ USAFA-AH
U.S. Air Force Academy, CO 80840-5461
O 719.333.4008/ F 719.333.3798
hans.mueh@usafa.af.mil

FALCONS PLAYERS

Player	YB	GR	Ht/Wt	P	Hometown/Last Team
Bryan Becker	84	08	6'1"/190	F	Moorhead,MN/Billings Bulls (NAHL)
Matt Charbonneau	83	08	5'10"/175	D	Lakeland,MN/Billings Bulls (NAHL)
Billy Devoney	84	07	5'10"/185	D	Buffalo Gr,IL/Danville Wings (USHL)
Eric Ehn	84	08	5'10"/170	F	Dexter,MI/Green Bay Gamblers (USHL)
Matt Fairchild	85	10	5'10"/175	F	Ashburn,VA/Walpole Stars (EJHL)
Greg Flynn	86	09	6'1"/200	D	Lino Lakes,MN/Billings Bulls (NAHL)
Peter Foster	83	07	5'10"/170	G	Canton,MI/Wichita Falls Rustlers (AWHL)
Josh Frider	85	09	5'9"/170	F	Moorhead,MN/Alexandria Blizzard (NAHL)
Brian Gineo	83	07	6'0"/195	D	S Windsor,CT/Capital District Selects (EJHL)
Jeff Hajner	85	10	5'9"/185	F	Las Vegas,NV/Melfort Mustangs (SJHL)
Ian Harper	84	08	6'3"/185	G	Eagle,ID/Springfield Blues (NAHL)
Chris Hepp	87	10	6'1"/195	D	Burnsville,MN/Omaha Lancers (USHL)
Brandon Johnson	85	10	5'11"/180	D	Duluth,MN/Santa Fe Roadrunners (NAHL)
Michael Johnson	85	10	6'0"/185	D	Eagle Rvr,AK/Fairbanks Ice Dogs (NAHL)
David Martinson	86	10	6'0"/190	F	St. Louis Pk,MN/New England Huskies (EJHL)
Michael Mayra	84	09	6'2"/200	D	Anchorage,AK/Billings Bulls (NAHL)
Jay Mendenwaldt	82	07	5'10"/175	F	Monticello,MN/Wichita Falls Rustlers (AWHL)
Brett Nylander	85	10	5'10"/175	F	Baudette,MN/Bozeman Icedogs (NAHL)
Brent Olson	85	09	6'0"/190	F	Baudette,MN/Fargo-Moorhead Jets (NAHL)
Mike Phillipich	84	09	5'10"/175	F	Lansing,MI/Fairbanks Ice Dogs (NAHL)
Josh Print	83	08	5'10"/175	F	Timberlake,OH/Billings Bulls (NAHL)
Andrew Ramsey	85	07	5'8"/165	F	Noblesville,IN/Culver (PS)
Brian Reese	83	07	6'0"/190	F	Brainerd,MN/Billings Bulls (NAHL)
Josh Schaffer	84	08	5'10"/175	F	S Lyon,MI/Fargo-Moorhead Jets (NAHL)
Frank Schiavone	83	08	6'0"/195	D	Oceanside,NY/Chilliwack Chiefs (BCHL)
Andrew Volkening	85	10	6'2"/175	G	Genoa,IL/Wasilla Spirit (NAHL)
Ben Worker	84	07	5'9"/165	G	Thief River Fls,MN/Lincoln (HS)
Theo Zacour	82	07	5'10"/160	F	Oslo,Norway/Cobourg Cougars (OPJHL)

ROSTER ANALYSIS (SCHOLARSHIPS - N/A)

Class		Country		Last Team				
Fr	8	USA	27	US JR A	20	CDN JR A	3	ACHA
So	5	Canada		US JR B	3	CDN JR B		NJCAA
Jr	7	Europe	1	US PS	1	CDN PS		NCAA
Sr	8	Asia		US HS	1	CDN HS		USNDT
Gr		Other		US Midget		CDN Midget		Other

ADMISSIONS, ENROLLMENT & CAMPUS INFORMATION

Founded 1954	Average acceptance rate - 13 %	Rolland Stoenman - Admission Director
Public, suburban campus	Freshman financial aid - 100 %	HQ USAFA/RR
3,462 men / 812 women	Early decision application deadline - Jan 31	2304 Cadet Drive - Suite 200
Tuition, room & board - $ 0	Regular application deadline - N/A	U.S. Air Force Academy, CO 80840-5025
Avg SAT - 1,290 / Avg ACT - 30	Financial aid deadline - N/A	O 719.333.2520/ F 719.333.3012

UNITED STATES MILITARY ACADEMY

Division 1

BLACK KNIGHTS PLAYERS

Player	YB	GR	Ht/Wt	P	Hometown/Last Team
Aaron Anderson	84	08	5'10"/195	F	Muskegon,MI/Soo Thunderbirds (NOJHL)
Casey Bickley	82	07	5' 9"/170	D	Faribault,MN/Cedar Rapids RoughRiders (USHL)
Chris Blair	86	08	6' 0"/180	D	Appleton,WI/Appleton (HS)
Chris Colvin	84	08	6' 2"/205	D	Brunswick,OH/New Hampshire Monarchs (EJHL)
Brady Dolim	83	07	5' 9"/180	F	Walnut Crk,CA/Chicago Freeze (NAHL)
AJ Drago	86	09	6' 0"/175	G	Guttenberg,NJ/New Jersey Hitmen (EJHL)
Jeff Fearing	83	08	6' 2"/175	F	Roseville,MN/Fargo-Moorhead Jets (NAHL)
Luke Flicek	83	08	5'10"/185	F	Burnsville,MN/Texas Tornado (NAHL)
Lyle Gal	84	08	5'11"/200	F	Amherst,MA/New England Coyotes (EJHL)
Matt Hickey	86	09	5'11"/185	F	Mendota Hgts,MN/Cretin-Derham (PS)
Bryce Hollweg	84	08	5'11"/185	F	Langley,BC/Surrey Eagles (BCHL)
Josh Kassel	85	09	6' 1"/195	F	Greensburg,PA/Bozeman Icedogs (NAHL)
John Kearns	10		6' 0"/190	D	Park Ridge,IL/Bay State Breakers (EJHL)
Bill Leahy	84	09	6' 1"/200	F	Gilmer,TX/Bozeman Icedogs (NAHL)
Tim Manthey	85	09	6' 3"/200	D	Anoka,MN/Alexandria Blizzard (NAHL)
Ian McDougall	85	08	5'11"/195	D	Boxborough,MA/Junior Bruins (EJHL)
Zach McKelvie	85	09	6' 2"/195	F	New Brighton,MN/Bozeman Icedogs (NAHL)
Biff McNally	84	08	5'11"/185	F	Ridgewood,NJ/Apple Core (EJHL)
Owen Meyer	10		6' 2"/185	F	Dundee,IL/Mahoning Valley Phantoms (NAHL)
Mike Migliaro	85	09	5'11"/210	F	Wallingford,CT/Choate (NEPSAC)
Michael Picone	83	07	5' 9"/165	F	Johnston,RI/Boston Harbor Wolves (EJHL)
Chase Podsiad	84	08	5'10"/170	D	Wyandotte,MI/Springfield Blues (NAHL)
Ken Porter	84	08	5'10"/180	F	Delmar,NY/Capital District Selects (EJHL)
Robb Ross	83	08	5' 9"/185	F	N St. Paul,MN/Fairbanks Ice Dogs (NAHL)
Ken Rowe		08	6' 0"/195	F	Faribault,MN/Des Moines Buccaneers (USHL)
Will Ryan	85	09	5'10"/175	F	Bloomfield Hls,MI/Green Mountain Glades (EJHL)
Eric Sefchik		10	5'10"/185	F	Lakewood,OH/Cornwall Colts (CJHL)
Joey Spracklen		10	6' 0"/195	G	Kennewick,WA/Minnesota Ice Hawks (MnJHL)
Mark Tilch	85	09	5'11"/175	D	Ft Washington,MD/Boston Harbor Wolves (EJHL)

ROSTER ANALYSIS (SCHOLARSHIPS - N/A)

Class		Country		Last Team			
Fr	4	USA	28	US JR A	12	CDN JR A	3	ACHA
So	9	Canada	1	US JR B	11	CDN JR B		NJCAA
Jr	13	Europe		US PS	2	CDN PS		NCAA
Sr	3	Asia		US HS	1	CDN HS		USNDT
Gr		Other		US Midget		CDN Midget		Other

ADMISSIONS, ENROLLMENT & CAMPUS INFORMATION

- 528 -

UNITED STATES NAVAL ACADEMY

Division 1

HOCKEY STAFF

HEAD COACH
Rick Randazzo *(USMA '93)*

ASSISTANT COACHES
Mike Fox *(Ohio '73)*
Brendan Curley *(Ohio)*
Pat Eliason *(USNA)*
John Bogdan *(USNA)*

HOCKEY OFFICE
8210 Folden Leaf Way
Chesapeake, MD 20732
O 410.286.5448 / H 410.286.3987
F 443.646.0268
richard.randazzo@verizon.net

HOCKEY MEDIA CONTACT
Ray Feldmann - Sports Information Dir.
O 410.507.7714
navyhockeypio@hotmail.com

HOCKEY RINK
Dahlgren Hall Ice Rink
103 Fullam Ct.
Annapolis, MD 21402
Size 200' x 85', Capacity 800
O 410.293.2350

ATHLETIC DIRECTOR
Chet Gladchuk
O 410.293.2700X110
gladchuk@usna.edu

MIDSHIPMEN'S PLAYERS

Player	YB	GR	Ht/Wt	P	Hometown/Last Team
Jay Alspach	07		5'9"/170	F	Milton,VT/Taft (NEPSAC)
Eric Anderson	10		5'10"/165	G	Sartell,MN/Sartell (HS)
Nolan Anliker	09		6'0"/180	F	Brooklyn Park,MN/Park Center (HS)
Chandler Brewer	10		5'11"/175	D	Darien,CT/Phillips Exeter (NEPSAC)
Charlie Daniel	09		5'9"/180	F	Notingham,MD/Westminster (NEPSAC)
Jimmy Doherty	07		6'1"/210	D	Elkridge,MD/Mt. St. Joseph (PS)
Aaron Erzinger	09		5'10"/170	F	Stevens Point,WI/St. Paul Lakers (MnJHL)
Jeremey Estevez	10		6'0"/165	G	Grand Rapids,MI/East Kentwood (HS)
Brian Gleason	08		6'2"/210	F	Auburn,NY/Auburn (HS)
Matt Gross	09		5'10"/180	D	Parma,OH/Normandy (HS)
Patrick Heitmann	10		5'11"/200	D	Imperial,MO/Seckman (HS)
Nick Hinkley	10		6'2"/180	F	Orlando ,FL/Park Tudor (PS)
Donnie Horner	08		6'2"/200	F	State College,PA/Canterbury (NEPSAC)
Charlie Hymen	09		5'11"/180	F	Chicago,IL/Deerfield (NEPSAC)
Derek Johnson	08		5'9"/165	F	Champlin,MN/Champlin Park (HS)
Keegan Kinkade	10		5'7"/150	F	Indianapolis,IN/Culver (PS)
Kevin Krmpotich	07		5'9"/180	F	Minneapolis,MN/Holy Angels (PS)
Joe Liles	08		6'0"/170	D	Zionsville,IN/Culver (PS)
Jeff Martin	09		6'0"/195	F	Columbia Heights,MN/Totino Grace (HS)
Calen Mims	10		6'0"/185	F	Albuquerque,NM/Albuquerque (PS)
Andrew Ochalek	10		6'1"/200	D	Milan,MI/Milan (HS)
Alex Sandroni	07		5'9"/190	D	Granger,IN/Penn (HS)
Nick Schwob	08		5'10"/175	F	Buffalo,NY/Wheatfield Blades (GHJHL)
Adam Sheppard	07		5'9"/180	D	Minneapolis,MN/Minnehaha (PS)
Adam Shields	08		5'10"/165	D	Grosse Ile,MI/Grosse Ile (HS)
Andrew Stoner	08		6'2"/205	F	South Bend,IN/Culver (PS)
Patrick Sullivan	07		6'0"/200	F	Milwaukee,WI/Marquette (HS)
Matt Swezey	09		6'2"/185	D	Albany,NY/Shaker (HS)
Sean Ublacker	08		5'8"/170	G	Freedom,WI/Freedom (HS)
Alex Wallis	10		6'0"/205	F	Milwaukee,WI/Marquette (HS)
Jon Westerman	09		5'6"/150	F	Gaylord,MI/St. Mary's (PS)
Zach Williamson	09		6'1"/175	F	Portland,ME/Portland (HS)

ROSTER ANALYSIS (SCHOLARSHIPS - N/A)

Class		Country		Last Team			
Fr	9	USA	32	US JR A		CDN JR A	ACHA
So.	9	Canada		US JR B	2	CDN JR B	NJCAA
Jr	8	Europe		US PS	14	CDN PS	NCAA
Sr	6	Asia		US HS	16	CDN HS	USNDT
Gr		Other		US Midget		CDN Midget	Other

ADMISSIONS, ENROLLMENT & CAMPUS INFORMATION

Founded 1802	Average acceptance rate - 10 %	Col. David A. Vetter
Public, rural campus	Freshman financial aid - N/A %	United States Naval Academy
3,479 men / 870 women	Early decision application deadline - N/A	117 Decatur Road
Tuition, room & board $ 0	Regular application deadline - Jan 31	Annapolis, MD 21402
Avg SAT - 1,290	Financial aid deadline - N/A	O 410.293.4361 / F 410.293.4348

UTICA COLLEGE

ATHLETICS

HOCKEY WEST

Division 3

HOCKEY STAFF

HEAD COACH
Gary Heenan *(Hamilton '97)*

ASSISTANT COACHES
Jason Lefevre
Geoff Noyes
Sean Weiman

HOCKEY OFFICE
Utica College Hockey Office
1600 Burrstone Road
Utica, NY 13502
O 315.792.3726 / F 315.792.3211
gheenan@utica.edu

HOCKEY MEDIA CONTACT
Chris Kent - Sports Info Director
Utica College
1600 Burrstone Raod
Utica, NY 13502
O 315.792.3772 / F 315.792.3211
ckent@utica.edu

HOCKEY RINK
Utica Memorial Auditorium (Off Campus)
400 Oriskany Boulevard
Utica, NY 13502
Size 200' x 85', Capacity 4,000
O 315.738.0614

ATHLETIC DIRECTOR
Jim Spartano - Athletic Director
Utica College
1600 Burrstone Road
Utica, NY 13502
O 315.792.3051 / F 315.792.3211
jspartano@utica.edu

PIONEERS PLAYERS

Player	YB GR Ht/Wt	P	Hometown/Last Team
Jared Allison	07 5'9"/175	F	Blairsville,PA/Cranbrook (PS)
Randy Bauer	07 6'0"/200	D	Gibsonia,PA/Pittsburgh Forge (NAHL)
Phil Boots	07 5'10"/175	F	Cornwall,NY/National Sports (PS)
Bryce Dale	09 5'10"/195	F	Fresno,CA/Williams Lake Timberwolves (BCHL)
Adam Dekker	08 6'3"/200	G	Muskegon,MI/Soo Indians (NAHL)
Matt Fitzgibbons	10 6'0"/195	F	Natick,MA/Junior Bruins (EJHL)
Aaron Jeffery	10 6'0"/180	F	Brighton,MI/Billings Bulls (NAHL)
Matt Jimenez	10 6'1"/195	D	Santa Rosa,CA/Pembroke Lumber Kings (CJHL)
Gregg Johannesen	07 6'2"/215	D	Kalamazoo,MI/Wexford Raiders (OPJHL)
Colin Kingston	09 6'1"/185	F	Vail,CO/Springfield Blues (NAHL)
Kevin Krogol	07 6'0"/215	F	Livonia,MI/Soo Indians (NAHL)
Brandon Laidlaw	10 5'9"/180	F	Pleasonton,CA/Nanaimo Clippers (BCHL)
Mike Lane	10 6'2"/195	D	West Chester,PA/Green Mountain Glades (EJHL)
Anthony Luvkow	10 6'0"/170	G	Shelby Twnsp,MI/Strathroy Rockets (WOJHL)
Nick Lynch	08 6'2"/190	F	Buffalo,NY/Capital District Selects (EJHL)
Sean McKevitt	10 6'1"/195	F	Clinton,NY/Gunnery (NEPSAC)
Josh Merson	09 6'1"/210	D	Hanover,MD/North Bay Skyhawks (NOJHL)
Vincent Nucci	10 6'1"/185	F	Rochester,NY/Capital District Selects (EJHL)
Steve Nutty	07 5'9"/180	F	Whiteboro,NY/Whitesboro (HS)
Jeff Pappalardi	10 5'11"/195	F	Delmar,NY/Capital District Selects (EJHL)
Scott Phelps	10 6'0"/205	F	Old Lyme,CT/Springfield Blues (NAHL)
Aaron Raymo	10 5'9"/180	F	Massena,NY/National Sports (PS)
TJ Schneider	09 6'4"/200	F	Spring City,PA/La Ronge Ice Wolves (SJHL)
Kyle Sibley	08 5'9"/175	D	Hanson,MA/Salisbury (NEPSAC)
Jon Starr	09 5'10"/165	G	Grosse Pt,MI/Brantford Golden Eagles (MWJHL)
Joe Watson	08 6'2"/205	F	St. Louis,MO/Toledo IceDiggers (NAHL)
Dave Werner	10 6'0"/180	F	Milwaukee,WI/Capital District Selects (EJHL)
Tony Wiseman	08 5'10"/200	D	White Lake,MI/Cleveland Barons (NAHL)

ROSTER ANALYSIS (SCHOLARSHIPS - 0)

Class		Country		Last Team					
Fr	12	USA	28	US JR A	8	CDN JR A	6	ACHA	
So	5	Canada		US JR B	6	CDN JR B	2	NJCAA	
Jr	5	Europe		US PS	5	CDN PS		NCAA	
Sr	6	Asia		US HS	1	CDN HS		USNDT	
Gr		Other		US Midget		CDN Midget		Other	

ADMISSIONS, ENROLLMENT & CAMPUS INFORMATION

Founded 1946	Average acceptance rate - 80 %	Patrick Quinn - Director of Admissions
Public, urban campus	Freshman financial aid - %	Utica College
1,064 men / 1,107 women	Early decision application deadline - N/A	1600 Burrstone Road
Tuition, room & board - $ 32 K	Regular application deadline - Jan 15	Utica, NY 13502-4892
Avg SAT - 965 / Avg ACT - 21	Financial aid deadline - Feb 15	O 315.792.3006 / F 315.792.3003

www.utica.edu

www.utica.edu/athletics/

UNIVERSITY OF VERMONT

Division 1

HOCKEY STAFF

HEAD COACH
Kevin Sneddon *(Harvard '92)*

ASSOCIATE HEAD COACH
John Micheletto *(Dartmouth '88)*

ASSISTANT COACHES
Willie Mitchell *(Western Ontario '93)*
Terry Lovelette *(Johnson State '98)*

HOCKEY OFFICE
University of Vermont
Hockey Office
Patrick Gymnasium
Burlington, VT 05405
O 802.656.1414 / F 802.656.0949
kevin.sneddon@uvm.edu

HOCKEY MEDIA CONTACT
Chris Wojcik - Sports Info Director
University of Vermont
Patrick Gym #226
Burlington, VT 05405
O 802.656.1110 / F 802.656.8328
chris.wojcik@uvm.edu

HOCKEY RINK
Gutterson Fieldhouse (On Campus)
Spear Street
Burlington, VT 05405
Size 200' x 90', Capacity 4,035
O 802.658.0653

ATHLETIC DIRECTOR
Robert Corran - Athletic Director
University of Vermont
Patrick Gym #148
Burlington, VT 05405
O 802.656.4052 / F 802.656.0949
robert.corran@uvm.edu

CATAMOUNTS PLAYERS

Player	YB	GR	Ht/Wt	P	Hometown/Last Team
Jay Anctil	85	10	5'10"/185	F	Wolfeboro,NH/Boston Bulldogs (AtJHL)
Chris Atkinson	88	10	5'10"/170	F	Sparta,NJ/USNDT (NAHL)
Corey Carlson	85	09	5'10"/175	F	Two Harbors,MN/Omaha Lancers (USHL)
Tom Collingham	84	07	6' 0"/175	F	Yonkers,NY/Apple Core (EmJHL)
Andy Corran	81	07	6' 1"/195	F	Burlington,VT/Wisconsin Stevens Point (NCHA)
Patrick Cullity	87	10	6' 2"/200	D	Tewksbury,MA/Berkshire (NEPSAC)
Joe Fallon	85	08	6' 3"/195	G	Bemidji,MN/Cedar Rapids RoughRiders (USHL)
Art Femenella	82	07	6' 7"/255	D	Annandale,NJ/Sioux City Musketeers (USHL)
Tim Geverd	87	09	5'11"/220	D	Hooksett,NH/New England Monarchs (EJHL)
Ryan Gunderson	85	07	5'10"/170	F	Bensalem,PA/Holy Ghost (PS)
Jonathan Higgins	86	10	6' 1"/180	F	Stratham,NH/Green Mountain Glades (EJHL)
Jeff Hill	85	08	5' 8"/160	G	Cranston,RI/South Kent (NEPSAC)
Brayden Irwin	87	10	6' 5"/205	F	Toronto,ON/St. Michael's (PS)
Kyle Kuk	86	09	5'11"/170	D	Monroe,MI/Tri-City Storm (USHL)
Peter Lenes	86	09	5' 6"/160	F	Shelburne,VT/Sioux City Musketeers (USHL)
Mark Lutz	83	08	6' 2"/190	D	Stevens Pt,WI/Soo Indians (NAHL)
Kenny Macaulay	84	07	5'10"/195	D	Baddeck,NS/Findlay (CHA)
Torrey Mitchell	85	08	5'11"/190	F	Greenfield Pk,QC/Hotchkiss (NEPSAC)
Chris Myers	83	07	5'11"/185	F	S Boston,MA/Salisbury (NEPSAC)
Dan Owens	84	07	5' 9"/195	F	Clinton,NY/Northwood (PS)
Brian Roloff	86	10	5'10"/180	F	W Seneca,NY/Green Bay Gamblers (USHL)
Mike Spillane	86	10	5'10"/185	G	Bow,NH/Omaha Lancers (USHL)
Viktor Stalberg	86	10	6' 2"/195	F	Gothenburg,Sweden/Frolunda Indians (SEL)
Evan Stoflet	84	07	6' 1"/185	D	Madison,WI/Des Moines Buccaneers (USHL)
Dean Strong	85	09	6' 2"/170	F	Mississauga,ON/Vernon Vipers (BCHL)
Slavomir Tomko	83	08	6' 0"/200	D	Zvolen,Slovakia/St. Louis Eagles (USHL)
Colin Vock	85	10	5'11"/175	F	Plymouth,MI/Des Moines Buccaneers (USHL)
Reese Wisnowski	84	08	5'10"/175	F	E Middlebury,VT/New Hampshire Monarchs (EJHL)

ROSTER ANALYSIS (SCHOLARSHIPS - 18)

Class		Country		Last Team					
Fr	9	USA	22	US JR A	11	CDN JR A	1	ACHA	
So	5	Canada	4	US JR B	5	CDN JR B		NJCAA	
Jr	6	Europe	2	US PS	6	CDN PS	1	NCAA	2
Sr	8	Asia		US HS		CDN HS		USNDT	1
Gr		Other		US Midget		CDN Midget		Other	1

ADMISSIONS, ENROLLMENT & CAMPUS INFORMATION

Founded 1791	Average acceptance rate - 76 %	Donald Honeman - Admissions Director
Public, urban campus	Freshmen financial aid - 82 %	University of Vermont
3,670 men / 4,486 women	Early decision application deadline - Nov 1	194 South Prospect Street
Tuition, room & board - $18 K / $31 K	Regular application deadline - Jan 15	Burlington, VT 05405
Avg SAT - 1,150 / Avg ACT - 25	Financial aid deadline - Feb 10	O 802.656.3370 / F 802.656.8411

www.uvm.edu

www.uvm.edu/athletics/

UNIVERSITY OF VIRGINIA

VIRGINIA

ACC/HL
ATLANTIC COAST COLLEGIATE HOCKEY LEAGUE

EST. 1991
ACHA
Division 2

HOCKEY STAFF

HEAD COACH
Rob Boyle *(Concordia '94)*

ASSISTANT COACHES
Roger Voisinet *(Miami-Ohio '72)*
Gary Jones
Rich Price

HOCKEY OFFICE
rjboyle@adelphia.net

HOCKEY RINK
Charlottesville Ice Park (Off Campus)
230 West Main Street
Charlottesville, VA 22902
Size 185' x 85', Capacity 500
O 434.817.2400
www.icepark.com

HOCKEY PRESIDENT
David Parisian - Team President
dlp3h@virginia.edu

HOCKEY MANAGER
Roger Voisinet - General Manager
1907 East Market Street
Charlottesville, VA 22902
O 434.974.1500 / H 434.979.7648
F 434.974.7750
roger@cvilleproperties.com

CAVALIERS PLAYERS

Player	YB	GR	Ht/Wt	P	Hometown/Last Team
Dave Adelman	07		5'10"/165	G	Oakton,VA/Oakton (HS)
Alex Bronson	07		5'11"/160	F	Arlington,VA/Washington (Midget AAA)
Michael Brown	09		5'11"/170	F	Roanoke,VA
James Buonato	09		5'11"/175	F	Columbia,MD
Doug Fletcher	10		6'0"/190	D	Pittsburgh,PA
Doug Franken	09		6'0"/190	D	
John Gelb	09		5'11"/165	D	Riverside,CT
Pat Giesecke	07		5'11"/170	F	Annandale,VA/Trinity Pawling (NEPSAC)
Alex Glaser					
Adam Hermida	08		5'11"/170	D	Miami,FL/Florida (Midget AA)
Risto Keravuori	07		6'0"/180	F	Fairfax Station,VA/Exeter (NEPSAC)
Wyatt Kupperman	07				
Ye Liang	08		5'8"/155	F	Herndon,VA/Thomas Jefferson (HS)
Edward Lindquist	09		5'7"/140	F	Richmond,VA
Kevin Miller	09		6'2"/225	F	Annandale,VA
David Pettibone	07		6'0"/165	D	Chalfont,PA/Glaciers (Midget AA)
Andrew Potter	10		5'11"/160	F	
Sean Rada	09		5'6"/130	G	Fredricksburg,VA
Andy Rallis	08			G	
Sam Rosen	07			D	
Ricky Schoepke	09		5'8"/170	F	Richmond,VA
Andrew Sufka	09		5'11"/170	D	Minneapolis,MN
Tyler Teass	08		5'7"/160	G	Roanoke,VA
Michal Vydrzel		GR	5/10"/185	F	
Ian Yang	07		5'4"/150	F	Vancouver,BC/Bears (Midget AA)

ROSTER ANALYSIS (SCHOLARSHIPS - 0)

Class	Country	Last Team		
Fr	USA	US JR A	CDN JR A	ACHA
So	Canada	US JR B	CDN JR B	NJCAA
Jr	Europe	US PS	CDN PS	NCAA
Sr	Asia	US HS	CDN HS	USNDT
Gr	Other	US Midget	CDN Midget	Other

ADMISSIONS, ENROLLMENT & CAMPUS INFORMATION

Founded 1819
Public, suburban campus
6,086 men / 7,145 women
Tuition, room & board $ 13 K / $ 29 K
Avg SAT - 1,330 / Avg ACT - 23

Average acceptance rate - 39 %
Freshman financial aid - 94 %
Early decision application deadline - Nov 1
Regular application deadline - Jan 2
Financial aid deadline - Mar 1

Office of Admissions
University of Virginia
P. O. Box 9017
Charlottesville, VA 22906-4160
O 434.982.3200 / F 434.924.3587

Looking for Success?
~success on the ice, success in school, success in life.....
You've found it at UVAHOCKEY.COM

VIRGINIA POLYTECHNIC INSTITUTE

Division 2

HOCKEY STAFF

HEAD COACH
Michael Spradlin

ASSISTANT COACHES

HOCKEY OFFICE
125 War Memorial Hall
Blacksburg, VA 24060
O 540.982.1998
aglick@vt.edu

HOCKEY MEDIA CONTACT
Alan Glick - Rec. Sports
aglick@vt.edu

HOCKEY RINK
Roanoke Ice Station (Off Campus)
O 540.265.1505

HOCKEY DIRECTOR
Henry Eickelberg - President
O 703.587.4735
hecklbrg@vt.edu

HOKIES PLAYERS

Player	YB	GR	Ht/Wt	P	Hometown/Last Team
Jon Allen			5'10"/200	G	Huntington Valley,PA
Kenny Bensman	07		6'1"/165	D	Stafford,VA/Prince William
Mike Brennan	09		6'0"/160	F	Manassas,VA/Osbourn Park (HS)
Ryan Chafe	10		6'1"/165	D	Richmond,VA
Matt Clements	10		6'1"/165	F	Arlington,VA
Mitch Cline	07		6'1"/190	D	Blue Point,NY/New York
Ryan Cole	07		5'11"/215	D	Canonsburg,PA/Canon McMillan (HS)
Marc Dudzinski	07		5'11"/175	G	West Chester,PA/Bozeman (AWHL)
Henry Eickelberg	07		6'1"/203	D	Chicago,IL/Potomac Falls
John Farrell	10		6'2"/190	D	Duluth,GA
John Fratello	09		6'2"/205	D	Hampton,VA/Hampton Christian (PS)
Matt Harrison	09		5'11"/185	F	Clifton Park,NY/Shenendehowa (HS)
Nolan Horowitz	09		5'11"/165	G	Middletown,NJ/Middletown South (HS)
Matt Hulse	07		5'11"/175	F	Herndon,VA
Mike Hulse	09		6'2"/185	F	Herndon,VA/Oakton (HS)
Michael Hultberg	09		6'1"/180	D	Newport News,VA/Denbigh (HS)
Matt Lidd	08		5'11"/190	F	Silver Spring,MD/Hempfield (HS)
Zach Malone	07		5'7"/165	F	Pittsburgh,PA/Junior Penguins
Todd Minetree	10		5/11"/165	F	Woodbridge,VA
Jimmy Pope	09		6'2"/192	F	Woodbridge,VA/Forest Park (HS)
Justin Reid	08		5'11"/175	F	Annapolis,MD
Kenny Richards	08		5'11"/185	G	Mechanicsville,VA
Ryan Rickley	10		5'10"/195	D	Virginia Beach,VA
Russell Schlafer	10		5'10"/150	F	Trumansburg,NY
Michael Sorensen	10		5'10"/165	F	Oak Hill,VA
Jack Wydler	10		5'8"/140	F	Chantilly,VA
Zack Zaremski	09		6'4"/210	D	Manassas,VA/Osbourn Park (HS)

ROSTER ANALYSIS (SCHOLARSHIPS - 0)

Class	Country	Last Team		
Fr	USA	US JR A	CDN JR A	ACHA
So	Canada	US JR B	CDN JR B	NJCAA
Jr	Europe	US PS	CDN PS	NCAA
Sr	Asia	US HS	CDN HS	USNDT
Gr	Other	US Midget	CDN Midget	Other

ADMISSIONS, ENROLLMENT & CAMPUS INFORMATION

Founded 1872	Average acceptance rate - 71 %	Admissions Director
Public, rural campus	Freshman financial aid - 71 %	Virginia Tech University
12,550 men / 8,722 women	Early decision application deadline - Nov 1	201 Burruss Hall
Tuition, room & board $ 12 / $ 23	Regular application deadline - Jan 15	Blacksburg, VA 24061
Avg SAT - 1,195	Financial aid deadline - Mar 11	O 540.231.6267 / F 540.231.3242

WAYNE STATE UNIVERSITY

Division 1

HOCKEY STAFF

HEAD COACH
Bill Wilkinson *(St. Lawrence '70)*

ASSISTANT COACHES
Chris Luongo *(Michigan State '89)*
Frank Novock *(Western Michigan '99)*

HOCKEY OFFICE
Wayne State University
101 Mathaei Athletic Complex
5101 John Cabot Lodge
Detroit, MI 48202-3489
O 313.577.9173 F 313.577.9176
william.wilkinson@wayne.edu

HOCKEY MEDIA CONTACT
Jeff Weiss - Sports Info Director
Wayne State University
5101 John Cabot Lodge
Detroit, MI 48202-3489
O 313.577.7542 / F 313.577.5997
jeff.weiss@wayne.edu

HOCKEY RINK
State Fairgrounds Coliseum *(Off Campus)*
8 Mile & Woodward Avenue
Detroit, MI 48203
O 313.366.3300

ATHLETIC DIRECTOR
Rob Fournier - Athletic Director
Wayne State University
5101 John Cabot Lodge
Detroit, MI 48202-3489
O 313.577.4280 / F 313.577.5997
ai.5611@wayne.edu

WARRIORS PLAYERS

Player	YB	GR	Ht/Wt	P	Hometown/Last Team
Derek Bachynski	83	08	5'10"/165	F	Belle River,ON/Leamington Flyers (WOJHL)
Jason Baclig	82	07	5' 8"/165	F	Leamington,ON/Leamington Flyers (WOJHL)
Ryan Bernardi	87	10	5' 8"/160	D	Etobicoke,ON/Milton Icehawks (OPJHL)
Jordan Black	83	08	5'11"/185	F	Canton,MI/Merrimack (HEA)
Jason Bloomingburg	82	07	5'10"/200	F	Canton,MI/Providence (HEA)
Matt Boldt	82	07	6' 1"/205	D	Burnsville,MN/Billings Bulls (NAHL)
Brett Bothwell	86	10	5'10"/170	G	Red Deer,AB/Yorkton Terriers (SJHL)
Jeff Caister	85	10	6' 2"/185	D	Mississauga,ON/Milton Icehawks (OPJHL)
Mark Cannon	82	07	6' 0"/225	F	River Rouge,MI/Compuware Ambassadors (NAHL)
Brian Cooke	85	10	6' 2"/190	D	Los Angeles,CA/Bridgewater Bandits (EJHL)
Taylor Donohoe	82	07	6' 3"/205	D	Richmond,BC/Powell River Kings (BCHL)
Adam Drescher	82	07	6' 4"/240	D	Bellville,MI/Wexford Raiders (OPJHL)
Mike Forgie	83	07	6' 3"/215	F	Scarborough,ON/Stouffville Spirit (OPJHL)
Jon Grabarek	84	09	5'11"/175	F	Sterling Hgts,MI/Cedar Rapids RoughRiders (USHL)
Nate Higgins	82	07	5'10"/205	F	Calgary,AB/Green Bay Gamblers (USHL)
Will Hooper	83	07	6' 2"/185	G	Woodbridge,ON/Findlay (CHA)
Dan Iliakis	82	07	5'11"/195	D	Scarborough,ON/Georgetown Raiders (OPJHL)
Jared Katz	85	10	5' 8"/145	F	St. Clair Shores,MI/Bay State Breakers (EJHL)
Matt Krug	85	09	6' 0"/230	D	Livonia,MI/Texas Tornado (NAHL)
Tylor Michel	84	08	5'10"/195	F	Sudbury,ON/Owen Sound Greys (MWJHL)
Mark Nebus	82	07	6' 0"/200	F	S Lyon,MI/Texas Tornado (NAHL)
John Nogatch	85	08	6' 3"/205	D	Redmond,WA/Lake Superior (CCHA)
Bryan Olds	83	09	6' 0"/185	F	Duluth,MN/Wichita Falls Rustlers (NAHL)
Stavros Paskaris	84	08	6' 1"/195	F	Dearborn,MI/Soo Indians (NAHL)
Derek Punches	84	09	5'11"/190	F	Manchester,MI/Texas Tornado (NAHL)
Adam Smith	85	09	5' 6"/165	F	W Bloomfield,MI/Springfield Spirit (NAHL)
Dan Vasquez	86	10	5'10"/195	G	Grosse Pt,MI/Helena Bighorns (NAHL)
Ryan Ward	86	10	6' 0"/175	F	Saline,MI/Cleveland Barons (NAHL)

ROSTER ANALYSIS (SCHOLARSHIPS - 18)

Class		Country		Last Team					
Fr	7	USA	17	US JR A	12	CDN JR A	7	ACHA	
So	5	Canada	11	US JR B	2	CDN JR B	3	NJCAA	
Jr	5	Europe		US PS		CDN PS		NCAA	4
Sr	11	Asia		US HS		CDN HS		USNDT	
Gr		Other		US Midget		CDN Midget		Other	

ADMISSIONS, ENROLLMENT & CAMPUS INFORMATION

Founded 1868
Public, urban campus
8,410 men / 10,703 women
Tuition, room & board $ 12 K / $ 19 K
Avg ACT - 20

Average acceptance rate - 63 %
Freshman financial aid - 53 %
Early decision application deadline - N/A
Regular application deadline - Aug 1
Financial aid deadline - Mar 1

Michael Wood - Admissions Director
Wayne State University
656 West Kirby Street
Detroit, MI 48202-3489
O 313.577.3577 / F 313.577.7536

www.wayne.edu   www.wsuathletics.com

WENTWORTH INST. OF TECHNOLOGY

HOCKEY
NORTHEAST

Division 3

HOCKEY STAFF

HEAD COACH
RJ Tolan *(Massachusetts Lowell '02)*

ASSISTANT COACHES
Michael Bertoni *(UMass-Boston '02)*
Kevin Crowder *(Northeastern '06)*

HOCKEY OFFICE
Wentworth Institute of Technology
550 Huntington Avenue
Boston, MA 02115-5998
O 617.989.4149 / F 617.989.4150
rjtolan13@wit.edu

HOCKEY MEDIA CONTACT
Bill Gorman - Sports Info Director
Wentworth Institute of Technology
550 Huntington Avenue
Boston, MA 02115
O 617.989.4147 / F 617.989.4150
gormanb@wit.edu

HOCKEY RINK
Matthews Arena (Off Campus)
238 South Botolph Street
Boston, MA 02115
Size 200' x 90', Capacity 6,000
O 617.225.3533

ATHLETIC DIRECTOR
Lee Conrad - Athletic Director
Wentworth Institute of Technology
550 Huntington Avenue
Boston, MA 02115-5998
O 617.989.4146 / F 617.989.4150
conradl@wit.edu

LEOPARDS PLAYERS

Player	YB	GR	Ht/Wt	P	Hometown/Last Team
Andrew Affronti	86	10	6' 2"/190	F	Neconset,NY/Bridgewater Bandits (EJHL)
Matt Buono	84	07	5' 9"/195	F	Ashburnham,MA/Cushing (NEPSAC)
Greg Demerjian	86	09	5' 9"/180	D	Cary,NC/Northwood (PS)
JT Fortier	85	09	6' 0"/225	D	Somersworth,NH/Portland Pirates (MJHL)
Phil Gabriele	84	08	6' 0"/215	D	N Stonington,CT/Curry (ECAC NE)
Matt Gilman	85	09	5' 8"/165	F	Groveland,MA/Hebron (NEPSAC)
Russ Hanson	86	09	6' 0"/180	F	Braintree,MA/Bridgewater Bandits (EJHL)
Brendan Healey	88	10	5'10"/160	F	Salem,NH/New Hampshire Monarchs (EJHL)
Jay Kalafatis	87	09	6' 1"/200	F	Littleton,MA/Bishop Guertin (PS)
Alan Keeso	83	08	5'10"/160	G	Listowel,ON/Sarnia Blast (WOJHL)
Matt Koehler	84	08	5'11"/205	F	Pembroke,MA/Walpole Stars (EJHL)
Dave Lewandowski	84	09	6' 1"/210	F	Glenmore,PA/Wichita Falls (NAHL)
Justin Marriott	85	10	5'11"/175	G	St. Clair Shores,MI/Valley Warriors (EJHL)
Doug Martin	88	10	5'10"/190	F	Trumbull,CT/Fairfield (PS)
Michael O'Brien	85	10	5'10"/190	F	Royersford,PA/Philadelphia (AtJHL)
Jeff Oddleifson	83	08	6' 3"/210	F	N Vancouver,BC/Prince George Spruce Kings (BCHL)
Jeff Olitch	85	10	5'11"/180	F	Calgary,AB/Helena Bighorns (NAHL)
Stephen Owens	85	09	5' 9"/175	F	Boston,MA/Walpole Stars (EJHL)
Rob Pagani	86	09	5'11"/190	D	Spencerport,NY/New England (EJHL)
Dillon Rioux	86	09	6' 2"/195	D	Rocklin,CA/Texarkana Bandits (NAHL)
Derek Rupert	86	09	5' 7"/175	F	Louisville,NY/South Grenville Rangers (EOJHL)
Joey Sides	86	09	5'11"/180	F	Sun Valley,ID/Avon (NEPSAC)
Ryan Singer	82	07	6' 0"/205	F	Kamloops,BC/Alberni Valley Bulldogs (BCHL)
Dean Smith	86	09	6' 1"/185	G	Wilmington,MA/SUNY Morrisville (NJCAA)
Jan Vastl	86	09	6' 2"/205	D	Salem,NH/Salem (HS)
Neil Walsky	87	10	5' 8"/165	F	Anchorage,AK/Wasilla Spirit (NAHL)
Martin Winzer	84	10	6' 2"/215	D	Nuremberg,Germany/ETC Crimmitschan ()
Adam Ysosi	82	07	6' 4"/210	F	Phoenix,AZ/Phoenix Polar Bears (WSHL)
Dan Zabkar	85	10	6' 0"/175	D	Bethel Park,PA/Bethel Park (HS)

ROSTER ANALYSIS (SCHOLARSHIPS - 0)

Class		Country		Last Team					
Fr	9	USA	24	US JR A	4	CDN JR A	2	ACHA	
So	13	Canada	4	US JR B	10	CDN JR B	2	NJCAA	1
Jr	4	Europe	1	US PS	6	CDN PS		NCAA	1
Sr	3	Asia		US HS	2	CDN HS		USNDT	
Gr		Other		US Midget		CDN Midget		Other	1

ADMISSIONS, ENROLLMENT & CAMPUS INFORMATION

Founded 1904	Average acceptance rate - 63 %	Keiko Broomhead - Admissions Director
Private, urban campus	Freshman financial aid - 40 %	Wentworth Institute of Technology
2,878 men / 719 women	Early decision application deadline - N/A	550 Huntington Avenue
Tuition, room & board - $ 19 K	Regular application deadline - May 1	Boston, MA 02115-5998
Avg SAT - N/A / Avg ACT - N/A	Financial aid deadline - Mar 1	O 617.989.4000 / F 617.989.4010

www.wit.edu

www.wit.edu/athletics/

WESLEYAN UNIVERSITY

Division 3

CARDINALS PLAYERS

Player	YB	GR	Ht/Wt	P	Hometown/Last Team
Tim Archibald		10	6' 4"/195	G	Wellesley,MA/Tilton (NEPSAC)
Kevin Armstrong		08	6' 1"/195	F	Palm City,FL/Canterbury (NEPSAC)
Mike Barbera	84	07	6' 2"/205	D	Cos Cob,CT/Greenwich (HS)
Jeff Beck		10	5'10"/185	F	Warrington,PA/Taft (NEPSAC)
Will Bennett	84	07	6' 3"/210	F	Boston,MA/Phillips Exeter (NEPSAC)
Dallas Bossort		09	6' 0"/195	D	Bismarck,ND/Shattuck-St. Mary's (PS)
Scott Burns		09	6' 3"/210	D	Wallingford,CT/Bishop Sheehan (PS)
Sam Campbell-Decock		10	6' 3"/200	D	Hamilton,NY/Hamilton Central (HS)
Anthony Christiano		10	5' 9"/185	D	Andover,MA/Andover (NEPSAC)
Derek Davidson		08	5'11"/200	F	Southington,CT/Choate (NEPSAC)
Brian Dew		09	5'10"/175	F	Freeport,NY/Portledge (PS)
Mike Dorsey		08	5'10"/180	F	Weymouth,MA/Berkshire (NEPSAC)
Brian Erensen		08	5' 8"/165	F	Greenwich,CT/Hill (PS)
JJ Evans		09	5'10"/170	F	Orland Pk,IL/Deerfield (NEPSAC)
Taylor Evans	84	07	6' 0"/190	D	Milton,MA/Phillips Exeter (NEPSAC)
Jarred Gagnon	84	07	5' 9"/200	F	Manchester,NH/Lawrence (NEPSAC)
Sean Gallagher		08	6' 0"/195	F	Chaska,MN/Blake (PS)
Gary Garofalo		10	6' 1"/180	F	Ridgefield,CT/Ridgefield (HS)
Chris Graceffa	84	07	6' 1"/205	F	Waltham,MA/Waltham (HS)
Ryan Hendrickson	84	07	5' 9"/175	F	Georgetown,MA/Pingree (NEPSAC)
Edward Klein		08	6' 1"/190	D	New Rochelle,NY/New Rochelle (HS)
David Layne		10	6' 3"/205	F	Flourtown,PA/William Penn (PS)
Dusty Mones		09	6' 0"/185	D	Trumbull,CT/Notre Dame-Fairfield (PS)
Mike Palladino		09	5'10"/165	G	Litchfield,CT/Taft (NEPSAC)
Woody Redpath		10	5' 7"/165	F	Norwich,VT/Taft (NEPSAC)
Sam Robinson		10	5'10"/170	F	Winchester,MA/Winchester (HS)
Dave Scardella	83	07	5'10"/175	G	Princeton Jctn,NJ/Milton (NEPSAC)
Alex Shklyarevsky		08	6' 1"/185	F	San Jose,CA/Northwood (PS)
Brenton Stafford		08	6' 2"/205	D	Cranston,RI/Kimball Union (NEPSAC)
John Wierzba		09	5'11"/185	F	Mequon,WI/Trinity-Pawling (NEPSAC)
Brent Winship		09	5' 9"/165	D	Manhattan Bch,CA/Mira Costa (HS)
Ryan Zemel		10	5' 6"/160	F	Miami,FL/Holderness (NEPSAC)

ROSTER ANALYSIS (SCHOLARSHIPS - 0)

Class		Country		Last Team				
Fr	9	USA	32	US JR A		CDN JR A		ACHA
So	8	Canada		US JR B		CDN JR B		NJCAA
Jr	8	Europe		US PS	25	CDN PS		NCAA
Sr	7	Asia		US HS	7	CDN HS		USNDT
Gr		Other		US Midget		CDN Midget		Other

ADMISSIONS, ENROLLMENT & CAMPUS INFORMATION

WEST CHESTER UNIVERSITY

Division 1

HOCKEY STAFF	GOLDEN RAMS PLAYERS			

HOCKEY STAFF

HEAD COACH
Mark Gonsalves

ASSISTANT COACHES
Gregg Rudinsky

HOCKEY OFFICE
1109 Foster Street
Philadelphia, PA 19116
O 610.384.1237 / F 610.384.6078
H 215.676.1380
domwcu@aol.com

GENERAL MANAGER
Dom Bellizzie
1109 Foster Street
Philadelphia, PA 19116
O 610.384.1237 / F 610.384.6078
H 215.676.1380
domwcu@aol.com

HOCKEY RINK
Ice Line Arena (Off Campus)
Capacity 75
O 610.436.9670

FACULTY REPRESENTATIVE
Dr. Thomas Treadwell - School Rep.
West Chester University
Peoples Building #33
West Chester, PA 19383
O 610.436.2723

GOLDEN RAMS PLAYERS

Player	YB	GR	Ht/Wt	P	Hometown/Last Team
Will Averona	08		5'11"/185	D	Malvern,PA/Malvern (PS)
Luke Benner	07		6'0"/190	D	West Chester,PA/Malvern (PS)
Ken Bergeron	08		5'9"/150	F	Egg Harbor,NJ/Hollydell (Midget AA)
Robert Bushman	09		6'1"/195	F	Stafford,VA/Central Florida (ACHA)
Matt Chandik	09		6'0"/225	F	Allentown,PA/Bethlehem (Midget AA)
Ed Devine	09		5'10"/160	F	Wayne,PA/Philadelphia (Midget AAA)
Ryan Fenyves	10		6'2"/250	G	Hummelstown,PA/Norwich (Jr)
Jason Ferrell	07		5'10"/215	F	West Chester,PA/Iindiana PA (ACHA)
Dan Flynn	10		6'2"/200	F	Drexel Hill,PA/Monsignor Bonner (PS)
Jim Gehring	09		5'10"/200	F	Chester Springs,PA/Mercyhurst (ACAHA)
Corey Hackney	10		5'10"/160	G	Watford,ON/Lucan Irish (Jr)
Pat Johnson	10		5'9"/165	F	Vankleek Hill,ON/Char-Lan (EOJHL)
Bob Jones	07		5'11"/210	F	Denville,NJ/Morris Knolls (HS)
Adam Jordon	09		5'10"/180	F	Center Hall,PA/Hershey (EmJHL)
Ryan Jordan	10		6'2"/175	D	Media,PA/Valley Forge (CHA-S)
David Karcher	09		5'8"/155	D	Hatboro,PA/Ice Dogs (Midget AA)
Eric Keene	10		5'11"/170	F	North Wales,PA/Raiders (Midget AA)
Bob Kenworthy	07		6'2"/205	D	Brookhaven,PA/Des Moines (USHL)
Bob MacLaughlin	09		6'0"/206	F	Havertown,PA/Haverford (HS)
Joe Mango	09		5'10"/170	D	Boothwyn,PA/Philadelphia (AtJHL)
Patrick McMahon	10		5'8"/160	F	Marlton,NJ/Jaguars (Midget AA)
Drew Mervin	10		5'8"/160	F	Yardley,PA/New Jersey (Jr)
Jason Munter	08		6'1"/180	D	Springfield,PA/Valley Forge (MJHL)
Chris Orlando	09		5'10"/180	D	Ivyland,PA/Nichols College (ECAC NE)
Louis Perez	08		5'9"/170	G	Flourtown,PA/Germantown (PS)
Jesse Petrillo	09		5'7"/160	D	Philadelphia,PA/Valley Forge (MJHL)
John Povey	09		5'10"/165	F	Havertown,PA/Philadelphia (AtJHL)
Andrew Reuter	10		5'7"/140	F	Chalfont,PA/Philadelphia (MJHL)
Jeff Shockley	10		6'3"/170	D	Magnolia,NJ/Jaguars (Midget AA)
Jeremiah Trostle	09		6'1"/180	F	Tork,PA/Robert Morris University
Rob Troxell	07		5'7"/135	F	Warrington,PA/LaSalle (PS)
Tom Waite	09		5'8"/150	F	Perkasie,PA/Valley Forge (MJHL)
Ben Wirjosemito	10		6'1"/165	G	Westmont,NJ/Hun (PS)

ROSTER ANALYSIS (SCHOLARSHIPS - 0)

Class		Country		Last Team					
Fr	8	USA	29	US JR A	1	CDN JR A		ACHA	4
So	13	Canada	1	US JR B	11	CDN JR B		NJCAA	
Jr	3	Europe		US PS	5	CDN PS		NCAA	1
Sr	6	Asia		US HS	1	CDN HS		USNDT	
Gr		Other		US Midget	7	CDN Midget		Other	

ADMISSIONS, ENROLLMENT & CAMPUS INFORMATION

Founded 1871	Acceptance rate - 51 %	Marsha Haug - Admissions Director
Public, suburban campus	Freshman financial aid - %	West Chester University
3,535 men / 6,565 women	Early decision application deadline - N/A	Admissions Office
Tuition, room & board $ 9 K / $ 15 K	Regular application deadline - Jun 1	West Chester, PA 19383
Avg SAT - 1,030	Financial aid deadline - Mar 1	O 610.436.3411 / F 610.436.2907

www.wcupa.edu   www.wcuhockey.com

WESTERN MICHIGAN UNIVERSITY

Division 1

HOCKEY STAFF

HEAD COACH
Jim Culhane *(Western Michigan '87)*

ASSISTANT COACHES
Chris Brooks *(Western Michigan '96)*
Brendan Kenny *(Western Michigan '97)*
Matt Barnes *(Western Michigan '99)*

HOCKEY OFFICE
Western Michigan University
Lawson Arena
2009 Howard Street
Kalamazoo, MI 49008-3899
O 616.387.3050/ F 616.387.3051
jim.culhane@wmich.edu

HOCKEY MEDIA CONTACT
Daniel Jankowski - Hockey Info Director
Western Michigan University
218 University Arena
Kalamazoo, MI 49008-5166
O 616.387.4122/ F 616.387.4139
daniel.jankowski@wmich.edu

HOCKEY RINK
Lawson Arena (On Campus)
2009 Howard Street
Kalamazoo, MI 49008
Size 200' x 85', Capacity 3,667
O 616.387.3065

ATHLETIC DIRECTOR
Kathy Beauregard - Athletic Director
Western Michigan University
Gary Center
Kalamazoo, MI 49008
O 616.387.3061
kathy.beauregard@wmich.edu

BRONCOS PLAYERS

Player	YB	GR	Ht/Wt	P	Hometown/Last Team
Nathan Ansell	86	08	5'11"/195	D	Sarnia,ON/Sarnia Blast (WOJHL)
Daniel Bellissimo	84	08	6' 2"/170	G	Toronto,ON/Stouffville Spirit (OPJHL)
Brian Bicek	85	08	5' 8"/170	F	Downers Gr,IL/Cleveland Barons (NAHL)
Chris Clackson		10	5'11"/195	F	Pittsburgh,PA/Chicago Steel (USHL)
Matt Clackson	85	09	6' 0"/190	F	Pittsburgh,PA/Chicago Steel (USHL)
Jordan Collins		10	6' 1"/220	D	Novi,MI/Trail Smoke Eaters (BCHL)
Chris Frank	86	09	6' 1"/240	D	Lynnwood,WA/Cowichan Valley Capitals (BCHL)
Patrick Galivan	86	09	5'11"/170	F	Oak Park,IL/Texarkana Bandits (NAHL)
Riley Gill		10	6' 2"/200	G	Northfield,MI/Texarkana Bandits (NAHL)
Trevor Heffernan		09	6' 0"/195	G	LaGrange,IL/Western Michigan (ACHA)
Brett John	83	07	5'10"/195	F	Plymouth,MI/Chicago Freeze (NAHL)
Dave Krisky	84	09	5'10"/180	F	Westbank,BC/Williams Lake Timberwolves (BCHL)
Kevin Labatte	84	07	6' 2"/190	F	Ogden,UT/Elmira Sugar Kings (MWJHL)
Mike Lesperance	85	08	6' 1"/195	F	Newmarket,ON/Newmarket Hurricanes (OPJHL)
Mark Letestu		10	5'11"/195	F	Elk Point,AB/Bonnyville Pontiacs (AJHL)
Jeff LoVecchio	85	09	6' 2"/195	F	Chesterfield,MO/Omaha Lancers (USHL)
Tyler Ludwig	85	09	6' 1"/205	D	Colleyville,TX/Texas Tornado (NAHL)
Jonathan Lupa	83	08	6' 0"/200	D	London,ON/Stratford Cullitons (MWJHL)
Ryan Mahrle	85	07	5'11"/175	D	Troy,MI/Leamington Flyers (WOJHL)
Jason Moul	83	07	5' 8"/170	F	Livonia,MI/Sioux Falls Stampede (USHL)
Kevin O'Connor	84	09	5'11"/180	D	Trenton,MI/Omaha Lancers (USHL)
Jeff Pierce	83	08	6' 0"/180	F	Troy,MI/Petrolia Jets (WOJHL)
Steve Silver	86	09	6' 2"/225	D	Brighton,MI/Cleveland Barons (NAHL)
Paul Szczechura	85	07	5'11"/175	F	Brantford,ON/Brantford Golden Eagles (MWJHL)
Cam Watson		10	6' 0"/190	F	Cambridge,ON/Cambridge Winterhawks (MWJHL)
Sean Weaver	84	09	6' 0"/200	F	Victoria,BC/Merritt Centennials (BCHL)
Julian Zamparo		10	6' 2"/200	D	Toronto,ON/St. Michael's (PS)

ROSTER ANALYSIS (SCHOLARSHIPS - 18)

Class		Country		Last Team					
Fr	6	USA	17	US JR A	11	CDN JR A	7	ACHA	1
So	10	Canada	10	US JR B		CDN JR B	7	NJCAA	
Jr	6	Europe		US PS		CDN PS	1	NCAA	
Sr	5	Asia		US HS		CDN HS		USNDT	
Gr		Other		US Midget		CDN Midget		Other	

ADMISSIONS, ENROLLMENT & CAMPUS INFORMATION

Founded 1903
Public, urban campus
11,168 men / 11,168 women
Tuition, room & board - $13 K / $21 K
Avg ACT - 22

Average acceptance rate - 85 %
Freshman financial aid - 66 %
Early decision application deadline - N/A
Regular application deadline - rolling
Financial aid deadline - Apr 1

John Fraire - Admissions Director
Western MichiganUniversity
Seibert Building
Kalamazoo, MI 49008
O 616.387.2000/ F 616.387.2096

WESTERN MICHIGAN UNIVERSITY

Division 1

HOCKEY STAFF

HEAD COACH
Wayne Pushie

ASSISTANT COACH
Matt Kakabeeke

HOCKEY OFFICE
O 269.343.6919
wayne.pushie@wmich.edu

HOCKEY MANAGER
Gregory Korbecki - General Manager
519 Argyll Lane
Schaumberg, IL 60194
H 847.490.1609
O 773.714.3876
rhkorb@aol.com

HOCKEY RINK
Lawson Arena (On Campus)
2009 Howard Street
Kalamazoo, MI 49008
Size 200' x 85', Capacity 4,500
O 269.387.3076

CLUB PRESIDENT
Eric Korbecki - Team President
O 847.809.0728
eric.korbecki@wmich.edu

STALLIONS PLAYERS

Player	YB	GR	Ht/Wt	P	Hometown/Last Team
Sean Baltazar	08		6' 3"/210	D	Plymouth,MI/Brownstown Bombers ()
Scott Cortwright	09		5' 9"/170	F	LaGrange,IL/Huskies (Midget AA)
Nick Cross			5'11"/170	F	Kalamazoo,MI/Portage Central (HS)
Joe Diebold	07		5' 8"/170	F	Lisle,IL/Darien Huskies (Midget AA)
Tony Genualdi			6' 0"/185	D	Naperville,IL/Robert Morris (ACHA)
Mike Guentner	09		6' 0"/195	F	Butler,PA/ ()
Jim Guzzardi	09		5' 7"/150	F	Elk Grove,IL/Chicago Flames (Midget AA)
Kyle Johnson			5' 8"/180	G	Arnold,MO/St Louis (ACHA)
Andrew Karie			6' 1"/195	G	Shelby Township,MI/Motor City Chiefs (CSHL)
Steve Koich	08		5'10"/175	F	Chelsea,MI/Victory Honda (Midget AAA)
Derek Krause	08		5'10"/180	D	Shelby Township,MI/Belle Tire (Midget AAA)
Kevin McAvoy	08		5'11"/180	F	Naperville,IL/Chicago Mission (Midget AAA)
Mike McMahon	07		6' 0"/190	D	Barrington,IL/Peoria Mustangs (CSHL)
Sean McWhorter			5'11"/180	F	Grand Ledge,MI/Bismark Bobcats (NAHL)
Chris Meegan	09		5' 8"/195	D	Oak Park,IL/Twin Bridges Lightning (Midget AA)
Aaron Moss	09		5'10"/160	F	Linden,MI/ ()
Bryan Moss	08		6' 0"/190	D	Linden,MI/West Virginia (ACHA)
Michael Podelnyk	08		6' 0"/185	F	Fenton,MI/Compuware (Midget AAA)
Nick Roberts			5' 9"/155	G	Schoolcraft,MI/Kalamazoo Eagles ()
Ben Ruffolo			5' 8"/160	D	New Boston,MI/Huron (HS)
Jack Sandmeyer			6' 2"/205	F	Portage,MI/Portage Central (HS)
Chris Serra	08		5'10"/180	G	Clinton Township,MI/Metro Jets (CSHL)
Michael Sholler			5' 9"/200	F	Orland Park,IL/Peoria Mustangs (CSHL)
Ricky Simmons	09		6' 0"/185	F	Wheaton,IL/Chicago Huskies (Midget AA)
Dan Smyth	08		6' 4"/185	D	Rochester Hills,MI/Rochester United (HS)
Ryan Tallon	08		6' 1"/210	F	Kalamazoo,MI/West Michigan Warriors (Midget AAA)
Jerry Taylor	09		6' 1"/200	D	Clinton Township,MI/Grosse Pointe (HS)
Jason TerAvest	09		6' 0"/185	F	Battle Creek,MI/West Michigan Warriors (Midget AAA)
Teddy Theodoroff	09		5'11"/185	F	Ferndale,MI/Hill (PS)
Evan Visuri	09		5'11"/190	F	Saginaw,MI/Nouvel Catholic Central (PS)

ROSTER ANALYSIS (SCHOLARSHIPS - 18)

Class	Country	Last Team		
Fr	USA	US JR A	CDN JR A	ACHA
So	Canada	US JR B	CDN JR B	NJCAA
Jr	Europe	US PS	CDN PS	NCAA
Sr	Asia	US HS	CDN HS	USNDT
Gr	Other	US Midget	CDN Midget	Other

ADMISSIONS, ENROLLMENT & CAMPUS INFORMATION

Founded 1903
Public, urban campus
11,168 men / 11,168 women
Tuition, room & board - $ 13 K/ $ 21 K
Avg ACT - 22

Average acceptance rate - 85 %
Freshman financial aid - 66 %
Early decision application deadline - N/A
Regular application deadline - rolling
Financial aid deadline - Apr 1

John Fraire - Admissions Director
Western MichiganUniversity
1903 West Michigan Avenue
Kalamazoo, MI 49008-5211
O 269.387.2000 / F 269.387.2096

www.wmich.edu

www.rso.wmich.edu/stallions

WESTERN NEW ENGLAND COLLEGE

H O C K E Y
NORTHEAST

Division 3

HOCKEY STAFF

HEAD COACH
Chris Bernard *(Clarkson '98)*

ASSISTANT COACHES
Bryan Musa *(Elmira '95)*
Clay Strahan *(W. New England '99)*

HOCKEY OFFICE
Western New England College
1215 Wilbraham Road
Springfield, MA 01119-2684
O 413.796.2283 / F 413.796.2121
cbernard@wnec.edu

HOCKEY MEDIA CONTACT
Ken Cerino - Sports Info Director
Western New England College
1215 Wilbraham Road
Springfield, MA 01119-2684
O 413.782.1227 / F 413.796.2121
kcerino@wnec.edu

HOCKEY RINK
Olympia Ice Center (Off Campus)
125 Capital Drive
West Springfield, MA 01089
Size 200' x 85', Capacity 1,200
O 413.736.8100

ATHLETIC DIRECTOR
Mike Theulen - Athletic Director
Western New England College
1215 Wilbraham Road
Springfield, MA 01119-2684
O 413.782.1202 / F 413.796.2121
mtheulen@wnec.edu

GOLDEN BEARS PLAYERS

Player	YB	GR	Ht/Wt	P	Hometown/Last Team
Mike Amato	84	07	5'10"/170	F	Mt Laurel,NJ/New Jersey Jaguars (Midget A)
Joe Balog	86	09	5' 9"/175	D	Ludlow,MA/Springfield Falcons ()
Ross Bennett-Bonn	85	08	6' 0"/195	F	Warwick,RI/Rhode Island (ACHA)
Tyler Campbell	84	07	6' 0"/160	D	Dowingtown,PA/Philadelphia Little Flyers (MJHL)
Tim Cutshaw	88	10	5'10"/165	F	Hampton,NJ/Bethlehem Blast (MJHL)
Andrew Dinkelmeyer	86	10	5'10"/190	D	Hicksville,NY/Syracuse Stars (EJHL)
Connor Fallon	87	09	5'11"/190	F	Springfield,MA/Cathedral (PS)
Brandon Gervais	86	08	5' 8"/190	G	Lewiston,ME/St. Dominic's (PS)
Chris Girardi	85	07	5'10"/160	F	Easton,CT/Fairfield (PS)
Justin Graziano	88	10	5' 8"/170	F	N Haven,CT/Connecticut Wolves (MJHL)
Mike Haddock	86	10	5' 8"/175	F	Hillard,OH/Capital District Selects (EJHL)
Nick Klassen	86	08	6' 0"/170	D	Parker,CO/Colorado Outlaws (Midget AAA)
Philip Lamy	86	09	5'11"/160	F	Manchester,NH/Kents Hill (NEPSAC)
Hank Levin	84	09	5' 8"/165	F	Lido Beach,NY/Apple Core (EJHL)
Shawn Longley	85	08	5' 7"/155	F	Lewiston,ME/St. Dominic's (PS)
Mike Majesty	85	09	5' 8"/145	F	Chicago,IL/Toledo Cherokee (CSHL)
Glenn McCaffrey	85	08	5' 9"/150	G	Londonderry,NH/Londonderry (HS)
Joe Nobilio	86	08	5' 8"/155	F	Hillsborough,NJ/St. Joseph's (PS)
Zach O'Steen	84	07	6' 1"/210	F	Chelmsford,MA/Massachusetts Lowell (HEA)
Jason Remsbecker	87	09	5'10"/165	F	Farmingdale,NY/Long Island Gulls ()
Jake Rinaldo	86	09	5' 7"/160	D	Union,NJ/New Jersey Rockets (MJHL)
Andrew Rosser	86	09	6' 0"/195	D	Herndon,VA/Mass.-Conn. Braves ()
Kyle Sagnella	85	09	5' 9"/190	G	E Haven,CT/Connecticut Wolves (MJHL)
Nick Sampson	85	08	6' 3"/180	F	Reading,MA/Reading (HS)
Dean Smith	87	09	5'10"/155	F	Warwick,RI/Toll Gate (HS)
Pat Tamez	86	08	6' 0"/210	D	Mt Laurel,NJ/New Jersey Jaguars (Midget A)
Drew Vrolyk	87	10	5'11"/165	D	Boylston,MA/New England Falcons (EJHL)
Joe Willard	87	09	5' 9"/170	F	Holliston,MA/Marian (PS)

ROSTER ANALYSIS (SCHOLARSHIPS - 0)

Class		Country		Last Team				
Fr	5	USA	28	US JR A		CDN JR A	ACHA	1
So	11	Canada		US JR B	12	CDN JR B	NJCAA	
Jr	8	Europe		US PS	7	CDN PS	NCAA	1
Sr	4	Asia		US HS	3	CDN HS	USNDT	
Gr		Other		US Midget	4	CDN Midget	Other	

ADMISSIONS, ENROLLMENT & CAMPUS INFORMATION

Founded 1919	Average acceptance rate - 79 %	Dr. Charles Pollock - Admission Director
Private, suburban campus	Freshman financial aid - 67 %	Western New England College
1,872 men / 1,148 women	Early decision application deadline - N/A	156 Wilbraham Road
Tuition, room & board - $ 32 K	Regular application deadline - rolling	Springfield, MA 01119-2684
Avg SAT - 1,055	Financial aid deadline - Apr 1	O 413.782.1321 / F 413.782.1777

www.wnec.edu | www1.wnec.edu/athletics/

WILLIAMS COLLEGE

Division 3

HOCKEY STAFF

HEAD COACH
Bill Kangas *(Vermont '82)*

ASSISTANT COACHES
Jesse Desper *(Hobart '05)*
Charles Bellows *(Williams '06)*

HOCKEY OFFICE
Williams College
Chandler Athletic Center
Williamstown, MA 01267
O 413.597.2036/F 413.597.4272
william.r.kangas@williams.edu

HOCKEY MEDIA CONTACT
Dick Quinn - Sports Info Director
Williams College
Chandler Athletic Center
PO Box 676
Williamstown, MA 01267
O 413.597.4982/F 413.597.4429
dick.quinn@williams.edu

HOCKEY RINK
Chapman Rink (On Campus)
Latham Street
Williamstown, MA 01267
Size 200' x 85', Capacity 2,500
O 413.597.2433

ATHLETIC DIRECTOR
Harry Sheehy - Athletic Director
Williams College
Chandler Athletic Center
Williamstown, MA 01267
O 413.597.2366/F 413.597.4272
harry.c.sheehy@williams.edu

EPHS PLAYERS

Player	YB GR	Ht/Wt	P	Hometown/Last Team
Dan Bergan	09	6' 0"/195	F	Newtown,PA/Deerfield (NEPSAC)
Will Bruce	08	5'10"/185	F	Nashville,TN/Thornhill Islanders (OPJHL)
Steve Bruch	08	5' 8"/150	F/D	London,ON/Hotchkiss (NEPSAC)
Kevin Colwell	07	6' 1"/200	F	Wellesley,MA/Thayer (NEPSAC)
Chris DeBaere	09	5' 8"/165	F	Natick,MA/Belmont Hill (NEPSAC)
Matt Draheim	09	5' 8"/165	F	Costa de Caza,CA/New England Falcons (EJHL)
Christopher Fahey	09	6' 5"/240	D	Milton,MA/Northfield Mount Hermon (NEPSAC)
Ben Fields	09	6' 0"/200	D	Winnetka,IL/Deerfield (NEPSAC)
Colin Greenhalgh	07	6' 0"/195	F	Paxfield,MA/Nobles (NEPSAC)
Brett Haraguchi	09	5' 8"/160	F	Cupertino,CA/Lawrenceville (PS)
Owen Holm	10	6' 0"/190	F	Wayzata,MN/Blake (PS)
Brandon Jackmuff	08	6' 2"/180	F	Woodbury,NJ/Hotchkiss (NEPSAC)
Andrew Lepore	10	5'11"	F	Clarence,NY/Nichols (PS)
Steve Lunau	07	5' 9"/160	F	Bergenfield,NJ/Salisbury (NEPSAC)
Matt McCarthy	07	6' 0"/180	D	Tonawanda,NY/Nichols (PS)
Zach Miller	10	5' 9"/175	F	Bridgeton,NJ/Groton (NEPSAC)
Mark Pulde	10	6' 0"/180	G	Lexington,MA/B B & N (NEPSAC)
David Ramsay	09	5' 9"/170	D	Exeter,MN/Exeter (HS)
Rick Redmond	09	6' 2"/180	G	Winnetka,IL/Deerfield (NEPSAC)
Greg Schultz	08	6' 6"/230	F	Avon,CT/New England Coyotes (EJHL)
Evan Seely	10	6' 3"/205	D	Woodstock,VT/St. Paul's (NEPSAC)
Alex Smigelski	10	6' 2"/195	F	Mt Lakes,NJ/Delbarton (PS)

ROSTER ANALYSIS (SCHOLARSHIPS - 0)

Class		Country		Last Team			
Fr	6	USA	21	US JR A		CDN JR A	1	ACHA
So	8	Canada	1	US JR B	2	CDN JR B		NJCAA
Jr	4	Europe		US PS	18	CDN PS		NCAA
Sr	4	Asia		US HS	1	CDN HS		USNDT
Gr		Other		US Midget		CDN Midget		Other

ADMISSIONS, ENROLLMENT & CAMPUS INFORMATION

Founded 1793	Average acceptance rate - 19 %	Richard Nesbitt - Admissions Director
Private, rural campus	Freshman financial aid - 100 %	Williams College Office of Admissions
946 men / 985 women	Early decision application deadline - Nov 10	988 Main Street
Tuition, room & board - $ 41 K	Regular application deadline - Jan 1	Williamstown, MA 01267
Avg SAT - 1,325	Financial aid deadline - Feb 1	O 413.597.2211/F 413.458.2158

www.williams.edu   www.williams.edu/athletics/

UNIV. OF WISCONSIN - EAU CLAIRE

Division 3

HOCKEY STAFF

HEAD COACH
Luke Strand *(Wisconsin-Eau Claire)*

ASSISTANT COACHES
Matt Loen
Bob Thorp

HOCKEY OFFICE
University of Wisconsin-Eau Claire
McPhee Physical Education Ctr. #223
Eau Claire, WI 54702-4004
O 715.836.4516/ F 715.836.4074
strandls@uwec.edu

HOCKEY MEDIA CONTACT
Tim Petermann - Sports Info Director
University of Wisconsin-Eau Claire
McPhee Physical Education Center
Eau Claire, WI 54702-4004
O 715.836.4184/ F 715.836.4074
petermta@uwec.edu

HOCKEY RINK
Hobbs Ice Center (Off Campus)
915 Menomonie Street
Eau Claire, WI 54703
Size ' x ', Capacity 1,100
O 715.836.2992

ATHLETIC DIRECTOR
Scott Kilgallon - Athletic Director
University of Wisconsin-Eau Claire
McPhee Physical Education Center
Eau Claire, WI 54702-4004
O 715.836.5858/ F 715.836.4074
kilgals@uwec.edu

BLUEGOLDS PLAYERS

Player	YB	GR	Ht/Wt	P	Hometown/Last Team
Sam Bauler		09	6'1"/180	F	Apple Valley,MN/Eastview (HS)
Ben Bosworth		09	6'5"/220	F	Hudson,WI/Hudson (HS)
Peter Bracker		09	5'9"/165	F	Albert Lea,MN/Albert Lea (HS)
Tyler Brigl		10	5'10"/185	G	Eagan,MN/Bismarck Bobcats (NAHL)
Evan Byers		09	6'0"/185	D	Eagan,MN/Eagan (HS)
Dave Coleman	83	07	6'2"/205	F	Whitby,ON/Father Austin (PS)
Steve Dus	84	07	6'2"/205	F	Onalaska,WI/Onalaska (HS)
Dan Fina		09	6'1"/195	F	Fontana,WI/Glenbard South (HS)
Kyle Garner	84	07	5'11"/205	D	Sun Prairie,WI/Sun Prairie (HS)
Sean Garrity		08	6'2"/205	F	N St. Paul,MN/St. Cloud State (WCHA)
Mike Gatzke		08	6'1"/190	G	White Bear Lk,MN/Hill-Murray (PS)
Ben Hendrick		09	5'9"/185	F	Andover,MN/National Bandy ()
Andrew Johnson		09	5'11"/195	F	Andover,MN/Green Bay Gamblers (USHL)
Kevin Knapp	82	07	6'0"/215	D	Minneapolis,MN/Spring Lake Park (HS)
Joe Krahn		10	5'8"/180	F	Greenfield ,WI/Bridgewater Bandits (EJHL)
Dan Krenn		08	6'1"/210	F	Madison,WI/Norwich (ECAC East)
Nicholas Kugali		10	6'2"/200	D	Pittsburgh,PA/Wellington Dukes (OPJHL)
Brooks Lockwood	83	07	5'10"/180	F	Hudson,WI/Hudson (HS)
Dan Lohr	81	07	5'10"/195	D	Middleton,WI/Middleton (HS)
Ryan Mensing		09	5'11"/190	G	Langley,BC/Western Michigan (CCHA)
Greg Peterson		09	6'2"/200	D	Maple Gr,MN/Robert Morris (CHA)
Mike Schneider		09	5'9"/180	F	Owatonna,MN/Owatonna (HS)
Nate Smith		10	6'1"/195	F	Clayton,WI/Minnesota Owls (MnJHL)
Tyler Trudell		10	5'10"/175	D	Waukesha,WI/Texarkana Bandits (NAHL)
Jesse Vesel		09	5'9"/170	F	Hibbing,MN/St. Thomas (MIAC)
Jeremiah Weber	84	08	6'1"/205	F	Hayward,WI/Northwest Wisconsin Knights (MnJHL)
Tyler Weigel		10	6'0"/195	F	Madison,WI/Madison Capitals (Midget AAA)

ROSTER ANALYSIS (SCHOLARSHIPS - 0)

Class		Country		Last Team				
Fr	6	USA	25	US JR A	3	CDN JR A	1	ACHA
So	11	Canada	2	US JR B	3	CDN JR B		NJCAA
Jr	4	Europe		US PS	2	CDN PS		NCAA 5
Sr	6	Asia		US HS	11	CDN HS		USNDT
Gr		Other		US Midget	1	CDN Midget		Other 1

ADMISSIONS, ENROLLMENT & CAMPUS INFORMATION

Founded 1916	Average acceptance rate - 66 %	Robert Lopez - Admissions Director
Public, urban campus	Freshman financial aid - 96 %	University of Wisconsin-Eau Claire
3,751 men / 6,120 women	Early decision application deadline - N/A	112 Schofield Hall
Tuition, room & board - $ 10 K / $ 20 K	Regular application deadline - rolling	Eau Claire, WI 54701-4004
Avg SAT - 1,120 / Avg ACT - 24	Financial aid deadline - Apr 15	O 715.836.5415/ F 715.836.2409

www.uwec.edu

www.uwec.edu/Athletics/

UNIVERSITY OF WISCONSIN - MADISON

Division 1

HOCKEY STAFF

HEAD COACH
Mike Eaves *(Wisconsin-Madison '78)*

ASSISTANT COACHES
Mark Osiecki *(Wisconsin-Madison '90)*
Kevin Patrick *(Notre Dame '92)*
Bill Howard *(Colorado College '67)*

HOCKEY OFFICE
University of Wisconsin Athletic Dept.
Kohl Center
601 West Dayton Street
Madison, WI 53715
O 608.262.3932 / F 608.262.8959
mge@athletics.wisc.edu

HOCKEY MEDIA CONTACT
Paul Capobianco - Hockey Info Director
University of Wisconsin Sports Inf. Office
1440 Monroe Street
Madison, WI 53711
O 608.263.1983 / F 608.262.8184
phc@athletics.wisc.edu

HOCKEY RINK
Kohl Center (On Campus)
601 West Dayton Street
Madison, WI 53715
Size 200' x 97', Capacity 15,237
PB 608.265.4336

ATHLETIC DIRECTOR
Barry Alvarez - Athletic Director
University of Wisconsin Athletic Dept.
1440 Monroe Street
Madison, WI 53711
O 608.262.5068 / F 608.262.9212

BADGERS PLAYERS

Player	YB	GR	Ht/Wt	P	Hometown/Last Team
Zach Bearson	87	10	6' 2"/195	F	Naperville,IL/Waterloo Blackhawks (USHL)
Aaron Bendickson	86	10	5'11"/170	F	Thief River Fls,MN/Des Moines Buccaneers (USHL)
Andy Bohmback	87	10	6' 2"/190	F	Hudson,WI/Waterloo Blackhawks (USHL)
Andy Brandt	83	07	6' 1"/190	F	Wausau,WI/Pittsburgh Forge (NAHL)
Ross Carlson	82	07	5'11"/185	F	Duluth,MN/Waterloo Blackhawks (USHL)
Shane Connelly	87	09	5' 9"/180	G	Cheltenham,PA/Chicago Steel (USHL)
Michael Davies	86	10	5' 8"/170	F	Chesterfield,MO/Lincoln Stars (USHL)
Jake Dowell	85	07	6' 0"/205	F	Eau Claire,WI/USNDT (NAHL)
Davis Drewiske	84	08	6' 1"/210	D	Hudson,WI/Des Moines Buccaneers (USHL)
Brian Elliott	85	07	6' 3"/190	G	Newmarket,ON/Ajax Axemen (OPJHL)
Josh Engel	84	08	6' 3"/205	D	Rice Lake,WI/Green Bay Gamblers (USHL)
Matthew Ford	84	08	6' 1"/205	F	W Hills,CA/Sioux Falls Stampede (USHL)
Blake Geoffrion	88	10	6' 2"/195	F	Brentwood,TN/USNDT (NAHL)
Tom Gorowsky	86	09	6' 0"/195	F	Lino Lakes,MN/Sioux Falls Stampede (USHL)
Ben Grotting	86	10	6' 1"/195	F	Birmingham,AL/Lincoln Stars (USHL)
Jeff Henderson	86	09	6' 2"/180	G	Menomonie,WI/Menomonie (HS)
Ryan Jeffery	86	09	6' 1"/175	G	Madison,WI/Memorial (HS)
Andrew Joudrey	84	07	5'11"/190	F	Bedford,NS/Notre Dame (PS)
Kyle Klubertanz	85	08	6' 0"/185	D	Sun Prairie,WI/Green Bay Gamblers (USHL)
Jeff Likens	85	07	5'11"/180	D	Barrington,IL/USNDT (NAHL)
Jamie McBain	88	10	6' 0"/190	D	Faribault,MN/USNDT (NAHL)
John Mitchell	86	10	6' 5"/210	F	Neenah,WI/Indiana Ice (USHL)
Matt Olinger	83	07	6' 1"/200	D	Madison,WI/Cedar Rapids RoughRiders (USHL)
Joe Piskula	84	08	6' 3"/210	D	Antigo,WI/Des Moines Buccaneers (USHL)
Jack Skille	87	09	6' 1"/205	F	Madison,WI/USNDT (NAHL)
Ben Street	87	09	5'11"/190	F	Coquitlam,BC/Salmon Arm Silverbacks (BCHL)
Nigel Williams	88	10	6' 5"/220	D	Aurora,IL/USNDT (NAHL)

ROSTER ANALYSIS (SCHOLARSHIPS - 18)

Class		Country	Last Team					
Fr	9	USA	24	US JR A	16	CDN JR A	2	ACHA
So	6	Canada	3	US JR B		CDN JR B		NJCAA
Jr	5	Europe		US PS		CDN PS	1	NCAA
Sr	7	Asia		US HS	2	CDN HS		USNDT	6
Gr		Other		US Midget		CDN Midget		Other

ADMISSIONS, ENROLLMENT & CAMPUS INFORMATION

Founded 1848
Public, urban campus
12,415 men / 15,802 women
Tuition, room & board - $13 K / $27 K
Avg SAT - 1,265 / Avg ACT - 27

Average acceptance rate - 66 %
Freshman financial aid - %
Early decision application deadline - N/A
Regular application deadline - Feb 1
Financial aid deadline - N/A

Keith White - Admissions Director
UW - Peterson Office Building - Rm 140
750 University Avenue
Madison, WI 53706-1400
O 608.262.3961 / F 608.262.1429

www.wisc.edu

www.uwbadgers.com

UNIV. OF WISCONSIN - RIVER FALLS

Division 3

<table>
<tr><td colspan="2">HOCKEY STAFF</td></tr>
</table>

HOCKEY STAFF

HEAD COACH
Steve Freeman *(Wisc.-Stevens Pt '81)*

ASSISTANT COACH
Bob Ritzer *(Wisconsin-Superior '86)*

HOCKEY OFFICE
University of Wisconsin
W.H. Hunt Arena
410 South Third Street
River Falls, WI 54022
O 715.425.3252 / F 715.425.4486
steven.c.freeman@uwrf.edu

HOCKEY MEDIA CONTACT
Jim Thies - Sports Info Director
University of Wisconsin - River Falls
24 South Hall
410 South 3rd Street
River Falls, WI 54022-5001
O 715.425.3846 / F 715.425.4486
james.g.thies@uwrf.edu

HOCKEY RINK
WH Hunt Arena (On Campus)
1110 South Main Street
River Falls, WI 54022
Size 200' x 80', Capacity 1,800
O 715.425.3381

ATHLETIC DIRECTOR
Rick Bowen - Athletic Director
University of Wisconsin
Karges Center
River Falls, WI 54022
O 715.425.3246 / F 715.425.3696
rick.h.bowen@uwrf.edu

FALCONS PLAYERS

Player	YB	GR	Ht/Wt	P	Hometown/Last Team
Joe Adams	83	08	5'10"/180	F	Roseau,MN/Bismarck Bobcats (NAHL)
Cory Baldwin		10	5'10"/190	F	St. Adolphe,MB/Dauphin Kings (ManJHL)
Pat Borgestad		07	6' 3"/200	F	St. Paul,MN/Des Moines Buccaneers (USHL)
AJ Bucchino		09	5'10"/185	G	Bow,NH/Des Moines Buccaneers (USHL)
Skylar Christoffersen		10	6' 0"/175	F	Langley,BC/Southeast Blades (ManJHL)
Tyler Dahl	84	08	6' 0"/195	F	Burnsville,MN/Des Moines Buccaneers (USHL)
Carver Dowhan		10	6' 1"/195	F	Selkirk,MN/Swan Valley Stampeders (ManJHL)
Tom Flikeid		09	6' 0"/180	F	Lakeville,MN/Alberni Valley Bulldogs (BCHL)
Derek Hansberry		09	6' 0"/190	F	Arvada,CO/Wichita Falls (NAHL)
Wade Harstad	83	08	6' 1"/185	F	Moorhead,MN/St. Louis (USHL)
Jim Henkemeyer	85	08	5'11"/180	D	St. Cloud,MN/Bismarck Bobcats (NAHL)
Jim Jensen		08	6' 1"/190	D	Maplewood,MN/Waterloo Blackhawks (USHL)
Mitch Kerns		10	5'11"/185	F	Stoughton,WI/Billings Bulls (NAHL)
Tyler Kostiuk	83	07	5'10"/170	F	Cranbrook,BC/Fernie Ghostriders (NAHL)
Lance Malark		09	5'10"/180	F	White Bear Lk,MN/Fargo-Moorhead Jets (NAHL)
Jordan McIntyre		10	5' 9"/185	F	Grand Forks,ND/Portage Terriers (ManJHL)
Josh Meyers		09	6' 0"/190	D	Int'l Falls,MN/Bozeman Icedogs (NAHL)
Dustin Norman		09	6' 2"/175	F	S Delta,BC/Neepawa Natives (ManJHL)
Matt Page		10	5'10"/210	G	New Richmond,WI/Wisconsin Mustangs (ManJHL)
Sean Pettinger		10	6' 0"/190	D	Elgin,MB/Swan Valley Stampeders (ManJHL)
Chris Robinson		09	5'11"/185	D	Brooklyn,NY/Lincoln Stars (USHL)
Jared Sailer	82	07	6' 3"/220	F	Fernie,BC/Fernie Ghostriders (NAHL)
Tony Stoehr		10	6' 1"/190	G	DePere,WI/Michigan (NOJHL)
Jeff Stone		10	6' 3"/210	D	Wyoming,MN/Sioux Falls Stampede (USHL)
Matt Szypura		09	6' 1"/210	D	Warrenville,IL/Springfield Blues (NAHL)
Devin Underwood		09	6' 3"/190	F	Wasilla,AK/Helena Bighorns (NAHL)
Jason Usher	84	08	6' 0"/195	D	Eden Pr,MN/Fairbanks Ice Dogs (NAHL)
TJ Warkentin		10	5'10"/190	F	Fork Rvr,MB/Dauphin Kings (ManJHL)

ROSTER ANALYSIS (SCHOLARSHIPS - 0)

Class		Country		Last Team					
Fr	10	USA	22	US JR A	18	CDN JR A	9	ACHA	
So	9	Canada	6	US JR B	1	CDN JR B		NJCAA	
Jr	6	Europe		US PS		CDN PS		NCAA	
Sr	3	Asia		US HS		CDN HS		USNDT	
Gr		Other		US Midget		CDN Midget		Other	

ADMISSIONS, ENROLLMENT & CAMPUS INFORMATION

Founded 1874	Average acceptance rate - 85 %	Alan Tuchtenhagen - Admissions Director
Public, suburban campus	Freshman financial aid - %	University of Wisconsin - River Falls
2,143 men / 3,214 women	Early decision application deadline - N/A	112 South Hall - 410 South 3rd Street
Tuition, room & board - $ 9 K / $ 19 K	Regular application deadline - Feb 1	River Falls, WI 54022
Avg ACT - 22	Financial aid deadline - Mar 15	O 715.425.3911 / F 715.425.3304

www.uwrf.edu   www.uwrf.edu/sports/

UNIV. OF WISCONSIN - STEVENS POINT

Division 3

HOCKEY STAFF

HEAD COACH
Wil Nichol *(Wisc. Stevens Pt '98)*

ASSISTANT COACHES
Matt Interbartolo

HOCKEY OFFICE
University of Wisconsin-Stevens Point
118 C Berg Gymnasium
Stevens Point, WI 54481-3897
O 715.346.3332 / F 715.346.3626
wnichol@uwsp.edu

HOCKEY MEDIA CONTACT
Jim Strick - Sports Info Director
103 Berg Gymnasiun
Steven Point, WI 54481-3897
O 715.346.2840 / F 715.346.3626
jstrick@uwsp.edu

HOCKEY RINK
KB Willett Arena (Off Campus)
1000 Minnesota Avenue
Stevens Point, WI 54481
Size 195' x 85', Capacity 1,700
O 715.344.1781

ATHLETIC DIRECTOR
Frank O'Brien - Athletic Director
University of Wisconsin-Stevens Point
Quandt Fieldhouse - 4th Street
Stevens Point, WI 54481
O 715.346.3888 / F 715.346.4655
fobrien@uwsp.edu

POINTERS PLAYERS

Player	YB	GR	Ht/Wt	P	Hometown/Last Team
Brett Beckfeld	85	09	6' 0"/170	F	Plymouth,MN/Bozeman Icedogs (NAHL)
Matt Buha	85	09	5'10"/180	F	St. Louis,MO/Soo Indians (NAHL)
Nick Bydal	84	09	6' 2"/230	D	E Grand Forks,MN/Bismarck Bobcats (NAHL)
Josh Callenja	86	10	5' 7"/180	F	New Richmond,WI/Wisconsin Mustangs (MnJHL)
Andy Cankar	84	09	6' 1"/190	F	Lockport,IL/Springfield Blues (NAHL)
Brett Coburn	82	07	5' 9"/175	F	Addison,IL/Springfield Blues (NAHL)
Chris Conway	85	10	5' 9"/185	F	Westminster,CO/Springfield Blues (NAHL)
Sean Fish	85	09	5' 6"/165	F	Ramsey,MN/Alexandria Blizzard (NAHL)
Shane Foster	84	09	6' 4"/210	F	Madison,WI/Springfield Spirit (NAHL)
Dan Francis	81	07	5' 9"/190	F	Roseville,MI/Findlay (CHA)
Vince Goulet	85	09	6' 0"/185	F	Denver,CO/Providence (HEA)
Taylor Guay	84	09	6' 1"/170	F	Boulder,CO/Springfield Spirit (NAHL)
Marc Hale	83	09	5' 9"/195	D	Chesterfield,MO/New England (ECAC East)
Ross Johnson	84	09	6' 0"/180	F	Int'l Falls,MN/Wisconsin River Falls (NCHA)
Reed Lally	85	10	5'10"/180	F	Duluth,MN/Wasilla Spirit (NAHL)
Karl Larsen	85	09	5'10"/180	D	Princeton,MN/Alexandria Blizzard (NAHL)
Russel Law	84	09	5' 9"/165	F	Bay City,MI/Northern Michigan Black Bears (NOJHL)
Pat Lee	84	10	5' 8"/190	F	Schaumburg,IL/Springfield Blues (NAHL)
Ryan Miech	84	09	5'10"/175	G	Stevens Pt,WI/Twin Cities Northern Lights (MnJHL)
Jordan Neamonitis	84	10	5' 8"/175	G	Kirkland,QC/Syracuse Stars (EJHL)
Anthony Noreen	83	07	5'11"/180	D	Chicago,IL/Springfield Blues (NAHL)
Marcus Paulson	85	09	5'10"/165	G	Eden Pr,MN/Alexandria Blizzard (NAHL)
Adam Setten	82	07	5'10"/185	D	New Hope,MN/Wichita Falls (NAHL)
Nate Sorenson	82	08	6' 2"/230	D	Tomah,WI/Wichita Falls (NAHL)
Matt Stendahl	84	09	5' 9"/175	F	Forest Lk,MN/Springfield Blues (NAHL)
Rolf Ulvin	82	07	6' 0"/205	F	Edina,MN/Michigan Tech (WCHA)
Tom Upton	85	10	6' 1"/210	D	Austin,TX/Mahoning Valley Phantoms (NAHL)
Tom Vernelli	83	08	5'11"/175	F	Sault Ste. Marie,ON/Soo Thunderbirds (NOJHL)
Nick Zebro	82	07	6' 2"/205	F	Mosinee,WI/Springfield (NAHL)

ROSTER ANALYSIS (SCHOLARSHIPS - 0)

Class		Country		Last Team				
Fr	6	USA	27	US JR A	19	CDN JR A	2	ACHA
So	15	Canada	2	US JR B	3	CDN JR B		NJCAA
Jr	2	Europe		US PS		CDN PS		NCAA	5
Sr	6	Asia		US HS		CDN HS		USNDT
Gr		Other		US Midget		CDN Midget		Other

ADMISSIONS, ENROLLMENT & CAMPUS INFORMATION

Founded 1894	Average acceptance rate - 75 %	David Eckholm - Admissions Director
Public, urban campus	Freshman financial aid - 94 %	University of Wisconsin-Stevens Point
3,756 men / 4,780 women	Early decision application deadline - N/A	102 Student Services
Tuition, room & board - $ 9 K / $ 19 K	Regular application deadline- rolling	Stevens Point, WI 54481-3897
Avg SAT 1,053 / Avg ACT - 23	Financial aid deadline - Mar 15	O 715.346.2441 / F 715.346.2558

www.uwsp.edu

www.uwsp.edu/athletics/

UNIVERSITY OF WISCONSIN - STOUT

Division 3

<table>
<tr><td colspan="2">

HOCKEY STAFF

HEAD COACH
Terry Watkins *(Wisconsin-Stout '72)*

ASSISTANT COACHES
Ed Roethke *(Wisconsin-Stout)*
Paul Frank *(Colorado)*

HOCKEY OFFICE
University of Wisconsin Stout
Johnson Fieldhouse
Menomonie, WI 54751
O 715.235.5423 / F 715.796.2243
watkinsd@uwstout.edu

HOCKEY MEDIA CONTACT
Layne Pitt - Sports Info Director
Johnson Fieldhouse
Menomonie, WI 54751
O 715.232.2275 / F 715.232.1684
pittl@uwstout.edu

HOCKEY RINK
Dunn County Ice Arena (On Campus)
800 Wilson Avenue
Menominee, WI 54751
Size ' x ', Capacity 800
PB 715.232.4016

ATHLETIC DIRECTOR
Steve Terry - Athletic Director
University of Wisconsin-Stout
205 Physical Education Building
Menomonie, WI 54751
O 715.232.2161 / F 715.232.1684
terrys@m1.uwstout.edu

</td></tr>
</table>

BLUE DEVILS PLAYERS

Player	YB	GR	Ht/Wt	P	Hometown/Last Team
Adam Boche	07		6'2"/185	D	S St. Paul,MN/St. Paul Lakers (MnJHL)
Derrick Bohn	10		6'1"/205	F	Stillwater,MN/Fargo-Moorhead Jets (NAHL)
Pat Conrad	10		6'0"/205	F/D	Centerville,MN/St. Paul Lakers (MnJHL)
Kyle Crable	08		6'0"/185	F	Bemidji,MN/Alexandria Blizzard (NAHL)
Jeff DeFrancesca	07		5'11"/170	D	Mt Prospect,IL/Lowell Loch Monsters (EJHL)
Jake Erickson	08		5'8"/165	F	Rochester,MN/Wichita Falls (NAHL)
BJ Garczynski	07		6'1"/200	D	Sun Prairie,WI/Rochester Americans (EmJHL)
Jake Gullickson	10		6'0"/210	D/F	Apple Valley,MN/Holy Angels (PS)
Derek Hanson	10		5'8"/175	F	Bemidji,MN/Winnipeg Saints (ManJHL)
Andrew Hasbargen	10		6'2"/210	D/F	Warroad,MN/Bismarck Bobcats (NAHL)
Scott Hellquist	07		6'1"/190	D	Bemidji,MN/Bismarck Bobcats (NAHL)
Paul Henderson	10		6'2"/210	F/D	Menomonie,WI/Alexandria Blizzard (NAHL)
Nick Klaren	09		6'1"/195	D	N St. Paul,MN/Wichita Falls (NAHL)
Matt Koenig	09		6'1"/190	G	Lakeland,MN/Billings Bulls (NAHL)
Bobby Kuehl	10		6'2"/195	D	St. Paul,MN/Alexandria Blizzard (NAHL)
Matt Mlynarczyk	07		6'0"/175	F	Oakdale,MN/St. Paul Lakers (MnJHL)
Scott Motz	10		6'1"/205	F	Lake Elmo,MN/Alexandria Blizzard (NAHL)
Cory Mozak	09		5'10"/165	F	Sioux City,IA/Helena Bighorns (NAHL)
Rob Mueller	09		5'9"/160	F	Buffalo,MN/Buffalo (HS)
Luke Schroeder	08		5'11"/180	F	Minneapolis,MN/Minneapolis (MnJHL)
Scott Sikkink	08		6'0"/200	F	Chippewa Fls,WI/Fargo-Moorhead Jets (NAHL)
Andrew Stearns	07		6'2"/220	F	Wadena,MN/Wisconsin Superior (NCHA)
Preston Stearns	10		6'1"/205	D/F	Wadena,MN/Deer Creek (HS)
Andy Sternberg	10		5'11"/175	F	Duluth,MN/Wasilla Spirit (NAHL)
Mike Stone	08		6'0"/170	G	W St. Paul,MN/Minneapolis (MnJHL)
Glenn Walker	08		5'11"/165	G	Verona,WI/Verona (HS)
Jeff Wheeler	09		5'10"/190	F	Bainbridge,WA/Dubuque Thunderbirds (MnJHL)
Andy Wiesner	07		5'10"/210	F	Rochester,MN/Chicago Freeze (NAHL)
Jack Wolgemuth	09		6'3"/185	D	Anchorage,AK/Wichita Falls (NAHL)
Todd Wynia	08		5'11"/170	D	Minneapolis,MN/Dubuque Thunderbirds (MnJHL)

ROSTER ANALYSIS (SCHOLARSHIPS - 0)

Class		Country		Last Team					
Fr	10	USA	30	US JR A	15	CDN JR A	1	ACHA	
So	6	Canada		US JR B	9	CDN JR B		NJCAA	
Jr	7	Europe		US PS	1	CDN PS		NCAA	1
Sr	7	Asia		US HS	3	CDN HS		USNDT	
Gr		Other		US Midget		CDN Midget		Other	

ADMISSIONS, ENROLLMENT & CAMPUS INFORMATION

Founded 1891	Average acceptance rate - 80 %	Cindy Jenkins - Admissions Director
Public, rural campus	Freshman financial aid - 87 %	University of Wisconsin-Stout
3,375 men / 3,512 women	Early decision application deadline - N/A	Admissions Office
Tuition, room & board $ 10 K / $ 20 K	Regular application deadline - Jan 1	Menomonie, WI 54751
Avg ACT - 21	Financial aid deadline - Apr 1	O 715.232.1411 / F 715.232.1667

www.uwstout.edu   www.uwstout.edu/athletics/

UNIVERSITY OF WISCONSIN - SUPERIOR

Division 3

HOCKEY STAFF

HEAD COACH
Dan Stauber *(Wisconsin-Superior '88)*

ASSISTANT COACH
Chris Bell *(Wisconsin-Superior '02)*

HOCKEY OFFICE
University of Wisconsin-Superior
Wessman Arena
1800 Grand Avenue
Superior, WI 54880-2898
O 715.394.8362 / F 715.394.8110
dstauber@uwsuper.edu

HOCKEY MEDIA CONTACT
David Kroll - Sports Info Director
University of Wisconsin-Superior
1800 Grand Avenue
Superior, WI 54880-2898
O 715.395.4614 / F 715.394.8110
dkroll@uwsuper.edu

HOCKEY RINK
Wessman Arena (On Campus)
2701 Catlin Avenue
Superior, WI 54880
Size ' x ', Capacity 2,500
O 715.394.8044

ATHLETIC DIRECTOR
Steve Nelson - Athletic Director
University of Wisconsin-Superior
1800 Grand Avenue
Superior, WI 54880-2898
O 715.395.4619
snelson@uwsuper.edu

YELLOWJACKETS PLAYERS

Player	YB	GR	Ht/Wt	P	Hometown/Last Team
Eric Bausano	84	09	5' 6"/165	F	Laurium,MI/New Hampshire Monarchs (EJHL)
Chad Beiswenger		09	6' 3"/190	G	Moorhead,MN/Helena Bighorns (NAHL)
Aaron Berman	84	09	6' 1"/210	D	Surrey,BC/Langley Hornets (BCHL)
Chris Berry		10		F	Calgary,AB/ (AJHL)
Brian Bina		10		D	Grand Forks,ND/Lincoln Stars (USHL)
Joe Bluhm		10		F	Red Wing,MN/Fairbanks Ice Dogs (NAHL)
Baron Bradley	07		6' 1"/180	G	Neepawa,MB/Dauphin Kings (ManJHL)
Dane Bushey		10		F	Duluth,MN/Fargo-Moorhead Jets (NAHL)
Anthony Casmano		10		F	Wheaton,IL/Helena Bighorns (NAHL)
Art Clark		10		F	Bloomington,MN/Jefferson (HS)
Dustin Cosgrove	08		5'11"/200	D	Neepawa,MB/Cowichan Valley Capitals (BCHL)
Braden Desmet		10		F	Strathmore,AB/ (AJHL)
Eddie Fischermann		10		G	Costa Mesa,CA/Shattuck-St. Mary's (PS)
Jeff Herman	84	09	5'10"/200	D	Cranbrook,BC/Prince George Spruce Kings (BCHL)
Ryan Kuntz	84	09	5'11"/205	F	Regina,SK/Weyburn Red Wings (SJHL)
Matt Lamirande		10		F	Calgary,AB/ (AJHL)
Jamie Lazorko	08		6' 0"/195	D	Kelowna,BC/Fernie Ghostriders (NAHL)
Corey Lennartson	82	07	6' 0"/185	F	Cloquet,MN/Wisconsin River Falls (NCHA)
Andrew MacKenzie	84	09	6' 0"/175	F	Terrace Bay,ON/Neepawa Natives (ManJHL)
David Moncur	84	09	6' 5"/215	D	Burnaby,BC/Surrey Eagles (BCHL)
Derek Paige	08		5'10"/190	D	Logan Lake,BC/Coquitlam Express (BCHL)
Myles Palliser	07		6' 1"/190	F	Lake Cowichan,BC/SUNY Potsdam (SUNYAC)
Seth Reda	81	09	6' 1"/200	F	Palmer,AK/Fairbanks Ice Dogs (NAHL)
Nate Rein	84	09	5' 9"/185	F	Shakopee,MN/Helena Bighorns (NAHL)
Josh Seifert		10		D	Superior,WI/Bismarck Bobcats (NAHL)
Corey Stark		10		F	Chanhassen,MN/Santa Fe Roadrunners (NAHL)
Rob Turnville	84	09	6' 0"/200	F	Olds,AB/Brooks Bandits (AJHL)

ROSTER ANALYSIS (SCHOLARSHIPS - 0)

Class		Country		Last Team					
Fr	11	USA	13	US JR A	10	CDN JR A	12	ACHA	
So	10	Canada	14	US JR B	1	CDN JR B		NJCAA	
Jr	3	Europe		US PS	1	CDN PS	1	NCAA	2
Sr	3	Asia		US HS	1	CDN HS		USNDT	
Gr		Other		US Midget		CDN Midget		Other	

ADMISSIONS, ENROLLMENT & CAMPUS INFORMATION

Founded 1893
Public, urban campus
1,069 men / 1,419 women
Tuition, room & board - $ 10 K /$ 20 K
Avg SAT 1,160 / ACT - 23

Average acceptance rate - 77 %
Freshman financial aid - %
Early decision application deadline - N/A
Regular application deadline - rolling
Financial aid deadline - Apr 15

John Wojciechowski - Admissions Dir.
University of Wisconsin-Superior
1800 Grand Avenue
Superior, WI 54880-2898
O 715.394.8230 / F 715.394.8407

WORCESTER STATE COLLEGE

HOCKEY
NORTHEAST

Division 3

HOCKEY STAFF

HEAD COACH
John Guiney *(Worcester State '76)*

ASSISTANT COACHES
Bob Thebeau *(Notre Dame '86)*
Marvin Degon *(Worcester State)*

HOCKEY OFFICE
Worcester State College
Athletic Department
486 Chandler Street
Worcester, MA 01602-2597
O 508.929.8510 / F 508.929.8184
jguiney@worcester.edu

HOCKEY MEDIA CONTACT
John Meany - Sports Info Director
Worcester State College - Athletic Dept.
486 Chandler Street
Worcester, MA 06102-2597
O 508.929.8730 / F 508.929.8128
jmeany@worcester.edu

HOCKEY RINK
Horgan Rink (Off Campus)
400 Oxford Street North
Auburn, MA 01501
Size 185' x 85', Capacity 1,500
O 508.832.7201

ATHLETIC DIRECTOR
Susan E. Chapman - Athletic Director
Worcester State College - Athletic Dept.
486 Chandler Street
Worcester, MA 01602-2597
O 508.929.8034 / H 508.929.8184
schapman@worcester.edu

LANCERS PLAYERS

Player	YB	GR	Ht/Wt	P	Hometown/Last Team
Ed Achilles	08		5' 7"/165	F	Horsham,PA/Nichols (ECAC NE)
Chris Austermann	10		5'11"/175	F	Littleton,MA/Littleton (HS)
Matt Auwarter	08		5' 9"/170	F	Malverne,NY/Suffolk PAL (MJHL)
Derek Banks	10		6' 0"/215	D	Ellicott City,MD/Mount St. Joseph (PS)
Lee Belisle	10		5' 7"/140	F	Chicopee,MA/Chicopee (HS)
Mark Bucci	08		6' 1"/210	F	Sellersville,PA/Wyoming (PS)
Andrew Burrill	09		5' 8"/170	D	Uxbridge,MA/Uxbridge (HS)
Dan Drinkwater	10		6' 0"/195	F	Walpole,MA/Walpole Stars (EJHL)
Tom Ford	09		6' 3"/200	F	N Grafton,MA/St. John's (PS)
Christopher Gramlich	08		5' 7"/150	F	Philadelphia,PA/Hudson Valley (NJCAA)
Chris Hanson	10		5'11"/215	F	Chelmsford,MA/Chelmsford (HS)
Mark Holman	07		6' 1"/195	G	Lincoln,NE/Lincoln Southeast (HS)
Timothy Hunt	10		6' 0"/190	D	Sterling ,MA/St. Bernard's (PS)
William Knauber	09		6' 0"/190	D	Cheektowaga,NY/Maryvale (HS)
Chris Krawczyk	07		5' 8"/170	F	Marlborough,MA/Massachusetts Boston (ECAC East)
Josh McClellan	07		6' 0"/220	D	Tyngsboro,MA/Tyngsboro (HS)
Dan McLaughlin	08		6' 0"/205	D	Medford,MA/Exeter Seawolves (AEHL)
Brian Miga	10		6' 1"/190	F	Kensington,CT/Berlin ()
Josh Morgan	08		5'10"/185	F	Mountaintop,PA/Wyoming (PS)
Ian Nadeau	10		5' 9"/200	G	Tolland,CT/Rockville ()
Jack Nagle	10		5' 8"/185	D	Weymouth,MA/Archbishop Williams (PS)
Steve Nims	09		5'10"/210	D	Worcester,MA/St. Peter-Marian (PS)
Nathan Perreault	08		6' 1"/190	F	Smithfield,RI/Bridgewater Bandits (EJHL)
Jason Richardson	09		5'11"/185	G	Perkasie,PA/Wyoming (PS)
Mark Rintel	10		6' 0"/205	F	Oakland Gardens,NY/Benjiman Cardozo ()
Michael Smith	10		6' 1"/205	F	Bourne,MA/Bourne (HS)
Dave Szydlowski	07		5' 9"/185	D	Islip Terr,NY/Nichols (ECAC NE)
Will Walsh	09		6' 0"/200	F	Arlington,MA/Arlington (HS)

ROSTER ANALYSIS (SCHOLARSHIPS - 0)

Class		Country		Last Team					
Fr	11	USA	28	US JR A		CDN JR A		ACHA	
So	6	Canada		US JR B	4	CDN JR B		NJCAA	1
Jr	7	Europe		US PS	8	CDN PS		NCAA	3
Sr	4	Asia		US HS	9	CDN HS		USNDT	
Gr		Other		US Midget		CDN Midget		Other	3

ADMISSIONS, ENROLLMENT & CAMPUS INFORMATION

Founded 1874
Public, urban campus
1581 = men / 2,277 women
Tuition, room & board - $11 K / $17 K
Avg SAT - 1050 / Avg ACT 21

Average acceptance rate - 56 %
Freshman financial aid - 75 %
Early decision application deadline - N/A
Regular application deadline - Jun 1
Financial aid deadline - Mar 1

Michael Backes - Admissions Director
Worcester State College Admissions
486 Chandler Street
Worcester, MA 01602-2597
O 508.929.8040 / F 508.929.8131

YALE UNIVERSITY

Division 1

HOCKEY STAFF

HEAD COACH
Keith Allain *(Yale '80)*

ASSOCIATE HEAD COACH
CJ Marottolo *(Northeastern '89)*

ASSISTANT COACHES
Mike Richter
Kyle Wollack

HOCKEY OFFICE
Yale University
Department of Athletics
PO Box 208216
New Haven, CT 06520-8216
O 203.432.1478 / F 203.432.1417
keith.allain@yale.edu

HOCKEY MEDIA CONTACT
Steve Conn - Hockey Info Director
Yale University - Department of Athletics
PO Box 208216
New Haven, CT 06520
O 203.432.1455 / F 203.432.1454
steven.conn@yale.edu

HOCKEY RINK
Ingalls Rink (On Campus)
73 Sachem Street
New Haven, CT 06520
Size 200' x 85', Capacity 3,486
O 203.432.0778

ATHLETIC DIRECTOR
Tom Beckett - Athletic Director
Yale University - Department of Athletics
PO Box 208216
New Haven, CT 06520-8216
O 203.432.4747 / F 203.432.7772
thomas.beckett@yale.edu

BULLDOGS PLAYERS

Player	YB	GR	Ht/Wt	P	Hometown/Last Team
Mark Arcobello	88	10	5' 9"/165	F	Milford,CT/Salisbury (NEPSAC)
Sean Backman	86	10	5' 8"/165	F	Cos Cob,CT/Green Bay Gamblers (USHL)
Greg Beller	87	10	6' 2"/200	F	Vancouver,BC/Green Bay Gamblers (USHL)
Billy Blasé	87	10	6' 0"/190	G	Santa Monica,CA/Salmon Arm Silverbacks (BCHL)
Jean-Francois Boucher	85	08	6' 0"/205	F	Rosemere,QC/Upper Canada (PS)
Patrick Brosnihan	86	09	6' 4"/220	F	Worcester,MA/Worcester (NEPSAC)
Robert Burns	84	07	6' 1"/200	F	Belmont,MA/Deerfield (NEPSAC)
Chris Cahill	87	10	5'11"/185	F	Haverhill,MA/Andover (NEPSAC)
Matt Cohen	85	07	6' 2"/220	D	New York,NY/USNDT (NAHL)
Thomas Dignard		10	5'11"/190	D	Reading,MA/Andover (NEPSAC)
Ryan Donald	86	10	6' 3"/205	D	St. Albert,AB/Camrose Kodiaks (AJHL)
Will Engasser	85	08	6' 2"/240	F	Chanhassen,MN/Blake (PS)
David Germain	85	08	6' 0"/200	F	Quincy,MA/New Hampshire Monarchs (EJHL)
David Inman	87	09	6' 0"/210	D	San Diego,CA/USNDT (NAHL)
Michael Karwoski	86	09	5' 9"/185	F	Greenlawn,NY/Apple Core (EJHL)
Bill LeClerc	84	07	6' 0"/200	D	Acton,MA/St. Paul's (NEPSAC)
Brad Mills	83	07	6' 0"/200	F	Olds,AB/Fort McMurray Oil Barons (AJHL)
Matt Modelski	82	07	5'11"/180	G	Brighton,MI/Chicago Freeze (NAHL)
Shawn Mole	85	07	6' 1"/195	D	Mississauga,ON/Burlington Cougars (OPJHL)
Matt Nelson	86	09	6' 0"/200	F	Westwood,MA/Nobles (NEPSAC)
Robert Page	85	08	6' 2"/205	D	Eden Pr,MN/Blake (PS)
Alec Richards	87	09	6' 4"/190	G	Robbinsdale,MN/Breck (PS)
Matthew Thomey	86	08	6' 0"/205	F	Harbour Grace,NF/Niagara Falls (GHJHL)
Brennan Turner	86	09	6' 3"/220	D	Winnipeg,MB/Notre Dame (PS)
Blair Yaworski	85	08	6' 3"/210	F	Calgary,AB/Sioux City Musketeers (USHL)

ROSTER ANALYSIS (SCHOLARSHIPS - 0)

Class		Country		Last Team					
Fr	7	USA	17	US JR A	4	CDN JR A	4	ACHA	
So	6	Canada	8	US JR B	2	CDN JR B	1	NJCAA	
Jr	6	Europe		US PS	10	CDN PS	2	NCAA	
Sr	6	Asia		US HS		CDN HS		USNDT	2
Gr		Other		US Midget		CDN Midget		Other	

ADMISSIONS, ENROLLMENT & CAMPUS INFORMATION

Founded 1701
Private, urban campus
2,740 men / 2,528 women
Tuition, room & board - $ 42 K
Avg SAT - 1,480 / Avg ACT - 33

Average acceptance rate - 10 %
Freshman financial aid - 100 %
Early decision application deadline - N/A
Regular application deadline - Dec 31
Financial aid deadline - Mar 1

Michael May - Admissions Director
Yale University - Office of Admissions
P. O. Box 208234
New Haven, CT 06520-8234
O 203.432.9316 / F 203.432.9392

www.yale.edu

yalebulldogs.collegesports.com/

Athletic Guide
Publishing Titles

ATHLETIC GUIDE PUBLISHING TITLES

TITLE	LIST PRICE
College Hockey Guide Men's Edition (Keegan)	45.95
College Hockey Guide Women's Edition (Keegan)	42.95
Junior Hockey Guide (Keegan)	45.95
Pro Hockey Guide (Keegan)	32.95
Prep School Hockey Guide (Keegan)	42.95
Power Play: Mental Toughness for Hockey and Beyond (Smith)	29.95
Prep School Baseball Guide (Keegan)	42.95
Prep School Basketball Guide (Keegan)	42.95
Prep School Bowling Guide (Keegan)	42.95
Prep School Fencing Guide (Keegan)	42.95
Prep School Field Hockey Guide (Keegan)	42.95
Prep School Football Guide (Keegan)	42.95
Prep School Golf Guide (Keegan)	42.95
Prep School Gymnastics Guide (Keegan)	42.95
Prep School Hockey Guide (Keegan)	42.95
Prep School Lacrosse Guide (Keegan)	42.95
Prep School Rifle Guide (Keegan)	42.95
Prep School Rowing Guide (Keegan)	42.95
Prep School Skiing Guide (Keegan)	42.95
Prep School Soccer Guide (Keegan)	42.95
Prep School Softball Guide (Keegan)	42.95
Prep School Swimming & Diving Guide (Keegan)	42.95
Prep School Tennis Guide (Keegan)	42.95
Prep School Track / Cross Country Guide (Keegan)	42.95
Prep School Volleyball Guide (Keegan)	42.95
Prep School Water Polo Guide (Keegan)	42.95
Prep School Wrestling Guide (Keegan)	42.95
Boarding School Guide (Keegan)	29.95
The Student-Athlete & College Recruiting (Wire)	24.95
Athletic Recruiting & College Scholarship Guide (Scott)	29.95
How to Market Your Student-Athlete (Scott)	29.95

Athletic Guide Publishing
PO Box 1050
Flagler Beach, FL 32136-1050
www.athleticguidepublishing.com
agp@flaglernet.com
386.439.2250 phone
800.255.1050 order line
386.439.2249 fax

Athletic Guide
Publishing Titles

ATHLETIC GUIDE PUBLISHING TITLES

TITLE	LIST PRICE
College Hockey Guide Men's Edition (Keegan)	45.95
College Hockey Guide Women's Edition (Keegan)	42.95
Junior Hockey Guide (Keegan)	45.95
Pro Hockey Guide (Keegan)	32.95
Prep School Hockey Guide (Keegan)	42.95
Power Play: Mental Toughness for Hockey and Beyond (Smith)	29.95
Prep School Baseball Guide (Keegan)	42.95
Prep School Basketball Guide (Keegan)	42.95
Prep School Bowling Guide (Keegan)	42.95
Prep School Fencing Guide (Keegan)	42.95
Prep School Field Hockey Guide (Keegan)	42.95
Prep School Football Guide (Keegan)	42.95
Prep School Golf Guide (Keegan)	42.95
Prep School Gymnastics Guide (Keegan)	42.95
Prep School Hockey Guide (Keegan)	42.95
Prep School Lacrosse Guide (Keegan)	42.95
Prep School Rifle Guide (Keegan)	42.95
Prep School Rowing Guide (Keegan)	42.95
Prep School Skiing Guide (Keegan)	42.95
Prep School Soccer Guide (Keegan)	42.95
Prep School Softball Guide (Keegan)	42.95
Prep School Swimming & Diving Guide (Keegan)	42.95
Prep School Tennis Guide (Keegan)	42.95
Prep School Track / Cross Country Guide (Keegan)	42.95
Prep School Volleyball Guide (Keegan)	42.95
Prep School Water Polo Guide (Keegan)	42.95
Prep School Wrestling Guide (Keegan)	42.95
Boarding School Guide (Keegan)	29.95
The Student-Athlete & College Recruiting (Wire)	24.95
Athletic Recruiting & College Scholarship Guide (Scott)	29.95
How to Market Your Student-Athlete (Scott)	29.95

Athletic Guide Publishing
PO Box 1050
Flagler Beach, FL 32136-1050
www.athleticguidepublishing.com
agp@flaglernet.com
386.439.2250 phone
800.255.1050 order line
386.439.2249 fax